BEYOND CAMELOT

BEYOND CAMELOT

RETHINKING POLITICS AND LAW
FOR THE MODERN STATE

Edward L. Rubin

PRINCETON UNIVERSITY PRESS   PRINCETON AND OXFORD

Copyright © 2005 by Princeton University Press

Published by Princeton University Press, 41 William Street, Princeton, New Jersey 08540

In the United Kingdom: Princeton University Press, 3 Market Place, Woodstock, Oxfordshire OX20 1SY

Library of Congress Cataloging-in-Publication Data

Rubin, Edward L., 1948–
    Beyond Camelot : rethinking politics and law for the modern state /
Edward L. Rubin.
       p.   cm.
    Includes bibliographical references and index.
    ISBN 0-691-11808-6 (cloth: alk. paper)
      1. State, The—History.   2. Political science—Philosophy.   3. Public administration—
History.   4. Bureaucracy—History.   5. Rule of law—History.   6. United States—
Politics and government.   I. Title.

JC11.R83   2005
320'.01—dc22

                                                                2004045860

British Library Cataloging-in-Publication Data is available

This book has been composed in Galliard

Printed on acid-free paper. ∞

pup.princeton.edu

Printed in the United States of America

10   9   8   7   6   5   4   3   2   1

Contents

Acknowledgments

THIS book grew out of my experience teaching administrative law at the University of California, Berkeley School of Law (Boalt Hall), and at the University of Pennsylvania Law School. When I began, in the early 1980s, the student radicalism of the prior decade, with its concern for social equality, was beginning to fade, and my most vociferous students were free-market conservatives who wanted the regulatory state dismantled. In trying to explain to them why their ideas were neither just nor practical, I noticed that I was continually fighting against the terminology of legal and political theory. It was easy for them to assert that regulatory government was undemocratic, illegitimate, and overly discretionary, that it violated separation of powers, human rights, property rights, and the rule of law. It was difficult for me to explain that these terms could not be taken at face value, that they were reflecting views that most people no longer held, and that there were other, more compelling considerations that they tended to obscure.

By the 1990s, free-market conservatism among my students had faded away, to be replaced by a sort of torpid liberalism. I was thus relieved of the obligation to justify the regulatory state, but I still had to explain it to students whose loss of an impassioned desire to change the world had left them with an intensified anxiety to understand that world as it exists. Once again, I found that the very terms in which I thought about the political and legal worlds were betraying me. They turned out to be just as inadequate for describing the modern state as they were for justifying it. It then occurred to me that instead of using basic political and legal concepts to interrogate the existence of the administrative state, perhaps it would be more productive to use the existence of the administrative state to interrogate these political and legal concepts. The concepts, after all, were mental furniture, which could be refurbished, moved around, or even donated to outmoded philanthropic institutions. The administrative state was the foundation and superstructure of our present government; it could not be moved, and it was not going to go away.

My initial thanks for this book, therefore, must go to all my administrative law students (by now, some two thousand of them), who served as the book's unwitting inspiration, and as the victims of some very idiosyncratic lectures that I gave while thinking it through. I also want to thank my colleagues at Boalt Hall and Penn, who were more conscious contributors. Both these institutions provide an amazing intellectual environment, brimming with ideas and crackling with mental energy; in many cases, they were the sources of the book's ideas. Other ideas came from the faculty workshops at the law schools where I presented preliminary versions of the book's various chapters: Boston College, Chicago-Kent, City University of Hong Kong, Columbia, Cornell, Duke, Emory, Florida State, Georgetown, Hong Kong, New York Law School, Ohio State, Oxford Center for Law and Society, Rutgers-Camden, Temple, State University of New York at Buffalo, University of Arkansas (Fayetteville), University of Chicago, University of Colorado, University of Illinois, University of Kansas, University of Minnesota, University of North Carolina, University of San Diego, University of Texas, University of Wisconsin, and Vanderbilt. Finally, although I hesitate to single out individual faculty members among the many who helped, I must give special thanks to Guyora Binder, Jacques deLisle, Geoffrey Hazard, Cynthia Farina, Sanford Levinson, Kim Scheppele, Peter Strauss, and David Westbrook.

I am grateful to the Smith Richardson Foundation for providing a grant that enabled me to start this project, to Mark Steinmeyer, my program officer at Smith Richardson, and to the two deans during my time at Penn, Colin Diver and Michael Fitts, for providing funds that enabled me to devote my summers to the book's continuation and completion. I am also grateful to my research assistants, Bronwen Morgan, Lauren Bishow, Sherri Kaplan, and Anna Perng, and to my editors at Princeton University Press, Charles Myers, Kevin McInturff, Jennifer Nippins, Eric Schramm, and Nathan Traylor, for their assistance and encouragement in its later stages.

Finally, I want to thank my family: my children, Greg, Tim, Juliette, and Alex, and my wife, Ilene, for their forbearance and their devotion.

One

Introduction

The Thesis

Social Nostalgia

OVER the course of the last two centuries, we have developed a new mode of governance—the administrative state—and it makes us feel miserable. We rail at the bloated bulk and dreary pragmatism of our public institutions. We condemn the uninspired, cumbersome rigidity that, despite such pragmatism, makes those institutions ineffective. We yearn for times that were not only simpler but more joyous and more integrated, when our individual experience was directly connected to the collectivity and we inhabited a political world that was suffused with moral values. This set of attitudes can be described as social nostalgia.

Social nostalgia pervades both our political and our popular culture. Citizens complain that government has become too large, too bureaucratic, too remote. Politicians, even when they are incumbents, regularly campaign against the prevailing administration, promising to restore the virtues of some prior period, to bring the government "closer to the people," or to "return to normalcy."[1] In the movies, anyone with an ordinary administrative role—an office supervisor, university dean, or government official—is either an actual villain or, at the very least, an impediment to justice and good sense. How often have we seen our hero, a police officer, for example, slam his badge down on the captain's desk and say, "I've had it with your rules; now I'm going to take care of things myself."[2] Indeed, the romance of life outside the administrative state rivals sex and violence as the dominant theme in contemporary cinema. The Wild West, the Middle Ages, the urban ghetto, outer space, and Earth after a nuclear or environmental holocaust all serve as settings where heroism and adventure flourish in the absence of bureaucracy. One might imagine that the planetary and interplanetary regimes in *Star Wars* would require a good deal more administrative resources than the small segments of our own planet that constitute contemporary nation-states, yet planets are ruled by queens and princesses, the evil intergalactic empire is controlled by Darth Vader's personal commands, and political conflicts are resolved by individual combat between opposing leaders.[3]

   The thesis of this book is that many of the basic concepts that we use to describe our current government are the products of social nostalgia. The three branches of government, power and discretion, democracy, legitimacy, law, legal rights, human rights, and property are all ideas that originated in pre-administrative times and that derive much of their continuing appeal from their outdated origins. Of course, they are sedimented with many centuries of subsequent thought,[4] and are so central to our prevailing theories that they themselves have become causal factors, structuring our institutions and our interactions. But in the final analysis, it will be argued, these concepts are simply not the most useful or meaningful ones that we could find to describe contemporary government. Our thoughts fare like Miniver Cheevy, who "grew lean while he assailed the seasons."[5] They reveal an abiding distaste for our current situation, a distaste that is sufficiently profound that we have difficulty confronting the reality of the government we actually possess.

   Social nostalgia may seem like an odd notion, almost an oxymoron. The term 'nostalgia' generally refers to an individual experience, the longing that people feel for some previous period in their lives. It is often ascribed to the experience of loss—a village destroyed, a neighborhood transformed, a baseball team transferred.[6] Nostalgia of this sort can be a collective phenomenon if a group of people share the same experience, such as the conquest of their homeland by a foreign power. Raymond Williams notes a permanent pastoralism in English literary culture, as each generation mourned the loss of the rural world that its members knew in their own childhoods.[7]

   But the social nostalgia that generates our collective yearning for the pre-administrative state seems different, since no living person who has grown up in a contemporary Western nation can remember any different mode of governance. It must be based instead on a collective memory, in Maurice Halbwachs's terms,[8] an image of some prior era that is preserved and yet constructed by the written texts and continuing traditions of society. Such memories are common, but they are not self-activating; history also provides numerous examples of texts discarded, traditions abandoned, and entire epochs or social experiences consigned to oblivion. Our present yearning for the pre-administrative past seems motivated by our collective dissatisfaction with the particular system of governance that we have created, and in which we find ourselves inextricably immersed.[9]

   One should not imagine, however, that social nostalgia is a unique affliction of these unpoetic, overcomplicated times, or that in other eras, when the world was younger, people were better integrated and more optimistic. That would be social nostalgia. People always feel that their era is the oldest in the world—as indeed it always is—that life is dreary, and that the difficulties they confront are particularly severe. Their yearning for the past regularly dominates the present, dictating taste in art and architecture, and teaching virtue through archaic, misinterpreted examples. For the entirety of the past millennium, images of classical antiquity have held the Western world in thrall; Burckhardt found this to be the defining mentality of the fifteenth and sixteenth centuries,[10] Charles Homer Haskins then identified it as equally central to the twelfth century,[11] and R. W. Southern discovered the same inclination, albeit in somewhat more diluted form, in the tenth and eleventh centuries.[12] The stranglehold of classical antiquity was partially broken in the nineteenth century, and then only because it was displaced by a newfound yearning for the Middle Ages[13]—those same Middle Ages that had themselves been yearning for antiquity. Similar attitudes, of course, prevailed in antiquity itself. The Imperial Romans, the Republican Romans, the Hellenistic Greeks, even the Periclean Greeks were all persuaded of their own degeneracy. If we go back to the very dawn of the written tradition in the West, the time when, by all subsequent accounts, the world was young, we find this same ever-unrequited yearning.[14] In the eighth century B.C., *Works and Days*,[15] Hesiod's famous tantrum against his deadbeat brother, recounted four long eras that precede the present one, with golden people who never age and obtain food without working, silver people who enjoy a hundred-year-long childhood, bronze people made out of ash trees who have no need for agriculture, and "the godly race of the heroes who are called demigods,"[16] all of this leading up to Hesiod's own iron age, where people "will never cease from toil and misery by day or night, in constant distress, and the gods will give them harsh troubles."[17]

In a sense, then, the particular era that serves as the source of social nostalgia is irrelevant to the phenomenon itself; people will always find some prior period, whether real or imaginary, which they can use to flagellate the present. But in another sense, the choice is an important one, for the specific features of a prior, partially or entirely imagined past both reveal and influence the attitudes of those who yearn for it. This choice is rarely unconstrained, of course, since one period's nostalgia necessarily becomes incorporated into the cultural heritage of its successors. Thus, the same era may serve as the object of nostalgia for a number of successive periods, each period repainting the familiar image with the coloration of its own afflictions. Over time, the image becomes richly sedimented, and thus a source of real continuity. Such nostalgia-driven images exercise a profound effect upon the conceptual structure of society, becoming ever more difficult to analyze because they constitute the pre-empirical foundations on which the society's methods of analysis are based.

The Middle Ages

Our present nostalgia for the pre-administrative state venerates a variety of prior eras, including ancient Greece and Rome, pre-Columbian America, the Wild West, and Enlightenment Europe. Its most common object, however, is the era in which the past millennium began, and which we now describe as medieval. Many of the concepts that structure our theories of government developed in that period and derive their continuing appeal from our yearning for its perceived simplicity, poetry, faith, sense of adventure, and youthful vitality. These yearnings, of course, are generally not explicit, and present themselves as condemnations of the present rather than as invocations of the past. Nonetheless, the Middle Ages, or rather our socially constructed image of the Middle Ages, is frequently the silent but implicit element in the comparison, the collective memory that infuses our present theories about government.[18]

The legacy of the Middle Ages is complex, however. To some extent, this era's influence on modern political and legal concepts rests upon a firm foundation, for, as Joseph Strayer and, more recently, Alan Harding have observed,[19] many of our public institutions originated at that time. Medieval society created the first representative legislatures and established national courts that took evidence and dispensed justice according to pre-established rules.[20] The Magna Carta, our earliest codification of political rights, specified that these included trial by jury and due process of law.[21] The nation-state itself, a secular, centralized regime that commands the primary political loyalty of its subjects, emerged during this period, replacing the empire, the city-state, the feudal hierarchy, and the tribe.[22] Thus, the continued survival of the medieval mode of thought that spawned these institutions is not surprising, even though the nature of the institutions themselves may have been transformed by subsequent developments.

But there is much more to the Middle Ages and to our contemporary image of them. During this period, Europe's rude military encampments and rustic villages grew into cities, trade increased, and mercantile fortunes were amassed on a scale that had not been known for some eight hundred years.[23] Universities were founded and rapidly developed into institutions that dominated many of the newly developed cities and sent ideological shock waves rolling across the continent.[24] Vast cathedrals were constructed, great monasteries were established, stone castles sprang up everywhere. The military classes not only fought among themselves, but launched invasions against common enemies, expanding the boundaries of Christian Europe as they conquered Spain, the Mediterranean islands, Pomerania, Prussia, the eastern Baltic, and, however temporarily, the Holy Land.[25] Royal governments consolidated their control, and replaced their casually organized councils of leading warriors with staffs of tax collectors, record keepers, financial advisors, lawyers, and judges.[26]

These developments generally made people feel miserable. They railed at the bloated bulk and dreary pragmatism of their institutions. They con-

demned the uninspired, cumbersome rigidity that, despite such pragmatism, made those institutions ineffective. They yearned for times that were
not only simpler, but more joyous and more integrated. In other words,
they suffered from social nostalgia.

This feeling sometimes attached itself to Ancient Greece and Rome, and
sometimes to the more recent Carolingian Empire, but its most common,
most distinctive object was King Arthur's court at Camelot. From the
twelfth century to the fifteenth, a vast body of literature was created that
celebrated the adventures of King Arthur and his knights. Perhaps the
religious literature of the era was ultimately more extensive, but the
Arthurian literature is certainly the most sustained political fantasy of the
entire period.[27] Much of it was specifically designed to satisfy people's social nostalgia. It was set at the time when Roman rule was disappearing,
and the historical record disappearing with it, to produce a marvelously
empty space, an entrancing nothingness to be filled with unexplored for-
ests, mysterious castles, and a life of adventure free of all the dreary realities and disconcerting developments of medieval society.[28] The political
complexities of medieval times are nowhere to be found at Camelot.
Arthur is the ruler of Britain, but he never devotes any time to administration; he never does anything as drearily mundane as collect taxes, appoint judges, or issue promulgations. He certainly never employs a lawyer.
The annoyances of manufacturing and commerce are also absent; there are
no merchants to contend with, no peasants to control, no crops to manage, and virtually no money.[29] In a very real sense, therefore, Camelot
served as an escapist fantasy from the initial development of the administrative state in Western European nations.

It is perhaps this very feature that has preserved its appeal over the many
years which followed. The legend of Camelot was still vibrant enough to
be taken seriously by Malory[30] and several Spanish writers[31] in the late fifteenth and early sixteenth centuries. There was a subsequent decline in interest, marked by the satire of Cervantes,[32] but the fascination re-ignited
in the nineteenth and early twentieth centuries, as indicated by the pre-
Raphaelite painters,[33] the music of Richard Wagner,[34] the writings of Lord
Tennyson,[35] Matthew Arnold,[36] Walter Scott,[37] Algernon Swinburne,[38]
Benjamin Disraeli,[39] Mark Twain,[40] and Edwin Arlington Robinson,[41] and
by the explicitly Arthurian imagery invoked by the creator of the Boy
Scouts.[42] In our own times, the theme lives on in popular novels,[43] a
Broadway play,[44] a variety of motion pictures,[45] a chain of pizza restau-
rants, and a Las Vegas hotel,[46] while its more general influence lies heavily
on the entire genre of contemporary fantasy. The six long, very popular
Star Wars movies, although ostensibly science fiction, are heavily
Arthurian in atmosphere and spirit, while the *Lord of the Rings* trilogy[47]—
which recently became three very popular and even longer movies—was

actually written by a medieval scholar. When Jacqueline Kennedy sought to characterize her husband's administration, a week after his assassination, it was not the economic revival that he engineered, not his successful resolution of the Cuban missile crisis, not his tireless campaign for civil rights legislation, not the Peace Corps, and certainly not his efforts to increase employment, alleviate poverty, and modernize governmental operations through administrative action that she chose to accentuate. Nor did she use the New Frontier, Kennedy's own forward-looking and very American sobriquet. No, the image that Mrs. Kennedy insisted that her family's favorite journalist, Theodore H. White, invoke to describe the Kennedy administration in his exclusive *Life* magazine interview was that "one brief shining moment that was known as Camelot."[48]

It is a further thesis of this book that our theories about government are not only derived from the Middle Ages, but represent a mixture of the political thought of the Middle Ages and the political fantasies of that era, in particular the legend of Camelot. Our social nostalgia for the pre-administrative state, as specifically focused on the medieval world, thus preserves that period's own social nostalgia. It does so because realism and fantasy were fused, profoundly and inextricably, in the alembic of people's minds at the time, and thus projected forward as a single body of thought. In addition, when we look back upon a prior era, driven by our own social nostalgia, we tend to forget that people then felt miserable, that they sought relief in their own nostalgic fantasies, and so we assume the linkages they forged represent a coherent, integrated vision. And finally, we preserve this mixture of realism and fantasy because the fantasy, a sedimented image communicated across time, appeals to us as profoundly as it appealed to its bygone originators.

The Nature of the Thesis

This thesis bears a certain resemblance to Raymond Williams's idea of keywords in Western culture,[49] to W. B. Gallie's and William Connolly's essentially contested concepts,[50] to Daniel Rodgers's contested truths,[51] and to Terence Ball's critical conceptual history.[52] It shares the view that words shape our concepts and that concepts shape our theories, and also agrees that these words and concepts possess inherent ambiguities because they encompass our deepest value conflicts, and are sedimented with the multiple meanings that have been attached to them over many centuries of use. It further agrees with Connolly that these concepts generally possess an identifiable core, that their multiple meanings bear a Wittgensteinian family resemblance.[53] But this thesis goes on to assert that each concept's identifiable core is so replete with prior meaning that it dumps those meanings indiscriminately into any setting where it is invoked. As a result, our conceptual categories bear the indelible imprint of the prior era when they took shape[54] and control our current controversies in ways that we neither desire nor expect.

Of course, most words in our language have pre-modern origins, and we use them without serious disadvantage, even when their underlying concept has been transformed by subsequent developments. From classical to relatively recent times, for example, people believed that physical reality was composed of four essential elements: air, water, earth, and fire.[55] This taxonomy, however evocative, is now regarded as lacking any scientific value. Nonetheless, we have been able to adapt the word 'element' for contemporary scientific purposes, and even occasional references to the older meaning of the term do not create confusion. Journalists can speak of a mountain climber braving the elements without anyone thinking that they are challenging the validity of the Mendelevian system. But as Wittgenstein insisted, basic terminology reflects the forms of life that generated it.[56] The contention in this book is that our continued use of pre-modern concepts for modern government embodies the thought processes of a prior era, its way of conceiving the world, of creating categories, and of determining the relative significance of different issues. As such, these concepts are an impediment to understanding, and control our current thinking in ways that are genuinely counterproductive. It is as if we never quite managed to formulate a verbal description for substances whose atoms have a given number of protons, and were induced by the pre-modern meaning of the word 'element' to lose track of our own best theories and keep searching for physical regularities among air, water, earth, and fire.

Even if this admittedly controversial contention is correct, however, it seems implausible to suggest that we can actually abandon the keywords and contested concepts that have been developed and deployed during the preceding millennium. In fact, all the evidence that argues for their obsolescence simultaneously makes their abandonment unlikely, for if pre-modern concepts possess such durability when contradicted by events, how could they be so quickly overthrown? To observe that they are dysfunctional, or that they experience increasing strains as the administrative state progresses, is hardly a sufficient answer. The force of social nostalgia sustains them, and the range of historically meaningful debates that they embody ensures their continuing survival.

It would also be implausible to suggest that our political science and legal concepts could be displaced by something called reality, that is, by an accurate, unmediated description of the modern state. Terms such as branches of government, the social contract, power, even rights, are metaphorical, of course, but all thought is metaphorical. The effort to replace metaphor with some objectively demonstrable theory is what Hilary Put-

nam describes as the fallacy of metaphysical realism.[57] Even if one does not
want to accept Putnam's analysis with respect to the physical sciences, it
seems unavoidable with respect to the human sciences, for at least two reasons. First, the events studied by the human sciences rarely yield to quan-
tification, and can only be rendered comprehensible by more impression-
istic models. Second, these events engage our emotions more intensely,
thus setting off associations between the subject under study and a wide
range of collateral and equally emotion-laden issues. Any theory built on
such impressions and associations will necessarily be metaphorical in character.[58]

Consequently, this book does not suggest that we should abandon our
current political science and legal concepts, nor that these concepts can be
replaced by objectively valid ones. Its purpose is considerably more modest; it is, in essence, an extended thought experiment. As such, it is directed to scholars, policy analysts, and judges, that is, to those whose role
is to regard modern government from a conceptual and at least partially
detached perspective. What would happen, it inquires, if we were to
bracket, or hold in abeyance, our existing concepts, if we were to perceive
them as the much-embellished relics of a prior era rather than the building
blocks of contemporary political science and legal analysis? Would we gain
any insights into the nature of the administrative state that we have
created, and in which we find ourselves immersed? What would happen,
moreover, if we were to search for a new set of metaphors, ones that were
the products of our own era rather than a prior one? Could these alternative conceptions provide ways to clarify our thoughts, and thereby free us
from the unnecessary implications of our inherited ideas? Could they help
policy analysts and academics achieve new perspectives on which they
could base recommendations for improving governmental operations?
Could they help judges reach decisions that better achieved their intended
purposes?

The idea of bracketing a concept is taken from Husserl's phenomenology. It is the process of setting aside the validity claims of the "sciences
which relate to this natural world."[59] This does not involve refuting such
validity claims, but simply suspending them for a delimited period of time.
"[T]hough they stand never so firm to me," Husserl writes, "though they
fill me with wondering admiration, though I am far from any thought of
objecting to them in the least degree, I disconnect them all, I make absolutely no use of their standards, I do not appropriate a single one of the
propositions that enter into their systems."[60] The term 'disconnect' is an
evocative one, and suggests an analogy to an electrical appliance such as a
television set. Ordinarily, the television sits in the middle of the living
room, a source of news and entertainment for the entire family. If Mom
and Dad decide to disconnect the set, it will still be there, just as it always

was. But as long as it remains unplugged, or disconnected, it can be regarded as an object. Suddenly, one perceives the play of reflected light across the screen, the scratches on its side, its contrast with the living room's traditional decor. One also becomes aware of the amount of time the family spends in front of it, the way it structures family life, and the kinds of information and entertainment one obtains from it. These insights into a thing's appearance and one's relationship to it are the sorts of insights that we obtain from the phenomenological process of disconnecting the thing's normal operation. Without actually extirpating it from our minds—a practical impossibility for the basic and familiar terms under consideration here—we can bracket it, that is, suspend its claim to validity and pursue the thought experiment of considering alternatives.

Bracketing our inherited ideas—setting them aside entirely and trying to describe the underlying subject in other terms—may seem like an extreme solution. But these ideas are so influential, so historically sedimented, that it may be the only way for us to obtain control over their claims, their imagery, and their insinuations. It should not be argued, in response, that our inherited ideas have some uses, regardless of their inaccuracies, that they should not be bracketed because they retain some meaningful application. Of course they have some uses—they are a thousand years old, and have been continuously reinterpreted throughout their long existence. But "some use" is not a valid justification for descriptive metaphors. The point of such metaphors is to create a comprehensive framework for analysis and evaluation, to provide an instrumentality of thought that functions across the whole range of its application. The theory that the earth is flat has some use—one needs nothing more to design a garden or to build a house—but it is not a useful conception because it fails in other aspects of its asserted range. Progress was made by bracketing the idea of a flat earth and trying to conceive alternatives.

The difficulty with saving inherited ideas because they have some use, or trying to refurbish them so that they can be retained despite the felt need for redecoration, is that these ideas are far too potent to be domesticated in this fashion. They are the genii and demons of our mental landscape, creating, transforming, and distorting it before our eyes and beyond our will. Terms like democracy, legitimacy, law, or rights structure our conception of government in highly specific ways, making conceptual incisions that cannot easily be reconfigured. Consider, for example, the idea of rights. It proclaims an organic unity between moral constraints on government and legal claims established by statute, and it divides these constraints and claims from the policy initiatives of the general populace and their elected representatives. At the same time, it generates an image of individuals as possessing some inherent ability to impose such constraints or present such claims, thus advancing strong assertions about people's relationship to government and to each other. None of this can be readily controlled by definition because the scholar's invocation of an idea such as rights calls forth the cumulative voices of our entire intellectual tradition, a booming chorus that will drown out any judicious comments and careful qualifications that the individual scholar might suggest.[61]

In fact, many scholars do not try to cabin the influence of inherited ideas with definitions, but rather rely on these ideas as arguments. After all, it is always nice to have a booming chorus on one's side. Even the most insightful and systematic thinkers frequently succumb to this temptation, whether because they are consciously drawing on the force of these ideas, or unconsciously allowing themselves to be controlled by that same force. Alexander Bickel opens his famous book with the sentence: "The least dangerous branch of the American government is the most extraordinarily powerful court of law the world has ever known."[62] But the dramatic irony of this statement depends on the implicit comparison of the Supreme Court to Congress, and to the president and all the federal departments and agencies taken as a unit, and Bickel fails to explain why this is the proper comparison, relying instead on his use of the term 'branch.' Michael Mann begins his magisterial discussion of social power by defining it as either the "mastery exercised over other people" or the ability of people to exercise joint control "over third parties or over nature,"[63] without pausing to consider why one would treat the varied relationships comprised by this definition as a single entity. Amy Gutmann and Dennis Thompson, in their leading discussion of deliberative democracy, declare that democracy is "a natural and reasonable way" to live with moral disagreement "since it is a conception of government that accords equal respect to the moral claims of each citizen, and is therefore morally justifiable from the perspective of each citizen."[64] But the authors fail to explain why they define this twenty-five-hundred-year-old term in a manner that excludes any government prior to the twentieth century, and that incorporates a highly controversial assumption that democracy either implies, or inevitably achieves, the universal moral approbation of its citizens. Jürgen Habermas declares that the "legitimacy of statutes is measured . . . according to whether they have come about through a rational legislative process"[65] without considering why such legitimacy should serve as a standard for either moral or effective government.

With respect to the concept of law, Theodore Lowi condemns liberalism as "hostile to law,"[66] but fails to tell us why such hostility merits condemnation. H.L.A. Hart, while rejecting the idea that law is equivalent to a coercive order from the sovereign, states, nonetheless: "where there is law, there human conduct is made in some sense non-optional or obligatory."[67] He never discusses why it is important to distinguish such actions by the government from other governmental actions that are regularly implemented by statutes, or "laws," such as creating institutions, providing benefits or subsidies, allocating resources, and issuing hortatory or honorary declarations. Ronald Dworkin defines rights as "political trumps held by individuals" and continues by saying that "individuals have rights when, for some reason, a collective goal is not a sufficient justification for denying them what they wish, as individuals, to have or to do."[68] He does not tell us why rights must be held by individuals, as opposed to groups, or why a right is something that is capable of being "held" in the first place. Robert Nozick states that the "central core of the notion of a property right in X . . . is the right to determine what shall be done with X"[69] and argues for severe restrictions on the authority of the administrative state so that this right is not impaired. But he never explains what is important about the ability to determine what is to be done with something, nor does he ever tell us the limits or extent of X. To be sure, one cannot question every concept, or aspire to the rigor of quantum electrodynamics in political science and legal studies. But the concepts listed here are so redolent with ancient meanings, and play so prominent a role in the arguments being advanced, that they often appear to be speaking through the scholar, and imposing the imagery and norms of a prior, bygone era on our efforts to understand the government we actually possess.

Nor is this a problem that is restricted to the realm of scholarship. Few elected or appointed officials read contemporary academic literature, and even fewer cite it, but that is not necessarily a measure of the scholarship's importance. Scholars strongly affect what is taught in school; while contemporary politics also plays a role, and a large one in totalitarian societies, the basic curriculum is largely a redaction of scholars' cumulative work. Going beyond such causal influences, scholarship can be understood as an explicit expression of the conceptual process by which a modern society understands itself, and formulates its policies and plans. When we look at political science and legal scholarship, we are not seeing the self-contained ceremonies of a cloistered, recondite elite, but rather the visible and audible manifestations of comprehensive social efforts to determine and achieve a good life for ourselves. All such efforts are affected by concepts like democracy, legitimacy, law, and rights. Besides, these concepts are not restricted to scholarly works, the way more specialized and arcane concepts such as functionalism or ethnomethodology may be. Political participants use them regularly in debate, in collective planning efforts, and in their own less visible but hardly nonexistent thought processes.

The basic point is that we enter this third millennium with a set of concepts about government that were developed in the first few centuries of the preceding one. Those concepts, moreover, were cobbled together from ones that developed during the first millennium, and during even earlier times when people did not know that they were living in any millennium at all. Worse still, it can be said, in defense of the people at the beginning of the second millennium, that they were at least being true to their own values when they allowed themselves to be controlled by earlier ideas. They believed in the sanctity of tradition; for them, the past was directly applicable to the present and possessed the validating quality of age. We believe in progress, not tradition, and we recognize the enormous differences between prior societies and our own. We have no reason to be bound by previous ideas. The millennium we are entering offers great opportunities and poses great dangers—opportunities and dangers that we now know, unlike our predecessors at the beginning of the previous millennium, that we can neither predict nor imagine. To prepare ourselves for these vast developments, we need, at the very least, a set of concepts that accurately depicts our current reality and reflects our own genuine values about our relationship to the past and to the future.

The Method

Doubt and Bracketing

With the thesis presented, it is now necessary to say something about this book's methodology. The central element in this methodology, so central that it needed to be stated above as part of the thesis, is to bracket some of the concepts we have inherited from the pre-administrative era, to set them aside and conduct the thought experiment of describing the government we actually possess without relying on them. But how should the concepts to be subjected to this process be selected? Once again, we can look to Husserl, who employs a technique that he calls Cartesian doubt.[70] Descartes decided to begin by doubting everything, but quickly retreated from this stance, first by relying on thought itself, and second by relying on God.[71] Husserl adopts a more unalloyed form of Cartesian doubt, arguing that we can initiate a process of bracketing all reality by the conscious mental exercise of doubting it.[72] The present inquiry is not designed to call all reality into doubt, of course, but only to challenge the centrality of certain inherited ideas. Like reality itself, however, these ideas present themselves to us as "given," that is, as part of an established order that we generally accept without reflection. In most cases, we simply assume that concepts like the three branches of government, power, discretion, law, rights, and democracy represent useful categories; even when we are trying to define them with precision we do not doubt their existence or utility. To call them into question requires real mental effort. It requires us to nurture doubt—not the Cartesian doubt that Husserl describes, because we are not questioning all reality, but quasi-Cartesian doubt, because we are questioning particular concepts that, within a delimited field of inquiry, have a quality of givenness analogous to that possessed by reality in general.

This study will treat a familiar political or legal concept as eliciting quasi-Cartesian doubt if it displays two characteristics. The first is that it evolved in the pre-modern era, and was organically connected to the general conception of the state, or government, that prevailed at that time. The second is that its usage in contemporary accounts of government seems to produce a sense of dissonance or incongruity, a grinding of intellectual gears, when applied to a modern administrative state. The point is not to disprove the concept, or to marshal arguments against it, since these concepts, given their essentially metaphorical character, cannot really be disproved. Rather, analysis will be directed to the concept's fit or feel. Does it carry with it pre-modern associations that lead scholars to condemn administrative government on pre-analytic grounds, or to make distinctions that run counter to the structure of the government we actually possess? If a concept displays these characteristics, doubts about its continued utility should arise in our minds; we should begin to question its analytic value, no matter how basic and familiar it appears.

Once a concept elicits this quasi-Cartesian doubt, the next step is to bracket it, to set aside its validity claims, as discussed above, and explore the possibility that we might describe its subject matter differently. The alternative descriptions that will be suggested in this book are drawn from modern business practices and from mechanical and electrical engineering. Of course, government is neither business nor machinery; the proposed alternatives are heuristics, designed to provide illumination, not demonstrable truth. They have been chosen because they are aggressively contemporary. There is no point bracketing our medieval and Arthurian concepts of government only to replace them with images that carry the very same implications that we are trying to excise. Using contemporary images is a means of protecting ourselves against the beckoning voice of our collectively remembered past.

The search for these new concepts does not lead into a conceptual abyss. Instead, it provides validation for many of the existing efforts of contemporary scholars and political participants. During the past several decades, numerous scholars in political science, sociology, and law have managed to master our collective distaste for modern times and look at our existing system of governance with calmer, more sustained attention. Their work has begun to expose the prosaic machinery of public administration, the grimy devices and convoluted circuits that constitute our means of managing ourselves. But this work has placed itself, quite consciously, at the level below general political science and legal theory. To some extent, moreover, it has been constrained by that theory's long-established categories. Among political participants, the same few decades have seen impressive creativity in the development of governmental strategies and programs, but these developments, constrained by those same categories, have been limited in scope, and have not been recognized in general political debate. Holding our inherited categories of thought in abeyance will reveal that the seemingly mundane scholarship of public administration constitutes a new political science and legal theory for modern government, while certain political developments point the way toward far-reaching solutions to our present quandaries.

The Criteria for Alternative Imagery

After contemporary imagery has been used to generate a new heuristic, the next question is whether this alternative description is superior to the existing concept it is designed to displace. It certainly resolves the quasi-Cartesian doubt that attaches to this existing concept because of its premodern origins, but does it also remove the doubts generated by the awkward fit between the existing concept and the situation it describes? To determine whether the thought experiment truly provides new insights into the nature of modern government, the alternative concept needs to be systematically evaluated. The criteria that this study will employ are whether the alternative captures our emotional commitments, whether it reflects the heuristic character of theory, and whether it facilitates a mode of explanation that will be referred to as microanalysis. While these criteria can be derived from the application of phenomenology to social science,[73] they are presented here as intuitively plausible ways to evaluate a conceptual or metaphorical image of political reality.

The requirement that an explanatory concept reflect our emotional commitments is derived from the idea that all theory is socially constructed. While this view remains controversial with respect to natural science, it has become sufficiently widespread to serve as a working premise in the social sciences.[74] Because social science theories cannot aspire to objective or transcultural veracity, any theory we develop should serve our culturally determined, or intersubjective purposes;[75] it should explain things that we believe are important to explain, and do so in a way that enables us to improve our lives.[76] In order to make this determination, it is necessary to identify our commitments.[77] The commitment that will guide this inquiry is the one that has been regarded as central to our political morality since the Middle Ages: that the government's purpose is to benefit its citizens. This principle can be operationalized by considering the nature of the benefits. Scholars as diverse as Henry Shue and Robert Cooter suggest that these benefits are security, prosperity, and liberty.[78] Shue, who is describing rights rather than benefits, identifies subsistence rather than prosperity as the third value. Since the effort here is to identify policy goals, not basic rights, the minimal goal of subsistence should be replaced with the related, but more aspirational goal of prosperity, or affluence. The manner by which these goals are reached is important as well. We want the government to be effective in achieving its goals, we want it to do so efficiently, which means with the lowest possible expenditure of resources, and we want it to do so fairly, which means that benefits are reasonably distributed, and limits are placed on the sacrifices individuals are required to undergo.

No effort will be made in this study to justify these commitments, which is the reason they will be described as merely emotional, and not as normative, that is, as elements of a coherent moral system.[79] Providing such a justification would involve the entire field of political philosophy, which is far beyond the limits of this study. Instead, the existence and centrality of these commitments will be taken as empirical fact about our own society, and used as a criterion for evaluating the concepts under consideration without further analysis.

Another commitment, it has been argued, that strongly motivates academic inquiry is social nostalgia. This book is designed to separate social nostalgia from our genuine commitments and to reject it as a basis for selecting research projects or framing recommendations. While social nostalgia possesses a certain aesthetic appeal, it lacks the intensely felt and widely held character of our commitments to security, prosperity, and liberty. It is a clandestine commitment that few scholars or political participants would admit to in this pragmatic, instrumental era, a sort of conceptual narcotic that is smuggled into scholarship or policy analysis to assuage our distress about modernity. Alternative descriptions of the modern state will thus be judged not only by their ability to fulfill our genuine emotional commitments, but also by their ability to interdict intellectual contraband such as social nostalgia.

The second major criterion for judging the value of alternative concepts is the extent to which these concepts signal their heuristic character. Virtually all the terms and concepts that we employ in political and legal theory are heuristics, or metaphors, rather than observable features of the world. The power that our muscles produce, or that surges through electric lines, can be safely treated as a real thing; the power exercised by political leaders is a metaphorical characterization. Statutes are real enough, but law is a metaphor; elections are real but democracy is a mental image; the president, Congress, and the federal judiciary are certainly observable entities, but the three branches of government exist only in our minds. The problem is that such well-established concepts, which we have developed and employed over the course of many centuries, tend to become reified. People in Western culture have been writing, talking, thinking, and arguing about power, democracy, law, and the three branches of government for hundreds of years, and this ubiquity of usage tends to make these concepts seem like naturally occurring categories. Moreover, since everyone wants to claim that their own theory fits within, or captures the essence of, these blessed categories, many different arguments become coagulated into a single concept. The result is not only reified metaphors, but awkward, counter-intuitive metaphors that owe their continued impression of coherence to this conceptual coagulation.

A related difficulty is that these reified metaphors induce observers to overinterpret their data, to offer explanations that are not justified by the evidence on which the observer purports to rely. This tendency is motivated by the effort to find meaning, the intensely felt desire to place events in a framework that seems coherent to the observer. Because intelligent observers can always devise explanations that support their pre-empirical interpretive theory, the use of such interpretations reveals only the potential limits of the theory, and the intellectual power of the theorist. It does not necessarily provide the most plausible explanation for the information available. Reified, conceptually coagulated metaphors are engines of overinterpretation because these metaphors impose unnecessarily elaborate explanations on the data, and demand still further explanations to maintain their rigid, awkwardly shaped boundaries.

It is therefore a criterion of a concept's value that it announces its heuristic character, that it declares itself to be an image or a metaphor, thus repelling reification, conceptual coagulation, and overinterpretation. This is partially achieved by the mere novelty of the alternative, its separation from a culturally embedded intellectual tradition. Beyond this, metaphors concede their heuristic character when they are relatively dull and unimaginative, when they lack the vividness that makes them seem like real entities. Thus, a collateral advantage of the commercial and mechanistic metaphors that will be offered in this book, in addition to their modern character, is that they are sufficiently mundane to discourage reification. They present themselves as convenient ways of thinking about complex relationships, and nothing more.

The problem of overinterpretation can be further minimized by employing heuristics that are not only uninteresting, but also uninformative and naive. While neither uninformativeness nor naivete is generally regarded as a conceptual virtue, they serve as methods of self-restraint, reminders to proceed with caution in the explanatory process. An uninformative category is one that uses its distinctive term as a placeholder, rather than attempting to define it. The more informative and sophisticated the definition, and the more pre-analytic assertions it incorporates, the greater the danger of overinterpretation; the weaker and more uninformative the term, the more it serves to simply demarcate the subject matter of the particular analysis, and the less overinterpretation it involves. Heuristics whose boundaries are demarcated by uninformative categories are less likely to be regarded as naturally occurring entities.

A naive heuristic is one that relies on ordinary language, more specifically the language used by the participants in the activity under discussion. This does not preclude the invocation of specialized theories of human behavior, but it demands that such theories be specifically introduced and justified, rather than serving as a starting point for the analysis. What will tend to be precluded are false consciousness arguments, that is, claims that social actors are deluded about their own genuine interest and advantage. Such assertions stray too far from naive, uninformative categories, and indulge in excessive overinterpretation. Once an observer is unencumbered by his subjects' own identification of their interests, he is unlikely to discern those interests accurately and much more likely to project his own predilections onto them through the interpretive process.

While the danger of reification suggests that bracketing familiar terms, and replacing them with more modern alternatives, will always be conceptually advantageous, the virtue of naive heuristics suggests an exactly opposite approach. In a field such as politics, existing concepts, precisely because they are existing, are the ones that social actors employ to characterize their own behavior. The conceptual coagulation that characterizes many of these concepts may encumber them with multiple meanings and uncertain boundaries, but it also provides a continuity and emotive depth that encourages their use. When scholars, policy analysts, or judges share that usage, they are taking the actors' explanation of their behavior at face value; when they impose new concepts, they run the risk of overinterpretation. It is certainly invigorating to recharacterize social behavior in terms that dissolve existing concepts, scrape away the past's encrusted sediments, and advance into a new clear space that stands at some remove from ordinary language. Having done so, however, there is nothing to stop the scholar from drifting off into the speculative stratosphere of overinterpretation.

One way to avoid this difficulty is to replace the existing concepts that have been bracketed with naive alternatives, that is, equally familiar ones from other contexts. Such familiarity provides some assurance that the new concepts are also ones that social actors use and understand. Naive alternatives that serve this purpose are often available because ordinary discourse is complex, containing many different strands that are separated for some purposes and combined for others. In fact, if one chooses sufficiently familiar concepts, it may turn out that social actors sometimes think about the particular subject in those terms, even if they ordinarily use the more traditional, historically sedimented ones. It may even turn out that the traditional concepts are invoked in public settings because of their historical associations, but that other concepts are used more frequently for daily problem solving. That is another reason why the alternative descriptions offered in this book are drawn from our contemporary experience in business and technology.

The third criterion is that alternative concepts for describing government can be regarded as preferable to the existing ones if they provide the framework for a mode of explanation that will be described in this book as microanalysis.[80] A study of modern government is necessarily concerned with institutions. The microanalysis of institutions attempts to trace the actual pathways of individual decision making and related action through an institutional structure. Abjuring generalizations and attributions of behavior to the institution as a whole, it begins with individuals, identifying their specific actions that are relevant to the subject under study. It describes these actions in terms of the individuals' actual positions in the institution—their assigned tasks, the scope of their authority, the forces acting on them, the information that is available to them, and the consequences of their actions. In assessing individuals' response to their position, it avoids highly contestable claims about their motivations, such as the claim that they are entirely rational or that they are not rational at all. Rather, it acknowledges that people act from a mixture of rationality and irrationality, self-interest and altruism, ideology and convention. Its only strong assertion is that this mixture also includes the phenomenologically derived motivation that people desire to create meaning for themselves, and will sometimes sacrifice other values in pursuit of this objective.

The microanalytic approach to institutions offers a solution to the famous macro-micro problem that has long bedeviled social science, that is, the problem of creating explanatory linkages between individual action and collective behavior.[81] Microanalysis begins from the premise of methodological individualism but recognizes the existence of emergent institutional behavior. It acknowledges that some emergent institutional behaviors arise because similar forces act upon each separate individual, just as rational actor theory claims. But it also suggests that other behaviors arise from the ideological, conventional, and ritualized beliefs that are intersubjectively communicated to individuals by others in the institution, and then expressed through coordinated action. In addition, individuals' desire to achieve meaning, their need for belonging and a sense that they are doing something useful, often leads them to act on the institution's behalf, and to think in institutionally established ways, even absent any conscious effort at coordination.

Normative Considerations

The methodology suggested above is not intended as an intellectual game, but as a means of improving our understanding of the government we actually possess, and thereby increasing our ability to improve that government itself. From this perspective, the methodology may raise several normative concerns that are important to address: first, that developing more accurate descriptions of government only reinforces the status quo and forecloses comprehensive criticisms; second, that such improved descriptions are purely verbal changes, with no normative significance; third, that inherited concepts protect important underlying values that would be endangered by their suspension, even as a thought experiment; and fourth, that the particular alternatives suggested create a mechanistic, technocratic image of government that ignores important values. These objections will be considered in turn.

Of these normative concerns, the first must be partially conceded. This book does not offer any general critique of the administrative state; its premise, rather, is that the essentially administrative character of the modern state is irreversible.[82] Many modifications are possible within that basic framework; certain functions can be privatized,[83] the level of regulation can be altered,[84] and command and control regulation can be replaced by more flexible modalities,[85] but none of these will alter the state's basic character. To recommend that we abandon the administrative state in its entirety is so unrealistic a proposal that it can only be saved from risible irrelevance by being treated as a dramatic way of stating more delimited critiques. The same may be said for the recently fashionable position that globalization will make the nation-state irrelevant. While there is much evidence for globalization, there is little indication that it is producing this effect. Moreover, as Philip Bobbitt suggests, even if the nation-state is replaced by other forms of governance, these novel structures are likely to be as administrative as their predecessor.[86] This concession to brute reality, however, does not preclude less sweeping criticisms. In fact, a better understanding of the government we actually possess serves as a useful predicate to either condemnation of specific practices or constructive recommendations for reform. Certainly, the vast range of existing practices and possible alternatives that exists within the ambit of administrative government allows ample room for wide-ranging normative debate. The proposed methodology thus accommodates condemnations and recommendations that are as comprehensive as the critic chooses, so long as they do not rise to attacks on the administrative state in its entirety. Administrative governance represents the horizon of our present political experience,[87] and genuine efforts to attack or improve our government, as opposed to self-indulgent ululations of social nostalgia, can be formulated only within its extensive, albeit finite confines.

The benefits of improved understanding for normative discourse serves as a response to the second concern as well. This study, while primarily descriptive, is not designed to purify our language, but to formulate usable and productive ways for thinking about our collective enterprise of governance. Because our theories are socially constructed, description and prescription are not the mutually exclusive modalities of Humean epistemology. Rather, they are permeable categories, different styles of analysis that serve related purposes. Descriptions are inevitably committed descriptions. They are motivated by our emotional commitments because we will choose to describe only those things about which we care, and they are controlled by our culturally contingent vision of the world. Thus, the effort to describe our government simultaneously implies, at the very least, a potential strategy for improving it—indeed, even the effort to describe past governments is often motivated by a desire to improve the present one. Conversely, prescriptions, at least in scholarship, are not merely declarations of the author's will but possess a cognitive component because they engage our commitments and provide insights about the subject matter they attempt to alter. Thus, a prescription is often an effective way to describe a given situation; by recommending improvements in a statute, for example, the scholar develops and communicates a deeper understanding of the statute's present character. This latter point is related to Weber's insight that understanding, or *verstehen*, in the human sciences at least, cannot be achieved by distant observation, but requires participation in the subject matter.[88]

The third objection to the approach adopted in this study is that familiar concepts such as democracy, law, and rights may provide rhetorical bulwarks for values with which they have been traditionally associated, values that would otherwise be open to assault. To bracket them, even as a thought experiment, thus threatens to undermine their continued vitality. It is all very well to say that scholars or policy analysts could achieve greater understanding of modern government if they replaced existing concepts with novel ones. But suppose political participants undertook a similar thought experiment, or were otherwise convinced by the thought experiment undertaken by observers. Would this create a risk that these participants, having been convinced that the historically sedimented concepts connected with our cherished values are analytically unsound, would then reject the values themselves? Would it therefore be preferable to leave our familiar concepts undisturbed?

This is essentially an argument for continued mystification of political actors, and there are at least two serious difficulties with it. First, it is inherently retrograde, because any social concept, no matter how detrimental, possesses some connection to other concepts that we deem desirable. If this becomes an argument for the concept's retention, then we have forbidden conceptual developments in our theory of government. The fear that we will throw out the baby with the bathwater can ultimately leave us waist-deep, at the very least, in dirty bathwater, probably a much greater risk than the risk that we will actually discard a baby. Second, at the epistemological level, deciding to purposefully mystify another person for that person's own good implies that one is much more knowledgeable or mature than that other person. It is a stance that adults often take toward children, or that therapists take toward the disturbed. But why is a scholar or policy analyst justified in treating political participants in this fashion? In most cases, the participants are just as intelligent, just as knowledgeable, and just as concerned about genuine social values. There is no obvious reason to believe that they will become so confused by reconceptualization that they will succumb to arguments that undermine their basic commitments.

Finally, it might be objected that microanalysis has a tendency to sound mechanistic and inhuman, particularly since business and engineering concepts will be invoked in this study to facilitate its application. But it must be recalled that one of the core premises of microanalysis is that individuals are motivated by a multitude of different desires, including the desire to create meaning, that they are thinking individuals, not bundles of self-interest or cogs in a machine. The mechanistic character of the analysis that will be presented in this book comes from another source—the effort to bracket the familiar terminology of government. This effort has a mechanistic or inhuman quality because it reflects the transition to a modern administrative state, a transition, it must be admitted, where something genuine and appealing has been lost. Small towns that governed themselves possessed a true integrity, a sense of homey coherence that was lost when they were ripped apart by freeways, strip malls, and telecommunication networks. The literate and lively political debate of coffee houses and town councils was truly more engaging than the radio talk shows, sound bites, and staged interviews that have replaced it. And to go further back, and deeper down, a reigning monarch can confer a sense of temporal redemption on a government official or a private person that is simply not available in contemporary times. It is nice to get a letter, or an appointment, from the president, but to be recognized, trusted, or commended by a king is an infinitely more profound experience. The intensity of that experience is reflected in the literature and fairy tales of our predecessor eras, and exercises a continuing if dimly felt appeal to the present day.

But no matter how appealing the world that we have lost, the point is that we have lost it, and it cannot be retrieved. To mourn is one thing, but to immolate ourselves upon our sorrow is another thing entirely. It is not only impractical, but ultimately unrewarding. A revival of the past is not the past itself; what was beautiful in its original and genuine existence becomes monstrous when one attempts to bring it back to life. Many horror movies are based on this principle. Robert Musil depicts a related horror in *A Man without Qualities*, set in 1913, when he describes the home of Paul Arnheim, a Prussian plutocrat. Arnheim, who turns out to be Jewish, has a room filled with Baroque and Gothic sculpture:

As it happens, the Catholic Church (for which Arnheim had a great love) depicts its saints and standard-bearers of Goodness mostly in poses of joy, even ecstasy. Here were saints dying in all kinds of postures, with the soul wringing out of the body as if it were squeezing water out of a piece of laundry. All those gestures of arms crossed like sabers, of twisted necks, taken from their original surroundings and brought together in an alien space, gave the impression of a catatonics' ward in a lunatic asylum. . . . [Arnheim] felt how morality had once glowed with an ineffable fire, but now even a mind like his could do no more than stare into the burned-out clinkers.[89]

The Administrative State

Defining the Administrative State

Having stated the thesis and the method, one final requirement before proceeding is to clarify the empirical claim on which the thesis depends in its entirety, namely, the claim that our society has experienced a qualitative change in government, a change so profound that it renders many of our well-established, treasured concepts obsolete. Like Twain's Connecticut Yankee, who began by building a railroad from Camelot to London and introducing other modern conveniences, and ended up using the technology he introduced to slaughter all the knights of England, the administrative state has annihilated its predecessor.[90] But what was the precise nature of this change, and when, precisely, did it occur? It has been argued above that administrative governmental mechanisms began to evolve during the Middle Ages, and were sufficiently prominent at that time to produce the abreaction of Arthurian fantasy. In what sense, then, can the administrative state be treated as a subsequent development? And how can our current circumstances demand a reconceptualization of government and law that would not have been necessary during the earlier centuries when the administrative state was taking shape?

Obviously, there was no day or year or decade when government suddenly and definitively became administrative. One way to reconcile this observation with the claim of qualitative change is to identify continuous trends, acting over long periods of time, whose cumulative effects produce a palpable change at some defined and delimited juncture. As the homespun image of the straw that broke the camel's back suggests, decisive moments do occur, but they are made decisive by the process that proceeded them and the events that follow, just as the significance of the crucial straw is not attributable to any of its inherent features, but only to its impact on the unfortunate ungulate. Following Thomas Schelling, this process may be described as a tipping trend.[91] The trend operates, in some defined direction, over an extended period, but at some point, when it becomes more dominant than the counterbalancing or predecessor tendencies, a qualitative change can be discerned.

The idea that contemporary government is administrative, and for that reason qualitatively different from its predecessors, is a central tenet of Max Weber's sociology. Weber uses the term bureaucracy, for which he offers two separate definitions. The first is that bureaucracy is characteristic of the rational, or rational-legalistic mode of legitimate domination.[92] Rational behavior, according to Weber, occurs when an actor chooses strategic means, based on natural events or human behavior, that will best achieve an objective that actor judges to be in his own self-interest.[93] Legalism is "a consistent system of abstract rules which have normally been intentionally established."[94] Weber's second definition consists of a list of characteristics, many of them quite precise, that the typical bureaucracy displays.[95] The primary ones are a continuously operating set of agencies with defined areas of jurisdiction and defined authority within each area, a clearly established hierarchy of offices within the agency, generally dependent on a single chief administrator, a management system based on written documents "preserved in their original or draft form," and a staff of officials who work full-time for their agency, are paid fixed salaries rather than receiving property, privileges, or fees, possess specialized training, and are selected on the basis of their credentials.[96] Bureaucracy, in Weber's view, is technically superior to any other form of organization: "Precision, speed, unambiguity, knowledge of the files, continuity, discretion, unity, strict subordination, reduction of friction and of material and personal costs—these are raised to the optimum point in the strictly bureaucratic administration."[97]

Although Weber's account of bureaucracy is seminal, his particular definitions present difficulties that are best avoided. The claim that bureaucracy is a rational-legal mode of governance involves two terms that are freighted with innumerable controversies. Rationality is one of the most contested concepts of modern times; for some, it implicates collective aspirations for objective truth or social emancipation, while others regard it as the essence of Eurocentric oppression of the third world or the human spirit. Even worse, it serves as the basis of microeconomic analysis, which has attempted to lay claim or lay waste to such disparate fields as law, political science, and sociology, and has become the subject of raging academic battles in every one of them.[98] The concept of legality is almost equally contested, having been the focal point of jurisprudential debate for at least two centuries. It fact, it is so encumbered with inherited and supernumerary connotations that it is one of the concepts that will be bracketed in a later chapter of this book. Weber's second definition, although free of such contested concepts, suffers from the opposite problem of being undertheorized and overly precise. As frequently observed, it bears

the imprint of the managerial theories of Weber's day about the most efficient way to design an organization,[99] and only poorly describes more contemporary developments such as Post-Fordism, New Public Governance,
or New Public Management.[100] Beyond these difficulties with his specific
definitions lie two more general ones. The very term 'bureaucracy,' although simply a French-language synecdoche for the *bureau*, or desk,
where public officials worked, was an insult from its outset in the eighteenth century, and has only become more of an imprecation over time.[101]
In addition, Weber's definition of bureaucracy relies on his notion of ideal
types, and is thus purposefully ahistorical.[102] While this methodology enables him to generate tremendous insights, its brightly delineated categories consciously ignore the jumbled process of transition; we never
learn, for example, precisely when the predominantly bureaucratic state
came into being.

For all these reasons, it would appear that Weber's definition, and indeed, the terms 'bureaucracy' and 'bureaucratization' themselves are best
avoided in a study that attempts to recharacterize our concepts of government in a modern administrative state. Instead, we need more uninformative terminology that makes fewer assertions, raises fewer hackles, and can
be applied to what has been called a tipping trend. Modernization theory
may seem like a promising source.[103] Samuel Huntington, for example,
identifies three components of the modernization process: the differentiation of structure, the rationalization of authority, and the expansion of political participation.[104] Participation, however important, hardly seems to
be a defining feature of the process. The first two are more basic, but they
are virtually restatements of Weber's theory of bureaucracy in dynamic
or teleological terms and present many of the same problems. They are
complex concepts that have reverberated through the entire corpus of social and political theory, creating various echoes, static, and noise along
the way. Differentiation implies the specialization or division of labor,
which is linked to pre-analytic notions about the loss of community and
the oppression of industrial workers, while 'rationalization' is simply another form of rationality.

The term that will be used in this book for the tipping trend that produced a qualitative change in Western governance is 'articulation.' One of
the ordinary meanings of this word is the connection of discrete elements
by visible ligatures or joints in a manner that preserves their separate identities; another is the expression of something in explicit verbal form. Both
usages are found in contemporary scholarship; the first is one of the images employed in Deleuze and Guattari's *A Thousand Plateaus*,[105] while
the second figures prominently in Derrida's *Of Grammatology*[106] and
Polanyi's *Personal Knowledge*.[107] Despite its familiarity, the term has not
acquired any strong connotations, and is thus bland enough to describe

long-term trends in governance without implying any controversial normative claims or asserting any unsubstantiated empirical ones. Thus, the first
meaning of articulation—to connect discrete elements—will be used in
place of Huntington's idea of differentiation or Weber's list of characteristics, and will be called the articulation of structure. The second meaning—
to express something in coherent verbal form—will be used in place of rationality or rationalization, and will be called the articulation of purpose.
These two uses of this relatively bland term are sufficient to distinguish between the administrative and the pre-administrative state. To state the
matter more precisely, a continuing process in Western society reached its
tipping point when both the structure and the purpose of the state became
predominantly articulated, and this tipping point represents the transition
to a mode of governance that we recognize as distinctively administrative.
Any implications of this process, such as whether it produces a state that is
more differentiated, more rational, more open to participation, or more
destructive of the human soul, must be argued for rather than assumed or
insinuated by virtue of a definition.

The Articulation of Structure and Purpose

Both uses of the term 'articulation' need to be elaborated in a bit more detail. To begin with the articulation of structure, there has been a gradual
development, throughout the past millennium, of the *bureau* after which
bureaucracy was named, that is, the desk-filled office of government agents
performing a specific task. At the beginning of this process, government
was generally not organized into the specialized ministries or agencies that
seem so characteristic of the modern state. Officials often had their own
job assignments, to be sure, but rather than being members of an agency,
they also had their own personally hired staff, their own source of revenue,
and their own physical location.[108] The tax collector bought his position
for a lump sum, hired whom he chose, and kept what he collected; the
clerk was responsible for issuing all the licenses for marriage, or the im-
portation of goods, or the operation of hackney coaches in a given area,
and received a fee for each license he issued; the military officer raised and
provisioned his own regiment, again for a fee, even though the soldiers
then fought under a unified command. These positions were essentially little self-contained institutions of their own and resembled medieval fiefs,
rather than components of an administrative hierarchy. Being private
property, they could be bequeathed and inherited, or bought and sold,
like landed estates. Baron Montesquieu, for example, inherited the presidency of the Bordeaux *Parlement* from his uncle and sold it for a substantial sum when he decided to live a more fashionable life in Paris.[109] And
just as the owner of landed property was free to hire someone else to man-

age his estate, paying a fixed salary and retaining the remainder, office-holders could appoint a salaried deputy to fulfill their office's responsibilities, while retaining its emoluments. In England during the 1780s, the King's Remembrancer paid £1500 to his deputy and retained £991, while the Exchequer's Clerk of the Pipe paid £100 to his deputy and retained £720.[110]

The self-contained character of government offices contrasted with the fluidity of the structure in which these offices existed. The king's personal household merged imperceptibly into the general government, so that, in England, the Master of the Horse or the Lord Chamberlain were regarded as equivalent positions to the Lord High Chancellor or the Secretary of State.[111] The Church merged into the state, so that acting clerics like Richelieu, Mazarin, or Wolsey could simultaneously serve as the king's chief minister, while the right to appoint abbots and priests was as central to royal authority as the right to appoint ministers and military officers. Of course, private affairs merged into public affairs; great lords with no official position often controlled the central government the way elected representatives or appointed ministers do today, and the king governed through these great lords as much as through his own officials.[112] Specially appointed royal officers were often reabsorbed into the locally–based nobility, as occurred with France's *noblesse de la robe*.[113]

In a contemporary administrative state, the semi-independent officials of pre-modern times have been replaced by employees whose positions are defined as interlocking parts of a hierarchically organized ministry or agency. As Weber points out, and as modernization theorists emphasize, these employees are not remunerated with fees, but with a prescribed salary; their responsibilities and relationships with one another are fixed by the hierarchic structure, and their performance is monitored and evaluated by their superiors within the hierarchy.[114] These ministries or agencies, moreover, are themselves articulated. They are conceived as separate entities within a clearly delineated public or governmental realm, and their internal hierarchy is independent of the status hierarchy that prevails in society at large. Their boundaries tend to be fixed, rather than fluid, and their relations with other ministries or agencies is defined by elaborate rules that create a larger and equally articulated hierarchy.

A second millennium-long trend in the governance of Western society is the articulation of purpose. In the medieval era, government was not conceived as implementing specified goals or purposes. Most of the mechanisms by which society was governed relied on what Weber described as traditional modes of domination.[115] Their authority was ascribed to some force that ran back into the misty past, or up into the heavens, but certainly beyond the reach of existing temporal decision makers.[116] The leaders of the government, everyone recognized, could make war and peace, collect taxes, dispense benefits, and impose sanctions, but they were not regarded as having the power to issue basic laws regulating ordinary social or economic relations. These laws were regarded as transcendent, and the task of government decision makers was to discover, interpret, and enforce them. Thus all government officials were seen as fulfilling what we now describe as a judicial role.[117]

This conception of government may be described as sacerdotal, in that the ruler was supposed to mediate between the divine and human worlds. To some extent, it was the sedimented belief of an earlier pre-Christian era, when the purpose of human life was seen as serving a divine ruler or the gods whom a divinely ordained ruler represented. By the Middle Ages this belief's remaining force was animating people's attitudes toward the Church, not toward the government. In the political realm the dominant view was that the people constituted an end in themselves, and the role of government was to benefit them and serve their needs. This was clearly stated by John of Salisbury, generally regarded as the West's first political theorist,[118] and strongly championed by many others, including Dante.[119] But medieval people also believed in an unquestioned supernatural order, and it was in this realm that their most important benefits, most notably salvation, were to be obtained. The governments of the time were considered just, or moral, to the extent that they could confer benefits flowing from this supernatural realm upon their people—hence their sacerdotal character.

In order to mediate between the divine and human worlds, and thereby facilitate the salvation of its subjects, a government needed to partake of each world's nature. This is the image of Moses, who spoke to God and man, of Jesus, who was both God and man, and of Arthur, a secular, non-priestly ruler who was infused with divine grace. The ruler, typically the king, was regarded as chosen by God and as exercising his authority with God's approval. Thus, the mystic force of justified power, or legitimacy, flowed from God into the sovereign and thenceforth out into the expressions of the sovereign's power—his subordinates, the law, and the legal rights that law created. Because its origins were divine, this force had always functioned in this manner; thus tradition—the way things had been done in the past—possessed the same sacerdotal character. It deserved respect because it embodied the collective experience of prior eras, but it was the sacerdotal element itself that supplied its moral status.[120]

In the contemporary view, government traces its authority to some explicitly established ordering that has been declared by a particular ruler, or, more commonly these days, established by a written constitution. Government decision makers create the laws that regulate the relationships among the citizens in exactly the same sense that they make war, raise taxes, or confer benefits. As such, they are comprehensive policy makers, carrying out explicitly identified purposes, not adjudicators or interpreters. There remains, of course, the need for the judicial function of interpreting the laws, but the laws are regarded as humanly created products, and the task of interpretation is to identify the intention or purpose of their human originators.[121]

The subtraction of the transcendental realm from political debate has led to a reinterpretation of the moral purposes of government. While the idea of glorifying or propitiating God no longer makes sense, the idea that government should benefit the people remains entirely applicable; indeed, as stated above, it serves as the moral premise of this study. But benefit is no longer defined in supernatural terms; rather it refers to purely secular advantages, not necessarily material, but almost exclusively identified with the welfare of individuals, specifically their security, liberty, and prosperity. Government is thus regarded as an instrumentality, a mechanism for providing secular benefits for those who live under its control. This is sometimes described as the eudaemonic state, the state whose purpose is to maximize the personal happiness of its members. It is not quite the same as a utilitarian approach to government, since it does not specify how happiness is to be measured or aggregated with as much precision, but it can fairly be described as the related political philosophy of welfare consequentialism.[122] What is important, for present purposes, is that government is regarded as fulfilling explicit, or articulated purposes, defined by a secular process of some sort.

Shifting to an instrumental conception of the state is not the thoughtless, mechanistic tropism of contemporary Morlocks who have forgotten the meaning of morality. Rather, it is a morality of its own. The idea that government should be a pure instrumentality, an entity that possesses no independent moral force, and should be judged according to its ability to benefit the people, is an organizing moral principle. This does not mean, of course, that every actual administrative state is necessarily a moral one. Rather, it suggests that the conception of an instrumental administrative state provides us with the criteria we use in contemporary society to make political judgments. Hitler's Germany, an administrative state, is something we deplore, but it is our morality—a morality that has evolved in an administrative context—that forms the basis of our judgment. Thus, recognition of the new political morality does not preclude condemnation of any particular administrative state; what it does preclude is a condemnation of a modern administrative state simply because it is administrative, or instrumentally conceived, and does not fit the model of its sacerdotal predecessor.

The two types of articulation that have been identified—structural and purposive—may seem like separate concepts, linked only by an adventitious overlap of English words. But, without adopting the Heideggerian conceit that language itself whispers secret verities in our ears, it can nonetheless be suggested that this linguistic correspondence reveals a more substantive relationship—the co-causal interaction of structure and intention. Structures of government affect the way that people think, and the way they think in turn affects those structures. In the case of the administrative state, the articulation of government into functionally defined and hierarchically integrated agencies naturally contributed to articulating the specific purpose of those agencies, while the recognition of such purposes enabled people to reorganize the government along more functional, articulated lines.

The Advent of the Administrative State

If this dual meaning of articulation is an accurate description of the two trends that generated the contemporary administrative state, it should be possible to use this term to locate these two trends' tipping points in historical time. The general consensus among scholars who have addressed this question, after Weber left it unresolved, is that the transition occurred during the last quarter of the eighteenth century and the first quarter of the nineteenth century.[123] In fact, articulation of structure and articulation of purpose turn out to be effective descriptions of developments in governance during this critical half-century.

With respect to structure, two great transitions occurred during this period. First, the overlap of public offices with private property, and of public officials with the land-owning nobility, was replaced by salaried, non-hereditary positions that were not conceived as property, and certainly not as nobility. Second, the quasi-independent, traditionally established government agencies were reconfigured into interconnected, functionally defined institutions. These transitions occurred throughout Europe, but can be illustrated by events in France and England.

Prior to the Revolution, French civil and military administration displayed the typical pre-modern pattern of self-contained and quasi-independent offices, even though Louis XIV had worked so hard to fill these offices with non-noble occupants. The French crown's practice of selling offices to raise money, and then demanding an annual fee from the officeholder, quickly transformed appointed positions into private property and their occupants into a new but nonetheless hereditary nobility, the *noblesse de la robe*.[124] Between 1789 and 1793, however, the Revolutionary government instituted salaries, pensions, and a fixed chain of command to replace the fees and favors that had previously constituted the primary compensation for so many government positions. The individuals who previously held these positions were purged. The Convention asked each existing ministry to submit lists of all their members, partially to facilitate the purges, but also to establish the staff members' status as salaried officials, answerable to the central government.[125] To further reduce the independence of the administrators, special committees were set up to oversee their efforts; at one point, the Committee of Public Safety had a substantial staff divided into sections for monitoring each of the ministries.[126] The general conscription eliminated privately raised regiments, and a state-run distribution system replaced the private contracts for military supply.[127]

The Revolution also reorganized the government, dividing it into separate, clearly defined units. During the last decades of the *ancien regime*, major administrative functions had been parceled out among four secretaries of state and the *Contrôle Général*.[128] Attempted reforms yielded equally irregular alignments; Bertin's department, for example, which was specially organized to take advantage of his economic talents, was responsible for agriculture, mining, postal communications, provincial affairs, secretarial matters, and stud farms.[129] The largest unit in the government was the *Contrôle Général*, which Clive Church describes as "a rambling agglomeration of commissions, services, semi-independent functionaries, and others, all held more or less together by a small and still very personal team of clerks."[130] Many public functions were performed by the *Maison du Roi*, which was responsible for running the king's household.[131] The revolutionaries abolished the *Contrôle Général* and distributed its component parts among different agencies. They transformed the *Maison du Roi* into the Ministry of the Interior, with responsibility for the king's household first confined to a single section, and later abolished together with the king. By spring of 1791, the Convention had passed an organic statute that stated each ministry's responsibilities; by 1792, the ministries had acquired a distinctively contemporary structure, being divided into Foreign Affairs, War, Navy, Interior, Justice, and Finance, and subdivided into a number of functionally defined bureaus, usually five or six.[132]

England was well past its revolutionary phase by the last quarter of the eighteenth century, and had entered into its long-lasting era of stable parliamentary government. Nonetheless, it went through a rather similar process of articulating its administrative structure. Beginning in 1782, permission to exercise one's office through a deputy was gradually withdrawn. Numerous laws were passed during the 1780s and 1790s to eliminate offices that drew their income from fees, or to replace those fees with salaries and pensions.[133] When Parliament failed to enact one such law, Pitt implemented its provisions, to the extent possible, by executive action.[134] Lacking the convenience of a revolution, the English reforms had to proceed more slowly than the French. The offices were regarded as private property, and Parliament could not simply abolish them or displace the current officeholder. In some cases, therefore, the officeholder was bought out with an annuity. This could be expensive; the two Auditors of the Imprests were each paid £7,000 a year for life when their offices were abolished in 1785.[135] In other cases, the office was simply allowed to lapse upon the death of the holder. Although relatively lengthy, the process had become government policy by the 1790s, and was essentially complete by the 1820s. The last Teller of the Receipt to be paid by fees, Lord Camden, held his office until 1834, but he was clearly an anachronism by that time, something he acknowledged by relinquishing the bulk of the fees to which he was entitled.[136]

The positions that were thus freed from their quasi-independent status were combined, as in France, into ministries and subministries with functionally defined responsibilities. Prior to 1782, for example, there were two secretaries of state. They had originally been the king's personal secretaries, but their responsibility for use of the signet had gradually involved them in a wide range of public affairs. By the eighteenth century, they were jointly responsible for domestic matters, one for northern England and the other for southern England, and divided foreign affairs between them on a rather loopy geographic basis, the Northern Secretary handling relations with northern European nations and with Scotland, the Southern Secretary handling southern Europe and, until 1762, North America. In 1782, Parliament separated their functions, making one the Home Secretary, with jurisdiction over domestic affairs, and the other the Foreign Secretary. The Home Secretary continued to be responsible for both war and the colonies until 1801, when a separate War Secretary was established.[137]

A related change was the creation of a Consolidated Fund in 1787 to replace England's complex system of special taxes with a unified account. Partial merger of the seven revenue boards that were responsible for collecting specified taxes was proposed as early as 1781, and the idea began to be implemented in 1798. It was not completed, however, until the formation of the Board of Inland Revenue in 1849, a quarter-century past the period in question. Similarly, the Parliamentary allocation to the king for his personal expenses, the Civil List, was also the source of salaries and pensions for many high officials. An Act of 1782 imposed some fiscal discipline on these expenditures, and complete separation between the personal expenses of the monarch and the expenses of the civil government was finally achieved in 1831.[138]

The same half-century also saw the purposes of government become articulated; arguments from tradition were explicitly rejected and the idea that government is an instrumentality of consciously developed social policy took hold. This process can be illustrated in the areas of public ideology, law, and, somewhat surprisingly, traditionalism itself. With respect to public ideology, France once again provides the most dramatic illustration. The central tenet of the revolutionaries was the rejection of tradition, a visceral aversion for doing things the way they had been done before. They not only abolished the privileges of nobility, but abolished the entire concept; they not only deposed the king, but beheaded him; they not only disestablished the Catholic Church but closed its facilities, seized its assets, and tried to replace it with a new religion. They divided and renamed France's ancient provinces, renumbered the years, changed the week from seven days to ten, renamed the months on the basis of the weather, and, most bizarre of all, invented a new system of weights and measures based on the quadrant of the Earth's circumference.[139]

Amid all this institutional carnage, the revolutionaries also developed a positive theory of government. Government, they believed, was not supposed to preserve tradition or the status quo, but to secure the happiness of all in the most logical and efficient manner. The Convention's organic statute was designed to transform administration into an instrument of public policy, as was the Committee on Public Safety's organized supervision of the ministries.[140] It was as characteristic of the Convention to proceed by statute as it was characteristic of the Committee to proceed by terror-backed surveillance, but both were seeking mechanisms to articulate the purposes of government. However far this effort proceeded during the tumultuous years of the Revolution, there can be no doubt that it was essentially completed by Napoleon,[141] which places the transformation securely within the same fifty-year period.

Once again, events in France may seem too dramatic to be generalized, as much a product of the Louis XVI's fecklessness and the frenzy of the *sans-culottes* as the tipping point in a thousand-year-long trend. But a very similar process occurred in other European countries. Perhaps the most intriguing case is Habsburg Austria, the archenemy of the French Revolution. During the decade prior to the Revolution, the Austrian emperor was Joseph II. The eldest son of Maria Theresa, Joseph had grown up chafing under his long-lived, devout, domineering mother, and ascended to the throne in 1780 determined to carry out his own ideas as rapidly as possible.[142] Although a member of one of Europe's most ancient and traditionalist families, he explicitly conceived his program as the extirpation of tradition.[143] He was content to retain the names of the months and the numbers of the years but he tried to abolish many of the privileges of the nobility. All positions in the government were to be based on merit, educational academies were to be open to worthy students of any background, and criminal justice was to be administered without regard to rank. He closed the monasteries and secularized their property, using it to pay pensions to the displaced monks and nuns, but also to establish educational and charitable institutions.[144] He abolished serfdom, allowing the former serfs to marry at will, choose a profession, and substitute cash payments for their required work.

Government officials were forbidden to have outside occupations—

Joseph would have liked to forbid them from having outside interests—and guaranteed a pension after ten years of service to secure their economic independence. They were required to fill out a fifteen-item questionnaire every six months, stating their abilities, years of service, conduct, and accomplishments.[145] Proclamations, at a rate of more than seven times the number issued by his mother's government, poured forth from these officials, prescribing rules for virtually all aspects of social, economic, and religious affairs. A centralized police force was organized to monitor compliance with these orders, but also to monitor the provincial administrators and ensure that they were implementing the required policies.[146] All this was conceived by Joseph as a means of creating a rational, instrumental government that served the interests of the citizens. In a statement critiquing the status quo in his Hungarian possessions, he declared, quite independently of Bentham or the French Revolution, that the form of government "must be in accordance with the general good of the greatest number."[147]

Like these changes in public ideology, the enactment of comprehensive legal codes between 1775 and 1825 also illustrates the articulation of purpose. These codes were designed to replace the mass of localized, customary provisions in each nation with a single, organized system that achieved the explicit purposes of government—the protection of property, the encouragement of trade, the suppression of crime, and, at least in some cases, the protection of human rights. The most influential, of course, was the Napoleonic Code of 1806.[148] Scholars have concluded that this was not the Newtonian reconceptualization that it purported to be, but a relatively conservative compromise between Roman and medieval law that consolidated several prior projects.[149] Nonetheless, the claims asserted on its behalf are significant, for they indicate a decisive watershed; legal rules were no longer to be justified by tradition but by logic, no longer celebrated because they were autochthonous and particularized, but because they implemented a nationwide regime of public order, commercial efficiency, and social justice. The Napoleonic Code was carried into Belgium, Poland, and the Rhineland principalities by the victorious French armies, and was voluntarily adopted by progressive regimes in Italy, Spain, Romania, and Argentina,[150] but its success does not represent the limit of legal articulation in this period. Prussia introduced a comprehensive legal code in 1794, after a period of development unrelated to the French Revolution.[151] Joseph II, as might be expected, initiated a wide-ranging law reform project shortly after his accession, designed to abolish customary law and establish a new system based on general principles and devoted to achieving public purposes.[152]

It might appear that England was an exception to this pattern, since it retained the common law over Bentham's strident call for codification.[153]

But England's common law had been organized and systematized in 1776 by Blackstone's Commentaries, which presented it as a coherent system designed to achieve the recognized purposes of government.[154] Of course, the publication of a book is not necessarily a political event, but Blackstone's was no ordinary book. An immediate success, it won a central place on every English and American lawyer's shelf, where it was treated as the final word on the content and meaning of Anglo-American law.[155] Much of Bentham's fury sprang from his adversary's evident success in systematizing and justifying England's traditional legal system, thereby insulating it from more radical reform.[156]

One final illustration of the late-eighteenth- and early-nineteenth-century articulation of purpose involves the reconceptualization of traditionalism itself by the enemies of reform and the defenders of religion—Burke, Herder, Maistre, and Bonald. In the aftermath of the Revolution, these thinkers found that the old order could no longer be defended simply because it was old, or because it was right, or because it was sanctioned by God. Instead, they argued that tradition and religion were necessary to secure social stability and to avoid a descent into sanguinary chaos.[157] In thus offering a nontraditional argument for tradition, they reflect the conceptual transition to the contemporary world of articulated policies.[158] Maistre, though a sincere Catholic, was so perspicacious in analyzing the social utility of religion that the founders of secular social science, Comte and Saint Simon, drew heavily upon his work.[159] Bonald, an equally passionate proponent of political conservatism and ultramontanism, went still further, striving to justify his views by means of systematic, scientific analysis. This ultimately led him to propose a new set of rituals that were consciously designed to reinvigorate and improve those that the Revolution had displaced.[160] They included, as David Klinck describes, his Temple to Providence, a pyramid-shaped structure to be placed at France's geographic center and surrounded by statues of great public heroes. The Dauphin would live there, together with young nobles who had graduated from specially organized schools and wore gold rings betokening their status. Coronations, royal burials, and meetings of the Estates General would be held at the Temple, and the populace, having attended these august rituals, would return home inspired to maintain the status quo.[161] One expects such elaborate, overheated fantasies from socialists like Fourier or Owen, but to find a Catholic conservative proposing rituals as radically new as Robespierre's Cult of the Supreme Being indicates how fully the defense of tradition had been reconceptualized.

There remains the case of the United States, which will be of central concern in this study. In some ways the United States was a full participant in the late-eighteenth-century transition to administrative government, and the clarity of the example it provided may rank along with the invention of the lightning rod as America's first contributions to Western culture. From its outset in 1789, the national government, with its separate departments of State, Treasury, War, and the Post Office, was as structurally articulated as any in Europe. Fee-supported sinecures, hereditary offices, and the welter of loosely and traditionally structured institutions that characterized pre-administrative Europe were entirely absent. Nor did American political leaders experience any difficulty in articulating the general purposes of government. Indeed, they did so at least as early as any European nation—if not in the Declaration of Independence, then certainly in the Constitution and the Federalist Papers. On the other hand, economic and social regulation in the United States evolved somewhat more slowly than in Europe, particularly at the national level.[162] While the new nation quickly developed a postal system, land offices, a customs service, a standing army, and a navy, its skittishness about regulation[163] led to at least two major political decisions—the veto of the Second Bank of the United States and the ultimate rejection of Henry Clay's American System[164]—and to at least one genuine social tragedy—the failure of the understaffed, underfunded Freedman's Bureau to enforce the rights of the former southern slaves during Reconstruction.[165]

Stephen Skowronek attributes the delayed development of regulatory government in the United States to federalism, and to the small scale of the federal government during the antebellum era.[166] In addition, one can always invoke the Turner thesis,[167] which has the additional advantage of having been anticipated by Hegel,[168] or one can cite the lack of any serious military threat that demanded large, well-organized armed forces.[169] The question is certainly an interesting one, but of no great significance for present purposes. It is incontrovertible that the United States became an administrative state some time between its Revolution and the beginning of the twentieth century. That means that America's transition to administrative governance occurred after the concepts that will be bracketed in this study were developed and before the contemporary period when those concepts, despite their pre-modern origins, continue to be applied.[170]

The thesis of this book can be elaborated once again in light of these considerations. The advent of the administrative state, resulting from the articulation of structure and purpose that reached their tipping points about two centuries ago, has rendered the concepts that we use to describe our government outdated. We retain these concepts due to social nostalgia; because they carry moral implications, however, we imagine that we retain them to provide criteria for evaluating our government. But our existing concepts are as outdated in the moral realm as they are in the descriptive one. They emerge from a sacerdotal conception of government that we no longer maintain, and that conflicts with our current view of government as instrumental, or eudaemonic. Consequently, we can express our moral values more clearly, and implement them more effectively, if we conduct the thought experiment of setting aside the pre-modern concepts that we currently employ, and replace them with more contemporary alternatives.

It can thus be said that the purpose of this book is moral as well as descriptive, but, in fact, these two purposes are inextricably connected. From the descriptive point of view, the concepts we have inherited from the sacerdotal state fail to describe our current moral attitudes, just as they fail to describe our government itself. They fail, moreover, in exactly the same way because the government that we possess is a product and a source of our morality. From the moral point of view, continued reliance on these concepts is a political wrong; it is wrong to misdescribe our government because we must understand that government if we want it to serve as a eudaemonic instrumentality, a means of providing us with desired benefits. It is our moral responsibility to squelch our social nostalgia, and come to terms with the government we actually possess, no matter how dreary its pragmatism seems, how painful the individual's apparent alienation from the collectivity may feel, how vast and grim modernity appears to be. For these are only moods, however deeply felt. In fact, the modern administrative state, in its articulation and its instrumentalism, is the way we take collective action to solve the enormous problems and achieve the even more enormous promises of modern life. As we advance into this new millennium, we need to reconcile ourselves to its existence, understand its underlying structure, and make it work.

Part I:

THE STRUCTURE OF GOVERNMENT

Two

From Branches to Networks

The Government as Body and Branches

The Human Body Metaphor

THE most basic question about our government, as opposed to the state or the society in general, involves its structure, its principal components and their interrelationship. Our prevailing description of governmental structure is that the government is made up of three branches—executive, legislative, and judicial. This notion is the topic of the present chapter. The next question concerns the human attitudes and relationships that animate this governmental structure and that are generally described by the terms 'power' and, secondarily, 'discretion' (Chapter 3). We can then ask how the government relates to its citizenry. The standard concepts used in this discussion are democracy, monarchy, and dictatorship, with democracy being the one of greatest interest at the present time (Chapter 4). Finally, we can explore human attitudes and relationships that animate this second aspect of structure and that are typically discussed in terms of political legitimacy (Chapter 5).

What is our conception, or image, of our government's overall structure? Surprisingly, only a few such images have been widely employed in the Western political tradition. The first of these is that government is like the human body. Strictly speaking, this is an image of society in general, but it divides society into different components, many of which correspond to the individuals or institutions that we now identify as governmental. In Western culture, the human body image received its decisive formulation in the early part of the second millennium from John of Salisbury who, as previously mentioned, is generally regarded as the first political scientist in our tradition.[1] The idea of society as human body served as the principal image of government throughout the Middle Ages and the Renaissance. It lasted long enough to be relied upon by Rousseau and Blackstone,[2] and, as Antoine de Baecque describes, to figure prominently in the popular rhetoric of the French Revolution.[3]

According to John's great work, *Policraticus*, which was addressed to his patron Thomas Becket, the Church is the soul of society and "ought to be esteemed and venerated like the soul in the body."[4] The head of society is the prince, or king, who is "subject only to God and to those who act in His place on earth."[5] The position of the heart is occupied by the Senate, which John envisions as a body of wise elders.[6] He describes them as counselors or advisors, but then identifies a separate group of people, the courtiers, who assist the prince and constitute the flanks of the state.[7] The eyes, ears, and tongue of society are "the governors of the provinces," who carry out their duties by "conferring legal right."[8] Society has two hands, one armed and one unarmed. Soldiers are the armed hand and are described, with notable directness, as being "occupied with marching and the blood-letting of war."[9] Officials, particularly tax collectors and advocates, comprise the unarmed hand described, again rather directly, as soldiers who take action "against the citizen" rather than against external enemies.[10] Treasurers and record keepers, but not "those who supervise prisoners," are analogous to the stomach and intestines. "If they accumulate with great avidity and tenaciously preserve their accumulation," John observes, they "engender innumerable and incurable diseases so that their infection threatens to ruin the whole body."[11] Last come all those who "exercise the humbler duties," including "peasants who always stick to the land," weavers, blacksmiths, and others whose management "does not pertain to the public authorities."[12] At this point, John loses track of the way analogies work, and observes that since there are many such occupations, the state must have innumerable feet, thus transforming his image from a well-proportioned body to a hideous centipede.[13]

John Morrall observes that John of Salisbury elaborates his metaphor "with a thoroughness sometimes bordering on indelicacy."[14] As a framework for analyzing the actual operation of the government, however, the difficulty with the metaphor is that it is not indelicate enough. Quite apart from his failure to specify the political equivalent of the body's reproductive organs, or even the gender of the body that is being used, John says virtually nothing about the way that the organs he discusses actually carry out their functions. Instead, once he identifies the bodily organ to which a particular individual or group of people corresponds, he immediately launches into a moralistic malediction of corruption and dishonesty. The prince must not indulge in luxury, the senate must not succumb to greed, the soldiers must foreswear pillaging, the magistrates and courtiers must not sell benefits for gifts, although—these are pre-bureaucratic officials, after all, who derive their income from fees—they may "lawfully accept presents so long as these presents are not impudently extorted."[15] Violation of these precepts will produce a diseased or distorted body, whose head is the image of the devil, whose heart consists of iniquitous senators, and whose hands are violent and unjust.[16]

Such Christian sermonizing represents a tradition that was well-established

by John of Salisbury's time, the so-called "mirror of the princes" literature.[17] One does not need John's elaborate corporeal metaphor, however,
to urge uniform virtues upon different state officials; in fact, the uniformity of his recommendations seems to run counter to differentiated analysis that his metaphor promises to provide. John could have developed a
much more effective account of governmental operations had he paid
more attention to the way a human body really functions. This is not to
charge him with ignorance of twenty-first-century physiology, but rather
with ignorance, or lack of interest in, twelfth-century physiology. John
knew the functions of the eyes, ears, and tongue as well as we do, yet, having compared the provincial governors or magistrates to these organs, he
failed to discuss the way in which they provide the king with information
about outlying regions, or pronounce his laws within these regions. He incorrectly thought that the heart was the seat of the emotions, but there is
still much he could have said about the relationship of church and king as
heart and head, about the way they work together or compete to control
the armed and unarmed hands. While he seems to understand what the
stomach and intestines do, he never states that the treasurers and record-
keepers who serve as their equivalents digest funds and information, thus
providing the state with its needed nourishment. He analogizes the dishonesty of these officials with constipation, but fails to explain what
purgative or emetic can correct this ailment, or to be still more indelicate,
which of the two hands can most effectively administer the remedy.

One reason that John overlooks the analytic possibilities of his own
metaphor lies in the committed character of political description. John,
like all subsequent practitioners of the field he is credited with initiating,
was motivated to develop his account of society and governance by his
emotional concerns. The first of these is that all the parts of society have
their appointed place, and need to remain in that place for the state in its
entirety to function—another version of the great chain of being.[18] John's
second, closely related commitment is that society can function smoothly
and eliminate conflict if the obviously appropriate ordering of its components is maintained.[19]

We can see, in these commitments, John's reaction to the stresses that
convulsed medieval society and made people yearn for Camelot. The revival of commerce disrupted the medieval social hierarchy, at both the collective and individual level, creating truculent towns that did not fit into
the feudal system, wealthy merchants who wanted to buy their way into
the nobility, impecunious noblemen who were only too anxious to sell
their hereditary privileges, and upwardly mobile artisans and peasants who
made everyone else feel uncomfortable. The continued weakness of the
royal governments led to dynastic struggles for control of the monarchy,

warfare between monarchies for control of territory, warfare among the nobles within monarchies for control of taxes, fees, or servitudes, and violence by these same aggressive nobles against townspeople, peasants, traveling merchants, and virtually anyone else who lacked a sword and a horse. In fact, the stable, irenic character of John's human body metaphor not only represents his committed effort to deny both the dynamic and disruptive features of his society, but also to deny the effect of this dynamism and disruption on his personal life. Becket, his friend and patron, had risen from a modest merchant background to become Chancellor of the realm and Archbishop of Canterbury,[20] while he himself had ascended from equally modest origins to the bishopric of Chartres.[21] Less positively, England had been in the throes of a devastating civil war between King Stephen and the Angevins for half his lifetime,[22] while his entire life was dominated by the conflict between the European monarchs and the papacy over the control of ecclesiastical offices—the so-called Investiture Controversy—that twice led to his banishment from England, as well as to the assassination of his patron.[23]

The committed character of John's descriptions helps explain a striking feature of *Policraticus*—the fact that its extended metaphor does not actually refer to the political regimes that existed when he was writing. He speaks of the senate, or a council of elders, as being separate from the courtiers and assistants who represent the flanks, yet no such separate entity existed in Angevin England or Capetian France. Neither were there appointed governors of provinces; the feudal system, with its hereditary fiefs, provided the machinery of local governance in Western Europe. Finally, there were no standing armies of the sort that John describes, and certainly no heavy, intensively trained infantry. All these are clearly instrumentalities of the ancient Roman state. Their prominence in John's account was partially a product of his belief that ancient Rome would serve his didactic purpose and partially a product of his formidable erudition.[24] But the underlying motivation seems to be social nostalgia: John's visceral distaste for his own—modern—time and his inability to confront its dreary and complex realities.

The point of all this is not to level harsh judgments at a man who was both a pathbreaking scholar and an admirable individual, but to illuminate the dangers of political imagery, dangers that we can more readily discern with an image that is no longer our own. From our current vantage point, we can see that the human body metaphor fits poorly with the society it was intended to describe; we can hear the grinding of its conceptual gears. The problem is not that it was a committed description—all descriptions are—but that the commitments that animated it were partially antiquarian and partially clandestine. Rather than describing the society that existed at the time, it served to express its author's discomfort with that society in the guise of a description.

The Three-Branch Metaphor

During the past few centuries, the image of society as human body has been gradually replaced by the more secular image that government is divided into three branches—the legislative, executive, and judicial. This is our dominant conception of governmental structure, a conception that has become so sedimented into our political culture that we perceive it as a description of objective reality, rather than a heuristic akin to John of Salisbury's human body image. Surprisingly, there do not seem to be any other images in general use. Marxist and Marxist-inspired theory, which conceives society as a collection of discrete, economically based classes engaged in a continued struggle for control, views the government as either an agent of the dominant class or as an arena where class conflict is played out, but does not provide a separate image of governmental structure.[25] There is also the occasional image of the state as a machine,[26] which seems promising in its modernity, but has not been used with any regularity or developed in any significant detail.

The branch imagery itself emerged at the end of the eighteenth century, but the underlying concept that the government is composed of three distinguishable components—one that makes the law, one that enforces it, and one that applies it—goes back much further. It can be found in Aristotle's *Politics*, where three elements of government are identified: the deliberative element, "which discusses everything of common importance," the official element, either elected or chosen by lot, and the judicial element, which includes criminal courts, civil courts, and inquiries of public officials.[27] This conception of government was given its modern form by the political thinkers of the English Civil War, specifically James Harrington, George Lawson, and Algernon Sidney.[28] Their opposition to the monarchy led them to discern different components of government and to champion the separation of the monarch from the others on the theory that these other components, once separate, would provide an antidote to absolutism. To this notion that the various components of government could restrain each other was linked the much older notion of mixed government, a favorite of classical writers, including Aristotle, Polybius, and Cicero.[29] Cicero's account, loosely adapted from Aristotle, begins from the premise that there are three basic forms of government—an autocracy dominated by a single ruler, an aristocracy dominated by the nobility, and a democracy dominated by the general populace. The most stable government, he concludes, for familiar reasons, is a mixture of the three. This theory is not logically connected with the theory of separated powers, but its Trinitarian structure and underlying aspirations created conceptual associations between the two ideas.[30]

As M.J.C. Vile recounts, the Civil War writers generally agreed that the number of separate components in the government was three, but did not always agree upon the identity of the three, or the extent that they should remain separate from one another.[31] Locke follows this pattern, identifying the three "powers" of government as the legislative, the executive, and the federative, or foreign relations power.[32] Montesquieu, at the beginning of his discussion of the English constitution, identifies the three components as the power to make laws, the power over foreign affairs, and the power "of judging the crimes or the disputes of individuals."[33] He thus includes the judicial power, which Locke excluded, but omits the power to enforce the laws and retains foreign relations as a separate power. Within two paragraphs, however, he reintroduces the judiciary, and by the time he proceeds to his analysis of the Roman constitution, his categorization has settled down into the now-familiar pattern of legislative, executive, and judicial.[34]

There is nothing clandestine above the commitments that motivate Montesquieu's description; he explicitly declares that he is trying to determine the distribution of powers that will most reliably secure the people's liberty.[35] Oddly, but perhaps not surprisingly, he concludes that the optimal distribution is precisely the one that existed in England when he visited there between 1728 and 1731. This leads him to favor a partial separation of powers, with a number of highly specific imbrications. The executive must not participate in the process of enacting legislation but, to protect its autonomous existence, must be able to veto legislative proposals. The legislature must not "have the right to check executive power," but it must have the ability to examine the way in which that executive power has been used. It must not exercise the power to judge individuals, except in cases where the accused person is a noble or a public official, or the law is too severe for the specific case. It must not have the power to convene itself, that power being reserved to the executive. The legislature must possess the sole power to raise funds, but it must exercise that power only on a year-to-year basis, or it will confer too great an authority on the executive.[36]

The Framers of the United States Constitution used the tripartite conception of government to organize the principal provisions of their document. To say that they were influenced by Montesquieu is something of an understatement, for they appear to have swallowed him in his entirety.[37] In fact, they were probably as strongly influenced by their own recollection of early to mid-eighteenth century English government as they were by Montesquieu, but since Montesquieu based his own theory on this same governmental model, the two influences served only to reinforce each other. The result, as no less a person than Woodrow Wilson observed,[38] is that the Framers codified the arrangements that prevailed in England during their youth or the youth of those who taught them. These arrangements, in turn, owed their conceptual origins to the Civil War period, Tudor England, and the Middle Ages, as other scholars have often pointed out.[39] The Framers substituted an indirectly elected president for the king, and an upper house representing the states for one representing the nobility, but aside from expanding the role of the upper house, they made few changes. America's most important conceptual innovation—the authority of the judiciary to invalidate legislation on constitutional grounds—does not appear explicitly in the constitutional text, of course.

The use of the term 'branches' to describe the three components of the government evolved around the time the Constitution was drafted. The Civil War writers tend to speak of power flowing in different streams, while Locke and Montesquieu both rely on the term 'powers' for the component parts of government. By the time Blackstone wrote his commentaries, however, the image of three branches seems to have been familiar.[40] Today, it constitutes the standard formulation of the image; Alexander Bickel, to be reassuring, described the judiciary as the "least dangerous branch,"[41] and Joseph Clark, to be critical, described Congress as "the sapless branch."[42] Although Great Britain no longer maintains any juridical distinction between its legislature and executive, the two are still treated as separate functions, and the differences between them are as readily perceived in Britain as they are in the United States.

The Problem with the Three-Branch Metaphor

Just as John of Salisbury's human body metaphor is more applicable to ancient Roman government than to his own, the three-branch metaphor applies to the government that existed prior to our current one. About seven hundred years ago, the government of European states, or proto-states, consisted of three groups of relatively equal size—the legislature, the judges, and the king's household. A centralized administration, staffed by university-trained lawyers and clerics, was already beginning to develop, but it was still small enough to be combined with the king's household, yielding three components of roughly commensurate size. Today, of course, this is no longer the case. While the size of the legislature, the judiciary, and the chief executive's personal staff have increased only incrementally and in rough proportion to the increasing population of their subject territories, the central administration has grown to gigantic proportions. In the United States, it numbers several million people—two orders of magnitude larger than the remainder of the government.

It is difficult to capture this reality in a meaningful or useful way by relying on the three-branch metaphor of governmental structure. Where are
these millions of administrators to be placed? The traditional answer is that
they are part of the executive branch, but the reference to branches suggests that we are envisioning a tree, and what tree has one branch that is a
hundred times larger than the others? Moreover, it is well known that administrative agencies regularly perform legislative and judicial functions in
addition to executive ones,[43] which means that pieces of this one edema-
tous branch must now reach over and intertwine with the two other, tiny
ones. Worse still, many American administrative agencies are not under the
president's direct control; they are independent agencies, which means
that the president appoints their leading officers but cannot remove those
officers without a showing of good cause.[44] The Brownlow Commission,
established by Franklin Roosevelt, was highly disconcerted by this "hap-
hazard deposit of irresponsible agencies and uncoordinated powers," describing it as "a headless fourth branch."[45] This addition to the three-
branch metaphor halves the size of the overgrown executive branch, and
produces another of roughly equal proportions, but it suggests the somewhat grotesque idea, perhaps reflecting an unconscious reversion to the
human body metaphor, that the other three branches have heads appended at their ends. The resulting image is even uglier than John of Salisbury's centipede.

Thus, the problem with the three-branch metaphor is that it denies or
underemphasizes the reality of the administrative state, just as John of
Salisbury's human body metaphor denied the instability of the medieval
social hierarchy and the pandemic conflicts that convulsed it. We all know
that the officials whom we deal with on a daily basis and who make decisions that govern our lives are not elected but appointed; that they are not
chosen from among the general population, but on the basis of specialized
training and internal promotion; that they are not supervised or controlled
by elected officials, or by the traditional constraints of common law, but
only by other appointed officials like themselves. But we seem to be clan-
destinely committed to the belief that we still live in the kind of democracy
that seventeenth and eighteenth century thinkers envisioned, that elections give us complete control over our government, that appointed officials are constrained by law, that each branch can check the others and
thereby protect us from government oppression or excess. We want to
condemn and reject the all-too-obvious divergences from this image.
While we no longer ascribe such divergences to the devil, as John did, we
treat them as the products of our own bêtes noires—narrowly focused
interest groups, Washington politicians, and, of course, the bureaucrats
themselves.

The three-branch metaphor is not only inappropriately bucolic, but also inappropriately static. While it certainly proclaims the notion that the executive, legislature, and judiciary are supposed to be separate, it obscures the principal purpose of this notion, which is the control of governmental abuse. The branches of a tree do not control each other, but simply sit there separately. Control, which is crucial in the modern state, involves a complex, dynamic interaction among different parts of government that the three-branch image does little to illuminate. In addition, the image coagulates each part that it identifies into an opaque, woody mass, rather than revealing its articulated structure in a way that would enable specific decisions and communication pathways to be traced, evaluated, and, if necessary, reconfigured.

An additional difficulty with the three-branch metaphor is that its historical sedimentation, and its embodiment in our Constitution, makes it appear to be an intrinsic feature of our governmental system. When John and his successors used the human body metaphor, as reified by tradition, its artificial vividness obscured the nature of existing government and encouraged them to overlook discordant features they might have otherwise been willing to confront. The reified, nonheuristic character of the three-branch metaphor produces fruit of a similarly addictive nature. As a general matter, it induces us to underemphasize the administrative character of our government and overemphasize the value of political and judicial controls.

Perhaps the image would serve as a more useful heuristic if more attention were paid to plant biology, just as John's image could have been operationalized by attending more to human physiology. After all, what tree consists exclusively of branches?[46] Virtually all trees have a trunk, and the trunk is generally far larger than any branch. The trunk, then, is the missing element that serves as the analogue of our massive administrative apparatus. Introducing it into the metaphor resolves virtually all the aesthetic difficulties that the advent of the administrative state creates. Administrative agencies can be pictured as combining executive, legislative, and judicial functions, since all three of the branches that represent these functions feed into, and grow out of, the trunk. The independent agencies are not a branch at all, but part of this same trunk; they are headless only in the sense of having no definitive endpoint, since the trunk terminates, quite naturally, by dividing into branches. Most important, the addition of the trunk eliminates the disproportion among branches by enabling us to remove the presidentially supervised agencies, as well as the independent agencies, from the executive branch. What remains in this branch is the chief executive and his immediate staff—in the United States, the so-called Executive Office of the president that includes his personal staff, his immediate advisors, White House counsel, and the Office of Management and Budget.[47] Thus reduced, the executive branch is now approximately the same size as the other two, and produces a much more harmoniously proportioned tree.

Nifty as this solution may appear, it represents only a marginal improvement. While it acknowledges the central role of the administrative apparatus, its continuing Arcadianism remains an inducement to social nostalgia and an ongoing denial of the complex, instrumental character of the modern state. In addition, the image fails to conform to our commitments because a tree trunk's primary purpose is to supply and elevate the patulous branches, while the administrative apparatus is the basic operational component of our governmental system. The branches that the trunk holds aloft, moreover, are still the reified branches of the predecessor image, and thus continue to obscure their heuristic nature. Most important, the image fails to explain how branches would control the trunk, just as it fails to explain how they would control each other, while the trunk itself appears to the mind's eye as a uniform, impenetrable mass. Perhaps the metaphor could be developed further through a more technical use of plant biology. We might inquire about the correlative of the roots that are appended to the lower end of the administrative trunk, or trace the operations of the agencies in terms of xylem, bark, and annual growth rings. But plant biology is too technical to possess much intuitive appeal, and it is highly unlikely that any political participants think in these terms unless they work for the National Forest Service.

The Modern Image of a Network

The Network as Hardware

There is thus good reason to bracket the metaphor that government is divided into three distinct branches, and thereby disconnect its claim to descriptive validity. This requires some mental effort, since the metaphor has become virtually instinctive, and is widely used by political participants as well as scholarly observers. But the purpose of bracketing a concept is to set these habits of thought aside, to hold our inherited and sedimented images at a distance from ourselves and consider them anew. We can thus proceed with the thought experiment of developing an alternative description for the comfortably familiar but now bracketed concept, and inquire whether this alternative heuristic would provide a superior description of modern administrative government.

The alternative image of governmental structure that will be suggested here, and used through the remainder of the book, is the network. This usage follows the political science analysis of Karl Deutsch,[48] and the modern organization theory of Paul DiMaggio, John Meyer, Walter Powell, and Richard Scott.[49] While the term itself is not new, its associations are distinctly contemporary, ranging from broadcasting to engineering to the electronic connections among computers. We can readily envision those whose lives convey our yearned-for feeling of romance—the Framers, King Arthur's court at Camelot, the ancient Athenians—talking about trees and branches, but it is difficult to imagine them discussing networks. Thus, the network image provides an antidote against social nostalgia, and focuses our vagabond attention on the realities of our political existence. With its multilevel, articulated, mechanistic structure, the image embraces the administrative state, just as our society has embraced it over the course of the previous two hundred years.

A network, at its simplest level, is a set of interconnections between particular localities. In the elegant terminology of engineering, the localities are called lumps,[50] while neural network theory uses the equivalent but slightly more euphonious term 'units.'[51] A unit is a discontinuity in the network, a region where matter, energy, or information is generated or altered for transmission through an interconnection. These units generally possess a definitive physical reality and a boundary that separates them from other components of the network. The interconnections transmit the matter, energy, or information between pairs of units. To describe a network, one must identify both its architecture and its content, or, in terms of current computer technology, its hardware and its software. A description of the architecture, or hardware, specifies the units and the connections among them; a description of the content, or software, indicates the operations that each unit carries out, and the types of matter, energy, or information that are transmitted through the linkages.

When the network concept is used as a metaphor for government, the most essential aspect of its architecture involves the identity of its constituent units. That depends upon the scale of observation. Different levels of observation represent horizontal cross-sections of the network at various heights, revealing different types of units and interconnections. At the lowest level of the network, the units are individual human beings, a conclusion that follows from either phenomenology or the methodological individualism of microeconomics. The level above the individual might consist of offices, that is, physical locations where groups of individuals work in daily, face-to-face contact. It is possible that the Internet will ultimately eliminate this level, but the more likely scenario, for the foreseeable future, is that it will simply diminish its physical component. Above the office level are departments of agencies and still further up are agencies themselves and other units that are defined as separate entities, such as the Federal Reserve Board, the Department of Agriculture, Congress, or the federal judiciary. The highest level that is useful for political analysis is presumably the one where the units are nation-states or associated groups of nation-states. Alternatively, the internal structure of any institution can be examined by taking a vertical slice or cross-section of the network, starting at the level on which the institution appears as a unit and working downward. This would reveal connections between different levels of the institution, as opposed to the interconnections between the institution and other units at its particular level.

Before proceeding to describe the content, or software, of the network, several features of its architecture or hardware are worth noting, namely, its depiction of status, of hierarchy, of the concept of government, and of the nation-state. To begin with status, the different horizontal levels, although they are described in terms of the up-and-down imagery that George Lakoff and Steven Winter have discussed,[52] do not represent status rankings but physical size. Thus, the second highest level includes all large government institutions, regardless of status; the lowest level includes all individuals within the government, the chief executive and the file clerk, the janitor and the judge. Status is determined by the number of interconnections between a given unit and other units, and by the content of the information that flows through those interconnections. Such a determination requires microanalysis of both the network's structure and its software.

Closely related to the metaphor's depiction of status is its characterization of hierarchy. John of Salisbury's human body image, in which the head controls the other organs, portrays government, and society in general, as a unified hierarchy, with all political authority flowing from a single source. The network image carries no such implication. Rather, it portrays modern government as a complex apparatus, where commands can come from multiple sources, and where units are potentially autonomous or semi-autonomous. It is possible, for example, that the entire government will cease functioning if its leadership is overthrown, but it is also possible that its separate units will continue their quotidian operations. The network metaphor neither privileges nor disfavors either of these possibilities. Instead, it emphasizes that the choice among them and their various intermediate positions depends on the particular character of the connections among units, something that, once again, can only be determined by microanalysis.

A third structural feature of the network metaphor is that it acknowledges the uninformative nature of the term 'government' as a category of social organization and behavior. Branches of a tree, and even a tree's trunk, are self-contained entities having crisply delineated boundaries and delimited points of contact with the surrounding environment. The network that constitutes the government, however, is readily conceived as simply one region of a larger, more comprehensive social network. At any given level, a boundary can be defined, separating governmental and nongovernmental institutions, or public employees from private individuals, but the significance of this boundary will depend upon a microanalysis of the interactions that occur across it, and on either side. Between judges and litigants the line may be definitive; judges interact extensively and informally among themselves, but only in occasional and highly formalized ways with any litigant. Between agencies and the firms they regulate, the line may be much less clear because on-going, two-way interactions may essentially efface any operational distinction, leading to cooperative governance or a corporatist state where policy is extensively formulated by nongovernmental parties.[53] The solidity of the boundary between public and private, or even the existence of this boundary, is a variable feature, and this variability is highlighted by the network model. Ironically, the boundary between government and private actors was less clearly delineated in the pre-modern era than it is at present, which suggests that the tree metaphor, like the human body metaphor, was not even a good description of the situation when it was first developed.

Finally, the network model neither privileges nor disfavors the nation-state. There has been much discussion recently of globalization—so much so that one wonders why those funny-looking colors still appear on our maps. To some extent, the idea is a dangling comparative, an inherently comparative claim that fails to identify the other element in the comparison. Finance and production may have been more international in twelfth-century Europe than it is today; in John of Salisbury's time, for example, all educated people in Europe wrote in exactly the same language, and trade moved across political boundaries with as much ease, or difficulty, as it moved within them.[54] But the network metaphor enables us to leave this question open and to assess it through microanalysis. Nation-states appear as the units at the highest horizontal level of observation, to be sure, but the metaphor allows us to look down one level, or several, at the way that institutions and individuals within nation-states interact with one another. It may turn out, for example, that government officials maintain regular contacts with their opposite numbers from other nations, in a manner that tends to dissolve the boundaries between them, but it may also turn out that they do not.

The Network as Software

While the architecture or hardware of the network metaphor provides a way of modeling the relationships among individuals or institutions in the government, the content or software of the metaphor provides a way of modeling the actual operations that are carried out through these relationships. For this second purpose the metaphor is very rich; mechanical engineering, electrical engineering, and neural network theory each provide an elaborate set of concepts for describing network operations. Indeed, the real challenge is not the task of generating analogies for government behavior—that can be achieved with disarming ease—but the task of keeping the analogies naive enough to avoid overinterpretation. It must always be recalled that the entire image is a heuristic, to be justified by the insights about government that it provides, and not by the seductive complexity with which it can be elaborated.

Generally speaking, the operation of each unit in a network is described by the types of matter, energy, or information that flow through its connections to other units, and by the operation that the unit itself performs. These two features can be collectively described as the design, or operational scope of the unit, while the flow is generally described in terms of inputs and outputs. An input is an independent variable, that is, one that originates outside the unit under consideration, while an output is a dependent variable determined by the operation of that unit. In the administrative state, some of the inputs and outputs involve physical material. Paper, pencils, and computer terminals must be delivered to government offices; garbage, diseased animals, and disruptive visitors must be physically removed from nature preserves. Of greatest interest, however, are the various verbal statements that constitute the major portion of the governmental process.

J. L. Austin's classic categorization of verbal statements identifies them as locutionary, illocutionary, and perlocutionary.[55] A locutionary statement transmits information, that is, it describes the existing state of the world. An illocutionary statement, or performative, carries out an action or function in the world, such as making a promise or issuing a command. A perlocutionary statement produces an effect upon its audience. In view of the well-known difficulty distinguishing illocutionary and perlocutionary statements, Habermas redescribes these categories as strategic action, which is designed to produce a particular effect upon its recipient, and communicative action, which is designed to reach an understanding between the recipient and the speaker.[56] For present purposes, Austin's categories can be recharacterized, more simply, as information, performatives and judgments. Performatives can then be further divided into commands, requests, promises, and suggestions, while judgments can be divided into approval and disapproval. This is a bit complex, but it is designed to capture the complexities of contemporary governance. There is, for example, a longstanding tendency in political theory, intimately connected to the medieval concepts of power, legitimacy, and law, to discuss communication within government, and between government and private citizens, exclusively in terms of commands. It seems clear, however, that information, requests, promises, and judgments flow through the governmental network as frequently as commands, and are as important in understanding governmental action.

Having characterized the connections between units, the second step in elaborating the network metaphor is to characterize the operations that the units perform. In some cases, units generate a signal on the basis of their internal program, that is, the part of their design that determines the action of their components. In other cases, they perform operations on incoming signals, operations that can be identified as scaling, summing, and integrating.[57] Scaling is the proportional increase or decrease in an input variable. Summing is the combination of two separate input variables. Both are described as feed forward functions, since they transform an input into an output variable without any further operations. Integrating is the combination of an independent input variable with a dependent output variable that has been generated by the unit, a process generally described as feedback. Because the operational implications of feedback are often quite complex, this aspect of the analogy, despite its apparent familiarity, will be used sparingly in the subsequent analysis.

The unit's response to inputs is described as activation, which can be either continuous or binary.[58] Continuous activation means that the unit's output will change incrementally in response to incremental changes in the input, like a car engine controlled by continuously depressing or releasing the accelerator. Binary activation means that the unit will respond to inputs by switching on or off, like the car's headlights. Continuous and binary activation can be combined by applying a bias—a constant input from a separate source—to the unit in question.[59] If this is done, the original input must exceed a certain level to overcome the bias and activate the unit, after which the input activates the unit in a continuous manner.

The Advantages of the Network Model

The network metaphor provides an alternative image of government to the bracketed image of three separate branches. But as noted in Chapter 1, replacing a familiar image with a novel one is not, by itself, of any particular value. The question is whether the new image provides a superior way to describe our modern administrative state. As discussed, the criteria for making this determination are whether the heuristic corresponds to our emotional commitments, whether it announces its heuristic character, and whether it provides a framework for microanalysis.

One of our most basic emotional commitments in government is to the administrative state itself. Despite all the condemnation that has been leveled at administrative government, and all the dismay and social nostalgia that it elicits, it is the form of government that we have chosen, that we maintain, and that we rely upon to solve our social problems. Thus, an image of governmental structure that captures the reality of the modern administrative state, rather than obscuring or denying it, comports more fully with our prevailing emotional commitments. The extent to which the image of a network captures this reality can be seen by considering the defining features of the administrative state, features that have been described in Chapter 1 with the purposely bland term of articulation.

The first meaning of articulation is the division of government into a set of functionally defined agencies or departments. Conceiving of the government as composed of legislative, executive, and judicial branches captures part of this process, and constitutes the essence of Montesquieu's recommendations. But most of the articulation that is so characteristic of our contemporary state occurs within and among administrative departments, that is, in an area that the arborescent metaphor envisions as a single, grotesquely hypertrophic branch. The network metaphor allows us to depict this articulation as interconnections among separate but interdependent units, each with its own defining function. Moreover, it emphasizes the fact that articulation occurs at various levels. The principal departments of government are articulated, but each department consists of numerous divisions, which are similarly articulated, and the divisions consist of similarly articulated offices. This reproduction of the basic structure at each successive level, described by new institutional sociology as institutional isomorphism,[60] is also captured by the network metaphor.

The second form of articulation is the self-conscious implementation of social policy by government. Here too, the arborescent metaphor fails to capture the reality that embodies our emotional commitment to the administrative state. A tree is a natural object, and not a particularly conscious one; in fact, given their size, trees may have less intelligence per pound than any other living thing on earth. They can be pruned, shaped, even miniaturized, but they cannot be ordered to carry out a task. A network, in contrast, is something that is quintessentially designed to serve a purpose, and that can be issued specific and varying instructions. Moreover, it can be designed and programmed to learn on its own.[61] Thus, it provides an image of government as an instrumentality and as a self-contained adaptive mechanism. Both these possibilities may cause us discomfort, as they force us to confront the unpleasant possibility that the wrong people can gain control of the governmental apparatus, or that it can generate its own self-serving goals and wreak havoc on the citizenry. Trees, on the other hand, are natural, benign, and reassuring; that is still another reason not to use them as a committed description of modern administrative government.

With respect to the second criterion for political imagery, the difficulty with the three-branch metaphor is that familiarity has reified it to the extent that people think of government as truly separated into three observably distinct components. In the United States, where ambivalence about the administrative state runs unusually high, and where the three-branch metaphor is viewed as being codified in the Constitution, the reified character of this metaphor has led both judges and scholars to perceive the separation of the branches as a normatively grounded doctrine that should be enforced by the judiciary. While courts, which are after all composed of politically astute people who sense the importance of the administrative state, have generally been wary of this notion, they have struck down a number of major federal statutes on these grounds.[62] The rationales that they have offered are typically described by scholars as either formal or functional,[63] but the weakness of both rationales suggests that the decisions are being at least partially driven by the reified force of the metaphor itself.

The formal rationale, which is based on the language or original intent of the Constitution, confuses the incontrovertible fact that the Framers conceived of government according to the three-branch model with the questionable claim that they intended to maintain a strict separation among these components. There is little support for this latter proposition.[64] The Constitutional text is notoriously ambiguous, but historical evidence of the Framers' intentions strongly contradicts any notion of strict separation. Several states, including Virginia and Pennsylvania, had followed the more radical Civil War writers and enacted constitutions that specifically declared the three branches of government to be entirely separate.[65] The authors of the federal Constitution were certainly aware of these provisions, but they were more immediately concerned about the ineffectiveness of the central government than about its potential threat to liberty,[66] and never seriously considered a provision of this sort. Indeed, the First Congress, in which many of them sat, rejected a separation of powers amendment when James Madison, apparently experiencing regrets about his original draftsmanship, proposed it together with the Bill of Rights.[67] But the reified nature of the three-branch image has induced the Court to turn what was essentially a topic outline into a moral declaration that extends two centuries into a different era.

The functional rationale looks to the purpose, rather than the provenance, of maintaining the separation among branches. In essence, it asserts that the different components of government can best restrain each other, and prevent abuses of authority, if strict boundaries among these components are maintained. But most of the statutes invalidated on separation of powers grounds were designed to increase legislative control over administrative agencies—the very goal that separation of powers is supposed to achieve. In *Bowsher v. Synar*, for example, a statute by which Congress tried to restrain the growth of the federal budget was invalidated because the statute assigned the task of determining when budget overruns occur to a legislative officer.[68] In *Buckley v. Valeo*, the Federal Election Campaign Act, which established an administrative agency for the politically sensitive task of supervising federal elections, was partly invalidated because it provided for legislative appointment of the agency's members.[69] And in *INS v. Chadha*, a closely related case, the legislative veto, which gave Congress the authority to cancel administrative regulations, was invalidated on the grounds that Congress could only exercise such authority by legislation.[70] One might have thought that a commitment to the functional rationale for separation of powers would have led the Court to approve these legislative efforts. But the reification of the three-branch metaphor had separated it from its recognized purpose, and transformed into an end in itself, a conceptual entity that, Saturn-like, was devouring its children.

In contrast, the network metaphor is less likely to be reified because it is free from historically sedimented meanings that could grant it a normative force that it does not merit on formal or functional grounds. What is novel is also frequently arcane, however, and thus violates the criterion that heuristics ought to be naive. The idea of a network, however, is familiar and widely comprehended. Although people's primary associations with the term reside in technical areas, they regularly apply the image to social and political phenomena as well, and often use it to capture the complex, interconnected character of situations that they associate with modernity. In his study of the way white collar workers get new jobs, for example, Mark Granovetter concluded that personal contacts were the single most important factor.[71] This was almost certainly true in the Middle Ages as well, and would have been conceived in terms of recommendation, reference, and family background, but Granovetter uses the term 'network' for its modern avatar. What renders his image judiciously naive is that participants in the labor market think in similar terms; they commonly conceive of a group of close and remote acquaintances as a network, and describe the effort to extend this group, or obtain information from it, as "networking."

The third virtue of the network metaphor is that it provides a framework for microanalysis, that is, an analysis that begins from individual behavior, that recognizes the spatial and temporal context of those individuals, that accounts for the full range of human motivations, and that attempts to trace actual pathways of communication or decision that these situated individuals create. This final claim can only be demonstrated by developing the metaphor itself in greater detail and then applying it to some exemplary situations.

Applying the Network Model

The Tectonic Structure of Government

The advantages of the network model in providing a framework for the microanalysis of modern governmental architecture, or hardware, can be illustrated by considering the operative relationships among various governmental units. Of particular interest is the relationship of each of the traditional units of government—the chief executive, the legislature, and the judiciary—with the welter of administrative agencies that characterize the modern state. In the U.S. government, the three-branch metaphor places the president in the same branch as the agencies, but places Congress and the federal courts in separate branches. Thus, the president and the agencies are seen as linked by the organic relationship of superior and subordinate, whereas Congress and the agencies, or the courts and the agencies, supposedly stand on opposite sides of an organizational divide. This oversimplifies the first relationship, problematizes the second and third, and obscures the essential similarity among all three.

By placing the chief executive in the same branch as the agencies, the prevailing metaphor suggests that the president can control the agencies by simply issuing commands. The fact that this is obviously not the case is then seen as an institutional failure of some kind, either a lack of presidential competence or a mephitic expansion of the administrative apparatus.[72] Generalizations and judgments of this nature preclude microanalysis of existing practices and problems. Once the three-branch metaphor is bracketed, the realities of the situation become more apparent. First, as many observers have noted, the brobdingnagian scale of the administrative apparatus means that no single person can comprehend or control it in any meaningful way.[73] Each of the Cabinet agencies that is juridically subject to the president's control is in fact a separate unit of the government. Thus, any commands the president issues must traverse a significant institutional divide, another reality that is distorted by the metaphor that places the president and these agencies in a single branch of government. The proliferation of independent agencies that are not subject to the president's direct control only makes this problem more severe. In response, every modern president has relied on White House staff—a group of advisors and small, informally organized agencies—to gather information and transmit instructions to his own cabinet members and their myriad subordinates.[74] By Kennedy's time, which, despite his wife's subsequent characterization, was a long time after Camelot and its decision making by the Knights of the Round Table, presidential staff members were among the most important and publicly recognized members of the government. Theodore Sorensen, himself a leading staff member, noted that the president had to expend exceptional amounts of energy to supervise even his own personal staff, or he might have become "merely a clerk in his own office, caught up in the routines and recommendations of others."[75]

The confusion engendered by the idea that the president and the administrative agencies are part of the same branch has not only affected legal and political science scholarship, but may have affected practical politics as well. The crucial role of the White House staff has been underappreciated, and the staff itself too fluid in its structure and uncertain in its role. Moreover, it was not until the 1970s—at least one hundred years after the advent of the American administrative state—that a specially designed governmental unit, the Office of Management and Budget (OMB), was developed to facilitate presidential control of the agencies. As its current name suggests, this unit grew out of efforts by the president and his advisors to design a budget that reflected the president's policy priorities.[76] Because such policies could only be implemented by administrative agencies, the agency role in this design process grew increasingly more prominent. When the need for a specialized governmental unit to implement presidential control over the agencies became apparent, the president turned to OMB.[77] Perhaps by association of ideas, and perhaps because of the ideological predilections that prevailed at the time, OMB's mission was defined as controlling the cost of regulation, rather than ensuring its general effectiveness.[78] The unit was given only one policy tool, cost benefit analysis, and was encouraged to develop an anti-regulatory ethos inconsistent with its general mission.[79] This narrow orientation has begun to change as the underlying function becomes better understood; OMB now issues "prompt letters," urging agencies to regulate, as well as "return letters" that reject regulations on cost-benefit grounds.

With the three-branch modeled bracketed, the alternative image of a network can be used to understand the president's relationship to the administrative agencies. At the most basic level of the network, the president appears as a single individual with a wide range of linkages to other individuals. At the next level up, which is probably a more useful perspective, the president and the individuals and small agencies described as White House staff constitute a unit. This unit communicates with other units by issuing and receiving signals, but it is simply inaccurate to think of these signals as consisting exclusively of commands. Commands are only one kind of performative that issues from the president's office; in addition, the president and his advisors make requests, threats, promises, and suggestions, and they transmit a variety of positive and negative judgments. It is equally inaccurate to imagine that all the relevant signals flow, as commands do, from the president's office to the agencies. The president cannot command an agency effectively unless he receives a good deal of information about it, nor can he formulate substantive policy without such information. Thus, information outputs from the agency, predominantly in the form of locutionary statements, flow through the linkages and become valued inputs for the president's office.[80]

From this perspective, OMB's role in supervising administrative agencies is neither a surprise nor a disruption of the government's established structure, but rather a virtually inevitable development. Microanalysis of the president's relationship to the administrative apparatus, using the network model, would indicate that the president's office can only issue a limited number of signals, so that the signals flowing to many agencies will be too intermittent or cursory to produce any significant effect. In addition, the locutionary signals flowing from the agencies to the president's office become more voluminous and complex with every passing year, overwhelming that unit's processing capacities. OMB represents a means of increasing the president's ability to transmit and receive the signals necessary for effective control of the administrative apparatus. The president's office puts out signals to OMB, and OMB issues a much larger number of signals to the agencies; many of the signals that the agencies put out flow to OMB rather than the president's office. Going further, one might observe that some of the signals flowing from the president's office to OMB represent commands, requests, suggestions, and judgments whose effect is to alter or reinforce OMB's internal programming. This enables the president to exercise comprehensive control over the agencies with a relatively small number of signals, essentially using OMB to scale up his general statements into more detailed instructions to individual agencies. Of course, the process has its costs, disadvantages, and inefficiencies, but the network model facilitates analysis of these as well.

Microanalysis also facilitates an understanding of the extensive but much-debated development of independent agencies, such as the Federal Trade Commission, the Federal Communications Commission, and the Federal Reserve Board. The idea that the president and the administrative agencies are part of the same branch has led some observers to conclude that independent agencies, that is, agencies whose leadership cannot be removed by the president, represent an illegal distortion of the Constitution's structure—a hideous, headless fourth branch.[81] But the evidence for this position, from either the text of the Constitution or the intent that lay behind it, is extremely thin.[82] The real arguments for the unitary presidency are structural, which is to say that they are emanations of the three-branch model. Microanalysis, as facilitated by the network model, allows us to free ourselves from global judgments about governmental branches and focus on the actual consequences of agency independence. In essence, independence means that the president or his office may not issue a direct command to a particular agency. It can still issue other types of signals, including requests and judgments, however.[83] Moreover, independent agencies send locutionary signals to the president's office, and in some cases to OMB, at a similar rate as the executive agencies, and such information provides a basis for control. From this perspective, agency independence appears as a particular governance technique that forbids one type of signal from flowing from the president to certain agencies, not as a violation of the central organizing principle of American government.[84] The impact

of this prohibition is a complex question that cannot be answered by saying that executive agencies are under the president's control while independent agencies are not. This does not preclude normative opposition to
agency independence, of course, but it removes the sense of unnaturalness
that attaches to this mechanism, and demands more specific, functionally
oriented criticisms.

In contrast to the chief executive, the legislature is regarded, in the
three-branch metaphor, as belonging to a different branch. Its basic task,
in enacting statutes implemented by administrative agencies, is then regarded as a delegation of power from one branch to another. For some,
this delegation represents the initial lapse of legislative courage that spawned
our current political degeneracy.[85] For others, it is the lifeline of legitimacy,
the essential link between the legislators that citizens send off to the capital and the administrative government that they get back.[86] Once the
three-branch metaphor is bracketed, however, the delegation issue appears
as another artifact or exhalation of that metaphor, rather than an accurate
description. We speak of delegation, and attach so much significance to it,
because we regard the legislative authorization of an administrative agency
as an action that crosses an interbranch boundary. Moreover, we imagine
that some actual substance, generally described as power, is being transferred across that boundary. If we view the government as a multilevel network, the force of these impressions tends to dissipate, and what we now
describe as delegation becomes the ordinary and essential task of issuing
assignments to one's institutional subordinates within the governmental
structure. It is thus equivalent to the president's effort to control the administrative apparatus.

According to the network model, Congress is not delegating its authority in any unusual or suspect manner when it enacts a statute that instructs
an administrative agency to implement some function. It is simply exercising that authority by sending well-recognized types of signals through established linkages. For example, prior to the passage of the Federal Reserve Act in 1913,[87] the federal government had no ability to extend loans
to banks, to accept deposits from them, to issue nonredeemable notes, or
to regulate state banks. By enacting the statute, Congress authorized these
functions. The fact that they were to be carried out by an administrative
agency, the Federal Reserve Board, does not mean that Congress relin-
quished its newly created authority at the moment of its creation, like
some exotic subatomic particle that decays a nanosecond after it appears.
Rather, the process of enacting a statute and assigning its operation to an
agency is precisely the way that a policy-making entity like Congress is expected to function in an administrative state. The network metaphor thus
implies that there are no inherent presumptions against broad, open-
ended assignments of authority. This is in fact the conclusion that the fed-

eral courts have reached,[88] and indicates their acceptance of the administrative state's reality.

The network model thus enables us to look at the role of the legislature clearly, rather than through the dusty and distorting lens of delegation. Enacting statutes is a legislature's most characteristic task, and generally its most important one. These statutes can be modeled as feed forward signals issued from the legislature to other governmental units, such as administrative agencies, that exist at the same level of generality. Typically, a statute takes the form of a command, but it can also include other performatives, such as suggestions, by using language that is vague, ambiguous, or explicitly precatory, hortatory, or advisory. Statutes are not the only signals that issue from the legislature, however. After the statute is enacted, the legislature monitors its implementation by issuing other signals to the implementing agency. Some of these are themselves legislation, and thus commands, such as amendments to the statute or changes in the agency's budgetary allocation. In addition, there are many more informal mechanisms, including resolutions issued by one chamber or two, oversight hearings, communications from an individual legislator or her staff to the administrative agency, and public announcements by the legislators in hearings, on the chamber floor, or elsewhere.[89] These are generally not commands, although they may be phrased as such if the legislator is sufficiently irate. Rather, they are other performatives, such as suggestions or threats, or they are positive and negative judgments with a vague sense of threat attached. As in the case of the president, information from the agencies, in the form of locutionary signals, is crucial to this process of control, and Congress can command the production of such signals, as well as generating them by threat, suggestion, or request.

This network model facilitates microanalysis of the legislature's relationship to administrative agencies, providing an analytic framework in which the complex and continuous contacts that characterize this relationship can be understood. In this model, the delegation issue disappears; legislation, no matter how broadly worded, is simply part, and far from the entirety, of the way Congress issues signals to an agency regarding a specified subject. There is something further to be said about this issue, however,[90] because the most convincing criticisms of broadly worded statutes are not based on the formal structure of government, but on functional considerations.[91] Broadly worded statutes, critics argue, enable legislators to evade political accountability by deferring politically difficult decisions to the administrative agencies.[92] Because they recognize that the outright prohibition of broadly worded statutes is politically impossible, and perhaps even theoretically undesirable, many critics have proposed that nondelegation be treated as a subconstitutional principle that should inform statutory interpretation.[93] Such concerns are certainly important ones, but the generalizations about their connection to broadly worded statutes is as much an artifact of the three-branch model as the formal objection to such statutes. This becomes apparent from the microanalysis of the drafting process facilitated by the network model.

Claims about the motivations of legislators, such as those that critics of broadly worded statutes advance, direct attention to the lowest level of the network, where the functional units are individuals. Individual legislators, like everyone else, experience a range of motivations that they try to integrate into a coherent totality.[94] These different motives, such as self-interest and ideology, do not translate neatly into a particular strategy or preference. Rather, the legislators' strategies depend on their empirical assessment of the situation and the nature of the particular task being assigned by means of the legislation in question. When a legislator is motivated by the desire to maximize his chance of reelection, his drafting strategy will depend upon a variety of factors, including the issue's political valence, the character of the administrative agency, and the prevailing political configuration of the government in its entirety. If he believes that the legislation, on balance, will aid his reelection, but alienate an important special interest group, he may prefer a broadly stated statute that assigns extensive rule-making authority to the administrative agency. But if he feels that the risk is low, and the potential political payoff high, he may favor more precisely worded legislation that holds the agency to a specific course of action. The legislator will also be influenced by the character of the agency itself. As Robert Cooter points out, much will depend on the legislator's estimate of the agency's loyalty or responsibility;[95] broad phrasing is preferable if the individuals who control the agency can be expected to obey the legislative enactment or respond to the same political interest groups to which the legislator does, but specific requirements may be preferable in the absence of such expectations.[96] The legislator's preference for generality or specificity will also be influenced by the similarity between the chief executive's political preferences and his own.

When the legislator is motivated by her ideological commitments, she will be guided by a different but not entirely dissimilar set of considerations. If she feels that she knows exactly how to achieve her policy goal, she will favor a precisely worded statute. If she is certain of her goal, but lacks the knowledge necessary to devise an effective strategy, she may prefer to assign extensive rule-making authority to the agency.[97] As in the case of the reelection maximizer, her decisions will also be heavily influenced by the character of the agency and the overall political configuration. She will favor broad assignments to an agency whose leaders share her ideology, or that is controlled by a chief executive who does so, but prefer narrowly tailored ones if she regards the agency or the chief executive as ideologically unreliable. In short, legislation is a complex signal whose design depends upon the particular goals that the legislator is attempting to achieve, and upon a wide range of empirical information about the signal's recipient. Generalizations, of the sort that critics of broadly worded statutes have advanced, may be accurate in some cases but will be inaccurate in others. The motivation to insist upon such generalizations comes from a nostalgia-driven desire to restore the three-branch metaphor by refurbishing it in contemporary terms.

The network metaphor does not imply that there can be no limitations on a governmental unit's ability to issue assignments to other units. But those limits must be specifically argued for, not derived from an outmoded, pre-analytic image of government. One important limitation emerges from the structure of the network itself, in that each unit is linked only to certain other units. Thus, the network's design may provide that a given unit may only issue assignments over certain pathways, and only to certain other units that are generally designated as its subordinates.[98] Indeed, the identity of an individual or unit as the subordinate of another individual or unit generally depends on the ability of the second unit to issue assignments to the first. As Elizabeth Magill suggests, this intrinsic dispersal of government authority provides much of the protection to which separation of powers doctrine aspires, but does so in a manner consistent with the realities of an administrative state.[99] Moreover, the design may prohibit the assignment of specific tasks, which means that the unit is expected to perform that task itself. For example, Congress, according to the prevailing interpretation of our written Constitution, and Parliament, according to the understanding of Britain's unwritten one, are expected to conduct impeachments of leading executive officials themselves. It would be regarded as improper to assign the matter to a respected judge. The Federal Reserve Board is expected to make the final decisions regarding monetary policy. And one type of restriction on assignment is central to the operation of a modern administrative state: an individual who holds a government position is not permitted to assign the entire position and go hunting. The contemporary official, unlike the Clerk of the Pipe or the King's Remembrancer, is not a property holder; she is expected to perform her job herself, although she is generally not prohibited from assigning specific functions to her subordinates in doing so.

Like the legislature, the judiciary is regarded as a separate branch of government. In this case as well, the network metaphor provides a more promising basis for microanalysis of the judiciary's relationships to other governmental units. The idea that the judiciary is a separate branch only impedes our understanding, obscuring these relationships with outdated generalities—that courts are the primary interpreters of the law, that they are also the primary adjudicators of disputes, that their proper role is limited to these two functions, and that the independence that they need to implement these functions requires them to be placed in a separate branch of government.

The idea that courts are the primary interpreters of law is misleading because the task of interpreting a statute does not depend upon whether the decision maker is a member of the judiciary, but on whether the decision maker is subject to a preexisting legal statement as a result of the government's authority structure. If an administrative agency—or the chief executive, for that matter—is bound by a particular statute, it must interpret that statute in order to perform its role.[100] In fact, administrative agencies are generally the primary interpreters of statutes in the modern state, and most of these interpretations are never reviewed by the judiciary.

A related distinction, also of arborescent provenance, is that the courts adjudicate while the legislature makes public policy. The distinction, which predates the administrative state, was central to the efforts of the American legal process school to ascribe some sort of institutional essence to the courts. As administrative law scholars such as Jerry Mashaw have pointed out, however, the great bulk of adjudications in the modern state is performed by administrative agencies, not by the judiciary.[101] This is hardly surprising, since agencies engage in ongoing supervision of organizations and individuals in many areas, and the adjudication of disputes is usually a central feature of such supervision. In the pre-modern state, where there were many fewer agencies and little social regulation, supervision and its attendant adjudication could be largely limited to the judiciary, but this is no longer the case.

Of course, the judiciary of a modern state continues to interpret and adjudicate, but it also engages in roles supposedly limited to other branches, such as making policy and supervising administrative agencies. Courts have always made public policy—and the three-branch image has always tended to obscure this—but this role becomes more prominent, and thus more difficult to deny, in an administrative state, where the cases that come before the courts increasingly involve complex governmental institutions. In fact, as Malcolm Feeley and I have argued at some length, policy making is an ordinary and fully justifiable aspect of the judicial role.[102] Policy making is generally required when judges create new legal doctrine, a process that has been responsible for much of the Anglo-American common law, most American constitutional law, and even a fair number of statutorily–based doctrines, such as the rule reason doctrine under the Sherman Act.[103] The structural position of the courts demands that they make public policy in many instances, just as the structural position of the agencies demands that they interpret statutes.

In addition to functioning as a policy maker, the modern judiciary serves as an important supervisor of administrative agencies. Rather than being viewed as a separate branch, it should be viewed as one unit of an interacting network that, like the chief executive and the legislature, issues signals to other units in that network. It differs from these other units because it derives its authority from legal doctrine, rather than elections, but this does not necessarily alter its structural role. One mode of judicial supervision is to take individual appeals from agency adjudications. This gives the losing litigant a second chance to argue its position, but it also serves to supervise the agency's adjudicatory function. The reversal of an adjudication sends a signal to the agency that will thereafter be summed with the agency adjudicator's own interpretation.[104] The judiciary also supervises the agency's statutory interpretations by hearing challenges to agency rule making or other actions based on statutory authorizations. If the court disagrees with the agency's interpretation, it may invalidate the action on the grounds that it violates the statute. The most important American administrative law decision of the last several decades, *Chevron, USA v. NRDC*,[105] involved the standards that courts should apply in this situation. Finally, the judiciary supervises the policy decisions of the agency through a variety of less direct, but equally important means. If it finds the agency decision questionable, it may apply a more demanding interpretive standard or search assiduously for procedural defects—the so-called "hard look" doctrine in administrative law.[106]

A final distortion of the three-branch metaphor involves judicial independence. According to the traditional view, the independence of the judiciary is regarded as desirable because it is, after all, a separate branch, while the independence of the agencies is regarded as undesirable because it makes them a fourth branch and there are only supposed to be three.[107] The network metaphor provides a way to analyze this issue in terms of our genuinely felt values rather than our unexamined trinitarian mind-sets.[108] When the status of an individual is being adjudicated, fairness generally demands that the adjudicator, whether a judge or agency hearing officer, be independent of any other governmental unit except another adjudicator.[109] But adjudication is not the only situation where independence is desirable. Most economists, for example, believe that governmental effectiveness increases when the monetary control authority possesses a similar level of independence.[110] In contrast, when courts supervise agencies on complex policy-making matters, they might be more effective if they received input from a wider variety of sources and their independence were less carefully maintained. When courts promulgate rules of procedure for themselves, or frame recommendations to the legislature, their independence is often unnecessary, and sometimes counter-productive.[111] Thus, as Peter Strauss suggests, independence is a political resource, to be deployed when it can be specifically justified by normative or practical concerns, not an inherent feature of any particular governmental unit.[112]

Independence, moreover, is not secured by declaring that a particular unit is in a separate branch, but by the nature of the interaction among units. The standard methods of securing a unit's independence are to deny any other unit the authority to issue commands to it, to restrict the informative or locutionary inputs that other units are allowed to provide, to minimize the impact of judgments and threats by giving the decision makers job tenure and salary protection, and to apply a bias to limit the unit's activation, often in the form of professional training requirements. Precisely how these methods are to be deployed is a matter that can be resolved only by microanalysis. In the United States, federal judges are given a specially defined status, while some state judges are separately elected; in Europe, judges are treated as administrative agents, and insulated by ordinary administrative means.[113] These methods may work well or poorly, depending on circumstances,[114] but it is simply not correct to assume that an adjudicator characterized as part of the executive is necessarily subordinate, or that one characterized as part of a separate branch is necessarily independent.[115] The point of the network metaphor is to avoid condemnation or complacency on the basis of pre-empirical categorizations, and to facilitate the more tedious but useful process of microanalyzing the need for independence and the methods by which it can be achieved.

The Process of Controlling Administrative Apparatus

As the foregoing, and necessarily abbreviated, discussion of the tectonic relationship among the various components of a modern administrative government makes clear, the traditional units of government—the chief executive, the legislature, and the judiciary—can all be viewed as engaged in a common enterprise: the control of the administrative apparatus.[116] This apparatus constitutes our primary means of governance, and, once set in motion, tends to operate autonomously. The process of control involves initially setting it in motion and subsequently redirecting its otherwise autonomous behavior. Public policy, legal doctrine, and moral imperatives are implemented through this process of control. This does not mean that the agencies will be blind to such considerations if they are left to their own devices; their internal programs and external contacts with nongovernmental entities incorporate a range of policy, legal, and moral considerations. But if elected officials are to affect public policy in response to the voters' desires, and if the judiciary is to implement legal doctrine according to its own interpretation, they must do so through the process of controlling the administrative apparatus. The natural question to pursue, therefore, is how this process of control actually occurs.

The three-branch metaphor provides a rather poor conceptual framework for this inquiry. Its pre-modern generalizations only impede the ability of scholars to focus on the complex dynamics of the interaction of the chief executive, legislature, and judiciary with the bureaucratic apparatus. This problem has been partially remedied in recent years by the positive political theory scholarship of Matthew McCubbins, Mark Moran, Roger Noll, Thomas Schwartz, Barry Weingast, and others[117] but the arborescent image continues to impinge on their descriptions, while delegation issues prevent legal scholars from integrating such descriptions with their normatively oriented analysis. A major advantage of the network model is that it shifts attention from the arid issue of delegation toward a micro-analysis of these more relevant concerns.[118]

According to the network model, one unit of government controls another by issuing feed forward signals to that unit. The controlling unit must make a variety of choices in designing these signals, including the choice between specifying procedures and specifying input or output, the choice between commanding the agency and encouraging it to learn, and the choice between initial instructions and continuous monitoring. Such choices confront all controlling units, whether executive, legislative, or judicial in character, and the nature of the choice is often rather similar, despite the different modalities that these units employ. The network model not only provides a framework for microanalysis of these efforts, but also illuminates their underlying similarity.

The first choice is whether the signals issued by the control unit will specify the inputs, the outputs, or the internal program of the unit being controlled. In the United States, all the control units have tended to focus their efforts on controlling the agency's internal program. This may reflect the legal or procedural predilections of American public officials, or it may indicate their lack of the social science skills that are needed to measure outputs or results. With respect to Congress, some scholars have asserted that this predilection is required by the Constitution. David Schoenbrod, for example, argues that a statute specifying the goals the agency is supposed to reach, as opposed to the procedures it is supposed to use, represents an impermissibly broad delegation.[119] But the conclusion seems driven by the pre-analytic, pre-empirical nature of the terminology, and the three-branch metaphor that underlies it, rather than by an analysis of real government control functions. Specifying the agency's output might not represent an abdication of congressional responsibility but a higher level of control, one that requires the agency to confront and overcome the refractory nature of reality rather than merely dressing itself up in the procedural specifications of the statute.

Presidential and judicial orders also display a tendency to specify procedures, rather than outputs. OMB, for example, requires agencies to engage in cost-benefit analysis, often rejecting regulations because the agency failed to perform the analysis correctly. Courts invalidate regulations because the agency failed to follow the statutorily required procedures. Robert Katzmann, Thomas McGarity, Shep Melnick, and others have expressed concern over the extent to which the outputs of this procedural supervision by the federal judiciary are scaled up within the agency, disrupting its regular operations.[120] But executive and judicial supervision need not be limited to this approach. OMB can reject regulations because the cost actually exceeds the benefit, the president can order the Department of Defense to produce a weapon with a specified success rate, and courts can issue injunctions that require a prison to provide meals with a specified caloric content.

In fact, both the specification of procedures and the specification of output have advantages that will vary from one situation to another and that can only be discerned by microanalysis. A unit might choose to specify procedures if it thinks that the procedures are likely to achieve a particular goal. Alternatively, it might be uncertain how the goal should be defined, but sense that specified procedures will move the agency in the desired direction. In contrast, a control unit might be clear about the goal it wants, but uncertain which internal procedures are most likely to achieve it. As James Q. Wilson points out, different agencies have different structures; in some agencies, such as a mental hospital, the procedures are observable but the outcome is not, while in others, such as the Army Corps of Engineers, the outcome is observable but the procedures are not.[121] This will influence, if not determine, the preferable mode of control. If the goal can be clearly identified and no countervailing values such as fairness intervene, specification of that goal would seem to be the most effective method, since it would be directed to the precise results that the controlling unit wants.

Another possible option is to specify the agency's input. By itself, this does not seem very promising; it would prescribe the kind of signals that the agency could receive, but not its internal procedures or the results it was expected to produce. Combined with other methods of control, however, input control is a valuable option, implicating the structural issue of independence discussed above. Agencies can be required to receive signals from other units in the network, or they can be forbidden to do so, and these specifications clearly affect the agency's operations and results. To take just one example, most administrative agencies receive inputs from private parties, and are expected to sum these inputs with inputs from other governmental units. But certain agency actions, such as the Federal Reserve's monetary control function, are supposed to be insulated from this political process, a result that is achieved by blocking the ordinary connections through which input from private parties is received.[122] Since these connections cannot be blocked entirely, at least in an open society like our own, Congress has also applied a bias to the Federal Reserve that is intended to increase its activation level, and thereby scale down any political inputs that are nonetheless received. This bias takes the form of professional training; there is a general view that the governors and other leading officials of the Federal Reserve are supposed to be trained economists, and that the decisions they reach are to be conceived and justified in economic terms.[123] Inputs to agency adjudicators, from either private parties or other branches of government, are similarly restricted by both Congress and the courts.[124] In contrast, relatively little control is exercised over inputs from private parties to agency policy makers during the rule-making process because our notions of fairness do not demand the insulation of that process from external influences.[125]

The second crucial choice is between command and learning. Quite apart from attempting to control the input, output, or program of the agency, the control unit can also attempt to establish a program within the agency that enables it to learn. Learning is preferable to command when circumstances are likely to change, when the control unit that can issue commands knows the result it is trying to achieve but does not know the means for achieving it, or when the control unit does not even know what result it desires. The first situation is relatively well understood and well accepted; administrators are "on the ground" or "in the trenches" or in some other low-lying metaphorical position where they regularly receive information that is unavailable to the control unit, or not known to anyone at the time the control unit issues its original signal. The second situation, where the control unit cannot determine the means of achieving a desired result, is sometimes treated as a failure of technical knowledge or political nerve by the control unit,[126] but can also be seen as an honest, empirically oriented approach to the problem of governance. Certainly, our sense of both public policy and legal doctrine allows for the existence of goals that non-administrative units can identify without knowing how to accomplish. When Congress decided, in 1927, that the radio spectrum should be allocated in an orderly fashion, when a federal court decided that conditions in an Arkansas prison must be altered to meet constitutional requirements, and when President Kennedy announced that the United States would put a man on the moon by the end of the decade, they could reasonably expect that the implementation strategy could be left to the expertise of the relevant administrative agencies.[127] The third situation, where the control unit simply defines the area of concern, and instructs the agency to develop its own goals through a learning process, may seem the most problematic. But as scholars such as Michael Dorf, Susan Sturm, and Cass Sunstein note, a control unit can fulfill its function by engaging other institutions in a dialogue about desirable norms.[128] That is, the control unit need not regard itself as the sole source of policy initiatives, but may view itself as participating in a mutual learning process with those units subject to its authority.

Intriguing theories about learning within networks have been developed in the fields of cognitive psychology and artificial intelligence.[129] For present purposes, the important point is that a control strategy that encourages an agency to learn is not necessarily equivalent to one that defers to agency decision making. Instead, it can specify procedures or identify criteria that are designed to establish a feedback loop within the subject agency. Lisa Bressman has proposed that the delegation doctrine be reinterpreted to allow broadly worded statutes that permit agency learning, but require the agency to embody what it has learned in explicitly stated regulations.[130] Alternatively, agencies might be required to report back to the legislature, to achieve certain benchmarks by certain times, or to engage in specified forms of evaluation. If mechanisms such as these seem more suitable to executive supervision, that is because we are accustomed to viewing the chief executive as part of the same branch as administrative agencies, while we view the legislature and the courts as located in different branches. In fact, control mechanisms that encourage learning are general instrumentalities of governance.

The third crucial choice is that the control unit, like any hierarchical superior, must decide how much control it will exercise by issuing instructions in advance, and how much it will exercise by monitoring the subordinate's performance. Ashutosh Bhagwat discusses this as the choice between ex ante and ex post regulation,[131] while McCubbins and Schwartz describe it as the choice between "police patrol" and "fire alarm" modes of legislative oversight.[132] Issuing instructions in advance generally possesses the virtue of clarity, but suffers from the vice of inflexibility, while continuous monitoring exhibits the opposite features. One can ameliorate the rigidity of instructions stated in advance by making these instructions open-ended, but only at a partial sacrifice of clarity. One can ameliorate the oppressiveness of continuous monitoring by following a pattern that is transparent to the subordinate, but then one has sacrificed a certain amount of flexibility. Of course, the two approaches can be combined, which either amplifies their individual virtues, amplifies their individual vices, or produces previously unimagined difficulties.

This choice between instructions stated in advance and continuous monitoring is quite separate from the choice between specifying procedures and specifying output, since the control unit can specify either the procedures or the output in advance, and monitor either the procedures or the output on a continuous basis. These choices are not separate from the choice between control and learning, however. Advance instructions are generally more conducive to learning than continuous monitoring, and the specification of output is more conducive to learning than the specification of procedures. Combining these factors, it can be said that the best way to encourage learning is to issue advance instructions regarding output, so that the agency must figure out the best way to achieve a specified goal, while the best way to preclude it is to monitor procedures on a continuous basis, so that the agency's day-to-day actions are being regularly revised by its superior.

To a significant extent, the choice between instructions and continuous monitoring determines whether there will be an ongoing relationship between the control unit and the agency. Here again, the three-branch metaphor creates a misleading distinction. While the sort of ongoing relationship that results from continuous monitoring is regarded as normal for the chief executive's control over administrative agencies, it is often seen as exceptional, even improper, for the legislature and the judiciary. But in this case as well, the three-branch metaphor, like John of Salisbury's human body image, does not really apply to the government it purports to describe. The legislature is the structural superior of the agencies and, like many superiors, it supervises its subordinates on a continuous basis. It does so primarily through the oversight process, the process to which the network model directs attention, as described above.

One recently controversial element of this oversight process is the legislative veto, by which one House of Congress, or one congressional committee, invalidates an agency regulation. In *INS v. Chadha*,[133] as already mentioned, the Supreme Court struck down all the legislative veto provisions in federal statutes—there were over two hundred—on the ground that they constituted legislation, and thus needed to be approved by both Houses and signed by the president.[134] This rigid conception of the legislature's role, however, is merely another emanation of the three-branch metaphor. The alternative heuristic of a governmental network suggests that continuous monitoring of administrative agencies is an essential role of modern legislatures. From this perspective, a statute is not a fixed set of rules that the legislature enacts by the constitutionally prescribed procedure and then ignores. Rather, it represents the initiation of an ongoing process in which the meaning of the statute evolves continuously as the situation governed by the statute changes. The implementing agency is the primary mechanism by which a statute thus propagates itself through time, but the legislature can exercise at least partial control over this process by monitoring the agency. To do so, however, it must act by some means that is less elaborate than the initial enactment of the statute, and the legislative veto is one such means. That is the reason why Congress has continued to enact legislative veto provisions despite the *Chadha* decision[135] and why it enacted a comprehensive "report and wait" statute governing all major regulations.[136] The U.S. Congress does not typically make such concerted efforts to circumvent a Supreme Court decision, but *Chadha* speaks with the voice of the three-branch model that is no longer relevant to modern government, and Congress, in its effort to govern, has been compelled to disobey it.

Courts engage in the same sort of continuous monitoring as do the chief executive's office and the legislature. The most obvious example occurs when they do so within the context of a single case, retaining jurisdiction until a complex remedy is implemented.[137] In the prison reform cases, the federal district courts often retained jurisdiction for years, sometimes appointing a special master to exercise direct, on-the-scene supervision of the prison's daily operations.[138] The courts adopted this approach for the same reason that hierarchical superiors often do; state prison officials had proven themselves disloyal, in Cooter's terms[139]—unwilling to follow instructions and unwilling to learn. But continuous monitoring by courts also occurs in a less dramatic, more pervasive manner when the courts decide a series of cases in a particular area. Assume one court issues a landmark decision, declaring the existence of a new cause of action, such as the tort of emotional distress. Private parties will then proceed to assert such claims, simultaneously attempting to expand their scope, while other private parties who are defendants to these claims will resist these efforts. The cases will be tried, and the courts, in deciding them, will define and adjust the boundaries of the new cause of action over time.[140] This represents another form of continuous monitoring by the judiciary. Although no injunctions have been issued, and no single case has continued for any significant length of time, the cumulative impact of the decisions represents the same sort of ongoing supervision that a hierarchical superior might exercise within the purported executive branch.

This discussion of the relationships among the chief executive's office, the legislature, the courts, and the administrative agencies is only a preliminary consideration of a complex topic. For present purposes, the main point to be noted is that the three-branch metaphor has become so historically sedimented that we regard it as a self-evident description of external reality. In fact, it is a less than useful way to describe the relationships that are crucial to the effectiveness, efficiency, and fairness of modern government. It should not be used by courts to strike down or interpret legislation; its obsolescence renders it undesirable, on policy grounds, and, as discussed above, its invocation is not compelled by the Constitution's text or history. For similar reasons, it should not be used by policy analysts. And even if these actors, and other participants, use the term, it should be avoided by scholars as a method of description, since it does not capture the realities of modern government.

At the time of John of Salisbury, the principal task of government was to establish and maintain civil order. England was at best only a conquest-forged collection of self-sufficient baronies, each with its own laws and its own armed forces. During John's lifetime, even that precarious unity had dissolved; the barons split between two rival claimants to the throne, Stephen and Maud, and fought each other for twenty years.[141] While John's image of government was outdated even at the time, it at least reflected a felt need for stable structures, permanent institutions with well-defined responsibilities, a clear chain of command, and a willingness to work together as parts of a unified governmental structure. But these are not our problems or our tasks today. Modern government is articulated, hierarchical, and generally cohesive. The principal danger is not that it will dissolve into warring principalities, but that it will become inefficient or oppressive, that its massive, stable structure will become too self-contained to devote its efforts to the people's needs, and that it will either ignore the people or persecute them. To avoid these dangers we have developed administrative agencies to manage our social processes and we have assigned elected policy makers and doctrinally oriented judges to monitor those agencies. Thinking about government in conceptually coagulated terms—as a series of fixed structures that touch only at defined points, or as three branches growing from the ground or floating in the air—will not assist us in this task. The network metaphor, although just as much a metaphor as the three branches, is much more likely to generate a microanalysis of our government that enables us to accept its existence, comprehend its complex operations, and generate practical ideas for its improvement.

Three _____

From Power and Discretion to Authorization and Supervision

Power and Discretion

The Pre-Modern Concept of Power

WHEN Arthur, with his unsuspecting hand, pulled the sword out of the stone, he was revealed, in Malory's words, as the "rightfully-born king of all England."[1] We would say that he acquired power. For us, power is the force that animates the governmental structure described in the preceding chapter; it constitutes the purpose for which that structure is created, and the effect that it produces. Other institutions in society also exercise power, it is said, but the government is generally described as the most powerful, and power is more central to its purpose and its operation than it is for any other institution. To discuss the nature of government without discussing power would be regarded as naive or, worse still, as a false apologia, an effort to conceal the harsh realities of government behind a haze of high school civics bromides.

But power, a very old term and a very old concept, elicits quasi-Cartesian doubt about its applicability to the contemporary administrative state. As employed in the Western political tradition, it is not simply pre-modern, like the three branches of government, but distinctly medieval.[2] It reflects the sacerdotal conception that human rulers mediate between the divine and human worlds, and are infused with power as a result of this intermediate position. Priests, for example, were described as possessing a sacerdotal office derived from the keys to the kingdom of heaven that Christ gave to St. Peter.[3] A standard view was that one of these keys represented power (*potestas*) while the other represented knowledge or judgment (*scientia* or *discretio*).[4]

Another equally medieval concept of power involved the bodily role of the king and the corporate personality of social institutions. To begin with the king's bodily role, the Middle Ages inherited from more primeval times a conception of the king as possessing two distinct types of power. The first was his physical strength, his ability to lead his tribe into battle waving his sword and fighting as its leading warrior, like Achilles, Hector, or, of course, King Arthur, who personally leads his troops against the eleven kings who challenge his succession, against the Roman legions, and against the forces of the rebellious Mordred.[5] The second was his mystical or sacerdotal strength, which enabled him to intercede with the supernatural realm on behalf of his tribe, bringing it the good health and good harvests so essential for its tenuous survival.[6] Both types of power were contained within his body, and thus readily regarded as his personal possessions. Because he possessed this power personally, he could distribute fragments of it among his subordinates, just as he distributed land under the feudal system. And as with land, these distributed fragments were regarded as the only valid, that is, divinely sanctioned form of power.

Reverberations of the physical conception of sovereign power continue into contemporary times. In the movie *Independence Day*, aliens attack the Earth in gigantic spaceships.[7] The president of the United States organizes the air force's counterattack, and, having been a military pilot in the Gulf War, mans one of the planes himself. To a bewildered general, who sees him putting on a flight suit when he is supposed to be coordinating a worldwide military action, he explains, "I'm a fighter pilot, Bill. I belong in the air." In *Air Force One*, the president's airplane is taken over by terrorists.[8] Fortunately, as one of the generals back at the White House explains, the president is a medal of honor winner. "In Vietnam, he flew more helicopter rescue missions than any other man in my command. He knows how to fight." And, indeed, the president proceeds to physically overpower three hulking young terrorists and a disloyal secret service agent, kill three more terrorists with a gun he has grabbed from their hands, and pilot Air Force One past six attacking military jets.

While political thought in the Middle Ages was clearly influenced by the concept of the king's bodily role, it did not remain restricted to that concept. This primeval image was joined by another, entirely medieval one involving the nature or personality of collective entities. Although more abstract, this latter concept was also developed in relation to the human body. As Ernst Kantorowicz discusses, medieval theologians described the consecrated host as Christ's true or natural body, perhaps as a way of clarifying transubstantiation doctrine. The Church then came to be seen as the mystical body of Christ, reflecting the increasingly abstract way that collective institutions were regarded. St. Thomas Aquinas went one step further, referring to the Church as a mystical body in its own right, rather than Christ's mystical body. Like so many other theological and ecclesiological concepts, this was soon borrowed by the secular world, which began to designate the commonwealth, or proto-state (*res publica*), as a mystical body of its own. Over time, the christological connotations of the concept faded, and the commonwealth came to be called a mystical person; still later, it was called a fictitious person, which completed the pro-

cess of secularization.[9] This concept became linked, by a natural association of ideas, with the human body metaphor discussed in Chapter 2, so
that the king was now the head of the commonwealth's mystical body or
person.

Clearly, these conceptual developments reflect the efforts by political
thinkers of the High Middle Ages to conceptualize collective entities.[10]
The commonwealth, they recognized, was more than the king's family,
and its government was more than the king. It was something eternal in
time and extensive in space, something made up of many different individuals, whose actions could not necessarily be ascribed to any single one
of them. As thinking along these lines progressed, political theorists ceased
to derive the king's power from his sacerdotal role as a mediator between
heaven and earth, and began to regard it as emanating from his political
role as a representative of society's collective will. The overall conception
remained sacerdotal, however, because the collective will was seen as a
mystical unity that linked society to the supernatural order. Thus, the
king's role became partially secularized in this conception, although full
secularization did not occur until the Renaissance or later. He was now regarded as a representative, his power came from his position, and only his
appointment to that position came from God.[11] But kingship, although
now integrated into a more secular, political conception of government,
was still regarded as a personal possession by virtue of the king's divine appointment, and the mystic unity of the political realm that he commanded.
Symbolically, he was still seen as wielding the sword of power.

Relational Theories of Power

Despite these primeval and medieval origins, power appears to be a term
of contemporary relevance. Its secular and systematic use by Machiavelli,
Hobbes, Locke, Madison, and other founders of modern political theory
seems to have cleaned the slate of all the vivid, visceral imagery that
characterized medieval thought. If not, then the extensive discussion by
twentieth-century social scientists such as Weber, Mills, Parsons, Dahl,
Arendt, Foucault, Lukes, Giddens, Connolly, and Blau must certainly have
cleared the screen. With all this contemporary thought pouring content
into the term, there would appear to be little benefit to bracketing it and
attempting to develop an alternative description for the relationships that
it describes.[12]

But the sedimented, categorical, and ultimately elusive quality of this
term reawakens quasi-Cartesian doubt. The bodily conception of power
survives most obviously in ordinary political language, where, as Steven
Winter points out, it is generally treated as a tangible possession.[13] We say
that the president has it, the Supreme Court has abused it, or a narrow

elite monopolizes it. While the doubts about the legality of legislative delegation that were discussed in the preceding section result, in part, from
the belief that these delegations are crossing some fixed institutional
boundary, they also result from the conceit that some tangible thing,
called power, is being transferred across that boundary. It may seem unfair
to charge a social science term with responsibility for its informal usage,
but the same tendency to reify power, to treat it as a personal possession,
appears in the work of several major theorists. No one, of course, claims
that power exists in isolation; what is generally at issue is power over other
people. But it has been regularly asserted that power emanates from the
intrinsic capabilities of individuals, so that the mere existence of individuals, combined with some principle of interaction, explains how one person
exercises power over another. Hobbes expresses the classic version of this
view, using a mechanistic principle of interaction.[14] It makes a surprising
reappearance in the later work of Talcott Parsons, who uses an economic
principle of interaction by analogizing power to money.[15]

Treating power as a possession is a metaphorical approach that, like any
metaphor, cannot be either proved or disproved, but it appears to be an infelicitous description of our administrative state. The dual articulation that
characterizes modern government means that public offices are defined in
institutional terms and designed to implement specific functions. In other
words, the office has become separated from the person occupying it. A
talented and energetic individual will generally do a better job than one
who is ignorant or indolent, but the authority and influence of a given position is a feature of the office, not the individual. There is something personalistic, almost physical, about the possessory approach to power that
does not comport with contemporary practice.

Not all contemporary definitions of power, however, treat it as a physical possession. The most influential definition, here as in so many other
areas, was developed by Max Weber. Power, Weber states, "is the proba-
bility that one actor within a social relationship will be in a position to
carry out his own will despite resistance."[16] Michael Mann adopts this
same definition in his extensive historical survey of the subject, although
he also recognizes other types of power.[17] Bertrand Russell's variation on
this theme is that power is "the production of intended effects,"[18] while
Robert Dahl's is that "A has power over B to the extent that he can get B
to do something that B would not otherwise do."[19] At the other end of
the political spectrum from Dahl, Michael Oakeshott defines power as
"the ability to procure with certainty a wished-for response in the substantive conduct of another."[20] Peter Blau advances a microeconomic theory of power, but does not employ an analogy to a possessible entity like
money; rather, he treats power as a product of social exchange, and defines
it as "the ability of persons or groups to impose their will on others despite

resistance."[21] And Wesley Hohfeld, in his classic theory of legal rights, defined a power as the volitional control of legal relations.[22] To follow Carl Friedrich, these may all be described as relational theories of power, in contrast to the possessory theories of Hobbes and Parsons.[23]

Relational theories of power might appear exempt from the charge of medievalism that can be so readily leveled at the possessory approach. What could be more contemporary than describing power as a social interaction? In fact, however, these theories are heavily dependent on the second medieval concept of power. They avoid the idea of power as personal possession but rely on medieval notions about collective entities. The inapplicability of this relational theory to the internal structure of the modern state can be explored by considering the elements that a relational theory necessarily implies: the entity that exercises power, the entity that receives it, and the interaction between the two.[24]

With respect to those exercising power, the relational theory treats the assertion of power as an act of will or of intention. But where precisely does this will reside? Most orders in an administrative state issue from multimember institutions such as legislatures or regulatory agencies, and the problem of identifying the intent of such institutions is widely recognized.[25] Following Adolph Berle's suggestion,[26] or the principle of methodological individualism, one can focus on the individuals within the institution, but this renders the concept of intent even more problematic. When a legislature enacts a statute, or an agency promulgates a regulation, after months of lobbying, testimony, negotiation, staff work, and strategic compromises, precisely which individual's intent does such a statute or regulation represent?

The concept of will is equally central to a relational theory's description of the recipient, or addressee of the assertion of power, since that is what generates the resistance, and what is presumably being overcome. Once again, however, the term seems too personalistic to be applicable in an administrative setting. Administrative orders not only issue from institutions, but are often addressed to institutions, whether public or private. Many policy initiatives developed by the legislature or the chief executive require agencies, not individuals, to implement them; within the agency, commands flow from superior offices or divisions to subordinate ones. To be sure, a substantial portion of these commands, having been processed through various levels of the governmental system, are ultimately addressed to the citizenry, but even then, the recipient is often a firm, a labor union, or a school. Precisely what does it mean to say that the will of these governmental or private institutions was overborne? It may seem more natural to say that they resisted, or were compelled to do something they otherwise would not have done, but the personification involved again obscures more than it reveals. To say that an individual resists an order describes a recognizable subjective feeling of unwillingness. To say that an agency or a firm resists only raises questions about whether the perceived resistance involves a coordination problem within the institution, some attitude of the institution's membership or leaders, or a formally adopted stance voiced by the institution's representatives.

Relational theories of power are not only too personalistic in describing the originators and recipients of commands in an administrative state, but also too dramatic and emotive. Sometimes decision makers, particularly those in policy positions, may regard the commands that they issue as an act of will, but they are more likely to view such commands as a way to carry out their role, or do their job. At the operational level, this is even more frequently the case; a citation from an occupational health and safety agency instructing a factory to modify the shielding on one of its machines is rather poorly described as an act of will. Similarly, the mid-level functionary in a government or private organization who receives a command and alters his behavior in accordance with its tenor is rarely being compelled to take action contrary to his will. Most often, he has no specific will regarding the subject matter in question. He is waiting to be told what to do and, on receiving instructions, he will act accordingly. Of course, a functionary might be recalcitrant or lazy, in which case he will have countervailing inclinations which may be—or may not be—overcome. But a theory of governmental structure that depends on actual recalcitrance or laziness to be comprehensible is not a generally applicable one.

In addition to its overly personalistic and emotive approach to both the initiator and the recipient of power, the relational concept of power is also too personalistic and emotive in describing the connection between the two. The concept implies A's capacity to tell B what to do,[27] but hierarchical relations in an administrative state often follow specified pathways that place barriers between A and B. The president of the United States could be reasonably described as the most powerful person in the U.S. government, but as the discussion of political insulation in the preceding chapter suggests, there are many people—federal judges, members of independent agencies, hearing officers of executive agencies—to whom he cannot give direct commands.[28] Even with respect to the members of executive agencies directly under his control, he may not be able to give commands that contravene the prevailing interpretation of a statute, and it would be regarded as inappropriate, at best, for him to circumvent the chain of command and give orders to a subordinate official.[29] When a person in a modern state wants another person to carry out some particular task, she rarely achieves that goal by giving that second person a face-to-face instruction that overcomes his will. More commonly, she issues a complex series of successive instructions that ultimately make their way to a recipient whom she will never see.

A further difficulty with the will-based approach in describing the relationship between the superior and subordinate in an administrative structure is that many commands do not order the subordinate to carry out a specific task at all. Rather, they give that subordinate a new assignment, instructing it to implement some program that it did not previously perform. Whose will was overborne when the Federal Reserve Board was created?[30] Whose will was overcome when its open market operations were codified, or when it was given the new, and previously unexpected, assignment of administering the Truth-in-Lending Act?[31] The will-based approach to power seems applicable only to a pre-modern, unarticulated government that was pictured—incorrectly—as making minor adjustments to a fixed political and social structure. In the modern articulated state, new areas of government control are commonly established and constitute some of the government's most important impacts on society. This represents a cooperative public enterprise, a continuous augmentation of the government's ability to control previously unregulated areas. Both Talcott Parsons and Michael Mann explicitly acknowledge this process in their theories of power,[32] but then attempt to salvage the relational approach by saying that the government is using power to create more power. This formulation, however, possesses an impenetrable, mysterious quality that carries us back to the image of the sacerdotal king, communing with supernatural forces on his tribe's behalf. It does not seem to be a meaningful description of the process in which superiors give new assignments to their subordinates.

Using the concept of power to describe relationships among government officials is also problematic because it conflicts with the three-branch image that supposedly models the organization of those officials. Branches are stable, rather placid things that do not seem to possess inherent power and never overcome each others' wills; to add power and control to the image would transform the branches of our bucolic tree into the tentacles of a slimy cephalopod. To be sure, we speak of the relationship among the branches being stabilized by the separation of powers, but this is a different use of the term, namely, power as a set of specified functions, rather than as a personal possession or an exercise of will. Thus, the separately developed images of three branches and of power not only fail to describe the modern state, but also fail to align with one another into a coherent metaphorical framework.

It might be argued that relational definitions like Weber's or Dahl's refer primarily to the government's interaction with the citizenry, rather than its internal operations. That would be a serious limitation, however, since it necessarily coagulates the entire government into a single entity, to which one can ascribe behavior only by adopting a rather extreme form of medieval corporatism. The way in which actions are generated within the government is of equal interest to the way the government, in its entirety, takes action affecting private parties. To limit the relational theory of power to the connection between government and private parties, therefore, precludes the use of this concept to describe the affective aspects of the government's internal structure, and thus renders it irrelevant to the present chapter. The relationship between government and citizens will be discussed in Chapters 4 and 5, with the structural aspects of the issue addressed in Chapter 4, and the affective aspects, to which this second use of the term 'power' relates, addressed in Chapter 5.

The disjunction between the relational approach to power and the realities of modern administrative government has not gone unnoticed. Many contemporary scholars have rejected this approach for more modulated, microanalytic accounts. At the level of general theory, however, the perceived disjunction has not led to the rejection of the concept but to various efforts to expand it in order to maintain its plausibility. These efforts, which may be characterized as diffuse relational theories, draw upon a variety of theoretical frameworks, among them neo-Marxism, post-structuralism, and feminism. All three regard power as more extensive than the standard relational theories do because of their emphasis on social structures—class structure and elite domination in the case of neo-Marxism, sources of patterned or repetitive social behavior in the case of post-structuralism, and the gendered character of ideology and institutions in the case of feminism. But they tend to circumvent the pitfall of medievalism only by succumbing to the closely related one of coagulating widely disparate social relations. Once the ideas of power as a physical possession or a relationship among personalized collective entities are jettisoned, there is very little left. Without these medieval meanings, the concept is something of an empty shell, given substance by social nostalgia and by the desire to appropriate the term, with all its emotive force, for polemic purposes.

Steven Lukes, in his well-known neo-Marxist discussion, identifies three levels of power.[33] The first is the relational idea that one person can compel another to act against his own desires, the second is control over the political agenda,[34] and the third involves control over the populace's attitudes and beliefs. This third level extends power beyond its traditional boundaries, but only at the expense of a rather aggressive false consciousness argument. Absent such an argument, Lukes's third level, like his second, personalizes government to an implausible extent. It suggests that the entire government possesses important knowledge that no one else in society comprehends, and that it maintains this intellectual superiority over long periods of time. A smart, secretive individual might be able to achieve this difficult feat in a delimited setting, but it is difficult to imagine it being done by a complex institution like a government, which is divided from society only by a vague and permeable boundary. Whereas relationship theories of power personalize government actors in a manner inconsistent with the modern state, Lukes's theory personalizes the government in its entirety, coagulating it into an imaginary individual in a manner reminiscent of medieval conceptions of monarchy.

Foucault, who can be regarded as one representative of post-structuralism, offers a theory of power that bears a certain resemblance to Lukes's, but instead of viewing power as one group's dominance over another, he treats it as a complex "grid" or "network" of relationships that permeates the entire social structure.[35] Having conceptualized power in such vague terms that it applies to everything, however, it is hardly surprising that he can find it everywhere.[36] Anthony Giddens, who can also be regarded as a post-structuralist, treats power as "the transformative capacity of human action . . . the capability of the actor to intervene in a series of events so as to alter their course."[37] He goes on to define power "in the narrower, relational sense . . . as the capability to secure outcomes where the realization of these outcomes depends upon the agency of others."[38] The difficulty, as with Foucault, is that defining the concept of power in this manner merges it into the general pattern of social relations.[39] But what is the point of defining power so broadly that it applies to virtually all social relations and, more important for this discussion, how does that assist us in understanding the structure of modern government?[40] Why assert that a woman's sexual appeal at a cocktail party is the same phenomenon as the communication of instructions through a governmental hierarchy, as Dennis Wrong does, unless one wants to advance some complex rhetorical argument that should be explicitly stated, and subjected to analysis?[41]

The feminist analysis of governmental power comprises at least two separate arguments: first, that relations between men and women involve patterns of domination and subordination that can be usefully described in terms of power,[42] and second, that governmental action is part of the same pattern.[43] The first argument is a convincing one, and its use of the term 'power' is probably coherent, particularly since male domination is often achieved by using physical force. But the second argument is subject to the same critique as the diffuse relational theories of Lukes, Foucault, or Giddens—namely, that a relationship between distinct phenomena like government action and social relations must be argued for, and cannot be established merely by labeling them both with a single term. Are the ways in which male and female identities are constructed in the social world truly related to the ways in which government officials are organized? Is there any obvious relationship between the way male doctors define, diagnose, and treat women's complaints and the way that one government official issues commands to another?

If claims about the gendered character of government are freed from
the connection with the concept of power, and are argued for directly,
they become much more convincing. To begin with, the traditional concept of the king as warrior is an unalterably male one. In addition, there is
the simple but significant fact that most leaders, most of their advisors, and
most subordinate officials have been and continue to be male. Women
have historically been denied the opportunity to serve as government officials, a situation that was not remedied at those times when accidents of
heredity brought women to the throne, and that has been only partially
remedied at the present time. Of course, such discrimination within government obviously reflects broader social attitudes, and contributes to
them as well, but that connection can be delineated in much more concrete and productive ways than by reference to overarching constructs
about power.

These observations can be safely made because they are apparent to the
participants, and understood by them in the same terms that feminists assert. To go further, and claim some deeper connection between social relations and governmental organization that is captured by the concept of
power, risks overinterpretation.[44] Consider, for example, one of the most
ubiquitous topics in feminist literature, namely the penis. The penis played
a central role in the medieval understanding of kingship because that
organ's operational capacities were of direct concern to the king's subjects,
as the source of an heir who would provide an orderly succession. But its
symbolic and mythical associations should be invoked with caution. The
sword, as an insignia of royal power, is an obvious phallic symbol to our
Freudianized minds, and the scepter is another. But the most common,
well-known symbol of kingship was the crown, essentially a hole surrounded by a circle of gold. Of course, the king puts his head into his
crown, and often points his scepter at it. All of this is so much fun that we
cannot trust ourselves to apply it in a consistent or disciplined manner as
an explanation of the government's essential character.

There is, however, another implication of the feminist claim that
yields real insights. Whatever the nature of the government itself, it can
be argued that theories about government, specifically theories phrased
in terms of power, are inherently male. All this talk about possession,
about asserting one's will, and about overcoming other people's wills
conveys the impression of teenage male sex fantasies. Perhaps this is the
reason why the term 'power' has survived so long, despite our general
inability to agree upon a definition, and despite its poor fit with the
administrative state. Power, after all, is generally a negative term, and
one might imagine that it would fail to elicit the kind of social nostalgia
that would ensure its survival. But it does invoke fantasies of triumph,

dominance, and sexual prowess, and thereby possesses a counterbalancing appeal.

Discretion

The sprawling theoretical debate about the meaning of power has encompassed many ancillary terms, including domination, force, coercion, authority, and influence. Discretion has not figured prominently in this debate, although it would appear to be power's closest relative—its kid brother, in effect—but power figures heavily in debates about discretion.[45] As the term is generally used, discretion refers to the latitude, scope of action, or slack that a public official possesses. The major differences between power and discretion, largely tonal in nature, are that discussions of discretion do not emphasize assertions of will or of resistance, and that they extend only to the condition of being unconstrained, and not of being absolute. Thus, discretion might be regarded as the exercise of power by a subordinate official. Many observers regard the discretion possessed by public officials as the central problem of the administrative state.[46]

Like the term 'power,' the term 'discretion' was used extensively during the Middle Ages; it was, for example, the second of the keys that provided priests with their sacred office. As it evolved, it acquired at least two distinguishable meanings. First, in conformity with the sacerdotal model of government, it was something possessed by subordinate officials, a small fragment of the sovereign's divinely granted power that he distributed among his subordinates. Second, it was associated with the circumspection of the trusted advisor who stands behind the throne, whispering in the sovereign's ear, or perhaps that of the confidential courtier, arranging assignations in the back rooms of the palace. These pre-modern origins generate quasi-Cartesian doubt, and contemporary usage deepens it. In ordinary language, discretion, like power, remains a personal possession. We say that public officials have high levels of discretion, that they have been granted discretion, and that they use their discretion wisely or unwisely. In addition, discretion continues to be associated with judicious circumspection. We also say that officials acted with discretion, or that they displayed discretion in carrying out their tasks. Neither of these usages bears any particular relation to actual decision-making processes in a modern administrative state. Their coalescence in a single term is equally problematic. It remains unclear whether there is any organic relationship between the power and judgment aspects of discretion, or whether the linkage is nothing more than a remnant of the medieval modes of thought.

There are numerous descriptions of discretionary action in political science and sociology that seem to bypass the atavisms and ambiguities of ordinary discourse by addressing actual government practices. But systematic definitions that attempt to replace the associations of this concept with a more precise formulation are, somewhat surprisingly, found more often in legal literature. According to Kenneth Davis, who wrote a pathbreaking work about the ubiquity of discretion in public decision making, a "public official has discretion whenever the effective limits of his power leave him free to make a choice among possible courses of action."[47] Similarly, Denis Galligan describes discretion as "powers delegated within a system of authority to an official, or set of officials, where they have some significant scope for settling the reasons and standards according to which that power is to be exercised."[48] Henry Hart and Albert Sacks, two of the founders of the legal process school, define discretion as "the power to choose between two or more courses of action, each of which is thought of as permissible."[49] Carl Friedrich adds a normative component by requiring that the choice must be justifiable by reasons.[50]

The most elaborate definition, and the one that is probably most widely invoked, is Ronald Dworkin's.[51] Dworkin identifies three different meanings of discretion, which is itself a sign of conceptual trouble. He begins by noting that any use of the term applies only "when someone is in general charged with making decisions subject to standards set by a particular authority"[52]—essentially the theme of subordinate power. He then states that discretion can be either weak or strong. Weak discretion can mean two different things: first, that the person "has final authority to make a decision and cannot be reviewed and reversed by any other official,"[53] or second, that the person is required to exercise judgment in reaching a decision.[54] Strong discretion means that the actor "is simply not bound by standards set by the authority in question."[55] Presumably, the operative distinction between weak and strong discretion is that the actor is bound by standards in the former case, but not in the latter.

Does the concept of discretion, as it has been used by political scientists and defined by legal scholars, describe a useful category of behaviors for scholarship, policy analysis, or judicial decision making in a modern administrative state? There can be little doubt that administrative agents regularly make choices, as Davis, Friedrich, and Hart and Sacks suggest, but the question is whether their choices can be usefully identified as a single category and whether the term 'discretion,' with its implicit combination of power and judgment, is a useful description of that category, assuming it exists.

Since the idea of choice is so impenetrably general, it seems best to turn to Dworkin's more specific definition. The two forms of weak discretion he identifies are the absence of review and the need for judgment, a formulation that appears to reiterate the medieval duality between power and judgment. Seven hundred years later, the task of unifying them into a single operative concept has still not been accomplished; Dworkin's two forms of weak discretion seem to lack any organic relationship with one another. The first describes the structure of a governmental hierarchy, while the second describes the internal process that the decision maker is expected to employ. The existence of review is certainly not an invitation to cease using one's judgment, nor does a decision maker's use of judgment, by itself, eliminate the desirability of reviewing his decision. Relying on a single, sedimented term to describe these disparate features of administration seems confusing, and thus a less than satisfactory strategy for committed description.

Not only does the concept of discretion seem unsatisfactory in describing the relationship between the absence of review and the deployment of judgment, but it seems equally unsatisfactory in describing either of these features when considered separately, at least in the context of an administrative state. The issue can be approached from the dual perspectives of the superior and the subordinate. Beginning with the absence of review, which presumably reflects the superior's decision, the concept of discretion fails to capture the superior's phenomenological situation, her subjectively perceived reasons for dispensing with review. These reasons include resource constraints, confidence in her subordinate, or indifference about the outcome.[56] If the reason is resource constraints, such as the amount of time the superior can devote to reviewing her subordinates, or the number of intermediate subordinates she can employ to do so in her place, then whatever freedom the subordinate possesses is simply a by-product of these constraints. If the reason is that she has confidence in the subordinate, and regards review as unnecessary, then the subordinate's freedom is again distinct from a grant of discretion; the superior is not forgoing review because she affirmatively wants her subordinate to make choices, but because she expects the choices that the subordinate makes to parallel her own or to achieve her goals more effectively than she herself could by specifying her subordinate's actions. Finally, if the reason for dispensing with review is indifference to the result, the subordinate's freedom is also poorly described as a grant of discretion. A matter about which the superior is indifferent lies outside the institution's ambit of concern, and thus outside the category of discretion Dworkin has defined. It is pointless to say that an employee has discretion about the color of his clothing, for example. If there are no rules about clothing color, the matter is better described as being irrelevant to the organization's objectives and concerns.

Discretion does not reflect the phenomenological experience of a subordinate exempted from review any more than it reflects the superior's experience in creating the exemption. The term is simply too coagulated to capture the complex realities of modern government. To begin with, Keith Hawkins notes that unsupervised actions often appear to administrative agents as part of their quotidian task performance, rather than as a decision that demands discretionary action.[57] Often, such actions, whether delineated or diffuse, are governed by standards that come from other units of government, from formal or informal norms, and, most important of all, from the need to achieve particular results.[58] The cumulative effect of these standards will be to eliminate the sense of freedom that the term 'discretion' tends to imply. Because the administrative state is doubly articulated, each unit will have an identifiable function, and that function will be defined in largely instrumental terms. There may be no review of that function in the short run, but the unit will ultimately be answerable for its performance. Individual officials are aware of this, both consciously and intuitively. All sorts of things that are absolutely crucial for them—salary, promotions, job security, the respect of their peers, a sense of purpose, and a sense of self-worth—depend on their ability to perform in the expected manner. When they are exempted from review, one constraint—direct supervision by a particular superior—may have been removed, but many others still remain. Consequently, the official is not likely to think, "How wonderful—I can make a choice," but rather, "I have a decision to make—now I need to get it right."

If discretion is an infelicitous description for exemption from review, from either the superior's or the subordinate's perspective, it might appear more promising as a way to describe the other form of Dworkin's weak discretion, namely, the subordinate's need to use his judgment. From the superior's perspective, the term 'judgment' does possess a certain degree of relevance because it is a dictionary synonym for rationality, or reasoned decision making. Does the superior want her subordinate to use his judgment to decide a matter that has been assigned to him? Of course she does; as Martin Shapiro points out, judgment is a necessary and inextricable element in any administrative decision.[59] After all, what else could the subordinate possibly use in reaching a decision? He could roll dice, or abjure his judgment and do something insane, but what is the point of a descriptive term that excludes only these possibilities? Neither judgment nor discretion is a complete description of the superior's desires; what the superior really wants is that the subordinate employ the decision-making process that is most likely to produce the best result. The mere use of judgment would be regarded as insufficient, because the superior expects a certain level of effective performance, an ability to achieve the desired goal, whether precisely specified or only vaguely outlined.

From the subordinate's perspective, the notion of discretion as judgment is an equally inadequate description of administrative practice. Like the concept of power, it does not apply very well to institutions. While it is possible to speak of an agency's decision-making process, discretion, in the sense that is synonymous with judgment, seems like a quality that individuals exhibit. Even if this difficulty is ignored, the actual decision-

making processes that agencies employ are often too technical and rou-
tinized to be usefully described as judgment. Many agencies reach decisions by using standard policy analysis, that is, the agency will define the
problem, identify the possible solutions, assess each solution, and select
the most promising possibility.[60] Often, and particularly since the advent
of OMB's regulatory review, it will adopt cost-benefit analysis as a specific
variant of this procedure.[61] To be sure, agencies sometimes rely on less formal methods, and might even "muddle through," to use Charles Lindblom's term.[62] In this case the terms 'judgment' and 'discretion' become
more descriptive, although practical reason is probably a better formulation. In any event, such an approach is only one of several decision-
making strategies, and, significantly, it is regarded as less modern than
more systematic alternatives.

In addition to weak discretion, Dworkin also identifies a strong variety,
where the actor "is simply not bound by standards set by the authority in
question." There is, however, a serious ambiguity about this definition.
Does Dworkin mean that the actor is not bound by any standards at all, or
only that he is not bound by standards set by his direct superior? The latter situation is not truly distinct from weak discretion, as Kent Greenawalt
points out.[63] Administrative agents, to reiterate, are regularly subject to
standards set by units other than their supervisor, by formal or informal
norms, and by the expectation that they produce particular results. These
standards can be just as constraining as standards emanating from a hierarchical supervisor. The difference between the two describes one specific
aspect of governmental structure, but a categorical distinction between
these related modes of action does not contribute to our understanding.

The other possible meaning of strong discretion is that the actor is not
bound by any standards at all. To distinguish it from the previously discussed category, this could be called super-strong discretion. The most interesting feature of super-strong discretion is that it is essentially unknown
in an administrative state. To be given license to do anything one chooses
on a given subject matter is to exercise the authority of an absolute
monarch, like Louis XIV, or an absolute dictator, like Stalin. One could
then declare that one was reaching a decision "because it is my sovereign
will." In fact, it is unlikely that any political leader, including Louis XIV
and Stalin, was actually so unconstrained. In any case, the notion is risible
in connection with the Assistant Secretary of the Treasury, who is, after all,
a high-ranking official; it is even risible in connection with the chair of the
Federal Reserve Board. In the modern articulated state, government officials are always subject to supervision or control by some other component of the much-divided government. Second, they must always act in a
manner instrumental to some public purpose, their range of choices is always limited, and they are always subject to standards based upon that

guiding purpose. Even elected officials rarely exercise super-strong discretion. They are constrained by the views of those who elected them and will decide whether to reelect them, as well as by their colleagues, other governmental actors, and the instrumental conception of the government in its entirety as a means for achieving certain identified goals. The legislator who declared that he has voted for a measure "because it is my sovereign will" is not likely to be reelected by his constituency or taken seriously by his colleagues.

One possible exception in American government is the chief executive's ability to pardon, that is, to exempt a designated individual from criminal punishment. This can be traced directly to the powers of medieval monarchs.[64] Partially for this reason, and partially because of its more general connection with forgiveness and grace, pardoning has been traditionally regarded as unbound by any standards at all, and thus may be one area where the concept of super-strong discretion provides an accurate description. It is therefore quite significant that this approach to pardons has been largely undermined in modern government. The massive number of pardon requests that a president or governor receives, that is, the very same problem of scale that was so important in creating the administrative state in general, has induced these chief executives to adopt an administrative approach to pardons. Thus, an agency or bureau is established, which receives pardon requests and makes decisions according to pre-established criteria.[65] The chief executive retains the ability to issue pardons directly in important cases, but, as Gerald Ford's pardon of Richard Nixon and Bill Clinton's pardon of Marc Rich suggests, the arbitrary or partisan use of this device can come at a high political cost, a cost that a Congress dominated by the opposing party will strive to increase.[66] Here again, the voters will often punish an elected official for what they perceive as an act of sovereign will, that is, indulgence in the atavistic exercise of super-strong discretion.

Perhaps the reason we retain the term 'discretion,' despite these descriptive difficulties, is because of the normative roles it plays in accounts of modern government. For some, discretion justifies that government by securing flexibility and opening a space for empathy.[67] The administrator with discretion can respond to unexpected circumstances and to the equities of an individual case that our inevitably overinclusive or underinclusive general rules cannot incorporate.[68] She is not a pod person or a borg; she has "a human face." For other observers, probably the larger number, discretion condemns modern government because it violates the rule of law.[69] The administrator with discretion can maximize his own something-or-other—perhaps his salary, perhaps his agency's budget, or perhaps that very discretion—to the detriment of the public, or he can oppress honest, law-abiding citizens from either unmotivated animus or a warped sense of the public good.[70]

Modern bureaucracy possesses both these features, but neither is central to its promises or to its dangers. The real possibilities of bureaucracy, for good and evil, lie in the area discussed by Weber. Weber recognized that bureaucracy, as a purposive-rational mechanism of governance, creates unprecedented possibilities for the mobilization of social resources and the exercise of political control.[71] But such action fulfills our commitments only to the extent that the individual or the society can identify its purposes; if that does not occur, then efficiency becomes a purpose of its own, and the bureaucratic apparatus turns into an enclosed, self-sustaining system that imprisons its society in an iron cage.[72] Weber saw this imprisonment as virtually unavoidable, and bureaucracy itself as an "escape proof" social development.[73]

In actuality, both the proponents and the critics of discretion are invoking the concept as a means of combating Weber's bleak prognosis. For the proponents, discretion humanizes the bureaucracy, leavening its hierarchical, mechanistic structure with the flexibility and empathy that characterized—at least in theory—the traditional governments of pre-bureaucratic times. Thus, the path of escape from the iron cage lies in more humane and diverse administrators, who can empathize with a broader range of clients, in more pragmatic administrators, who can vary their instructions humanely and intelligently, or in more progressive administrators, who can combat the oppressive features of bureaucracy from inside the system. For the critics, discretion permits the bureaucracy to follow its own goals and ignore or frustrate those that the people have chosen through their democratically elected leaders.[74] The path of escape lies in reasserting democratic control, eliminating or at least strictly curbing that discretion so that the bureaucracy's actions reflect the decisions made by the chief executive or the legislators, who are accountable to the electorate.

Neither of these implied solutions is promising, however, and neither represents the genuine escape from Weber's iron cage that our own value system supplies. With respect to humanizing the bureaucracy, any relaxation of formal controls seems likely to amplify the effects of the informal norms that control so much of institutional behavior. These informal norms may be either more or less humane, pragmatic, and progressive than their alternatives. They may embody greater empathy for the clients, but they may also embody annoyance, prejudice, and contempt. In any case, they will proliferate out of the superior's control, and the ability of policy level officials to achieve predictable results will be reduced. Because we have no reason to think that the subordinate is more humane, pragmatic, or progressive than the superior, this seems like a less-than-promising strategy for bureaucratic reform.

The critics' image of discretion is equally unrealistic. Of course, administrators exercise extensive control over society in modern governments, but this cannot realistically be decreased by elected officials. The administrators and judges are not exercising that control on their own, as a result of some surreptitious, quasi-conspiratorial power grab. They were granted control by the elected officials because it is essential for an administrative state, and an administrative state is what those officials want, and ultimately what the people want as well. That state has been developing for two hundred years, simultaneously with the growth of the democracy that is supposed to control it, because it is our society's response to the complexities of modern industrial life. The image of the bureaucrats as exerting authority through an act of will, in disobedience of the hapless chief executive and legislature, is again unrealistic. Like the image of the humane, discretionary bureaucrat, it diverts us from our genuine commitment, which is to accept the reality of administrative government and use it to achieve our articulated social goals.

Authorization and Supervision

The Concept of Authorization and Supervision

Because the concepts of power and discretion seem to misdescribe the government we actually possess, the quasi-Cartesian doubt generated by their pre-modern origins appears to be well placed. This suggests that it may be valuable to bracket these concepts, to disconnect them from their validity claims, set them to the side, and explore alternative ways to characterize the animate structure of our modern administrative state. As already argued, a network is a more preferable image for the hardware, or structure of government, than the three branches and the separation of powers. This same image can serve as a starting point in the thought experiment of searching for alternative descriptions of the network's software, that is, the relationships among governmental units that we now describe in terms of power and discretion. The network image, of course, is not unrelated to Foucault's concept of a power grid, and it is even more closely related to Stewart Clegg's image of power as an electronic circuit.[75] For reasons already stated, however, the image will be employed here to replace the concept of power, rather than to expand it.

As described in Chapter 2, each unit in a network is designed to perform a particular function, responding to inputs and scaling, summing or integrating those inputs with other inputs and its own internal program to generate a set of outputs. This design can be described as the unit's range of operation, or to use Hans Kelsen's more familiar term, its authorization.[76] The signals that flow from one unit to another for the purpose of controlling the second unit's outputs, either by creating its initial authorization, altering that authorization, or providing particular inputs, can be described as supervision. Authorization and supervision, taken together, serve as an alternative to power and discretion for describing the animate structure of modern government. They explain the actions that each individual or institution within government is allowed to perform, and the way each one controls, or fails to control, any other individual or institution. They do so, moreover, in the articulated terms that are appropriate to an administrative state. Authorization establishes a delineated identity and role for each governmental unit, and indicates that these features are established to achieve an explicit and identifiable purpose. Supervision provides the means by which the unit's ability to achieve that purpose can be monitored and measured. Rather than being sacerdotal or personalistic, the resulting image is an instrumental, mechanistic one.

The term 'supervision' is relatively unproblematic. While familiar enough to be deemed naive, it is also largely modern in its connotations, and does not necessarily imply any particular theory of governance. 'Authorization,' however, is more troublesome because it is derived from the term 'authority,' which is far from modern: it appears, essentially in its present form, in the writing of Gelasius, who was the pope at the time of King Arthur,[77] and like so many other concepts of such august vintage, its meaning is highly contested.[78] Perhaps most serious, modern definitions of authority depend on the concept of power, and on the equally problematic concept of legitimacy that will be discussed—and bracketed—below. According to the standard definition, authority, while not equivalent to power,[79] is a mode of power that is based on a claim of legitimacy, or right.[80] Weber points out that the claim of right, if accepted, renders the leader's power more effective because it means that many of his subjects will obey simply because they accept this claim, thereby obviating the awkward and extensive use of force.[81] David Easton's formulation is that a statement is authoritative when "the people to whom it is intended to apply or who are affected by it consider that they must or ought to obey it."[82] According to Joseph Raz, an authoritative statement is not supposed to be evaluated as one reason among many to determine whether it serves as the proper basis for action; rather, once the leader's claim is accepted, his subjects will obey his commands without taking countervailing considerations into account.[83] Thus, authority is thought to be midway between coercion and persuasion; as Hannah Arendt suggests, "[a] father can lose his authority either by beating his child or by starting to argue with him, that is, either by behaving to him like a tyrant or by treating him as an equal."[84]

The term 'authorization,' as opposed to 'authority,' has been chosen to avoid these implications, while remaining familiar enough to be deemed naive. It makes no claim about whether government commands will be obeyed by citizens, or whether they are morally justified. These issues will be addressed in Chapter 5. Rather, it simply indicates the core idea that each unit of government has a specified range of operation. Using the term 'authorization' has the additional advantage of distinguishing political or institutional authority from theoretical authority. Theoretical authority is a mode of influence that is explicitly based upon a person's intrinsic qualities, most frequently his personal knowledge or expertise in a specific area. Thus Professor Scales is described as an authority on reptiles because of the knowledge he possesses, not because of his hierarchical position. People will accept his statements, without investigating their empirical basis, because they believe that if they were to investigate, he would always turn out to be correct. It is generally agreed that institutional and theoretical authority are different concepts,[85] although some scholars argue that one ought to depend on the other.[86] The passive voice provides a convenient means of making the distinction, since only institutional authorities can be said to be authorized or issue authorizations.

Reliance on the concept of authorization, particularly in the passive voice, naturally raises the question of ultimate authority. In most cases, the source of a governmental unit's authorization is clear enough; the legislature authorizes, or designs, administrative agencies, and each agency typically authorizes a variety of subsidiary offices. But what about the legislature's authorization? Is it not necessary, from the conceptual perspective, to trace this authorization, and all other subsidiary authorizations, back to some initial source that is more properly described in terms of power? For a modern administrative state, this question can be answered in the negative. The reason is that the question derives its force from the principle of sovereignty, which asserts that the authority of subsidiary governmental institutions necessarily flows from some ultimate sovereign who serves as the source of power.

As its name suggests, the principle of sovereignty is a residue of the medieval era. It rests on the sacerdotal idea that all power comes from God, and must be channeled through a single ruler whose relationship to his subject reiterates God's relationship to humankind. This idea was partially secularized by Renaissance and Reformation thinkers, most notably Jean Bodin, who were inspired by the absolute monarchs of their day.[87] Legal positivists such as Kelsen retained the notion in the still more secularized form of an impersonal *Grundnorm*, perhaps because it was so useful for their theory.[88] H.L.A. Hart dispenses with it in the process of rejecting Kelsen's idea that laws consist exclusively of sanctions, and thereby recognizes that the authorization of the units that compose a modern state is generally derived from a multiplicity of sources.[89] These sources can include a constitution, a revolutionary declaration, tradition, and even, as Melvin Eisenberg points out, nongovernmental actors such as scholars and practicing attorneys.[90] All that is necessary is that the populace accept the established authorization of the governmental units in question, as it exists in the state's ongoing practice. In a functioning modern state, moreover, the most authoritative units will be authorized to change their own design, or a group of units will be authorized to change each other's, thereby achieving adaptability without the need for an ultimate authority that stands above the rest.

Closely connected to the idea that all government authority must be derived from a single source is the pre-modern idea that government authority must be traced back to a single definitive event, a sort of juris-political Big Bang. Origin myths of this sort made sense for the sacerdotal state that was regarded as having been created by the supernatural force that it continued to serve. In fact, as modern social science demonstrates, governments either evolve over time or owe their origin to acts that are illegal according to both their own rules and the rules of the predecessor government. More important, however, any account of the state's origins is only of historical interest in a modern, administrative setting. Regardless of the way it was created, the government exists at present as an organized, extensive entity. Critical judgments about it are based upon its current operation, its ability to serve the instrumental function that constitutes the essence of political morality in an administrative state. Thus, once the government is in place, its animate structure can be fully described, evaluated, and critiqued in terms of the authorization and supervision of its units, without reference to either an ultimate source or historical origin of the varied authorizations that define its contours.

The Emotional and Heuristic Advantages of Authorization and Supervision

The main advantage of bracketing the concepts of power and discretion and, as a thought experiment, replacing them with the alternative concepts of authorization and supervision, is that the alternatives facilitate a microanalysis of the relationships that animate the governmental process. Before proceeding to demonstrate this claim, the extent to which these concepts satisfy the other two criteria for alternative concepts—that is, the extent to which they correspond to our emotional commitments and reflect the heuristic character of thought—need to be considered. For the sake of brevity, the applicability of these two considerations to both authorization and supervision will be considered together. Their advantage as a framework for microanalysis will then be considered separately in the section that follows.

To begin with our emotional commitments, the principal advantage of concepts such as authorization and supervision is their blandness, their dull, technocratic quality that conjures up an image of grumpy bureaucrats sitting in a bullpen behind metal desks, underneath fluorescent lights. Most of the inherited medieval concepts that are bracketed in this book enjoy intensely positive associations. As a result, the modern state's failure to display the features we associate with democracy, legitimacy, law, human rights, or property rights engenders rapid condemnation. Power and discretion often possess negative associations, and no one seems to doubt that the administrative state amply displays these features. Thus, condemnation follows just as rapidly. But such condemnation is a dangling comparative; it does not tell us whether a particular government possesses more or less power or discretion, whatever that may mean, whether it is more or less oppressive, whether it supports or violates our political values more or less than others. The concepts of authorization and supervision are relatively free of these strong associations that are sedimented into power and discretion. They thus enable us to evaluate the government we actually possess in terms of our genuine commitments to security, prosperity, and liberty. To take just one example, what we would describe as the government's assertion of power over private citizens sounds like a limit on their liberty, but it may increase the liberty of many citizens if the governmental action is directed against oppressive employers or abusive parents. To say, using the alternative terminology, that the legislature has authorized its subordinate agencies to issue commands to employers or parents tends to leave these normative questions open, to be resolved through careful consultation with our genuinely felt values.

A second way in which the concepts of authorization and supervision reflect our emotional commitments lies in their link to instrumentalism. We want our government to function instrumentally, to serve the interests of its citizens rather than generating emergent interests of its own. Describing the animate aspect of its structure in instrumental terms facilitates judgments about whether it is conforming to that basic value. When we describe government institutions or officials as possessing power and discretion, the usage provides no metric for judging whether they have too much or too little, and whether their actions are proper or improper. In contrast, when we describe governmental structure in terms of authorization and supervision, we are naturally led to questions that reflect our instrumentalist values. Did the unit act with or without authorization? Did it succeed or fail in its authorized mission? Was this success or failure the result of satisfactory or faulty supervision?

With respect to the heuristic character of thought, few terms are as misleading as power, and discretion is only marginally better. The possessory approach to power implies that there is really something there, some enigmatic substance that can be acquired, squandered, or retained. Relational theories of power seem to avoid this implication, but tend to reify the concept nonetheless. There always seems to be something in addition to the relationship itself that gives one party the ability to overcome the other party's will. This becomes more evident in diffuse relational theories, where power, now detached from the dyadic relationship between parties, turns into a grid or substrate, like the electricity supply or sewage system, that underlies the entire society. Authorization and supervision avoid these implications because they clearly describe processes, not entities. While they are sometimes treated as naturally occurring categories, it is relatively easy to recall that they are simply ways to characterize the relationships between institutions and individuals in modern government. Their blandness, and their lack of historical associations, serves to secure their heuristic character. At the same time, they are naive heuristics, regularly used by the people whose actions they describe. Their familiarity offers some protection against overinterpretation, since the scholarly observer's use of the concepts will be at least partially disciplined by ordinary meanings. This is the reason why the term 'authorization' has been pried away from its premodern definition and employed in this context, despite its complexities of connotation, in preference to using a neologism or an idiosyncratically defined expression.

The Microanalysis of Intra-Governmental Relations

Authorization

The emotional and heuristic advantages of the proposed alternatives, as stated, are secondary to their principal advantage: to facilitate the microanalysis of the government's animate structure, or software, by dissolving the coagulated categories that litter our description of that structure. These categories may seem organic to us, living things that we are reluctant, from both squeamishness and pity, to dissect. In fact, they are black boxes that preclude detailed inquiry. As we trace the patterns of authorization and supervision in an administrative state, the internal operation of these boxes opens up, in all its flickering and twittering complexity. The result, while bewildering and not particularly pleasing, is a good deal less gruesome than we may have feared.

In order to explicate the microanalytic advantages of the authorization concept, it is necessary to describe this concept in a bit more detail. According to the metaphor presented in the previous chapter, each unit of government is organized by means of a specific design. This design consists of the signals the unit is instructed to receive, the signals it is instructed to transmit, and the internal program by which it generates new signals and by which it sums, scales, or otherwise transforms its input into output. As the previous chapter also discussed, the signals that flow through the network are descriptions (Austin's locutionary acts), performatives (Austin's illocutionary acts), and judgments (roughly, Austin's perlocutionary acts). Performatives are statements that constitute action by virtue of their declaration, and include commands, requests, and promises. Authorization can be defined as the maximum scope of a unit's operations, the total range of activities, whether receiving, transmitting, or transforming signals, that is specified by the unit's design.

Sociologists and political theorists generally take great pains to emphasize that power does not necessarily involve the use of force, but may achieve its purposes by other means.[91] The need for this reminder is itself an indication of the term's pre-modern origins, since contemporary administrative agencies rarely employ physical force in carrying out their functions. More significantly, while the concept of power has been distinguished from force, it remains bound, by its pre-modern origins, to the idea of command: to exercise power is generally regarded as the ability to issue a command that others will obey. This creates at least two serious descriptive difficulties. First, commands, although important, are only one of the many different signals that compose the modern governmental process; to isolate this signal and grant it such exaggerated prominence distorts the nature of the process, and thus acts as an impediment to understanding. Second, the association of commands with power distorts the character of commands themselves in an administrative state, thus leading to further descriptive inaccuracies and misunderstandings.

The network-based model of authorization resolves these difficulties, and provides a better description of the government we actually possess. It recognizes that the performative statements that governmental units issue include not only commands, but also requests and promises. Much of the communication between individuals, offices, or agencies, for example, does not involve a superior and a subordinate, but collegial or coordinate entities. The actual drafting of regulations is often carried out by a group of colleagues within a given agency.[92] The turf battles that are so characteristic of modern agencies are not fought with swords—which are of little use against turf—but negotiated by interagency communication.[93] Even the relationship between a legislative committee and its corresponding agency is not truly hierarchical, but heavily negotiated.[94]

A microanalysis of operations in an administrative state, therefore, must incorporate performatives such as requests and promises as well as commands. It must be able to explain how coordinate entities ask each other to carry out certain tasks, and how they can elicit positive responses to their requests by various means—appeals to a common purpose, appeals to the recipient's self-interest, threats to withhold their own cooperation, threats to report to a superior, offers of unrelated services that the recipient might value, and so forth.[95] It must describe the way that the unit issuing the request can make credible threats and offers by issuing a promise about its own behavior. Since these promises are usually not legally enforceable, which merely means that the promisees cannot go to court for breach, the analysis must explain how they can be enforced by retaliation, trust, settled habit, or a sense of common purpose.

In addition to performatives of various kinds, the signals that flow through a governmental network also include locutionary statements, or information. A unit will often produce its effects upon another unit by these means, rather than by issuing commands or performatives of any other kind. Sometimes, subordinate units in a hierarchy will engage in primary information gathering, and will be instructed to report that information to their superior by means of descriptive statements. Sometimes superior units will receive information from their own superiors, or from other units, and will transmit that information, in whole or part, to their subordinates. In other cases, coordinate units will transmit information to each other in exchange for other information, or to facilitate some other type of signal. Without an effective model that incorporates these information flows, a microanalysis of modern government is virtually impossible.

Judgments also flow through a governmental network, producing notable effects. The judgments of a superior that is authorized to issue commands will generally influence the subordinate, but this is far from the only type of influential judgment. Very often, a high-status individual can affect a unit that she is unable to command by transmitting judgments based on general values. For example, the president of the United States is not authorized to issue commands to an independent agency, but because the president appoints the chair, and is generally recognized as the nation's chosen leader, the judgments he communicates to the chair will often constitute inputs that the agency will scale up dramatically.[96] Similarly, the politically appointed leader of a government agency is often affected by moral disapproval voiced by career officials.[97] Even if one wants to be cynical and attribute this effect to the staff's implicit threat to undermine the leader's efforts, it is difficult to reconcile with the concept of power. And the cynicism may itself be driven by a pre-empirical commitment to that concept. After all, social disapproval is a well-recognized force that explains many phenomena, from the rules of courtesy to the development of norms to the effects of voodoo, and there seems little reason to exclude it from the governmental process. In fact, as Peter Shane suggests, a breakdown in the informal norms that link disparate governmental units can lead to a chaotic situation that undermines the effectiveness of the entire enterprise.[98]

Even if the range of inquiry is restricted to commands, the authorization pattern that emerges from the structure of a network provides a much better framework for microanalysis than the concept of power. This point can be illustrated by considering the institutional nature of modern government, its articulated character, the variable forms of government commands, and the variable effects that they produce. To begin with the institutional nature of government, the relevant actor in many governmental processes is an organization at a level of the network that lies above that of the individual. As previously mentioned, it is awkward to describe an institution as exercising its will, or having its resistance overcome. The idea of an institution issuing or responding to signals in the form of a command is much more natural. Rather than agglutinating the agency into a single entity, this perspective facilitates and encourages microanalysis of the way that the command was generated and received. Precisely which person in the agency issued the actual words of the command? How was she authorized to do so? To whom was her command communicated, and what changes occurred in the receiving institution as a result of it? These questions can be pursued with the terminology of power, but the terminology impedes, rather than facilitates, the analysis, and exercises a continual temptation to convince oneself that discussion of an institution's intention, resistance, or desire is a real explanation.

The discourse of authorized command is also preferable to power as a means of microanalyzing the ways that groups of institutions are related to each other in the articulated structure of a modern administrative state. It focuses attention on the fact that units are only authorized to issue commands that follow a specified, often tortuously branching path. If the president wants to establish a task force to reform the bank examination process, he can issue a command to his direct subordinate, the Secretary of the Treasury, or to the Secretary's subordinate, the Comptroller of the Currency. As a practical matter, he is probably not expected to issue commands to a lower-level official. In many cases, moreover, even officials with the broadest scope of authorization are forbidden to issue commands along particular paths. Such prohibitions serve many purposes. When they are defined functionally they can insulate an institution from certain forms of political influence; as noted in Chapter 2, much of the federal judiciary's independence, for example, is achieved by simply prohibiting any elected official to issue commands regarding its decisions.[99] When prohibitions are defined geographically, they can create a federal structure that allocates specified decisions to regional or local administrators.

In addition to their institutional nature and their articulated form, the commands issued in the administrative state diverge from the traditional concept of power because they go beyond simple instructions to carry out a defined act, or even a series of defined acts. The authorized commands issued by the legislature to administrative agencies are often the broadly worded assignments described in the preceding chapter. Such commands create new agencies or offices that are then authorized by the command to issue commands, descriptions, and judgments of their own. Since it is counterintuitive to describe this process as exercising power over the authorized agency, or crushing its resistance, the usual image is that the legislature is transferring power to that agency. As discussed above, this reifies the concept of power in a conceptually confusing manner; as discussed in the preceding chapter, it misdescribes what actually occurs. By granting an agency control over some aspect of society, the legislature has not transferred its preexisting power or authority but increased its own control. That control that can be exercised by specifying the agency's output, or by issuing subsequent commands, or by expressing judgments about its operation.

A fourth aspect of command that is essential in describing the modern administrative state, or the pre-modern, pre-administrative state for that matter, is that commands vary in effect. The terminology of power portrays this as the result of resistance or a clash of wills. In many situations, that is not an accurate description, but even if it were, it does not capture the complexity of the process very well. A federal agency, for example, is subject to a multitude of signals.[100] The president is authorized to issue direct commands to it, but Congress is authorized to alter the agency's budget or its standing authorization to act.[101] To be sure, Congress is not authorized to issue commands to the agency, but it can certainly communicate its judgments—more precisely, those members of Congress who are authorized to initiate proposals to change the agency's budget or statutory authorization can communicate their judgments—through oversight hearings or individualized contacts.[102] The network model, and the concept of authorization that has been derived from it, allows for the microanalysis of these interactions. They indicate that the two sets of signals are likely to be summed within the agency, with the result that the amplitude of the president's command will be reduced by Congress's countervailing judgment signal.[103] Alternatively, the agency may be authorized or designed to scale down the effect of the president's command because the legislation that created the agency requires it to consider specified factors—environmental impact, for example—before taking action.[104] Similarly, the legislation might cause the agency to scale down a presidential command by applying the rules of professionalism to that agency.[105] The solicitor general, for example, is an attorney; she might accede to a presidential command to make a legally unsupportable argument to a federal court, but the impact of the command is likely to be scaled down by her specialized knowledge.[106] The complex process by which commands are summed and scaled in a modern state is difficult to describe as the product of resistance, or in any related terms that involve the idea of forcing someone, or something, to do what it otherwise would not have done.

One possible objection to the concept of authorized command, and the more general network imagery in which it is embedded, is that the description is not complete, that there is really something left over in the unit issuing the commands that can be effectively described as power. This objection might take at least five specific forms: that the concept of authorized command ignores the irreducible element of physical force that stands behind all governmental action, that it ignores the informal, collegial and atmospheric constraints described above in the criticism of discretion, that it ignores illegitimate influences on official behavior, that it ignores the role of extraordinary or charismatic individuals, and that it does not extend to absolute dictators. These are, indeed, all areas where the term 'power' is employed, but they all represent imprecise, and in most cases outmoded, usages. The concept of authorization, and the network model from which it is derived, serves to clarify the description of each area.

There can be little dispute that the modern administrative state, like its traditional, sacerdotal antecedent, sometimes deploys physical force to obtain compliance with its commands. This is not, however, a description of governmental structure, but rather a description of the government's effects upon its subjects.[107] Within the government, physical force is rarely used, and resort to it would be taken as a sign of imminent collapse. Its use was prevalent in the less settled times of the pre-modern state, when the central government was first asserting its authority over truculent, semi-autonomous principalities, but is now restricted to rare cases of open secession. Authorization, which lacks this implicit connection to force, is thus a superior description of the government's internal structure. Between government and citizens, where physical force is deployed, power might conceivably be a serviceable term. But, as described in Chapter 5, most government commands, particularly the multitudinous, quotidian commands of an administrative state, are followed because they emanate from an authoritative source. It seems better to avoid the ambiguities of power, in this situation, and speak of authorized commands, only some of which are backed by the physical ability of authorized governmental agents to catch a person and restrain him or to put a bullet in his brain.

As far as informal or collegial constraints on the action of government officials are concerned, most of these are fully accommodated by the concept of authorization. One reason is that the authorization to a unit of modern administrative government is always instrumental; it always incorporates a specified purpose that structures and constrains its exercise. A second reason is that such authorizations enable many modern governmental units to do much more than issue commands to their hierarchical subordinates. As subsidiary policy makers, rather than mere functionaries, they can issue a wide variety of other performatives, such as advice and requests, and they can also issue judgments that express opinions and establish standards. One of the descriptive advantages of the authorization and supervision model is that it provides a framework for incorporating such standards, requests, and hortatory interactions into a description of the government's internal structure.

There are, however, other constraints on government officials that lie outside the boundaries of authorization. These include corrupt and otherwise illegal interactions within government, as well as influence from private parties, both legal and illegal, and more general social norms. In the pre-modern state, these constraints were not necessarily regarded as separate from the governmental process. As discussed above, offices were regarded as private property, the king's household merged into the general government, and private affairs merged into public ones due to the quasi-public role of the nobility. The modern administrative state separates these functions through its articulated structure, and the concept of authorization describes that separation. Of course, this does not mean that corrupt practices do not occur within the government, or that private actors do not exercise an influence on governmental policy. But to describe these unauthorized effects as power, and to then use the same term to describe the authorized internal structure of the government, elides two types of action that are conceptually and functionally distinct.[108] It is simply inaccurate to say that a wealthy person's ability to convince or bribe public officials to give him a contract is the same sort of thing as an authorized command to give him the contract because he meets established programmatic criteria. To be sure, this means that the constraints on administrative decision making that make discretion an inaccurate description do not stem solely from authorized action, but also from illegal, external, and underlying social influences. But the disjunction is intentional; authorization and supervision are designed as alternative descriptions of the government we actually possess, not the broader set of social practices that constrain government decision makers and are encompassed by the concept of power. As stated above, the tendency of the term 'power' to coagulate governmental action with more general behavior is one of the features that renders it a poor description of administrative government.

These considerations lead naturally to the next objection, namely the role of extraordinary or charismatic individuals. The existence of such individuals among elected officials, or even among administrative agents, is not inconsistent with the terminology of authorized command. As Weber recognized, elected politicians often depend on charisma for their success,[109] while the idea that bureaucrats are a group of faceless automatons who thrive on anonymity and mediocrity is a pop-political canard.[110] In modern government, as elsewhere, intelligence, imagination, and personal charm are valuable assets that enable individuals to excel in carrying out their assigned tasks.[111] The results can be adequately described in the network-derived concepts suggested here. It is true that exceptional individuals often produce effects that go beyond the boundaries of their assignment, and in some cases, function independently of the established structure, but their impact can be treated as a set of informal signals whose pathways can be traced as readily as formal ones. It is also true that extraordinary individuals outside the governmental structure may influence governmental action. Whether the source of this influence can be usefully described as power is a question that lies beyond the scope of this discussion, which is an effort to describe and understand modern government, not society in general. Certainly, their impact on government can be readily described as a set of signals that serve as inputs to the governmental units they affect.

A final objection involves dictators, particularly dictators like Hitler, Stalin, or Mao, who attain their position by overthrowing established institutions, and seem to hold it without direct constraints upon their actions. This discussion focuses on elected, legally structured governments such as those in the present-day United States, Western Europe, and Japan; if it is applicable only to those governments, it will have served a useful purpose. In fact, the proposed analysis is more general, although its application to dictatorships will not be extensively explored. On the precise issue of a dictator's role, the proposed alternative of authorization is in fact preferable to the concept of power. However natural it may seem to describe a dictator as possessing absolute power, the description obscures more than it reveals. Of course the dictator is able to do a great deal of will-imposing and resistance-overcoming, but how precisely does one physically unimposing middle-age man get to do so? Certainly, no dictatorial leader of a modern, bureaucratic state has been able to rely on the veneration of his physical being that supported the ascendancy of medieval kings. A microanalysis of modern dictatorships would reveal that their leaders were in fact authorized to act by a complex, albeit recondite, informal network.

To take just one example, Stalin established his dominant position during the years when Lenin was the leader of the Soviet state. He did so by immersing himself, as Isaac Deutscher says, "in the party's daily drudgery and in all its kitchen cabals."[112] As Commissar of Nationalities, he appointed or approved the administrators and local leaders for most of the non-Russian population of the Soviet Union; as Commissar of the Workers' and Peasants' Inspectorate, he determined the success or failure of the existing civil service; as General Secretary of the Central Committee, he controlled the appointments, promotions, and demotions of the entire Communist Party apparatus.[113] Thus, Stalin's ascendancy as party leader, and his subsequent control of the Soviet state, can very plausibly be regarded as informally authorized by the large group of functionaries who owed their positions to him, and who in turn were authorized by the institutional structure to issue commands to the citizenry. This characteriza-

tion certainly opens up a more useful line of inquiry than the simple assertion that Stalin possessed absolute power.

Supervision

Supervision occurs when a superior attempts to control a subordinate's
behavior. It can refer either to one governmental unit's effort to control
another, or a unit's effort to control a private party. The latter situation
will be discussed in Chapter 5, when the animate aspect of the government's relationship with its citizens is explored. Here the concern is with
intra-governmental supervision, which is a crucial aspect of the government's animate structure. Virtually any action by a unit of government involves supervision of some other unit. In many cases, attention focuses on
the result the decision maker is attempting to accomplish, and the supervisory element of its decision goes relatively unnoticed. The decision to
spend a few billion dollars on a new national park or a particle accelerator
requires the decision maker to control its subordinates in certain ways, but
those controls are unexceptional, whereas the decision itself is highly controversial. In many other cases, however, the process of supervising subordinates is absolutely central to the success or failure of the entire governmental effort. No crime can be punished unless the government controls
the police, and no regulatory goal can be achieved unless the initiator of
the regulation can control those charged with its implementation.

Although authorization is being proposed, in this thought experiment,
as an alternative to the concept of power, supervision is not intended to
serve as a direct alternative to discretion. Rather, the idea is that the concepts of authorization and supervision, taken together, provide a unified
model of the government's animate internal structure that can substitute
for our current ideas about both power and discretion. With respect to
discretion specifically, the assertion is that a figure-ground reversal is in
order, and that the decision-making process for subordinate units should
be described by the authorizations and controls imposed upon it, not by
the freedom of action that remains. Dworkin virtually concedes this point
by comparing discretion to the "hole in a doughnut."[114] He then goes
on to identify his three varieties of discretion, that is, to ignore the doughnut and describe the hole. This seems like a questionable way to address
the issue. If one can describe the doughnut, what is gained by an independent description of the empty space that constitutes the hole? If one
has described the governmental network, located the channels of authorization, and identified the modes of supervision, what is gained by using
the term 'discretion' to describe the area left over once that description is
complete?

Although supervision is not a direct substitute for discretion, the figure-ground reversal that would replace discretion with a comprehensive account of government authorization requires that the term 'supervision' be employed, and that it display the same advantages over discretion that authorization displays in comparison with power. Again, the criteria for making this comparison are its correspondence with our emotional commitments, its identifiability as a heuristic, and its ability to provide a framework for the microanalysis of government. The first two criteria were discussed at the beginning of the previous section, in conjunction with power; the remaining question involves microanalysis. From this perspective, the great advantage of supervision is its derivation from the network model and the degree of specification that the model facilitates. The concept of discretion generates no analytic strategy except the one employed by Goldilocks—is it too big or too little or just right? The concept of supervision, in contrast, facilitates the microanalytic project of tracing the actual pathways of administrative decision making.

Because authorization and supervision constitute a unified model of government's internal structure, the methods that the two concepts employ are closely allied, particularly from the perspective of microanalysis. When the legislature enacts a statute enforced by an administrative agency, it is authorizing the agency to act, but it can also be regarded as controlling the agency's operations. As discussed in Chapter 2, legislation involves specification of the agency's outputs, inputs, or operations, a choice between controlling the agency and allowing it to learn, and a choice between stating rules in advance or monitoring performance on a continuing basis. Supervision within the administrative apparatus involves these same considerations. The major difference is the complexity or variability in the latter case. The legislature in a given government is typically a single unit, and it typically provides instructions directed only to the highest levels of the agency. In contrast, supervision within the administrative apparatus occurs between every pair of levels and in a wide variety of contexts. It includes the extremely remote relationship between the agency head and its lowest functionary in some distant local office, and the intensive relationship between an official and her immediate subordinate, with whom she is in daily or hourly contact.

The choice among various strategies for supervision will depend on a range of factors that are relatively easy to list and virtually impossible to quantify. One is the goal that the superior wants to achieve for his own reasons, or for emergent reasons intrinsic to his institution. A second factor involves the demands of the superior's superior, demands that the superior can often satisfy only by controlling the behavior of his subordinates. Third, the superior must assess the capacity, loyalty, and tractability of his subordinate and—again emphasizing the complexity of an administrative hierarchy—the subordinate's ability to make these assessments of its own subordinates. Still another factor are the resources available to the superior; the level of supervision can be increased by adding staff, but this always has a cost, and the supervisory staff must itself be supervised.

A brief survey of the issues involved in administrative supervision can begin with the choice between specifying or monitoring the subordinate's outputs and specifying or monitoring its operations. Specifying outputs is a more familiar strategy in this context than in the legislative one, with its most extensive form being management by objective. The superior's choice of this strategy clearly does not indicate any desire to grant the subordinate discretion; rather it requires the subordinate to choose the most effective approach. The operations may be left unspecified because there is only one possibility, or because the superior does not know what will be effective, or because he prefers to control the procedures through subsequent monitoring. Similarly, specifying the operations rather than the output does not imply that the subordinate has discretion to choose whatever output it desires. Usually, it means that the superior thinks that the best way to control the output is to specify the procedures. Sometimes, as in the case of dispute resolution, it may mean that the operations are important to the superior, but the particular outputs are not.

A second consideration in designing supervision strategies involves the choice between control of any sort—whether of operations or output, for example—and authorizing the subordinate to learn. Learning may appear to be akin to discretion, but it is not; it is a cognitive process, not an exercise of will. When applied to an administrative agency, as opposed to a human being, both terms are obviously heuristics. Discretion, however, personalizes the agency along medieval corporatist lines, coagulates its operations into a single reaction, and carries an implicit condemnation. Learning, in contrast, invites a microanalysis of an agency's decision-making processes, the way that the agency sets goals, develops strategies, monitors its output, and feeds that information back into its operations. It replaces condemnation with an invitation to consider whether the superior is choosing learning over control because it cannot clearly define its goal, or because it cannot determine the best way to achieve that goal, or because it trusts the agency, or because it cannot resolve its own internal disagreements, or for some other reason. The concept of learning thus recognizes that a superior's low level of control over a subordinate is a standard strategy of administration, and not necessarily a lapse in attention or a failure of nerve.

Finally, in deciding on a supervision strategy, the superior must also decide between rules stated in advance and subsequent monitoring. Here the question of supervisory resources, which is generally not central to the choice between controlling output and controlling operations, looms large. Stating rules in advance requires the superior to obtain more information at the time the decision is made, but requires fewer staff resources at subsequent times. Monitoring generally demands a relatively extensive staff, although economies can be achieved through reporting requirements of various kinds. These are difficult choices, and they are not illuminated in any way by treating them as a grant or restriction of discretion. As stated above, one of the conceptual difficulties with Dworkin's two forms of weak discretion—the absence of review and the need to exercise judgment—is that there is no organic relationship between them. Reconceptualizing them in terms of supervision reveals an underlying regularity. The idea of discretion based on the absence of review is better described as the extent to which supervision by means of subsequent monitoring leaves the subordinates's actions unobserved. The idea of discretion based on the exercise of judgment is better described as the extent to which rules stated in advance leave the subordinate's actions unspecified. But these possibilities are not typically the result of an affirmative decision to grant the subordinate discretion, nor do they necessarily result from the other behaviors that the term 'discretion' implies, such as a lapse of attention of the superior or a power grab by the subordinate. Rather, they are part of the ordinary administrative process, and depend on the usual factors that determine the level of supervision within that process, such as the superior's goals, the subordinate's capacities, and the resources available for supervision.

The concept of supervision facilitates a microanalysis of the manner in which agencies, offices, and individuals in modern government are controlled by their superiors. In place of crude determinations of too little or too much discretion, the model leads us to ask whether a superior's commands are being scaled up or scaled down by the subordinate, whether a bias is being applied to raise the activation level of these commands, or whether such commands are summed with inputs from other agencies. Under what circumstances are these operational specifications more effective than specifying the result? Under what circumstances should operations or results be specified in advance, as opposed to being imposed by continuous monitoring? What will induce an agency to learn, and when will this learning be superior to supervisory control? These kinds of questions, which are being asked by organization theorists today, are encouraged, and integrated into political theory, by the network model.

As in the case of power, the objection to bracketing the term 'discretion' may be that something real is left over, this time in the unit subject to a command rather than the unit that has issued the command. This objection can take at least three specific forms: that the lack of supervision reflects the superior's affirmative reliance on the subordinate's judgment or discretion; that discretion indicates that the person said to be possessing it has a wide range of permissible choices; or that, from a normative per spective, discretion serves identifiable and important purposes and creates identifiable and important dangers. The first of these objections has been answered earlier. Of course the superior wants the subordinate to exercise judgment, in the sense of acting sanely and intelligently, but it wants the subordinate to exercise judgment in furtherance of the output it has demanded or the procedures it has specified. In other words, the superior does not want the subordinate to exercise some general quality of judgment, but to act effectively in carrying out the specified assignments. Demands for a general quality of judgment are characteristic of the premodern state. As indicated, they do not reflect an exalted moral vision, but only that state's lack of articulation, and its consequent need to rely on exhortation rather than articulated structures.

With respect to the second objection, there are certainly many agencies in a modern administrative state that have a wide range of permissible choices, and every agency has at least a few. But this condition simply describes the nature of the agency's authorization or design, as discussed in the preceding section. It is neither useful nor phenomenologically accurate to say that an agency is authorized to make choices. The agency is authorized to achieve some articulated purpose, and the choices that it makes are simply the unsupervised portion of its efforts to fulfill its mission. If the agency's authorization involves large-scale purposes, and the structure of the hierarchy gives it few supervisors and many subordinates, the agency will certainly be confronted with more decisions than a narrowly circumscribed agency with many supervisors and no other governmental unit to command. We might then want to describe the agency as a policy maker, a concept that will be discussed in Chapter 6. Once again, the statement that this agency possesses more discretion tells us relatively little about the range or limitations of its choices.

But as the final, normatively based objection asks, is discretion not a separate quality, desirable as a means of making government agencies more humane and empathetic? And is it not a quality that induces those agencies to venture beyond their legally established limits? The answer is that we need not seek any such quality, but only need consider different modes of supervision that, in our inevitably imperfect world, offer particular advantages or disadvantages. If we want to make agencies more flexible, so that their actions will be more humane, we cannot rely on simplistic formulations such as "more discretion." If we want agencies to be more mechanistic, so that their actions will remain properly delimited, "less discretion" is an equally inadequate prescription. Instead, we need to decide precisely how the agency will be supervised to produce the desired mode of operation.

The association between discretion and a key is a forgotten detail of medieval thought, but the key, a pre-modern device soon to be replaced by magnetic-strip cards, voice recognition, and eye scans, is an appropriate symbol for the outmoded concept of discretion, just as the sword is an appropriate symbol for the outmoded concept of power. It conjures up an image of the trusted functionary opening his private office or storeroom, where he will work in an isolation made necessary by the government's lack of communications facilities and supervisory capacities. In contrast, the symbol of the modern administrative official's authorization is the portfolio. It contains her job description, its performance criteria, an account of her agency's procedures, and a list of required, permitted, and forbidden contacts with other offices and agencies. Soon this portfolio, essentially a Weberian file, will be replaced by a computer program, and the official will be seen as deriving her authorization from a network that mirrors, and perhaps embodies, the hierarchical administrative structure where she actually performs her appointed tasks. This suggests that the functionally articulated units of a modern state are best described by focusing on the instructions in the portfolio or the computer—the unit's authorization and the way it supervises or is supervised by other units. We will gain clarity and understanding if we set aside the sword of power and the key of discretion, if we try to describe a modern agency in network terms and treat those metal artifacts, together with the concepts that they symbolize, as elements of the medieval fantasy games that the officials play on their computers when their supervisor is out of the room.

Four

From Democracy to an Interactive Republic

The Pre-Modern Concept of Democracy

Aristotle's Legacy

THE discussion thus far has been exclusively concerned with the government's internal organization. That organization is traditionally divided between structural and animate components, with the former being envisioned as three branches, and the latter as the exercise of power and discretion. It has been suggested that both these descriptions can be replaced with the image of a multilevel network that unites them and describes each one with greater emotional, epistemological, and analytic realism. Thus, the internal structure, or hardware, of government is represented by the network's overall design, rather than three branches, and the more animate relationships among the units—the software—is described as the authorization and supervision of each unit, rather than as power and discretion.

The next issue involves what may be called the external structure of government, that is, the relationship between the government and its subjects, or citizens. In the standard account, this too is divided into structural and animate components. The structure of the government's relationship with its citizens is generally described as monarchy, aristocracy, dictatorship, or democracy, while the human attitudes that animate the relationship are described in terms of legitimacy. The question is whether either description is accurate and useful with respect to a modern administrative state. Democracy is discussed in this chapter and legitimacy in the following one.

Although there are many different structural relationships between government and its citizens, including monarchy, oligarchy, and dictatorship, democracy is the only one considered here. This study is not a general inquiry into the nature of government, but an exploration of whether the concepts that we currently use to describe our existing government remain applicable in the contemporary world. While various forms of governance have been previously lauded as ideal or acknowledged as acceptable, democracy is the only one that receives such approbation at the present time. Reducing the taxonomy of government to a single category simplifies the inquiry, but also adds a serious complexity for purposes of this dis-

cussion. Since everyone believes in democracy these days, the only debate
is whether the lordly edifice needs cleansing, and whether it is being pro-
faned by the hands of particular leaders who worship at its altar. Few people have gone to war to make the world safe for the tripartite structure of
government, or marched under a banner of administrative discretion, but
we regard democracy as something that we will fight and die for. In waving the mundane gadget of quasi-Cartesian doubt before the edifice of
democracy, therefore, one is potentially defiling sacred ground. The point
of the following inquiry, however, is not to attack our current form of government, or to endorse the policies of Stalin. Rather, it is to ask whether
the concept of democracy really serves as a good description of the government we actually possess, or whether this concept, with its Ionic
columns and its sculptured architraves, is really a papier-mâché facade that
conceals a different actuality.

The term 'democracy' comes from ancient Greece, of course,[1] which is
sufficient to raise at least the initial stirring of quasi-Cartesian doubt. It
disappeared as a practice with the rise of the Roman Empire, and as a concept with the Empire's decline, and it reentered European thought only
when Aristotle's *Politics*[2] was translated into Latin by William of Moer-
beke, sometime around 1260.[3] Discussion of democracy sprang into Western culture at that moment, and has continued in an unbroken and ever-
expanding stream until the present day. Medieval writers such as Marsilius
of Padua and St. Thomas Aquinas follow Aristotle's definition of the term
quite closely;[4] modern writers, although they have developed an enormous and sophisticated literature on the subject, remain curiously fettered
to his underlying concept.

That concept, in essence, is direct democracy. According to Aristotle, a
democratic city-state, or polis, is one ruled by poor citizens, rather than a
single person or a small group of nobles.[5] Since the poor generally out-
number the wealthy, Aristotle says, this is equivalent to rule by the majority.[6] He then derives the characteristic features of democracy from this feature of majority rule; some of the main ones are "that the appointment to
all offices, or to all but those which require experience and skill, should be
made by lot; . . . that no one should hold the same office twice, or not
often, except in the case of the military offices; that the tenure of all offices, or of as many as possible, should be brief; . . . that the assembly
should be supreme over all causes, or at any rate over the most important,
and the magistrates over none or only over a very few."[7] When these conditions are not satisfied—when most offices are filled by election, or are
held for long terms, or involve an extensive policy-making role—the government is not a democracy but an oligarchy, even if all the citizens participate in the elections. Sparta's constitution is a mixed one in Aristotle's
view, because in addition to its democratic elements, such as the fact that

all the citizens eat the same food and wear similar clothing, it has a number of oligarchic elements: "That all offices are filled by election and none by lot, is one of these oligarchic characteristics; that the power of inflicting death or banishment rests with a few persons is another."[8]

To this definition, Aristotle adds another, one that may reflect Greek ambivalence toward democracy or Aristotle's own ambivalence toward the Athenian democracy where he resided as a foreigner. Democracy, he says, represents a perverted version of a *politeia*.[9] This term, unlike the ones that he uses for other forms of government, namely monarchy, aristocracy, tyranny, oligarchy, and democracy, has not come into modern usage; it is, of course, the origin of our word 'polity,' but we use that term to describe any government, not one particular variety.[10] For Aristotle, a *politeia* is a mixture of democracy and oligarchy. While people might call this mixture an aristocracy, he notes, aristocracies add the element of virtue, whereas a *politeia* is simply a government that attends to the interests of both the rich and poor.[11]

It has been frequently observed that Aristotle's theory is designed for the diminutive city-states of ancient Greece,[12] and also that his concept of the citizenry excludes both women and slaves.[13] But the real difficulty with Aristotle's theory is that it envisions a direct democracy that has no relationship to any government that has ever existed in the Western, postclassical world. As Benjamin Constant and, more recently, Giovanni Sartori have noted, the Greek polis was really a community, rather than a modern state.[14] At the time the *Politics* was translated, there were a few small republics, such as the Swiss cantons and the city-states of northern Italy and the Netherlands, that bore a superficial resemblance to Aristotle's democracies, but their governmental structure was quite different and, in any case, they proved to be a dead-end in the development of Western government.[15] The modern nations that we now call democracies owe their political structure to an entirely different source—medieval corporatism and the concept of representation.

Medieval people, as noted in Chapter 3, struggled to conceptualize their collective organizations, such as guilds, trading companies, universities, towns, and, ultimately, nation-states. Once they had done so, they needed a further conception if these entities were to play a role in governance. The nobles could participate directly and the clergy could participate either directly or through hierarchical assignments, but the towns, and the growing bourgeoisie that inhabited them, needed a more particular mechanism. The mechanism they evolved was representation, and its basic elements, as Gaines Post and Arthur Monahan point out, came from Roman civil law.[16] One element was the principle—useful for resolving joint interests in a single subject matter—that "what touches all similarly is to be approved by all." A second was that a procurator, or proctor, could act in another's place, or represent that person. When these and other conceptual elements were combined, it generated the idea that a collective entity could select a person, by the joint action of its members, who would then act on the entity's behalf. The result was the representative assemblies that flourished in almost every European monarchy during the Middle Ages. Thomas Ertman argues that the assemblies whose members represented local territories, rather than status groups, were better able to resist the subsequent trend toward monarchical absolutism, and thus became the progenitors of modern republican government.[17] Certainly, the legislatures with this type of representative structure were the ones that maintained a continuous existence from the medieval era to the present, and that served as the template for the reestablishment of legislative assemblies in nations that had succumbed to absolutism, such as France and Prussia.

These representative assemblies, which are clearly central to modern republican government, owe virtually nothing to the classical conception of democracy. All the assemblies that existed in the ancient world, and that are discussed by Aristotle, are gatherings of the entire citizenry where each citizen speaks for himself and casts his own vote on the substantive issue. Had the example of representative legislatures been available to Aristotle, he would have regarded them as a case of people being ruled by others rather than themselves—exactly the position taken by Rousseau, whom he so profoundly influenced.[18] Elections, which Aristotle regards as an instrument of oligarchy, serve only to fill functional offices in his account,[19] and he never considered the idea that a group of people could elect an individual to speak for them.

Representative government, moreover, does not end the list of political developments in post-classical Western republics; a further transformation has occurred due to the advent of the administrative state. Our government now consists primarily of a vast number of appointed, specially trained officials, employed full-time and organized into hierarchical institutions. They are not representatives whose task is to reflect the desires of a group of citizens, and they are certainly not Aristotle's randomly selected citizens who would serve for short periods of time. Among contemporary institutions, only a jury—that most unadministrative of governmental institutions—is organized according to these principles. In short, even the traditional Western concept of representative democracy is itself out of date, and Aristotle's concept is as foreign to our reality as the Inca Empire or the Khanate of the Golden Horde.

The fact that Western nations are not democracies, according to Aristotle's definition of that term, may not seem like such a bad thing; after all, who really wants to be a political pervert? Even if one rejects Aristotle's harsh judgment of democracy, Athens, an over-aggressive, domineering, self-destructive, leader-punishing, slave-owning, woman-scorning little state, seems to be a poor model for us, given our present values. The Athenians produced great art and literature, but it is a lot more pleasant to read them than it was to live with them. Being a *politeia,* or mixed government, would seem preferable. In fact, mixed government, not direct democracy, was regarded as the primary rival of absolute monarchy throughout the five centuries after Aristotle's *Politics* was translated into Latin. The particular theory of mixed government that was in vogue was drawn more directly from Cicero's and Polybius's adaptation of Aristotle than from Aristotle himself, in that it added monarchy to the ideal mixture of oligarchy and democracy.[20] As such, it was able to incorporate the conflict between monarchical authority and representative assemblies that loomed so large in Western history.

It might appear that it would do no harm to retain the term 'democracy' and use it to describe the concept of *politeia,* or mixed government. While the Western concept of mixed government was gradually developing, the term 'democracy' was undergoing one of those transformations of keywords that Raymond Williams has described.[21] Its original association with direct democracy and ancient Athens had led writers to use it as we would use the term 'mobocracy'; it referred to the rule of an uncontrolled populace or of unscrupulous demagogues. But more radical thinking during the English Civil War led to its compurgation. James Harrington, who incorporated several Athenian features into his utopia of Oceana, coined the word 'anarchy' to describe mob rule, and reserved democracy for any regime where the populace possessed the leading role.[22] A greater influence was Montesquieu, who used democracy to mean a republic ruled by the "people as a body," and contrasted it with republics ruled by aristocracies.[23] According to Jennifer Roberts and Gordon Wood, the American revolutionaries began with the standard admiration of mixed government and distrust of democracy.[24] But by the time they adopted the Constitution, they were beginning to reject mixed government, with its implicit recognition of nobility and monarchy, and, with Montesquieu's encouragement, embrace the fearsome term 'democracy.'[25] This usage spread throughout Europe during the nineteenth century. Tocqueville used it in his description of America,[26] and George Grote supported it with his scholarly rehabilitation of ancient Athens.[27]

Given this evolution, the disjunction between Aristotle's use of the term 'democracy' and our own use of that term would not seem problematic. Finding the terms *politeia* or mixed government a bit awkward, we have simply replaced them with the term 'democracy,' a term that was available because the kinds of governments for which Aristotle used it no longer exist. All that is needed to achieve verbal clarity is to remember that some time in the early nineteenth century the usage switched, and what had been called mixed government until that time was subsequently described as democracy.

But this is not a satisfactory solution. It is true that the mixed or middle constitution Aristotle describes as characteristic of a *politeia* may combine oligarchic elements with democratic ones, thus allowing more extensive reliance on elected officials, and that the Cicerorian addition of the monarchy accommodates the addition of a chief executive. None of this, however, comes any closer to modern representative government. In fact, the reason Aristotle's discussion of the way the two elements of oligarchy and democracy can be mixed—which is that one can combine them, average them, or take parts from each—sounds more like a mathematical formula or a cookbook recipe than a political theory is precisely because he cannot conceive of strategies such as representation or indirect elections.

Moreover, Aristotle's concept of a *politeia*, or mixed government, is just as distant from an administrative state as his concept of democracy. The more extensive use of elections would allow some specialization of functions; even Athens elected all its military and some of its financial officers.[28] But while an administrative state is also specialized, it does not choose these specialized officials by election. Conversely, Aristotle makes no allowance for a hierarchy of appointed salaried officials, and he seems adamantly opposed to specialized training that would separate a person from the general run of citizens on the basis of knowledge rather than virtue. The state that best embodies the features of mixed government, in Aristotle's view, is Sparta, which was even more unadministrative than Athens, and bears a closer relationship to someplace the Starship Enterprise would come across than to any modern Western nation.[29]

Modern Theories of Democracy

Theories of democracy do not end with the eighteenth century, of course. Contemporary theories are legion, and many have received sophisticated theoretical elaboration and extensive empirical support. These theories have not freed themselves from their Aristotelian origins, however, because the imprint of those origins is sedimented into the very concept of democracy itself. It is all very well to say that we will simply set aside Aristotle's outmoded definition and use the term for a modern theory of our modern state. But when we pick up this scintillating object—and why would we bother reaching down for it if it didn't glitter so—the embedded social memories that it contains sing secret songs in our ears. We may think that we have appropriated the term for our own uses, and that we control its meaning, but as soon as our attention drifts, it will whisper to us: "Shouldn't all your decisions be made by an assembly of the entire populace? Shouldn't public officials be selected by lot, so that each of you may rule and then be ruled in turn?"

Reverberations of this siren song can be found in a wide range of modern theories of democracy, including self-government, participatory democracy, deliberative democracy, elitism, and pluralism.[30] As noted by many observers, perhaps most forcefully by Carl Schmitt, the term 'self-government' is an oxymoron because the basic concept of governance is that one person rules over another.[31] Modern Western states are certainly governed, in this sense; according to their own theory, they are ruled by elected representatives, not by the populace.[32] Whatever difficulties political representation creates for the theory of self-government, the administrative state increases those difficulties enormously. Not only is the state governed by elected representatives at the most general level, but most of the quotidian tasks of government are carried out by officials who are appointed, specially trained, and hierarchically organized. As a result, the control that the people themselves exercise over governmental operations, being doubly attenuated by the intervening representatives and administrators, is far removed from anything that could plausibly be described as self-government. The fictions that had been devised to stretch the fig leaf of self-government so that it somehow covered a representative regime no longer provide even minimal decency—the little leaf simply cannot conceal the overdeveloped apparatus of a modern administrative state. In short, the liberal theory of self-government appears to be driven by polis envy, rather than by any effort to grasp the realities of modern government. Athens is the Camelot of democratic theory.

The current support for participatory democracy, frequently described as civic republicanism, can be seen as an effort to concoct an aspirational antidote to these disconcerting realities.[33] Some proponents of this idea assert that citizens can only fulfill themselves as human beings through active political participation in the governmental process. For others, participation is required to make the government responsive to the people's needs and to combat its leaders' tendency toward self-aggrandizement, self-absorption, or outright oppressiveness. Most agree with both positions, and regard the minimally active voters of the modern state as simultaneously endangering their personal integrity and their political liberty. But this view, whatever its normative appeal, is necessarily grounded on a false consciousness argument, because the majority of people in Western nations choose to avoid active participation in government, even when the opportunity is readily available, and continue to support the specialized, appointed hierarchies of the administrative state. As discussed in Chapter 1, false consciousness arguments are epistemologically suspect, since they demand a strong interpretive overlay. Moreover, these arguments deconstruct themselves quite rapidly when applied to the idea of self-government. The basic justification for self-government is that people know their own interests, and should be able to choose a government that will be responsive to those interests. To argue that their lack of desire to govern themselves fails to reflect their real interests is a contradiction; if the claim is true, it undercuts the reason why one would want them to govern themselves in the first place.

There is, moreover, a certain perspicacity in the public's general apathy. Participatory self-government is incompatible with the administrative state, which is not staffed by citizens, but by experts with specialized, often highly technical training. This expertise, while fashionable to dismiss, is supported by our theory of knowledge in its entirety, our belief in the cumulative transmission of skills and information that has generated modern science, social science, and technology. We expect the government officials who design bridges to be trained engineers, the ones who monitor pollution to be trained chemists, and the ones who manage the economy to be trained economists. We would be scandalized if a political leader appointed ordinary citizens to these roles on a rotating basis to increase participation. In fact, when something goes wrong, there is often a general demand for the appointment of public officials with better training or credentials.

The concept of deliberative democracy is closely allied to participatory democracy, and suffers from a similar affection for the Aristotelian image of direct democracy. Its central claim is that democracy is defined by the existence of a free, inclusive, rational debate among citizens that determines the basic thrust of public policy. In the course of this debate, citizens exchange views, persuade or are persuaded on the basis of sound reasons, and reach conclusions that represent a mutually agreeable position at the very least, and perhaps a vision of the common good.[34] But this notion of deliberation must be recognized as a metaphor when applied to the political realm of a modern administrative state. It describes an intensive pattern of statement, response, and counter-response, where the speakers are in direct contact of some sort and can answer or accept each other's arguments. This certainly occurs among individuals, and within some organizations, but can it really be said to occur within civil society at large? In a modern state, with its millions of people, thousands of interest groups, and hundreds of administrative agencies, any sort of unified, collective debate is inconceivable, and citizens are more likely to be engaged in intensive interactions with a particular agency than they are with each other. The metaphor of deliberation among the members of civil society in general seems inspired by a yearning for Aristotle's assembly, where all the citizens meet to debate and decide "all causes, or at any rate . . . the most important."[35]

A second premise of deliberative theory is that public deliberation must be rational. Contemporary political debate obviously fails to achieve this standard, something one can readily confirm by spending a few minutes listening to political talk radio. Moreover, the idea that political issues have consensus solutions that can be perceived by reason is another outmoded Aristotelian notion. Modern social science teaches us that people often have genuinely incompatible views based on both their interests and their ideology, that these views are generated by, and generate, intense emotional responses, and that these conflicts are resolved by compromise or suppression, rather than persuasion. It would be difficult to view American presidential election campaigns, including the most recent one, in any other light. This does not mean that citizens are incapable of reasoned argument, or even that reason cannot triumph over emotion under certain circumstances. But reason operates in particular regions of political discourse, while interest or emotion prevails in others. In fact, the virtue of our modern governmental system is not that it displaces people's emotions with rationality, but that it displaces people's natural response to those emotions, which is to kill each other, with an orderly governmental process. That process is not persuasion, or the formulation of public policy by reasoned argument, but compromise among elected representatives, non-majoritarian protection of minorities, and the assignment of most governmental tasks to appointed administrative agents.

Two other, more structural theories of democracy, one critical, the other laudatory, bear the imprint of direct democracy as well. The first, elite theory, has two major strands—an analysis of elected leaders and an analysis of the electorate. The essential claim regarding the leaders, developed by Robert Michels, Gaetano Mosca, and C. Wright Mills,[36] is that these leaders, although elected by a large proportion of the populace, are drawn from a narrow social group and generally reflect that group's ideological commitments. The second strand, originated by Joseph Schumpeter,[37] and to a lesser extent, Walter Lippmann,[38] is that the voters are often uninformed about the issues at stake in an election and that their views are readily shaped or altered by the rival candidates. These observations are astute and, to a certain extent, incontestable, but the critical interpretation that has been given to them results from dangling comparatives. Modern government is controlled by elites, but what government has not been—medieval France, the Han Dynasty, the Inca Empire? Modern voters are not fully informed about political issues, and rely on leaders to provide both emphasis and information, but precisely when has the entire populace been knowledgeable and self-directed?

Once these questions are asked, the answer seems apparent. The only regime that is obviously superior to our own in these respects is the Aristotelian image of democracy. In this Hellenic Camelot, there is no political elite because the officials who control the state are selected by lot, the same person may not hold the same office twice, and each person serves for only a fairly brief and clearly delimited period of time. Moreover, these officers do not even constitute a temporary, situationally defined elite, because the assembly of the entire populace is "supreme over all causes, or at any rate over the most important, and the magistrates over none or only over a very few."[39] In such a democracy, moreover, the citizens will be well informed, and resistant to manipulation, for each is as likely as the other to hold office, and each participates in the assembly where all major issues are debated and decided. Thus, reliance on our inherited concept of democracy transforms elite theory's plausible but unsurprising observations into a condemnation, and that condemnation into a descriptive theory. Michels characterized the patterns of behavior that he observed in political parties as the iron law of oligarchy. It was oligarchy because it did not conform to Aristotle's concept of democracy, it was characterized as iron because it seemed grimly modern in its divergence from that concept, and it was characterized as a law because that declaration of its inevitability supported Michels's condemnation.

Pluralism is a more laudatory theory of democracy, but it is equally beholden to inherited, outdated notions. Against liberal theory, pluralism asserts that the citizenry cannot be regarded as an undifferentiated mass that governs itself through the electoral process. As Robert Dahl, James Buchanan, and Gordon Tullock point out, elections do not effectively aggregate individual preferences.[40] Even if they could, they occur only intermittently, and do not address the full range of political issues. Thus, people must express their preferences by contributing and campaigning during elections and by communicating in various other ways with government officials during the relatively long intervening periods. Usually, all this activity occurs through the medium of organizations, and it is thus organizations, not the electorate in general, that exercises control over the government. Against elite theory, pluralism notes the multiplicity of organizations and their varied strategies for exercising influence. Dahl and Nelson Polsby have shown, through careful empirical work, that most American governments are not dominated by a single, independently defined elite, but by shifting alliances of organizations.[41] William Riker points out that the political strength of organizations is often not attributable to the social status of their members, but to their ability to mobilize resources and votes.[42] Social movement theorists such as William Gamson, Anthony Oberschall, and Sidney Tarrow in the United States and Donnatella Della Porta, Alberto Melucci, and Alain Touraine in Europe have demonstrated the manner in which politically active organizations emerge from broadbased popular concerns and attitudes.[43]

But in the work of Dahl, Polsby, Earl Latham, and David Truman,[44] pluralism goes beyond these important, widely accepted observations, and advances the further claim that the patterns it has discerned constitute a theory of democracy. This claim is based on the contention that all political interests in society, or perhaps the primary political interests of all members of society, are reflected in the organizations that vie for political control. In addition, the thought is that these groups will exert sufficient force to balance out each other, so that each one will secure at least minimal recognition of its members' interests, but no group will become dominant enough to take control of the state and tyrannize the remainder of society. Dahl traces this concept of democracy back to Madison and Hamilton, and describes it as the rule of the minorities, rather than the rule of the majority.[45]

As critics have regularly observed, this homeostatic account of pluralism's operation is empirically implausible, most notably because there is no mechanism to ensure that all interests will be recognized.[46] Some individuals may find that their interests are not represented by any politically active organization, or that the organization that represents them might be systematically excluded from the governmental process by a majority that defines itself as "us," and the excluded group as "other."[47] As a result, the oppression of racial, religious, or linguistic minorities, or any other readily identifiable subgroup, becomes a real possibility, and a real danger to the values of fairness and liberty. In their effort to deny this possibility, the polyarchic pluralists have resorted to the old Athenian image, depicting American democracy as a *politeia* of organizations. America becomes the modern equivalent of Athens, or Camelot-Athens, with organizations occupying the place of idealized Athenian citizens. Like these idealized citizens, the organizations are fully informed, they participate enthusiastically in governance, and there is only a relatively small, manageable number of them. They do not gather in an assembly, to be sure, but the shifting alliances that Dahl and Polsby found enable all of them to rule and to be ruled in turn.[48] This carries the delicious implication that the administrative apparatus is epiphenomenal, a reflection of the collaboration among the meta-citizens who constitute the real essence of our government. Like self-government, participatory democracy, deliberative democracy, and elite theory, it is political fantasy whose judgments, whether positive or negative, are driven by embedded images of a yearned for but long-lost regime.

Electoral Interaction

The Interaction Model of Elections

As in the case of power and discretion, the quasi-Cartesian doubt raised by the pre-modern origins of democracy is amplified by its use in political theory. If we want to explain the process by which a modern government relates to its citizens, it would seem preferable to bracket this concept, disconnecting its claim to provide an accurate description of the system that we presently possess, or to establish an emotionally satisfying and cognitively useful norm. We should then seek an alternative conception that will help us fulfill our emotional commitments, reflect the heuristic quality of thought, and provide a framework for microanalysis. That conception, for reasons given below, will be described as interactive republicanism. It acknowledges the republican nature of modern government, that is, the fact that it is a government where representatives elected by the citizens, and not the citizens themselves, make basic policy decisions. But it is not civic republicanism, which attempts to restore direct democracy's element of participation with the unrealistic assertion that citizens need to, or ought to, become involved in public activities. Rather, it also acknowledges the administrative nature of modern government, a complex, technical process carried out by appointed officials. Citizens do participate in this process, but they do so through specified channels that include elections and professional or quasi-professional interaction with the administrative apparatus. Hence, the proposed alternative is not described as democracy, or civic republicanism, but interactive republicanism.

In the previous chapters, the internal structure of the government was described in terms of a network metaphor, and it was argued that this metaphor generates descriptions that better satisfy the stated criteria. The question now is whether that same metaphor can provide a better account of the relationship between the government and its subjects than the bracketed concept of democracy. As stated, the network metaphor envisions government as a multilevel network of interconnected units. Each level is defined by the size of the unit, with the lowest level being individuals, the highest being nation-states. The role, authority, and status of the units on a given level are determined by the nature of the connections among them. It is easy enough to imagine this network as extending outward into the general society, which can then be envisioned as precisely the same kind of network as the government; stated differently, the government can be considered as simply one particular region of the general social network. With this image in mind, a government's relationship with its citizenry can be described as a set of interactions that occur across the boundary separating the governmental region of the social network from the remainder of that network.

Elections have often been regarded as the defining condition for democracy. With the concept of democracy bracketed, and the network model used in its place, they appear as simply one particular, albeit very important, type of signal between the government and citizens of a republic. Contrary to the implications of many democratic theories, elections cannot be modeled as signals generated by citizens to control the government. Citizens do not, as autonomously acting individuals, determine government policy in the manner of ancient Athens, or select their leaders in the manner of the legendary German tribes. Rather, an election is an output signal from citizens responding to an input to those citizens that is generated by the government itself. Some administrative organization within government is authorized to generate this input. It must specify the time and place for voting, set up polls, and list the issues for decision. Various individuals, who are sometimes inside the government and sometimes outside it, will then campaign for the result they want, thus providing additional input to the citizenry. The citizens respond to these inputs—one can say that they are intersubjectively programmed to respond—by going to the polls and casting votes; these votes then constitute an output signal which is transmitted to and collated by a governmental mechanism that is designed to respond to them. To elicit this signal in a truly effective manner, the government needs rather substantial administrative capacities, which is at least one reason why the evolution of large-scale elections generally parallels the evolution of the administrative state. In short, elections are not an act of self-governance by the populace, but a highly structured interaction between a group of voters and a government that has defined their role and their identity.

In this interaction model of the electoral process, concepts such as the populace, the popular will, and public opinion disappear, as coagulated concepts often do. There can never be an autonomously generated signal from the populace to the government because only an individual or organization can generate a signal, and the populace is neither. Elections consist of a signal generated by the government that elicits a responding signal from a large group of citizens, acting individually. This administrative mechanism constructs the populace, or more specifically, it constructs a particular kind of populace by virtue of its operations. Public opinion polls, focus groups, and social movements of various kinds construct different populaces. There are, of course, regularities among the lifeworlds of the individuals who constitute each structured populace. But as Cynthia Farina points out,[49] there is no such thing as public opinion in the abstract, just as there is no assembly, be it actual, conceptual, or virtual, where the citizens meet to debate the issues of the day.

Our Aristotelian expectations of self-government often lead us to overestimate the significance of elections. In fact, the role of elections, although exceedingly important, is delimited. Their most crucial function in a modern, interactive republic is to determine the identity of a particular category of government officials, generally those who exercise the broadest and most complete authority. In other words, elections serve to authorize those individuals who then issue authorizations and exert policy control over the administrative apparatus, and supervise that apparatus in the manner that was described in Chapter 3. This arrangement falls far short of self-government, public participation, or deliberation, but it does represent a partial solution to three endemic problems of governance—the problems of the succession, competence, and responsiveness of governmental leaders.

The problem of replacing subordinate officials can be readily resolved in any governmental hierarchy; once they serve a specified term, or misbehave, or become decrepit, their superiors will appoint another person in their place. But the replacement of the policy-making officials who have no superior is much more difficult. Elections, when fully institutionalized, solve the problem of succession so decisively that the significance of their achievement can be easily forgotten. The threat of a succession crisis hovered over every medieval monarchy, as it must over every government that relies on the hereditary principle. As noted in Chapter 3, the stability of the succession in a hereditary regime rests on the ruler's physical ability to produce an heir. One sees the reflection of this problem, and the depth of people's anxiety about it, in accounts of the chaos that preceded Arthur's reign, when there was no recognized successor to Uther Pendragon, and the chaos that resulted from his war with Mordred, which left the succession equally uncertain.[50] Elections resolve this problem through an orderly procedure that can be used either at defined intervals or upon the leader's death. It is impressive that not a single drop of blood has been spilled during the past century in world powers such as the United States or the United Kingdom over the potentially incendiary issue of succession. The calmness with which Americans reacted to the badly botched vote count in the 2000 election underscores this observation. Of course, elections do not guarantee this happy outcome; the American Civil War was triggered by the results of the 1860 election,[51] while other nations have dissolved into chaos over disputes about an election's procedural validity. All in all, however, elections are probably the best solution to the problem of succession that has been devised.

A second role of the electoral signal is to alleviate the problem of competence. Neither heredity nor random selection provides any guarantee that a successor will be competent; sadists, sybarites, and imbeciles are just as likely to succeed under these systems as intelligent and conscientious leaders. The electoral signal, in contrast, generally incorporates a judgment about the competence of the successor. It does not guarantee that the most competent person will be chosen, of course, but it eliminates those who are too lazy to campaign, too stupid to convince, or too perverted to behave. In addition, hereditary regimes, as noted in Chapter 3, are hostages to the physical body of their ruler. Even if they are fortunate enough to obtain a competent ruler, that person will often go through a period of debilitation before death installs his successor. The same, of course, is true for electoral regimes if the leading officials are elected for life, like the pope or the Holy Roman Emperor. But elections held after a term of years, or upon a loss of confidence, alleviate the problem. Admittedly, the ruler can fall ill before the term runs out or the next election can be organized, as Woodrow Wilson did, but the likelihood that this will occur is substantially reduced by regular elections for relatively short terms. Candidates must be reasonably healthy when they run for office, and so are likely to fulfill their term, or wear out their welcome, while their minds and bodies are intact.

Finally, electoral signals play an important role in solving the problem of making government responsive to its citizens. Unlike succession and competence, this is not a universal problem, but it is a problem for any government whose purpose is to benefit its people, and a particular problem for an administrative state committed to the moral principle of instrumentalism. Elections tend to render government responsive because the voters' selection of a candidate generally incorporates a judgment about their policy preferences. Despite the well-known role of demagoguery, charisma, photogenic looks, and a sound-bite sensibility, people tend to choose a candidate whose views correspond to their own. In addition, the signal from the electorate contains information to which the elected official who wants to be reelected is likely to respond. To be sure, elections are not a complete solution to the problem of nonresponsiveness. The electorate may represent only a portion of the citizenry, even in a government that we would be willing to describe as a democracy. The English property qualification, for example, led to the election of representatives who were singularly unresponsive to the poor, while American racial exclusions produced similarly predictable results. There are, in addition, the familiar inaccuracies and distortions of the electoral process that favor the views of the wealthy, the well-organized, and the vociferous. Nevertheless, the use of the electoral mechanism for selecting leaders does provide at least some likelihood that the leaders will be responsive to the views of their constituents.

Elections thus offer imperfect, but often satisfactory solutions to the problems of succession, competence, and responsiveness. These advantages, though subject to the inevitable qualifications that attend any humanly designed device, are considerable, and argue strongly for the value of elections in achieving our commitments. That is, however, all that can be achieved by this particular mechanism. Elections do not implement self-governance by the electorate, they do not provide personal fulfillment through political participation, they do not ensure that government will be responsive to organizations representing all sectors of the population, and they do not generate collective deliberation within civil society. Most of all, they do not transform the dispersed, vaguely disaffected citizens of a modern administrative state into a decision-making assembly, or allow them to rule and to be ruled in turn.

The gap between elections and self-government became apparent to the American people in the 2000 election. The Supreme Court seems to have interpreted this revelation as a crisis of legitimacy, taking quick and doctrinally incoherent action to resolve the matter in *Bush v. Gore*.[52] But even granting the Court this charitable interpretation, its decision was wrong; the controversy merely revealed to the populace a long-suspected, half-recognized truth that the concept of democracy tends to conceal, namely, that elections are not the essence of self-government, but an imperfect mechanism for achieving specific political goals. The resulting public reaction was one of abashed acknowledgment, not the revolutionary rage that would have justified the Court's unconcealed butchery of legal doctrine.

Advantages of the Interaction Model

The advantages of using the interaction model of elections to describe the relationship between the government and its subjects in Western administrative states can be assessed by considering the extent to which it conforms to our emotional commitments, announces its heuristic character, and facilitates microanalysis. One of the most serious disadvantages of the concept of democracy is that it belies our genuine emotional commitments and appeals to clandestine ones. In particular, it appeals to social nostalgia—not our nostalgia for the medieval era, nor the medieval era's nostalgia for Camelot, but to our yearning for the equally alluring image of ancient Greece, with its heroic voyages, walled cities, marble temples, and debate-filled agorae. Describing the relationship between the government and its subjects as an electoral interaction conjures up only the unromantic process that it actually describes.

The genuine commitments that the concept of democracy belies are to security, prosperity, and liberty. Of these three commitments, we achieve at least two—security and prosperity—through the mechanisms of the administrative state that compose our basic means of governance. As discussed in Chapter 1, the norm that underlies this state is that the government is supposed to be an instrumentality, serving the interests of the people. To effectuate this norm, we need to solve the problems of succession, competence, and responsiveness, and the election of the highest-ranking public officials has served as a reliable means of doing so. The anti-administrative undercurrent in democratic theory—the myth of self-government, the condemnation of policy elites, the image of public deliberation, and the subterranean preference for selection by lot and direction by public debate—implicitly rejects our only path to realizing these commitments.

Democracy is most commonly linked with the third of the commitments that have been identified, namely, the commitment to liberty. To
some extent, this connection is the result of purely stipulative definitions;
if democracy is defined as a system of government where all citizens have
the right to speak freely, then democracies undoubtedly provide freedom
of speech. The instinct behind a usage of this sort, however, is a pre-
analytic commitment to the term 'democracy' itself. It results in an agglutinated discourse that forestalls analysis of the real connection between
governmental structures and their consequences. If we want to know
which structures secure liberty, we should bracket the concept of democracy, with its embedded normative associations, and ask directly how such
structures operate. This turns out to be a complex empirical question that
is best answered by using the alternative description of electoral interaction. The answer is that such interaction secures liberty to some extent, by
making government somewhat responsive to the electorate and requiring
a certain level of free speech so that the electorate can make a genuine
choice. But as both theoretical analysis and historical experience readily
demonstrate, electoral interaction does not preclude severe restrictions on
free speech, as occurred in nineteenth-century Britain, or enslavement of
one portion of the population, as occurred in nineteenth-century America, or the subordination and disenfranchisement of women, as occurred
in both. The metaphor of electoral interaction avoids bootless debates
about whether such regimes are truly democratic, and focuses attention on
the extent to which elections secure the liberty of the populace, and the
extent to which that liberty must be secured by other means.

A second advantage of describing the government's relation to the populace as an interactive republic is that this description is more obviously a
heuristic. Democracy, like any concept that has been used for a few thousand years, tempts us to regard it as a real entity, rather than recognizing
its heuristic character. In the case of democracy, one danger—already evident in Aristotle's work—lies in the assumption that governments fall into
natural, preexisting categories, rather than being complex, socially specific,
and historically situated political arrangements. This danger becomes greater
still when the governance structure is explicitly created, through the
mechanism of a constitution, or consciously borrowed from another nation. Another danger, which has emerged well after Aristotle, stems from
democracy's distinctive status in the modern world as the only morally acceptable form of government. This leads nearly every nation to declare itself a democracy, and every nation to dispute the application of that term
to its opponents. The result is that democracy is treated as a political
apotheosis, a definitive condition that each nation strives to attain. On reflection, most people would agree that governments are ad hoc, disorderly
responses to the political and social problems of the day, and that cate-

gories such as democracy are conceptual conveniences that we attach to them. But the term 'democracy' is so evocative, so often the banner under which very real armies march, that there is a constant tendency to imagine it as a unified, self-evident entity that political actors either accept or reject.

The alternative idea of electoral interaction, and an interactive republic generally, avoids much of the reification that afflicts the concept of democracy. There is, admittedly, a certain amount of reification that attaches to the idea of a republic, but this familiar term has been selected to avoid the countervailing disadvantage of neologism. While the term does imply a certain categorization of governments, it possesses fewer associations than democracy, and a much vaguer emotional or normative contour; it refers, most commonly, to a government ruled by elected representatives, as opposed to a hereditary monarch, a dictator, or the citizens at large. That is precisely the way it is being used in this chapter. The term 'election,' although familiar, is similarly unadorned. To provide more descriptive accuracy, but also to add a sense of unfamiliarity, the idea of interaction has been attached. This decreases the naivete of the proposed alternative, which is unfortunate, but also dispels some of the sense of familiarity that attaches to the term 'republic,' thus producing a compound that more clearly announces its heuristic character.

The third advantage of the interaction model is that it facilitates microanalysis of the government's relation to its subjects. With respect to elections, it reveals both the instrumental character and the inherent limits of this mechanism in a manner that the concept of democracy tends to obscure. To begin with, it underscores that elections are not the voice of the people or the apotheosis of self-government, but merely one mechanism, designed and operated by the government itself, which generates a certain set of outputs from the citizens. They are, moreover, a limited mechanism, particularly in an administrative state. The concept of democracy holds out an implicit promise that the people can use elections to effect the comprehensive control of the administrative apparatus. This is not the way any Western government operates, nor the way any such government could operate, because the limits that preclude the electoral mechanism from controlling the administrative state are inherent ones. Citizens can vote for only a small number of government officials, perhaps as many as five or six, perhaps only one or two. Perhaps the number depends upon the number of candidates who are competing, or the education level of the voters, or the intensity of political controversy at the time. But the limit is real, and it means that elections can be used to select only a few officials who will necessarily interpret their role in political terms, and who can govern, if at all, only by issuing broadly defined assignments to the administrative apparatus. Citizens simply will not, and perhaps cannot, absorb the information necessary to elect the hundreds of currently appointed officials who constitute the leadership of the administrative state. It would be possible, of course, to include candidates for these positions on a ballot, but this would only expand the bewilderment experienced by most Americans when confronting a ballot that lists candidates for city council, local school board, state judiciary, municipal water district, and a variety of other institutions to which they have never devoted any thought.

The same is true for referenda, where citizens decide specific issues that would otherwise be resolved by legislative or administrative action. Such referenda have become common in several American jurisdictions, most notably California.[53] The narrow-minded selfishness that their results reveal has proven disconcerting to many observers who had been willing to confer some normative priority on this direct expression of the voters' views. As a result, a scholarly literature has developed to recount the deficiencies and inaccuracies of referenda—that they are subject to the same interest group pressures that operate in elections for representatives, and add the further difficulty of asking voters to understand complex, abstract issues, rather than more comprehensible choices between rival human beings.[54] These are useful points, but the sense of surprise or dismay that underlies them is misplaced. A referendum, like an election, is simply a mechanism by which citizens interact with the government. Like any mechanism, it possesses both virtues and defects, but it cannot be regarded as a direct conduit to some mystical source of political justification, or a means for replacing the administrative state with a participatory or deliberative one.

The Meaning and Promise of Electoral Interaction

Bracketing the concept of democracy and replacing it with the network-derived idea of electoral interaction does not mean that elections should be regarded as merely a mindless selection among competing elites or blind expressions of material self-interest. Microanalysis, it will be recalled, incorporates a behavioral theory based on the search for meaning, rather than rational action. Consequently, a microanalysis of electoral interaction not only elucidates the instrumental, delimited character of elections, but also emphasizes the meaning with which participants infuse this mechanism. For elected officials, election is a source of status in addition to their actual authority, an indication to these officials that they are central to the governmental process. Elections play their most important role in determining the identity of officials who have no direct superiors, and therefore cannot be chosen by the convenient process of appointment. These are generally the primary policy makers in the government, that is, the most authoritative officials. As a result, selection by means of an electoral process serves as an indication that one has no superior, and is responsible for making important decisions. In addition, the official's election means that a majority of the voters have decided that she is competent and that her policies reflect their own opinions.

Beyond this, popular election places the official in an interesting middle ground between expertise and politics. The usual account is that an elected official—a legislator, paradigmatically—can either be a conduit, transmitting the views of her constituents, or a trustee, chosen by her constituents to exercise her own best judgment.[55] Empirical evidence, however, suggests that most legislators construct a meaningful account of their professional lives by integrating their role as an elected representative and their role as a government official.[56] This requires them to sum a variety of complex inputs from the electorate with an equal or greater variety of complex inputs from other persons in the governmental structure. Elected officials tend to view the meaning of their role as connected to precisely this process of summing inputs from two distinctly different sources. Lower-level officials can take refuge in technical tasks, or internal government relations, but they—the elected—must balance public opinion, governmental operations, and the broadest policy considerations.

For voters, elections also possess a variety of meanings.[57] Perhaps the most important are that the government is supposed to serve their needs, and that they are allowed to evaluate and criticize its performance of that function. These may seem to be rather rudimentary entitlements, far less gaudy than self-government or popular sovereignty. But if we begin with the administrative norm that the government is an instrumentality for meeting its citizens' needs, then the responsiveness that elections help secure is central to our entire morality of government.

A second meaning of elections, as a device for solving the problems of succession, competence, and nonresponsiveness, is that the voters are part of the same political system as the government. While elections do not transform the voters into rulers of the polity, they enable them to see themselves as members of it. At the individual level, making a choice and casting a vote means that one is responding to the government's output signal, and in some sense functioning as part of that governmental structure. In addition, it often creates an emotional bond with one's selected candidate. This is important in securing the enthusiasm of those who favored the ultimate victor, but even more important in securing the quiescence of those who favored the loser. At the institutional level, any group that participates in the electoral process, no matter how marginal its origins or radical its political philosophy, is likely to modify its message to attract more votes. Thus, the group will tend to organize its efforts around electoral politics to an increasing extent as time progresses. In Charles Tilly's view, this is an aspect of modernization, as localized, traditional actions such as peasant uprisings or appeals to paternalistic authorities are replaced by nationwide mobilization to present claims as part of a proactive program.[58] Over time, moreover, groups that participate in national elections tend to develop an internal structure that is homologous with mainstream groups, a phenomenon described as institutional isomorphism.[59] Elections are thus an effective means of defusing opposition to the government, even more effective than oppression. This is often a source of frustration to those observers who would like to see disadvantaged or marginalized groups serve as the shock troops of revolution, but the members of those groups generally decline to play that role once they are involved in an electoral system.

Further insight into the functions of the electoral mechanism in an administrative state can be obtained by considering cognitive prescriptions for its improvement. For example, as long as voter participation levels remain relatively low,[60] which remains the case in the United States despite higher turnouts in the most recent election, elected officials will not be responsive to those segments of the population who do not participate. The U.S. Motor Voter Law addressed this problem by facilitating registration.[61] A more effective strategy would be to rely on a technological device that allows low-cost, instantaneous communication. That device is not the Internet—although the Internet may ultimately be the instrument of choice[62]—but the lowly telephone. It is remarkable that during a century of widespread distribution, the telephone has not been utilized as a convenient means of increasing voter participation levels. There are certainly problems of authentication, but private firms authenticate credit cards over the telephone and ship thousand-dollar items on that basis. Moreover, authentication problems are not exactly unknown in elections using paper ballots or voting machines. Perhaps our dogged retention of these physical mechanisms results from the very fact that they require voters to travel to polling places, thus enabling us to maintain a vague sense of connection between modern elections and the assembly of ancient Athens.[63]

Elections also need to be more fairly organized; at present, fund-raising ability and personal wealth play far too large a role. Campaign finance reform, of the sort provided by the Federal Election Campaign Act of 1971,[64] is an obvious response. In the long run, government funding of major candidates at a level that would render additional spending otiose is probably the most promising strategy, but restrictions on the expenditure of private funds would also be of value. The Supreme Court struck down the Act's expenditure provisions in *Buckley v. Valeo*[65] by equating monetary expenditure with free speech and arguing that such expenditure may not be restricted in connection with elections, where free speech must prevail.[66] The Court conceded that free speech is subject to time, place, and manner restrictions, but argued that "expenditure limitations impose direct quantity restrictions on political communication and association."[67] As Edwin Baker points out, however, this argument analogizes an election to society in general, an analogy supported by the idea that the society is a democracy and an election is constitutive of that society.[68] If an election is regarded as one particular mechanism by which the government and the citizens interact, a different analogy suggests itself. From this perspective, an election resembles a trial, that is, a specific, highly structured mechanism by which we implement a particular function in our system. Fairness demands that both sides in a civil trial be given the opportunity to state their case, but it also demands that their statements be limited and channeled to create a rough equality between opposing parties. Similar considerations of fairness suggest that limits should be placed on the expenditure of funds so that the leading candidates for a particular position can state their cases in a roughly equal manner.

Prescriptions regarding international relations shed further light on the contrast between the electoral interaction model and the concept of democracy. Throughout the Cold War, the United States seemed to regard democracy as a complex, mysterious conception, the particular creation of the Anglo-Saxon *volk*, sprung from the soil between Kent and Chester, and capable of transplantation only to new lands where English-speaking people have exterminated or suppressed the native population. Even when we freed ourselves from this Anglo-Saxon master-race mythology, we maintained the view, expressed by Dahl and other leading theorists, that fair elections are part of an elaborate, sophisticated, somewhat fragile governmental system that can only be implemented, and perhaps only merited, by a well-educated populace that is already committed to its underlying morality. Consequently, we assumed that this system could not be exported to the non-Western World, that the only thing we could demand of Third World nations was anti-Communism, that we could not prevail by urging the adoption of our own values and our own ideals. But what would have happened had we regarded our system as being based on the quotidian mechanism of elections, rather than the transcendent mystery of democracy? What would have happened had we decided to fight the Cold War by supporting free and fair electoral regimes instead of anti-Communism?

Administrative Interaction

The Role of Administrative Interaction

If the foregoing discussion seems reductionist, despite its references to social meaning, the reason is that it addresses only one aspect of the electoral process—the election itself. Traditional theories of democracy generally focus on this same event, although they tend to treat it as an apotheosis rather than a signal.[69] But contemporary analysis is more sophisticated, and includes the multiplicity of interactions that accompany elections. One is lobbying by private groups, itself a complex process that includes threatening, begging, cajoling, testifying, supplying information, and drafting legislation.[70] Another is the various vote-gathering, support-building, and opposition-blunting activities in which elected officials engage, such as campaigning, providing information to constituents, negotiating with interest groups, and casework, that is, intervening with other parts of government on behalf of influential groups or individuals.[71] Using the network model, these activities can be depicted as additional signals flowing between private parties and elected officials. Many of these signals are subsidiary to elections, and some flow from government to citizens, but they are not qualitatively different from the electoral signal. Like elections, they represent part of the interaction between the government and its citizens.

In fact, these non-electoral signals between private parties and elected officials amplify some of the advantages of elections by transforming the intermittent signal that elections provide into a continuous one. Although they have no direct effect on the problems of succession or competence, they reinforce elections' role in achieving responsiveness and they strengthen the social meaning that those elections possess. With respect to responsiveness, the information flow provided by lobbying and inter-election campaigning is more consistent and detailed than that provided by the election. With respect to meaning, lobbying and campaigning provide additional ways of interacting with the government beyond casting a vote, and thus provide citizens with a greater sense of connection to the political system. Of course, these activities may favor some groups over others, but elections are also subject to distortions. The point is simply to understand the way these mechanisms operate before proceeding to normative judgments that may be based on outdated commitments.

While traditional theories of democracy generally incorporate the multiplicity of signals that accompanies the electoral process, discussion tends to be restricted to this set of signals and does not include the equally dense and varied set of signals that pass between citizens and non-elected officials, specifically the officials in administrative agencies. Yet private groups and individuals lobby agencies with equivalent assiduousness; they threaten, beg, and cajole, they testify, supply information, and draft regulations just as they do with elected legislators and executives. Conversely, agency officials are often as assiduous as elected ones in building support or blunting opposition. They do so not to gather votes, but to obtain cooperation in program implementation and to avoid appeals from the public to superior authorities. Appointed officials do not campaign, in the literal sense, but they certainly give speeches, provide information, negotiate with interest groups, and issue administrative indulgences that are equivalent to casework. This flow of signals between citizens and administrative agencies can be referred to as administrative interaction.

Recent scholarship in political science, sociology, and law provides an illuminating discussion of this interaction and its contribution to the relationship between citizens and government.[72] To some extent, however, even this more sophisticated body of scholarship has often been distracted by continued reliance on the concept of democracy. Discussion often focuses on whether interaction between citizens and administrative agencies contributes to or derogates from democratic values, with the term 'democracy' typically being undefined, treated as an unquestionable good, and inevitably sedimented with all its pre-modern, Aristotelian implications.[73] Once we bracket this concept, however, we can bypass many of these anguished questions and focus on the reality of modern government. As Peter Schuck has suggested,[74] this interaction is then revealed as similar, in both structure and meaning, to the interaction that occurs between the citizenry and elected officials; it involves the same sorts of signals and generates the same sorts of results. This complex process of administrative interaction is currently being explored by a new approach to regulatory policy, sometimes described as New Public Governance.[75] When combined with electoral interaction, it establishes the structural relationship between modern government and its citizens that can be described, for purposes of this thought experiment, as an interactive republic.

There is no need to demonstrate that the concept of administrative interaction fulfills the criteria of reflecting our emotional commitments, signaling its heuristic character, and facilitating microanalysis better than its traditional alternative, since no traditional alternative exists. Our inherited models of government's structural relationship with its citizens largely ignore the relationship between administrative agents and the citizenry. This cannot be attributed to the absence of these agents in the pre-modern state, since they not only were present, but present in sufficient numbers to make people yearn for Camelot. Rather, it is the conceptual sequestration of the administrative apparatus within the executive branch, the fact that standard models of government developed before the process of articulation reached its tipping point, and the tremendous influence of Aristotle's pre-administrative *Politics* that have all combined to exclude what has become our basic mode of governmental operations from our theories of government-citizens relations. To bring administrative interaction into view, and integrate it into these theories, represents an increase in descriptive accuracy that is sufficient, by itself, to justify this concept's introduction. Nonetheless, it is a concept, not a reality, and should be judged by the criteria that have been applied to other concepts in this study.

The concept's acknowledgment of its heuristic character need not be belabored. Clearly, administrative interaction is a neologism, and while it

aspires to a certain naivete—the administrative nature of the modern state
is hardly an unfamiliar idea—it lacks any of the historical associations that
would invite reification. The ability of this concept to facilitate microanalysis, which is discussed in the final section of this chapter, can also be
treated fairly briefly, since the concept, with no inherited antecedent to
contest, was specifically designed for this purpose. But its ability to reflect
our emotional commitments raises some complex issues, to which the following section is addressed.

Administrative Interaction and Our Emotional Commitments

The primary emotional commitment that administrative interaction embodies is the government's responsiveness to the desires of its citizens. In
the absence of a broadly accepted transcendental creed, specific governmental goals, such as the goals of security, liberty, and prosperity identified
in Chapter 1, derive their social value from the general norm that government is supposed to benefit its citizens, and from the citizens' own conception of what constitutes a benefit. In order for the government to achieve
this norm, it must be responsive to the citizens' desires. Elections deal
with this problem, but they do so much less successfully than they deal
with succession and competence. One set of reasons involves their intermittent character, their reduction of all voter preferences to the choice between a few individuals, and their vulnerability to wealth and special interests. Another involves their inability to control the administrative
apparatus. Elected officials are necessarily few in number and, despite their
election, impossibly remote from ordinary citizens. The subordinate officials whom they appoint, or their appointees appoint, while much more
numerous and vicinal, are not directly answerable to the electorate. This,
plus the demands of their positions and the incentives generated by the hierarchy in which they operate, often leads to the image of administrators
as soulless or spineless apparatchiks, deaf to logic, blind to experience, and
insensible to human feeling. The Very Important Person of Gogol's *Overcoat*,[76] the law court officers of Kafka's *Trial*,[77] the EPA official in *Ghostbusters*,[78] and the rule-bound automatons of Philip Howard's *Death of
Common Sense* all embody this idea of bureaucratic evil.[79]

Modern democratic theory offers no solution to either the limits of elections or the insensitivity of administrators. It only stamps its foot and demands that people participate more assiduously, that elected officials listen
to them more carefully, and that these officials exercise more control over
administrative agencies. This inability to incorporate the administrative apparatus into our view of the relations between government and citizens is
reflected in our imagery of government structure. The three-branch image
discussed in Chapter 2 packs the entire administrative apparatus into the

executive branch, where the chief executive is expected to ensure its responsiveness to citizens. It is difficult to envision direct contact between the citizens on the ground and the interior of that gigantic, lofty branch. This difficulty afflicts efforts to ground the idea of legitimacy on the concept of deliberation, which is discussed more fully in Chapter 5.[80]

If we adopt the proposed image of modern government as a network of interacting units, then citizen interactions with the administrative apparatus can be incorporated into our general vision of government-citizen relations. Virtually all governmental units, including administrative units, are connected to various nongovernmental units in society, as well as to each other, through a variety of complex linkages. These linkages are the mechanism that modern government employs to increase the responsiveness of the administrative apparatus by combating the dual problems of electoral limitations and administrative insulation. Bracketing the concept of democracy, and substituting the alternative of an interactive republic, enables us to view this administrative interaction as combined with electoral interaction to form a unified structure. From this perspective, administrative interaction counts, along with electoral interaction, as a means of securing the responsiveness of government. This captures our genuine emotional commitment to the responsiveness of government, and the role of citizen interaction with administrative agencies in securing that responsiveness.

John Rohr argues that the integration of electoral and administrative interaction is part of America's constitutional design.[81] As originally conceived, the Senate was a quasi-executive body, possessing expertise and stability, while the House of Representatives was expected to maintain direct contact between the people and the government.[82] The Framers were worried that the House districts were too large for the representatives to fulfill this function, and reduced these districts from 40,000 to 30,000 people on the last day of the Convention.[83] At present, of course, House districts have grown to half a million, which is one-seventh the population of the entire nation at the time the Constitution was ratified. Their intended function has fallen to the administrative agencies, the one part of government numerous enough to maintain direct contact with a population of nearly 300 million people. The fact that agency officials are unelected may seem to divide them from the original representatives, but, according to Rohr, both the federalists and anti-federalists agreed that elections are irrelevant to the process of representation. Since the people are sovereign, any government officers who are selected in accordance with a constitution ratified by the people can be counted as their representatives.[84]

Rohr's account seems a bit overstated, primarily because it relies too heavily on the origins of our government, rather than its ongoing operation. The initial ratification of a governmental design does not guarantee that it will fulfill our norms on a continuing basis. Elections have proven to be a crucial mechanism for selecting the most authoritative government officials, and it seems unlikely that we would be able to solve the problems of succession and competence through any other means. But Rohr is correct in noting that the Framers, although they may have been motivated largely by tradition in their use of elections, were sophisticated enough to look through this tradition to its underlying purpose. They recognized that elections are indeed a mechanism, and might well have searched for other mechanisms in the radically different setting of the modern state to achieve their goals.[85] In fact, as Jody Freeman, Philip Harter, Jerry Mashaw, Robert Reich, Susan Rose-Ackerman, Mark Seidenfeld, and others have suggested, the interaction between administrative agents and the citizenry is an essential means by which those goals, most notably the goal of making government responsive to its citizens, are currently achieved.[86] It also constitutes much of the social meaning that modern government possesses for its citizens. It is not the same as elections, but it provides a substitute when the electoral process has expanded to its natural limits. Seidenfeld connects his discussion to democratic theory by suggesting that administrative interaction fulfills many of the goals of civic republicanism.[87] This is insightful, but the discourse of civic republicanism only encumbers the analysis because of its pre-modern associations. The suggestion here is that democratic theory can be bracketed in its entirety, and administrative interaction treated as an independent and essential feature of our modern administrative state. It secures responsiveness, and conveys a sense of connection to the government, in a variety of ways that include information flow, compliance, and participation.[88]

To begin with, governmental unresponsiveness frequently results from a mere lack of knowledge, an ignorance born of the institutional insulation of government agencies or the social distance between public officials and the private persons whom they regulate. Interaction provides administrative decision makers with valuable information, in a quantity that tax-supported government officials could not realistically collect.[89] Of course, interaction also provides government decision makers with lies, half-truths, and distorted interpretations motivated by the mind-sets and material self-interest of the participating private parties. But exaggerations are readily discounted by experienced administrators and outright lies are frequently discovered, with serious consequences for the credibility of their originators. Moreover, one does not need to subscribe to pluralism's homeostatic theory to recognize that the presence of multiple interests and multiple sources of information gives the process a certain self-corrective quality.

Second, administrative interaction simultaneously contributes to responsiveness and to the social meanings that support political stability by facilitating compliance strategies based on cooperation. Virtually no government can achieve a reasonable level of compliance from an entirely recalcitrant populace; even one that recruits its forces from foreign lands and is prepared to use unlimited amounts of violence, like the Mongols or the Mamelukes, will quickly be hobbled if the populace will only respond to direct compulsion. While simple, nonregulatory rules such as criminal law can rely on generally held moral principles to achieve cooperation from the populace, the complex regulatory statutes that characterize an administrative state require interaction. The agency must typically negotiate the levels of compliance, provide guidance, allow exceptions, and excuse minor violations.[90] All this provides a measure of responsiveness. The signals that the agency has received from the legislature, and that are partially responsive to the people as a result of the electoral interaction, are being summed with the signals it receives from the parties that it has been instructed to regulate, and this makes the agency responsive to these parties as well. At the level of social meaning, such responsiveness makes regulated parties feel that they are part of the regulatory process, rather than being its victims. Just as electoral interactions bind people to the political system, thereby increasing social stability, these administrative interactions bind regulated parties to both the political system in general and to the particular regulatory system to which they have been subjected. In some cases, the parties become proponents of the regulation, which may be a cause of discomfort for the regulation's original proponents. Even when regulated parties take the more reassuring stance of continued opposition, they tend to feel that they can live with the regulation, and do not need to devote extensive resources to its repeal, or to undermining the political regime that enacted it.

Finally, administrative interaction, like electoral interaction, provides people with an opportunity to participate in government—not the Aristotelian participation that is necessary for every citizen to qualify as a respectable human being, but the modern participation that constitutes an opportunity for those inclined to take advantage of it. In fact, administrative interaction greatly increases the possibilities for such participation. Elections are intermittent, and participation is often controlled by political parties, leaving only menial tasks for ordinary citizens. In contrast, administrative interaction occurs continuously, and often involves social movement organizations that not only display a wider variety, but also give individuals an opportunity to participate more centrally by attending meetings, writing letters, and speaking directly with public officials. Perhaps this type of participation seems mundane when compared to the idea of an aroused electorate unseating unresponsive legislators, or presenting petitions to the chief executive, but it also conveys to the participants a sense that they are part of the governmental process.

None of this is meant to suggest that the interaction between government and citizens at the administrative level is free of disadvantages. In fact, these disadvantages are substantial; public choice analysis suggests that the process can privilege well-organized special interests, so that the government operates to benefit those interests, rather than the populace at large. Moreover, as Cary Coglianese and James Rossi point out, even public-oriented interaction can distort the decision-making process through the sheer volume of political noise that it creates.[91] Particular mechanisms for interaction must be designed to mediate between these disadvantages and the advantages discussed above. Sometimes the disadvantages are so great that they warrant radical constriction of the interactive process, typically by means of formal rules. When the status of an individual is being adjudicated, for example, our general view is that the only relevant considerations are the preexisting rules that establish the status in question and the preexisting facts that determine the rule's application.[92] Consequently, the interactive linkages are highly formalized and tightly constrained. The extent to which such constraints should be imposed in other settings is a complex question of institutional design. Restriction of interaction, like interaction itself, is a specific mechanism of governance that should be deployed on the basis of our consciously identified commitments and a microanalysis of the decision in question.

Although administrative interaction has not been treated as central to theories of state-citizen relations, questions about these relations have been extensively explored in the more detailed inquiries of administrative law scholarship. Prior to the New Public Governance movement, these questions were generally framed in terms of the conflict between expertise and pluralism.[93] Expertise is, in essence, the Weberian principle of bureaucracy—decision making by credentialed experts organized in a self-contained hierarchy—while pluralism is decision making that attempts to respond to, and compromise among, the multitude of private actors that interact with the administrative agency. Many observers have concluded that pluralism is increasing at the cost of expertise, that the agency's elaborate machinery that was supposed to manufacture optimal results is being dismantled, and that the ground is being cleared for combat between the opposing interest groups.[94] But this interpretation of modern developments, and the lugubrious conclusions that are often drawn from it, is partially determined by the belief that only electoral interactions are part of the legitimate, democratic process and that administrative interaction undermines this process. Once the term 'democracy' is bracketed, and administrative interactions are treated, like elections, as an element of the general relationship between government and society, both the trend and its interpretation can be reassessed.

With respect to the trend, the idea that nongovernmental input into agency decision making is increasing is a dangling comparative. This input has always been high in the United States, the only recent change being the developments in civil society that have increased the influence of organized social movements and public interest groups. Besides, its quantity is not something to be necessarily condemned, since this input plays a role in making government responsive to its citizens. The dichotomy between this interaction and expertise is equally misleading. When there is widespread social consensus about the proper way to carry out some function, like the way to build a bridge, that consensus is likely to prevail because political opposition to it would lack meaning. But many technical issues are in fact contested; the proper method of valuing bank assets, the level of a specified substance that is dangerous to human health, the effectiveness of a particular medicine, or the economic impact of insider trading are all subjects of intense debate. The reason for this debate is not that the irrationalities of politics have invaded an otherwise rational process. Rather, debate arises because these issues, technical though they may seem, implicate contested social values that are regularly debated in the political arena. As Seidenfeld suggests,[95] if deliberation of the sort envisioned by the advocates of deliberative democracy exists anywhere in our political system, it is here, in the decision-making process of administrative agencies that interact with a wide range of private organizations. The issue, as the image of an interactive republic emphasizes, is not to insulate expertise from politics, but to ensure that expertise is used in a manner responsive to the citizens' desires.

Administrative Interaction and Microanalysis

Aside from reflecting our emotional commitments, the concept of administrative interaction also facilitates microanalysis. As mentioned, this contention can be briefly presented, since democratic theory tends to ignore the entire subject, rather than offering a rival notion that must be bracketed before proceeding. The microanalysis itself is enormously complex, and represents a major theme in contemporary political science and legal scholarship. The only point to be made here is that the model of an interactive republic, unlike the model of democracy, accommodates this scholarship within a comprehensive image of the relationship between modern government and its citizens.

Administrative interactions exhibit an enormous range and variation. Some of these interactions are legally created, others are legally controlled, and others are largely informal. In the United States, many legally created interactions are the products of the Administrative Procedure Act,[96] which requires federal administrative agencies to provide the general public with notice of proposed rules and to allow a period of time for comments re-

garding the proposal.[97] In addition, the Act provides for various procedural protections, such as notice and a hearing, in adjudicating the status
of private parties.[98] These mechanisms can be regarded as adding an additional input to the agency that must be summed with the ones it receives
from the legislature or from other agencies. Subsequent amendments to
the Administrative Procedure Act include the Freedom of Information
Act,[99] giving citizens access to agency files, and the Government in the
Sunshine Act,[100] giving them access to agency meetings under certain circumstances. Both can be regarded as interactions in their own right, because mere observation functions as a supervisory input; in addition, while
their effectiveness has been a matter of controversy,[101] it does appear that
they give citizens the information necessary to render other interactions
more effective.

These interactions were legally established, in part, because they relate to
areas of the administrative process that are analogous to pre-administrative
modes of governance. Regulations resemble statutes, administrative adjudication resembles civil trials, and information about government files or
meetings is the sort of information that would be revealed in the discovery
associated with such trials. The Administrative Procedure Act provides,
moreover, that all these requirements are to be supervised by the courts,[102]
again because courts have been the traditional means of supervising government performance. In less familiar areas, administrative interactions are
equally intensive, but they have developed informally, and either remain so
or become subject to intermittent legal control.

When engaged in economic regulation, the agency is in direct and continuous contact with the regulated industry; it interprets existing rules, enforces those rules, investigates potential infractions, demands information
about general industry conditions, supplies information about legal compliance or technical requirements, provides employees to the industry and
draws its own employees from that source, opposes the industry's legislative initiatives or joins in those initiatives. During this process, it is con-
stantly receiving signals from the firms it regulates, signals consisting of
information, suggestions, complaints, threats to appeal to the agency's administrative or elected superiors, promises to comply, and threats to sue.[103]
The agency can sometimes scale these signals down, and must sometimes
scale them up, but will almost always sum them with other signals in generating its outputs.

Nor are these the only signals that the agency receives from nongovernmental sources. In situations where the regulated parties opposed the initial statute—and this is not always the case, by any means—there will be
other groups that favored the enactment; if there were no such groups,
there probably would have been no statute. These groups, moreover, are
often connected with, or generated by, broad-based social movements.[104]

The political importance of such groups and the general norms that support those who can claim to be acting in the public interest often impel the agency to scale up these signals. The result, it can be said, is that a regulatory agency will receive strong signals from civil society as well as from the economic system represented by the regulated firms.[105] The meaning-based, intersubjectively communicated attitudes of the agency's members, as well as those who supervise and observe it, will cause these signals to be summed with those from regulated parties, and from the agency's legislative and hierarchical superiors, in generating the agency's output. Moreover, as Robert Katzmann and Shep Melnick have demonstrated in detailed case studies, both industry and public interest groups regularly engage in litigation as well as lobbying, and thereby interact with agencies by invoking judicial supervision of the agencies in support of their position.[106]

These cursory observations are intended to indicate that the idea of administrative interactions can function as part of an overall, network-based model for the structure of government-citizen relations. The concept of democracy tends to suggest that elections are the sine qua non of moral government, and that public contacts with appointed officials are at best irrelevant, and at worst a disruption of the self-governance that elections secure. With this concept bracketed, contacts with appointed officials are revealed as an additional source of the same sort of participation, one that can amplify or substitute for elections in securing the responsiveness of modern government. Some further insights into the similarity between electoral and administrative interaction can be obtained by cognitive prescription. Consider three exemplary government activities in the United States—environmental protection, public welfare, and foreign intelligence. For all three, the goals of security, prosperity, and liberty would be advanced by a more active and regularized interaction process.

In the environmental area, the proponents of development possess an impressive capacity to present their claims to both electoral and administrative officials. Contrary to the predictions of public choice theory, however, those who favor environmental protection have generated social movements and political organizations that have often been equally effective in presenting the opposing view.[107] The problem in this area is to develop mechanisms by which these two well-organized alliances can negotiate with the agency, and each other, to produce acceptable compromises and perhaps even optimal solutions.[108] A promising step in this direction is the Negotiated Rulemaking Act, which establishes a procedure whereby interest groups can participate in designing agency regulations.[109] Its success has been quite mixed, however,[110] and it clearly represents only the first small, clumsily built encampment upon virgin legal territory. Another such experiment is Project XL, which involves comprehensive planning of a plant's entire industrial process from an environmental perspective.[111] In general, mechanisms need to be developed to integrate the essentially ad-versarial confrontation between developers and environmental groups with an instrumentally rational planning process designed to achieve re-sponsive and effective government. The concept of democracy provides little guidance in this enterprise.

Public welfare programs are perennially regarded as abject failures, with the originators of each program being excoriated for their naivete or inep-titude at the time of its replacement.[112] But we are asking too much of the experts. In the United States, public policy is generated by a familiar, if un-stable, mixture of expertise and public input, and real progress may de-pend on our ability to improve this complex process. This would require that groups representing welfare recipients play a role in the policy process that is analogous to the role played by environmental groups. Encourag-ing the poor to participate in program planning and implementation was a feature of Lyndon Johnson's War on Poverty, and its unfortunate results have been documented by Daniel Patrick Moynihan.[113] But the plan was far too grandiose, in that it aspired to create a sense of community among the poor, to mobilize them politically, and to grant them direct control over the government programs that affected them. The debacle of this one attempt tells us more about the defects in our concept of democracy than about the viability of the underlying inspiration. Clearly, interaction be-tween welfare recipients and government depends on organized groups representing the interests of the recipients; such groups exist, but they are underdeveloped, and would require positive encouragement and funding from the government. But to treat such groups as the democratic voice of America's oppressed will render them both threatening and ineffective. Rather, they need to be regarded as a mundane mechanism to improve the design of social welfare through administrative interaction.

Strictly speaking, military intelligence has no clients other than the citi-zens in general, and relatively few private groups have taken a direct inter-est in its subject matter. The rationale for its insulation from the citizenry, however, lies not in this lack of clients but in the need for secrecy that its appointed officials proclaim, and that elected officials join with varying de-grees of enthusiasm. Certain intelligence functions must be kept secret, of course; obviously we cannot reveal the identities of our spies. But there is nothing particularly unique about this, as prosecutors must keep their tar-geting strategy secret, tax agencies must not disclose their audit policies, and public hospitals must maintain patient confidentiality. The need to keep specific information secret does not justify the insulation of an entire agency from public interaction.[114] Rather, that insulation has been based on our democracy-derived belief that citizen participation is a mode of self-governance. Since an espionage agency demands both expertise and secrecy, such participation seems inappropriate when viewed from this perspective. In fact, participation serves the more mundane, but thereby more generally applicable purpose, of making government effective. Some separate agency needs to encourage the development of private institutions committed to monitoring and assessing intelligence activities, and those institutions then need to be given specific linkages to the decision-making process in this area. This is not an encumbrance that our system imposes on us as a price for other liberties; it is our basic means of governing effectively, and to exclude it in this situation represents both a loss of faith and a failure of nerve.[115]

In the final analysis, of course, the concept of democracy is too familiar, and too emotionally resonant, to be abandoned. Concepts such as the three branches of government, power, or discretion are used primarily by scholars, who are consciously committed to linguistic precision. Democracy, in contrast, is common parlance among political participants, where it serves as a means of expressing their basic values and commitments. We have no other word for the form of government found in modern Western nations; the proposed alternative of an interactive republic is obviously not intended as an addition to public discourse. Its purpose, rather, is as a label for a new heuristic that reflects our emotional commitments, declares its heuristic character, and facilitates microanalysis more effectively than the concept of democracy. Democracy should be regularly bracketed as an operative term for political analysis, and scholars, policy analysts, and judges should avoid it in the interest of conceptual clarity. The clandestine commitments and pre-modern images that it incorporates create unrealistic expectations and blind us to the nature of the government we actually possess.

Five

From Legitimacy to Compliance

The Pre-Modern Concept of Legitimacy

Descending Theories of Legitimacy

THE relationship between government and its citizens, like the government's internal organization, possesses an animate as well as a structural aspect. Democracy, or electoral and administrative interaction, characterizes the structural aspect of this relationship. But how do people feel about the government? Do they regard it as good or bad, justified or unjustified, protective, neutral, or oppressive? The answers to these questions are crucial for a committed description of the modern administrative state. If the purpose of the state is to benefit its citizens, the way people feel about the state's actions clearly constitutes an important part of what we mean by benefit. One might be willing to accept the notion that small children are benefited by things they hate, like tetanus shots and homework, but it pushes false consciousness beyond most people's endurance to make the same assertion about adult citizens. Moreover, as a practical matter, the effectiveness of government, specifically its ability to achieve security and prosperity, depends heavily on people's willingness to comply with the policies that it advances.

In political theory, people's attitudes toward the government, and their willingness to obey its commands, are generally described in terms of legitimacy.[1] We speak of a government being legitimate or illegitimate, of increasing its legitimacy by just and effective measures, or squandering that legitimacy by ill-considered action. We speak of citizens who accept the government as legitimate, reject it as illegitimate, or question its legitimacy in a variety of circumstances. The government's control over its citizens is commonly described as the exercise of legitimate authority, which suggests that authority is the mere exercise of control, while legitimacy describes the animate aspect of control, the citizens' attitudes toward coercive governmental action.

But what exactly do we mean by legitimacy, at least in the context of a modern state? As soon as one squints at this term a bit, it triggers quasi-Cartesian doubt. The underlying concept is obviously, almost risibly, medieval, since it refers to the status of the king's heir in a hereditary monarchy. If the king had a child by a woman with whom he was joined in a Church-sanctioned marriage, that child was regarded as legitimate. If the child was male, and the eldest male, he was then the acknowledged successor to the throne.

In his *History of the Kings of Britain,* which was published just as King Henry I's death without a legitimate male heir was plunging England into civil war, Geoffrey of Monmouth takes care to ensure Arthur's legitimacy.[2] Uther Pendragon, he recounts, had fallen prey to an adulterous passion for Igrayne, the Duke of Tintagel's wife, and laid siege to the duke's castle. During the siege, Uther has Merlin transform him into a likeness of the duke, goes to visit Igrayne, and sires Arthur. But this is not adultery; fortunately for England, the duke had sallied forth from his besieged castle several hours earlier and had been killed by Uther's forces.[3] Uther's subsequent marriage to Igrayne made Arthur the rightful heir, as Merlin explains at length in Mallory's version.[4] It was this status that entitled Arthur to pull the sword from the stone and become the "rightfully-born king of all England."

The importance of legitimacy in a hereditary regime is clear—it is a general principle of family law that determines who can succeed to a person's title and inherit his property.[5] This principle acquired vast political significance in the case of the person whose title was king and whose property was the entire realm. By determining who could inherit this great estate, familial legitimacy constituted the prevailing response to the crucial problem of succession.[6] It did not justify monarchical rule; the prevailing justification was divine right,[7] but as Fritz Kern points out, this was often regarded as a kin right or a blood right, that is, God's grant of authority to a person and his heirs.[8] In any event, once that rule was established, the principle of legitimacy determined how it could be justifiably transferred from one person to the next. As the royal line continued, and developed an independent grounding in tradition, the legitimacy of the king's heir became tantamount to a justification of his sovereignty.[9] Conversely, the lack of a legitimate heir, the fact that the king had no surviving sons, or that his only surviving sons were illegitimate, could lead to civil war and social chaos as it did in Geoffrey's time.[10]

The quasi-Cartesian doubts raised by legitimacy's obviously medieval origins are not sufficient, by themselves, to justify bracketing such a familiar concept. As employed in modern political theory, the concept is far removed from hereditary monarchy, and refers to the moral justification for any type of regime. Rodney Barker states the common definition: "legitimacy is precisely the belief in the rightfulness of a state, in its authority to issue commands, so that those commands are obeyed not simply out of fear or self-interest, but because they are believed in some sense to have moral authority, because subjects believe that they ought to obey."[11] Accepting for the moment that the real issue involves the issuance of commands, this definition means that legitimacy refers to something that originates from outside the government's mere existence as a set of authorized entities, and justifies those entities as a totality. Authorization, as that concept was developed in Chapter 3, defines the jurisdictional and hierarchical structure of the government; in network terms, it describes the program of the governmental units and the connections among them. Legitimacy, as a separate concept in political thought, refers to a source of justification that confers a general imprimatur on that authorized structure in its external relations with its citizens. By what right, it asks, does the government exercise authority over a group of individuals; what general principle gives the government the moral prerogative to employ coercive force?

Typically, this imprimatur is viewed as attaching to the entire government, but that is not an essential aspect of the concept. Individual institutions within government, such as the courts, the legislature, the chief executive, or even an administrative agency, can also be described as legitimate. David Easton distinguishes between these usages by calling the first a diffuse concept of legitimacy and the later a specific one.[12] But whatever the scale of the institution, the imprimatur attaches to that institution in its entirety, and not simply to its separate actions.[13] The rationale behind this terminology is an eminently practical one. A rule for judging governmental actions on a case-by-case basis, and not on the basis of their institutional origin, is simply a rule of critical morality, and can be described as such. Thus, if a person decides that she will only obey governmental actions that maximize wealth, or that conform to the teachings of Christ, she simply has a moral rule for determining her obedience. No other description is necessary. The term 'legitimacy,' in political discourse, refers to the concept of a general imprimatur that would otherwise have no commonly understood designation.[14] In any event, it is this standard concept of legitimacy that is analyzed in the present chapter. Other concepts to which this word may be applied, such as the moral acceptability of particular governmental acts, are discussed on their own terms, and not conflated with the concept of a general imprimatur.[15]

Walter Ullmann's division of medieval theories of legitimacy into descending and ascending approaches follows naturally from the basic definition.[16] Since legitimacy is an additional factor that stands outside the government's authority structure, it must be derived from some source external to that structure. A descending approach ascribes the legitimacy of government to a general principle or higher force, while an ascending theory ascribes it to the agreement or approval of the citizens. The fact that modern theories of legitimacy fit so well within Ullmann's classification of medieval thought might itself be taken as a source of quasi-Cartesian doubt. In order to avoid using pre-analytic categories for analytic purposes, however, these categories will be treated as uninformative, that is, they will be used only to organize the discussion, and no significance will be attributed to the category into which a particular theory of legitimacy falls.

To the extent that one is interested in describing people's relationship to government, both descending and ascending theories ultimately reside in the belief system of the citizens, since these citizens are the ones who will obey or disobey the governments's commands. According to descending theories, the citizens believe that the government is justified by a principle that stands outside themselves, as well as standing outside the government's authority structure. In ascending theories, the citizens believe that the government is justified by some process that involves their own beliefs or actions. An observer can also, of course, explore her personal beliefs about government justification, which is typically called a normative, as opposed to a descriptive theory of legitimacy. As noted in Chapter 1, descriptive and normative discourse is inevitably interconnected, but since the primary purpose of this study is to describe modern administrative government, citizen beliefs about descending and ascending theories of legitimacy constitute the primary focus of discussion.

The classic example of a descending theory of legitimacy is the divine right of kings. This was the dominant, although not the exclusive theory, in the Middle Ages.[17] It remained a leading theme in political thought through the seventeenth century, although the elaborate defenses of it by King James I and Robert Filmer in that period suggest that it was already falling victim to demands for secular theories of government.[18] Contemporary writers have advanced various secular versions of the descending approach, but, in subtracting God, these versions tend to conflate the mere authority of the state with its legitimacy. That is, they take the fact of a command structure for the existence of a moral imprimatur. Weber's account of rational-legal domination, for example, while presented as a theory of legitimacy, only describes the way commands are conceived and generated.[19] As Alan Hyde points out, it cannot explain why people would regard the government as an entity that possesses some generalized justification, nor can it explain the reason why they would obey any commands it issued.[20] In fact, the modern state's positivization of law and its instrumentalization of reason dissolves the justificatory force that law and reason played in the pre-modern state, and precludes these principles from serving as a descending source of legitimacy.

H.L.A. Hart's account of legitimacy, which he developed in response to Hans Kelsen's positivist theory of law, suffers from a similar defect. According to Kelsen, law is simply a command backed by a sanction, and a state is an institution that can promulgate such sanction-backed commands throughout a given territory.[21] Hart responds by observing that a state relying solely on force is merely "the gunman situation writ large."[22]

This is not the way the state is regarded by its citizens, he argues. Rather, citizens recognize that government commands are issued by those in authority, and he distinguishes authority from force by observing that people obey an authority because of its identity, not because of a particular harm that it can threaten or impose.[23] Hart goes on to observe that an authority is identified by a rule of recognition, that is, a generally accepted principle that identifies it as authoritative.[24] In short, he formulates a positivist view of law based on an assertion of authority and not mere use of force.

In equating this assertion of authority with the concept of legitimacy,[25] Hart, like Weber, is conflating the state's authority structure, the sinews of its mere existence, with a normative principle for the exercise of that authority. Surprisingly, Alexander Bickel, Charles Black, and other writers of the American legal process school make a similar assertion,[26] although they did not think of themselves as positivists. It is true, to be sure, that legitimacy bears a structural similarly to authority in that it bases obedience to commands on their origin rather than their content. Citizens regard a command as authoritative because it issues from a recognized source, and they regard a command as legitimate because it issues from a justified one. But this does not make authority and legitimacy equivalent, nor recognition identical to justification. Authority describes a structural principle that assigns particular responsibilities to particular units of government; it identifies the pathways through which a government's commands, as well as other types of communication, can flow, the position of different units as superior or subordinate for purposes of supervision, and the task each unit is expected to perform. Legitimacy, in contrast, is a justificatory principle that attaches to this authority structure in its entirety, or to specific components of this structure, such as the legislature or the courts. It cannot be derived from the mere description of that structure.[27] Moreover, the asserted equivalence is not only theoretically defective, but, as Brian Tamanaha points out, it is also empirically inaccurate; many legal rules that are recognized as authoritative are regularly disobeyed.[28] Hart has interpolated an additional, unexplained element in moving from authoritative to legitimate commands, a moral imprimatur whose source and character he fails to explain.

Social Contract Theory

Ascending accounts of legitimacy, which view the state's moral imprimatur as arising from an agreement of the people, include social contract theories and deliberative democracy. Social contract theories are the dominant account of political legitimacy in modern Western thought. In one form or another, they provide the core of many of our normative theories of government, including virtually all those that are associated with philo-

sophic liberalism. Their essential elements are that people begin, historically or conceptually, in some sort of pre-political condition, that they
agree to establish a political regime, where some of them are designated as
rulers who exercise suzerainty over the others, that the others are obligated to obey the rulers' orders, and that the rulers are obligated to frame
those orders in accord with the original agreement.[29]

Social contract theory flows rather directly from two central aspects of
medieval thought. First, the Bible says that people once existed in a pre-
political condition and that government is a subsequent development.
When this temporal sequence was combined with the prevailing view that
the purpose of government was to benefit the people, it led to the conclusion that pre-political people had established governments to improve
their lives and safeguard their salvation.[30] Second, the king and his subjects, most important his free or noble subjects, were regarded as being
bound by the contractual arrangements of the feudal system. It was therefore natural to conclude that government in general was a contractual
agreement between a ruler and the people. Additional support for social
contract theory came from the Aristotelian notion of people's natural sociability, from the biblical account of Saul's selection as king of Israel, and
from independently evolved medieval practices such as the election of the
Holy Roman Emperor.

Modern social contract theory was built upon these dual foundations—
the Christian concept of pre-social human origins and the feudal concept
of contractual agreement. It is generally regarded as a product of the Reformation, beginning with the work of Calvinists such as George Buchanan and Johannes Althusius.[31] Their essential innovations were to
combine the contractual conception with the account of political evolution and to secularize the entire process, so that neither God nor religious
inclination played any significant role in the account. The great figures of
the seventeenth century—Grotius, Hobbes, Locke, and Pufendorf—then
contributed the idea that the contract was not formed between the ruler
and the people, but among the people themselves, thus constituting the
political system in its entirety.[32]

This theory was attacked by Hume as a fanciful account of human history,[33] a charge that was probably unfair to Locke, as Jeremy Waldron
points out.[34] In response, Kant dehistoricized it, presenting the social contract as the terms on which rational persons would willingly submit to government control.[35] Kant's approach was decisively critiqued, in turn, by
Hegel, who argued that it reduced the state to a quasi-commercial bargain.[36] A comprehensive answer to this critique, and a revival of social contract theory, appeared only with the publication of John Rawls's *A Theory
of Justice* in 1971.[37] Just as Kant dehistoricizes the theory, Rawls decom-
mercializes it, thereby avoiding much of Hegel's criticism.

For Rawls, the social contract that establishes a legitimate state is not derived from any concept of exchange, any surrender of one's liberty in return for security, prosperity, or even social freedom. Rather, the contract represents the terms of association under which rational people would agree to live if they were creating their political system from the outset. Instead of offering a quasi-historical account of this process, Rawls imagines that the future citizens of a given state, in their original or pre-political position, stand behind a "veil of ignorance,"[38] where "no one knows his place in society, his class position or social status; nor does he know his fortune in the distribution of natural assets and abilities."[39] Under these circumstances, Rawls argues, people would rationally agree to a set of principles he identifies as the nature of justice and the essence of legitimate government. These include equal human liberties, equality of opportunity, and an economic structure that secures everyone's minimum needs and endorses inequalities only when they increase the wealth of the least advantaged group.[40] Michael Sandel has criticized this theory on the grounds that it assumes that human beings are capable of separating themselves from their community and social context.[41] As Rawls points out in response, however, his theory does not claim that people can actually place themselves behind a veil, but rather offers a methodological device, a thought experiment, by which the reader—the actual reader in her current social context—can interrogate her own views about justice and government legitimacy.[42]

This response, however, suggests a basic problem with Rawls's theory and the entire contractarian account of government legitimacy. From a phenomenological perspective, the whole thing is so hypothetical, so obviously constructed by elaborate speculation, that it suffers from overinterpretation. By varying the terms of the imaginary narrative, one can prove virtually anything, as indicated by the prodigious variety of political arrangements that have been derived from contract theory, and by the tendency of each writer's personal norms to leak over into his account of a supposedly independent process of agreement. Thus, Hobbes's contracting parties choose to escape from their nasty, brutish, and short existence by establishing an absolute monarchy; Locke's parties not only retain the right of revolution but the protection of their private property; Kant's opt for gradual republicanism; while Rawls's, from behind their veil of ignorance, manage to generate the domestic program of the Kennedy administration.

This consideration is sufficient to raise quasi-Cartesian doubt about the entire enterprise, but it also points to a still deeper difficulty. To function as either a normative argument or a committed description, a hypothetical account should evoke a sense of familiarity or recognition. Social contract theory, once it is considered from this essentially phenomenological perspective, feels wrong; in fact, it has virtually nothing to do with the experience of living in a modern state. The problem, as Hegel noted, lies in its medieval origins.[43] It is an accurate, almost visceral account, of social attitudes in a different society, and no matter how far it is abstracted from its origins, no matter how far the original idea is dehistoricized and decommercialized, it retains that basic character. Its continuing appeal resides in its ability to evoke social nostalgia, not to capture the relationship between the modern state and its citizens. These medieval origins are apparent from the components of the theory itself, but they can be more vividly illustrated by considering one of the finest Arthurian poems, *Sir Gawain and the Green Knight,* written in the late fourteenth century by an unknown English author and first translated into modern English by J.R.R. Tolkien.[44]

Arthur and his knights are assembled for a feast at Camelot on New Year's Day when a knight of gigantic stature suddenly appears in the hall. He is dressed in green, has long green hair, and rides on a green horse. Unarmored, but carrying an enormous ax, he challenges any of the knights at the Round Table to exchange ax strokes with him; his adversary is to strike the first blow, and he will strike a single return blow a year and a day later. After an astonished silence, which elicits an expression of contempt from the green knight, Sir Gawain accepts the challenge. The green knight speaks to him—"I'd know first, sir knight, thy name; I entreat thee to tell it me truly, that I may trust in thy word"—and he is pleased to discover that his challenger is the well-known, well-regarded Sir Gawain.[45] Gawain takes hold of the great ax and with a single stroke cuts off the green knight's head. But the remainder of the green knight strides forward to retrieve the head, which is being kicked around by the assembled company, and, holding it by its green hair, remounts his horse. The head then reminds Gawain of his promise, and instructs him to go to the Green Chapel the next New Year's Day to receive the return blow.

On the morning following All Saints' Day, Sir Gawain sets forth from Camelot to search for the Green Chapel. After an arduous journey, which lasts till Christmas Day, he comes upon a magnificent castle, where he is greeted by the baron, a big man with a "beaver-hued" beard. "You are welcome at your wish to dwell here," the baron says. "What is here, all is your own, to have in your rule any sway."[46] After being graciously entertained for three days, Sir Gawain tells the Baron that he must resume his quest for the Green Chapel. But the baron informs him that the Green Chapel lies only two miles away, so he can safely set forth on New Year's Day itself. In the meantime, the baron proposes a "bargain." He will go out hunting, and "whatever I win in the wood at once shall be yours, and whatever gain you may get you shall give in exchange."[47] Sir Gawain, apparently not a man to turn a proposition down, agrees.

The next day, the baron goes deer hunting while Sir Gawain, sleeping late at the castle, receives a visit from the baron's exquisitely beautiful wife. She tells him, "To my body will you welcome be, of delight to take your fill."[48] But Gawain rejects her advances—courteously, of course—and accepts only a single kiss. When the baron returns he delivers all the venison from his successful hunt to Sir Gawain, who responds by giving him a kiss. That may be the better gift, the baron observes, if Gawain will tell him where he got it. "That was not the covenant," Gawain replies. "Do not question me more!"[49] Acknowledging the justice of the answer, the baron then offers to renew their bargain for another day. Off he goes to the hunt again, where he bravely kills an enormous boar, while Gawain deflects another amorous advance and accepts another kiss. After the exchange of the spoils, the baron offers to extend the bargain one more day. This time, however, his hunt produces nothing but a fox, which in the wilder and hungrier days of medieval England was regarded as a disappointing prize. Meanwhile, at the castle, the baron's wife tries once again, this time in a revealing gown, but Gawain remains steadfast. She offers him her ring as a love token, and then her green silk girdle (her belt, not underwear), both of which he declines. He should not be so quick to reject the girdle, she informs him, for it possesses the magical property of rendering its wearer invulnerable to any blow. That indeed appeals to Sir Gawain, and after further urging he accepts it, promising, as she asks, to conceal the gift from her husband. She then kisses him three times and departs. When the baron returns with his paltry fox, Sir Gawain goes out to meet him, declaring that "in this case I will first our covenant fulfil that to our good we agreed" and kisses him three times in exchange for the fox.[50]

Early the next day, which is the New Year's, Sir Gawain sets out from the castle, journeying through wild, uninhabited countryside to an even wilder ravine. The Green Chapel turns out to be an empty pagan barrow in the middle of this desolate landscape—in other words, a long way from Camelot. Sir Gawain calls out and the green knight appears, intact and carrying his ax. Gawain removes his helmet and awaits the blow. The green knight feints twice with his ax, making fun of Gawain for flinching the first time, and then brings the ax down on Gawain's neck, giving him nothing more than a slight scratch. Gawain springs away, puts his helmet back and brandishes his sword, declaring that the covenant is now fulfilled. The green knight readily and cheerfully agrees. He informs Sir Gawain that he is the baron who has just been entertaining him. The two fake blows were for Gawain's honorable behavior with his wife on the first two days, and the scratch wound was for his duplicitous but understandable behavior on the third. Sir Gawain, now mortified, confesses his cowardice, casting the girdle away. But the green knight forgives him, saying, "I hold thee purged of that debt."[51] He gives the girdle back to Gawain, who agrees to wear it as a "token of my trespass."[52] Gawain then returns to a hero's welcome in Camelot; how he transported the venison and the pork is not recounted.

The real problem with social contract theory, as an account of legitimacy, is that it depends on a relationship between the individual and the state that is much better reflected in *Sir Gawain and the Green Knight* than by modern political experience. As Kent Greenawalt suggests, the essential feature of the theory's conception of individuals is not that they are originally presocial, or rational, or that they can conceive of themselves behind a veil of ignorance, but that they feel a moral obligation to keep their promises.[53] They may find themselves starving, or oppressed, or subject to unequal treatment, but they remain obligated to fulfill their initial agreement. If they do not—if they feel justified in changing their moral commitments once they experience their actual position in society—then the whole point of social contract theory is lost and—since there is no actual contract or agreement—it should be replaced by something different, such as a theory of evolving and particularized attitudes toward government.

Sir Gawain exemplifies this moral obligation to promise keeping. Once he has given his word, he is not merely resigned to finding the green knight and having his head chopped off, but positively desperate to do so. As he tells the baron, he would not miss his appointment at the Green Chapel "on New Year's morning for all the land in Logres [England]," and he will look on the green knight, "if God will allow me, more gladly, by God's son, than gain any treasure."[54] At the climax of the poem, his mortification when he realizes that he has broken his word to the baron is extreme, and he makes no excuses for himself, despite the circumstances. Only the baron, now in the guise of the green knight, has the power to forgive him.

It is quite clear from the poem, and from what we know about medieval society in general, that this fanatical commitment to promise keeping sprang from an ethos of chivalry, or honor. Honor secured status in society; it was the basic mechanism by which one invested one's life with meaning.[55] As Dante insisted, it was personal, to be determined by one's comportment with an accepted set of social norms.[56] Noble birth, in theory, was a prerequisite for status, but only actions could establish, maintain, and perhaps increase one's honor. That honor attached to one's name; this is the first thing, indeed the only thing, that the green knight wanted to know about his challenger. To keep one's promise was the most important way that one achieved one's good name and preserved one's honor.[57] It was also important, in the bellicose society of medieval Europe, to accept challenges and confront one's enemies, but, as the poem indicates, a person could make choices; the assembled knights do not feel compelled to accept the green knight's challenge. What the code of chivalry made absolutely compulsory was the obligation to keep one's word.

Breaking promises meant losing one's honor, one's reputation, one's status in society, and one's meaning in life. It was better to die.

This is simply not our contemporary social ethos. A gap has opened between people's sense of meaning and their social role, so that our view of ourselves has become simultaneously more individualized and more collective. We tend to construct our sense of meaning individually, on the basis of our life experiences, our achievements, and our social or economic progress, not on the basis of our socially recognized reputation. On the other hand, our relationship to society is not determined by our individual comportment, but by our membership in a nation, an ethnic group, and an economic or occupational class. In this context, promise keeping ceases to be an absolute and central obligation as a means of securing honor, and becomes just one of many private virtues. In fact, many would recognize it—and criticize it—as the sort of abstract, decontextualized approach to human relations that is specifically male in its orientation.[58]

When social contract theorists construct their thought experiments, they build a pre-analytic preference for the medieval idea of promise keeping into their theory by placing the decision point at the time society is being initially established. Rawls explicitly acknowledges this, but he treats it as a general requirement of rationality.[59] Suppose, however, we add a second decision point at the later time when the consequences of the initial decision have become apparent. This is what Jon Elster identifies as the freedom of choice available to people's "later selves."[60] In the social contract context, it possesses an additional appeal, since the later decision is the only one that people actually make.[61]

So now, as a further thought experiment, suppose we say to people: "You have turned out to be a loser in the society to which you thought you would agree. You are poor while others are rich, oppressed by your employer while others are treated with dignity, restricted to minimal satisfaction of your basic needs while others can indulge their most extravagant and otiose desires. Do you still think your original decision was rational?" And they will answer: "No. Promise keeping is not that important. Finding myself enmeshed in the reality of a constrained, unsatisfactory existence, I feel differently. Indeed, I am different, having been changed by my experiences. Although Rawls had me convinced when he first asked me the question, I have now had a chance to think more clearly about it, and I realize that it was irrational for me to agree with his argument. To use a far-fetched analogy, I think Gawain should have rescinded his promise once he saw that the green knight was a supernatural being." In other words, a rational person would not agree to keep her promises at the expense of her subsequent well-being. Rather, she would agree to a different principle, one providing that whatever promises she made without knowing her ultimate fate could be revised to redistribute resources in her favor if she ended up too disadvantaged.[62] That is, in fact, roughly how the modern administrative state was born. People simply refused to play by the rules of capitalism and sacerdotal government when they found themselves so disadvantaged, and they demanded the doubly articulated structure of administrative government. This willingness to reevaluate one's commitments on the basis of one's current position corresponds to our current notions of rational behavior much more closely than the obsessive commitment to promise keeping that characterizes Gawain and the hypothetical citizens of social contract theory.

A second concept that is embedded in social contract theory, closely related to the idea of promise keeping, is that the relationship between the individual and government, or among the pre-political individuals, can be conceived as a fixed and delimited bond. The individual is absolutely committed to keeping his promises, and his promisees are equally committed, but those obligations extend only to the limits of the agreement and no further. When the baron asks Gawain where he got his first kiss, Gawain tells him, "That was not the covenant." When the green knight scratches Gawain's neck, Gawain jumps back, declares that his obligation has been fulfilled, and prepares to fight. This apparent legalism in fact defines the essence of a contract; obligations are fixed in advance before the parties become entangled in their interaction with each other. Precisely where a guest in one's house got a kiss is a very interesting question, but in a contractual relationship, one is not entitled to know the answer unless one obtained the right to such information in advance.

For the pre-modern state, the notion of fixed obligations is a meaningful one. The state's authority was limited to certain specified functions, such as taxation, management of critical resources, coinage, foreign affairs, and internal security. Extension of this authority into areas administered by the Church, the local magnates, the cities, or the ascribed custom of the locality, was precisely what a lawful ruler was expected to abjure. To say the king was absolute ruler meant only that he was sovereign, in Bodin's sense, and related to the question of civil order. It did not mean that he could invade those areas reserved to the control of other authorities. When an aggressive ruler such as Louis XIV or Joseph II in fact extended his control in this manner, it was conceived as a breach of ancient understandings. The recrudescence of the *parlements* following Louis XIV's death[63] and the widespread baronial and peasant rebellions against Joseph[64] were justified, if not motivated, by this quasi-contractarian belief system.

The modern administrative state, in contrast, exercises plenary authority over its society. While its articulation of structure assigns each official a specific jurisdiction, the highest-ranking officials are typically authorized to carry out a general policy making role. As such, they will often measure their success by the new programs they have developed and the new areas they have brought under governmental supervision. In the nineteenth century, these areas included economic production, education, public health, and poor relief; in the twentieth, they were labor relations, the environment, consumer affairs, and civil rights; in the following century, they may involve the climate, human heredity, family relations, and interpersonal communications. The moral element of instrumentalism, discussed in Chapter 1, means that the articulation of purpose is not merely a demand that the state justify its policies by giving instrumental reasons, but also a mode of thought that renders government a mechanism of social transformation. In the transition from traditional to administrative governance, therefore, the idea that past practices should be maintained yields to the idea that society, through government, exercises plenary control over itself, and can reshape itself through collective action. In this sense, government enables society to become self-conscious, that is, to subject its entire structure to evolving, consciously developed policies.[65] The static conception of government's role and range of action that a contractual bond implies misrepresents the dynamism and self-constructed character of the administrative state.

Thus, social contract theory's account of the state's legitimacy seems inapplicable, on both descriptive and normative grounds, to a modern administrative state. Of course, one cannot definitively disprove either a descriptive metaphor or a normative argument. But social contract theory feels very wrong for either purpose, not only because it relates to our present society so poorly, but because it relates to a previous society so well. It seems to emerge directly from the sensibility reflected in *Sir Gawain and the Green Knight*—from an ethos of honor and promise keeping, and from a concept of the relationship between the two as pre-arranged and stable. The sensibility is not an unattractive one, but it is not our own.

In fact, the problem with social contract theory is even more severe. The contrast that has been presented between modern and pre-modern social norms was not established by comparing modern society with medieval society, but by comparing modern society with a medieval poem. Social contract theory is wonderfully good at describing the world of the poem, but that was not the real world of the time when the poem was written. By the late fourteenth century feudalism was virtually dead, and the code of chivalry was subsiding into arid antiquarianism.[66] Feudal obligations had been commuted into monetary payments, so that most of the soldiers who marched with such paragons of chivalry as William the Conqueror, Richard the Lion-Hearted, Edward III, and the Black Prince were paid professionals.[67] In many areas of Europe, royal regimes had replaced the bonds of mutual obligation with at least a rudimentary form of comprehensive civil government. Administrative staffs, often consisting of low-born law school graduates, were growing steadily, and government was beginning to assume the impersonal, instrumental, and continually evolving form that characterizes it at present. Thus, the poem partially reflects the reality of the fourteenth century, but more fully reflects that era's social nostalgia for the more adventuresome period that preceded it. Social contract theory's account of legitimacy is thus doubly nostalgic. It not only incorporates the sensibility of a prior era, but the sensibility it incorporates was itself filled with nostalgia for still earlier times.

Deliberative Democracy

There is, however, another ascending theory of legitimacy, deliberative democracy, that does not depend on the metaphor of a social contract. Its essential idea is that the deliberative process, by which all citizens debate policy issues in reasoned terms, is not simply an account of democracy, as a specific type of government, but a theory of government legitimacy. A government that is constituted by such debate, the theory goes, is normatively justified in its entirety, and will be perceived as such by its members.[68] In describing the structure of government-citizens relations, this theory escapes medievalism, but only through its pervasive social nostalgia for Ancient Greece. These descriptive difficulties were discussed in the preceding chapter and need not be repeated here. For present purposes, the issue is whether deliberative democracy, however unrealistic as a description of the government's structural relationship to its citizens, can confer contemporary meaning on the concept of legitimacy.

In order to transform the concept of deliberative democracy into an account of political legitimacy, the mere existence of public debate or discussion is not sufficient. Rather, this debate must be deliberative, that is, it must be based on reason and reach a definitive consensus. If it is not based on reason, then it lacks the normative force that proponents of deliberative democracy wish to ascribe to it; if it does not reach a definitive consensus, then other principles must be invoked to govern society, and those principles require their own justification. In addition, treating deliberative democracy as a theory of legitimacy demands that some mechanism exists, or can be realistically envisioned, for translating the reasoned consensus generated by public deliberation into the institutional structures that govern society. The first requirement runs into serious psychological and epistemological difficulties, while the second is subject to equally serious institutional concerns.

As a psychological matter, the problem with any ascending theory is that it is inherently open-ended. In a descending theory of legitimacy, like the divine right theory of the Middle Ages, the content of the theory—the substantive values that the theory generates—are established by God, and accessible to human beings through their use of reason. With an ascending theory, in contrast, the content, or substantive implications of the theory, depend on the particular interactions among citizens. As Robert Post observes, since many people, all of whom lay claim to reason, disagree quite vociferously, an observer who endorses deliberation as a measure of legitimacy must recognize the possibility that the process of public deliberation will produce results that disagree with his present views.[69] Very few people can accept this divergence; instead, they simply assume that the deliberative process will produce conclusions that agree with their own. This assumption has already been noted with respect to social contract theories, and it raises a suspicion that the contracting process that the observer is hypothesizing possesses very little substance. With deliberative theories, there is no substance at all; they are entirely procedural. If one rejects the reasoning process, one eliminates any claim that public deliberation can serve as a source of legitimacy.

Even if one avoids this psychological problem, and truly accepts the open-ended character of an ascending theory of legitimacy based on rational discourse, there remains a closely related epistemological difficulty with the concept of reason. Legitimation of a government based on reasoned deliberation assumes that there always exists a consensus position on contested issues that can be reached by reasoning, a claim very closely allied, if not equivalent, to the age-old yearning for definitive political truths and unambiguously optimal solutions. But people's personal interests and ideological commitments might both diverge in a manner that precludes consensus, as Madison asserted.[70] This may be because they are subject to "passion" or "interest,"[71] but it may also be because there are no optimal solutions that reason would reveal. As discussed in Chapter 4, this is one reason why our interactive republic does not rely on deliberation to reach decisions, but rather reaches decisions by taking a vote among the eligible decision makers. Such a procedure, however effective as a matter of political practice, has no value for a theory that attempts to derive legitimacy from democratic deliberation. But unless there exist political solutions that can be discerned by reason, and are not subject to unresolvable emotional or normative disagreements, this notion of legitimacy cannot be sustained.

In the unlikely event that consensus on contested political issues could be achieved through reason, it would only be possible to translate this consensus into the institutional structure that governs society in simpler, pre-administrative times. The tasks of modern administrative government are too complex, technical, and numerous to be determined by general public debate. Of course, it is easy enough to assume that public debate would establish the general contours of government policy, leaving professional administrators to implement this policy by filling in the technical details. But in any realistic scenario, those general contours would be so broad, and the area to be filled in by specialized administrators would be so vast, that the legitimating force of the consensus would be open to serious question. Moreover, unless we assume that deliberation would effect a basic change in human character, the vast area that was left to administrative implementation would tempt many people to circumvent the consensus to which they had acceded and extract special benefits by lobbying the administration, thereby undermining the system's deliberatively based legitimacy. The legitimacy of our present government, where administrative agents are supervised by elected representatives, is frequently attacked because it delegates excessive power to administrative agents, as discussed in Chapter 2. How much more frequently would such an attack be voiced if all such supervision had to be generated by general public debate? In short, the idea that deliberation could legitimate governmental operations seems to arise from the nostalgic image of a simpler, pre-administrative state with many fewer operations.

This difficulty afflicts Jürgen Habermas's *Between Facts and Norms,* certainly one of the leading efforts to ground a theory of legitimacy on deliberative democracy.[72] For Habermas, deliberation is achieved through communicative action—verbal interchanges designed to achieve understanding between people by means of a decentered rational discourse.[73] In an earlier work, Habermas recognized that such communicative action would be difficult to institutionalize in contemporary politics because of what he vividly described as the colonization of the individual's lifeworld—the problem that economic and political matters in modern society are determined by large systems that lie beyond the experience, or lifeworld, of the individual, and so are not accessible to the understanding generated by communicative action.[74] *Between Facts and Norms* responds to this concern by envisioning society as consisting of three concentric circles—elected officials, the administrative apparatus, and civil society at large, and then locating communicative action in civil society, the nongovernmental, non-economic realm composed of "more or less spontaneously emergent associations, organizations, and movements."[75] For this communicative action to guide government, there must be some mechanism to "distill and transmit such reactions in amplified form to the public sphere."[76] Unfortunately, as Habermas concedes, much of the public sphere consists of administrative agents who are guided by instrumental rationality, a perspective that conflicts with true communicative action. So he suggests that the results of the national discourse in civil society can be transmitted by "sluices" past the administrative apparatus and directly to the elected officials in the inner circle, who will respond to the civil society's deliberative decisions.[77] But Habermas never really explains how communicative action, which involves an intensive, almost intimate interaction between two individuals, can become a means for eliminating the interest-based and ideological divisions of a mass society. And his sluices are virtually a concession that he cannot incorporate the administrative character of the modern state into his design. Civil society, in his view, can only transmit its communicatively generated insights to elected officials, but elected officials do not exercise sufficient control over the administrative apparatus to make this circuitous mechanism a satisfactory account of the modern state's legitimacy.

The Compliance Model

Components of the Compliance Model

Both ascending and descending theories of legitimacy, when applied to the government of a modern administrative state, induce quasi-Cartesian doubt. Descending theories overlay an additional, unnecessary term on the state's authority structure, while ascending theories overlay a social contract or a deliberative process on the citizenry's behavior. Both are a bad fit with the administrative state. Perhaps the reason is that the concept of legitimacy refers to nothing—more specifically, that it describes a relationship that simply does not exist in our era. This possibility can be explored by bracketing legitimacy. Suppose we set aside the entire concept, with its medieval origins, its divine right, its social contract, and its rational deliberation. Can we find an alternative way to describe the animate aspect of the state's relationship with its citizens that better accommodates our emotional commitments, the heuristic character of political theory and the process of microanalysis?

Once again, the network metaphor can be used to generate the proposed alternative. Its essential implication is simple—that the relationship between government and its citizens consists of a set of signals being transmitted from various governmental units to various private individuals, either as independent actors or as members of organizations. In Chapter 3, the concept of power was bracketed and replaced with the authority structure of the state to explain the manner in which signals from the government are generated. The concept that can be used as an alternative to legitimacy is the manner in which such signals are received. Since the question involves the animate aspect of people's relationship to government, it can be analyzed in terms of the phenomenological experience of the citizens receiving the signals. Thus, legitimacy's quasi-sacerdotal force, which somehow inheres in the government as a totality, would be replaced with the ordinary reactions of ordinary individuals to signals from various governmental units. The question would no longer be whether the govern-

ment possesses legitimacy, but simply whether its subjects will comply with
its commands, suggestions, and requests. Their compliance would be
manifested as a set of signals transmitted from private individuals or organizations to the relevant governmental units. This approach may be described as the compliance model for the animate aspect of government-
citizen relations.

   Citizen attitudes regarding compliance can be regarded as the internal
program of each citizen, considered as a political actor. These attitudes
may be divided between those based on self-interest and those based on
non-self-interested motivations. Self-interest, or more precisely the rational pursuit of self-interest, is the basis of public choice analysis, and is
probably the first attitude toward government that comes to mind for
many contemporary observers. The ability of government officials to visit
unpleasant consequences on citizens who disobey their commands, or
even their suggestions, is extensive, and often constitutes a sufficient explanation for observable levels of citizen obedience. This impact on the individual is often amplified by the actions of other private citizens, at least
in a generally well-ordered society. If other people disapprove of disobedient behavior, on the basis of their own self-interest or for some other reason, they may impose sanctions that are more serious than those imposed
by government authorities.[78] The business person who breaches a contract
because she is willing to risk the damage remedy a court might impose
may find her business ruined if no one will contract with her thereafter.
And while it is generally a punishable offense to take one's clothes off in
public, most people would regard the resulting social opprobrium as far
more serious than any officially established punishment. Thus, people
rarely commit this offense on city streets, but do so regularly on beaches
where nudity is officially prohibited but socially accepted.

   Even if most people will approve or collude with an illegal undertaking,
signaling theory indicates that the cost of illegality may be higher than
such general opposition may suggest. How is one to find allies for one's
acts of disobedience?[79] One can never be sure how the other party will
react, and even a single mistake may vitiate all the advantages of illegality;
nine people may collude in an illicit undertaking, but the tenth will call the
police. In larger corporate structures, moreover, there are often individuals who stand to benefit from a governmental rule that others prefer to
evade. For example, those minority group members already hired by a firm
have an interest in the firm's compliance with discrimination law, as do the
other employees, minority or not, who have been hired to monitor compliance.[80] It is, moreover, relatively easy for the government to take advantage of this differential willingness to disobey by imposing specially
tailored sanctions on people in particular positions.[81] Consequently, the

transaction costs in organizing disobedient activity may be high enough so that entirely self-interested corporate actors will nonetheless choose to avoid violations of prevailing rules.

Self-interest, moreover, is not limited to the avoidance of unpleasant consequences, but also includes the quest for positive advantage. All governments, and particularly administrative ones, distribute benefits as well as burdens, and many people will be motivated by rational self-interest to obtain these benefits by obedient behavior. This is particularly true in the modern, eudaemonic state, the state that obtains compliance by catering to its citizens' needs and satisfying their desires, and that achieves public order with the carrot rather than the stick. The carrot-stick dichotomy, moreover, is too simple. The government's intensive interaction with its citizens often includes a complex mixture of veiled threat, conditional benefits, informal promises, and vaguely defined possibilities that combine to make obedience both a prudent and enticing prospect.[82] Thus, self-interested actors, enmeshed in a situation whose precise contours, as a matter of lived experience, cannot be determined, often find themselves being beaten with a carrot.

When rationality is recognized as bounded, additional reasons for obedience emerge. A state, at least when it is reasonably stable, creates a comprehensive context in which citizens exist; it becomes a component of, and indeed a partial creator of, the individual's lifeworld. As a result, following rules becomes habitual. Weber identified habit as a ground for obeying the government quite separate from legitimacy,[83] but the distinction tends to suggest that habitual behavior is automatic, that is, beyond the individual's conscious control. In fact, people are generally able to conceive of the possibility of violating any rule when it is in their self-interest, but, as Robert Cooter points out, doing so often involves certain psychological or coordination costs that are as real as any benefits that may be gained.[84] The classic example is whether a driver will stop for a red light at an empty intersection. Drivers who have better things to think about than traffic laws or political theory are likely to stop at the light habitually, because it is so often in their self-interest to do so that it has become part of their general pattern of behavior. By the time the driver becomes aware that there is no police car around in the particular instance, and has craned his neck from side to side to avoid an accident, the light will have turned green. People who run through red lights in these circumstances may be motivated more by an emotional desire to prove to themselves that they are tough-minded nonconformists than by a rational desire to save time. Similarly, business executives often obey regulatory laws because the expense of searching for loopholes and altering their internal practices accordingly may exceed the costs incurred by settled patterns of compliance.

But human beings are not motivated solely by material self-interest; as suggested in Chapter 1, a more plausible model of behavior is that they want to live meaningful lives. They respond to a wide range of motivations that they try to integrate into a coherent sense of self. These additional motivations, which include affection, cooperativeness, and concurrence, are also part of the compliance model, and provide additional reasons why citizens obey governmental signals in the absence of some overarching judgment of legitimacy. Several social scientists, including David Beetham, E. Allan Lind, and Tom Tyler, have drawn attention to these non-self-interested motivations.[85] They tend to identify them as a belief in government legitimacy, but this is a sort of abreaction to public choice doctrine. The motivations they have documented can be described on their own terms, and the mere fact that such motivations go beyond self-interest does not mean they constitute the categorical, morally based approval of government that the concept of legitimacy invokes.

To begin with, most people are strongly motivated by feelings of affection for their family, for their friends, for members of their religion, and for members of their ethnic group. The same feelings of affection can be directed toward one's country as well, and toward that country's government. In the modern world, such sentiments tend to be identified with nationalism. While some theorists view nationalism as an instinctive human sentiment,[86] and others take the opposing position that it is a rational response to circumstances,[87] the more general view is that it is a means by which people construct their sense of identity,[88] or have that sense constructed for them.[89] The strength of such affection will depend on a variety of factors, but it generally seems to be sufficient, in most modern nations, to induce a modicum of compliance with government commands.

Some extreme forms of nationalism may involve an unconditional, unswerving commitment to the nation and its government that is essentially equivalent to legitimacy, because it means that every government command will be obeyed on the basis of its origin alone. This level of commitment is sometimes described as loyalty.[90] But it is simply an error to assert that affection for government, even when based on nationalism, regularly leads to such unconditional commitment or unswerving loyalty. Nationalist sentiments often attach to an ethnic group or culture, and not necessarily to the government and its commands. As a result, they can motivate people to reject the nation or disobey the government if the ethnic group or culture is an oppressed minority, or simply a minority, within the larger polity.[91] Even when the boundaries of one's ethnic group correspond to the government's jurisdiction, commitment to that group does not necessarily imply obedience to government; the more intensely one feels commitment to one's group, the more critical one might be of the government that controls its fate or regulates its traditions. Beyond this, loyalty is typically limited in scope, however great its intensity within a relatively narrow range of operation. It may induce people to fight and die for their country, but such self-sacrifice is typically generated by a sense of external threat or internal conflict. In the quotidian, mundane relationship between people and an administrative government in times of peace, intense commitments of this sort are likely to be dissipated. Stalin was able to elicit fantastic devotion from the Soviet people in resisting the German invasion during World War II,[92] but he was unable to obtain obedience for his peace-time economic policies, despite a savage and relentless use of force.[93] In short, affection for one's government, whether born of nationalism or some other sentiment, is typically one part of the subject's motivation structure. It is often present, but its level and effect will vary just as other motivations do.[94]

A second non-self-interested motivation for compliance is the old Aristotelian and Thomistic idea of sociability—a natural inclination to cooperate with other human beings, a desire to be regarded as a helpful, congenial, and reliable member of one's group. Some theorists, such as David Gauthier, treat this as an aspect of self-interested rationality,[95] but the more natural description is that the desire to cooperate represents a separate impulse. This impulse is often linked with communitarianism, that is, the bonds that people experience within a small, interacting group that defines, and is defined by, their sense of self-identity.[96] Unlike affection, which can attach to an abstract entity like a nation, cooperativeness, at least in this communitarian sense, probably extends no further than the group of people with whom an individual has ongoing contact of some sort.[97] But cooperative attitudes are not necessarily restricted to the intimate communities from which they arguably originate, particularly in this complex, modern world.[98] As discussed in Chapter 4, interactive republics offer many opportunities for groups to interact with and influence the government through either the electoral process or the process of lobbying administrative agencies. Such interaction tends to enlist people's sense of cooperativeness on the government's behalf by allowing personal contacts of relative equality between private actors and public officials. It binds people to the existing government and creates an emergent institutional commitment to further interaction, thereby inducing additional compliance. Totalitarian regimes, despite their fearsome levels of compulsion and indoctrination, often suffer an endemic instability because they have forgone reliance on these forms of human sociability. The widespread corruption that characterized Soviet society may have resulted from precisely this omission.[99]

Still a third reason for people to comply with the government is concurrence—the government's requirements conform to general principles, whether procedural or substantive, to which individuals independently subscribe. With respect to procedure, Tom Tyler has determined on the basis of empirical observations that people are more likely to obey governmental rules that they regard as fairly administered.[100] For example, the losing party in an adjudication—always a fecund source of disaffection and disobedience—will tend to comply with the decision if the procedures used to reach that decision are congruent with his conception of fairness. As for substance, citizens will tend to obey decisions they regard as being designed to achieve an objective that they share.[101] People who ascribe importance to clean streets are more likely to obey anti-littering laws than those who attach little value to this goal. People who believe that the government provides valuable services are more likely to pay their taxes than those who believe that it is oppressive or irresponsible.[102] As Paul Robinson and John Darley point out, people are more likely to obey criminal laws when the sanctions for violating them are consistent with their sense of justice.[103]

In addition to providing an alternative to the ill-fitting concept of legitimacy, the compliance model also provides an alternative to the equally ill-fitting concept of power, as that concept is applied to government-citizen relations. These two concepts, in fact, are often connected, since government is frequently described as exercising legitimate power. Chapter 3 argued that power was a poor way to describe the internal structure of modern administrative government, but it deferred, for uninformative reasons, the use of that concept to describe the government's control over its citizens. The compliance model indicates that the concept of power, and more particularly the relational theories of power, are inadequate in this area as well. Relational theories assert that one actor overcomes the will of another. While the difficulty with describing government actors in this fashion have already been discussed, government-citizen relations involve citizens as individuals who can be plausibly described as having a will. But the idea that the government exercises legitimate power over citizens, like the idea of legitimacy in general, coagulates a complex, interactive relationship into a simplified, adversarial one more appropriate to the medieval times when both concepts originated.

The concept of power privileges the adversarial approach to regulation that is generally described as command and control. Recent scholarship, sometimes known as New Public Governance, points out that this emphasis is not only an ineffective strategy, but an inaccurate description.[104] As the compliance model indicates, most people do not have their wills overcome in their interaction with government. Rather they negotiate this complex relationship by intermixing self-interested motivations with deontological ones such as affection, cooperation, and concurrence. Moreover, the government's relationship with its citizens in a modern state not only extends beyond the use of force, but also extends beyond the issuance of commands to include temptations, suggestions, threats, promises, cajolery, and recursive examination of its own strategies and goals, all of which leaves the concept of overcoming the citizen's will behind. The question, once again, is not the binary one of exercising power, or possessing legitimacy, but the continually varying level of compliance that the government obtains.

Advantages of the Compliance Model

The compliance model, then, rejects the idea that government possesses any generalized justification or imprimatur arising from some external source, and asserts that citizens' willingness to obey governmental orders is the cumulative result of ordinary motivations of individuals, as phenomenologically self-conscious units. These motivations include instrumental rationality directed to material self-interest and deontological reactions such as affection, cooperativeness, and concurrence. While this model seems to describe the animate aspect of government-citizen relations more accurately than legitimacy, it is nonetheless a model. Its preferability depends on whether it corresponds to our emotional commitments, reminds us of its heuristic character, and facilitates microanalysis.

With respect to our commitments, the compliance model focuses attention on the instrumentalism of the administrative state and the morality associated with that stance. Because it carries no generalized approval, the modern state must prove itself to its citizens on a continuous basis; it must deliver the goods. In particular, it must provide the very things, most notably security and prosperity, that citizens demand and to which they are committed. Thus the compliance model corresponds to our eudaemonic conception of the state, while legitimacy, like power, hearkens back to a world where the state, having obtained its generalized imprimatur and secured its moral authority, felt free to ignore the welfare of its citizens, to pursue military triumph or architectural grandeur at the expense of the people's more unpoetic and mundane desires.

Our commitment to liberty is also captured by the compliance model and obscured by the traditional concept of legitimacy. It is tempting to assert that liberty is best protected by granting legitimacy to a just regime, and thus embedding this virtue in the regime's continued existence. That may be sufficient to express our rejection of totalitarianism, but it fails to address the more subtle problems of an articulated administrative state. We rely on an extensive administrative apparatus for our security and our prosperity, and no other means of satisfying those commitments in a mass technological society have been devised. But the scale and intrusiveness of this apparatus renders it a potential instrument of oppression, quite apart from any dictatorial inclinations of its leaders. To express our simultaneous commitment to these partially conflicting goals, we need a conceptual framework that allows us to make particularized assessments, to find ways that government can perform complex administrative tasks while preserving our liberties. We need to know how government can obtain the compliance that is necessary for its instrumental purposes without oppressing individuals or discouraging collective interaction through electoral and administrative channels. Attaching the term 'legitimacy' to a particular regime coagulates these complex calculations into a single judgment that masks the real situation.

This focus on the issue of compliance with individual commands, requests, or guidelines might seem to favor the political status quo and thereby threaten our liberties by foreclosing inquiry into the general justification for the government's existence. Many people might be inclined to agree with Nozick that "the fundamental question of political philosophy, one that precedes questions about how the state should be organized, is whether there should be any state at all."[105] But the administrative state is not a contingent alliance or a feudal lordship; it is a comprehensive, complex apparatus, so intertwined with our worldview and well-being that its non-existence is virtually inconceivable. If the fundamental question that we ask is whether this state should exist, the answer will almost always be yes. If we then conclude that the state is, in its entirety, legitimate, we have cast a moral benediction over the entire apparatus, conferring an unnecessary and perhaps undeserved approval on all its multitudinous activities. This is the real threat to our liberties.[106] The compliance model facilitates a moral discourse that challenges the propriety of each separate governmental action and allows us to bring morality to bear within the ambit of the ongoing relationship between citizens and government. It thereby effects a sort of figure-ground reversal from the concept of legitimacy. Instead of finding a justification for the state in its entirety, and then casting that approval over all the state's particularized actions, it begins by questioning each action, and then deriving the citizens' overarching attitudes from the cumulation of their separate judgments.

The concept of legitimacy is also problematic because it fails to remind us of the heuristic character of political theory. There is a tendency to treat legitimacy as a thing, a tangible possession of the government. Sometimes, this possession is imagined as a single adamantine jewel, while at other times it is described in terms that evoke the idea of male potency and hearken back to beliefs about the physical power of the king. More sophisticated discussions treat it as a quiver of arrows that can be lost in its entirety, squandered gradually through careless use, or left unattended, in which case it can be found and seized by others—perhaps those who already own a bow. This discourse of possession, loss, gradual waste, and sudden acquisition obscures the fact that legitimacy is not a tangible or even intangible entity, like buildings or bank accounts, that governments possess. The concept simply refers to the manner in which individuals, acting individually, through organizations, or as part of social movements, relate to governmental institutions. Describing such relationships as entities is an unnecessary and distracting reification, particularly in an era when social science provides us with more sophisticated methods of analysis. The compliance model resolves this problem, while at the same time avoiding any complex, conceptually unmanageable neologisms. In place of a coagulated entity, it offers a list of ordinary language attitudes that combine to produce a pattern described by the equally ordinary term 'compliance.'

Finally, the way in which the compliance model facilitates microanalysis of the animate relationship between citizens and their government can be illustrated by considering the character of the citizens themselves, the character of government, and the interaction between the two. To begin with citizens, the concept of legitimacy is limited to politics. We never say that one person regards another as legitimate except in the literal sense that her mother is married to her father, and even that usage is becoming obsolete.[107] We rarely say that a person regards a nongovernmental organization as legitimate. We may declare an argument legitimate, but we hardly ever use the concept to describe an entity. Thus, legitimacy does not reflect real human attitudes, but simply projects an abstract theory onto human beings, providing a fudge factor necessary to turn an outmoded way of thinking about government-citizen relations into a plausible account of human behavior.

In contrast, the compliance model possesses a recognizable relationship to modern people's phenomenological experience. We often relate to each other on the basis of material self-interest; we also feel affection for each other, cooperate with each other, and concur with each other's judgments. We relate to private organizations with this same mixture of motivations. There is no reason to assume that the motivations that animate people's ordinary relationships to each other and to private organizations do not apply to their relationship with government. It is true, of course, that the administrative state is vast, impersonal, and remote, but modern people's experience includes many other institutions with these charming attributes, such as their employer, their union, or their religious organization. To assume that one particular relationship, namely the relationship with government, elicits a set of attitudes among people that are not found in any other setting creates a grave danger of overinterpretation. The opposing assumption that human motivations remain essentially the same, but must be adapted to the specific circumstances of the interaction, seems more plausible, and places more control on the explanatory process. If it appears that legitimacy is more applicable when describing the attitudes of organizations toward government, it is only because organizations are themselves abstractions. Once those organizations are factored into their individual members, as microanalysis demands, the same explanatory problems with the concept of legitimacy will arise.

With respect to the character of government, the second component of the government-citizen relationship, the compliance model, is also more amenable to microanalysis. The problem with legitimacy is its binary or coagulated character—a particular government is either legitimate or illegitimate. One can say, of course, that the government has become less legitimate, or is losing its legitimacy, but it does so on its way toward becoming illegitimate, to crossing some sort of qualitative boundary. Such formulations seem relevant to a government that is struggling to be recognized, a government whose principal concern is civil order. Pre-modern European governments were faced with precisely these concerns; not only did they experience frequent crises of succession, but their main task, even in periods of relative stability, was to establish their authority over their purported subjects. The landed nobility's assertion of their feudal rights amounted to partial but continuous declaration of independence, and much of the history of the pre-modern European state involved the king's countervailing assertion—successful in the case of France, unsuccessful in the case of the Holy Roman Empire, and successful with qualifications in the cases of England and Austria—that he was the definitive authority in his entire realm.

Civil order was not only a dominant concern of European monarchs, but also the primary benefit that they could deliver to their subjects. The pageantry of feudal conflict and the drama of religious and dynastic war received their intense coloration from the blood of ordinary citizens.[108] Since pre-modern armies, lacking organized logistics, lived off the land, their arrival in a particular locality was generally an economic disaster at the very least.[109] If the locality was hostile, this disaster was often accompanied by unspeakable brutality. The very fact of discord, moreover, generally shattered the flimsy structure of the pre-modern economy, producing stagnation, decline, or outright starvation. It is revealing that the most fecund period for social contract theory came in the seventeenth century, following the religious war that had convulsed and often devastated the leading European states—the War of the Three Henrys in France, the Civil War in England, and the Thirty Years' War in the Empire. The writings of these social contract theorists are suffused with a yearning for civil order; all agree that this is the greatest benefit to be derived from the formation of a government, and many, such as Grotius and Hobbes, argue that people should relinquish virtually all their natural liberty to secure it.[110]

In a modern administrative state, however, civil order is not the principal concern. Except for an occasional uncertainty regarding its frontiers, the state's control over its subjects is usually definitive. Conflicts about its authority structure tend to involve subsidiary issues such as federalism or agency independence, not basic matters of allegiance, and are typically resolved by ordinary governmental mechanisms. Moreover, the administrative state performs many tasks beyond the maintenance of civil order; it regulates the economy, educates its citizens, redistributes income, assists the poor, protects the environment, and operates large numbers of institutions. Under these circumstances, the sort of binary or coagulated determination that the concept of legitimacy implies fits as badly as the adversarial relationship implied by the concept of power. What we need instead, in order to microanalyze the relationship between government and citizens, is a means of assessing the government's varying rules and differential performance across an innumerable variety of tasks, a conceptual framework that enables us to make distinctions among these policies, to explain why they possess different levels of public support and induce different levels of citizen compliance.

One of the central insights of the New Public Governance model is the recognition that compliance with a rule is never total, and that the rulemaking unit, whether chief executive, legislature, agency, or court, does not truly expect it to be total.[111] This is always true as a matter of fact, but it is also true in the administrative state as a matter of theory. It is apparent to any modern rule maker that compliance cannot be achieved by mere declaration of the rule, but rather will require implementation or enforcement. The level of compliance, that is, the signals coming from private individuals or groups regarding their obedience to governmental policy, will depend on the resources allocated to this implementation or enforcement function. These resources are virtually never sufficient to obtain total compliance. Rather, as Daniel Farber points out, some lesser level of compliance is implicitly accepted.[112] Social nostalgia, however, makes us reluctant to acknowledge this reality; we have an abiding affection for the sacerdotal state, where law was promulgated with an authority derived from God, and everyone was expected to obey. It would be interesting if a rule maker were to acknowledge the realities of the modern administrative state in passing a rule and to specify the level of compliance that it expected the agency to achieve.[113] This might decrease the *in terrorem* impact of the rule, but it might also provide a more realistic and effective way for the agency to measure its performance, and for other governmental units to supervise that performance.[114]

In addition to providing a more realistic picture of both citizens and government in the modern state, the compliance model provides a means of capturing the complex interplay between the two. It indicates that the various components of the citizens' attitude toward government can assume different orientations. Thus, citizens may feel affection for their government, but fail to concur with some of its decisions. Alternatively, they may concur with government decisions, or act cooperatively with their neighbors, but feel no affection for the government itself. A particularly conplex permutation is that they may be motivated to comply by feelings of affection, cooperativeness, and concurrence, but be oppositely motivated by self-interest. The phenomenological model of behavior suggests that the first three motivations are intersubjectively established and constitute a significant part of the individual's lifeworld, but it also suggests that these motivations must be activated within each individual, and can therefore be counteracted by self-interest at virtually any time. This interplay of deontological attitudes and self-interest displays both temporal and spatial variation. Generally speaking, deontological attitudes like affection, cooperativeness, and concurrence change relatively slowly and carry over from one set of governmental actions to another. In contrast, behavior based on self-interest varies rapidly, in response to more immediate circumstances. As a result, self-interested attempts to circumvent legal rules seem to dominate when citizen behavior is studied at short range, but become less important when such behavior is viewed over long periods of time.

Even more significantly, citizens may have different attitudes toward different parts of government. One cannot really say that Americans regard their government as legitimate but the Internal Revenue Service as illegitimate. The IRS was properly authorized, and the whole point of legitimacy is to confer the governmental imprimatur on authorized subordinates. But one can certainly say that the same feelings of affection, cooperativeness, and concurrence that attach to the armed forces do not extend to tax collectors. In short, the compliance model explains interactions between government and citizens that seem contradictory when interpreted in terms of legitimacy. As Malcolm Feeley has suggested, it tells us why genuinely patriotic individuals smoke marijuana and cheat on their taxes,[115] why people will sacrifice their lives for their country while being dissatisfied with its leaders, and why business executives who vote for increasingly punitive criminal laws will assiduously search for ways to circumvent regulatory requirements.

The Large-Scale Application of the Compliance Model

Large-Scale Attitudes

By dissolving the coagulated concept of legitimacy into particularized motivations, the compliance model facilitates a microanalysis of each citizen's relationship to government. But can this model explain large-scale or macro features of that relationship? To pursue this question, it is helpful to distinguish between large-scale attitudes and large-scale behavior. The former refers to beliefs about government in general that are held by each specific individual, while the latter refers to the action of large groups of individuals, like a revolution or a period of government stability. Of course, the two are far from unrelated. It is quite likely, for example, that people will act in concert when the attitudes they share are large-scale ones such as approval or disapproval of the entire government. Nonetheless, the distinction between attitudes and behavior is a useful one for analytic purposes.

The simplest large-scale attitude or general belief about government held by an individual is that the government in its entirety is good or bad, moral or immoral, acceptable or unacceptable. The concept of legitimacy is certainly sufficient to explain such general attitudes, since a legitimate government, almost by definition, is a good or a moral one in the eyes of the person who regards it as legitimate. But the correspondence of these attitudes does not mean that the concept of legitimacy is needed to account for global judgments of this sort, since these judgments can also be based on some or all of the motivations that compose the compliance model of government-citizen relations. A government that the individual regards as regularly satisfying her self-interest and to which she regularly experiences feelings of affection, cooperativeness, and concurrence will also be regarded as generally good or moral. Thus, global judgments can represent conclusions, or generalizations, from separate responses to varied government actions.

Not only does the compliance model account for global judgments about government as well as the concept of legitimacy, but it is more plausible from the psychological or phenomenological perspective. In deciding whether someone is a good or moral person, people tend to generalize from particular behaviors that they have observed, rather than concluding that the person bears the signs of an externally established goodness. This is also likely to be true for similar decisions about government. The formation of global judgments without any intermediate assessment of particular actions is characteristic mainly of religious faith. It may be applicable to political judgments in the era of the sacerdotal state, but seems implausible in our secularized, administrative times. Admittedly, these belief patterns would be difficult to measure, but the main point is that the mere existence of global judgments about the state does not prove that legitimacy is a useful theory from the psychological perspective.

Global attitudes toward government are not limited to simple judgments about whether the government is good or bad, however. In addition, there are more complex beliefs about the way that government in its entirety is constituted and about its underlying sources of justification. The first section of this chapter argued that neither descending nor ascending theories of legitimacy reflect the attitudes of people in a modern administrative state. Nonetheless, it seems clear that individuals often hold fairly specific beliefs regarding the moral basis of the government in general. These are often derived from constitutionalism, the idea that government is justified because it follows the rules set forth in a particular organic document. An alternative view, found most notably in Great Britain, is that the government is justified because it evolved as part of an indigenous political tradition. In either case, the concept of legitimacy may appear to be the most accurate way to describe these beliefs; bracketing it, however convincing in theoretical terms, would appear to ignore a basic element of people's actual belief systems.

The contemporary significance of constitutionalism is open to question, however. In the Middle Ages, the origin or constitution of government was a highly salient subject, since governments were often alliances among landed nobles, or fiefdoms that had been granted within living memory. Many functions that we now regard as governmental were carried out by the Church, which of course was divinely ordained, or were based on custom, which was regarded as unchanging. In contrast, political associations often seemed to be flowing lambently across this stable base, changing with each conquest, marriage, or feudal alliance, and justified by the relatively recent agreement that gave rise to them. But the modern administrative state constitutes a comprehensive context for its citizens, a substantial proportion of their lifeworld—"the world in which I find myself and which is also my world-about-me"[116]—and its existence is taken for granted. People are born into it, they live in it, they depend on its continuation for their survival, and they make their political choices within its capacious boundaries. As a result, questions about the origins or constitution of the state tend to fade from view, to be replaced with questions about its day-to-day performance.

There are a number of reasons why the modern administrative state acquires this all-encompassing, taken-for-granted character—its correspondence to the nation-state, the range of services it provides, and its articulation of purpose. The result is a shift away from arguments based on tradition or the origins of government to arguments based on the satisfaction of the people's current needs. To be sure, political debates often feature conflicting claims about the meaning of the Constitution and the intent of its Framers, but these claims are typically driven by current disagreements about government performance. A genuine commitment to tradition, a willingness to sacrifice one's current preferences out of a sense of veneration for the past, is foreign to the modern mindset. In the United States, where constitutional questions often seem decisive, the rhetorical nature of these questions is generally reflected in the correspondence between people's political preferences and their constitutional interpretations. Opponents of gun control have suddenly discovered in the Second Amendment, unused and differently interpreted for nearly two centuries, an original understanding that opposes current legislative efforts in this area.[117] Proponents of prison reform discovered, and the federal courts actually relied upon, an interpretation of the Eighth Amendment that had gone unnoticed for nearly the same length of time.[118] This is the opposite of tradition, of an agreed-upon belief about the origin of the state that controls its present policy. It is the use of a creation myth in a contemporary debate whose opposing positions are so intensely felt that they obscure any serious commitment to inherited or time-honored practices.[119]

Here again, it is the compliance model, and not the concept of legitimacy, that provides a convincing description of people's general attitudes in a modern state. Legitimacy focuses attention on the way the state was constituted; both descending and ascending theories treat the government's creation as the decisive moment, and evaluate its subsequent performances in terms of their fidelity to that seminal event. In contrast, the compliance model treats the state as an ongoing experience. Instead of focusing on the state's origin, it focuses on the way people respond to specific actions taken at the present time. While the concept of legitimacy certainly figures in political debate, the compliance model more accurately captures the ongoing commitments and reactions that this debate embodies. For people confronted with a massive modern government that is co-extensive with their nation, that delivers essential services, and that implements consciously articulated social policies, the legitimacy-driven question of origin fades from view, and the compliance-based question of performance fills their lifeworld.[120]

The here-and-now orientation of people's general attitude toward government that the compliance model implicates should not be regarded as philosophically naive. It is true that many philosophic systems are constructed from first principles. Modern political philosophy is often viewed as beginning with Hobbes precisely because he adopted this approach to politics, and the tradition continues through Kant and Rawls. But the procedure is not independently justified. In Husserl's view, which underlies Continental social theory and a large part of contemporary social science, our life experience, the world around us, is prior to any theory. There is no obvious reason why people cannot build their understanding of government directly upon that experience. Reliance on a creation myth for judging government is in fact a reflection of the sacerdotal concept of the state, the desire to connect the state to some power or principle that lies beyond its limits. It substitutes original virtue, in the political realm, for original sin in the individual realm, but regards this generative event as equally determinative of moral judgments. Theories that derive moral judgments from people's ongoing life experience reflect the instrumentalist conception of the state that is central to modern, administrative governance, and, in addition, are more congruent with modern sociological perspectives on human behavior.

This shift in the grounds for justification of the government finds a pragmatic correlative in judicial review, an important innovation of American constitutionalism and an increasingly popular provision in many contemporary constitutions. Medieval thinkers, beginning with John of Salisbury,[121] were fully aware that the king could act improperly and that the cumulation of such improper actions would render him a tyrant, but they perceived no recourse for the people other than the right of revolution.[122] This placed the people in the same intractable situation as a nation whose only weapon is a nuclear bomb, or a government whose only punishment is the death penalty: quite often, to have only an option with catastrophic consequences is to have no option at all. The genius of judicial review is that it provides an orderly mechanism, within the framework of existing government, through which actions by the dominant authorities can be struck down on moral grounds. It reflects a conceptual transition from the binary concept of legitimacy, where one must obey every government command or rebel against the government in its entirety, to the segmented concept of compliance, where particular governmental actions can be rejected within an ongoing structure. To be sure, the binding character of the Constitution in its entirety is based on an originating act—a remnant of pre-modern thought—but judicial review allows that claim to fade from view, and establishes a mechanism where moral judgment can be exercised in a contemporary context, using contemporary arguments, and without a totalistic attack on the government's original formation. It does not dispense with the origin myth, but it domesticates that myth's effect, thereby dissipating its importance.

Large-Scale Behavior

The issue of general behavior is separate from that of general attitudes; although the two obviously interact, people's behavior often falls into general patterns that do not necessarily reflect their conscious thoughts. The most notable general behaviors in the political arena involve stability and change. Modern administrative states tend to be stable, and those that make use of electoral and administrative interaction exhibit a striking, even spectacular level of stability. On the other hand, revolutions do occur and are often the most dramatic events in people's political experience. Both sets of behaviors are typically described in terms of legitimacy. We say that a government is stable when it possesses legitimacy, and that revolutions result when that legitimacy is lost.

In fact, the compliance model provides a better account of the administrative state's stability. The sacerdotal concept of legitimacy suggests either a powerful enchantment or a readily broken spell. Virtually all observers of modern politics agree that the enchantment has degenerated into a spell and the spell has been broken. This process, which occurred some time during the eighteenth or nineteenth century, and is variously described as rationalization, modernization, or secularization,[123] has been more blandly described in this study as the articulation of purpose. Its advent led to nearly a century of revolutions, which seemed to vindicate Marx's prediction about the imminent decline of capitalism. But Western nations surmounted these stresses and established stable regimes.[124] They did not do so, however, by restoring the moral authority of government, but by providing a steady stream of services that cater to citizen needs and thereby satisfy the demand for redistribution that Marx thought could only be provided by a socialist revolution. The state's eudaemonic character, which contributes to the sense that it is an all-encompassing reality, simultaneously secures its stability by appealing to the self-interest of its citizens.

This implies, however, that the state will only be stable if it delivers services effectively. The slogan of the post-Camelot, eudaemonically oriented citizen is "Ask not what your country can do for you, but what your country has done for you lately."[125] Western nations were able to achieve political stability because electoral interaction impelled political leaders to respond to the citizen's demand for services, and administrative interaction made these services reasonably efficient. Ironically, it is Marxist governments that proved unstable, an instability that stemmed, in part, from conscious reliance on the legitimacy model. The Soviet regime declared that it was a government of the working classes and claimed moral authority on this basis, a moral authority that Lenin and Stalin were actually able to deploy for brief periods of time. But its lack of electoral and administrative interaction ultimately made the government fatally unresponsive. While it could use its citizens as military and industrial canon fodder, it failed at the eudaemonic task on which the stability of modern government depends, and its claim to socialist legitimacy was incapable of saving it.

The state's ability to deliver services is more than an appeal to people's individual self-interest, however. Because of the instrumental morality of the administrative state that was described in Chapter 1, service delivery becomes a means of eliciting affection, cooperation, and concurrence. Administrative states, like others, can appeal to these motivations on non-eudaemonic grounds. They can induce affection by invoking ethnic solidarity, obtain cooperation by recruiting officials from all sectors of society, and draw upon concurrence by adopting popular policies. Their unique stability, however, derives from their ability to convince modern, cynical citizens that they are acting as an instrumentality to serve the citizens' own needs. Thus, citizens reach the global judgment that their government is basically good, not because it claims some generalized moral imprimatur, but because it delivers the goods.

While legitimacy does not provide a convincing account of modern government's stability, it may seem quite useful as a means of describing revolutionary change, the moments when new leaders seize authority against the wishes of the prior ones. The binary character of legitimacy, which misdescribes the quotidian operations of an administrative state, seems appropriate for these cataclysmic occurrences. It seems natural to say that the prior government has lost its legitimacy and that the revolutionaries have seized it. It seems even more natural, however, if one imagines the seizure of a physical symbol of power, and more natural still if one places this event in an attractively medieval setting. One moment, the king is sitting on his throne, holding his scepter and wearing his crown. Then the revolutionaries rush in and stab him with their rough-hewn swords. Their leader grabs that crown and scepter and sits down on the blood-stained throne. The multitudes are allowed into the chamber; they see the revolutionary leader wearing the crown and holding the scepter and they shout, "The king, the king" as they fall upon their callused knees. Thus, the old leader has lost his legitimacy, and the new one has acquired it.

The characterization of these dramatic events as a transfer of legitimacy works well as long as one coagulates the concept of legitimacy and authority, the way Weber does with his descending theory. Assuming that any such revolutionary moment occurs, it is the authority structure of the government that has changed. The concept of legitimacy claims to do more than describe the fact that authority has been transferred; it is generally regarded as an account of people's attitudes toward government. For that purpose, however, the description of revolution is far less convincing. A revolution is typically preceded by a gradual deterioration of people's affection, cooperativeness, and concurrence, or a growing sense that the government no longer serves their individual self-interest.[126] These attitude changes may not manifest themselves in outright disobedience of the government, but they lead to decreasing levels of compliance and prepare the citizenry for the ultimate conflagration. When the revolution comes—when, to shift to more modern scenarios, the troops refuse to fire, local officials no longer accept orders from the center, or angry crowds feel released from their ordinary habits of obedience and fear of injury—it is because a long period of disaffection has reached its tipping point. Conversely, the new government must generally struggle for some period of time to gain control of the nation. It must convince the populace, by force, bribery, or service delivery, that compliance is in their individual self-interest, and it must gradually win their affection, cooperation, and concurrence. The large-scale behavior of accepting a new government, like the large-scale behavior of rejecting an existing one, is best described by the compliance model and by the microanalysis that it facilitates. This model, moreover, accommodates the widespread phenomenon of partial

178

CHAPTER 5

revolutions, where the insurgents proclaim affection for one part of government but insist on displacing or slaughtering another.[127]

There is, in short, no need to resort to the concept of legitimacy to describe the attitudes of people about government in general or the general behavior of the populace en masse. While legitimacy may seem more applicable to global behaviors than the compliance model, it in fact merges a wide range of differentiated reactions into a sticky, agglutinated mass. The compliance model, although designed to describe the ordinary attitudes and behaviors of citizens in an administrative state, is in fact more useful. Citizens do form global judgments about government, but those judgments depend on the same mix of self-interest, affection, cooperativeness, and concurrence that determine their more particularized reactions. They do make claims based on political origin of government, but these claims tend to be rhetorical devices that use an available symbol system for purposes determined by that same mix of motivations. And it is this same mix that renders government stable or unstable, that explains the collapse of existing regimes and the survival of their successors. Perhaps in the small, sacerdotal state of the pre-modern era, general attitudes and collective behaviors could be based on the concept of legitimacy, but in a modern administrative state, with its intensive relationship to its citizens and its articulation of structure and purpose, these attitudes and behaviors are best elucidated by the mixture of self-interested and affective reactions that compose the compliance model. In the modern state, there is no divine right, no descending imprimatur, no social contract, and no definitive forum of rational deliberation. There is only the daily flux of innumerable interactions that, when taken together, define the contours of citizen obedience and generate its apparent solidity.

Conclusion to Part I

The four chapters in Part I of this book have argued that there are significant conceptual advantages to bracketing a number of the basic concepts that we use to describe the tectonic and affective structure of the modern state—the three branches of government, power, discretion, democracy, and legitimacy. They are awkward descriptions, inherited from a prior and distinctly different era, that divert us from our genuine commitments, mask their heuristic character, and impede microanalysis. A further disadvantage of these concepts is that they do not fit together. They thus fail to satisfy a fourth criterion as well, a criterion that can be called the metaphorical unity of committed description. It is desirable, on heuristic as well as aesthetic grounds, to derive descriptions of government's various aspects or components from a single source, to rely upon a unified, comprehensive metaphor for the entirety of government. The alternative descriptions that were proposed in the preceding chapter were all derived from the model of an interactive network, and thus satisfy this fourth criterion. This provides another argument for bracketing our inherited concepts and proceeding with the thought experiment of describing the modern administrative state in alternative terms.

The disjunctions among the concepts discussed in Part I can be illustrated by considering them in succession. There is, to begin with, no conceptual relationship between the three-branch metaphor that was discussed in Chapter 2 and the concepts of power and discretion that were discussed in Chapter 3. Three branches suggest separate and co-equal entities, each of which is stable and self-contained. Power suggests a command structure, with particular individuals or organizations able to issue orders to other individuals or organizations and overcome their will. In other words, the three-branch metaphor divides government into separate areas, whereas power determines who is in control within a unified structure. The point of contact between these two heuristics might appear to be the phrase 'separation of powers,' a common although not necessary aspect of the three-branch metaphor. But power, in the phrase 'separation of powers,' refers to an area of jurisdiction, not a hierarchy of command. The reason for assigning criminal trials to the judicial branch is not to give the judiciary power to overrule a trial verdict by the legislature, but to preclude the legislature from conducting trials in the first place. The reason for declaring that the American president is commander-in-chief of the armed forces is not to give him control over the strategic decisions of the judiciary, but to locate those decisions exclusively within the executive. Thus, the two heuristics seem consistent only when one exploits the ambiguity of the term 'power.'

One can argue, of course, that the purpose of dividing government into three separate branches is to distribute power among different institutions, so that each institution can control the others through its own hierarchical system of power. This idea, however, conflicts with both heuristics, since it is unclear how three branches can exercise control over each other, and equally unclear how such mutual control corresponds to the essentially hierarchical concept of governmental power as a whole. Because of these conflicts, we tend to invoke the entirely different image of checks and balances in order to describe this mutual control. The result is that our metaphorical mixture now contains a tree, a hierarchy, a negotiable instrument, and a balance beam.

This is more than a problem of mixed metaphors. Because government is such a complex process, scholars, policy analysts, and judges who are attempting to conceptualize its operation need to rely on images to assist their understanding. The metaphorical farrago that power, discretion, and the three-branch structure generate offers little assistance in this enterprise. In particular, it is unhelpful in modeling the actual operation of government, the way one institution controls, limits, or assists the actions of another. Since different governmental units interact so frequently, and in such complex ways, we need a coherent image to explain the multitudinous relations among these varied units.

Democracy, discussed in Chapter 4, adds another equally inconsistent theme. The original concept, as defined by Aristotle and sedimented into our present perspective, is that all major policy decisions would be the result of deliberation and majority voting in a general assembly of citizens, and that the officials who carry out these policies would be selected by lot. This seems to conflict with the three-branch metaphor, which generally envisions an elected chief executive, a representative legislature, and an appointed judiciary. It also conflicts with the concept of power; in a democracy, supreme power is supposed to be exercised by the assembly of citizens, but modern states contain no such assembly. The conflict can be partially resolved by recognizing the representative nature of modern democracy, which accommodates at least two of the three branches, the executive and legislature, and views power as being transferred from the citizens to these two branches. It is notable, however, that the more fully this representative process is recognized, the more pressure it places on this concept of democracy. When jurisdiction is divided among different branches, with different representational structures, and when power is delegated to public officials, the idea that the people are ruling becomes increasingly attenuated. We respond with jeremiads about the counter-majoritarian difficulty of judicial review, the excessive delegation of legislative power, the headless fourth branch of government, the iron law of oligarchy, and the iron triangle of policy making. These metaphorical monstrosities are generated largely by the disjunction between the concept of democracy, the three-branch image, and the concept of power. They arise from the conflict between our pre-analytic assumptions about the way government is supposed to work and our observations about its actual operation.

Legitimacy is an equally discordant concept. Attributing the state's legitimacy to an external imprimatur, coming from either above or below, circumvents and possibly conflicts with the internal features of the three branches, power, discretion, and democracy. There might appear to be an organic connection between descending theories of legitimacy and power, and also between ascending theories of legitimacy and democracy, but the homologous structures of these paired ideas is deceptive. As discussed in Chapter 5, legitimacy is a constitutive principle, relating to the origin of the state, not its ongoing operation. In a descending theory, the power relations in the state become legitimate by virtue of some principle or force that stands outside the government's command structure, and thus has no necessary connection with the power exercised within that structure. In fact, the two tend to diverge in most accounts; descending legitimacy typically derives from a moral principle or from the use of force, whereas the resulting power of government officials flows through established legal channels. In an ascending theory, the democratic government that the parties to the social contract authorize cannot provide the principle of aggregation among these contracting parties, since it is the contract that creates the government. Again, this disjunction is emphasized by most theories of ascending legitimacy, which are based on a unanimous agreement that binds the contracting parties in perpetuity, unless circumstances change. This is entirely different from both Aristotelian and representative democracies, which feature majoritarian decisions that are reconsidered either at any time or at regular and fairly frequent intervals.

If these natural alliances between legitimacy on the one hand and democracy or power on the other are in fact discordant, the reverse connections, which have been advanced by several leading thinkers, reveal an even more pronounced divergence. Rousseau attempted to derive democracy from the descending concept of a general will, but the conception of citizens whose liberty consists of complete obedience to government decisions bears little resemblance to our current image of democracy. Hobbes attempted to derive a theory of strict hierarchical power from an ascending social contract theory, but never convincingly explained why free, independent people would agree to such an absolutist contract. Both theories contained disjunctions between their legitimacy-oriented premises and their democracy- or power-oriented conclusion that left them open to convincing criticisms. These came from Hegel, who provided a power-based interpretation of Rousseau's general will theory, and from Locke, who provided a democratic version of Hobbes's social contract theory. Because their components are more homologous, Hegel's and Locke's approaches seem preferable to their predecessors, but the linkage is only an intuitive one. Both theories ultimately suffer from the disjunctions that have been described in the preceding paragraph. And to conclude this tour among the permutations of the concepts described in Part I, no theory of legitimacy has established an organic or even a metaphorical connection with the three-branch imagery of government.

Of course, connections among these disparate descriptions of our political system can be asserted, with arguments adduced to explain them and evidence marshaled on their behalf. The question, however, is whether all of this is merely overinterpretation, a product of our insistent drive toward meaning, rather than a source of useful insight into the underlying subject matter. The test is not whether an argument can be constructed—it almost always can be—but how much energy must be expended in the effort. The vast amount of effort required to bridge the gaps between the three-branch image, power, discretion, democracy, and legitimacy suggests that our current descriptions of the political system are a collection of unrelated or discordant elements, rather than a unified conception.

This situation can be contrasted with the one that prevailed when these heuristics were developed in the medieval era. At that time, government was conceived in sacerdotal terms, a means of mediating between the divine and human realms. The dominant image of governmental structure was not the three-branch image but the human body. As described in Chapter 2, the body image was intensely sacerdotal; Christ's body was the central feature of the Eucharist, the Church was explicitly conceived as His body, and the state was initially conceptualized as a similarly sacred body by analogy. Thus, the body image linked the human world with the divine through its mystic collectivity, its transformation of separate individuals into a Christian commonwealth. At the same time, it was naturally hierarchical—the head, or king, was at the top of government, the hands, or soldiers and officials, were in the middle, carrying out the king's commands, and the peasants, or feet, were at the bottom. Thus, the state's hierarchical ordering was a sacred ordering, a God-given structure that enabled it to exist as a collectivity and serve its mediating function.

Power flowed through this governmental structure, both sacerdotally and hierarchically. Sacerdotally, it flowed from God to the properly ordered state; hierarchically, it flowed through that proper ordering, from the king to his officials. The concept of power was thus entirely consistent with the image of the state as human body because both possessed the same divine origin, served the same mediating function, and used the same hierarchical structure to reflect that origin and achieve that purpose. The descending concept of legitimacy expressed the rightfulness of this coordinated image. Government was legitimate because it derived its structure from the mystic body and its power from God. Power was legitimate because it came from God, and was transmitted through a divinely ordained hierarchy. Taken together, the whole set of concepts possessed a tightly organized, recursive quality. God ordained a hierarchically ordered government, and only a hierarchically ordered government could draw its power and legitimacy from God.

The inclination to explain political ideas in terms of their origins was linked to this explanatory system. All these ideas—the structure of government, its power and its legitimacy—could be unambiguously and uncontroversially traced back to God, Who was, after all, the Creator and First Cause. Anything that lacked this origin would be false; a government that derived its structure from any other source would be an improper one, perhaps the work of the Devil, as John of Salisbury claimed. Power emerging from some other source would be similarly suspect, and legitimacy was impossible without divine initiation. The Thomist emphasis on reason, which rapidly became canonical, amplified this style of explanation because reasoned argument characteristically proceeded from first premises. Thus, one used reason to explain the structure, the power, and most of all the legitimacy of government by identifying its origin. Since this origin was the Originator of all things, Whose eternal law created and comported with reason, the conceptual development of political ideas and their normative justification merged once again into a tightly organized, recursive unity.

It was neat and it was pretty, but it was not realistic, particularly with government's increasing complexity and administrative character. As the Middle Ages yielded to the Renaissance and Reformation, the sacerdotal glue that bound these political ideas together started to dissolve. Where theological explanations for the state's nature and origin had once appeared self-evident, secular accounts were now desired and supplied. The human body image was succeeded by the concept of three branches, descending theories of legitimacy were succeeded by ascending ones, and power was conceived in more worldly terms, whether it was the unalloyed power of an absolute monarch, as in France, or the conditional power of a constitutional one, as in England. Democracy, a concept borrowed from the secular theories of the Greeks and Romans, evolved from an imprecation into an acceptable component of a moral government, and finally into the apotheosis of political morality.

But these revised, more secular conceptions were never reconfigured into a new unity, never combined to form a coherent heuristic of government. Retaining the structure of their predecessor concepts, they remained in the awkward quasi-isolation to which they had been banished by the breakdown of the sacerdotal model. Government was no longer depicted as a mystic body, but it continued to be described by a naturalistic metaphor that ignored the administrative apparatus. Power no longer came from God, but was still conceived as a mystic fluid that either pooled within specific individuals or coursed between them. Legitimacy no longer descended from above, but the concept of a government validated by some external imprimatur remained. Democracy, newly added as an acceptable mode of governance, was rooted in the practice of the Hellenic polis to an extent that precluded its integration into an account of Western politics. And each component not only shared the structure of its predecessor, but also joined these predecessors in searching for its origin, the first cause that was so obvious in the sacerdotal Middle Ages, and has become so obscure in the skeptical, anthropologically literate period that followed.

The preceding chapters, therefore, suggest that much can be gained from bracketing the familiar concepts with which we describe our government and conducting the thought experiment of developing an alternative description. This experiment, it was argued, generated superior descriptions of the government we actually possess, that is, descriptions that are more congruent with our genuine commitments, that more explicitly announce their heuristic character, and that more readily accommodate microanalysis. It may have appeared, however, that the overall structure of the argument is a sort of conceptual drive-by shooting, picking off one concept after another at their most vulnerable points. In fact, however, the proposed alternatives all derive from a unified conception of government, a conception as unified as the sacerdotal model, and considerably more unified than the set of concepts into which the secularized components of that model have devolved. These alternatives thus satisfy the criterion of metaphorical unity in a manner that our inherited concepts, in this post-sacerdotal age, do not.

Chapter 2 suggested that the most useful way to conceptualize modern government is not as a human body, nor as a three- or four-branched tree, but as a multilevel network of interconnected units. At the lowest level of the network, the units are individuals: at the highest, for all practical purposes, they are nations, although multinational institutions have begun to acquire the organizational integrity that might justify adding a still higher level. Between these levels lie agencies, sub-agencies, and offices, the institutional machinery through which modern government generally functions. Each unit, at each level, can be conceived as possessing an internal program of some sort, a program that is either imposed by an external unit, often at a higher level of the network, or that emerges from the actions of the units themselves. These units receive inputs of various kinds and transform them into outputs by virtue of their program. The inputs can be received from any level; the unit can scale up or scale down the input in producing its output, it can sum two or more inputs, it can feed its output back into itself as an additional input, or send it to another unit at any level of the network.

This familiar, contemporary, and naive heuristic describes the structural aspect of contemporary government's internal organization. The three-branch image fails to accommodate the administrative apparatus, generates a normative preference for separation of the branches that cannot be currently maintained, and casts suspicion on the ordinary process of administrative government by characterizing it as a delegation of legislative, executive, or judicial power. The network image eliminates these anti-administrative implications by presenting all units of government as presumptively capable of interacting with each other to implement affirmative governmental policies. It thereby corresponds more fully to our current emotional commitments, which demand an administrative regime. Because it is free of enticing historical associations, it announces its heuristic character. In addition, it facilitates microanalysis, encouraging us to trace the exact connections between the various governmental units and assess them, both normatively and descriptively, in a realistic fashion.

This very same network model also provides a preferable way to describe the animate aspect of government's internal organization. Our current description, which relies on power and discretion, suggests the paleolithic idea that power is an indwelling force or a personal possession, and the medieval idea that it consists of an exercise of will that overcomes the countervailing will of others. The proposed alternative describes relations among government officials in terms of the actions they are authorized to perform and the type of supervision under which they function. This is a direct outgrowth of the same network model where the design of each unit states its authorized functions, many of its outputs involve the supervision of subordinates, and many of its inputs constitute supervision by superiors. The actual experience of public officials in an administrative state consists of being authorized to implement a particular task, of supervising their subordinates to accomplish that task, and of being supervised by their superiors, not of being infused with some force of higher origin, or bending others to their sovereign will.

Again, the network model provides a description that satisfies the stated criteria more fully. Although the terms 'power' and 'discretion' may warn us that government is a potential threat to liberty, they fail to indicate that its affirmative actions are essential to our way of life, and specifically to our security and prosperity. In other words, government is not a hostile opponent of its citizens, as power and discretion suggest, but an instrumentality that essentially, albeit dangerously, implements their collective desires. The network model also reminds us that it is a heuristic for depicting complex relationships, whereas power and discretion are regularly treated as real entities in legal and political science scholarship. Finally, the model facilitates a microanalysis of the precise relationship between various officials, for whom their job assignment and their relationship to supervisors and subordinates constitute essential aspects of their role.

In terms of the government's structural relationship with its citizens or subjects, the concept of an interactive republic, which has been proposed to replace the term 'democracy,' is also derived from the network model. In place of the Hellenic notion that people are supposed to rule themselves, it focuses on the actual relationship between the units of the governmental network and the units of society. Again, the issue is the design of the governmental units, the inputs they receive and the outputs they produce. In the area that is currently described by the term 'democracy,' some inputs, generated by elections, come from the citizenry in general and determine the identity of public officials. Others come from organizations of various kinds and are sent to either legislative or administrative units. The quantity and effect of these inputs and the government outputs that they generate strongly affects the government's responsiveness to its citizens' desires.

While democracy has become the world's most widespread slogan, the implications of the term are quite remote from our genuine commitments. Few people really want to rule themselves, and still fewer would abandon the security and prosperity provided by the mass administrative state for the uncertain augmentation of their liberty that self-rule might secure. What people are genuinely committed to is a professional but responsive government, a chance to vote for leading government officials, and to influence leading and subordinate officials in a few areas of special interest. The network model captures these commitments. At the same time, it avoids the reification that the term 'democracy' invites, and facilitates microanalysis of the interactions between government and citizens. In place of vague generalities and fugitive images of a bygone era, it offers a framework for describing the precise ways in which citizens control and influence their governments at any level. It neither exalts elections nor denigrates lobbying and negotiation with administrators, but enables us to understand the complexities and consequences of each mode of interaction.

Finally, the animate aspect of government's relationship with its citizens, now described in terms of legitimacy, is preferably described by a compliance model that is also derived from the image of an interacting network. Legitimacy suggests some external approbation or imprimatur

CONCLUSION TO PART I

for government, either descending from a transcendental source or ascending from the populace. But this description, which applies to total obedience or outright rebellion, is relevant primarily to a pre-modern state whose essential responsibility was civil order. An administrative state achieves civil order readily, but it confronts its citizens with a vast array of rules and regulations to which they respond with varying levels of obedience. The compliance model captures this relationship by depicting the intersection between government and society in terms of network interactions. Units in society receive specific governmental outputs as their own inputs and process them into outputs that reflect varying levels of compliance. At the individual level, these outputs depend on a program composed of self-interest, loyalty, cooperation, and concurrence. At higher levels of organization, such as business firms, the outputs can be analyzed as the aggregate of individual responses.

This description avoids the term 'legitimacy,' which is so frequently treated as a real entity rather than the heuristic that it is. It also avoids outdated ideas of promise keeping, and outdated implications that government is sacrosanct or sacerdotal. Instead, it captures our dynamic, flexible relationship with modern government, where we evaluate its performance on a continuing basis and base our willingness to comply on its ongoing ability to meet our needs. This model, moreover, facilitates microanalysis of specific government initiatives, thus revealing the crucial issue of compliance levels, and explaining why generally loyal citizens disobey particular commands.

In short, the alternatives suggested for the now disjointed elements of current political theory form a unified image, as unified as the sacerdotal image that prevailed in the Middle Ages. Considered individually, each element satisfies the stated criteria for a preferable description. Taken together, they are additionally preferable because they are the same image, and thus fit together intuitively, and without resort to complex, unconvincing explanations. This is not surprising, of course; the reason our existing descriptions of the structural and animate aspects of the government's organization, and of its relations with its citizens, no longer mesh is that they do not describe contemporary government. Rather, they describe previous governments, and have evolved, or been adjusted, in the effort to adapt them to a world that they were never intended to inhabit. The network model, in contrast, is our own, drawn from current conceptions and based on current realities.

That model, moreover, liberates us from the medieval, sacerdotally based concern with the conceptual origins of government. As everyone knows these days, and no one has seriously questioned since David Hume, society was not pre-planned or agreed upon. It evolved, over centuries and millennia, through the efforts of people who knew what they needed, but not where they were headed. And what is false as history is otiose as either conceptual modeling or moral theory. We do not need to explain the original source of power, nor do we need to justify our government in terms of a hypothesized consent to surrender one's hypothesized liberty. The felt need for such myths or origin is merely a remnant of the sacerdotal model, and the construction of imagined origins only breeds confusion. Government, and our political system generally, is a reality in which each person finds herself immersed. It resembles, or is most usefully conceptualized, as a vast interacting network, ever-changing, extending backward and forward in time. It can be understood by microanalysis of its current status, and evaluated according to our present commitments, without reference to its imagined origins. An inquiry into the actual origins of society is interesting, and perhaps edifying, but hardly decisive as a basis for either explaining or evaluating the ongoing operation of our complex modern state.

As we move from a sacerdotal to an instrumental conception of government, highlighted by the network model, the moral locus shifts from past to future. Politics no longer appears as the elaboration of some initial premise, divine spark, or pre-political agreement, but as an ongoing process that generates new meanings and commitments. It is no longer a product of our essential and unchanging human nature, but an adventure of self-development and political evolution. Government is revealed as an instrumentality by which we not only implement our current values, but transform ourselves by virtue of the way those values become manifest. Our current commitments to equality, or freedom of religion, were as unimaginable in the Middle Ages as the airplane or the Internet, but, while that newness might have made them suspect then, it does not do so now. Of course, a certain courage is required to cast oneself into this swift-flowing current of continuous social change—and it should be conceived as an electric current, not a river—but that is exactly the virtue that we need as we go forward, as we must, into a new millennium.

Part II

LEGAL OPERATIONS

Six

From Law to Policy and Implementation

Law and Regularity

Natural Law

PART I discussed the way that government is organized, that is, the tectonic and affective aspects of its internal design and its relationship with citizens. This part discusses the way that structure operates, that is, the way modern government performs its functions. To discuss the entire range of functions that a modern administrative state performs, however, would be an overwhelming task, and not necessarily a productive one. Many governmental actions, in areas such as diplomacy, espionage, war, internal operations, and the management of institutions, are relatively free of the premodern concepts that constitute the subject matter of this study. Instead, Part II focuses on the large area of governmental operations that is conventionally identified as the legal system, an area where such pre-modern concepts run rampant. The distinction between legal and nonlegal, and, indeed, between structure and operations, is highly porous, but these terms are being used in an uninformative sense. They are not intended to yield any conclusions or to sustain any pre-analytic assumption that the topics covered under these rubrics are organically related to each other or distinguishable from others. Rather, any resemblances or differences that exist must be determined by analysis. The purpose of the term 'legal' is simply to identify the area of governmental operations where pre-modern concepts that are traditionally identified as legal are employed, and then to pursue the thought experiment of bracketing these concepts and replacing them with alternatives more consonant with the realities of the administrative state.

Although the legal system of our modern state, as traditionally defined, is complex, contemporary discussion of its general aspects tends to focus on two essential concepts—law and rights. In ordinary English usage, law is an amphibious creature with two separate meanings. First, it refers to government rules that control the conduct of citizens, rules that are typically regarded as subordinate to the political decisions that establish general policies. Second, it refers to rules, sometimes of extra-governmental origin, that control the leading government officials, limiting the policies that they are able to establish and the means that they may use to enforce them.[1] George Fletcher points out that most European languages other than English distinguish between these two usages. In German, law in the sense of rules is called *Gesetz*, while law in the sense of overarching principles is called *Recht*; in French, the terms are *loi* and *droit*.[2] English thus appears impoverished, like the language of a tropical tribe that fails to distinguish among snow, sleet, and hail. On the other hand, even if different words were to be used to describe these two concepts, the same scholars study them and address them as part of the same general subject. Consequently, any comprehensive consideration of the legal system in a modern administrative state must deal with both meanings of the term 'law.'

The term 'rights' typically refers to claims that individuals can assert on the basis of some legal principle or rule. Rights are regarded as coming in two separate forms, reflecting the two different kinds of law. Those based on the government's positive enactments, that is, the law designed to control citizens, are generally called legal rights. Those based on overarching principles that control government officials are generally called human rights. This first chapter in Part II considers the concept of law, the second chapter considers the concept of legal rights, and the third considers the concept of human rights. The final chapter then focuses on the right of private property, which is both legal and human in conception, and which raises concerns uniquely relevant to the administrative state. It will be argued that the concepts of law, legal rights, human rights, and property rights all derive from pre-modern notions of governance that no longer apply to our modern context, and that we could describe and manage our contemporary legal system better if we bracketed these terms and sought alternative descriptions.

Unlike the structural concepts discussed in the preceding part—the three branches, power, discretion, democracy, and legitimacy—the concept of law is explicitly recognized as having been transformed by the advent of the administrative state. Indeed, Weber, Habermas, Luhmann, and many others treat this transformation as a defining feature of the administrative state's emergence.[3] Their basic claim is that law has become positive; whereas it was previously regarded as the product of God or of tradition, it is now a conscious creation of political officials. But if such a transformation has occurred, how do we know that the positive law of the administrative state bears any significant relationship to the God-given or traditional law of its predecessor? What are we asserting when we use the same term to describe these distinguishable concepts? The question generates quasi-Cartesian doubt, leading us to wonder whether a pre-modern concept is being projected forward into the modern world, or whether a modern concept is being projected back into the traditional one, in order to establish the identity of the two. To determine whether this doubt is sufficiently serious to consider bracketing such a familiar concept as law, the meaning of the concept must be explored in greater detail.

In the pre-modern era, most legal thinkers, whether they were philosophers such as St. Thomas or treatise writers such as Gratian, connected law with reason.[4] Natural and human law are not merely a set of commands that govern human conduct, according to this view, but display a deeper regularity, a regularity analogous to that of the physical world. The physical world obviously exists independently of humans—having been created by God—but humans can perceive and understand it with their God-given faculties. These faculties will only provide access to the reality of the physical world if that world is constructed in a manner that allows them to do so, but, of course, that is what God has ordained. Similarly, the moral order exists independently of human beings, but they can understand it with their God-given mental faculties, specifically the faculty of reason. Reason will only provide access to the objective moral order if that order is so constructed that it is accessible to reason, and here too God has so ordained it through His eternal law.[5] That is why natural law can be discerned by human reason, and what St. Thomas meant when he said that natural law was promulgated by having been inscribed in every person's mind.[6]

In order to be accessible to reason, natural law must possess an essential coherence or regularity; its various provisions must fit together in a manner that can be described as logical. Were they not so connected, were they merely a set of separate rules promulgated by God's will, they could not be perceived by reason, but only by faith or revelation. The underlying conception is best conveyed by a popular T-shirt that reads: "Gravity: It's not just a good idea—it's the law." When we say that something is not just a good idea but the law, we are referring to a human artifact. Gravity is not a law in this sense, but a regularity of the physical world,[7] and the joke lies in describing this physical reality as an ordinary legal enactment.[8] But to St. Thomas, his contemporaries, and his successors for some five centuries to follow, this was not a joke at all. Moral precepts and physical descriptions were both law in roughly the same sense; they were regularities of the external world that were accessible to human perception and reason because they were so structured by God through His eternal law.[9]

With the exception of the London fishmonger who wrote *The Mirror of the Justices*,[10] no medieval legal writer believed that all actual laws could be directly derived from natural law.[11] According to St. Thomas's sophisticated and vastly influential formulation, human law, whether statutory, adjudicatory, or customary, was the product of secular decision making.[12] Nonetheless, St. Thomas argued, it comported with the natural law that God established and it displayed a related regularity.[13] The product of reason, human law represented an elaboration of its divinely ordained template. In the case of customary law, these regularities were established by the reason God had instilled in every human being; since this law was the product of many people's actions, over long periods of time, it reflected the cumulation of such reasoned efforts.[14] In the case of statutory or adjudicatory law, the internal coherence and the congruence with natural law resulted from the lawmaker's reason, again instilled by God.[15] Thus, the relationship among customary law, enacted law, and moral precepts did not seem as conflictual to St. Thomas as it appears to most contemporary scholars.[16] This irenic balance was achieved, however, by simply ignoring a multitude of budgetary, military, administrative, and genuinely reformist actions taken by the ruling monarchs of the day. The monarchs, and society in general, cooperated with St. Thomas to achieve this result by characterizing these actions as something other than law.[17]

The same belief in the universal applicability of reason, and the resulting regularity within and between the different types of law, enabled St. Thomas to link two other elements that do not appear conflictual to modern scholars because we link them still. This is the law's amphibious character, its role as a set of rules governing human conduct that are enforced by the sovereign and its role as a constraint on the sovereign himself. Natural law applies to everyone, whether ruler or subject.[18] Human law, derived from natural law by practical reason, displays this same universal applicability.[19] Because of the way human societies are governed, the sovereign can enforce the law against the subjects, but no one can enforce it against the sovereign. This creates a practical problem, which legal theorists generally sidestepped, but it does not alter the universal applicability of law.[20] St. Thomas's concept of a law as an internally coherent system, based on reason, thus explains the amphibious quality of law as a means of governance and a constraint on government.[21]

The idea of laws to which the sovereign voluntarily submits may seem like a pious fantasy at present, but it did not seem so in St. Thomas's time.[22] After all, it was not only the kings whose subjection to the law was voluntary. In large parts of Europe, barons, or even lesser nobles, could only be tried in a royal court if they agreed to the court's jurisdiction, a situation that had been even more widespread two or three centuries earlier.[23] Moreover, self-enforcing bodies of law or rules were common. The Benedictine Rule that governed many medieval monasteries was, in part, an administrative provision backed by Church authority, but included many instructions about personal humility, solitary prayer, and spiritual attitudes that could not be externally enforced.[24] The Code of Love, a set of judgments in legal form embodying the romantic sensibility of the era and possibly promulgated by informal groups of aristocratic women, could only have been conceived as self-enforcing.[25] The rules of chivalry, governing the battlefield behavior and personal comportment of the nobility, possessed the same self-enforcing character.[26] The ubiquity of self-enforcing

were so deeply felt by those they governed—so deeply internalized, to use our modern parlance—that they were perceived as truly natural. Although secular in origin, they seemed to be inscribed in the order of the universe itself, and to possess the logic and comprehensibility that was attributed to God's creation.

Natural Law and Modern Theory

In St. Thomas's work, God acts simultaneously by exercising His will and by establishing an autonomously operating system of reason. The two are equivalent because of eternal law, the system of reason by which God governs the universe. Later thinkers, who favored naturalistic explanations, were readily able to separate the two bases of action that St. Thomas had so assiduously joined without making many other changes in his theory of law. Once the supernatural order of eternal and divine law were removed from the upper part of St. Thomas's gigantic fresco, there remained a realistic, finely drawn depiction of natural and human law that, with a little brushing up, and the addition of perspective, was entirely appealing to seventeenth- and eighteenth-century thinkers. According to this redacted picture, natural law was the product of human reason and was thus apparent to anyone who followed the classical—or Thomist—ideal of living in accordance with such reason, whether or not that person was following the will of God. Many of the greatest legal thinkers of this era, including Grotius, Pufendorf, and Christian Wolff, adopted this position, and devoted their efforts to demonstrating that a comprehensive body of detailed human laws could be derived from the desanctified natural law that was based on reason.[38] As Thomas Browne explained. "Thus are there two books from whence I collect my divinity: besides that written one of God, another of his servant nature, that universal and public manuscript that lies expansed unto the eyes of all. Those that never saw him in the one have discovered him in the other."[39] It was because natural law was linked to human reason that it could be treated as a universal set of rules infusing public life with a sense of collective purpose and shared belief, and thus survive the demise of the religious unity that characterized the Middle Ages.[40]

According to most contemporary observers, however, natural law has now been replaced by positive law, and this positivization of law represents one of the crucial stages in the modern world's emergence from its medieval antecedents.[41] The transition is generally viewed as having occurred during the last part of the eighteenth century and the first part of the nineteenth, with the promulgation and widespread adoption of the Napoleonic Code[42] and of similar codes in Austria and Prussia.[43] The newly formed United States did not engage in any similar codification, but Morton Horwitz has documented a parallel development in its judge-made law. During this same period of time, he observes, American judges stopped justifying their decisions in natural law terms and switched to social policy. They "came to think of the common law as equally responsible with legislation for governing society and promoting socially desirable conduct."[44] To be sure, a number of contemporary scholars have championed natural law, including Randy Barnett, John Finnis, Robert George, Martin Golding, Heidi Hurd, Alasdair MacIntyre, Jacques Maritain, Michael Moore, Henry Veatch, and Lloyd Weinreb,[45] but they generally cast their work as a proposed revival, and acknowledge that their views oppose the prevailing mode of legal thought.

The concept of law as a coherent body of rules accessible to reason is not defunct, however. It lives on in the very same legal codes that supposedly displaced it, as well as in the thinking of most leading jurisprudentialists. With respect to legal codes, the sacerdotal concept of law persists in the view that regularity is not merely one of many virtues that a code might display, but the cardinal virtue, and that any code that cannot lay claim to it should be counted as a failure. European codifiers have dutifully advanced this claim to regularity on behalf of their work product, although they can do so only by resorting to distortion.[46] This insistence on the regularity of codes manifests itself in the European approach to judicial interpretation. It is obvious that no code can provide an explicit answer to every particular situation that arises under it, and that the language of the code must be interpreted to address unanticipated problems. But European jurists, particularly in France, have long maintained that all these problems can be resolved by reason, specifically by the logical extrapolation of the code's explicit language, without reliance on creative interpretation or judicial precedent.[47] Even in England, which not only has no comprehensive code but is the mother of the common law, judges maintain the same view with respect to specialized statutes.[48] Admittedly, this unwillingness to recognize judicial gap-filling is partially motivated by a political commitment to parliamentary supremacy,[49] but such determined insensibility would not be possible, it would not make any sense, without a conceptual belief in the underlying regularity of general codes or specialized statutes.

A more serious problem induced by our continued reliance on the concept of law is that the insistent belief in the regularity of codes or statutes can only be preserved if the code or statute is limited to rules regulating traditional legal subject matter. As J. B. Ruhl, James Salzman, and Peter Schuck point out, the administrative state has led to an explosive growth in the number and complexity of governmental rules.[50] The mass of detailed, technical, policy-driven statutes and regulations that administrative agencies enforce could not plausibly be regarded as exhibiting the regularity that remains central to the concept of law. As a result, the claim to, or demand for, legal regularity has banished all these administrative statutes and regulations to the vaguely charted frontiers of the legal realm. Although they are often more important, in their impact upon business, education, housing, health care, and the environment, than court-enforced provisions, they continue to be regarded as peripheral. Few comprehensive efforts have been made to organize them, to help businesses and individuals find their way through their complexities, to indicate which ones are relevant to specific social actions, to make them user-friendly or, as William Buzbee points out, to ensure that their coverage is comprehensive.[51] Great energy continues to be lavished on civil and criminal codes, while the more important, more complex, and enormously more massive body of administratively enforced statutes and regulations remains a disorganized and relatively impenetrable mass.

The same tendency to treat law as a coherent body of rules accessible to reason can be discerned in the work of contemporary legal theorists. Consider, for example, the most influential formulation of positivism, and perhaps the most influential theory of law in the English-speaking world, H.L.A. Hart's *The Concept of Law*.[52] The core of this work is the criticism that Hart offers of John Austin's and Hans Kelsen's positivist view that law is nothing more than the commands of the sovereign that are backed by sanctions.[53] But his criticism fails to confront the most basic difficulty with positivism, namely, that it is dominated by the same commitment to regularity and coherence as the natural law theory it is designed to refute. The reason for Hart's failure is that his own approach is also afflicted with this difficulty and thus cannot confront the reality of the administrative state.

First, Hart argues that the Austin-Kelsen formulation distorts law "as the price of uniformity";[54] law does not merely instruct officials to impose sanctions, but also instructs citizens how to behave. To describe law exclusively in terms of sanctions is like saying that the rules of baseball direct umpires to make declarations about the actions of some people running around on a field, rather than directing players how to play a game whose basic principles they understand.[55] For example, a law providing that "no vehicle may be taken into the park'[56] is not merely intended as an instruction to public officials; it also tells citizens not to drive their cars down the paths or across the grass.[57] But Hart's idea that the law tells citizens how to behave suffers from the same defect as the Austin-Kelsen definition of law as commands. Both theories fail to account for a large proportion of our actual laws, specifically those that are distinctive features of a modern administrative state. Just as St. Thomas and his contemporaries excluded royal legislation from their concept of law, Hart excludes administratively oriented legislation from that concept.

Hart's law against driving in the park fits the traditional model of an instruction to citizens regarding their individual behavior. But how did the park get there in the first place? This was not a particularly important question for a traditional state, which generally did not establish public parks, but it is central to an administrative government, which not only creates and operates parks, but also schools, universities, libraries, museums, airports, train lines, bus lines, prisons, hospitals, clinics, fire stations, hazardous waste dumps, oil storage facilities, research stations, wildlife refuges, housing projects, welfare offices, job-training programs, drug rehabilitation facilities, and neighborhood youth anti-drug, alcohol, and violence counseling centers. The park, and these other facilities, came into existence because some legislative body passed what we ordinarily call a law. That law, however, does not instruct citizens how to behave; instead, it provides services to citizens by creating public institutions.

Another type of statute that is characteristic of the administrative state, and that also falls outside Hart's conception of law, as well as Austin's and Kelsen's, is one that provides monetary or various in-kind benefits to citizens—income support, medical expenses, disability payments, veterans payments, vouchers, retirement income, disaster relief, or mass injury compensation. These statutes are not designed to control citizen conduct but to transfer resources to meet citizen needs. The distribution of benefits to the blind, for example, is intended to give blind people money, not to encourage blindness; the distribution of social security is not intended to encourage people to grow old, or even to stop saving on their own. Still a third type of statute that Austin, Kelsen, and Hart fail to consider is an appropriations bill, an allocation of the state's fiscal resources. All governments make such appropriations, but the process has become more important since the abolition of particularized fees and the creation of a centralized budget that occurred at the tipping point of the administrative state. The appropriations bill is always one of the most important pieces of legislation in any session of the U.S. Congress, and, in the absence of epochal legislation like the Civil Rights Act or the Clean Air Act, often the most important. Yet no jurisprudential theory of law, and certainly not Hart's, Austin's, or Kelsen's, takes account of such a statute.

Hart's second criticism of Austin and Kelsen reveals a similar unwillingness to confront the realities of a modern administrative state. The positivist claim that law consists of commands backed by sanctions, Hart argues, applies only imperfectly to rules that instruct public officials such as judges to fulfill certain roles, or that authorize private parties to take action such as making wills or contracts. Hart describes these as power-conferring rules,[58] and argues that Austin and Kelsen force such rules into a Procrustean bed of their positivist theory at the expense of plausibility. Neither rules conferring jurisdiction on government agents nor rules authorizing private parties to take binding legal action, he argues, are accurately described as orders backed by sanctions. But Hart's characterization of these rules as power-conferring has forced the multiplicity of intra-governmental communications into a Procrustean bed of its own. As discussed in Chapter 3, power is an atavistic term for a set of relationships that are more accurately analyzed in terms of authorization and supervision. Statutes are only one mechanism by which government officials are authorized and supervised. There are numerous other signals, including guidelines, suggestions, advice, information, and disapproval that fulfill precisely the same function. To cordon off one type of authorization and supervision from the others by describing it as law, and then to combine it with qualitatively different actions such as regulating citizen behavior, makes a strong assertion with no obvious justification.

Moreover, even if one ignores the difficulties with the term 'power,' describing intra-governmental provisions as power conferring suffers from the same artificiality that Hart condemns. In discussing contract law, which he describes as conferring rule-making power on private citizens, Hart rejects the idea that this law can be characterized as imposing the sanction of non-enforcement for failure to follow the specified rules. The law is not designed to sanction people, Hart argues, but to grant them the capacity to take legally binding action. If that is true, however, then it is surely true that most statutes creating institutions, providing benefits, or allocating fiscal resources are not designed to confer power on government officials but to grant them the capacity to provide government services to citizens. The creation of a public school is intended to educate children, not to employ or empower principals and teachers; the distribution of welfare benefits is intended to distribute money to the poor, not to create a welfare bureaucracy. The grant of power, like the limits on citizen behavior, is incidental to the service.

Hart's leading jurisprudential adversary is Ronald Dworkin, but Dworkin's approach to law is equally beholden to pre-modern, natural law–related concepts of regularity. Dworkin's theory of judicial decision making holds that law consists of general principles as well as specific rules.[59] He then asserts, contrary to the view of most other legal scholars, including Hart,[60] that there are definitive answers to all legal issues. To be sure, some issues are hard cases that rules cannot resolve, but definitive answers can be found by referring to general principles embedded in our system of law. These principles can be applied to specific cases by treating law as possessing the virtue of integrity. Dworkin defines integrity as a conceptual framework that "instructs judges to identify legal rights and duties, so far as possible, on the assumption that they were all created by a single author—the community personified—expressing a coherent conception of justice and fairness."[61] Judges might also decide hard cases by invoking social policy considerations, but that is a mistake, in Dworkin's view, because it represents an excursion beyond the limits of the law, an excursion that is both unjustified and, given the presence of embedded legal principles, unnecessary.

Although heavily criticized, this theory does succeed in embodying the aspiration of many American legal scholars to reconcile governmental action and law. For present purposes, the important point is that Dworkin's notion of integrity is virtually a restatement of the natural law conception that all law forms a coherent conceptual system that is accessible to reason.[62] Dworkin can plausibly advance this position because his idea of law centers on the judiciary, and takes adjudication as its modal action. His grandly titled book, *Law's Empire*, begins: "It matters how judges decide cases."[63] About midway through the book, however, after introducing his principle of integrity, it occurs to him that the modern legal system involves a great deal of statutory drafting as well as adjudication, and that the provisions that result from statutory drafting compose a large proportion of modern law. He then attempts to apply his natural-law derived theory of adjudication to the drafting process, or more generally, to the policy making process that defines the essence of the administrative state.[64] Legislatures, Dworkin argues, also strive to instantiate the principle of integrity. After all, they do not reach compromises between contending political forces by making arbitrary distinctions. We think it unacceptable, for example, to resolve a political conflict about racial discrimination by forbidding it on buses but permitting it in restaurants, or a conflict about abortion by criminalizing it for pregnant women born in even-number years but not for women born in odd ones. The rejection of such "checkerboard" statutes, Dworkin argues, demonstrates that the principle of integrity applies to drafting statutes or, presumably, although he makes no mention of it, to drafting administrative regulations, just as it applies to judicial decision making.[65]

Even if what Dworkin says were true, it would fail to prove his point. The fact that legislative or administrative drafters seek to achieve integrity only indicates that this is one of their values, one criterion for determining whether their efforts are successful. There are obviously other criteria, such as whether the statute achieves its basic purpose of providing security, prosperity, or liberty in a fair and efficient manner. But Dworkin's claim about the legislative process is not true; legislative and administrative drafters regularly enact arbitrary compromises between contending forces. This occurs, for example, nearly every time a number is selected for a statutory rule. Consumer groups want customer liability capped at fifty dollars, while banks want unlimited liability, so the statute sets liability at five hundred dollars.[66] What drafters rarely enact, however, are insane compromises, like Dworkin's checkerboard statutes. The problem with such statutes is not that they lack integrity, but that they lack any reasonable relation to the policy that the drafters are trying to achieve. If some people oppose abortion and others favor it, there is simply no sense in forbidding it to an arbitrarily defined group of women and permitting it for others. Rather, the drafters will settle on some compromise related to the substance of the disagreement, such as permitting abortions only in the first trimester, or requiring anti-abortion counseling before the procedure can be performed. The reason Dworkin thinks that the problem with checkerboard statutes is their lack of integrity is because he ignores the policy-making aspect of the modern state. Having declared that judges should not engage in policy making—a questionable but conventional assertion—he seems to forget that the same prohibition cannot possibly be extended to legislators and administrators. As a result, he loses track of the distinction between totally arbitrary compromises that seem unacceptable to everyone and sensible compromises, related to the underlying policy debate, that seem unacceptable only to Ronald Dworkin. In the final analysis, Dworkin's approach to law is heavily judicialized. It is at least two centuries out of date, but, like Hart's outdated view, it allows him to sustain his nostalgia-driven claim that the legal system should be governed by the inherited principle of conceptual coherence.

Policy and Implementation

Policy and Implementation as an Alternative to Law

The foregoing considerations suggest that we should bracket the concept of law, that we should suspend its claim to describe some aspect of our society in a useful or convincing way and explore the possibility of an alternative description. This alternative can be derived from the unified image of the administrative state that was presented in Part I. The governmental actions to which the concept of law refers can be characterized as signals that flow from governmental units to other governmental units or to units outside government. Various aspects of such signals have already been discussed, including their role in creating the government's internal structure (Chapters 2 and 3), and the willingness of private parties to conform to their requirements (Chapter 5). The concern here, and in the remainder of this part, is with the purpose, or meaning, of these signals. In essence, they are the mechanism by which government formulates and implements its policies, or, more precisely, the way government officials carry out their assigned role, as they conceive it. Thus, the bracketed concept of law can be replaced, in the administrative state, with the alternative concept of policy and implementation.

Bracketing the concept of law, it should be recalled, only means that this concept will not be used as an analytic category in describing modern gov-

ernment. No effort is being made to extirpate the term 'law' from the English language. Thus, it would be awkward to refer to the body of judge-
made rules that create and implement policy in various fields as anything
other than the Common Law (a term that will be capitalized from here
on). More obviously still, no effort will be made to rename antitrust law,
lawyers, law school, or the LSAT. The point is not to purify the language,
or to joust with definitions, but to identify useful ways of describing the
features of the administrative state that has become our all-encompassing
political reality.

   The division of the governmental actions into policy making and implementation captures that reality; in fact, it parallels the bipartite conception
of rationality that Weber identified as the essential feature of the bureaucratic state.[67] Each policy can be regarded as a goal, or end, that can be
evaluated by means of values rationality, while its implementation can be
regarded as the means, or mechanism, to which instrumental rationality
applies. Taken together, policy and implementation thus constitute the full
range of governmental action in a modern state. Despite this comprehensive quality, the terms, being nothing more than heuristics, must be used
with caution. Weber states that the formulation of goals through cost-
benefit analysis can constitute a form of instrumental rationality.[68] Hebert
Simon points out that the characterization of actions as policy making or
implementation is not absolute, but changes according to the institutional
context; that is, a means for a particular governmental unit may become an
end for its subordinate.[69]

   Recharacterizing the bracketed concept of law as policy and implementation offers a number of descriptive advantages. It connects legal scholarship with scholarship in other fields, it comports with the character of the
administrative state, and it encompasses the full range of actions that the
government takes in carrying out its functions. To begin with the connection between legal scholarship and scholarship in other fields, the categories of policy and implementation are central to modern political science
research about the functions of government. Policy making is featured in
the work of Steven Kelman, Charles Lindblom, Nelson Polsby, Herbert
Simon, Edith Stokey, Richard Zeckhauser, Aaron Wildavsky, and others.[70]
Implementation has become a subject of discussion more recently, as described in Chapter 5, but has achieved similar importance through the efforts of scholars such as Ian Ayres, Eugene Bardach, John Braithwaite,
Cary Coglianese, Keith Hawkins, Robert Kagan, John Scholz, and Wildavsky.[71] In fact, only rational choice scholars, who regard governmental
action as the result of individual efforts to secure personal advantage, have
consistently rejected the characterization of governmental action in policy
and implementation terms.[72] Even within this tradition, the policy and implementation approach has gradually appeared through positive political

theory, which treats institutions as single actors intent on achieving emergent goals.[73]

Legal scholars have long recognized that the continuing vitality and relevance of their field depends upon connecting it with other disciplines.
Recharacterizing law in policy and implementation terms facilitates this
connection by coordinating the discourse of legal scholarship with the political science approach to government. In fact, policy and implementation
has become a central concern for administrative law scholars such as Ronald
Cass, Colin Diver, Jody Freeman, Thomas McGarity, Mark Seidenfeld,
Peter Strauss, and Cass Sunstein.[74] But the concept of law, and the sense
that law is a distinctive category of governmental action in a modern state,
has operated as an impediment to all these efforts. As Brian Tamanaha
points out, the question "What is law?" continues to hover over interdisciplinary studies.[75] Much energy has been expended on the dubious assumption that the question has an answer, and that the answer will yield
valuable insights of some sort. Once law is bracketed, this inquiry can be
set aside, and the intellectual tools that have been developed during the
past century of social science research can be applied to the legal system as
part of a continuous field with the remainder of the social realm. This does
not mean that legal scholarship must abandon its distinctively prescriptive
stance, its efforts to recommend better rules and strategies to government
decision makers.[76] Rather, what it means is that these prescriptions can
draw more comfortably on social science and be applied wherever they are
justified by their own force, without being encumbered by the sense that
legal scholars are straying outside their field, or that they must define the
areas that they address as law.

Beyond its ability to facilitate the connection between legal and social
science scholarship, the recharacterization of law as policy and implementation provides a benefit for scholars in all fields because it comports with
the character of the modern administrative state. In pre-modern Europe,
government in its entirety was regarded as predominantly judicial; its purpose was to discern and apply the eternal verities that were conceived in
terms of natural law.[77] The transition to the administrative state replaced
this model with a policy-making approach. The articulation of purpose
that constitutes part of this transition means that government actions are
no longer being justified by tradition, or linked to natural law, but instead
are being viewed as conscious efforts to achieve specific goals that are publicly identified as social policy. As Bronwen Morgan suggests, these policy
efforts are a form of "non-judicial legality" grounded on regulatory and
governance strategies.[78] Modern government is eudaemonic; it exists to
solve social and economic problems, to provide citizens with an optimal
material environment, and to facilitate their individualized self-fulfillment.
The implementation of public policy is the mechanism by which this en-

terprise is carried out. Replacing law with policy and implementation thus reflects the shift from a sacerdotal to an instrumental conception of the state.

Finally, the concept of policy and implementation encompasses the broader range of governmental actions that characterize the modern state's effort to achieve its eudaemonic goals. This is true whether one considers the mode of discourse that government signals employ or the governance function that they fulfill. With respect to mode of discourse, our standard concept of law as a coherent set of rules governing private conduct has traditionally induced legal scholars to focus their attention on performative governmental signals, and more specifically on the subset of these signals that constitute commands.[79] The style of governance that results is typically described as command and control regulation. Emphasis on this approach has placed other types of signals outside the boundary of law, where they are often left uncategorized, and either ignored or condemned for their unlawlike character. In recent years, however, a different approach to the administrative process, sometimes described as New Public Governance, has drawn attention to the rich variety of signals that are found in modern government.[80] Very often, a superior influences or controls the actions of its subordinates by performative signals such as suggestions, guidelines, or judgments, rather than by command.[81] Almost invariably, the subordinate influences its superiors by these means.[82] Within government, this process contributes to the complex relationship between both hierarchically connected and unconnected units that is described in Chapter 3. Between government and citizens, it contributes to the interaction between regulated parties, other interest groups, and regulators described in Chapter 4. As those chapters also indicate, informative statements and judgments are equally important. Given that people are only boundedly rational, their access to information often determines the quality of their decisions and their capacity to affect the behavior of others. Subtle indications of approval or disapproval are often the best way to induce compliance, or to calibrate the precise effect that governmental officials are trying to achieve in a complex situation. There is no reason to assume that all these expressive, informative, and noncommand performative signals are less important than commands, particularly in the fluid, continuous, and comprehensive context of administrative governance. The matter should be determined by analysis, and our conceptual framework should encourage that analysis, rather than prejudging or precluding it.

With respect to the range of governance functions, the concept of policy and implementation is also substantially broader than law because it accommodates important governmental actions that do not control citizen conduct, and thus appear unlawlike in character. As Neil Komesar and Peter Schuck point out, government can sometimes achieve its goals by leaving their implementation to other mechanisms of control, such as social norms or the market, and perhaps support these mechanisms with informative or expressive signals.[83] When government acts directly, moreover, it often does so by creating an institution such as a park or other facility, by distributing benefits, or by allocating resources through an appropriations bill. Thus law, as we use the term, seems applicable only to that subset of governmental activities that attempts to achieve policy goals through the mechanism of generally stated rules, an important but far from exclusive approach in modern government.

Even when the government acts through rules, those rules are often part of the gigantic mass of technical, hyper-detailed regulations generated by administrative agencies. Literally speaking, they count as law, but they are not the sort of law that jurisprudential theories of the subject call to mind. In fact, judicial decisions, government's most quintessentially legal actions, are no longer particularly lawlike in the modern administrative state. To begin with, as Judith Resnik notes, judges increasingly avoid handing down decisions at all, preferring to settle cases in order to manage their massive dockets.[84] Moreover, because complex institutions are often involved, the opinions they do issue tend to produce their effects by initiating an ongoing dialogue, or generating indirect and subtle crosscurrents, rather than by declaration or ukase. Alexander Bickel noted this phenomenon, but he treated it as a device that courts could use to guard their own legitimacy, and the outmoded notion of legitimacy obscured the full consequences of his observation.[85] New Public Governance scholarship by Michael Dorf, Charles Sabel, William Simon, Susan Sturm, Cass Sunstein, David Zaring and others has drawn attention to the ways in which judicial decisions become part of the same recursive institutional process of threat, bargain, cajolery, reexamination, and negotiation that characterizes the unlawlike regulation of administrative agencies.[86]

As discussed in Chapter 3, the concept of power, like the concept of law, also has the effect of focusing attention on commands to the exclusion of other modes of discourse, and on control of human conduct to the exclusion of other governance functions. This overlap between the two concepts is hardly adventitious. Both developed during the era when the government was relatively small and primarily concerned with the maintenance of civil order. In such circumstances, it generally acted at a distance from the citizens; it established basic rules of conduct and enforced those rules by means of physical compulsion. Such delimited and dramatically enforced intrusions into private life could be readily conceptualized in terms of governmental power, and readily organized into a coherent pattern recognizable as law. Administrative government, in contrast, is comprehensive in scope and vast in scale. It maintains continuous contact with the citizens it regulates and requires continuous coordination among its numerous and widely dispersed components. In this context, it employs a much broader range of discursive signals, and carries out a broader range of functions, neither of which can be organized into a coherent pattern with an internal logic that comports with our concept of law.

One might attempt to retain the concept of law, as a useful analytic category, by explicitly identifying it with the idea of command and the governmental function of controlling conduct—in other words, the government's use of coercion or force. Alternatively, one might retain it as a description of the use of general rules as an implementation mechanism. This is a dangerous conceptual strategy, however, because the emotive force that attaches to the idea of law will tend to give these actions a priority in descriptive efforts, and a valorization in normative ones, that exceeds any analytic justification. An equally dangerous strategy is to expand the term 'law' to include the entire range of modern governmental action. The problem is that many of the actions that will be included bear no relation to law's established meaning. As a result, any resulting gain in terminological economy will be more than counterbalanced by the confusion that this term's conceptual coagulation will visit on our still fragile efforts to describe the government we actually possess.

Nor should the term 'law' be salvaged by using it to describe a realm distinct from politics. Most legal scholars have insisted on the existence of this difference, while political scientists and critical legal studies scholars have indulged or even wallowed in the cynical pleasure of denying it. In fact, the debate is generated, and the underlying issue distorted, by reference to the concept of law. Insulation from politics is a specific governmental mechanism that we use to implement particular policies in a fair or an efficient manner. We want adjudications of an individual's status to be decided fairly, that is, on the basis of the information presented in a hearing, and without being influenced by information from any other source.[87] We want the money supply to be managed efficiently, that is, to maximize economic growth, without being affected by elected officials' temptation to inflate the currency and reap short-term political advantages.[88] These are decisions about the design of the governmental network. They should be made on the basis of some identifiable concern, such as fairness or efficiency, not treated as an inherent requirement of certain governmental units. More important for present purposes, these concerns, and the mechanism of insulation that we use to secure them, can be understood as simply another aspect of policy formation and implementation. The felt need to insulate the functions of certain governmental units from other units does not correspond to our existing concept of law, and it is confusing to invoke that concept of law in deciding when that mechanism is best deployed.

The Advantages of the Policy and Implementation Perspective

The alternative description of governmental action as policy making and implementation, rather than as law and a bunch of other things, is not only a more coherent description of modern administrative government, but also superior, as a committed description, because it better satisfies the three criteria for such descriptions. First, it corresponds more closely to our emotional commitments. In the traditional state, law played a sacerdotal role and was expected to reflect the regularity of a transcendental realm accessible to reason. Thus, as already noted, law was regarded as something that human legislators discovered, rather than invented, while new statutes were regarded as disconcerting intrusions into an established order. The advent of the modern state heralded the rejection of this view, however long its reverberations echoed and its appeal persisted. With the articulation of governmental purpose, modern people—both citizens and officials— have become unimpressed by the idea of the law's sacerdotal coherence, and unwilling to preserve it. The European codes, which tried to retain this coherence in secular form, have been overlaid by specialized statutes legislation and administrative regulations. The Common Law has been reduced to scattered remnants by legislation, and the rear-guard action that the U.S. Supreme Court fought on its behalf during the substantive due process era has been decisively defeated. There is no Western nation where people will deny themselves desired legislation because it conflicts with tradition or disrupts the integrity of law. Instead, citizens and officials view government as an instrumentality, and evaluate legislation according to its effectiveness in achieving security, prosperity, and liberty.[89]

As far as the heuristic nature of theory is concerned, modern terminology and novel characterizations are generally preferable to traditional, historically sedimented terms, but this advantage is often counterbalanced by the inconvenience of neologisms, so that the heuristic nature of a traditional concept is sometimes better signaled by a simple reminder. In the case of law, however, reminders are inadequate. The concept of law, sedimented with nine hundred years of Western political theory and jurisprudence, has worked its way too deeply into our collective consciousness. Our lurking sense that it refers to a definitive something that we struggle to identify is amplified by the fact that the concept itself advances this same claim; it still resonates with assertions that law constitutes the voice of God Himself, and possesses the same in-built regularities as the physical world. This sonorous, resounding paean to regularity and reason is all so familiar, and so stirring, that it drowns out our ability to hear our own contemporary voices. The suggested alternative of policy and implementation is free of such grandiose associations. As the same time, it retains the advantage of naivete because policy making and implementation are familiar concepts that are regularly used by political participants. They enable us to describe everything that we currently describe as law, but discourage us from smuggling pre-modern concepts and nostalgia-driven condemnations of the administrative state into those descriptions.

Finally, and most important, the concept of policy and implementation facilitates microanalysis. It provides a framework for tracing the operation of modern government in a detailed way, revealing patterns and practices that the concept of law obscures. This point, which is worth considering in some detail, can be illustrated by the most basic steps in the standard policy-making and implementation process—the enactment of a statute by the legislature and its implementation by the assigned administrative agency. Of course, other governmental units are involved in these activities. The president makes policy, as do presidential advisors, agencies, and courts, while courts remain an important mechanism for policy implementation. Since the primary policy maker in Western nations is the legislature, however, and its primary means of doing so is by enacting statutes implemented by administrative agencies, the statutory process will be the focus of the following discussion.

We can begin with the debate among positivists regarding the essential character of statutes. Kelsen argues that all statutes are directed to government agents in the strictest sense.[90] Hart responds that some statutes enact primary rules, which prescribe particular conduct by citizens, and constitutes the classic concept of law, while other statutes are secondary rules, that is, instructions to government agencies.[91] This distinction, while providing clarity for certain purposes, obscures Kelsen's basic insight. Microanalysis indicates that all statutes, except for symbolic ones designating the state bird or dedicating a fraction of the calendar to an influential group of voters, are necessarily directed to government agents. The reason is that the legislature, by virtue of its institutional design, cannot implement its own enactments. Some statutes, which Colin Diver describes an internal, instruct other government agencies to carry out a task or transfer resources from one agency to another; others, which can be called external, instruct government agencies to impose restrictions or deliver benefits to private persons.[92] These latter types of statutes can either state the applicable rules explicitly or instruct the agency to formulate the rules in accordance with generally stated goals or guidelines.

The degree to which the statute states the rule that an agency is expected to apply to private persons is an important feature that has no common designation, but can be called the statute's degree of transitivity.[93] If the statute states the precise rule that the agency is expected to apply, it is transitive. In essence, it is a signal from the legislature that is received by the administering unit and transmitted unchanged to the relevant persons, passing through the agency without being scaled, summed, or integrated. In contrast, if the statute instructs the agency to develop rules or regulations, it can be called intransitive. The signal is received by the agency and, after a variety of agency actions, a new signal is produced. This occurs most commonly when the agency's input is summed with other inputs in accordance with the agency's internal program; as described in Chapter 4, such inputs often come from the private entities that will be subject to the promulgated rules or that have an ideological commitment to the underlying issue.

There is probably no such thing as a totally transitive statute. As Meir Dan-Cohen points out, whenever private persons do not understand the applicable rules in the same way that the implementing agency understands them, a gap or separation will appear between the two.[94] Nor is there such a thing as a totally intransitive statute; no matter how broadly worded the legislative signal may be, it is likely to contain some substantive element that will be perceptible to the people it will ultimately affect. But the range of transitivity levels is extremely wide, and constitutes one of the most crucial aspects of statutory design; in particular, it determines the type of supervision that the legislature exercises over agencies, as described in Chapter 3. If the legislature enacts a highly transitive statute, the agency's task is likely to revolve around the application of the stated rules to specific persons, either through adjudication or through various compliance strategies. Such statutes enable the legislature to exercise a relatively high level of advance control over the agency, but demand correspondingly high levels of information in the drafting process. Alternatively, the legislature can enact an intransitive statute, which requires the agency to engage in extensive rule making. This places fewer demands on the legislature, and allows the particular rules that affect citizens to evolve through an administrative learning process, but relinquishes advance control. Of course, the legislature remains free to select the level of subsequent control, or monitoring, a determination that is largely independent of the statute's transitivity.

Questions about the optimal transitivity level for a particular statute, or statutes in general, are often framed in separation of powers terminology. As suggested in Chapter 2, that is a dysfunctional approach to the issue. There is no reason, apart from pre-modern imagery of government, to treat a statutory enactment as crossing some qualitative institutional divide. Virtually all nonsymbolic statutes are signals issued to an implementation agency, so this supposedly perilous passage is really an intrinsic element of legislation. Moreover, the instructions issued from the legislature to an agency are not significantly different in structure from instructions issued from superiors to subordinates within an implementing agency. The same type of communication is involved and the same issues regarding transitivity arise.

Another equally common and equally problematic way to assess transitivity issues is in terms of power or discretion. Intransitive statutes are often described as transferring extensive power to administrative agencies, or granting them overly broad discretion. But as Chapter 3 discusses, power and discretion are outmoded images when treated as either per-

sonal possessions or as relationships involving individual volition and resistance. Again, the authorization of an implementing agency is an inherent feature of legislation; it does not represent a transfer or surrender of
the legislature's power, but the basic way in which the legislature acts. Nor
can such authorization be usefully regarded as a grant of discretion; the
purpose is never to confer some affirmative liberty on the agency, but
rather to achieve the optimal balance between legislative control and
agency learning. Here again, the transitivity of the signal, and other features suggested by the network model, facilitate a microanalysis of actual
practices that coagulated concepts like power and discretion only conceal
or confuse.

However problematic separation of powers, transfers of power, or
grants of discretion are as accounts of the legislative process, resorting to
the concept of law is still more troublesome. The other concepts tend to
favor transitive over intransitive statutes as a pre-analytic matter, but the
term 'law' seems to demand a certain level of transitivity. Only statutes
stating definitive rules for the citizenry fit most standard definitions of law,
and only these statutes can conceivably display the reasoned regularity that
is sedimented into our cultural understanding of this concept. Thus, intransitive statutes that give the agency general guidelines, or state a goal,
or authorize action that the agency will subsequently choose, appear law-
less in the dual sense of being both chaotic and immoral.

But the reason for these pre-analytic associations relates, once more, to
our discomfort with the administrative state. In the pre-modern state all
statutes needed to be transitive because the primary government agency
available to implement a legislature's declarations was the judiciary. Kings
had a certain number of royal agents, but these agents were largely occupied by collecting taxes and managing the internal operations of the government. The courts remained the primary implementation mechanism
until the tipping trend of articulation produced the current panoply of
modern administrative agencies. Courts, however, were not expected to
create new legal rules; their role was to discover and apply the Common
Law's embedded principles or to interpret and apply the legislature's
statutory language.[95] Only the advent of administrative agencies, with
their explicitly acknowledged authority to make rules, permitted the legislature to enact intransitive statutes. By then, however, the association of
law with a regular, coherent structure had been reinforced by the long
centuries during which the government's institutional pattern required
legislatures to enact statutes stating definitive rules for human conduct.
Modern critiques of intransitive statutes for being incoherent, particularistic, and an abdication of the legislature's role reflect and valorize this pre-
modern mode of thought.

Microanalysis suggests that the real basis for assessing the desired transitivity level of a statute—the basis that enables government to benefit the citizens in a fair and efficient manner—is the relative effectiveness of the legislature or the implementation mechanism in designing the implementation strategy for the policy embodied in the statute. Many factors enter into this determination, the most obvious being competence and knowledge. Agencies are generally viewed as more knowledgeable about implementation, both because the process lies within their acknowledged era of expertise and because they are in direct, often continuous contact with regulated parties. But their proximity to the situation often leads observers to conclude that they have been captured by the regulated parties, that they have resorted to formalistic approaches to avoid such capture, or that they simply lack perspective. To this may be added more specifically political considerations. The party in control of the legislature may feel that the agency is dominated by the opposing party. This provides an incentive for the legislature to exercise a greater level of direct control by specifying the implementation strategy. It is countered-balanced, however, by other political considerations, such as the difficulty of obtaining agreement about the details of the regulatory process at the legislative level.

Further possibilities for the legislative design of implementation strategies are opened up by a microanalysis of the agency's internal structure. For example, the agency will typically comprise many levels of organization, from individuals to offices to departments to the agency in its entirety. Allocating authority among these various levels will often involve complex issues that are similar to the initial choice between the legislature and the agency. The legislature may decide that it wants to influence this allocation and may specify procedures, by either advance instructions or continuous monitoring, that require decisions to be made at the agency's policy-making level, or that transfers these decisions to the operations level. Alternatively, the legislature may be uncertain about the best method to achieve its goals, or about any method for doing so, and may entertain similar doubts about the agency's level of knowledge. It can address this uncertainty by establishing a structure that encourages the agency to learn.

These design questions structure the agency to some extent, that is, they partially determine the internal program by which the agency transforms inputs into outputs. Unless the statute involved is the organic statute that establishes the agency, however, they do not determine the most basic features of the agency's program, and in virtually no case does a single statute determine the agency's program in its entirety. As a result, an ordinary, or non-organic, statute is best viewed as an input, or set of inputs, into an existing agency. This input will necessarily be summed with the agency's preexisting program, the emergent characteristics that result from that program, and the inputs from other sources such as private parties. The preexisting program will generally include generalized decision-making techniques, among them cost-benefit analysis, cost-effectiveness analysis, and incrementalism. These techniques have been extensively discussed in legal and political science literature.[96] The agency's emergent characteristics or patterns of behavior are generated through the intersubjective process by which separate individuals learn their expected roles and carry out those roles by cooperating with each other. Robert Kagan arranges the emergent characteristics of administrative agencies along two axes, one running from legalistic to conciliatory, the other running from zealous to ineffective.[97] John Braithwaite, John Walker, and Peter Grabosky, in a study of 101 Australian agencies, adopt a more Linnean approach, identifying seven distinct enforcement styles that they evocatively name Conciliator, Big Gun, Benign Big Gun, Diagnostic, Inspectorate, Token Enforcer, and Modest Enforcer.[98] Finally, the responses of private parties are part of the interactive process that has already been discussed in Chapter 4. This process will alter the selected implementation strategy by means of inputs from regulated parties and public interest groups that will be summed with the inputs from the legislature and the agency's emergent characteristics. In addition, emergent characteristics will themselves be affected by the interactive process, which creates a feedback loop between the characteristics and their political environment.

This microanalysis of the policy and implementation process, while cursory, suffices to illuminate a wide range of issues that the concept of law only obscures. In an administrative state, there is no category of action that corresponds to law; rather, there are policies that are implemented in various ways and achieve various levels of compliance. Bracketing law focuses attention on the detailed dynamics of this policy and implementation process, and thereby facilitates microanalysis, as well as accurately reflecting our emotional commitments and signaling the heuristic character of theory. Scholars and policy analysts will thus have a clear field where they can explore the interesting questions about the way a modern state carries out its operations and achieves its purposes without becoming mired in the tangled, antediluvian inquiry into the meaning and nature of law.

The Morality of Policy and Implementation

The Inherent Normativity of Law

Despite the descriptive disadvantages of law, it may appear that something important has been lost by bracketing this concept. Law is often regarded as possessing normative force and embodying essential social values. These emotional commitments, it might be argued, are ignored by a functional model of the sort suggested in the preceding section. While this model dissolves law into the separate elements of policy and implementation, so that it no longer looks like a coherent concept, a more normatively based description, it could be asserted, would restore the law's essential unity, revealing moral regularities that the functional approach obscures.

To assess this assertion, it is necessary to identify the normative claims made on behalf of law with more precision. These can be divided, at the outset, into two essential types—those asserting that law is essentially or inherently normative, and those asserting that law, whether inherently normative or not, plays a normatively important role in our society. Claims about the inherent normality of law vary greatly in the way that they conceive the relationship between law and morality. If we imagine positive law and morality as two sets of rules, then these claims can be placed along a continuum. The first, or strongest claim, would be that the two sets of rules correspond entirely; that all moral principles, to the extent feasible, must be enacted into positive law, and that all positive law must be directly based on moral principles. This position is virtually unknown in Western jurisprudence, its most notable representative being the fishmonger's *Mirror of the Justices*.[99] St. Thomas certainly did not subscribe to it; his view, which represents the next step on the continuum, is that positive law must implement some principles of general morality and that all law must be consistent with this morality. But many principles of morality—divine law, for example—need not be embodied in positive law, and all positive law need not, and indeed cannot, be derived from moral principles.[100] A third position is that law does not necessarily embody general morality, but that there are certain moral rules that apply specifically to law. Its best known proponent is Lon Fuller, who claimed that these principles were essentially structural, or procedural.[101] A fourth, weaker claim for the relationship between morality and law, most notably advanced by H.L.A. Hart, is that there is one single moral principle embodied in all law: namely, that law ought to be obeyed.[102] This gives law an inherent normativity simply because it is law, without prescribing any particular feature, substantive or procedural, that it necessarily possesses. Finally, the weakest claim is that law does not necessarily contain or obey moral principles, but that certain laws express the moral attitudes of the legislators, while others shape the moral attitudes of the citizenry by creating social meaning.[103] This view, which is currently described as the expressive theory of law, does not appear to deny the amoral positivism of the Austin-Kelsen theory regarding law in general, but insists that some laws serve a normative function.

The arguments advanced in support of these various claims about the normativity of law, and the responses to them, constitute a large portion of Western society's jurisprudential thought. But this debate, despite its sophistication and extent, does not establish a normative role for law that rescues it from its conceptual obsolescence. On the contrary, the obsolescent character of law undermines the relevance of the debate. The more that legal theorists try to debate the meaning of law, or use it to elucidate political morality, the more they will be arguing about normative issues that do not apply in contemporary circumstances. None of the claims for the morality of law is a coherent position in a modern state, regardless of one's moral views, none of them captures our real political morality, and none, therefore, provides any argument against bracketing the concept of law.

Substantive natural law, which St. Thomas championed, is not a widely held position these days.[104] If the concept of law depends on natural law for its relevance as a normative approach, it will not be regarded as particularly relevant by most contemporary observers. The well-known reason is that substantive values are open to dispute, that each natural law proponent projects his own values onto the eternal order, asserts that everyone agrees with him, and then brands the multitudes who disagree as lacking reason. In the context of an administrative state, substantive natural law suffers from an additional difficulty that can be illustrated by considering the work of John Finnis, a leading proponent of this position. Finnis attempts to derive the content of a legal system from a set of seven basic values; knowledge, life, play, aesthetic experiences, friendship, practical reasonableness, and religion.[105] Like natural law in general, any such list is disputable: this one reflects the sensibility of an academic philosopher, while omitting some of the coarser joys that the less brainy and less tenured might identify, such as money, employment, fame, and sex.

The problem relevant to the present discussion, however, is that Finnis's list is heavily oriented toward our commitment to liberty, and underemphasizes our commitments to security and prosperity. Liberty can be instantiated, particularly in Finnis's sense, by merely leaving people alone, but security and prosperity, in a mass, technological society, require an administrative state.[106] By constructing his list as he does, Finnis is able to derive a set of human laws that avoids the dreary tasks of economic, environmental, and social regulation, and conjures up the image of self-reliant citizens listening to philosophic discourses, exercising in the gymnasium, attending the theater, strolling through the forum with their friends, and—since Finnis is a christianized Aristotelian like St. Thomas—stopping by the church at the end of their otherwise Athenian day. Nor is this unique to Finnis; there is a pastoral quality to most substantive natural law theories, in part because nostalgia will tend to figure prominently in the sensibility of anyone who adopts a position that has been considered out of date for several hundred years, but also because it is difficult to claim that the complex, detailed, politically contingent, and frequently innovative provisions that characterize a modern state are derived from or consistent with transcendent virtues. In addition, the very existence of a list rejects, or ignores, the process by which an interactive administrative state creates and implements new norms. Like ascending theories of legitimacy, substantive natural law denies the disconcerting but ubiquitous dynamism of administrative governance. Overall, Finnis's theory is at least as anti-administrative as anti-positivist, achieving its coherence by ignoring the characteristic features of the modern state.

The idea that a certain set of moral principles are intrinsic to law is best represented by Lon Fuller's *The Morality of Law*.[107] Although Fuller wants to reject positivism and view law as embodying inherent moral rules, he also wants to avoid the charge of selecting his own values. Thus, he tries to identify those principles that are internal to law and to which virtually everyone will agree. There are, in his view, eight such principles: generality—the law must act through general rules; promulgation—the law must be readily available to citizens; clarity—the law must state rules that are clear enough to be followed; noncontradiction—the law must not give an order that requires violation of another law; non-impossibility—the law must not require an act that the subject is incapable of performing; nonretroactivity—the law must not impose punishment for past actions that were legal at the time; constancy—the law must not change with excessive frequency; and congruence—the law must be stated in such a way that its application bears a reasonable resemblance to its stated form.[108] This is an illuminating list, but it does not identify a general and inherent morality of law. At some level, Fuller is aware of this, since he acknowledges that his list applies only to "a system for subjecting human conduct to the governance of rules."[109] He concedes that not all statutes fit his description, and offers as an example a statute declaring the chickadee the official bird of Massachusetts.[110] This would appear to be a minor omission; in fact the types of enactments that fall outside his category go well beyond the chickadee. They include the creation of and organization of institutions, authorizations issued to administrative agencies, and the allocation of fiscal resources—all actions that characterize an administrative state. Creating and organizing institutions is necessarily specific, and violates Fuller's principle of generality; authorizations can be defined quite vaguely and concretized only over time by the implementing agency, thus violating the principle of clarity; fiscal allocations typically change every year, and thereby violate the principle of constancy. In fact, every single one of Fuller's principles is regularly violated by institution-creating, agency-authorizing, and resource-allocating statutes.[111] But it is difficult to perceive any moral problem with such enactments unless one believes in the immorality of the administrative state itself.

Fuller's principles, like Finnis's, do not even apply to all regulatory enactments that are part of "a system for subjecting human conduct to the governance of rules." In an administrative state, many statutes that are intended to govern human conduct do not actually enunciate the legal rules that citizens are supposed to follow. Rather, they are intransitive; they state general policies that will guide the agency in formulating those rules through its rule making or adjudicatory process. Intransitive statutes are not general—they are directed to the agency. They are not promulgated to the citizens; the agency promulgates the specific requirements. They need not be clear, because the agency will clarify them, and they need not be congruent, because only the agency's specification of them will affect the general public. As for impossibility, they are virtually all impossible because, as discussed in Chapter 5, they envision a 100 percent compliance rate.[112]

On reflection, the problem is that Fuller has not stated principles that apply to law in general, and reflect its internal morality, but rather principles that apply to the way the state controls the conduct of its citizens through transitive statutes—in other words, to the same traditional, pre-administrative category of enactments that positivists regard as law. Positivists focus on this limited category because it can conceivably be organized with the same degree of regularity as natural law. Fuller, in opposition, is astute enough to observe that we in fact possess strong moral intuitions where this category is concerned. But because he accepts the positivists' notion that this one particular type of legal action constitutes law in general, he imagines that these intuitions betoken an indwelling regularity of law. All he has done, however, is to restate the intersubjectively developed principles of fairness that we apply when punishments or burdens are imposed directly on citizens, that is, the principles that we ordinarily describe as due process. His principle of generality simply embodies the basic idea that when the state imposes burdens on a specific person, it must do so through some sort of adjudication, and that legislative punishment of specific persons—a bill of attainder—is unfair. Five of his remaining principles—clarity, promulgation, noncontradiction, constancy, and congruence—all derive from the due process norm of notice—that people must be able to understand the rules they are required to obey. The remaining two—non-impossibility and nonretroactivity—provide that people should be able to obey those rules.[113] These are important considerations, but they emerge from our moral intuitions about the way the government should treat its citizens. Fuller regards them as an inherent morality of law in general because, despite his opposition to positivism, he shares the positivists' pre-modern concept of law as limited to rules that directly regulate human conduct.

H.L.A. Hart's position on the inherent morality of law is less demanding. It rests only on the moral principle that the law is supposed to be obeyed, that law, as such, has a normative force. Hart develops this position as a criticism of the more relentless positivism of Austin and Kelsen, which asserts that law depends only upon sanctions, not on any moral principle.[114] He then defends it against Fuller, in a famous debate, where he argued that Fuller identifies too many moral principles.[115] In the context of an administrative state, however, Hart's one moral principle is one too many. It is an aspect of pre-modern thought, and not part of our modern moral sensibility.

As has already been discussed in Chapter 1, the sacerdotal concept of the state infused its various elements with the divine force that flowed through the sovereign, thus conferring a normative character on legal rules. Given the structural features of the pre-modern state, this inherent normativity was both necessary and practical. It was necessary because the government possessed only limited capacities for the ongoing supervision of its subjects. As a result, legal rules, like the rules of chivalry, depended for their effectiveness on mechanisms such as voluntary compliance, social disapproval, and the assistance of the Church, mechanisms that could only be deployed for inherently normative rules. This inherent normativity was practical because there were a limited number of rules, serving only a few basic purposes that corresponded to prevailing moral sentiments. In a modern state, the articulation of purpose detaches morality from the mechanisms of government and reveals these mechanisms as contingent instrumentalities, without any inherent normativity.[116] Normative considerations do not disappear, of course, but they attach to the purpose or policy that motivates the governmental instrumentalities, not to the instrumentalities themselves.[117] Contrary to the fears of many people who observed this transformation taking place, this loss of normativity for legal rules did not lead to social breakdown. There is no necessity for governmental instrumentalities to possess moral force in a modern administrative state because that state can compel obedience through ongoing supervision by administrative agencies and induce obedience through the eudaemonic provision of services. Besides, it would not be practical for a modern state to rely on the moral force of these instrumentalities, given the range, complexity, and technical character of the rules that it must implement to carry out its eudaemonic functions.

There is thus no category of governmental action that possesses the normative character that Hart attributes to law. Instead, there are a range of implementation mechanisms, each expected to achieve a certain level of compliance. As described in Chapter 5, compliance levels are determined by self-interest and by non-self-interested motivations such as loyalty, cooperativeness, and concurrence. The behavior patterns that Hart attributes to the inherent normativity of law are better explained as the compliance induced by non-self-interest motivations. Modern people obey a statute, apart from the fear of punishment, because they feel loyalty to the regime, or want to be cooperative, or agree with the policy underlying the command, not because they think all laws should be obeyed. When these motivations are absent or attenuated, they will not obey, which is the reason why compliance levels are nearly always less than total, and why governmental implementation strategies are so important. Hart's concept of inherently normative law cannot explain this, but he overlooks the problem because his notion of law is limited to traditional civil and criminal enactments, where law more often corresponds to morality, and levels of concurrence, although not necessarily obedience, are unusually high.

The final and weakest claim about the inherent morality of law is that some laws possess an expressive quality, that they constitute normative statements as well as positive enactments, or that they function as an important force in the creation of social meaning.[118] As an empirical observation, this position is hardly news to sociologists;[119] on the contrary, it would be truly remarkable if a major component of social life, such as the government's mode of action, could be insulated from moral considerations or deprived of moral impact. The claim that transforms these observations into a theory of law's morality is that this relationship is inherent to certain types of laws, that these laws can only be understood as expressions of a moral position. But this is simply not the case, as Matthew Adler has pointed out.[120] Our morality refers to the effect of a statute, or the intention of the legislator, not to the statute's linguistic character; as Adler says, "The connection between the linguistic meaning of a legal official's action and what truly matters, morally speaking, about that action, is a purely contingent connection. . . ."[121]

The contingency of this relationship between law and morality is a product of the particular political morality that accompanies the administrative state, namely, the instrumentalist morality discussed in Chapter 1. In pre-modern times, the linguistic form of the law mattered a great deal, because law was expected to constitute a coherent system that reflected both timeless tradition and the transcendental realm. From an instrumentalist perspective, however, the linguistic expression of a statute is merely a means to an end. In some cases, of course, the statute's linguistic form is part of its effect, but for most modern statutes, and particularly for intransitive ones, the language is too recondite or turgid to play any role at all. The fact that some statutes express moral sentiments is certainly worth noting, but it tells us very little about the character of statutory enactments in a modern state, and even less about the general concept of law.

This serial attack on law's moral claims should not be regarded as a general rejection of morality, or as submission to the cold embrace of a technocratic, soulless system. Modern government is suffused with morality and uniquely able to shape the moral beliefs of civil society, for good or ill. But the effort to locate our political morality within the concept of law imprisons it and debilitates its real force, or, worse still, conceals that force behind a facade decorated with outdated platitudes. The genuine morality of the modern state is revealed by bracketing the concept of law and substituting the concept of policy and implementation. It is the articulated policies of government that serve as the reflection of our greatest moral aspirations and concerns. And it is those same policies that possess the potential to inspire and recruit the citizenry.

Most of this morality, as the expressivists have sensed, is embodied in statutes that take the form of independent policy initiatives. They bear no necessary relationship to other legal enactments and cannot be integrated into a comprehensive code. William Eskridge and John Ferejohn have proposed the term 'super-statutes' for enactments that seek "to establish a new normative or institutional framework for state policy," and ultimately succeed in transforming the legal system and influencing public morality.[122] Their observation underscores the point that the interaction of the modern state with its citizens' morality involves the formation and implementation of public policy, and not any separate conceptual entity that can be identified as law. The articulation of purpose that characterizes the administrative state has made the verbal statements that were previously identified as law transparent to the policy choices that underlie them.

Law's Normative Function, or the Rule of Law

Apart from the various views about the inherent morality of law, it is also argued that law, whether linked to morality or not, plays an important normative role in government. This position is generally described as the rule of law. Like so many other historically sedimented terms, the rule of law possesses a variety of meanings.[123] Two of the most prominent and most relevant to this discussion, because they focus directly on the concept of law,[124] are first, that the government can only rule through law, that it must use enacted rules of general application as its means of governance;[125] and second, that law must rule the government, that there must be definitive rules controlling the behavior of leading officials.[126] These two positions are certainly not inconsistent, but they are not the same, and one does not imply the other; rather, they reflect the amphibious character of law described above.[127] The most important connection between them are that both are functional claims about the moral character of law. As such, they do not conflict with claims about the inherent morality of law, but neither do they depend upon such claims. Even Austin's and Kelsen's orders backed by sanctions, which are innocent of any inherent morality, might fulfill the requirement that government must act through law, or that government officials must be subject to it.

There can be little question that both versions of the rule of law idea capture important aspects of our political morality. But the difficulty with both versions, as an assertion of law's moral force, is that neither has very

much to do with law. The claim that government must legislate by means
of generalized commands that, at least in theory, could be part of a coherent system that is accessible to reason is essentially the same as Fuller's
principle of generality. But as discussed above, this requirement cannot
apply to an administrative state, since that state regularly acts in ways that
do not conform to it. In particular, modern government creates organizations, distributes benefits, and allocates resources. All of these actions can
be taken by the legislature, by means of the discursive category of commands, and yet be stated in specific terms. In fact, any intransitive statute
can be specific—and most such statutes are—without in any way offending our political morality.

What does violate our political morality is rule making by either a legislature or an agency that imposes punishment or other disadvantage on
private individuals, that is, the use of monitoring supervision by a rulemaking body for individual conduct. The reason, however, is not because
the government is obligated to act through law, but because the government may not impose penalties on individuals without specific procedural
protections that legislatures and administrative rule makers do not provide, such as notice, a hearing, and an impartial decision maker.[128] Again,
the normative principle is due process, a rather specific means of protecting liberty or achieving fairness that can be fully described without reference to the concept of law.[129] The rationale for this protection is directly
related to the morality of the interactive republic discussed in Chapter 4.
Interaction enables people to secure their liberty against the government,
by acting in groups that influence the government through electoral or administrative mechanisms. Individuals almost never have sufficient influence to protect themselves in this fashion, however. If government can act
against individuals, it can circumvent the interaction that is so central to
our political morality. Due process demands that government impose disadvantages on people only on the basis of a provision that has been subjected to this interactive political process, and only in a manner that offers
a reasonable likelihood that the individuals belong within the category
specified by the provision.[130] It thus gives individuals the protection of the
interactive process that they could not otherwise invoke.

One might assert that this requirement of prior statutory authorization
could be equated with the rule of law requirement that the state act only
in accordance with pre-established rules. There are, however, several important reasons why this equivalence does not obtain. To begin with, as
discussed above, the due process requirement is not coterminous with
governmental action generally, but rather applies only to those actions that
impose disadvantages on individuals. Rule of law theory is much more
general, and fails, both descriptively and normatively, in precisely those
areas, such as intransitive statutes, where it extends beyond the scope of

the due process guarantee. In addition, the asserted equivalence depends upon the claim that rules stated in advance definitively constrain the officials who apply the rules to individuals. This assertion, now associated with formalism,[131] has seemed unconvincing since the Legal Realist attack on it,[132] and few legal scholars regard it as sufficiently coherent to support the strong claim that rule of law theory asserts.[133] Due process depends on the much weaker and thus more sustainable claim that preestablished rules serve as a source of authority for officials who impose disadvantages on individuals, and that these rules provide general guidance about the kinds of issues these officials should consider in reaching a decision.[134] The bulk of the constraint is provided by the due process mechanisms of notice, a hearing, an impartial decision maker, and a decision on the merits, that is, on the relevant issues. This is the reason why these mechanisms are regarded as the essence of the due process guarantee, and why due process does not simply require that officials follow preestablished rules using whatever mechanisms they select.

The second meaning of the rule of law is that law rules the government, that the authority of each governmental unit is circumscribed and the procedures that it must use within that sphere of authority are prescribed with some degree of specificity. This principle is often connected with the idea of human rights, which are generally regarded as placing limits on governmental action.[135] If that is all this second meaning of the rule of law involves, however, then it is simply a theory of human rights, and ought to be discussed in those familiar terms, as will be done in Chapter 8 below. This is not a matter of mere terminological preference, but an important conceptual distinction. Human rights, in most people's view, are not law at all, but moral principles that stand outside the legal system and enable us to evaluate that system.[136] The only law that can be described as a source of human rights is natural law, but, as already discussed, the idea of natural law is largely defunct, and few modern human rights theorists rely on it. To allow varying and contestable notions of morality to count as law removes any specific meaning from the rule of law idea, and reduces it to an empty slogan.

If the rule of law, in its second sense, is not merely an awkward synonym for human rights, then it must refer to the other types of constraints that are typically imposed on governments, such as constraints on the authority and operations of governmental units. Such constraints are extremely important, but they cannot be properly described as creating a rule of law because the limits they establish cannot be properly described as law. As stated, the concept of law refers to a coherent body of rules that is accessible to reason, and is typically transmitted and enforced by command. The rules that define and delimit the authority of governmental units possess neither of these features. To begin with, these rules are historically contingent, particularistic, and often arbitrary. For example, the separation of powers principle that the same governmental unit cannot enact rules governing conduct and then apply these rules to individuals is historically contingent; as embodied in the American Constitution, it applies to institutions that developed during the pre-modern era, such as courts and legislatures, but not to administrative agencies. Our commitments to fairness and liberty only demand that an adjudicatory unit employ due process, which includes independent decision makers, when it applies its rules.

Many of the specifications of authority that appear in the U.S. Constitution are particularistic, such as those that authorize Congress to "coin money, regulate the value thereof, and of foreign coin, and fix the standard of weights and measures," that authorize the president to "fill up all vacancies that may happen during the recess of the senate," and that authorize the Supreme Court to decide "all cases affecting ambassadors."[137] These rules possess a rationale, to be sure, but that rationale is derived from specific policy decisions about the distribution of authority within the governmental structure, not from any general principle. Finally, many constitutional rules are arbitrary, as positive rules must often be. Why must a senator be at least thirty years old, as opposed to twenty-nine? Why are there two senators from each state, as opposed to three? Choices of this kind must always be made in designing a government, but only numerology, not logic, reason, or integrity, can determine the specific number.

This disjunction between constitutional rules and the concept of law is not adventitious, but follows directly from the social meaning of a constitution. The American Constitution, and the written constitutions of all other modern states, are products of the administrative era. They reflect one of the defining features of that era, namely, the articulation of governmental purpose. Their underlying concept is not the preservation of a time-tested status quo, or the discovery and application of some transcendent principle of governance, but the conscious design of governmental units to achieve identifiable goals such as security, prosperity, and liberty. This concept is explicitly stated in the Preamble to the U.S. Constitution, which reads, in full:

> We the People of the United States, in Order to form a more perfect Union, establish Justice, insure domestic Tranquility, provide for the common defense, promote the general Welfare, and secure the Blessings of Liberty to ourselves and our Posterity, do ordain and establish this Constitution for the United States of America.

What this passage says is that the reason why the Constitution states particularized, arbitrary rules is that it is trying to articulate a set of governmental units for an instrumental purpose, rather than trying to create a coherent legal structure. A constitution, however extraordinary its effect, is a typical administrative-era enactment. The constraints that it imposes on the government do not correspond to our concept of law, but simply to the authority structure described in Chapter 3.

Second, a constitution is not properly regarded as the sort of command that is generally associated with our idea of law. Commands imply the existence of a superior authority that can deploy force, persuasion, inducement, or habit to obtain obedience. The government stands in this sort of superior relationship to its citizens, but the government itself has no superior. Americans of the founding generation attempted to resolve this problem through the doctrine of popular sovereignty, which asserted that the people were sovereign, and thus the true superiors of government.[138] Whatever its value as political mythology, this notion is without functional significance. The Constitution itself was both drafted and approved by representative mechanisms, the drafters being appointees of elected state legislatures, and the approval being given by elected representatives at specially organized state conventions.[139] In fact, as Jack Rakove notes, the drafters specifically rejected popular sovereignty–based claims that the state conventions should be allowed to make their approval contingent on subsequent revisions, or even to propose such revisions.[140] Moreover, the document contains no direct democracy mechanisms, such as popular referenda, that are found in a number of state constitutions. As critics have pointed out, even these referenda do not reflect the direct voice of the people, but are simply a decision-making mechanism designed by government and subject to manipulation by elites.[141] Popular sovereignty may be important as political rhetoric, but the underlying reality is that the people do not serve as the superiors of government in any operative sense.

Consequently, constitutional rules are more correctly viewed as self-imposed constraints that the government accepts and applies to itself through legislative or judicial mechanisms. Such constraints are not enforced by any regular governmental mechanism, but rather by public attitudes, social movements, and periods of intense political mobilization, as Bruce Ackerman points out. They are essentially extra-legal and extra-governmental in character.[142] This is, of course, a disconcerting thought from which we tend to recoil, and our description of a constitution as law reflects our continuing uneasiness. It would be reassuring to believe, as John of Salisbury did, that law is a universal and continuous set of principles that apply to the rulers and the rules alike, that the absence of an earthly superior for the ruler was an unfortunate detail that did not derogate from this continuity, and that rulers who violated the law and could not be punished in this life would be punished in the next by the Almighty. It would be equally reassuring to believe that the people, as a collectivity, possess the mysterious mana of sovereignty that confers authority on government in some operative fashion. But we do not believe this; the rationalized worldview of the modern era compels us to acknowledge that we are all alone, without anyone to protect us from the government but our own, socially constructed system of beliefs. In short, the rules that constrain government are more accurately described as a means of implementing a self-imposed policy of structuring and constraining governmental actors, rather than as a rule of law.

Apart from the descriptive inaccuracies from which each of the rule of law's separate meanings suffer, there is the further problem that the same term is being used with these two separate meanings—in other words, the rule of law, in incorporating the term 'law,' is infected by that term's amphibious character. Amphibians are not a very successful chordate class these days. They did very well as dry-land pioneers, but they have since been outcompeted by the fishes, birds, and mammals that are willing to make a more definitive commitment to a single environment. Similarly, law's amphibious character served it well during its pioneering days in the Middle Ages, but it would be odd if more successful means of controlling society and rulers had not developed in the intervening centuries. In fact, they have; by bracketing the term 'law,' it becomes apparent that what seems like an amphibian is in fact two different animals. Control over the citizenry is exercised by external signals emanating from the government, while control over government agencies is exercised by a set of self-imposed constraints enforced by public attitudes, social movements, and political mobilization. Thus, there is no single entity, or concept, that is simultaneously walking on the dry land of governmental agencies and swimming in the ocean of citizen attitudes and action. Once again, it is better to bracket the term 'law,' and consider the mechanisms for achieving these two crucial but separate functions on their own terms.

_____

Seven

From Legal Rights to Causes of Action

The Concept of Legal Rights

Legal Rights and Adjudication

RIGHTS are central to our current conception of the legal system. Together with obligations, they constitute our idea of the way that the legal system, the system by which the government carries out a large portion of its functions, interacts with private parties. According to the traditional account, the obligations that the law imposes can be derived from the content of the law itself, and need not be considered separately, while rights, being claims that private parties can assert, possess an independent status that merits detailed consideration. Rights are generally divided into two basic types, legal rights and human rights, which roughly correspond to the two different aspects of the amphibious concept of law. Legal rights are claims generated by the process by which government rules the citizenry through law, while human rights are claims generated by the process by which law, or lawlike moral principles, rule the government.

As this distinction implies, legal rights are creations of positive law, and exist only because some governmental agent has taken authoritative action. Human rights, in contrast, are nongovernmental in their origin and act as a constraint, or limit, on governmental agents. There is virtually no controversy about this distinction. St. Thomas Aquinas, Hans Kelsen, and everyone in between—which is virtually everyone[1]—subscribe to it. The debatable issues have generally involved the relationship between the two categories of rights and the term 'law.' According to natural lawyers like St. Thomas, human rights are part of the law, while legal rights that violate these human rights are not.[2] According to positivists like Kelsen, human rights are not part of the law, but all legal rights are law, regardless of their moral status.[3] With the term 'law' being bracketed, this controversy can be avoided here, and the two concepts of rights can be considered on their own terms, as independently operating ideas.

The first question that arises is whether the two types of rights, legal and human, are really variants of a single concept, that is, whether the same term should be used to describe these two distinguishable things. Scholars often assume such a connection, and regard a theory's ability to account for both legal and human rights as a criterion of its validity or usefulness.[4] That is, however, a pre-analytic assumption, motivated by the sacerdotal conception of government, the pre-modern conceptions of law discussed in Chapter 6, and the dual meaning of the term 'rights' in the English language.[5] The existence of such motivations does not demonstrate that the assumption is unjustified, but does not supply a justification either. To begin the analysis by using the same term for two distinguishable concepts, particularly an emotionally charged, conceptually coagulated term like rights, risks serious confusion. With this in mind, the two concepts will be considered separately. To avoid prejudging the matter in the opposite direction, however, and the distinction between them will be treated as an uninformative one. This chapter considers legal rights, and the following one considers human rights.

Disputes about the existence and extent of legal rights were legion in the Middle Ages, and courts proliferated to adjudicate them. There were royal courts, baronial courts, ecclesiastical courts, chivalric courts, merchant courts, courts on each large manor, and courts at every trade fair.[6] The adjudications of these courts, whether they consisted of swearing contests among assembled serfs, the ordeal of burning iron, or armed combat in the lists, were major social events in people's daily lives.[7] Disputes about the authority to adjudicate disputes were equally common, and if not such a productive source of ordinary entertainment, certainly the basis of high political conflict and intrigue. A person's authority to declare rights was a source of prestige, since it betokened hierarchical superiority, as well as a source of remuneration, since the adjudicator—in consonance with the general structure of pre-modern officialdom discussed in Chapter 1—was entitled to retain the fees and fines collected by his court. In consequence, such authority itself became a right that was eagerly sought and jealously guarded.[8] Much blood was spilled in contesting the legal right to declare legal rights, and the growth of national monarchies in France and England was often achieved by consolidating these second-order rights in royal hands.

Despite the ubiquity and centrality of legal rights, no theoretical account of them was developed during the Middle Ages or the centuries that followed. While the theory of human rights can probably be traced back to the fourteenth century, the first person to offer a theory of legal rights seems to have been Jeremy Bentham.[9] The timing is suggestive of an explanation. Bentham wrote when the tipping trends of articulation produced the modern administrative state, and he was clearly a leading herald of this transformation. His ability to identify legal rights as a separate concept, and a subject for theoretical analysis, is related to the articulation of governmental purposes that was occurring at this time. Bentham realized that legal rules, in the ideology of the administrative state, were not derived from natural law, but were enacted to achieve specific public purposes. He was then able to perceive that legal rights were the mechanism by which these legal rules achieved their purposes, and not part of the substantive relationships that they secured. Thus, the features of legal rights could be analyzed by means of a general theory that would apply no matter what the content of the substantive law that they enforced.[10]

Bentham's theory divides legal rights into three major categories: those resulting from the imposition of a legal obligation, those resulting from the absence of a legal obligation, and those granting power over things or persons. Over a century later, Wesley Hohfeld proposed a related taxonomy that has become the best-known theory of legal rights.[11] According to Hohfeld, there are four fundamental categories of legal relations: rights, privileges, powers, and immunities.[12] Each possesses a correlative that serves to fix its meaning. The first legal relation is a right, in Hohfeld's terminology. This is a definitive claim, and its correlative is a duty; "when a right is invaded, a duty is violated."[13] If Jill has a right to exclude Jack from her house, then Jack has a duty to remain outside. Hohfeld's second category, a privilege, is a liberty or permission to perform a particular act, and expressly prohibits interference with that act, although not with any other act. For example, Jill can grant Jack the privilege of entering her house on Tuesdays. The correlative of this privilege is that Jill now has no right to prevent Jack from entering on the specified days. Hohfeld calls this a no-right, the only neologism in which he indulges. Jill's no-right does not stop her from selling her house or burning it to the ground, which effectively ends Jack's privilege, but only stops her from interfering with the specific act to which the privilege applies.[14]

A power, Hohfeld's third category, is the volitional control of legal relations. Jill has the power to extinguish her legal interest in her house—her right to exclude others from it and her privilege of entering it—by abandoning the place. She also has the power to transfer her interest in the house to Jack, extinguishing her interest and creating a new and corresponding interest in her transferee. If she offers to sell her house to Jack, Jack then obtains the power to effect the transfer by accepting the offer. The correlative of a power is a liability. Once Jill has made her offer, she subjects herself to a liability to transfer the house. That liability is not a duty; it will become a duty only if Jack accepts the offer, thereby converting her power to effect the transfer into a right to obtain various legal interests in the house.[15]

Finally, an immunity is the opposite of a liability, and means that the person is free from another's legal control. If Jill does not make an offer to Jack, despite intensive negotiations between them, then she is immune from Jack's desire to transfer the legal interest in the house. Jill may also be immune from certain types of taxation; perhaps she has obtained an immunity from the city's energy tax surcharge by installing solar heating.

The correlative is a disability; once Jill's immunity has been established, Jack is disabled from effecting a transfer and the city is disabled from imposing the tax surcharge.[16]

What is notable about Hohfeld's theory, for present purposes, is that, like Bentham's, it relates almost entirely to legal claims that are validated by privately initiated adjudication—that is, a nongovernmental party's presentation of a claim to a neutral government agent who will decide by weighing that claim against the contentions of an opposing party. It is only by means of such adjudication that the legal nature of these claims is definitively established. Hohfeld is quite explicit about this; the title of his work is "Fundamental Legal Conceptions as Applied in Judicial Reasoning."[17] He begins his analysis by distinguishing between legal relations and physical or mental ones. We can call an object property in ordinary speech, he points out, but the legal concept of property consists of interests that can be asserted in a court of law.[18] One can go to court to assert one's right to exclude another from one's property and obtain damages or an injunction. One can go to court to assert one's privilege to enter another's property, and the other, having granted this privilege, has no right, that is, a no-right, to oppose this claim. One can go to court to confirm one's power to transfer one's property if the validity of the power is challenged. And one can go to court to assert an immunity from another's intention to transfer the property, thereby imposing a disability on that other person. In other words, Hohfeld's categories consist of various types of claims, or assertions, that a natural or legally created person can present to an adjudicatory body. All his examples, which are sometimes more revealing than his abstract formulations, involve judicially enforceable assertions.

To be sure, the operative terms in Bentham's and Hohfeld's taxonomies are sufficiently capacious to include an administrative hearing, but that is about as far as these schema can be stretched. Power, as used by the two authors, might also include grants of jurisdiction to public officials, which are essentially the same as H.L.A. Hart's power-conferring rules.[19] But such rules are generally not regarded as legal rights. We do not say that a judge has the legal right to decide criminal cases in Nebraska, but that she has jurisdiction to do so; in effect, as discussed in Chapter 3, it is authorization—her job assignment. To assert the contrary, to characterize a public official's authority as a right, reflects the structure of pre-modern government when the ability to adjudicate legal rights was regarded as a species of personal property and provided remuneration through the fees and fines that the officeholder could collect. If Bentham and Hohfeld intend to embody this quaint idea in their theories, they would indeed be expanding these theories beyond the ambit of adjudication, but only at the expense of rendering them obsolete. Once the unproductive option of treating authorization or jurisdiction as a legal right is jettisoned, their notions of legal rights and of adjudication are essentially equivalent.

Theories of legal rights that rely on overall characterizations, rather than taxonomies, reveal the same underlying mindset. For example, Hart, in response to Bentham, describes legal rights in general as a legally respected choice.[20] This concept, according to Hart, accounts for three of Bentham's categories.[21] In discussing it, however, Hart focuses on the element of choice, and barely discusses the requirement that the choice must be legally respected. As a result, he never offers a definition of this second term. From the examples he gives, however, it seems apparent that he too is envisioning privately initiated adjudication as the mechanism of respect, that is, a choice is legally respected when it can be enforced in a judicial proceeding. In fact, the term 'legally respected' implies this association; had Hart been thinking of rights established by positive enactment, but not implemented by adjudication, he would presumably have said 'legally created.'

The connection between legal rights and adjudication is most explicit in Ronald Dworkin's work. Dworkin is so unembarrassed about conceptualizing the entire legal system in judicial terms that he does not even make an effort to generalize his definition of rights beyond the adjudicatory context. According to Dworkin, a right is an "individuated political aim" that prevails over social goals;[22] it is established by arguments of principle, and is thus distinguishable from these social goals, which are established by arguments of policy. Arguments of principle, in Dworkin's view, are the distinctive province of the judiciary.[23] While a legislator establishes public policy, the judge's task is to decide on the basis of principle because she is confirming or denying individual rights. From this follows his famous argument that there is always a correct or principled answer to a contested case dealing with individual rights, an answer that can be discovered through proper legal reasoning.[24] But the assertion that underlies this controversial claim is that legal rights are invariably being determined by a judge in an adversarial adjudication. Thus the concept of legal rights, whether used descriptively or normatively, is nothing more than an element of the adjudicatory process in Dworkin's view. "Its descriptive aspect explains the present structure of the institution of adjudication. Its normative aspect offers a political justification for that structure."[25]

Characterizations of rights in general, which are intended to encompass both legal and human rights, do not suffer from this same restriction to adjudication. Joseph Raz, for example, defines a right as "a sufficient reason for holding some other person(s) to be under a duty."[26] They indicate, he continues, "intermediate conclusions in arguments from ultimate values to duties."[27] Clearly, there can be an ultimate value, such as treating

others with respect, that would impose a duty on others, without any implication that the right could be enforced in court. But how does one
identify the subcategory of legal rights that he recognizes as distinguishable from moral rights within this overarching category of rights in general? According to Raz, legal rights are those recognized by law.[28] This
seems hard to argue with, but, as Raz is aware, it is rather unhelpful without an account of legal recognition. Consequently, he proceeds by noting
that law is an institutional system, and defining an institutional system as
something that "consists of rules which are subject to adjudication before
official bodies." Elsewhere, he says: "It is widely agreed (and by many natural lawyers as well) that a system of norms is not a legal system unless it
sets up adjudicative institutions charged with regulating disputes arising
out of the application of the norms of the system."[29] Clearly, Raz's account of what renders a legal right legal centers on the idea that the right
is enforced through adjudication.

The Limits of Adjudication

The fact that general theories of legal rights are a product of the administrative era, and were apparently inspired by the tipping trends that signaled
the advent of that era, would appear to vouchsafe the modernity of these
theories. But the association of legal rights with privately initiated adjudication triggers quasi-Cartesian doubt. Adjudication is certainly an important mechanism by which state policies are implemented, as Bentham perceived, but it is only one of many such mechanisms. The evolution of the
administrative state has brought other implementation mechanisms to the
forefront. The theory of legal rights has remained unchanged, however.
Conceptually, it is modern in perceiving adversarial adjudication as a
general mechanism that can be abstracted from its substantive context.
Operationally, it remains pre-modern in treating adjudication as the only
mechanism that can fulfill this role. Due to the perceived centrality of adjudication, the contingent nature of legal rights as one particular governmental mechanism has not been fully recognized. Instead, these rights, abstracted from their context, tend to be viewed as a necessary element in
the legal system, and an inherent feature of its operation.

   One difficulty that results from this unjustified emphasis on adjudication is that legal rights possess an apparent dignity that fails to acknowledge the ordinary, technical nature of adjudication. Use of the term
'rights' suggests the existence of some definitive result, some proper ordering of human affairs that is derived from our general, abstract idea of
right or rightness. Because legal rights are in fact linked to the mechanism
of adjudication, however, this suggestion can only be justified if adjudication were a definitive method for determining the truth. Precisely this

claim was advanced in the Middle Ages with respect to trial by combat. On the Continent, following the collapse of the Roman Empire, and in England, following the Norman conquest, serious criminal and civil cases were settled by judicial combat, that is, by a formally structured fight, with swords or clubs, between accuser and accused.[30] The two would fight all day, and the outcome was regarded as God's revelation of the just result.[31] Since women, children, the aged, and the incapacitated could not be expected to fight an able-bodied man, they would be represented by a champion, often a professional gladiator.[32] The more money one had, of course, the better a champion one could employ.

The defects, injustices, and general oddity of this dispute resolution mechanism are readily apparent to us. But the very similar difficulties with the thirteenth-century practice of adjudication that replaced judicial combat are less evident, since this practice remains the one we use today. Both practices were justified by the assertion that truth will emerge from a contest between opposing parties, with some or all of these parties acting through paid representatives. The difference is that we have less justification for our assertion, according to our own belief system.[33] The jury and inquisitorial trials that replaced judicial combat were never regarded as capable of invoking divine intervention, even in the Middle Ages. With the passing of the sacerdotal state, such a claim would be virtually inconceivable today. Thus, we have no general warrant for regarding adjudication as a source of truth or a guarantee of rightness; according to our own ideology, as Chris Sanchirico has pointed out, it can be nothing more than one mechanism, of variable value, for implementing public policy.[34]

Beyond its unjustified connection to the idea of truth and rightness, the concept of legal rights displays a second and perhaps more serious defect. It underemphasizes governmental actions that are implemented by non-adjudicatory means and it endows those actions that are implemented by adjudication with a significance that they do not necessarily deserve. In so doing, the concept is essentially inconsistent with the implementation patterns of the modern administrative state. The administrative state represents a massive shift away from adjudicatory enforcement mechanisms, and certainly away from adversarial adjudication. It relies heavily on regulations, advice, guidance, threats, negotiation, and education. In underemphasizing the importance of these typically administrative mechanisms, and overemphasizing the importance of their pre-modern antecedent, the concept of legal rights misrepresents the government we actually possess and reveals our social nostalgia for a bygone era.

The tendency of legal rights, as an operative concept, to underemphasize non-adjudicatory action can be illustrated by considering national defense. This is one of the most essential benefits that a government can provide to its citizens, and certainly one of its most characteristic roles. In the

United States and virtually all other nations, however, it contains no adjudicatory element, for no private party may bring a legal case to determine or affect the way that the nation is defended. Thus, it can be said, there is no legal right to national defense. If one were listing the legal rights of the citizenry, therefore, the right to retain one's possessions, to enforce one's contracts, and to be tried prior to conviction would appear, but security from foreign aggressors would not. In contrast, if one were listing the benefits that citizens receive, security would figure prominently, an obvious fact that the attack on the World Trade Center only emphasizes. What then is the distinction among these benefits, apart from the fact that the first three can be enforced in an adjudicatory proceeding and the last cannot be? Certainly, it is not their relative importance or their impact on political decision making. To confer the title of legal rights on the first three, and not on national security, only adds superfluous and confusing verbiage to a distinction that can be described directly as the presence or absence of adjudicatory implementation.

Perhaps the distinction seems supported by the fact that national defense is a public good, that is, a benefit that cannot be allocated to specific individuals.[35] Consider then the example of education and, to remove any sense of preexisting legal rights, consider an adult education program that the government has decided to initiate. This is not a public good, since it is necessarily provided on an individualized basis and, indeed, is sometimes provided by private profit-making institutions. As in the case of national defense, a publicly funded adult education program would represent an important benefit for citizens. Once again, however, it need not be implemented by creating legal rights. The decision to establish a facility in a particular area or to teach particular courses in that facility could be made exclusively by an administrative agency. The ability of citizens to challenge the agency's decisions in any adjudicatory forum could be rigorously precluded. Such an approach might detract from the efficiency or fairness with which the program was operated, or it might not. It would be a typical approach, however, and it certainly would not reduce the program to a nullity.

Once the program has been established, of course, there may exist a separate legal right to be allowed to attend if one meets the eligibility requirements. That does not alter the fact that both the facility itself and the eligibility requirements were established exclusively by agency action, with no adjudicatory intervention. Moreover, the legal right to challenge one's exclusion might also be precluded, and all decisions on eligibility might be assigned to an unreviewable decision of the agency. In the United States, that would probably invalidate the program for violation of the due process clause. But in theory, if the program were permitted to proceed, it might be deemed unfair, but it would still represent a valuable benefit for those citizens who were permitted to attend.

The concept of legal rights is not merely underinclusive, in that it applies only to those benefits that are enforced by adjudication, but overinclusive as well. It confers a misleading dignity on certain governmental actions that fail to provide any real benefits. This is not so much the problem of nominal rights as a problem of pragmatically unenforceable ones. A nominal right is a right without a remedy, that is, with no adjudicatory means of implementation. For example, the government might declare, by duly enacted statute, that every citizen has the right to adult education without taking any other action. This is not a legal right at all, in the traditional meaning of the term. It merely makes use of the word 'right,' with all its inspiring, historically sedimented meanings, to express a feeling or obtain a political advantage. It may represent an important moral statement by the government, as the idea of expressive law suggests,[36] or it may constitute a degradation of political discourse.[37] In any case, nominal rights are fairly rare, and readily recognized as such, so their designation as rights probably does not create a serious conceptual problem.

Pragmatically unenforceable legal rights are another matter, being more common and less often recognized. Since a legal right is essentially equivalent to a privately initiated adjudication, its pragmatic force, in any given case, will depend upon the availability of this particular implementation mechanism. In the United States, adjudication is generally provided by adversarial proceedings in state or federal courts. When the courts are closed to certain people, as this nation's courts were closed to women, African Americans, or Chinese Americans at various times, the proudly declared legal right is only a mirage for them. Such juridical exclusions have generally been eliminated but, as Marc Galanter, Stewart Macaulay, and others have demonstrated, significant financial barriers remain in force.[38] Litigation ranges from being rather expensive, to extremely expensive, to ferociously expensive, to make-your-hair-stand-up-on-end-knock-your-teeth-out-one-by-one expensive.[39] A person who cannot sustain such formidable expenditures has no legal right, since the right's only pragmatic role is to provide an adjudicatory remedy. Common Law, and the pre-modern state in general, were remarkably blind to this inconvenient fact. The sacerdotal quality of legal rights made their theoretical existence seem more significant than their practical effects, and the money that the court awarded in their name, partaking of their sacerdotal character, seemed more real, more significant, than the money spent in the adjudication process.

There are two principal reasons why a particular person might not be able to sustain the expenses of litigation. First, and most obviously, the person may not have enough money, a mundane little difficulty that besets the majority of the population. Most people are risk averse; even if a lawsuit ultimately promises to award them a significant amount of money, the uncertainty that they will prevail may make them reluctant to expend the sums necessary to prosecute their claim.[40] In addition, ordinary people incur higher search costs than the wealthy, or than corporations, in obtaining a lawyer because they do not keep one on retainer and may have the good sense not to have any as friends. Many people, moreover, are fearful of the legal system, sometimes with good reason. In short, as Einer Elhauge and Galanter point out, the inequalities of wealth and influence that pervade society are reproduced, not eliminated, by adversarial adjudication.[41]

A second difficulty is that many legal rights involve relatively small sums of money. If the cost of bringing a lawsuit to obtain this sum is greater than the sum itself, the right cannot be implemented, no matter how wealthy the rights-holder is. The right can be asserted, of course, and the defendant made to pay, which will provide psychological satisfaction to irrationally angry or vindictive individuals. But for the mentally ordinary, the right to recover a small sum is as illusory as the right to assert a complex claim for the financially ordinary.[42] Lawyers and legislators are aware of these problems, of course, and have instituted a wide range of strategies for solving them. Contingency fees, legal insurance, and attorney's fee provisions address the first problem,[43] while class actions, small claims courts, and statutorily liquidated damages address the second.[44] In the United States, the prevailing rule that denies attorney fee awards to prevailing plaintiffs has been altered by statute in a range of specific areas.[45] What the language of legal rights obscures, however, is that the existence of rights, as a pragmatic matter, often depends entirely on the availability of these particular strategies. Unless they are available, and unless they are effective, the legal right itself will be illusory. But the rhetorical implications of the term 'legal rights' do not suggest this possibility. Rights are described as being established by the legislature, as being granted to various persons, and as being possessed by those persons. They are not treated the way the administrative approach to governance suggests—as a specific implementation mechanism that may or may not operate effectively.

There is thus good reason to bracket the concept of legal rights. It is an unnecessary term, since it refers to something that can be described, more precisely, as an opportunity to obtain a remedy through adjudication. Admittedly, the present designation is more mellifluous and more historical, but it is also more misleading. It implies a link to truth, or definitive determinations, that is unjustified in practice. It emphasizes, indeed glorifies, one group of benefits for citizens that are no more valuable than other benefits, and it implies that these benefits are universally available to all possessors of the right, whereas in fact their availability depends on a variety of complex and often expensive procedural mechanisms. It is, in short, a coagulated concept, preserved by our social nostalgia for the pre-administrative era.

Causes of Action

Causes of Action in Context

In Chapter 6, the concept of law was bracketed and replaced with a network-based model of policy and implementation. Within the context of this model, legal rights, now bracketed as well, can be reformulated as one particular implementation mechanism. It is a mechanism that applies whenever adjudication, whether adversarial or inquisitorial, is employed as a means of achieving public policy objectives. The governmental unit or group of units assigned to conduct these adjudications is typically staffed by people with legal training, insulated from elected representatives by restricting signals from those representatives, and programmed with a set of specialized procedural rules. These rules allow private citizens to send a signal to the adjudicatory unit that will initiate the adjudication. If the moving party can make certain showings, again in accordance with procedural requirements, it will then be able to activate the unit and generate a signal of some sort in its favor, generally described as a remedy or sanction.

The content of the signal that initiates adjudication can be referred to as a cause of action, that is, a claim that a party can assert in an adjudication. This term, and its underlying concept, can be used to replace the bracketed concept of a legal right. It avoids the disadvantages of legal rights that were just described—the claim to truth, the underemphasis on non-adjudicatory means of implementation, and the overemphasis on adjudicatory ones. Instead it places adjudications, and the means of invoking and controlling them, in the broader context of policy implementation. The implications of using this alternative concept can be determined by considering the way different implementation mechanisms, both adjudicatory and non-adjudicatory, are deployed, distinguished, and combined in a modern administrative state.

When a legislature or other policy maker is deciding how to implement a given social policy, it can generally choose among a variety of governmental units. To choose the most effective one, it must consider various issues—the knowledge base of the various units, their capacity for learning, their ability to use existing resources or absorb new ones, their political proclivities, and so forth. Still another issue involves the role that private persons—natural or legal—should play in the implementation process. It is this issue that will generally determine whether the legislature will make use of the specific mechanism of adjudication, or causes of action, in implementing its policy. Causes of action are one of the mechanisms that allow private persons to participate in the process of implementing governmental policy. As such, they take their place among the other types of administrative interaction that were discussed in Chapter 4, and can be regarded as part of the process that is described as an interactive republic. They are not the only means of participatory implementation, however, nor is this mode of participation always regarded as desirable. In fact, modern governmental implementation mechanisms range from those that preclude participation to those that depend on it entirely.

Many implementation mechanisms afford citizens no role in the process; the implementing agency gathers all the necessary information and reaches the relevant decision by itself. In terms of the network metaphor, this means that the agency's implementation design does not instruct the agency to sum inputs from citizens with the other inputs it considers. National defense is one example. Citizens do not provide information about their needs to the armed forces and cannot demand military action. In practice, of course, a domestic firm may complain that its overseas operations are in danger of being seized by a foreign government and obtain armed intervention, or a community may exert sufficient influence to have a military base located within its borders, or to prevent an existing one from closing. But these inputs are not authorized parts of the implementation plan. Another example of an implementation plan that is closed to public participation is the adult education program envisioned in the previous section, which was designed so that an agency made all the decisions about the location and curriculum of the facilities. The agency would conduct its own research into the educational needs of the citizenry, and while it might interview individuals or groups in the course of that research, it would not grant citizens any role in its decision making.

The exclusion of citizens from the implementation process does not mean, of course, that citizens have no authorized input into the program at the earlier, policy formation stage. As described in Chapter 4, the United States and most other Western nations are interactive republics that feature participation at both the legislative and agency level. In the legislature, citizens may be influential or determinative in the overall design of the program. They may also be able to induce their representatives to influence the agency by jaw-boning or arm-twisting or ear-bending or applying force to some other part of the agency's metaphorical anatomy. At the agency level, citizens may participate in secondary policy making through mechanisms such as the notice and comment procedure or by more informal lobbying. Thus, excluding citizens from implementation does not mean that they have no voice; it simply means that a particular implementation mechanism has been designed to apply policy decisions to specific situations, and that citizens have no participatory role in the operation of that mechanism.

In contrast, if the policy maker wants citizens to play a role in the implementation process, it can generate a signal allowing them to appeal directly to an adjudicator, that is, a neutral decision maker authorized to provide a remedy if the moving party meets specified conditions. This implementation mechanism can be used when there is no agency with regulatory authority over the subject matter, as is the case with American contract law, or when the policy maker wants to provide an alternative to the agency's enforcement process. It operates by granting the private party a cause of action. In place of agency implementation, a cause of action enables that party to appeal to an adjudicator who is separated from the agency in some manner. Thus, in the modern state, considerations of justice may control or influence the underlying policy, but it is considerations of management, not justice, that determine whether causes of action are created to effectuate that policy.

From the perspective of a modern administrative state, therefore, a legal right, more usefully described as a cause of action, is merely one means by which a legislator or other policy maker can implement its policy. In the pre-modern state, it was the only mode of implementation that was generally available to legislators, since few administrative agencies existed. Under those circumstances, adjudicative remedies were naturally regarded as possessing some special moral or jurisprudential significance. To the extent that people thought in terms of law rather than policy, that is, in terms of an internally coherent set of rules that was accessible to reason, adjudicatory remedies seemed even more significant—indeed, sacerdotal. But since the legal system that we currently possess makes use of many other implementation mechanisms, and conceives governmental action generally in policy and implementation terms, the continued emphasis on adjudicatory remedies and their associated causes of action is little more than social nostalgia.

Recharacterizing legal rights as causes of action highlights the fact that a wide range of alternatives is available to policy makers in designing the adjudicatory process, and that they need not rely on traditional approaches inherited from the sacerdotal era. Two such choices, presented here as examples of a larger number, involve the identity of the parties and the identity of the adjudicator. Regarding the identity of the parties, a cause of action can be granted to a human being, a group of human beings, or an institution. These are often subsumed under the designation of a legal person, but the term 'legal person' simply refers to any group or institution that has been granted the cause of action. The U.S. Supreme Court, in cases such as *Sierra Club v. Morton*,[46] *Lujan v. Defenders of Wildlife*,[47] and

City of Los Angeles v. Lyons,[48] has restricted standing, that is, the ability to seek an adjudicatory remedy, to persons whose interests were directly injured. Thus, an environmental group raising a statutory challenge to pollution of a wilderness area must engage in the charade of asserting that one of its members has been cavorting, or intends to cavort, through that particular wilderness. In fact, as David Driesen, William Fletcher, and Cass Sunstein have argued,[49] the concept of standing is unnecessary; the operative question is whether the plaintiff has stated a claim, that is, whether she has a cause of action. Thus, there is no reason, on either constitutional or prudential grounds, for courts to restrict so-called private attorney general statutes, that is, statutes granting private persons a cause of action to enforce some public policy that has no direct relation to their own interests.[50] This is simply an alternative enforcement mechanism designed to achieve the same results as a statute enforced by an administrative agency. The only real limit on this mechanism is the one Lea Brilmayer emphasizes—that one person should not be granted a cause of action that would displace or impair the due process protection that should be afforded to another.[51] It is perfectly acceptable to grant a public interest group a cause of action to oppose whale hunting, but problematic to grant it a cause of action to oppose environmental damage to the property of individuals who are capable of asserting their own claims and controlling their own litigation strategy.

The special case of taxpayer standing can be used as an illustration of this point. The reason taxpayers may not bring suit against the government for an allegedly unconstitutional use of funds is not because they do not have standing, as the Supreme Court has held in *Frothingham v. Mellon*[52] and a variety of other cases,[53] but simply because they have no cause of action. The U.S. Constitution submits questions about the allocation of tax funds to the political process. None of the causes of action generated by the protections in the Constitution, such as free speech or due process, are affected when federal tax funds are used for a purpose that allegedly lies outside Congress's enumerated powers. But the Court has quite properly created an exception for tax funds used in violation of the establishment clause, because that provision grants citizens a cause of action to oppose government sponsorship of religion, and the allocation of tax funds for a religious purpose constitutes such forbidden sponsorship.[54] For the same reason, however, the Court was wrong to deny standing in *United States v. Richardson*,[55] where citizens challenged statutes keeping the CIA's budget secret as a violation of the accounts clause.[56] That clause requires that a "regular Statement and Account" of all expenditures be published, thus placing the government under a specific obligation to the citizens, and creating a cause of action to demand the information. There is no reason, moreover, why the government could not create a statutory cause of action that allowed individual taxpayers to challenge other government appropriations. If one thinks in terms of legal rights, one will be induced to conclude that there is something called a right, with a contour or content that is independent from the claim that it asserts, that can only be granted to certain categories of people. The concept of a cause of action clarifies that private-party adjudication is simply an alternative means of enforcing public policy, and no such limits exist.

The adjudicator who hears a cause of action can be either a judge or an administrative hearing officer, that is, a member of a separate governmental institution composed only of adjudicators or a member of the administering agency. In either case, the adjudicator needs to be insulated from non-adjudicatory governmental agents so that she can remain neutral between opposing parties, particularly when one party is itself a governmental unit. This neutrality is sometimes required by our concept of due process,[57] but not always. A statute might provide that decisions about building adult education facilities could be challenged by submissions to a neutral decision maker or to a policy level official at the agency. In the latter case, no due process violation would occur; the lack of neutrality would simply mean that the decision could no longer be described as an adjudication for taxonomic purposes, and the ability to elicit that decision would no longer be a cause of action. As discussed in the preceding chapter and in Chapter 2, neutrality, or insulation from the political process, is not required because the decision has some intrinsically legal character, but represents a conscious design choice. It is required by due process in certain situations, but it is optional in others.

Alternatives to Causes of Action

As just discussed, creating causes of action is a mechanism that a policy maker can deploy if it wants a relatively high level of citizen participation in the implementation process. If participation is not desired, as in the case of national defense or the hypothesized adult education program, then the policy maker will not create causes of action. But a policy maker who wants citizen participation is not compelled to create causes of action; there are a variety of other, non-adjudicatory mechanisms that can serve this same function, albeit in different ways. These alternatives are not fully developed in any Western industrial nation. Our eight-hundred-year tradition of adjudication tends to marginalize other means of participatory implementation, for the very good reason that we have a tremendous reservoir of cultural experience with adjudication, and for the very bad reason that social nostalgia makes us cling to familiar, pre-modern means of governance. Alternatives to adjudication are particularly underdeveloped in the United States, perhaps because of our particular cultural predilection

that Robert Kagan identifies as adversarial legalism.[58] Considering a few of
these alternatives will therefore serve as a useful cognitive prescription. By
recommending different and possibly more effective means of implementing government programs, it will provide a further characterization of the
causes of action that the alternatives could augment or replace.

The first alternative to adjudication is simply less formalized adjudications. The spirit of medieval trial by combat lives on in our nation, which
is supposedly so blessed by the absence of a feudal past. While valuable
efforts have been made, particularly in recent decades, to develop more
citizen-friendly alternatives, far too many social policies are still being implemented by prescribing full-dress trials. Even if the cost of a trial is not
so high that it precludes a remedy entirely, as discussed above, it is often
high enough to eat up much of the reward that a prevailing plaintiff wins,
or constitute real punishment for a prevailing defendant. Victims of our
own adversarialism, we continue to associate the oratory of opening and
closing statements, the drama of cross-examination, the welter of argu-
mentative objections, and the blizzard of briefs as the embodiment of justice.[59] Not only have we failed to fully recognize that most disputes cannot
be resolved in this manner, but, even within the narrow confines of trials
themselves, we have failed to recognize that all this jury-oriented bravura
is unnecessary for the majority of cases that are tried to a judge.[60]

There are many ways in which costs could be reduced if we were not in
thrall to the grandeur and ritual of dramatic, face-to-face confrontations
between opposing parties. Michael Seigel suggests that each side in a trial
could present its case by means of an edited videotape, containing selected
segments of the witnesses' depositions, rather than bringing all the witnesses into court, and having everyone sit through endless hours of in-
consequential sparring.[61] More extensive use could be made of telephone
testimony, internet communication, and, in the next few years, teleconfer-
encing. There would be some loss of accuracy, perhaps, but it would be
counterbalanced by the cost savings in many cases. To go one step further,
small cases could be tried entirely by telephone conference call. If businesses can make million dollar deals on the telephone, and resolve million
dollar disputes, the government should be able to adjudicate thousand
dollar cases by this means.

Our emphasis on legal rights and adjudication means that alternative
mechanisms often arise and pullulate outside the ambit of public scrutiny
or governmental supervision. The civil trials that our legal rights orientation induces us to provide, at the system design level, have proven so time-
consuming and expensive that everyone involved seems to do anything
they can to escape from the procedures that we ourselves have created.
Judges go to extraordinary lengths to induce parties to settle, divorcing

couples hire private mediators, business firms use arbitration and even more informal rent-a-judge arrangements to resolve disputes between themselves, and large enterprises establish arbitration systems to preclude their disaffected customers from going to court.[62] While many of these approaches offer real advantages on their own terms, they often exist in a recondite netherworld where decisions escape oversight and vanish without generating precedents.[63] If we could free ourselves from the concept of legal rights, and recognize causes of action as one of many implementation strategies, we might be more creative about dispensing with traditional procedures and developing adjudicatory mechanisms that meet people's needs.

Criminal trials present an analogous problem. In their combative formality, they are so expensive that no public jurisdiction is funded to try more than a small fraction of those whom it prosecutes, while no private party other than a mafioso or a corporate executive can afford a full defense. As a result, the overwhelming majority of criminal cases are resolved by fairly rapid plea bargains between the prosecutor and the defense attorney.[64] These are cheap, but they fail to satisfy some of the genuine fairness concerns that trials were designed to address; indeed, in the view of many commentators, they are a moral disaster.[65] Gerard Lynch suggests that we reconcile ourselves to the idea that trials are not, and cannot be, our modal method of resolving criminal cases, and pay more attention to plea bargaining itself.[66] Various forms of administrative and judicial supervision are possible; for example, the bargains could be subject to administrative review in the prosecutor's office, or judicially appointed magistrates could sit in on selected bargaining sessions. The legal netherworld in which plea bargaining presently exists results from regarding it as a lapse from our real method for determining guilt or innocence—the one that appears on *Perry Mason*, and even *Law and Order*. But plea bargaining is the dominant method in this undramatic, administrative mass society, and we betray our genuine values if we fail to ensure its fairness as a result of our nostalgia-driven wish that it did not exist.

In addition to the modifications of the adjudicatory process that the recharacterization of legal rights as causes of action would encourage, there are also alternatives to adjudication in its entirety. One such alternative is to authorize citizens to provide information to the agency through some established means, such as complaints. The agency is not required to act on these complaints, but it can do so if it chooses. Thus, citizen inputs are summed with inputs from other sources, such as the agency's own information gathering, the language of the controlling statute, and the expressed wishes of the legislators in the relevant committee. A standard example of an agency that sums citizen complaints with other inputs is the police. The police gather information about criminal activities through their own initiatives, such as patrols and investigations, but they also accept citizen reports. These reports can lead to investigations and arrests, but the police are not required to act on them, and often decide not to do so. Thus, citizens can complain, but they have no cause of action by which they can punish an offender.

Complaints are often a valuable source of information for the implementing agency, but there seems to be no general theory of complaint handling. In the United States, the subject is completely absent from the Administrative Procedure Act.[67] This does not mean, of course, that complaints do not play a role in the administrative process; many agencies respond to complaints, and have developed special forms or other procedures to facilitate their submission.[68] Federal agencies are generally scrupulous about providing opportunities for filing complaints on their websites.[69] Within recent years, innovative measures have been adopted, such as telephone numbers to report air pollution or whistle blower statutes to protect complainants against retaliation.[70]

Nonetheless, there is much more that could be done regarding citizen complaints. Monetary rewards could be offered, for example, but they are somewhat old-fashioned, and they create a danger of perverse incentives. A more promising approach would be to establish readily accessible facilities, or assign agency staff to interview the relevant population. This is resource-intensive, but its actual effectiveness can only be judged by comparing the expenditure of funds to the level of compliance that is obtained by virtue of that expenditure. One way to elicit complaints but economize on resources might be to rely on sampling, rather than comprehensive coverage of the relevant population. Private firms regularly use this technique to gauge consumer inclination or satisfaction;[71] its relative absence in public administration may result from thinking of complaints as diluted legal claims, where the complainant is seeking some personal remedy, rather than as sources of information for a non-adjudicatory implementation program.

A particular mechanism for eliciting and responding to citizen complaints is an ombudsperson, a government employee who, by various means, is rendered partially independent of other officials, and who is authorized to intervene in the administrative process on the citizens' behalf. The Scandinavian nations developed the idea,[72] the United Kingdom has made extensive use of it, and the European Union has recently adopted it.[73] In the United Kingdom, there are three separate groups of ombudspersons, one at the national level and having general jurisdiction, a second at the national level with jurisdiction over health-related matters, and a third for local government.[74] Moreover, the mechanism has proven so popular that many government agencies and even private firms have developed their own ombudspersons.[75] In order to complain to the national ombudspersons, citizens must file their complaints with a member of the House of Commons, who then transmits it to the ombudsperson. This somewhat unusual arrangement makes the mechanism appear to resemble casework in the United States, that is, interventions by legislators on behalf of important constituents.[76] In fact, the legislators in the United Kingdom perform only a very general screening or gate-keeping function and transmit most of the complaints to the ombudsperson, rather than serving as the means of redress.[77] The authority of the ombudsperson is limited, however, and the device, despite its popularity, appears to be in its infancy.

Social policy can also be implemented by authorizing private citizens to compel an agency decision. The citizen might be required to make specified assertions to the agency, or to demonstrate the existence of specified conditions. If the agency refused to act, the citizen could then appeal to some other government entity, which would be authorized to compel the agency action that the citizen requested. This entity could be the agency's superior, which would consider the citizen's assertions in the same manner that the agency did. In that case, the mechanism would be entirely non-adjudicatory. Alternatively, the citizen might appeal to an adjudicatory body, which would ask both the citizen and the agency to state their position, according to a set of specified procedures, and then render a decision about which party was correctly interpreting the authorizing statute. In that case, the citizen would have a cause of action to compel an agency decision, but the overall mechanism would still be essentially non-adjudicatory, and certainly a departure from the legal rights model.

The Administrative Procedure Act contains a pallid provision that allows citizens to petition agencies to issue or repeal a rule,[78] but the agency has no obligation to respond, and courts have generally been reluctant to impose such an obligation.[79] Similarly, there is no mechanism by which citizens can compel an agency to implement a statutory mandate, and even explicit statutory deadlines have proven difficult to enforce in court.[80] While there is an understandable reluctance to give individuals any authorization to commit agency resources, it is far from unrealistic to establish a mechanism that would require an agency to explain its implementation strategy, particularly when it is subject to a statutory mandate. Doing so would be one way to subject the kinds of compliance strategies described in Chapter 5 to a certain amount of citizen control. As stated, these strategies are generally unsupervised; in American law, they fall into the Administrative Procedure Act's residual category of informal adjudication, which means that they are subject to virtually no procedural requirements.[81] Complaints to an administrator or an adjudicator that would

challenge an agency's compliance strategy or compel the agency to under-
take certain efforts to achieve compliance could subject some of these
now-recondite decisions to external supervision.

Causes of Action v. Legal Rights

Emotional Commitments

Bracketing the term 'legal rights' and replacing it with 'causes of action' is
a plausible descriptive strategy. Our concept of legal rights is tightly bound
to the specific process of adjudication, a connection that is not severed by
any of the theoretical approaches to legal rights, no matter how abstract
they claim to be. The proposed alternative possesses the advantage of placing legal rights, recharacterized as causes of action, in the context of the
administrative state, where they are only one of many means by which
governmental policy is implemented. It thereby avoids the tendency to
underemphasize more administrative, non-adjudicatory means of implementation and to overemphasize the value and significance of adjudication. In addition, it encourages the development of various beneficial
alternatives to the adjudicatory process. But does the cause of action concept meet the stated criteria for a preferable descriptive term? Does it correspond more closely to our emotional commitments, signal the heuristic
character of theory, and facilitate microanalysis?

With respect to our emotional commitments, it might be argued that the
cause of action alternative fails to capture these commitments because it is
overly mechanistic. Even theories that retain the concept of legal rights, but
define these rights in functional terms, have been charged with this defect.
To take one leading example, Hart rejects Bentham's view that legal rights
result from the imposition of a legal obligation, which for Bentham meant
an order backed by a governmental sanction. Rights are not a residual category that describes the results of sanctions or obligations, Hart contends,
but an affirmative statement of individual entitlements. Bentham has failed
to perceive the ordinary language meaning of legal rights in his concern
with definitive sanctions. The law employs sanctions, Hart concedes, but its
principal purpose is to set behavioral standards, to tell citizens what they
should and should not do. Hart insists that a sense of normativity, of
"rightness," attaches to these standards and the rights they produce. Beneficiaries of these standards feel justified, not merely fortunate, in obtaining
their advantages, while violators are regarded as wrongdoers.[82]

Hart's ordinary language analysis of legal rights is essentially the same as
his ordinary language analysis of law, and it is problematic for essentially
the same reason. What Hart is discerning once again are the lingering reverberations of a bygone sensibility. The normativity that attaches to legal

rights is derived from the sacerdotal conception of the state, where government meditates between the divine and human worlds. In that conception, the power of divinity flows through government, from God to the legitimate ruler. It infuses the ruler with the ultimate political right, the right to rule, which naturally includes all subsidiary rights, and renders him immune from any other person's claims. By the process of making law or bestowing individualized largesse, the ruler then confers part of this right upon his subjects, and these humanly created rights give the beneficiaries a fragment of the ruler's powers and immunities.[83] He confers on Roger of Fussbudget Marsh the right to hunt in Finikin Forest, and he confers on all his subjects the right to exclude others from their property. He grants Bishop of Adelbrane immunity from taxation, and grants all members of the nobility immunity from suits by commoners. These legal rights, both particular and general, possess an inherent normativity because they are derived from the ruler's own rights, partake of his moral stature as God's deputy, and constitute part of a divinely sanctioned law. They define the proper way for subjects to behave toward one another, and they are supposed to be fully obeyed, just as Hart asserts.

Of course, as noted earlier, the abstract concept of legal rights was not current in pre-modern times, and the rights that possessed this sacerdotal character were conceived as a range of substantive entitlements. Benthams's insight that legal rights were simply one particular mechanism for implementing public policy should have extirpated these pre-modern associations, but because the mechanism was conceived in terms of rights, it retained its sacerdotal character. Thus, legal rights were not only perceived as a means of implementing public policy, but as a means that possessed some inherent normativity that arose from the general conception of rights or law. This inherent normativity, like the phantom appendage that the amputee continues to perceive after the physical original is gone, persists long after the sacerdotal character of law and legal rights has been rejected.

Apart from their pre-modern conceptual structure, legal rights continue to retain their phantom normativity because this normativity still seems applicable when one is referring to traditional, pre-administrative causes of action such as damages for breach of contract, conversion of funds, or tortious injury to property or person. But what about a cause of action to obtain twice the finance charge, but no less than $100 or more than $1000, plus attorney's fees and costs, if one's loan agreement contains a statement of the amount financed that fails to include one's prepaid finance charge?[84] It is certainly true, in this latter case, and for so many other modern regulatory enactments, that the statute or regulation that creates the cause of action is setting some sort of behavioral standard, but the element of normativity that seems so obvious in Common Law is now attenuated. These

relatively new causes of action do not reflect standards of behavior, linked
to a generally accepted social morality, but rather appear as efforts to implement specific social policies.

The administrative state, moreover, does not merely add new policies
and new causes of action to the existing Common Law, but also displaces
Common Law in many cases. Transportation and utility rates are set by
agencies, rather than by contract; injuries to employees are covered by
workman's compensation laws, which eliminate questions of causation and
negligence; environmental regulation displaces nuisance laws.[85] As a result,
prevailing rules become increasingly detached from intuitively grasped social morality. The causes of action that persons can assert seem less like
rights, or standards of behavior, and more like instrumentalities, more like
devices to achieve an underlying policy. This follows naturally from the discussion in the preceding section; causes of action are no longer some sui
generis category called legal rights, but simply one of many options for implementing the decisions of governmental policy makers.

As in the case of both legitimacy and law, Hart's argument contains an
unstated term, a phantom appendage, that he never adequately justifies.
The fact that a governmental signal is something more than an order
backed by a sanction does not necessarily confer upon the signal the normativity that Hart perceives. There is an intermediate position between
mere threats and full-blown normativity; the signal can serve as a behavioral standard, a command that people are expected to obey simply because it has issued from an authoritative source. It will only possess the
additional element of normativity if the authoritative source can claim a
generalized moral imprimatur, if it is, according to the standard terminology, legitimate. But as discussed in Chapter 5, legitimacy of this sort belongs to the sacerdotal conception of government and is absent from its
modern counterpart. A state that is justified in instrumental terms carries
no general imprimatur, and its signals are not seen as possessing some inherent moral force but as efforts to implement the social policies its citizens desire.

Morality is not absent from the administrative state, of course. As discussed in Chapters 1 and 6, however, it no longer attaches to specific
mechanisms of governance. With the articulation of purpose, public debate shifts to the choice of policies, and it is these choices that our sense of
public morality addresses.[86] Government in its entirety is regarded as an
instrumentality for implementing the choices that are made, and its particularized mechanisms, such as adjudication, are thus secondary or derived instrumentalities, partaking of the government's instrumental character just as pre-modern instrumentalities partook of the government's
sacerdotal character. Each mechanism, including courts and agency adjudicators, must demonstrate, through its performance, that it can fulfill its

assigned task, and will be judged on the basis of its ability to do so. This does not mean that causes of action never implement our deeply felt norms, that we must abandon our image of the heroic lawyer who uses the judicial system to defend the oppressed and bring privileged wrongdoers to justice. Those inspiring events can still occur, although we are more likely to see them in the movies than in reality.[87] But their inspirational content does not stem from the mere fact that the lawyer is going to court and invoking legal rights, as the widespread hostility to litigation demonstrates. Rather, its source is the underlying social policy that the lawyer is instantiating through his litigative efforts.

Are legal rights, or causes of action, supposed to be obeyed, as Hart suggests?[88] To reiterate the answer given in Chapter 6, it depends. In particular, it depends on the level of obedience that is required to achieve the policy that underlies the cause of action. According to many legal scholars, for example, contractual rules are not supposed to be obeyed in every situation. The social value that contractual causes of action implement is prosperity, and that value is sometimes served by breaching the contract and paying damages when the other party asserts its cause of action.[89] Regulatory rules that create governmental causes of action are not meant to be fully obeyed either. Rather, the agency is authorized to achieve the underlying social value by telling the regulated parties, through a complex set of signals, how much obedience is expected of them. This negotiated interaction regarding the compliance rate displaces the pre-modern, sacerdotal conception of uniform obedience to government commands. Once again, our sense of morality attaches to the underlying policy, not to the devices by which this policy is implemented.

Although our moral commitments involve the policies that government is expected to implement, the means that government employs to carry out this task are also subject to moral considerations. These moral considerations are generally described as procedural values; they provide that government should achieve its substantive values in an effective, fair, and efficient manner. Fairness is the value that seems more closely connected to a claim that legal rights possess some inherent normative quality, but the impression is illusory. Our actual sense of fairness, as it relates to the procedural issues that legal rights tend to implicate, is embodied in two separate principles, codified by the Fourteenth Amendment to the U.S. Constitution as the due process and equal protection clauses, and the concept of legal rights does not correspond to either principle.

Due process is best understood as a constraint on governmental action that requires the government to proceed by adjudication under certain circumstances, and then specifies the elements of the adjudication. As stated above, the concept of legal rights is dependent on adjudication, and would thus seem naturally linked to the due process guarantee. But legal rights are not presently conceptualized as a means of triggering adjudication; rather they are conceived as a norm inherent in our concept of law that adjudication enforces. This leads to the confusing idea that the ambit of the due process clause is established by the independent principle embodied in the concept of law and legal rights, and not by the need for adjudication. In other words, it interposes an additional and unnecessary concept into the organic relationship between due process and adjudication.

In the early decades of the previous century, the Supreme Court took the normativity of law and legal rights quite literally, holding that the causes of action created by Common Law had constitutional status and could not be altered or abolished by ordinary statutes. This constitutional status, the Court declared, was established and secured by the due process clause. Linking due process to this idea separated it completely from its adjudicatory basis and spawned substantive due process doctrine.[90] Ultimately, the doctrine proved incoherent and was abandoned.[91] It had political as well as conceptual origins, of course, but it would have been more difficult to formulate and to maintain had the Court been conceptually precluded from treating legal rights as an independent and inherently normative concept, and could only have regarded them as a means of triggering the mechanism of adjudication.

If designating causes of action as legal rights is confusing with respect to due process concerns, it is misleading with respect to equal protection. Equal protection focuses on the way people are actually treated, and the results they achieve; thus, the inequality of Southern schools led the Supreme Court, in *Brown v. Board of Education*,[92] to declare that school segregation violated the equal protection clause. When applied to adjudication, this principle requires citizens to have equal access to the courts and to be treated equally once they are involved in judicial proceedings. The idea that legal rights possess an inherent normativity, in contrast, suggests that the right itself is of positive value, and that social fairness is achieved if everyone is granted the same legal rights. It thus obscures, and possibly denies, gross violations of equal protection. For many years, Southern juries that regularly convicted blacks for minor or imagined offenses against whites, while exonerating whites who committed grievous offenses against blacks, were regarded as morally acceptable because whites and blacks had the same legal rights. While this problem has not been solved even today, as the disproportionate imposition of the death penalty indicates, we are at least aware of it. But the idea that legal rights are inherently fair has cast a deeper shroud of obscurity around the obvious inequality that afflicts poor people, or even middle-class people, when they go to court. The outdated idea that legal rights themselves have normative force, instead of being a mere implementation mechanism, has blinded us to the inequalities of our adjudicatory system, and the extent to which that system violates our genuinely held principle of fairness.

The Heuristic Character of Theory

The second criterion for evaluating descriptive terms is whether the term signals its heuristic character. Strictly speaking, neither legal rights nor causes of action are heuristics. They are not efforts by observers to describe social functions, but terms used by participants in carrying out those functions. Nonetheless, they present a similar conceptual dilemma. We cannot comprehend the world without heuristics, but we must remember that these heuristics are devices to facilitate our comprehension, not part of the objective world. In an analogous manner, we cannot create governmental functions without naming them, but we must remember that these names are ways of identifying and characterizing the function, and not the function itself. If the term is treated as equivalent to that which it describes—if it is reified—participants, and scholars who use the term in the same fashion, will be led astray. They will experience the conceptual coagulation that results when socially contingent relationships are treated as essential ones.

Legal rights terminology invites precisely this reification. The concept's claim to inherent normativity suggests that legal rights are an independent entity, rather than a means of describing a particular enforcement mechanism. Supreme Court procedural due process doctrine illustrates this confusion. The Court began, during the first half of the twentieth century, with the contention that due process protection—the constitutional requirement of notice, a hearing, an impartial decision maker, and a decision on the record—applies only to rights and not to privileges.[93] What the justices meant by rights were entitlements created by Common Law, most notably the rights associated with private property. Entitlements created by statute, such as government employment or welfare benefits, were not rights but privileges, and thus did not merit due process protection under the Constitution. The underlying idea was best stated by Oliver Wendell Holmes, Jr., when, as a state court judge in Massachusetts, he denied relief to a policeman who had been dismissed from his job for expressing political opinions when off duty. "The petitioner may have a constitutional right to talk politics," Judge Holmes wrote, "but he has no constitutional right to be a policeman."[94]

This doctrine seems plausible if one believes the substantive due process idea that Common Law causes of action are constitutionally protected from statutory alteration. It then follows, not by logic nor by experience, but by the association of ideas, that only these Common Law legal rights merit procedural due process protection of notice, a hearing, and an impartial decision maker. Thus, a recursive linkage between legal rights and Common Law not only rendered statutory enactments that altered Common Law constitutionally suspect, but also rendered the entitlements created by statutes constitutionally ephemeral. Such entitlements were merely privileges that the government distributed by some passing, soon-to-be forgotten fancy, and could therefore take away in any manner that it chose without offending the procedural requirements of the due process clause. Only Common Law, which reflected the transcendent principles that existed from time immemorial, and that could not be altered by quotidian legislation, possessed the inherent normativity that qualified as legal rights and merited procedural protection.

For some thirty years, the Court, bolstered by politically conservative appointments, clung to the substantive due process doctrine that Common Law causes of action could not be altered by statute, but the political and conceptual defects of this doctrine were obvious, and it was ultimately abandoned in 1937.[95] Everyone came to recognize that Common Law was merely another type of positive enactment, and that the legislature, as the primary policy maker of the state, could displace the Common Law's judge-made rules with its own rules when it chose.[96] But the related distinction between Common Law rights protected by procedural due process and statutory privileges that did not merit such protection persisted for another thirty years.[97] Even though Common Law causes of action no longer possessed constitutional status, judges believed that Common Law rights were an independent principle to which due process protection naturally and exclusively attached. They simply failed to perceive that their own doctrine no longer made a qualitative distinction between Common Law and statutory entitlements, that both were now perceived as positive enactments that were equally worthy, or unworthy, of due process protection.

Had the justices conceptualized the issue as involving causes of action, rather than rights, the result might have been different. A cause of action is the authority to obtain the adjudication of an issue by the government, and nothing more. The due process guarantee states the constitutional rules for fair adjudications. Consequently, the scope of the due process clause cannot be determined by some intrinsic quality of rights, or of causes of action, but must be determined by the extent to which the government is required to employ adjudication as its mechanism for implementing governmental policy.

Once the problem is framed in this manner, the resolution is a reasonably familiar one. Our sense of fairness demands that the government implement its policies through the mechanism of adjudication whenever its actions are directed against specified individuals, as opposed to general groups. The underlying rationale has already been introduced in Chapter 6, in connection with the rule of law. General groups, with some exceptions that are defined by other values or commitments, such as equal protection, have access to the political process and must take their chances in that process. The legislature, for example, possesses the authority to extract resources from groups such as doctors or automobile companies and distribute them to others; it can require doctors to see certain types of patients or to require automobile companies to make certain types of cars. If these groups are displeased with such burdens or restrictions, they can express their displeasure through elections, or through interaction at the legislative or administration level. This is our basic governmental structure, and, despite its defects, it satisfies our sense of fairness.[98] But individuals do not have any realistic recourse to the political process. When state officials impose burdens or restrictions on a particular person, that person's vote or interactive influence is too small to serve as a constraint on unfair governmental action. Adjudication provides the means of securing fairness in this situation. It prevents the government from acting unless it can demonstrate, to an independent decision maker in a structured procedure, that its actions are based on a legal rule, namely, on a governmental action that is directed toward a general group. The adjudication requirement compels the government to demonstrate that actions taken against specified individuals are consistent with general provisions for which the political process provides a guarantee of fairness.

What is interesting is that the Supreme Court identified this role of adjudication rather readily, at the height of the substantive process era. *Londoner v. City of Denver*, decided in 1908, held that taxes could not be assessed against specified individuals unless these individuals were provided with notice and a hearing.[99] *Bi-Metallic Investment Co. v. State Board of Equalization*, decided seven years later, held that a general tax increase, even if based on what purported to be specific factual determinations, was not subject to these due process requirements.[100] Thus, more than half a century before it abolished the right-privilege distinction in the 1970 case of *Goldberg v. Kelly*,[101] the Supreme Court had developed an alternative formulation of the due process clause's scope that could have entirely displaced that dubious distinction. Two decades after that, and still three decades before *Goldberg*, any political disinclination to make use of that formulation disappeared with the demise of substantive due process. But the justices failed to see the connection; they continued to think that due process related to legal rights, that is, rights created by Common Law and possessing an inherent normativity. They applied the *Londoner-Bi-Metallic* distinction only with respect to those rights rather than perceiving its universal relevance. The reification of legal rights created the idea that legal rights themselves possessed an inherent normativity that determined the scope of the due process clause, without reference to our structure of government or our societal sense of fairness.

More strikingly still, the justices of the *Goldberg* era remained unable to grasp this readily available solution when they realized that they needed some limiting principle to replace the one *Goldberg* abolished. Still transfixed by the reified concept of legal rights, they continued trying to use it to define the boundaries of procedural due process. In *Board of Regents v. Roth*, decided two years after *Goldberg*, they did so by going back to the Constitution's original language, which is generally a sign of conceptual confusion.[102] The Fifth and Fourteenth Amendments state that no person may be deprived of "life, liberty or property" without due process of law. Very well then, the justices reasoned, they need only identify liberty and property interests and they would have fixed the boundaries of the due process guarantee. *Roth* involved property, and property, of course, is created by state law. What courts should do, the Court declared, was to look to state law to determine the existence of a property right to which the federal guarantee of due process could attach. In *Roth* and its companion case, *Perry v. Sinderman*,[103] they held that a college professor who had been tenured under state law possessed the requisite property interest, but one who was a probationary employee could be terminated without due process.

Once again, the justices were reifying legal rights; once again, they were interposing this concept between due process and adjudication. The political instinct underlying this effort was undoubtedly the desire to limit the expansive doctrine they had launched. The conceptual instinct was the belief that some inherent principle in the content of legal rights determined the scope of the due process guarantee. Almost immediately, this doctrine ran into serious conceptual difficulties. If positive state law established property rights, why could it not also establish the procedures by which those rights were taken away? One member of the Court, Justice Rehnquist, was willing to embrace this idea; in *Arnett v. Kennedy*, he wrote, in a virtual paraphrase of Judge Holmes's opinion, that a government employee who accepts statutorily defined employment must also accept the statutorily provided procedures for dismissal; "he must take the bitter with the sweet."[104] But other justices balked at this conclusion, which would have permitted state and federal governments to eviscerate the due process guarantee by statute.[105] Property rights are created by state law, they concluded, but procedural protection then attaches to stated-created rights as a matter of constitutional law, and its content is to be derived from constitutional doctrine.[106]

This was not only a rather clumsy solution to the problem, but immediately raised another conceptual difficulty. It was easy enough to identify property rights created by Common Law, because these rights, by tradition, had always been granted due process protection. The controversial issue was statutory entitlements, the characteristic enactments of the administrative state. The whole point of abolishing the right-privilege distinction was to include these enactments within the ambit of due process. But administrative statutes rarely announce that they are creating property; they simply grant a benefit, or impose a restriction, sometimes specifying some of the procedures to be followed in implementing it, and sometimes not. How is a constitutional court to determine that a property right has been created? The Court finally settled on the idea that property is created by constraints on discretion: if the administrator is granted broad discretion, no property right has been created, but if constraints are placed on that discretion, then a property right exists, and due process applies.[107] As explained in Chapter 4, however, administrative statutes are not usefully characterized as grants of discretion because the legislature is not generally giving an administrator power as a sort of bequest. What the legislature generally does is to determine the type of supervision to which the authorized administrator will be subject. Trying to interpret these statutes as grants of discretion, therefore, will yield confused and uncertain results. The invocation of the term 'property,' moreover, will be of little use in resolving the quandary, for the analogy between Common Law property and administrative entitlements is likely to be an attenuated one that provides little intuitive guidance.[108]

Recharacterizing legal rights as causes of action could have resolved these conceptual complexities. It would have eliminated the intervening concept of legal rights and focused attention on the issue of adjudication. This is not a magic formula that immediately resolves all contested questions about the due process clause, but it does define the inquiry in a sensible way that reflects the realities of the administrative state and the value of governmental fairness that due process embodies. It suggests that the scope of due process protection depends on the extent to which the government is required to act by adjudication in implementing public policy. As discussed above, this requirement applies when the government is imposing disadvantages or burdens on specified individuals. Within the area of action taken against specified individuals, our sense of fairness may still allow implementation by non-adjudicatory methods. For example, denying an application for a job may not require notice or a hearing, whereas dismissing a person from a job generally does. There are innumerable intermediate cases, and people's judgment about them will differ. But asking whether the applicant or job holder has a property right in these situations does not advance the discussion at all; it merely restates the question in a more confusing form. One advantage of bracketing the concept of legal rights and using causes of action as an alternative is that it eliminates the unnecessary term that pre-modern attitudes have interposed between the organically connected concepts of due process and adjudication. As a result, it makes the analysis of due process cases more coherent, more realistic, more consonant with social values, and less confused by reified heuristics inherited from the pre-administrative state.

The Opportunity for Microanalysis

Finally, the cause of action concept is preferable to legal rights because it facilities microanalysis. Legal rights, as Bentham pointed out,[109] and Luhmann has reiterated, imply binary determinations.[110] Does a given person have a particular legal right or not? Can Roger hunt in Finikin Forest, does William have the right to receive rents from the estate of Blackacre, does Wesley have a legal claim against Ronald, does H.L.A. have a legally respected choice to exclude Jeremy from Whitefield? The sacerdotal quality of legal rights leads us to treat these determinations as the most important element in describing our legal system. Once they are made, moreover, they tend to forestall further inquiry—Roger or H.L.A. have obtained their legal rights, and the rest is mere detail.

Reconceiving legal rights as causes of action dissolves these coagulated determinations and invites us to trace the operation of our legal system with greater realism and precision. It draws attention to the fact that adjudication, invoked by a cause of action, is only one of many choices that are available for implementing social policy. This leads to an analysis of the way that choice is made, to an assessment of the effectiveness of adjudication as a means of implementing social policy, to a comparison of adjudication with other implementation mechanisms, and to cognitive prescriptions for making adjudication more effective in cases where it is deployed.

A good deal of this work has already been done by sociolegal, or law and society scholars. It began with the efforts of Marc Galanter, Stewart Macaulay, Ian Macneil, Laura Nader, and others to explain why consumers seemed to benefit so little from contract doctrines that appeared to protect their interests.[111] These scholars discovered the previously hidden world of law in action, where valid legal claims are regularly abandoned or ignored, where informal remedies are more effective than litigation, and where lawyers often serve their own interests, rather than those of the client. Law and economics scholars then built on this demystification of contract doctrine to analyze the effect of litigation costs and fee shifting arrangements, and the various strategic uses of the legal rules that govern the adjudicatory process.[112] At the same time, the conceptual agonies of the Supreme Court's due process decisions led public law scholars such as Malcolm Feeley, Jerry Mashaw, William Simon, and Lucy White to explore the effectiveness of adjudication in resolving disputes between the government and individuals.[113]

Insightful and significant as this work has been, it has not yet produced a reconceptualization of legal rights. We recognize the limitations and defects of adjudications, but somehow believe that legal rights, whose sole purpose is to invoke and govern these adjudications, are unaffected, and remain as conceptually important as they were before. We speak of legal rights—of their creation, their enforcement, and their abolition—as if they were a fixed, specific entity rather than a range of implementation mechanisms whose operation depends on the nature of the issue, the nature of the party, and the nature of the forum. Bracketing this concept for purposes of academic analysis, and replacing it with the notion of a cause of action as a means of triggering adjudication, would enable scholars to engage in a sustained microanalysis of adjudication, and of the alternative means of implementing social policy.

As in the case of John of Salisbury's human body image, it is easy enough to perceive the conceptual pathologies of bygone notions that are no longer part of our own thought process, that we perceive as separate because they lie across a gulf of quaintness. The predecessor of adjudication was trial by combat, where disputes were resolved by having the disputants, or their hired champions, fight each other until death or sunset. Not only can we readily perceive the inaccuracy, ineffectiveness, and unfairness of this mechanism, but we can also perceive the way that it emerged from feudalism, and the way it reflected a warrior society's unanalyzed beliefs about the connection between physical combat and moral virtue. We can also perceive the pragmatic defects in our own mechanism of adjudication, but what requires real mental effort is to perceive its underlying conceptual peculiarities, the unanalyzed connection it asserts between persuasion and veracity, and between going to court and obtaining a remedy for wrongs.

We like to regard ourselves as more rational, more creative, even smarter than our medieval predecessors, but it is they who shed their ingrained attitudes and generated our concepts, whereas we, living in a very different world, have not managed to shed the concepts we inherited from them. Perhaps we can learn something from them if we go back to their political texts, or better still their political fantasies, to watch their thought processes at work. In Chrétien de Troyes Arthurian romance, *Yvain (The Knight with the Lion)*,[114] the lord of Noire Espine has died, and the elder of his two daughters tries to take control of the entire manor, denying the younger one her fair share. When the younger one objects, the elder rushes off to Camelot and obtains the services of Sir Gawain as her champion. The younger daughter arrives to find Gawain, "the best man" at the court, already engaged to fight against her. When her sister insists that she find an opposing champion immediately, she appeals to King Arthur. Arthur, playing the role of judge, decides that this is an unfair demand and gives the younger sister forty days to find her champion. Yvain, the only equal to Gawain at court, has disappeared, but word has reached the court about the valorous deeds performed by an unnamed knight with a pet lion. The younger sister decides to seek that knight's assistance, unaware that he is actually Yvain, who has been fighting incognito.[115] After various vicissitudes, she finds him, and he agrees to help, arriving in Camelot just before the forty-day period has expired.

The two champions now take the field; although closest friends, they do not recognize each other, since they are covered entirely in armor, and set to fighting without uttering a word. Each is astounded to find himself facing such a formidable adversary. They belabor each other with resounding blows until their swords are blunted, their shields split, their armor dented, and their bodies bathed in blood. With night approaching and both collapsing from fatigue, they speak to each other for the first time to arrange a postponement of the fight, and discover the other's identity.[116] "Alas! What a tragedy," Yvain exclaims. "We've fought this combat in appalling ignorance, through not recognising one another, for had I known who you were, I would never have fought you."[117] Both then refuse to fight any further and—apparently forgetting the two sisters—insist that the other is the victor. King Arthur, very pleased with the chivalrous loyalty of his knights toward each other, now undertakes to settle the underlying dispute. "'Where,' he says, 'is the damsel who had expelled her sister from her land and has forcibly and pitilessly disinherited her?'—'Sire,' says she, 'I'm here'—'You're there? Come here, then! I've been aware for a long time that you were disinheriting her. Her right shall no longer be denied, for you've just admitted the truth to me.'"[118]

This contest is the third judicial combat portrayed in the romance. In the first two, Yvain's adversaries are evil, and he triumphs by God's grace and by the intercession of his lion, a symbol of divine justice. But in this third battle both combatants are good men and, in that coincidence central to every action or adventure story, formidable fighters. So Chrétien has confronted the basic contradiction of adversarial procedures: only one of their causes is just, but both champions are equally valorous and admirable. Had they known each other's identity in advance, they would have refused to fight and perhaps resolved the dispute in another way, but they were encased in armor and thus induced to slash away at one another until both become injured and exhausted.

Once the two heroes realize the error that their instinctive combativeness has led to, and refuse to fight each other any more, King Arthur decides the dispute between the sisters through a verbal interchange. It is not a trial, but it bears a resemblance to a trial, in that he is apparently getting ready to have each sister state her case. Chrétien probably would not have known how to depict this, even if he had wanted to, since neither inquisitorial nor adversarial trials were common at the time. So he resolves the situation quickly with a stratagem—a naive one, to be sure, although only a bit more naive than the ones used in many episodes of *Perry Mason*. But the sensibility that he reflects, the intimation that there is a more direct and accurate way than combat to decide the justice of a person's claim, would lead, in the two centuries that followed, to the creation of a range of new procedures whose use continues to the present day.

It is now two centuries since the tipping trend of articulation led to the advent of the administrative state. We like to regard ourselves as more rational, more conscientious, even smarter than our medieval predecessors, but we do not seem to have been equally creative. We have made some progress, but we are still thinking in terms of legal rights and the adjudications to which they are inextricably, though not explicitly, attached. Encased in the conceptual armor of an adjudicatory, often adversarily defined conception of legal rights, we slash away at each other in a manner that is often as thoughtless and unnecessary as the fight between Gawain and Yvain. If we could take off that armor, if we could bracket our pre-modern concepts, we might see ourselves and our practices more clearly, and perhaps achieve the kinds of conceptual advances that our predecessors did in the centuries following Chrétien.[119] The crucial question, in terms of the policy-implementation model that replaces the concept of law, is the way policy is implemented. In some implementation schemes, our sense of fairness demands that persons be granted causes of action so that they can invoke an adjudication of the way the government is treating them. In other settings, adjudications are ineffective or counterproductive, and different mechanisms should be used. Evaluation of these various options is always complex, and always requires detailed analysis. Relying on the pre-modern concept of legal rights, with its sacerdotal, combative implications, only encases us in rigid structures that obscure our real situation and our real options.

Eight

From Human Rights to Moral Demands on Government

Natural Rights and Human Rights

Natural Rights

CHAPTER 7 brackets the concept of legal rights, but its argument is inapplicable to human rights. Legal rights, by definition, are created by positive enactment and can be abolished by it; the concept should be bracketed, it was argued, because it refers to a specific implementation mechanism—privately initiated adjudication—that is only one of several in a modern administrative state. The concept of human rights, in contrast, belongs to moral theory.[1] It does not refer to an implementation mechanism at all, but to claims that human beings can assert against any form of governmental action. According to the general view, human rights cannot be abolished or significantly altered by the government because they embody values by which the government itself is judged.[2] Of course, proponents of human rights hope that the government will recognize these rights and implement them by creating causes of action; at the same time, they regretfully but readily concede that government action can violate these rights. But neither governmental recognition nor denial is thought to affect the existence of the rights themselves. The rights remain and determine our moral judgments about whether the regime is benign or malignant, just or unjust.

While the precise definition of human rights has been much debated, the concept involves two generally acknowledged elements that will be sufficient for purposes of this discussion. First, human rights must be human, that is, they must be based on considerations common to all human beings, rather than on those specific to individuals or groups.[3] Roger's claim to Blackacre is not a human right, nor is the right of freeborn Englishmen to liberty. Thus, human rights cannot be derived from any aspect of human beings other than their mere humanity, the traits that they possess in common. Second, human rights must be rights, that is, they must represent some claim or entitlement that can be asserted by the human beings in question on normative grounds.[4] If they lack this structure, then they are better viewed as interests, concerns, or attributes. As discussed in the preceding chapter, legal rights also possess the character of claims, but add the requirement that the right must be enforceable by an adjudicator of some sort, typically a court. Human rights are not subject to this additional requirement, as they are moral principles existing independently of governmental recognition. But to retain the general character of rights, as that term is generally understood, they must be conceived as claims or entitlements that humans can assert.

While previous chapters of this book have argued that several major concepts used to describe our political and legal system have become less relevant since the advent of the administrative state, the reverse would seem to be the case with human rights. An administrative state, whatever extensive benefits it may bestow upon its citizens, poses concomitantly extensive dangers to their liberty. Its articulation of structure creates an effective apparatus for the deployment of governmental compulsion by physical, political, or economic means; its articulation of purpose projects that apparatus into economic and social relations previously governed by traditional mechanisms that were arguably less coercive, and certainly less governmental. As a result, the government's capacity for oppression increases dramatically. The century just passed provides examples of administrative states that so comprehensively and efficiently oppressed their citizens, so hounded them by means of Weberian hierarchies and tracked them by means of Weberian files, that they replaced Dante's Inferno as our culture's predominant conception of Hell.[5] Thus, a vigorous concept of human rights would seem more important than ever before.

But the conceptual origin of human rights raises quasi-Cartesian doubt. The concept is a lineal descendent of natural rights, an idea that seems to have emerged from the interplay of the two dominant institutional and conceptual structures of the Middle Ages, feudalism and Christianity.[6] Feudalism generated the idea of personal rights, which consisted of either claims that a person could assert or entitlements that a person possessed.[7] In the absence of a centralized state and an effective system of civil order, these claims and entitlements, instantiated by physical force or litigation, defined the person's position in the world. Christianity then contributed the idea of natural law, and also of a pre-social era of human history when legal rights did not exist and only natural law prevailed.[8] These themes combined to generate the theory that human beings possess natural rights in their pre-social state, as a matter of natural law.[9] Modern scholarship has traced the origins of this theory to the fourteenth-century debate about apostolic poverty and identified William of Ockham as its first proponent.[10] Not surprisingly, Ockham's writings, and the debate in general, were phrased almost exclusively in terms of natural law.[11]

Early Protestant thinkers did not find much use for the doctrine of natural rights. As Quentin Skinner recounts, they viewed political authority as established directly by God and, when events began to turn against them, they viewed the right to resist that authority as derived from the same source.[12] But with the increasing secularization of political theory, and the resulting effort to derive both authority and resistance from natural law, rather than a specific command of the Almighty, the doctrine of natural rights became prominent once more. It owed its newfound popularity among Protestant thinkers to a refurbishment of medieval contract theory. As discussed in Chapter 5, the contract theory of government was based on the idea that promises were the most sacrosanct human relationship, and must be kept regardless of their consequences. Once people in the pre-social condition had agreed to establish a government, that government deserved their obedience and was thus legitimate. In developing this idea, medieval people were of course projecting the norms of their own society, or rather an idealized version of those norms, back onto the hypothesized pre-social world, or state of nature. They further projected the specific feature of their most important agreement, which was the feudal bond, onto that imagined world. Thus, in the constitutional contract theory of the Middle Ages, natural man was perceived as giving his personal loyalty to the king in exchange for monarchical protection.[13] Seventeenth-century social contract writers preserved the theory's basic reliance upon promise keeping, but modernized it by shifting the focus to the formation of society in general, and by altering the specific features of the hypothesized agreement. As C. B. Macpherson describes, the developing concept of possessive individualism led people to change the model from the feudal bond to a commercial agreement.[14] Thus, contract theory no longer envisioned an act of fealty between a subordinate and a superior, but an exchange of possessions between equal parties.

The result of this change, however, was a conceptual difficulty. If the contract was now being viewed as a quasi-commercial exchange, rather than a promise of loyalty and service, what did people in the state of nature possess that could be traded? Either they had no possessions or, if they did, the whole point of entering the social contract was to protect those possessions, not to relinquish them in a primordial distress sale. What they possessed, of course, were their natural, pre-societal rights, specifically their natural right to liberty. The concept of natural rights enabled contract theory to evolve from the fully medieval idea of a feudal bond to the partially modern idea of a quasi-commercial exchange by providing natural man with something to exchange, a personal possession that was described as natural liberty.[15]

The considerations that render these concepts out of date have already been discussed in the preceding chapters. As noted in Chapter 1, observers generally agree that natural law has been replaced by positive law in the modern administrative state. Chapter 6 argued further that the concept of law in its entirety is better described, in a modern state, as a process of policy making and implementation. Moreover, the primary setting in which natural rights theory was developed is similarly outdated; as described in Chapter 5, we no longer think in terms of a social contract or a general grant of legitimacy to the government, but in terms of compliance with specific governmental programs. That chapter, and the conclusion to Part I, also argued that the entire effort to justify government on the basis of its origins should be abandoned in favor of a justification based on the government's quotidian performance.

To this list may be added a more specific consideration that emerges from Hegel's critique of natural liberty, and that manifests itself in the administrative state. All natural rights theories treat natural liberty as a preexisting possession or quality of human beings, and Kant regards it as the only such possession.[16] Hegel argues, however, that liberty is not a quality that people naturally possess, but a consciousness that people gradually acquire, and that finds its greatest expression in contemporary nations.[17] Whatever one's opinion of Hegel's philosophical machinery, with its World-spirit, its Absolute, and its Thought thinking itself, his historical account of liberty seems unassailable in light of contemporary anthropology and social theory. Not only is it clear that pre-social human beings did not possess political liberty in any meaningful sense, but also that they did not possess the conception of political liberty. These things have developed over time; it seems incontrovertible that both our political liberty or our understanding of political liberty have increased dramatically between the Middle Ages and the present day.

This increased liberty in fact and thought is directly related to conceptual developments that involve people's interaction with the administrative state, as described in Chapter 5. One of the distinguishing features of that state is the articulation of purpose, the use of instrumental mechanisms to achieve consciously selected social policies. Liberty is such a social policy. Far from being a natural condition or possession, it is a complex and gradually evolving program, generated by insurrections and bitterly contested social movements,[18] and ultimately secured by a regulatory legislation such as married women's property acts, civil rights laws, voting laws, child labor laws and, depending on one's definition, a wide range of social welfare programs. One might argue, of course, that these historical and philosophical facts do not necessarily refute the philosophical position that human beings possess natural liberty. But if the very concept of liberty, as we currently understand that term, is the product of a historical process, the notion that it is a part of a transcendent natural law, which existed before human society began, seems like an arbitrary and extraneous assumption.

Human Rights

Contemporary human rights theories generally abjure reference to natural rights, precisely because the latter concept is so dependent upon natural law, and also because it is so indeterminate in content. Instead, human rights are regarded as consisting of specific protections against government—freedom of speech, freedom of religion, the prohibition of slavery, limits on the prosecution and punishment of criminals, due process, equality of legal treatment, and, sometimes, non-interference with private property. Various more abstract, philosophic theories have been advanced to support these protections,[19] but such theories are controversial. In contrast, the list of protections is largely a matter of consensus in contemporary thought and politics, although the specific contours of the individual protections are contested. Thus, as John Rowan suggests, the protections themselves, rather than any theory that attempts to unify them, may be taken as a starting point in the analysis.[20] This is, of course, an uninformative definition of human rights, which is exactly what a starting point should be.

We have become so accustomed to regarding specific protections against government as rights that it is difficult to describe them, or even imagine them, in any other terms. But with the single exception of property rights, to be discussed in the following chapter, this linkage is of relatively recent origin. All other human rights, as they originally developed in Western Europe, were not conceived as rights at all. Rather, proponents of policies such as toleration[21] or the abolition of slavery[22] argued for them in religious or pragmatic terms, that is, in terms of personal salvation, rather than natural law and natural rights. There were, to be sure, a few areas apart from property rights where some leading thinkers grounded considerations we now identify as human rights in natural rights theory. Hobbes identified protection again self-incrimination as an element of natural liberty at the same time that it was being adopted in English courts on pragmatic grounds.[23] Locke argued that natural rights included the requirement that government may act against individuals only in accordance with general rules adopted in advance.[24] These are fairly isolated correspondences, however, and what seems most notable is not that they occur, but that they occur so rarely, given that the same writers were often addressing both natural rights and protections against government.[25]

The link between the protections that we now associate with human rights and the natural rights tradition is largely a product of the late eighteenth century.[26] By that time, references to natural liberty had become so secularized and so abstract that this long-accepted concept could be pressed into service in the enlightenment campaign for legal reform.[27] Voltaire made this connection, although most of his rhetoric was derived from humanism,[28] and so did Beccaria in his influential treatise on criminal law, although Montesquieu remains his major inspiration.[29] But the connection was not established in any definitive way until the American Bill of Rights and the French Declaration of the Rights of Man were enacted by the legislatures of these nations.[30]

What appears to have happened, once again, is that late-eighteenth-century thinkers quailed at the onset of the secularized administrative state. Their social nostalgia made them cling to outmoded terminology, which they attached to the new situation they confronted in an effort to deny its newness. Just as they described policy as law, and causes of action as legal rights, they described protections against government as human rights. They did so because the natural rights conception was losing its force and revealing government as a purely human and potentially unconstrained creation, while simultaneously destroying the sense of collective purpose and shared belief to which the concept of natural law was linked.[31] Under those circumstances, it was reassuring to describe the protection that they championed as rights, rights that were related to the natural rights that people had been thought to possess when they could rely on natural law.[32] It thus became possible to envision a right to speak, to worship freely, to be free of slavery or torture, and to be tried by due process of law. Such rights, like natural rights, could be conceived as individual possessions, borrowing, by virtue of their form, the sacerdotal quality of their God-given predecessors. Like natural rights, these possessions were viewed as existing independently of government and controlling the government's proper relationship to individuals.

This new conception of protection against government was generally described as the Rights of Man. The term 'human rights' seems to have gained general currency immediately after World War II. It appears in the Charter of the United Nations, promulgated in 1945, and prevails in the Universal Declaration of Human Rights, adopted by the U.N. General Assembly in 1948.[33] The shift from "man" to "human" would seem, from our contemporary perspective, to reflect the desire for gender neutrality, and the preamble to the U.N. Charter does indeed follow this notion by affirming "the equal rights of men and women." The Universal Declaration speaks in terms of "everyone," and contains the substantive provision that everyone "has the right to equal pay for equal work,"[34] but it does not provide any explicit statement of women's rights, and it lapses into gendered language at certain points, such as the statement, "Everyone who works has the right to just and favourable remuneration . . . for himself and his family."[35] A more notable departure of the Universal Declaration from the preexisting Rights of Man formulation is the inclusion of positive or affirmative rights, such as the right to an education, the right to rest and leisure, and the right to "social security."[36] Consequently, 'human rights' is sometimes interpreted as betokening this broader concept. Positive rights are also described as second-generation rights, based on their later recognition. Our apparently innate trinitarianism then induces us to designate the next new category of rights, namely, rights asserted by groups or rights to collective benefits, as third-generation rights.[37]

These latter generations of human rights, however, do not represent an evolutionary theory, or any other theory, nor does the shift from man to human. Rather, the changes in terminology stem from the desire to include a longer list of rights in the existing category of protections against government. Like the more traditional or first-generation rights, they were born as part of a program for government reform, a program more likely to be political than religious these days, but equally disconnected from the natural rights tradition. Their identification as human rights succeeds only in invoking the sacerdotal force of this tradition, and provides little insight into the rationale or operation of the newly identified concerns.

Leading theories of human rights, despite their thoughtful exploration of our prevailing political morality, display this same lack of explanatory value. The problem is that these theories rely on the concept of natural liberty that generated natural rights, and that no longer possesses much intuitive meaning or appeal for us, apart from the specific issues to which it refers. Rawls, for example, uses a standard social contract argument to generate his list of necessary human rights. In a hypothetical pre-social condition—behind the veil of ignorance—people rationally agree to certain principles that will govern political life.[38] The first such principle, Rawls argues, is that "each person is to have an equal right to the most extensive basic liberty compatible with a similar liberty for others."[39] This liberty includes liberty of conscience, equality in political participation, due process, and freedom from impossible or retroactive criminal laws.[40] Few people in contemporary society would argue with this list, but whether Rawls's approach really adds anything to our general, deeply felt consensus on this subject is an open question. In any case, his approach depends upon two basic premises that underlie the conceptual pyrotechnics of his veil of ignorance. The first is that people are free to choose their form of government, and the second is that they must fulfill their promise to follow their initial choice.

Chapter 5 has already explored the outdated character of promise keeping as an element of political morality. The element of choice in Rawls's theory is equally outdated, for it largely restates the idea of natural liberty. Unless people have such liberty, unless they begin the contractual process by possessing some inherent freedom from political control that they can promise to relinquish or restrict, their choice lacks the moral value that Rawls wishes to ascribe to it. But precisely why are people regarded as possessing freedom of this sort? Surely, our prevailing conceptions of anthropology and history run counter to any notion of natural liberty and favor Hegel's view that liberty is socially constructed. It is simply not possible for modern people to imagine a pre-social world in any intuitive way, even as a thought experiment. Nor can Rawls justify his assertion in philosophic terms, for it is the initial premise of his political philosophy. This can be overlooked because liberty is presented as the very first choice that Rawls's people make behind the veil, but, as Rawls acknowledges, it is also a premise of the process by which this choice is made. His only justification for asserting this premise is that it is necessary in order to think rationally about the structure of government. But it is rational to begin the analysis from this position only if one assumes that there is such a thing as natural liberty, and that one can imagine oneself as free to choose the entire structure of the government under which one ultimately lives. To imagine doing so, however, one must reproduce the conceptual framework of the pre-modern natural law tradition, the idea that people begin with the natural liberty to choose their form of government.

Robert Nozick's theory of rights, while free of the contractarian dependence upon promise keeping, also depends on natural liberty. Unless people begin with natural or inherent liberty, state programs do not represent the intrusion on their will that Nozick finds so morally offensive. It is true, of course, that some people oppose redistributive taxes or public education, but there is no reason to count their preferences more heavily than the preferences of those who champion these programs unless one asserts that freedom from these programs is the starting point, a position that Cass Sunstein describes, and criticizes, as "status quo neutrality."[41] And this is precisely what Nozick asserts; he begins with Locke's state of nature, where people are in "a state of perfect freedom to order their actions and dispose of their possessions and persons as they think fit."[42] He further describes this state of freedom as a being's "ability to regulate and guide its life in accordance with some overall conception it chooses to accept."[43] The only justification that he offers for this premise is the individual creation of meaning.[44] Virtually no one who has addressed this matter during the past century, however, believes that meaning is created individually. As Husserl points out, it is created intersubjectively; while people certainly make life plans as individuals, their ability to do so, and the meaning that attaches to it, is part of a social process.[45] The conception of individual liberty that Nozick takes as his philosophical starting point cannot be justified by the kinds of psychological considerations he invokes. Rather, that conception simply reiterates the traditional idea of natural liberty. For Nozick, as for Rawls, this idea is so deeply embedded in our inherited conceptual framework that it is taken as a given starting point, even though they are trying to be philosophically systematic and the idea, once scrutinized, is clearly both contestable and pre-modern in its formulation.

The Concept of Moral Demands on Government

Moral Demands, Constraints, and Obligations

Because the concept of human rights originated with the now-rejected idea of natural law and natural rights, and remains dependent on it still, it seems promising to bracket that concept and approach the underlying issue from a new perspective. The issue that underlies the concept of human rights is the government's treatment of its citizens and, more specifically, the moral assessment of that treatment. With the concept itself bracketed, this issue can be recharacterized by means of the network model. According to this model, governmental action consists of various signals transmitted by the units we identify as constituting government. The signals that are relevant for this discussion are those transmitted to nongovernmental units, that is, individual citizens, groups of citizens, or private institutions. Moral positions regarding such signals could assume one of two basic forms: either the government is morally required to transmit a particular signal, or the government is morally forbidden to do so. A moral demand that requires the government to transmit a particular signal can be described, in the naive terms of ordinary language, as a government obligation. A moral demand that forbids the government from transmitting a particular signal can be described as a constraint on governmental action. Thus, the issue that is now conceptualized in terms of human rights can be recharacterized as the moral demands that we impose on government, with these demands taking the form of either obligations to act or constraints on action.

For most people, as a matter of their own critical morality, many signals will fall into neither category. This means that they are to be determined by the interactive political process described in Chapter 4, or by the administrative decision-making methods discussed in Chapter 6. The reason, in some cases, is that the people believe that no significant moral issue is involved; examples are so-called rules of the road, such as whether traffic should bear right or how to file a secured financing statement, and supererogatory governmental action, such as sending a camera to the moons of Saturn or adding organic chemistry to the fourth grade curriculum. In other cases, people do perceive a moral issue, and feel intensely about it, as described in Chapter 6, but also believe that disagreements should be resolved by the nation's ordinary political or administrative process, and that the resulting decision, although it may be distasteful, will lie within the bounds of morally acceptable action. But there will be at least some signals that most people in our society will regard as either obligations that the government is required to fulfill, or constrained in a manner that the government must not transgress. Since the subject under discussion is a theory of government, not a discussion of morality in general, the critical morality of government obligations and constraints must then be instantiated in a political structure of some sort. It might be argued that this is only possible in a democracy, or, in the administrative context, an interactive republic. More importantly, within the context of republican government, it means that some mechanism must be developed to prevent governing officials from making choices that disregard the applicable constraints and obligations. Tradition might fulfull this function, as it generally does in the United Kingdom, but the most common means of doing so is through a constitutional guarantee, enforced by judicial review. By virtue of this structure, the specified governmental signals are shielded from the ordinary political process, and, consequently, are not subject to the majoritarian decision making that governs rules of the road, supererogatory actions, and policy initiatives.

Obligations and constraints are only characterizations, not preestablished, mutually exclusive categories. In some cases, the two terms refer to distinctly different types of governmental actions. Providing education can only be described as a moral obligation; to say that the government is constrained from failing to educate its citizens tortures the English language for no useful purpose. Conversely, the prohibition against providing education in a discriminatory manner is best described as a constraint; while one could say that the government is obligated to provide equal, or nondiscriminatory education, it facilitates discussion if the benefit is separated from the manner in which it is provided. In other cases, however, the usages will tend to merge. Due process may be regarded as a constraint on the manner in which the government makes factual determinations regarding individuals, but as Jerry Mashaw, Frank Michelman, and Tom Tyler point out,[46] it is also an affirmative benefit, valuable for its own sake, that the government is regarded as being obligated to provide.

Recharacterizing human rights as the moral demands imposed on government effects another figure-ground reversal. Instead of viewing the moral aspect of government-citizen relations as primarily controlled by a feature of the citizens, that is, by the rights that humans naturally possess, it views the matter as primarily controlled by a feature of government, that is, by the obligations and constraints that are imposed upon its units. Of course, people have not been subtracted from the equation, since the moral demands depend on people's attitudes. Those attitudes retain the deontological origin that is generally associated with human rights. In an approach that focuses on government, however, as opposed to citizens, the moral attitudes of the citizenry will be determined by their own views, their overlapping consensus in Rawls's terms,[47] rather than by a philosophic inquiry into their real nature or their real interests. This does not represent a retreat from political philosophy, but an application of political philosophy to the nature of government rather than to the nature of human beings. The concept of human rights starts from some theory about human beings, while the concept of moral demands starts from a theory about government.[48]

The familiar idea that every right generates a corresponding duty effects a similar reversal, since it suggests that a right possessed by individuals implies a duty incumbent upon government. Bentham is probably responsible for the initial version of this observation.[49] More recently, Richard Fallon, Robert Nozick, and L. W. Sumner have advanced it in various forms,[50] and Nozick uses the term 'side constraints' to describe the character of human rights.[51] The U.S. Constitution seems to adopt this perspective as well. Article 1 prohibits bills of attainder and ex post facto laws in Section 9, which consists of a series of limitations on Congressional authority. The First Amendment states: "Congress shall make no law respecting an establishment of religion, or prohibiting the free exercise thereof; or abridging the freedom of speech, or of the press. . . ." As Joseph Raz points out, however, the correspondence is an incomplete one because many rights, such as a right to public safety or to education, can only be provided by complex governmental programs that are not reducible to duties.[52]

But the crucial question is not whether the concept of human rights can be formulated in a different way—of course it can—but whether there is any advantage to replacing so familiar and important an idea with a neologism, even within the delimited area of scholarship and policy analysis. It will be argued that the proposed recharacterization is advantageous because it resolves three conceptional problems, related to each of the three identified generations of human rights, that have long bedeviled the entire subject: the role of state action, the distinction between positive and negative rights, and the character of group or communal rights. In resolving these problems, the recharacterization also dispenses with the taxonomy of the three generations, replacing it with a four-box grid of constraints and obligations that operate in favor of either individuals or groups. This can only serve as an additional advantage, because the generational terminology contains an unanalyzed implication that the second and third generation are parvenus, and that there is some unspecified virtue in returning to the older and more pure conception of rights.

First-generation or negative rights are almost always addressed to the government. As Roderick Hills and Rex Martin have noted, freedom of speech, freedom of religion, freedom from self-incrimination, due process, the prohibition of torture, and the prohibition of slavery can only be secured by governmental action.[53] It is, of course, possible to include analogous claims against private persons in the concept of human rights, but such claims merge into considerations of general morality, and are not what people usually mean when they speak of human rights, particularly first-generation human rights. Even if one chooses to include such claims, they are typically translated into requirements for governmental action. For example, one can speak of rights against being enslaved by private employers, but, in terms of political morality, this is conceived as a requirement that the government abolish any statutes, regulations, or practices that facilitate slavery, and that it take positive action against private slaveholders.[54] As the example indicates, the requirement may go beyond first-generation rights, and include positive action of some sort, but it is nonetheless addressed to government.

The concept of human rights, however, fails to incorporate this necessary and perhaps exclusive relationship to government. When we speak of a person having a right, the image is one of an independent, self-contained possession that she can take wherever she goes, not of a relationship between her and the government. The concept, in other words, provides no intrinsic way to separate its generally accepted subject matter from broader questions of interpersonal morality. Elaborate arguments are then required to explain why the concept of human rights does not include the right to be treated with respect by one's children or to be told the truth by one's friends, while it does include contextual relationships with government such as the right of a news reporter to resist a subpoena or the right of a welfare recipient to a pre-termination hearing. The concept of moral demands on government puts the focus where it belongs—on the government and its relation to its citizens.

The status of second-generation rights, that is, positive rights such as the right to sustenance or to an education, is probably the most controversial issue in contemporary human rights theory. Vast rhetorical resources have been invested in establishing the distinction between these two types of rights[55] and arguing for the superiority of one over the other. Proponents of negative rights insist that positive rights are vague, that they cannot be translated into enforceable entitlements, and that they attenuate the protections that negative rights provide.[56] Isaiah Berlin goes further, asserting that positive liberty is a concept that justifies totalitarianism, because it allows the state to compel people to realize its own notion of their aspirations.[57] In contrast, proponents of positive rights claim that negative rights encourage alienation and self-absorption, that they diminish our sense of community, that they codify inequality by erecting presumptions against state intervention, and that they fail to respond to the full range of human needs.[58] What is required, in Alan Gewirth's phrase, is a community of rights, a collective effort to fulfill people's needs and provide them with the conditions for a meaningful existence.[59] The response, of course, is that the government's compassionate embrace is likely to become the python's grip.

This debate has produced some illuminating insights, but it is generated largely by pre-modern concepts, specifically the imposition of natural rights thinking on a separate and more relevant tradition of reform. The recharacterization of human rights as moral demands on government clarifies the issues at stake by conceiving of negative rights as constraints on governmental action and positive rights as governmental obligations. Thus, political morality can be viewed as containing two separate components, or perhaps expressing two separate moods. In some cases, morality may demand that the government take certain actions, that governmental units produce signals that are designed to achieve specified effects. In other cases, morality may demand that certain constraints on governmental action must be programmed into the software of these units. The precise scope of these obligations and constraints must be argued for in moral terms. There is no clear distinction between the two sets of demands, and certainly no fixed allotment of political morality that requires a zero-sum division between these alternative approaches. Indeed, as Seth Kreimer notes, the two categories are mutually dependent, since negative rights, such as free speech, can be infringed by merely cutting back on previously granted positive benefits.[60] It may happen, in certain cases, that implementing an affirmative obligation conflicts with a well-established, deeply felt constraint; for example, a moral obligation to provide medical care to all citizens may conflict with freedom to practice a religion that forbids certain types of treatment.[61] Such conflicts only remind us that we live outside the Garden, that our desires do not neatly fit into a tessellated plane, but grind against each other on occasion or with frequency. This does not reveal any systematic or intrinsic conflict, nor does it require us to choose between two conceptually incompatible regimes of negative and positive rights.

Third-generation rights involve community or group-based claims or entitlements, such as the right to preservation of a language or a culture, or affirmative action programs for members of a disadvantaged group.[62] Because rights are regarded as personal possessions of the individual, proponents of human rights are often said to choose the individual over the group, to recognize some region of human action that is immune to collective demands, to insist that considerations of individual autonomy trump, in Dworkin's phrase, considerations of social policy.[63] On this point, the proponents of positive and negative rights often stand united. Whether human rights are taken to include only such negative demands as the right to be free to speak or worship as one pleases, or whether they also include the right to be fed and educated, both contending camps agree that they are necessarily claims advanced by the individual in her own individual interest. The idea of communal rights represent a challenge to this view. It asserts that a group of people can assert a right that cannot be formulated as the right of its individual members.

Consider, for example, the difference between free speech rights and language rights. Even assuming, pace Wittgenstein, that there can be a private language,[64] a person's ability to indulge his linguistic idiosyncrasies is fully protected by the individual right of free speech. For example, there are apparently several hundred speakers of Klingon in the United States, but since they are all adults (sort of), who have voluntarily chosen to learn and speak this language as a matter of personal choice, they have no need of anything other than First Amendment protection. The right to the preservation of a minority language is a different matter. What is at issue, as Will Kymlicka points out, is not whether any individual has the right to speak the language, but whether the community of language speakers can demand that the government support its continued existence as a community.[65] This demand might be phrased as a negative right to resist social programs that would assimilate the speakers of the language into the majority culture and as a positive right to receive public education in the communal language. Rights of this kind can only be asserted by a group of people, and can only be granted to that group, because the purpose of these rights is not the individual's freedom but the group's continuing existence or prosperity.[66]

Communal rights of this sort create both conceptual and moral problems from the human rights perspective. The conceptual problem is that these rights fit poorly with the prevailing idea of human rights as claims that individuals assert on the basis of their common humanity.[67] Where does a communal right reside, and who exactly claims it? How can this claim count as a human right if it is based on the group's particularity, the traits that distinguish it from other groups? We grant rights, legal rights for the most part, to corporate entities such as business firms by reconceiving them as a unified individual that speaks with a single voice,[68] but an unorganized group of language speakers cannot be so conceived.[69] From the moral perspective, the difficulty with communal rights is that they often conflict with the individual rights asserted by those within the group, or those outside it. The essence of the group's right frequently involves its authority over individuals who, if left to their own devices, might choose to assimilate into the majority culture,[70] as noted by Justice Douglas's perspicacious dissent in *Wisconsin v. Yoder*.[71] Similarly, affirmative action, that is, granting preference to individuals because they are members of a group that merits favorable treatment, will often disadvantage those who are not members of a favored group.[72] Yet despite these conceptual and moral impediments, communal rights represent an important theme in contemporary political thought, and an insistent demand by many groups of people, including groups within nations that generally grant extensive political freedom, such as the French Canadians, the Basques, the Sami, the Flemish, and the Welsh.

Reconceiving human rights as moral demands on government resolves the conceptual difficulty with communal rights and clarifies the moral one. What is really at issue is not some special feature of the individual, nor is it some mystical construct that hovers over the group as an emergent entity. Rather, the issue is the moral aspect of the government's policy toward minority cultures. Is the government constrained from aggressive assimilationist efforts, such as outlawing the group's sartorial or dietary practices, or requiring its children to attend public schools that forbid the use of the minority language and scorn the minority culture? Is it obligated to engage in affirmative efforts to protect the culture, such as training teachers in the minority language, subsidizing publication of a dictionary, or allowing exceptions to neutral statutes and regulations on its behalf? The answer may depend upon empirical facts about the minority culture—is it indigenous, can it sustain itself, does it produce good music—but it will ultimately translate into constraints and obligations upon government. The fact that these constraints and obligations involve groups of people, rather than individuals, presents no conceptual difficulty from this perspective. Once rights are reconceived as moral demands, moreover, the nature of the conflict between the rights of groups and the rights of individuals is clarified. Assume, for example, that a particular minority group believes that girls should not receive a secondary education, and that the moral consensus of a particular nation is that the government is constrained from trying to force a particular minority group to assimilate, but simultaneously obligated to provide every individual with an adequate education. The idea that this dilemma involves a conflict of rights is not particularly helpful, and the solution that this idea suggests, which is that the two rights must be balanced against each other, is no solution at all, since we have no real metric or mechanism for striking such a balance. Shifting the focus to the government opens up a more promising line of inquiry— what kind of program can the government develop that will give girls in the minority group a genuine opportunity to continue in school, but minimize the impact on the group's culture? Kymlicka's leading analysis of the issue offers solutions of this kind; he states his conclusion in terms of rights, but most of his analysis turns on his conception of liberalism, which is actually a code of government behavior.[73]

Emotional Commitments

These conceptual advantages of recharacterizing human rights as moral demands on government provide an argument for bracketing the idea of human rights, but they are not sufficient. Not only is human rights a well-established concept, but it has served as a rhetorical rallying cry for social justice, and it defines the mission of some highly admirable organizations. A concept of this sort should not be bracketed, even as a thought experiment, unless it meets the stated criteria for an alternative approach, that is, it corresponds more closely to our emotional commitments, it announces its heuristic character forthrightly, and it facilitates microanalysis. Because human rights are primarily a matter of political morality, rather than an effort to describe the government, the most significant of these criteria is the correspondence with our emotional commitments.

With respect to these emotional commitments, the concepts of human rights and of moral demands on government are both equally effective in capturing the genius of constitutionalism and judicial review described in Chapter 5, namely, the idea that government actions can be invalidated on moral grounds without resort to revolution. Once legitimacy is bracketed, both these concepts are equally able to describe such intermediate mechanisms for disciplining the supreme political authority. The problem with human rights, however, is that it misdescribes the content of that discipline; it fails to capture the particular moral judgments that are deployed by those who accept the existence of an administrative state. Because of its pre-modern origins, it runs counter to the administrative state's essential function while simultaneously ignoring the real danger that this state creates.

The motive force for the creation and continuation of an administrative state is its citizens' desire to implement affirmative policies affecting the social and economic systems. The state, in their view, is an instrumentality to educate their children, provide health care, regulate the economy, and sustain people in times of misfortune or old age. Its articulation of purpose creates the conceptual framework for these programs by treating society as a human artifact subject to conscious alteration, while its articulation of structure provides the mechanisms by which such programs can be implemented. Since such extensive authority readily lends itself to oppression and abuse, citizens also demand, on moral grounds, that the state must be subject to certain constraints. As an instrumentality, the state cannot justify the violation of the citizenry's moral values, such as free speech or due process, except perhaps in the effort to achieve competing moral values. But the basic moral demand upon the modern state, and the dominant rationale for its existence in its present form, is that it provides economic and social programs to its citizens. The constraints, however valued, are primarily conditions imposed upon the manner in which the state fulfills its obligations. Conceptually, affirmative obligations are thus anterior to constraints in the modern state; morally, they are of equal importance.

From this perspective, the great difficulty with the concept of human rights, as Susan Bandes and Mary Ann Glendon argue,[74] is that it tends to favor negative rights, which are approximately equivalent to constraints, over positive rights, which are approximately equivalent to affirmative obligations. It grants a lexical priority, in Rawls's phrase, to the constraints.[75] This may have reflected people's emotional commitments in the pre-modern era, when a moral government was expected to establish civil order and otherwise avoid oppressing people, but it reverses the conceptual structure of the modern state and misrepresents the moral attitudes of its citizenry. The condemnation of positive rights, while often phrased in terms of verbal housekeeping, reveals a palpable distaste for the government we actually possess.

It is possible, of course, to argue that the concept of rights includes positive as well as negative rights. But the metaphorical playing field tilts upward against this approach. To begin with, the concept of human rights has been taken to mean negative rights, or constraints on government, for most of its two-hundred-year history. The legal reforms that became linked with human rights, once they shed their natural law origins, were largely constraints on government, thus adding the historical sedimentation of the pre-modern era. Second, the association of human rights with the idea of liberty, a product of this same historical experience, tends to favor negative rights. To be free, in common parlance, is to be left alone. Positive rights are typically demands for services, for things that could be alternatively obtained with money, and such things are not naturally associated with the idea of liberty. The U.S. Supreme Court illustrated this mindset in *Deshaney v. Winnebago County Department of Social Services*,[76] when it held that a child who was permanently injured by his father, after the Department of Social Services had been repeatedly notified that this might occur, had no constitutional remedy because "the Due Process Clauses generally confer no affirmative right to government aid." As Stephen Holmes and Cass Sunstein suggest, this is not a rationale; it is merely a recitation of the concept of rights that dates from the pre-administrative era when the state lacked social service agencies.[77]

Most serious, the rhetoric of rights favors negative rights because it incorporates the assumption that a right must be potentially enforceable in court. Once human rights are characterized as rights, they are taken to be one special case of a larger category that also includes legal rights. As discussed in the previous chapter, the concept of legal rights means causes of action, that is, authorizations to obtain a remedy from an adjudicatory body, typically a court. If human rights belong to the same category, then they must also be the sorts of things that can potentially be implemented by adjudicators. This adventitious verbal linkage works well enough for negative rights, or constraints on government. It is institutionally easy for a court to tell a legislative or administrative body to stop acting in some particular way—to stop interfering with a person's ability to express her opinions or practice her religion. But it is quite difficult for a court to tell legislators or administrators to design and implement a complex social program, even if they are given the authority to do so by the moral imperative of human rights doctrine.

The extent to which this inherent implication of judicial enforcement, or enforceability, betrays our genuine emotional commitments becomes apparent when one examines contemporary constitutions. As statements of the governmental functions that the drafters deem obligatory, these constitutions represent the political morality of the modern age. Almost invariably, they include a variety of social guarantees, including minimal subsistence, housing, health care, and education. These guarantees are frequently stated in terms of rights, since rights are thought to be the things that a constitution guarantees, and that form the sum total of the guarantees contained in the U.S. Constitution, the ur-constitution of the modern era.[78] But to declare something such as housing or education a human right forces the concept into an ill-fitting garb, and thereby makes it look impractical. How is a right of this kind to be provided? Who will supply the resources if a court insists on its enforcement? To what extent will the demand for these resources be balanced against other demands? Perhaps most important, since the right cannot be provided equally or universally, as a practical matter, how can it be said that it is ever truly implemented? These questions are important ones, but the reason that they seem to undermine the guarantee, instead of simply identifying the issues involved in its realization, is that the concept of rights strongly implies that the guarantee must be enforced by courts. Bracketing this concept and replacing it with moral constraints and obligations enables us to think of the guarantee as an obligation imposed directly on the government's administrative apparatus. As such, it might require the government to set certain budgetary priorities, or enact certain levels of taxation, or to adopt certain modes of benefit distribution. The obligation might be enforced by some independent unit within the administration, such as an ombudsperson, or by a court that could sanction the administration for noncompliance without being required to craft a remedy of its own.

There is, of course, an ongoing debate about the desirable level of affirmative governmental policies. Conservatives generally want to reduce that level, while progressives want to increase it. The argument against human rights discourse is not an effort to favor the progressive side of this debate, however, but an argument for freeing the debate, in its entirety, from the influence of a pre-modern, historically sedimented theory that neither side accepts. The debate should be pursued by asking what the affirmative obligation of the government should be, and what constraints should be imposed upon the government efforts to fulfill these obligations. Human rights discourse fails to reflect this important moral controversy; rather, it replaces meaningful arguments against expanded regulation with arguments that emerge from a distant and distinctly different era, when such intervention was not regarded as bad policy, but was simply beyond people's conceptual horizon.

Not only does human rights theory tend to ignore the positive role that an administrative state is expected to assume, but it also tends to ignore the real dangers that this state creates. The theory seems to establish a series of protections against governmental action, but it does so only by violating the core principle of modern political morality, the principle that ultimately disciplines the comprehensive authority and extensive implementation machinery that the administrative state commands. This principle, as stated in Chapter 1, is that government is an instrumentality, a means of benefitting its citizens. Rights theories violate this principle by inviting the government to adopt a deontological position about the essential character of human beings. More specifically, for the government to acknowledge human rights, it must authoritatively declare the essential character or purpose of humanity.

It is difficult to think of any theoretical position that could be a more productive source of government oppression. In the Middle Ages and the Renaissance, Western nations subscribed to the concept of Christian Man, and the afflictions that these pre-administrative states visited on Jews, Roma, Moslems, Manicheans, and Pelagians bear witness to the consequences. Administrative states, when armed with similar conceptions, are potentially more dangerous still. Even if one excludes the Nazi ideology of Aryan Man as the product of some bizarre collective mania, one still has Socialist Man. The Soviet Union, unlike Nazi Germany, was not a rogue state; Stalin, as Isaac Deutscher observed, differed from Hitler in that he was genuinely committed to improving people's lives.[79] But because he thought he knew what people really wanted, because he possessed a definitive conception of human purposes, he could justify the grinding oppressions that an administrative state is capable of imposing. He could slaughter the kulaks, transplant the Cossacks, suppress free speech, bowdlerize culture, and exterminate his rivals in the name of security, prosperity, and even, as Berlin says, liberty.

The recharacterization of human rights as moral demands on governmental action avoids any effort by the government to define humanity or the meaning of human existence. It shifts the focus of both consensus and critical morality from the kind of people we are to the kind of government we want. Of course, people have not been eliminated from consideration—how could they be?—but their moral commitments, not their essential natures, are the operative factor. From the perspective of consensus morality, people need only agree upon the nature of the government and need only treat that government as an instrumentality. They need not reach consensus about their own nature as human beings, nor need they grant the government any authority to adopt a deontological position of this sort. From the perspective of critical morality, the observer can just as easily begin with an inquiry about the nature of government as with an inquiry about the nature of human beings. There is no reason to assume that a theory of human beings is more primary or more principled than a theory of government.

It may be objected that the notion of a government that does not adopt a position about the nature of humanity is abstract and unrealistic. Of course the government, specifically the officials who staff various governmental units, make decisions in light of cultural attitudes regarding the nature of humanity, and of course they exercise considerable influence over those attitudes. Government is inevitably a major force in the process of opinion formation. Even if one distinguishes it from civil society, as a convenient heuristic, one must acknowledge that the two realms are intimately linked, and that the effects of each upon the other are profound. Those who are in an optimistic mood, or live in a nation that has treated them with kindness, may describe this governmental influence as education. Those who are more mistrustful, or who have felt the jackboot of authority press down upon their necks, may describe it as propaganda or indoctrination. But few people would deny that government, particularly the massive, comprehensive government of the administrative state, influences civil society's deontological debates about purposes and the character of human existence.

The recharacterization of human rights as moral demands on government is advantageous nonetheless, because the argument for it is normative, not empirical; it is an effort to identify our genuine commitments. We want government to act as if it did not exercise profound effects on citizen opinions, even though we must acknowledge that it does. From the empirical perspective, moreover, such a stance is neither fanciful nor ineffective. A government that conforms to a political morality that precludes it from imposing an image of humanity on its citizens, or affecting their deontological positions, will affect those positions nonetheless, but it will do so slowly. What it will avoid—what this political morality precludes—is the rapid, focused imposition of deontological positions as a matter of consciously developed social policy. And it is this difference in time scale that constitutes the largest part of the distinction between oppression and liberty. The gradual influences that transform people's views simply contribute to the process of intersubjective opinion formation. Since human beings are socially constructed, their opinions, although individually held, are never individually generated, but always derive from a complex social matrix. This process is experienced as ordinary life, not as oppression; in psychological terms, individuals internalize these gradual influences and perceive them simply as their own genuinely held opinions. Governmental imposition of deontological positions in brief periods of time, however, will be perceived by people as an external force that conflicts with their genuinely held views and their essential selves. They may resist or they may comply, but they will feel that they have been oppressed, that they have been denied their liberty.

One could argue, to be sure, that they have been denied their liberty in either case because a governing entity has imposed its views upon them. But this is essentially a false consciousness argument, and thus suffers from the epistemological weaknesses that have been previously described. To reiterate, there is no convincing definition of human liberty that does not involve people's ability to choose what they actually and presently desire. Moreover, people's experiences, how they actually feel, matter a great deal. Whatever other moral positions one adopts, the difference between feeling oppressed by government and not experiencing this feeling should be regarded as significant. Finally, an interactive republic, of the kind that exists in modern Western nations, will be strongly influenced by its citizenry over any substantial period of time. Elected officials must appeal to the populace, and appointed administrators, unless they occupy highly insulated positions, will be subject to a variety of pressures and pragmatic limitations. Thus, the deontological positions that such governments impose over extended periods will contain a large admixture of the citizenry's own desires, and, for this reason as well, will seem more like guidance than oppression.

The threatening aspect of human rights theory—its conclusion that the government may adopt an affirmative position about human nature—is often masked by our belief that this position consists only of recognizing and respecting the autonomy of human beings.[80] Rights, it is argued, demarcate a realm that is beyond the reach of government. Even if the boundaries are defined by definitive claims about people's basic nature, that realm's existence, once established, enables citizens to flourish without further interference, to make their own choices and pursue their own projects. The only claim about human nature that the government is asserting is that people want to be autonomous, that they want to be free.

Autonomy, however, is not an objectively observable phenomenon that can sustain an argument of this sort. Rather, it is a concept generated by human rights theory itself, and means nothing other than the particular combination of political protections that has become associated with human rights over the course of the preceding centuries. As an abstract or theoretical matter, human beings do not possess autonomy, but are subject to innumerable social and political controls. These controls cannot be regarded as having been imposed on previously autonomous individuals, the way natural rights theory imagined. Not only is there no historical period when social and political constraints did not exist but, more important, social and political controls are intrinsic aspects of the intersubjective process by which society, government, and thought itself is generated. The inevitable consequence is that the supposedly neutral concept of autonomy on which human rights theory relies is, in fact, the projection of a particularized view of human beings. Human Rights Man is a first cousin to Socialist Man; he is a specific and contestable image of humanity that the government imposes on the populace as a result of its prevailing ideology.

The particularistic character of Human Rights Man is illuminated by the current critique of human rights. This is not to suggest that the critique is justified, nor does it serve as an argument in this chapter for bracketing the concept of human rights. As discussed above, the concept has been bracketed because it is out of date, because it fails to describe the actual protections against government that we establish and the actual commitments we maintain. But the critique convincingly reveals that the image of humanity on which human rights theory relies is contestable, that one can readily conceive of alternative regimes that are at least arguably just.

To begin with, Human Rights Man is a man. As feminists have pointed out, his autonomy once included permission to rule his family as a virtual dictator, speaking for it in the political and social realms, controlling all its property, and using his superior physical strength to assault its other members with impunity.[81] Over the course of the past century, most human rights have been extended to women and, less extensively, to children, but the original conception was largely congruent with male domination. In the United States this conception was also congruent with overt discrimination against women. During the century following the Civil War, the Supreme Court upheld state enactments that precluded women from voting, practicing law, working in restaurants at night, or working as bartenders,[82] and it did not declare gender discrimination unconstitutional until its 1973 decision in *Frontiero v. Richardson*.[83] It did not allow women who became pregnant to decide whether they wanted to give birth to a child until *Roe v. Wade*, decided that same year.[84] Another closely related element of the feminist critique is that the entire idea of autonomy which human rights theory proclaims may be a gendered concept. The self-sufficient person who jealously patrols the borders of his private realm to repulse state interference is a man's idea of freedom. For women, a free person is one whose choices are not controlled by any outside entity, who has healthy, mutually respectful interactions with both private persons and the government.[85] Many feminists regard the private realm that human rights theory creates as one where social traditions of male domination continue undisturbed, and welcome state intervention to combat these traditions.[86] In their view, government programs to prevent spousal abuse, to redistribute money to single mothers, and to ensure equality of opportunity and pay are not intrusions upon freedom, as human rights theorists have often argued, but means by which freedom is established.

Human Rights Man is an individualist. According to communitarian and critical scholars, he adopts an adversarial, combative stance toward those who intrude upon the areas his rights protect, rather than trying to be conciliatory or cooperative.[87] He insists on his prerogatives and minimizes his responsibilities, particularly the responsibility to find cooperative solutions to interpersonal conflicts. He runs off to enforce his rights, in whatever forum is available to him, at the drop of a hat.[88] This belligerent individualism tends to shatter the public sphere, the shared moral space where conflicts are transcended, into a jagged, atomized collection of separate existences where these conflicts are merely compromised in a series of uneasy truces.[89] Feminist scholars often link the individualism of Human Rights Man to his essentially male character, arguing that the tendency to favor autonomy over relationship is an artifact of gender, not a universal moral truth.[90]

Human Rights Man is a heterosexual. It is difficult to understand why the sexual relations of a person with a consenting adult would not constitute a central component of autonomy. Yet homosexuality has been regarded as beyond the bounds of human rights until very recently.[91] The reason for this exclusion is the one given by Kant as part of his theory of natural liberty: that sexual union, "the reciprocal use that one human being makes of the sexual organs and capacities of another," is consistent with the natural liberty only in cases of monogamous marriage, where two people give themselves equally to one another. But this cannot be the case with homosexuality, which is unnatural and is consequently excluded from the realm of freedom.[92] This Kantian interpretation of human nature led to widespread discrimination against gays for most of American and, more generally, Western history.[93] It was central to the decision in *Bowers v. Hardwick*,[94] which was only recently overruled in *Lawrence v. Texas*.[95] Despite *Lawrence*, and other indications that discriminatory practices are being abandoned, gay couples still are not allowed to marry in our human rights regime.[96] Justice Scalia, dissenting in *Lawrence*, felt that his strongest argument against the decision was to place the apparently horrific possibility of gay marriage at the bottom of a slippery slope that began with decriminalization,[97] a stance that probably reflects a good deal of political, although not doctrinal or conceptual, acuity.

Human Rights Man is a property owner. The ability to protect one's property, and to use it as one wishes, was part of the natural law tradition,[98] and continues to be regarded as an essential human right by many people, including the U.S. Supreme Court.[99] This favors property owners over those who own little or no property and depend on wages for their sustenance. In an argument that runs parallel to the feminist argument against male autonomy, working people and their advocates assert that the protection of property against state interference subjects wage earners to private oppression.[100] True autonomy, they argue, requires the state to protect them by restricting their employers' use of property. It requires, in other words, that the state assume the affirmative duties that have been characteristic of the administrative era, and that have preserved market capitalism from the demise that Marx predicted. But this affirmative role is generally not regarded as a human right; rather, it has been established and maintained in the teeth of the property protection that human rights theory provides.

Human Rights Man is a European. Proponents of cultural relativism or cultural equality argue that he is the product of a distinctive historical experience, and that the European effort to impose his image on non-Western societies under the banner of universalism is no better than their quondam effort to impose Christianity or dinner forks on these societies under the banner of civilization.[101] To demonstrate the particularity of human rights, some scholars have suggested that Asian nations, particularly those with a Confucian tradition, offer a different conception of justice and human emancipation,[102] one that emphasizes economic development and collective social responsibility in place of rights. This conception is not only of equal pedigree and dignity, they argue, but it is more appropriate for the impoverished nations of the developing world.[103] People in the wealthy West may expend energy and resources to make sure that the government does not do anything that discourages the self-expression of its citizens, but nations where people are dying for lack of clean drinking water, sufficient food, and adequate medical care must direct their attention to these more pressing concerns.

To reiterate, the point of summarizing these critiques is not to assert that they are morally correct. In fact, they are highly controversial; many scholars have responded to them, arguing that human rights are invaluable for women, racial minorities, gays, and developing nations.[104] But the critique reveals, at the very least, that human rights and the autonomy they protect are not neutral concepts. It was asserted above that the various attributes of Human Rights Man reveal a bias against positive rights, or affirmative obligations, that is essentially anti-administrative. The further point is that these attributes violate an even more basic element of the administrative state—the moral principle that the state is a pure instrumentality. By the mere fact that he possesses specific features—whatever those features may be—Human Rights Man is revealed as much more than an abstract embodiment of autonomy. He is a particularized vision of human beings, and thereby threatens the liberty he is designed to protect by allowing the state to establish a deontological position about the true nature of humanity. This is precisely what we do not want in the administrative era. The modern, articulated state, with its specialized apparatus and its control of social relations, is too dangerous to be granted such a license. Our true emotional commitment is to restrict deontological positions to civil society, and to impose particular, historically developed demands upon the government. In other words, our political morality demands that public ideology be conceived as a theory of governance, not a theory of humanity.

Heuristics and Microanalysis

The remaining advantages of recharacterizing human rights as moral demands on government involve the heuristic nature of theory and its role in facilitating microanalysis. Because these criteria are less central to political morality, they can be discussed more briefly. With respect to the heuristic character of thought, human rights theory suffers from a tendency to reify those rights, to treat them as things. The clearest example, perhaps, involves the question of whether any human rights are absolute. "A right is absolute," Alan Gewirth says, "when it cannot be overridden in any circumstances, so that it can never be justifiably infringed and it must be fulfilled without any exceptions."[105] Gewirth argues that such rights exist; Justice Hugo Black, dissenting in cases such as *Konigsberg v. State Bar*, takes the position that free speech is such a right.[106] This debate is often regarded as raising troublesome issues, but much of it is an artifact of reifying rights, of viewing them as a preexisting conceptual entity rather than a heuristic for capturing certain moral and emotional commitments. If we recharacterize rights as moral demands on government, the issue's apparent difficulty dissolves. This alternative concept carries no implication of absoluteness, no reason to regard it as possessing a force transcending the values that support it. Ultimately, the scope and strength of our moral demands on government must depend on moral arguments; the historically sedimented image of a right only confuses the issue by presenting these considerations as independently existing entities that can potentially possess the quality of absoluteness. If the moral demand always remains as part of a governmental unit's program, if it blocks out any conceivable conflicting signal, that is because we cannot envision any policy or conflicting demand that can overcome its moral status, not because there is some inherent reason to regard that demand as absolute.

A final advantage of new, administratively oriented characterizations, and the one that this book has emphasized most often, is that such characterizations facilitate microanalysis. This methodology, as noted above, relates to committed descriptions, and not to moral arguments of the sort involved in discussions of human rights. But microanalysis becomes applicable once attention shifts from the existence of the right or the demand to the issue of its effective implementation. As stated above, the tendency to conflate human rights with the legal rights that create causes of action leads to the assumption that all human rights should be potentially enforceable by an adjudicator, generally a court. This tendency, which has been discussed as a discursive problem that disfavors affirmative obligations, presents an implementation problem as well. The problem is that it restricts human rights to a single implementation mechanism, and, in fact, to a traditional mechanism that faces institutional difficulty in confronting the administrative state. Once these rights are recharacterized as moral demands on government, possibilities for other, more contemporary implementation mechanisms come into view. Ideas for instituting these alternative mechanisms may be regarded as cognitive prescriptions that advance our understanding of the constraints and obligations that modern citizens impose on government.

To begin with the more familiar issue of constraints, courts are not the only governmental institution that can implement them. In an interactive republic, particularly one with an established tradition of political liberty, governmental institutions can voluntarily constrain themselves. The legislature can do so by keeping various constraints in mind when legislating, by enacting statutes that embody the constraints, or by establishing an internal review body to disapprove transgressions. The chief executive can constrain itself by analogous means, as can each administrative agency.[107] The United Kingdom, after all, relies on the legislature's self-imposed limits, rather than judicial review, yet its human rights record is not obviously worse than that of the United States; it abolished slavery sixty years earlier, for example.[108] When we rely on judicial review, after all, we expect the courts to constrain themselves, and while some legal scholars assert that courts can do this because their decisions are controlled by doctrine,[109] many others, and virtually all political scientists, question this assertion.[110] For them, any constraints on courts—and such constraints certainly exist— stem from the political process, that is, the same source that would produce self-imposed constraints on legislatures, the chief executive, and administrative agencies. The point is not that we should abandon judicial review, but that we should not allow the concept of human rights to focus all our efforts to constrain the government on this one mechanism.

In addition to self-imposed constraints, the legislature and the chief executive can impose morally based constraints on administrative agencies. As discussed in Chapter 3, they supervise the agencies to ensure the effectiveness of agency action, and there is no reason why they could not add moral issues to their existing list of supervisory concerns; in fact, they already do, to some extent. Admittedly, their lack of independence from majoritarian politics suggests that they might carry out this role less scrupulously than the judiciary. The countervailing consideration is that the judiciary has experienced serious difficulties in penetrating the administrative process. As government becomes more extensive and complex, the ability of citizens to combat its various abuses, particularly small, routine, technical, recondite ones, with judicial review seems to founder. In an interactive republic, the modern citizen's experience of oppression is not being burnt for heresy or drawn and quartered in the public square for criticizing the regime. It is standing in a long line at an overheated government office, under a malfunctioning fluorescent light, only to be told, upon arriving at the front of the line, that one must stand in another equally long line so that, when one reaches the front of that second line, one can be treated with off-hand disrespect and given incorrect advice. This is much less dramatic oppression to be sure, and we are entitled to feel wonderful that we do not draw and quarter anyone these days, but it is oppression nonetheless, and it is a form of oppression that judicial review seems incapable of addressing. Perhaps we should explore legislative and executive constraints on agencies that would require each agency to treat citizens with kindness and respect. Perhaps such constraints should be programmed into the agency's software by its hierarchical supervisor in advance, and monitored continuously on the basis of the agency's procedures or results. Perhaps the United States, having established an Office of Management and Budget to protect businesses for government oppression, should establish an equally high-level review agency—the Office of Decency and Fairness—to provide equivalent protection for ordinary citizens.

Even if we continue to rely on judicial review to impose moral constraints, we need not limit that review to the concept of rights. For example, review could be triggered by an ombudsperson, in addition to being triggered by a cause of action.[111] Ordinary citizens might enforce constraints on government more readily if they could go into a neighborhood office and engage in an informal discussion with an educated, experienced official, who could then investigate the issue, negotiate with administrative agents, and, if necessary, bring suit on her own authority, with government funds. Of course, this ombudsperson would be a government employee, but there is no reason why she could not be as independent as the judges, who are also government employees.

When we turn from constraints to obligations, the advantage of nonjudicial implementation becomes even clearer. Perhaps the simplest step, but a potentially effective one, would be for an executive or legislative unit to survey conditions regarding the obligations that have been established by statute. To what extent are enacted benefits not being provided due to ineffective implementation? To what extent are such benefits not being taken up due to lack of education or publicity? Beyond this, affirmative obligations, if embodied in the nation's constitution, could be implemented by similar executive and legislative supervision. This would not solve the resource issues that affirmative obligations implicate, since the legislature would still be required to allocate funds, but it would provide a means of ensuring that those funds, once appropriated, served their intended purpose. It would also be a means of publicizing the government's level of effectiveness in fulfilling its moral obligations, and thus enlisting the interactive process to increase that effectiveness.

A further means of implementation would involve a separate administrative agency, or an office within each agency, that could monitor the quality of service provided within each agency's area of jurisdiction and instruct the policy-making mechanism of the agency to take specified measures to fulfill its obligations. In the United States, this approach, which Eric Orts has described as reflexive environmental law,[112] has been adopted with respect to the environmental impact of agency action.[113] A similar approach, focusing on the human impact of the agency, is far from inconceivable. Moreover, as noted in the preceding chapter, this monitoring function could be triggered, in whole or part, by citizen complaints, thereby paralleling the structure of judicial intervention while avoiding many of its disadvantages.

Perhaps none of these alternative enforcement mechanisms would be as effective as the one we presently possess. That is not something we should assume, however, but something that we should determine by microanalysis. It may turn out, when the microanalysis has been undertaken, that legal rights, or causes of action, are the most effective means of implementing the moral demands that we impose on government, despite their medieval origins and obvious limitations in a modern administrative state. But it may also turn out, as New Public Governance theory suggests, that more interactive mechanisms which reflect contemporary political and social thought are at least equally effective.[114]

The Content of Moral Demands on Government

Moral Demands in General

The foregoing argument for recharacterizing human rights as moral demands on government is based on structural considerations, on the general operation of the two alternative conceptions. But what about the content of these conceptions, the particular protections that the two frameworks afford? Theories of rights often aspire to derive these protections from their general structure, and are often judged on their ability to do so. A convincing demonstration of this sort has been the Holy Grail of rights theorists, the admittedly difficult but unfailingly desirable goal toward which they strive.

As previously noted, however, the protections against government that we currently associate with human rights—due process, fair criminal procedure, free speech, freedom of religion, the prohibition against slavery, and so forth—developed independently of the natural rights tradition, and were not recognized as rights at all until the secularization of that tradition allowed the two themes to be merged. At a descriptive level, one must possess a rather robust sense of teleology to believe that these separately evolved protections fit together into a coherent pattern that could then be logically derived from a subsequent characterization. It seems more likely that they are separate emotional commitments, reflecting a generalized morality of politics, but lacking any deeper or more logical relationship. Normative considerations reinforce this historical experience. For most people in Western society, their commitment to the familiar protections against government is deeper, and more fixed, than their commitment to any general theory that purports to unify these protections. There is no conceivable argument about the architecture of human rights, for example, that could convince most people to abandon their commitment to free speech, or the prohibition of physical torture. In other words, we do not decide that there should be certain protections against government because we can derive them from a general theory; rather, we determine the value of a suggested general theory based on its ability to incorporate the protections against government to which we are already committed. This is not meant to suggest that debate about the choice or the relative importance of these protections is impossible, or that theoretical approaches cannot provide illumination, or even that these separate protections necessarily lack objective or transcendental validity. The point, rather, is that these protections possess independent deontological foundations, that they reflect basic commitments that are stronger than any commitment to their theoretical relationship to one another.[115]

From this perspective, a claim that our agreed-upon protections against government can be derived from some general characteristic of human beings such as their inherent autonomy or liberty appears to be a post hoc rationalization, an artificial construct designed to incorporate a set of protections that have independent historical origins and independent normative justifications. The concept of human rights is suspect on this ground. With its natural rights and natural law reverberations, it tempts us with the false promise of a unified theory that, upon discovery, will tell us precisely which protections against government are justified and which are not. The concept of moral demands on government avoids this difficulty. Being less reified, and essentially separate from the natural rights tradition, it implies neither a deep structure or an overarching logic. Instead, it invites us to identify and explicate the constraints and obligations that we want to impose on government by examining our particular historical experience and present-day emotional commitments.

While the concept of moral demands on government does not provide any basis for deriving our agreed-upon protections from a general theory, it does provide an explanation for one feature that all of these protections share. Although they address the way that government treats individuals, their specific contours often depend upon the structure of the government itself. The concept of human rights, that is, rights possessed by individuals, renders this consideration difficult to factor into the analysis; the moral demands concept, in contrast, facilitates it without derogating from the concern with individuals.

The point is most readily apparent for positive rights. Lists of such rights, which typically include rights to an education, to health care, and to basic sustenance, can certainly be connected to specific human needs, and might thus appear to have nongovernmental origins. But human beings have many other needs, such as love, sex, friendship, entertainment, and a feeling of superiority over others, that rarely appears in lists of rights. The idea that rights can be derived from needs, or from some other attribute of human beings, fails to explain the particular rights that are typically included in the list.[116] If positive rights are recharacterized as moral demands on government, however, the list can be more plausibly derived from the central element in the political morality of the administrative state, which is its instrumental character. Education, health care, and basic sustenance are citizen demands that can be collectively delivered; they are the sort of demands that modern governments, as presently conceived, can provide by the creation of a coordinated program. Administrative agencies can establish an education program, a health care program, or a welfare program, but it would be impossible for them to establish a love program, and impermissible, for other moral reasons, for them to establish a sex program. To be sure, no definitive list of obligations can be derived from the instrumental and collective character of government. Our particular choices depend on our historical experience, most notably the replacement of religious institutions with secular ones. But the shift of focus from human nature to governmental structure at least provides some explanation for the list of positive rights or moral obligations that most people would identify.

With respect to negative rights, this same shift of focus provides a more plausible account of our two most general constraints on government, due process and equal protection. What does it mean to say that an individual possesses rights of this nature? We can certainly identify the underlying values, such as fairness and equality, but due process and equal protection do not implement these values in any generalized sense. Just about everyone feels that the government's economic treatment of them is unfair—either too much money is being taken from them or too little money is being given to them—and virtually all legislation creates or preserves inequalities of one sort or another. Due process and equal protection do not reach these concerns, however; they refer to specific interactions between the government and its citizens. The Supreme Court, as discussed in Chapter 7, has created enormous conceptual difficulties for itself by trying to analyze due process in terms of a personal right to liberty or property. Equal protection has produced similar conundrums. Why can some groups, like doctors, be treated unequally, but not other groups like African Americans or Jews? And how can someone have an equal right to use a public golf course, as the Supreme Court held in *Holmes v. City of Atlanta*,[117] if there is no right to a public golf course in the first place?

Recharacterizing human rights as governmental constraints makes sense of these essential protections by shifting from claims or entitlements of the individual to demands on government, and the specific values that are associated with its administrative structure. An important implication of the basic value that government should be an instrumentality for satisfying citizen desires is that it should be responsive to its citizens, using their expressed desires as its goal in the policy and implementation process that was described in Chapters 6 and 7. The principle mechanism for achieving such responsiveness is the electoral and administrative interaction that Chapter 4 discussed. These interactions, of course, have purely instrumental functions; elections solve the problem of succession, while administrative interaction provides information and increases the compliance behavior that was described in Chapter 5. But they also serve a moral function in that elected officials will be responsive to citizen desires because they want to acquire and maintain their positions, while administrators will be responsive because they sympathize with the quandaries or fear the retaliation of those with whom they interact. Thus, these interactions not only serve specific instrumental functions, but also help secure our prevailing political morality, which demands instrumentalism of the government in its entirety.

Due process and equal protection can be understood as principles that bridge two gaps in governmental responsiveness, the first involving individuals, and the second involving excluded groups. With respect to individuals, the problem with electoral and administrative interactions is that they make public officials responsive only to groups of citizens, large organizations, or groups of organizations. Individuals cast but a single vote, command relatively few resources, and exercise minimal influence. Because individuals, considered separately, cannot affect the result of an election or impose sanctions on an agency, the interactive process generally fails them. This failure is resolved, and our political morality secured, through the constraint of procedural due process, the most general constraint on governmental action. As discussed in Chapter 7, the due process constraint applies whenever the government takes particularized action against an individual. It provides that the government may impose certain types of harms or punishments only when those actions are consistent with a preexisting authorization, that is, an authorization subject to the interactive process that secures government responsiveness. The specific components of due process—notice, a hearing, an impartial decision maker—are designed to enforce this congruence between particularized action and general rules.[118]

Treating due process as a constraint on government, rather than a right possessed by individuals, does not resolve any of the questions that have plagued this subject, but it does allow us to think about these questions with more clarity. It illuminates the primary value that informs due process—providing individuals with the protections that groups possess in an interactive republic. As discussed in Chapter 7, it also enables us to define the boundaries of the due process guarantee—action taken against individuals, not action that implicates some undefinable set of individual rights like liberty or property. In addition, the recharacterization clarifies the purpose of specific procedural protections—to ensure that individuals are treated in accordance with preexisting rules. This helps us determine the kind of notice or hearing that is appropriate in different situations. In addition, it explains why we are willing to allow agencies to treat regulated firms in a particularized, strategic way, as described in Chapter 5, but why that same treatment is regarded as inappropriate for individuals.

With respect to the equal protection guarantee, the explanation that has garnered the broadest support is the one suggested by the Supreme Court's decision in *U.S. v. Carolene Products*[119] and elaborated by John Ely.[120] Due process protection is premised on the belief that groups of individuals can make government responsive to their desires through electoral or administrative interaction, but this is obviously untrue in certain cases. The problem is not that some groups lose the competition to obtain favorable treatment from the government; that is an inevitable result of the political process and reflects its proper operation. Neither is the problem that some groups are too small, for their size reflects the prevalence of the position that they represent and their defeat, once again, signals political responsiveness, not its reverse. The real problem occurs when some specific group, defined on the basis of an immutable or relatively immutable characteristic such as race or religion, is regarded as Other, not as Us, by the majority. Such a group will be systematically excluded from the political process; no other group will form alliances with it, no politician will calculate its numbers, no compromises with it will be either necessary or possible for the dominant majority. In these circumstances, the constraint of nondiscrimination or equal protection is necessary to secure government responsiveness for the excluded group. This constraint, by precluding the government from taking actions to a group's specific disadvantage, merges that group into the general polity, for governmental purposes, so that the group benefits from the government's responsiveness toward other groups or toward the mass of citizens in general.

While Ely's theory characterizes equal protection as a human right, it is not truly congruent with this conceptual approach. Can someone be said to have a right to equal treatment because the group to which he belongs is excluded from the political process? How can the mere fact of exclusion of one's groups confer rights on an individual? It seems more coherent to say that the government is constrained from enacting policies that specifically disadvantage the excluded group. This perspective also explains the result in *Holmes*. There is no contradiction in holding that the government may not provide golf courses only for whites even though it is not required to provide any golf courses at all. The equal protection guarantee, viewed as a constraint, does not give anyone a right to a public golf course; rather, it limits the manner in which the government can take action of any kind, whether that action involves sacred liberties like freedom of worship, essential services like health and education, or merely the opportunity to play golf for a seven dollar fee. Our commitment to interaction allows us to rely on the political process to determine whether public funds will be used for golf courses or for some other purpose; equal protection prevents the government from implementing any of those functions in a manner that specifically disadvantages an excluded group.

Specific Freedoms

Other traditional protections are not derived from the political commitment to responsive government, but from separate values such as freedom of speech, freedom of religion, or humane treatment of the accused and the convicted. Because these values implicate individual experience as well as governmental structure, the difficulties with human rights discourse are less apparent in this context. It makes sense to say that individuals possess a right to free speech or freedom from torture; thus the advantage of recharacterizing human rights as governmental constraints does not reside in the description of these particular protections, but in the more generalized considerations discussed in the preceding section. As soon as these protections implicate the structure of government, however—as soon as they must take cognizance of the administrative state and its complexities—the account of them as individual rights runs into difficulty, and the advantages of recharacterizing them as moral demands on government appear.

Consider freedom of speech, for example. The Supreme Court has held that free speech must have "breathing space," that close or doubtful cases must be resolved in favor of protection to avoid producing a "chilling effect" on people's willingness to speak.[121] These vivid images work equally well with either characterization. One can say that the individual's right must have breathing space to avoid being chilled, or one can say that the government must grant breathing space to individuals and avoid chilling their free expression. But what about decisions such as *Grosjean v. American Press Co.*, holding taxes imposed specifically on newspapers unconstitutional in the interest of ensuring that the press is not chilled by such taxation?[122] This can hardly be regarded as a right of individuals, since it applies only to publishing companies, and since the entity that asserts the claim is not the one whose interests motivate its creation.[123] Such a right is more plausibly derived from considerations regarding the structure of government—the kind of authority that we want government to wield—than from any consideration about individuals.

A related but more significant aspect of free speech doctrine that possesses the same attributes is the public forum doctrine, the line of cases holding that in certain government-created spaces, such as streets or parks, all modes of speech must be permitted, while in others, such as schools, prisons, and military bases, speech may be restricted.[124] Does it make sense to assert that people possess a right to speak in public parks but not in other settings? What could we possibly learn from any moral analysis of human nature that could lead to this distinction between two types of governmental spaces? As Robert Post has pointed out, the doctrine depends on an analysis of the government's purposes in creating the setting, not on the character or needs of individuals.[125] This leads, however, to an analysis where the individual right and the governmental purpose frequently collide, a situation that is resolved by the unconvincing trope of balancing the two opposing forces. Recharacterizing rights as governmental constraints provides a more coherent approach. We can ask when government should be prohibited from restricting free expression, and when its valid purposes permit it to impose restrictions. The answer, in both cases, depends on the kind of government we want, not the kind of human beings we are. Significantly, this advantage of the governmental constraint approach occurs precisely where the administrative nature of the state becomes a factor. Any state can chill free speech by means of criminal punishment or civil liability, but only an administrative state creates so wide a range of governmentally managed spaces that the prohibition of free speech within those spaces represents a significant restriction. It is the purposive, managerial state whose relationship to citizens cannot be captured by an image of protections as individual possessions.

One more example within this vast and complex area is the prohibition against torture. This could be easily characterized as a right when the offending government behavior involved breaking people on the wheel or removing their intestines with a fork. However, when American courts confronted a pattern of prison management that resulted in barbarous treatment of the inmates, but lacked the interpersonal drama of systematic mutilation, they were unsure how to proceed.[126] It is not particularly coherent to say that a person possesses a right to have the government engage in a specified pattern of managing an institution. Finally, in *Talley v. Stevens*, a federal judge declared that the total conditions of confinement in an Arkansas prison constituted cruel and unusual punishment.[127] The decision ultimately led to an extensive series of cases where the federal courts engaged in comprehensive reform of entire state prison systems in the South, and particular prisons in other parts of the country.[128] The essential feature of these cases was to impose a series of obligations and constraints on government about the way it managed the institution of a prison.

Again, it is the administrative nature of the state that created difficulties for the individual rights perspective. Once the state is managing an institution, its patterns of management, not the nature of individuals, become the focus of our moral concerns. To protect individuals, one must identify the factors that operate in these managerial settings. Of course, it is not true, as Foucault asserts, that prisons were invented by the administrative state.[129] They existed well before, and were a factor in the abolition of judicial torture.[130] But the concept of a prison as a programmatic institution, rather than mere punishment, is distinctly a product of the administrative era. It is this conception that escapes the boundaries of individual rights discourse and demands that primary attention be directed to government behavior.

In summary, the thought experiment of bracketing the concept of human rights and replacing it with moral demands on government allows us to think more coherently about the content of protections against government. This recharacterization seems advantageous at the retail level of specific protections, as well as at the wholesale level of the overall conception. In both cases, the idea of human rights represents an effort to transfer traditional, sacerdotal modes of thought to protections against government that had evolved from separate sources, and that suddenly seemed both increasingly necessary and increasingly flimsy in the secular, administrative state. At the general level, the effort generates confusion, and risks precisely the danger that it was designed to avoid. At the specific level, it performs somewhat better, but does not succeed in explaining the content of the positive rights that people demand, or the operation of well-established negative rights in administrative settings.

Because the rhetorical force of human rights is so significant in modern politics, this thought experiment, whatever its conceptual virtues, may appear a dangerous one in practical terms. In its concern with government, rather than the rights or needs of individuals, it appears to abandon the moral high ground that is so essential to continued progress in this area. But the thought experiment possesses a morality of its own that makes it worth pursuing. Rather than invoking the romanticism of human rights to combat the equally romantic but ultimately dangerous image of a sacerdotal government, it deromanticizes government, and treats it as an instrumentality for the satisfaction of citizen desires. The deromanticized concept of moral demands on government is then a sufficient countervailing force, and possesses the advantage of being more conceptually coherent and more readily applied to an administrative state. It moves our political morality from the pre-modern world, or from nostalgia for the pre-modern world, into the environment where it is being generated, and where it must perform.

Nine

From Property to Market-Generating Allocations

Property as Control

The Problem of Property in the Modern State

THE previous chapter argued that human rights are better conceived, in the context of the modern administrative state, as a set of constraints and obligations upon governmental action that arise from the moral demands of the citizenry. Although the discussion extended to all other protections against government that are regarded as human rights, it specifically excluded the right to private property. This exclusion was not motivated by the desire to argue by verbal stipulation, or to avoid a complex subject, but rather by the idea that the concept of property raises distinct issues that merit separate consideration. Those issues are the subject of the present chapter.

There is no particular difficulty in translating the commonly understood idea of a property right into the moral demands framework suggested in Chapter 8. The right to property, for most theorists and in most Western constitutions, does not mean the right to a particular amount of property, but rather the opportunity to acquire valuable resources of various kinds, to retain some or all of the resources one has acquired, and perhaps do other things with the retained resource, such as transfer it, devise it, or destroy it.[1] Because both the desired guarantor and the potential violator of this human right is the government, the right can be readily recharacterized the way other human rights were recharacterized, that is, as a means of constraining or obligating the government in certain ways. Government, according to this view, would be constrained from taking someone's property away—taking the property of A and transferring it to B, in the standard formulation—and would be obligated to establish some scheme to protect people's property from private depredations, to provide them with the opportunity to obtain new property, and to do various other things that the right to property might be taken to include.

To be sure, not all the arguments presented in Chapter 8 to support the recharacterization of human rights apply to the right of private property. Chapter 8 argued that the concept of natural rights, from which our current concept of human rights arose, was unrelated to the protections

against government that we now associate with human rights. But this is
clearly not the case with the right to property, which was an essential part
of the natural rights tradition. The natural rights that theorists proclaimed
typically included the right to private property,[2] a view that prevailed well
into the nineteenth century.[3] Moreover, the right to liberty was often described, by Grotius, Overton, Locke, and others, as a property right in
one's own body.[4] But this does not mean that the arguments in the preceding chapter are inapplicable to the right of property. The disconnection
between natural rights and the currently recognized protections against
government was not treated in that chapter as an argument, but merely a
heuristic. Its purpose was to clarify the separate character of these two concepts, to illuminate the conceptual space in which the actual argument for
recharacterizing rights proceeded. This disconnection is not necessary to
the basic argument, however, which turned on the way protections against
government operated in the modern state, not on the historical origins of
these protections.

A second argument in Chapter 8 that may not seem applicable to property rights is the claim that protections against government are better regarded as relationships between the individual and government than as
possessions of the individual. Property rights, it would appear, have a great
deal to do with possession. As widely recognized, however, a right to acquire and possess things is more usefully regarded as a relationship between people and the state, rather than as a possession of its own.[5] The
idea of possession may seem relevant, with respect to property rights, because certain types of property, like land, can be intuitively described as
possessions.[6] But the right to possess land, unlike actual possession of
land, is an abstract set of relationships that must be obeyed and enforced
by government in order to be operative. Similarly, possession of an object
as one's property is often described as the right to exclude others from
using that object.[7] But the right to private property, unlike possession of
specific property, must be non-exclusive if it is to be a right at all; everyone, or at least every member of the polity, must have the right to acquire
and to retain what they acquire, just as everyone must have the right to
speak or to be free of torture.

This argument would still apply if one were to define the right of property in the very different manner suggested by Hegel,[8] C. B. Macpherson,[9]
Frank Michelman,[10] and Jeremy Waldron.[11] In their view, the right to
property is not merely the right to acquire and retain material objects, but
rather the right to own some particular amount of them. "A person must
translate his freedom into an external sphere," Hegel says; thus "property
is the first embodiment of freedom."[12] Despite its emphasis on the actual
possession of property, this notion of a right to property is just as relational
as the more traditional one. A universal right to have possessions is not it-

self a possession, but a relationship between the individual and the state. Once again, this can be readily recharacterized as a moral obligation on the state to provide or guarantee some specified amount of resources to each of its citizens.[13]

The reason the idea of a property right merits separate treatment, then, is not because it cannot be contained within the previously suggested recharacterization. Rather, separate treatment is required by the interaction of that right's substantive content and the administrative state. Chapter 8, in recharacterizing human rights as moral demands on government, abjured any effort to alter the content of these rights. In fact, it was argued there that the protections against government that arose in the pre-administrative era are, if anything, more important now because of administrative government's greater capacity to oppress its citizens, to insinuate itself into their lives, and to displace competing private institutions. Neither the advent of the administrative state nor the recharacterization of rights that the nature of this state suggests has any affect upon the substantive content of those protections, except possibly to make them more important.

This is not true for the right to private property, however. The administrative state displaces this idea, whether it is viewed in its traditional guise of a natural right, in its more contemporary guise of a human right, or in the proposed guise of a moral demand on government. Property does not receive any rights-based or morally based protection against government in the administrative state. The reason for this is that the essential nature of administrative government is to abolish the traditional idea of property itself, which means that there is no underlying or substantive feature to which a right or moral demand can be attached. Thus, the argument that will be advanced here for abandoning the idea of property is not based on Thomas Grey's observation that the idea is too uncertain to be comprehensible and too contentious to be useful.[14] Rather, it will be argued, as in prior chapters, that the idea, while clear enough at the time it arose, is essentially inapplicable to present circumstances. And, as in prior chapters, no argument will be advanced that this development is either right or wrong in some general or objective sense. The point is simply that it has occurred. One can have a modern administrative state, and reconcile oneself to the displacement of property that the advent of this state has effected, or one can opt to retain the concept of property and reject the administrative state. What one cannot do, it will be argued, is to have them both.

To perceive the inconsistency between the administrative state and our traditional idea of property, consider the familiar case of *Pennsylvania Coal Co. v. Mahon*,[15] decided by the U.S. Supreme Court in 1922. The case was a constitutional challenge to a Pennsylvania statute that forbade companies from mining certain coal deposits that they owned if such mining would cause separately owned land above the mine to subside.[16] There was no question that Pennsylvania was constitutionally permitted to enact the statute; the issue was whether the Fifth Amendment clause that "private property [shall not] be taken for public use, without just compensation" obligated Pennsylvania to reimburse the affected coal miners for the economic loss that resulted from the statute's application. Justice Holmes, writing for the majority, began by conceding that "government hardly could go on if to some extent values incident to property could not be diminished without paying for every such change in the law."[17] The Pennsylvania statute was unconstitutional, however, because the diminution in property values was too extensive. "The general rule at least is that while property may be regulated to a certain extent, if regulation goes too far it will be recognized as a taking."[18]

But what precisely does it mean to say that the diminution of value that results from regulatory legislation "goes too far"? The problem does not involve the well-known difficulties of judicial line drawing,[19] but rather the underlying theory that would explain the reason why the line is being drawn at all. One difficulty with this test for compensation is that it depends on a categorical but unexplained distinction between the diminution of value that results from regulation and the more traditional loss of value that results from the government's acquisition of a physical asset by means of eminent domain. When the government condemns a physical asset, such as ten acres of land, it is required to pay the market value of that acreage; when it reduces the value of the land by something short of "too far," it is not required to pay anything at all. A second difficulty is that Holmes's goes-too-far test depends on the equally categorical and unexplained distinction between the proportion of the loss and its absolute amount. Why should a person be compensated when a regulation eliminates the entire value of a little shed, but not when it eliminates half the value of a massive factory? Third, as Margaret Radin has pointed out,[20] the idea of total or extensive loss often depends on the "conceptual severance" of the property that has been totally devalued from other property whose value has remained. In *Mahon*, for example, the property whose value diminution had gone too far was the pillars of coal that had been left unmined to prevent surface subsidence. But the Court could just have readily concluded that the property at issue was the entire mine, in which case all the coal in the pillars would have represented only a fraction of the property's value.

The source of these problems is fairly easy to discern and, in fact, is virtually explicit in Justice Holmes's opinion. To require the government to compensate property owners every time a regulation diminishes the value of their property would hobble, and perhaps destroy, the administrative state, something no court and no developed country is prepared to do.[21]

Virtually every regulation that affects property owners causes some sort of economic loss to them; for coal mine owners, health and safety laws, environmental laws, and labor laws can be shown to cost them money and thus, in a very real sense, to produce economic loss.[22] On the other hand, permitting the government to simply seize a person's property without paying for it seems antithetical to our idea of a constrained and just regime. These conflicting instincts indicate that the concept of property suffers from an underlying instability in the modern administrative state. *Mahon* itself is an important case since the Supreme Court treats it as the wellspring of the regulatory takings doctrine,[23] although its actual holding may have been overruled in *Keystone Bituminous Coal Association v. DeBenedictis*, a 1987 decision.[24] But the real significance of *Mahon*, for present purposes, is that it raises quasi-Cartesian doubt about property, not only as an asserted human right, but as a legal category in the first place.

The Pre-Modern Concept of Control

These inherent conflicts in our concept of property can be traced to the concept's origins in pre-modern society. Although property now sounds economic to us, its origins, like the origins of money,[25] are more closely connected to ritual and status. Consider, for example, the story of Lancelot's origin told in the Vulgate Lancelot, a thirteenth-century prose epic.[26] Benwick, in the borderlands between Brittany and Gaul, was ruled by King Ban, an old man with a beautiful young wife and a little son named Lancelot. His neighbor to the east was Claudus, lord of Bourges. Both had been vassals of Aramont, the lord of Brittany, but Claudus had renounced his vassalage and taken as his overlord the king of Gaul. In response, Aramont made war on Claudus. When he found that he was suffering heavy losses because Claudus was receiving Gaul's support, Aramont went to King Uther Pendragon of Britain, Arthur's father, and made himself Uther's vassal on condition that Uther support him in his war. Uther and Aramont then invaded Bourges and took it away from Claudus; in the process, they ravaged it so badly that it was thereafter called the Waste Land.

After Aramont's death, Claudus recovered his land. When Uther died, Arthur became king of Britain, but many of the lesser British kings rejected his legitimacy and went to war with him. Claudus, perceiving an opportunity for revenge while Britain was in chaos, attacks King Ban because Ban is Arthur's vassal. With the help of an army from Gaul, commanded by a Roman consul, he conquers all of Benwick except its strongest castle, Trebe, which he besieges.[27] Realizing that he will have difficulty taking Trebe, he arranges a parley with King Ban and offers terms. "[G]ive me possession of this castle," he says, "and I shall hand it straight back to you, on condition that you immediately become my man, and hold all your land from me." " 'I will not do that,' King Ban replies, " 'for I should be breaking my oath to King Arthur, whose liege man I am.' "[28] Claudus then suggests that Ban send to King Arthur for help, and if it does not come in forty days, Ban can honorably surrender Trebe.

Although reluctant to make concessions, Ban finally accepts these terms and decides to appeal to King Arthur in person. He rides out of Trebe, which is being besieged on one side only, in the middle of the night, accompanied by his wife, his little son, and a single servant. Claudus, however, had secretly contacted King Ban's seneschal and promised to make him lord of Benwick if he would betray the castle. When the seneschal sees Ban depart, he opens the gates, and a fierce battle ensues between Claudus's invading forces and the defenders remaining loyal to King Ban, during which much of the town is burned. Meanwhile Ban, on the road to Britain with his wife and son, decides to ride to the top of a nearby hill to look back at the castle "which he loved so dearly."[29] Seeing the flames, he realizes that the castle has been betrayed. He falls from his horse, and "his heart broke in his breast."[30] The horse then bolts down the hill and his wife, observing it with great concern, sends the servant back up with it, and runs up herself when she hears his anguished cry, leaving little Lancelot beside a lake. Upon overcoming her first attack of grief after seeing her dead husband, she realizes she has left her child alone, and runs back down to find a young woman with him, who promptly picks him up and leaps into the lake. The lake, of course, is a magical illusion, and the young woman is Niniane, the Lady of the Lake, who proceeds to bring up Lancelot as her own son.

The war between Ban and Claudus is a struggle over land, which was clearly the most important form of property in the heavily agricultural society of the Middle Ages, but neither the author of the story[31] nor any of its characters thinks of the dispute in terms of property or economics. One might say, as J. H. Baker does, that the concept of property did not exist during the feudal period, or, as Laura Underkuffler does, that a different, "comprehensive" concept prevailed at the time.[32] What Ban and Claudus are fighting over is control. According to the ethos of feudal Europe, control of land makes them nobles, or free men; it gives them their identity and status.[33] To be a landowner was to exercise lordship—*dominium*—over the subject territory, a lordship that was not perceived as private property, but as a mode of governance, similar in kind and continuous in operation with the king's lordship over the entire country.[34] When Claudus is driven out of Bourges by Aramont and Uther, he does not simply lose the income from the land but his status as a member of the nobility, the society's ruling class. When he regains his territory after the death of Aramont, his status is restored, despite the fact that he is now the ruler of a "waste land." He is thus able to call upon the support of Gaul again, and this status gives him military power, even though his territory presumably could no longer support very many knights on its own. With Gaul's assistance, Claudus goes to war with Ban, his stated reason being to retaliate against Ban's overlord, King Arthur, because Arthur's father deprived him of his land, and thus his status. The devastation of his land is something that he does not bother mentioning.[35]

There was, moreover, a real economic and social reality behind this status-based concept of *dominium*. Anything more than a very small amount of agricultural land is valueless unless one can find other people to farm it, and there was no functional labor market in the Middle Ages. The medieval nobility, who were certainly not prepared to accept some Jeffersonian idea of small-scale, egalitarian holdings, solved this problem through the system of serfdom. Serfs were attached to the land and owed a variety of obligations to its overlord, including some of their laboring days and a portion of their produce from the remaining ones, when they labored on their own behalf.[36] To be a landowner, therefore, was to exercise control over a group of people, and while this control was designed, in part, to secure an income for the landowner, it also constituted the means by which these people were governed. Such control extended, on both social and economic grounds, to the seneschals, bailiffs, chamberlains, butlers, ostlers, and other servants who managed the lord's lands and household on his behalf.[37] It was for all practical purposes the only secular, or political, control over all these serfs and servants. While this control was constrained by custom and, more important, by religion—even the lowliest serfs were Christians, which gave them certain rights—it was the lord who policed their behavior, administered punishment, and resolved disputes.[38]

Another aspect of feudal *dominium*, very prominent in the story of Ban and Claudus, is the complex set of reciprocal obligations in which the lord's *dominium* was embedded. Each person was either a vassal of a greater lord, or a lord of lesser vassals, or, most commonly, a combination of the two. The vassal owed his lord military service, domestic service, or provisions. The overlord, in turn, promised protection to his vassals, which was often invaluable in an era when there were so many fighting men, so much honor, and so little central government.[39] This relationship could be established either by grant of land from lord to vassal, or by mutual agreement between existing landowners. The story of Ban and Claudus provides multiple examples of the latter method, and at least one example of the former. Claudus subordinates himself to the king of Gaul, repudiating his subordination to Aramont. Aramont subordinates himself to Arthur to obtain aid in a war against Claudus. Once Claudus regains his land, and the time is opportune, he calls on the support of Gaul, his overlord, again. Ban, of course, seeks the aid of his overlord, Arthur, to defend himself from Claudus. In the parley between Ban and Claudus, Claudus's only demand is that Ban become his man, that is, subordinate to Claudus, and Ban's only basis for refusal is that he is already sworn to Arthur. Instead, Claudus promises to grant Ban's land, which he has conquered, to the seneschal if the seneschal will betray the castle.

The fact that *dominium* was never absolute, but always embedded in a set of relationships with superiors and subordinates, did not alter its character as control because the mutual relationships that one entered into were regarded as an aspect of a landowner's control, not a diminution of it. Given the transportation, communication and managerial resources available during the early Middle Ages, one could only control a large amount of land by granting it to loyal subordinates, a process called subinfeudation. Having made such grants, to be sure, one was no longer the direct manager of the granted lands; one's vassal was now the lord and governor of the serfs who were attached to these lands. But serfs had no military role, nor was their loyalty prized on non-instrumental grounds. Their value lay in their ability to generate income, and the overlord enjoyed this value through the material and military obligations that his vassal owed. Thus, what the overlord gained, in making grants, was control over his vassals, who did have military value, and whose loyalty was valued on its own terms. These vassals were now the overlord's "men," bound to him by ties of fidelity, and thus by the morality of honor that, as described in Chapters 1 and 6, governed social relations in the Middle Ages.

As far as the vassals were concerned, their obligations to their lord did not detract from the *dominium* they exercised over the granted or subordinated lands. One reason for the subordinate's sense of freedom—and *dominium*—is that his obligations were treated as freely assumed, whether they arose from grants of land or agreements between existing landowners. But an even more important reason is that the subjective meaning of this control, for the people who participated in the feudal system, went far beyond its economic implications. It was an intimate human relationship, governed by the morality of honor. To be a great man's vassal did not decrease one's personal dignity but increased it, and to fulfill the obligations of that status was a sign of true nobility. Aramont goes to war with Claudus because Claudus committed the great offense of breaking his feudal vows. Claudus goes to war with Ban to avenge the insult of being driven from his land by Ban's two overlords, not to recoup his economic fortunes. The reader knows he is the villain of the piece because he betrayed his feudal bond to Aramont, and his efforts to subvert the seneschal's loyalty to his lord are thus very much in character. King Ban, father of the noble Lancelot, will not repudiate his bond to Arthur, even in circumstances of great peril.[40] His loyalty to his lord is an indication of his moral strength, not of his political subordination.

The Persistence of the Control Concept

With the gradual revival of commerce during the early and high Middle Ages, the feudal system, in its pure form, gradually disintegrated.[41] Noblemen were now able and willing to sell their land for money, thereby relinquishing their feudal obligations to their lord and vassals, while non-noblemen, the ever-increasing and prospering merchant class, were able to purchase land and to demand its transfer to them free and clear, without the attendant military obligations that they were unable or unwilling to fulfill. The growth of central government and political order, which made this commercial revival possible, concomitantly decreased the need to obtain military service from one's grantees, or military protection from one's grantors. As a result, the currently familiar concept of property gradually developed. Agricultural land became a commodity that could be bought and sold without incurring ongoing personal obligations to related land holders. The rules governing its retention and disposition became those of commercial activity, not of honor and fidelity. Serfdom was abolished and replaced by a true labor market; the large landowner could hire agricultural workers or lease land to tenant farmers, and no longer had to rely on holding human beings in bondage to the land. Moreover, other forms of valuable property, such as urban real estate, consumer goods, and financial intangibles, proliferated, to which the traditions of the feudal system were largely inapplicable.

But the feudal concept of *dominium* over land and people, which was so central to the entire fabric of early medieval society, could not be so readily displaced. The ownership of rural land continued to possess political significance; landowners, even if they had merchant origins, tended to become a local nobility by virtue of such ownership. More important, land ownership continued to serve as a form of governance as well as the allocation of an economic asset.[42] Any large landowner played an important role in regulating and controlling the lives of the common people who lived on his estate, or in the nearby village that supplied it with laborers.[43] This function was more explicit in England, with its Justices of the Peace, than in the more centralized regimes of France or Scandinavia, but it prevailed throughout Europe until the advent of the administrative state. Its late but still discernible existence is evidenced by Mr. Knightly's ministrations in Jane Austen's *Emma*, and by Eduard and Charlotte's management of their estate in Goethe's *Elective Affinities*.[44]

Still another means by which property owners continued their control of human beings in the post-feudal era was through the institution of slavery.[45] Slaves were not attached to the land, but, in accordance with the commercial character of post-feudal times, were a freely traded commodity, which, of course, made their predicament much worse.[46] It now seems impolite to treat slavery as an integral part of the pre-modern concept of property, but, in fact, every pre-modern property theorist, including Locke, believed that his theory extended to property rights in people.[47] The practice and theory of slavery, like the continued role of landowners in local governance, indicates that the property was still conceived as a mode of control, or *dominium*. To be a property owner was to exercise lordship over land and people, to lay down the law for these essential commodities and manage them according to one's desires.

Thus, as feudal rights and obligations gradually evolved into the property rights of a commercial culture, the sense of control, or *dominium*, that prevailed in the medieval period did not disappear, but survived in altered form. Additional attributes of property developed to meet the needs of a commercial culture and the consequent commodification of land, people, and other material possessions. To own property, in the post-medieval world, thus came to mean that one could transfer it, earn income from it, and use it as capital, as A.M.A. Honore suggests.[48] As time went on, and the economic system increased in specialization and complexity, these ownership-related benefits became increasingly separated from the owner's control. The wealthy property owner in the modern world is not the lord of a manor, ruling a territory filled with serfs, living in a castle filled with servants, and commanding the loyalty of vassals who rule other serfs and servants, but a person in a big house with a few employees who receives an income stream from stocks, bonds, and certificates of deposit. The ordinary property owner is not a small farmer who possesses and controls a bit of land, or a merchant who possesses and controls a little workshop, but a person in a small house who receives a salary and a pension.

But the sense of control, or *dominium*, the idea that property was one's own personal realm that one commanded, and that conferred the status on its owner that was independent of its economic value, proved as resilient as the Gothic cathedrals that still dot the European landscape.[49] Blackstone almost explicitly connects ownership with the medieval conception in his influential description of English Common Law. Ownership of property, he states, is that "sole and despotic dominion which one man claims and exercises over the external things of the world in total exclusion of the right of any other individual in the universe."[50] As Carol Rose notes, this mode of thought is reflected in the present day belief that possession lies at the center of our concept of property.[51] The continued centrality of control explains the sense of revelation that greeted Adolph Berle and Gardiner Means's observation that ownership is separate from control in the modern corporation.[52] Something that should have been long apparent seemed both astonishing and disconcerting due to the outdated but puissant expectation that property should involve control. Similarly, it was not until 1972, some eight or nine hundred years after the formulation of the Common Law, that Guido Calabresi and Douglas Melamed recognized that property and tort liability were simply alternative ways of protecting entitlements, with property rules forbidding nonconsensual private takings, and tort rules permitting such takings in return for payment of damages.[53] Recent scholarship has effaced this boundary still further by treating both as options with different prices.[54] The counterintuitive quality of these economically astute perceptions results from the same sense that property means control, not protection. Shifting to a different economic realm, Kevin Bales notes that modern forms of slavery in Brazil, India, Pakistan, and Thailand are recognizable as such although the slaveholders merely exercise control, without asserting ownership.[55]

While the ever-evolving notion of property undoubtedly incorporates a wide range of policies and themes,[56] the continuation of this conceptual connection between property and control can be perceived in all the major pre-modern theories about the origin and character of property, and a significant number of modern ones as well. Natural rights theory, a product of the Middle Ages, explicitly identified the God-given right of property as a right of control. William of Ockham, credited by some as the first proponent of natural rights, made an attempt to connect this God-given right with a mere right to use, rather than control, in order to extricate the Fransciscans from the most severe implications of their founder's teaching about apostolic poverty.[57] But the Church definitively rejected this idea and excommunicated its proponents. The right of property, Pope John XXII declared, is the right to control a thing, to exercise *dominium* over it.[58] One could only use it because one possessed such *dominium*, or had received permission from the possessor. When natural rights theory was expanded to include personal liberty, it conceptualized this more abstract idea as property in one's person. This makes sense only if property means control. As Richard Overton, the Leveller, wrote, "every one, as he is himself, so he has a self-propriety, else could he not *be* himself."[59]

Locke's modification of the natural rights tradition, perhaps the most famous theory of property in the Western political tradition, reveals this same mindset. He asserts that one acquires property rights in an unowned object by mixing one's labor with that object.[60] To mix one's labor with an unowned object, however, one must take control of it. If another person already has control, no amount of labor mixing will ever confer property rights on the laborer, according to Locke and the traditional conception of property. Construction workers, no matter how extensive and assiduous their labors, never acquire property rights in the structure they are building; tenant farmers never acquire property rights in the land. This conception is so deeply ingrained in our collective consciousness that it prevailed after the American Civil War, when those who had committed the moral crime of slave owning and the political crime of treason were permitted to retain their plantations, while their former slaves, who had such powerful moral and political claims to the land they had cleared and farmed, were given nothing, and left vulnerable to the restoration of their former servitude in the only slightly modified guise of the crop lien system.[61] If labor alone is the true determinant of property rights, then prior ownership should not count for so much, especially if the owner obtains it by grant, or inheritance, or merely staking a claim. In fact, prior ownership is determinative because Locke's theory actually turns upon control. When an object is unowned, mixing one's labor leads to ownership because it represents an assertion of control, not because ownership follows from the process of laboring itself.

These instincts continue to the present day. Suppose one goes to a supermarket, spends an hour or so putting various comestibles in one's cart, and then leaves the cart for a moment to use the bathroom. One would be infuriated, upon one's return, to find that someone else had taken the cart. "But that's mine!" one might very well say, and, if one had taken political science in college, one might add, "John Locke says its mine; I mixed my labor with it." On the other hand, no sane person in our culture would make the same argument to the cashier. The labor is the same—what differs is the extent of control. Vis-à-vis the other person, the shopper has taken control of those items; vis-à-vis Safeway, the shopper understands that Safeway has control of them, and is permitting the shopper to gather the items in order to purchase them, at which point statute or Common Law gives the shopper control.

The same notion of control that characterized the concept of property in both the natural rights and common law traditions remains the dominant theme in the work of modern scholars who treat property as a human right. Richard Epstein, for example, reiterates Blackstone's description as part of his argument that the state must compensate property owners for most forms of economic and social regulation.[62] Robert Nozick declares: "The central core of the notion of a property right in X, relative to which other parts of the notion are to be explained, is the right to determine what shall be done with X; the right to choose which of the constrained set of options concerning X shall be realized or attempted."[63]

Mahon and its progeny reflect this view. Judicial doctrine in the takings area is guided by what Bruce Ackerman calls the ordinary observer's point of view, that is, the idea of property that is found in nonlawyer's ordinary talk.[64] And the content of this notion, as argued above, has been shaped by the historical association between property and control. The government's exercise of eminent domain, no matter how small its absolute value or how small a proportion of the subject's total property is taken, is thought to demand compensation, while the diminution of value through regulation does not, because eminent domain, as opposed to diminution of value, removes property from the owner's control. But at some point, according to these decisions, the diminution goes too far. This desperately vague and largely unexplained criterion for compensation can also be understood as a survival of the medieval concept of property as *dominium*. The line is crossed—the government has gone too far—when it has taken so much of the property's value that it has effectively removed that property from the owner's control. The government may tax the income from mining pillars of coal, or impose heavy regulatory costs on mining them in the interest of health, safety, or the environment, but if it forbids the owner from mining them entirely, it has ended the owner's control, and this it may not do without compensating him. To deny such compensation is to commit the same offense, the same insult, that Aramont and Uther committed against Claudus when they ousted him from his land instead of merely devastating it.

Market-Generating Allocations

Markets as a Mode of Regulation

The prominence of the medieval notion of *dominium*, or control, in the contemporary theory and legal doctrine of property generates quasi-Cartesian doubt about whether the property concept continues to have value as a description of the governmental system that we actually possess. Nonetheless, the need to proceed with the thought experiment of bracketing this concept and exploring an alternative description is open to question. Unlike most of the other concepts discussed in this book, such as power, democracy, legitimacy, law, and rights, property is not one that we use reflexively, or that is so central to our mode of thought that we have difficulty extricating ourselves from its skein of connotations. In fact, the concept has been subjected to a withering critique in legal and economic theory since the beginning of the twentieth century. Legal realists attacked both the Common Law notion of title, which they condemned as artificial, inflexible, and unjust, and the concept of property in general, which they condemned as falsely reified.[65] Wesley Hohfeld disaggregated the concept in his analysis of legal rights discussed in Chapter 7,[66] and his realist colleagues described it, in a famous phrase, as nothing more than "a bundle of sticks."[67] Grey and Honore are the heirs of this tradition. Even more important, Ronald Coase dissolved the concept of property into a set of free-floating allocations that could attach anywhere, with equal effect but for the transaction costs of re-allocating them.[68] This perspective, as developed by Armen Alchian, Harold Demsetz, Douglass North, Oliver Williamson, and others, has become enormously influential in contemporary economic thought[69] and has exercised an only slightly less extensive influence on legal scholarship.

But the critiques, intellectually powerful though they may be, are not quite sufficient for present purposes. Their principal import is to suggest that the term 'property' is more properly regarded as a Wittgensteinian cluster of ideas than as a naturally occurring entity. All the revised approaches to property, however, include control, the persistent revenant of medieval *dominium*, as a central element. However else one transforms the concept, however many separate rights or sticks it is parsed or factored into, control remains a constant. It is precisely this element, however, that makes the concept clash with the realities of the administrative state.[70] As long as we rely on the idea of control to explain the difference between the loss of property through eminent domain and the diminution of value through regulation, as long as we retain the idea that regulation becomes equivalent to loss when it deprives the owner of control, we will not have a coherent account of the government we actually possess. For this reason, the thought experiment of bracketing property and exploring other metaphors for the underlying realities that it describes is worth pursuing.

As discussed in Chapter 2, a modern administrative government can be usefully regarded as a network of interacting units. This network has a boundary whose contour, as discussed in Chapter 3, is roughly defined by full-time government employment. Beyond it lies the society that is associated with this government. Government affects society by issuing a variety of signals, including commands, guidelines, suggestions, and information. In some cases, such as love or parenting, it issues relatively few signals, and allows people to act in a largely unregulated fashion. In other cases, such as banking or mining, it issues a great many signals, and attempts to exercise intensive control over people's actions. In still other cases, it issues an initial set of signals, and then allows a certain amount of unregulated action within the framework that its signals have established. One common framework of this nature is a market. As Neil Komesar has suggested, a market is simply an alternative mode of regulation to political or judicial regulation through direct or indirect command.[71]

Markets involve valued resources, that is, items whose supply is limited. Their essential feature is that they distribute such resources according to the expressed preferences of the participating individuals. They are generally thought to be the most economically efficient way to manage these resources, but they create serious distributional inequality that, in many people's view, leads to injustice. If the government, as a matter of public policy, wants economic efficiency in a given area, and is not overly concerned about distributional inequality, it will generally choose to rely on the market as its primary means of regulating human behavior; if it is concerned with the pattern of distribution, it will turn to some more intensive mode of regulation.

To establish a market in a particular resource, the government must issue signals that allocate to private parties certain specified economic relations to that resource. The minimal relations, as Coase argues, are that some economic benefit from each distinguishable portion of the resource in question must be assigned to specific parties, and that these parties must be able to transfer that benefit from one to another.[72] Without allocation, the self-interest of individuals will not be engaged. Without transferability, the individuals will not be able to reallocate the benefits in accordance with their changing preferences.[73] The terminology used within the financial community supports this view. In order to "make a market" in a particular item, one must be willing to buy however much of that item that individuals—that is, individuals to whom portions of the item are allocated—want to transfer: if the individuals cannot transfer their portions, no market in that item will exist.[74]

A true market in a particular resource requires that the benefits that are being allocated be those that are generated by the resource itself. Of course, if there is a general system of such allocations, and a money system to support trading in them, people can take a financial stake in things that are not allocated to them, but then the result is gambling, not a market. At a race track, people obtain a financial stake in the outcome of a horse race, but not in the income earned by the horse. This could lead to a secondary market in bets, but not to a market in horses. The betting at the race track would be essentially the same if the FHA (Federal Horse Authority) controlled all the horses, and simply raced them against each other for public entertainment.

It is allocation and transferability, not control, that are crucial for the creation of a market. While control over the item in question—the ability to determine how the item is used as opposed to transferred—is often granted as a convenient way to facilitate the market's operation, it is not a necessary element. There is, for example, a lively market in financial obligations, such as government bonds, corporate bonds, commercial paper, and credit card debt, but these items are pure income streams, and the owner of them can do nothing with them except receive the income or transfer the right to receive that income to some other party.[75] Berle and Means's great insight was that corporate stock, which theoretically confers the right to control the corporation, has become a mere right to a specified share of the corporation's profits in most cases, with no right of control.[76] This lack of control may affect the price of the stock, but it certainly does not impair its transferability and hence the existence of a thriving sec-

ondary market. Where control is involved, there are often a variety of limitations on it, and this does not impair the market's operation either.[77]
Zoning restricts the use of land, and while it certainly affects the price, it
does not preclude a fully operating market for the land's permitted uses.[78]
Legislatures and courts regularly restrict the ability of store owners to control access to their facilities,[79] but these facilities remain readily transferable. Federal legislation prohibiting those who buy artwork from destroying it[80] has left the art market pretty much intact, despite the apparent
exclusion of self-sacrificial Philistines.

Other characteristics associated with the traditional idea of ownership
are also not essential to the creation of a market, although they will often
make the market operate more smoothly. If individuals are not allowed to
devise their ability to derive economic benefit from the item in question,
or if the government can cancel the ability to benefit at some fixed or indeterminate time, end-game behaviors may occur.[81] These may disrupt the
market's operation, or make it less efficient, but they will not destroy it.
More generally, any of the characteristics of traditional ownership can be
established by itself or in connection with any other feature. It would be
entirely possible for the government to issue signals granting people the
ability to control assets from which they derive no economic benefit, or to
use assets they do not control, or derive income from assets from which
they have no other relationship. The reason that some of these combina-
tions are rarely seen is that they serve no useful public policy purpose.
Transferability combined with allocation is the most important combination because that is what is needed to regulate some matter through the
mechanism of a market.

As a means of regulation, markets are quite flexible with respect to what
Laura Underkuffler describes as their area of field, that is, the sorts of
items whose economic benefits they allocate.[82] In recent years, the Environmental Protection Agency has created a market in pollution limits in
order to distribute pollution abatement efforts in an efficient manner.[83] To
simplify, assume that limits are established for the amount of pollution that
each factory in a given industry is allowed to emit without paying a fine. A
by-product of this approach is that a factory emitting less pollution than
its limit would not be penalized for increasing its pollution to the limit.
But the EPA can create a market in pollution limits by allocating to each
factory the permission to pollute up to the limit, and then allowing the
factory to sell this permission. This may be more efficient because it gives
a factory that can reduce pollution cheaply an incentive to do so, allows a
factory that can only reduce pollution at great cost the ability to avoid
these costs by purchasing permission to continue polluting, and thus
achieves the same or greater pollution reduction with a lower economic

impact.[84] The market is created by allocating the limits and permitting their sale, without the need to confer other relations such as control, management, or derivation of an income stream.

Another area where the administrative policy of market regulation is widely utilized is services, that is, activities performed by human beings. Discussions of property tend to exclude services, although goods and services are invariably intertwined, and together constitute the core of our economic system. Once property is recharacterized as a regulatory policy designed to create a market by allocating economic benefits to individuals, services can be characterized the same way. It then becomes possible to provide a comprehensive description of the way both goods and services are treated in the modern state. The market for services—legal counseling, plumbing repair, weight training—reflects the same sort of regulatory policy, motivated by the same goal of economic efficiency, and using the same device of assigning economic benefit to individuals and regulating its use. Most typically, individuals are assigned the economic benefit of the services that they can provide, and then allowed to transfer those services to whomever they choose. This allocation has become so widespread that it seems too obvious to mention, but in fact it represents conscious social policy decisions. In the Middle Ages, many people were serfs, which meant that a large part of their services were assigned to their master, and there were limits on their ability to transfer the remainder. Even today, the economic benefit of children's services—consisting largely of stage and screen performance since the abolition of child labor[85]—is assigned to their parents.[86] The government can allocate people's services to itself, as in the cases of jury duty and the military draft. The Stalinist Soviet Union and Maoist China assigned the economic benefit of people's services to their factory or collective farm precisely because they did not want to create a market in these services.[87]

Market regulation is not only flexible with respect to the items it can cover, but it is also flexible with respect to the extent to which it applies to any given item, a feature Underkuffler identifies as stringency of protection.[88] For a given item, the public policy maker can choose to create a lot of market, a little market, or anything in between. Baseball cards are an item governed by a lot of market; there are virtually no restrictions on their production, sale, or resale, in part because they do not create externalities. Pharmaceuticals, on the other hand, are governed by much less market due to the administrative restrictions on their production and the prescription requirements for their consumption. Thus, it is somewhat inaccurate to speak about "the market" for a particular item; the question is how fully the policy makers want to rely on market-creating allocations and transferability, that is, how much market they want for the item in question.

This malleability of markets as a means of regulation can be most read-ily perceived when technology generates new products, or ways of bene-fiting from a previously unused resource. The invention of radio made a portion of the electromagnetic spectrum extremely valuable, but the U.S. government chose not to allocate this new-found resource the way land has been allocated since the Middle Ages. Instead, firms that wanted to ex-ploit the spectrum were given a time-limited license that could be renewed upon a showing that they were providing a valued service to the public.[89] There was some reliance on market regulation because the licenses could be bought and sold, subject to government approval, but it was very lim-ited. When player piano rolls were invented, Congress did not want to al-locate full control of these modalities to the owners of the music, for fear that they would refuse to transfer the recording rights to artists who wanted to perform the songs. Instead, they created a compulsory licensing system, where owners are required to license their music to performers for a designated fee.[90] Compulsory licenses are now used for sound record-ings, jukeboxes, cable television, noncommercial broadcasting, and satel-lite retransmission; they allow more market regulation than broadcast licensing, but less than copyright.[91] After the Internet was opened to com-mercial use, a more business-oriented Congress enacted the Digital Mil-lennium Copyright Act, which reasserted traditional copyright protection by prohibiting electronic circumvention of technological measures taken by copyright holders to restrict access to their works.[92] This meant that the market was being used as the primary means of regulating commerce on the Internet. Clearly, a wide range of ownership and transferability options exist. The basis on which this choice among alternatives is generally made, and should be made, is social policy, and not the concepts created by bel-ligerent medieval land holders.[93]

Despite the flexibility of markets with respect to both range and amount, there are, of course, limits on the use of markets as a regulatory mecha-nism. Some of these limits derive from moral considerations. History pro-vides lugubrious proof that it is perfectly possible to create a market in human beings, and, indeed, it still exists in certain places,[94] but it is no longer regarded as morally acceptable. Richard Posner proposes that a market be created to distribute desirable white babies on an efficient basis,[95] but most people find this equally offensive.[96] In the United States, many goods, such as morphine, and many services, such as sex, are con-sidered inappropriate for distribution by markets, although they are avail-able by others means, such as prescriptions and dating. Liberty considera-tions generally preclude assigning an adult's services to another person, although they do not prevent the transfer or prohibition of such services.

In addition, there are technological limits on the use of markets. The general view is that certain desirable goods or services, such as air and safety from foreign invasion, are public goods, which means that they cannot be supplied to particular individuals, and therefore that the mechanism of a market cannot be used for their delivery.[97] Other desirable features cannot be given the form of goods or services at all; it would be useful, and not morally objectionable, to create a market in physical courage, so that an accountant with no fear of heights could sell this quality to a construction worker who was having difficulty doing his job, but at the present time the thing cannot be done.[98]

This view of markets as a regulatory strategy resulting from a certain type of governmental signal enables us to bracket the idea of property. There is no private property according to this view, but simply a set of government signals that establish market-generating allocations. Thus, the medieval notion of control, or *dominium*, that clings to all definitions of the term 'property,' whether pre-modern or contemporary, can finally be extirpated. The crucial features for the use of market regulation are not control, but the allocations themselves and some rule providing for the transfer of those allocations. Control, in the sense that the person to whom the resource is allocated can exclude others, use the resource, transform it, or destroy it, may accompany the allocation, but it need not do so.

Bracketing the concept of property in this way is descriptively advantageous because property, and the control that it implies, is not a relevant category for administrative governance. Regulation regularly diminishes the value of resources that are under the control of individuals, but with the concept of property bracketed, there is no longer any implication that the government must compensate the individual for the resulting economic loss. Instead, these diminutions of value simply represent a public policy that alters the terms of a regulatory program. They are thus no different, in normative terms, from a public policy that decreases welfare benefits or raises the fee for a broadcasting license, although the pragmatic effectiveness of these measures will of course be variable. Numerous scholars have acknowledged this reality by qualifying 'property'; for example, Underkuffler has described the modern idea of property as operative, that is, "fluid in time, established and re-established as circumstances warrant," in contrast to the older notion of common property, which is protected against politically initiated change.[99] For Joseph Singer, this modern idea is entitlement, where all interests are balanced against each other, as opposed to ownership, where only the property owner's interests are considered.[100] John Christman distinguishes income ownership from the older notion of control ownership.[101] It would, in theory, be possible to retain 'property' and simply redefine the concept to which it relates,[102] since words do not have obligatory meanings, but the historical association of property with the concept of control renders such usage counterintuitive and confusing. The thought experiment suggested here is to bracket the concept of property in its entirety, and replace it with the idea of a market-generating allocation.[103]

The descriptive accuracy of the proposed alternative may appear to be contradicted by the Supreme Court's intermittent efforts to place limits on the government's authority over private property, and by Congress's equally intermittent efforts to legislate such limits.[104] The incoherence and inconsistency of these efforts indicates that they do not betoken the continued vitality of pre-modern property ideas, but rather the distress that the abandonment of these ideas engenders. Congressional efforts, while often introduced with great bravura, typically fail in the face of practical considerations, or pass in highly adulterated form. With respect to the Supreme Court, the incoherence of *Mahon*, has already been discussed. The Court's well-known decision in *Lucas v. South Carolina Coastal Council* provides a further example.[105] A developer who had purchased two lots on the South Carolina seacoast challenged a state statute that prohibited development of the lots, claiming that the statute had destroyed the entire value of his lots, and thus constituted a taking that demanded compensation. The Supreme Court, ruling in his favor, conceded that the state could regulate the use of land through zoning laws and similar restrictions, but concluded that this particular restriction, like the one in *Mahon*, had gone too far. Lucas, however, was but one of a large number of land owners who were affected by the statute, and who, it may be assumed, had lobbied against its passage and lost out to opposing interests. He lost money as a result, but a larger developer whose fifty inland lots were rezoned from industrial to residential use would have suffered greater loss. How is Lucas's situation to be distinguished from a general regulation that costs the regulated parties money, or from specific regulations that lead only to a partial loss? The only way, it would appear, is to appeal to the pre-modern notion of control.[106]

The Advantages of the Alternative

As in previous chapters, the next step is to demonstrate that the proposed recharacterization not only creates a more coherent account of current governmental practice, but also meets the criteria of reflecting our emotional commitments, announcing its heuristic character, and facilitating microanalysis. Emotional commitments are the most important of these criteria for present purposes, since the ability of alternative formulations to signal their heuristic character and facilitate microanalysis have been effectively discussed by Coase and those who follow him. Given the passion with which some people, such as Hayek, Nozick, and Epstein, defend the right of property, the various Supreme Court decisions on the subject, and the prominence of this concept in our legal system, it might appear that the abandonment of the term would violate, rather than reflect, our emotional commitments. But the fact remains that all these encomia to property have not impeded the continued development of the regulatory state. The value of property, or private allocations, is diminished every day without very many people, including those who own the property or possess the allocations, demanding that the government provide compensation for this diminution of value. Nor is this an oversight, a situation that modern people have stumbled into through some fit of collective absentmindedness. It is the essence of the administrative state, a mode of governance that has been steadily and inexorably evolving for the past two centuries in a wide variety of nations, including those interactive republics whose governments are more responsive to their citizens than any prior governments in Western history.

Would it really comport with our political morality for the government to cancel a widely recognized aspect of ownership, such as the ownership of automobiles, the way it canceled a benefits program such as Aid to Families with Dependent Children?[107] The answer is a definite yes. The horror that we feel about the idea of forbidding automobile ownership is not the same as our moral revulsion toward the Holocaust, or African slavery. Rather, it is a strong form of political opposition to an unwise, inefficient social policy. This sense of horror would prevent such a policy from being enacted, at least in an interactive republic like our own; any politician who proposed ending automobile ownership would be ending his own career instead. But suppose, some centuries from now, the clean, silent, instantaneous mode of transport that Captain Kirk uses in *Star Trek* is available, and the vast majority of citizens travel in this manner. It is entirely imaginable that a government like our own would then forbid automobile ownership to the cantankerous few who continued to utilize these filthy, obsolete machines, without providing compensation.

This study, as previously stated, does not attempt to enter into the age-old and interminable debate about the objective or transcultural morality of our administrative ethos.[108] Its only assertion is that the political morality that prevails in the modern state, and on which that state is premised, decisively rejects the idea that property is sacrosanct, and that those who are described as owning property should be compensated for the loss of economic value that results from regulatory programs. There may be some value, however, in explicating this morality at slightly greater length. Four arguments that proclaim the deontological value of property, and thus oppose the plenary authority of the government to decide how much market is to be employed in any given situation, are briefly canvassed here. These are the inherent morality of property, its role in protecting liberty, its role in creating responsible citizens, and its correspondence to the moral intuitions of the citizenry. To reiterate, the primary purpose for discussing these claims is not to refute them at the philosophic level, but rather to demonstrate their inconsistency with modern government. Claims about the manner in which the government may impair property interests through individualized action, as opposed to general regulatory policy, are deferred until the following section, and their separate treatment is justified in that section as well. Claims about the economic efficiency of property[109] need not be considered, as they are entirely consistent with the proposed perspective. Government regularly creates or approves the existence of markets because citizens and policy makers appreciate the enormous efficiency advantages that markets produce. Treating property as a market-generating allocation only emphasizes the centrality of this approach.

The claim that there exists an inherent morality of property, that there is a human right to acquire and retain property akin to the human right to speak freely, worship freely, or be free from slavery and torture, can be regarded, with some accuracy, as the most controversial issue of the last two centuries. It not only divides communism and socialism from free enterprise but also, within the more delimited arena of free enterprise societies, divides progressive from conservative opinion. For present purposes only one point about this claim needs to be made, and this can be advanced in response to Robert Nozick, perhaps the best-known proponent of the natural rights position. Nozick argues that taking property from any person, even in the form of taxes, is a violation of the person's rights.[110] But natural rights arguments of this sort, as discussed in Chapter 8, are outmoded in our modern state. In addition, they are arbitrary; one could just as easily argue, as Rousseau does, that people relinquish their individual claims to property when they become part of civil society, and then receive that property back from the state in undiminished but contingent form.[111] Moreover, as Waldron points out, Nozick's initial argument for holding property inviolate refers to property acquired by fair procedures. Since no current, real-world property fulfills this criterion, he must have recourse to the much weaker position that historically established holdings merit the same level of respect.[112]

This difficulty is concealed if one focuses on a person who earns his income by his current efforts, rather than as a return on capital. Nozick does precisely this in another passage, where he imagines that Wilt Chamberlain signs a contract providing that twenty-five cents from the price of each ticket goes to him, and people buy tickets knowing this to be the case.[113] But if the Chamberlain example conceals this defect, it exposes a different defect in Nozick's theory that is more central to modern political morality. Chamberlain obtained his splendid income, and concurrent fame, because he was seven feet tall and could put a ball through a hoop suspended ten feet off the ground. But in most societies besides our own, this skill would not have generated anything but passing interest and his height would have been a liability. Chamberlain's income-generating ability existed because civil society has created the game of basketball, organized a league, and generated popular interest, and because the government has created an economic and social environment in which so many resources could be devoted to so nonproductive an activity.[114] In general, our current political morality is based on the entirely plausible belief that wealth, and certainly the enormous wealth that some people have amassed, can only be obtained because of the advanced economy generated by collective efforts. Joseph Singer advances a similar argument in a different form when he points out that granting owners free use of their property is just as regulatory as restricting their use. For example, the government may decide that it does not want to intrude on the freedom of owners by passing an anti-discrimination law, but to do so it must enforce the trespass laws against those whom the owner wants to exclude.[115]

Regulation creates wealth. It establishes civil order—something that was lacking in the turbulent times when the Lancelot story was written. It enforces contracts, thereby obviating the need to enforce agreements by violence. It provides a stable financial system that keeps money in the country, forbids anti-competitive activity, ensures investor and consumer confidence, maintains worker health, and prevents destructive externalities. In short, markets only exist as a result of regulation.[116] Citizens are aware of this, of course, which is the reason that they have been voting for regulation, and for officials who favor regulation, for the past century at least. For the same reason, they tend not to be impressed by claims that the financial resources generated by regulation should now be shielded from the effects of further regulation.

This perspective is well illustrated by the admittedly extreme idea of deregulatory takings. As Western governments have moved from command and control to market regulation in fields such as trucking, airlines, electric power, and communications, some scholars have advanced the argument that firms which previously benefited from political regulation should now be compensated for the income that they will lose when subjected to market competition.[117] But the wealth-creating character of regulation is explicit in this situation; the income that these firms have earned and, indeed, their very existence, are the products of regulation. Why should they be protected from further regulation merely because it is less favorable to their interests? Every time the government alters a regulatory statute, some group loses out. The idea that the government may not change these laws without compensating the losers is inconsistent with the existence of the administrative state.[118]

The argument that property rights foster liberty appears in both individual and collective form. Property, it is said, establishes a refuge for individuals, a personal preserve where they are free from government control and from which they can sally forth to combat the government's more general depredations.[119] The collective version is that property ownership creates multiple power centers in society that counterbalance the monopoly on power that the government could exercise without them.[120] With regard to the first argument, it is probably true that property increases the liberty of certain people, specifically those people who own lots of property.[121] In the days when the Vulgate Lancelot was written, property owners were the only free men, and thus the only people that mattered. Now, however, we also regard the many people who do not own significant amounts of property as people, and these people find their liberty severely constrained by large property owners. Employers tell them when and where to work and what to do once there, landlords tell them where to live and how to maintain their homes, banks and insurance companies tell them how to manage their affairs, and merchants determine the kinds of goods that are available to them.[122] The small amount of property that most people own—a mortgaged home, a car, some furniture, some clothes, a wristwatch, and a cell phone—may be valued by them, but does not protect them from the control of owners or their managers. The choices that the market provides to consumers may also be valued, but, as Edwin Baker points out, such choices are constrained, manipulated, and often inadequate.[123] These former nonpersons, however, have obtained the vote, and they have used that vote to establish protection for themselves through government regulation. Thus, regulation not only creates wealth, but it protects the liberty of ordinary people. It does so, to be sure, by decreasing the liberty of large property owners, but it would require a strongly elitist sensibility to favor the interests of this small minority on the basis of their wealth, and our system does not do so.

One response to this observation is the collective argument for property, the idea that large property owners, whatever their effect on less fortunate individuals, perform a public service by creating alternative power centers that combat government oppression. But this idea that the wealthy speak for us all, though occasionally true, is more often a rather threadbare apologia for the retention of privilege. Rather than opposing government oppression of all citizens, economic elites typically seek to influence government in favor of their own particular interests. In fact, the influence their wealth confers can be plausibly regarded as an impediment to responsive government for the majority.[124] These elites have typically allied themselves with nonsocialistic dictatorships, and have opposed socialist dictatorships on economic grounds alone. The great force for the preservation and expansion of liberty has not been property owners, but social movements composed of ordinary individuals. The American Revolution, the abolitionist movement, the labor movement, the civil rights movement, the women's movement, and the gay rights movement are the events in U.S.

history that secured the liberties we currently possess.[125] While the people who created these movements were not necessarily poor, it was not their possession of property that made these movements possible, but their commitment, their organization, their leadership, and their numbers.

A third argument for the deontological value of property is that ownership of property produces mature political judgment, that it gives the person a stake in the state's survival and efficient operation that leads to wise decision making. Hegel's version of this argument leads him to conclude that every person should own at least some property.[126] The version that was more popular among propertied elites, and thus more important in historical terms, is not that everyone should have some property, but only that those who already had acquired property should have the right to vote.[127] Ever since Aristotle, the wealthy have worried that if the poor could exercise the franchise, they would use it to transfer resources from the wealthy to themselves, thus disrupting the economy.[128] Perhaps the wealthy have made this assumption because this is what they themselves would do if they were poor, being of the essentially rapacious character that enabled them to obtain their wealth. In fact, repeated historical experience indicates that the poor, when granted the franchise, rarely employ it in this manner, but take the need for stable economic relations as seriously as their more fortunate compatriots. Radical redistribution of property has generally been the work of dictatorships, not electoral regimes with universal suffrage.[129] There is virtually no evidence for the empirical assertion that property ownership makes a person more responsible, wise, or public-spirited than other, less fortunate citizens.

Finally, it is argued that the concept of property is deeply embedded in our intuitive sense of legality and political morality.[130] This is the grounds on which Ackerman's Ordinary Observer makes legal decisions.[131] There can be little doubt about the existence of such embedded moral notions; as discussed above, the medieval concept of *dominium* or control continues to govern our intuitions, at least in certain circumstances. Far from being a justification, however, this intuitive appeal means that property requires additional justification, as Jeremy Waldron points out.[132] Moreover, intuition is an uncertain guide, as the prior popularity of phlogisten theory, spontaneous generation, phrenology, and most of Aristotelian physics readily attests. The heavens, which used to be regarded as announcing the existence and glory of God, now announce the unreliability of human intuition through the big bang, cosmic inflation, black holes, evaporating black holes, and gravitational lensing. The reason, of course, is that our intuitions arise from our quotidian experiences, and interstellar phenomena lie beyond the range of that experience. Intuition is an unreliable guide to the structure and meaning of the administrative state for precisely the same reason. The modern state is not a Greek polis or a New England village that can be readily perceived and understood by all those subject to its authority, but a massive, complex, technologically sophisticated system, divided into many different, quasi-independent fields, each governed by elaborate rules and well-trained specialists. Habermas observes that no individual is likely to have intuitive access to these various fields and their rules.[133] What counts, therefore, is not intuition but consciously understood values or emotional commitments. Those commitments support redistribution and regulation, rather than the preservation of the private property owner's *dominium*.

Robert Ellickson's fascinating study of informal dispute resolution among Shasta County, California, ranchers should not be taken as demonstrating the continued significance of intuition.[134] His ranchers were clearly basing their behavior on inherited ideas about property, but they are a fairly elite group, and, as Neil Komesar points out, their situation is very simple, much too simple to be generalized to modern commercial relations.[135] They are, moreover, products of a society with a long legal tradition, and their instincts, far from being autochthonous emanations of the California soil, may simply reflect the positive and formerly nonintuitive legal enactments of preceding centuries that have subsequently been internalized.[136] Even more important, the task of governance is often to control popular inclinations, rather than reflecting them. Employers, particularly in the nineteenth century, instinctively believed that they could demand that their employees work twelve-hour days, without health benefits, pensions, or vacations, but the administrative state intervened to alter this belief, thereby saving capitalism from itself.

The second criteria for an advantageous political metaphor is that it announces its heuristic character, and discourages reification. As noted above, legal realists and transaction cost economists have argued forcefully against the reification of property. It could be said that this renders the thought experiment of bracketing the concept otiose, but the point of bracketing is to clear a conceptual space for an alternative metaphor, and here the existing legal and economic arguments are not fully realized. The metaphor that legal realists have proposed, of course, is the bundle of sticks, but it is more a critique than an alternative.[137] It emphasizes that property can be divided into its component parts, but it retains the same external boundary as the pre-modern concept, and only loosens the internal linkages. The alternative of market-generating allocations that has been suggested here demarcates a different region of legal relations, and provides a rationale for preferring this new demarcation.

A related and perhaps more serious difficulty, in terms of the heuristic criterion, is that retention of the term 'property,' and of the concept's preexisting boundaries, have enabled legal scholars, judges, legislators, and executive officials to maintain the pre-modern notion of property, and its essential element of control, without fully confronting the economic or realist critique. Thomas Merrill and Henry Smith have attempted to rehabilitate this position, at the theoretical level, by formulating an analytic defense that relies on information theory.[138] The bundle of sticks that has traditionally been described as property should not be unbundled, they argue, because its conventionally understood contour serves a real economic function. It makes property recognizable to all market participants, most notably those who have no prior connection with the property owner, thereby reducing transaction costs and facilitating commerce.[139] This is not sufficient to elevate property into a right, however. At most it argues for the economic efficiency of property; since the demise of substantive due process, Americans have accepted the idea that the polity is not compelled to implement the social policy of economic efficiency, as opposed to rival policies such as redistribution, health, or environmental protection.[140] Moreover, Merrill and Smith's argument does not establish the modern relevance of property as a concept. The recognition factor that they emphasize may operate in transactions among consumers, but it is unnecessary in the professional transactions that constitute the bulk of modern commerce. Business, like government, is a now complex, technologically sophisticated system run by specialists who do not need a stereotyped concept of property. In fact, the concept only impedes understanding of actual economic activities, which fractionate property into its different components.[141]

Microanalysis, which has occupied so much attention in earlier chapters, can be dealt with quickly here. Modern economics, particularly transaction cost economics, has fully performed the microanalysis of people's legal relationship to objects, intangibles, and, incidentally, services as well. The problem, once again, is that the retention of the term and conceptual boundaries of property has masked these conceptual advances, and allowed legal scholars and political participants to revert to prior usages of property as an operative unit of analysis. In *Mahon*, for example, the Court reached its conclusion by treating the challenged statute as destroying the coal company's entire property right in the coal pillars supporting the surface. A microanalytic approach would conclude that the coal company had been allocated underground coal through general legislation that created a market in this asset, and that subsequent legislation had altered this allocation by adding the restriction that removal of the coal could not cause the land above it to subside. This decreased the value of the coal company's allocation, just as requiring it to install safety equipment would decrease it. But there is no inherent contour, no essential property right, to the initial allocation that precludes its subsequent modification by a general statute. Rather, modern economic thought suggests that public policy should be formulated by considering the efficiency of each particular market-generating allocation.

The Protection of Individual Interests

Compensation for Takings

The previous section argued that our primary emotional commitment, in the area traditionally described as property, is to regulation based on collectively determined public policy, not on the preservation of existing property rights. But this claim applies only to general regulation; when the state impairs or eliminates the value of a particular individual's property, a different commitment appears to prevail. Most people in our society would regard government confiscation or destruction of a person's property as a form of unjustified oppression. Whatever our attitude toward general regulation, our reaction to particularized action seems to suggest that the concept of property still plays a role in our political morality, a role that has not been altered by the advent of the administrative state. This continued role for property would argue against the value of bracketing the concept and replacing it with the alternative conception of market-generating allocations.

In fact, our emotional commitments in this area are not described by the concept of property at all, but by a set of alternative conceptions that are fully consistent with the proposed alternative, and best expressed, surprisingly enough, by the language of the U.S. Constitution. The Fifth Amendment to the Constitution states, in part, that no person shall "be deprived of life, liberty, or property without due process of law; nor shall private property be taken for public use, without just compensation." As David Westbrook points out, the structure of this provision is to establish two alternative means by which the government can justifiably deprive a person of "property": first, by "due process of law," and second, with "just compensation."[142]

Although the due process clause includes the term 'property,' the Supreme Court's efforts to use this term to define the ambit of the clause's application have generated doctrinal incoherence.[143] This was explained in Chapter 7; the discussion in the present chapter about the antiquated character of our inherited idea of property adds to that explanation. In place of any effort to define the kinds of deprivations that would trigger due process protection, it was suggested that decision makers focus on the mode of governmental action. As Chapters 7 and 8 assert, when the government imposes some disadvantage on a particular individual, whatever the nature of the disadvantage, that individual must be given due process of law. This way of interpreting the due process clause connects it with our general theory of government. The imposition of a disadvantage on a group simply means that the group has lost out in the political process. The notion that the due process clause could be used to protect groups against the consequences of the political process was an idea that Americans decisively rejected with the demise of substantive due process.[144] Individuals, however, are vulnerable to a distinct set of illicit motivations and, generally speaking, they have no access to the political process. Government administrators can impose disadvantages on them because of particular actions they have taken, or because of personal animus against them, and there may be no one else in their position with whom they can ally themselves. For this reason, individuals need additional protection beyond that provided by an interactive political system, and this is what the due process clause provides. In our system, it does so by granting individuals a cause of action to argue that the disadvantage to which they were subjected was not authorized by a general legislative or administrative enactment. This precludes many illicitly motivated actions, and places the individual under the protection of a group.

Suppose that someone introduces a legislative measure that requires coal miners to pay one percent of their salaries into a fund that will compensate injured miners. The measure could be described, in traditional terms, as transferring some of the miners' property to injured workers, and thus a forbidden intrusion on their property rights. In the administrative state, however, it is more accurately described as a modification of the market-generating allocation of the miners' labor to themselves, and would thus be a permissible regulation, as in fact it is. The coal miners, or their union, might lobby against this measure, but they might lose, in which case they would be compelled to make the payments. Most regulatory legislation imposes costs on one group or another, and each group can rely only on its influence and arguments in the political process to oppose such costs. Now suppose, however, that the administrator of the program wants to take a sum of money from a particular miner because he injured a fellow worker. The miner is not likely to have access to the political process, certainly not to the same extent that all the miners do. Therefore, he is granted a due process right to oppose the administrator's action. In response, the administrator must demonstrate that she is authorized to act by general legislation, adopted through the political process, and that the particular amount she proposes to take from the miner is also authorized. Typically, this would be done by holding a hearing before a neutral decision maker and demonstrating that the miner fits into a statutory category that authorizes an additional percentage reduction in salary for workers who cause injuries.

It is this due process protection of specific individuals and firms that prevents the government from depriving them of their allocations. No reference to property is needed, and none would be coherent. The protection applies to any individual interest, whether it could be characterized as liberty or property or something else, and it applies to any penalty, whether it is a fine or prison sentence for an individual, or a fine or activity restriction for a firm. All that is required is that the governmental action constitute a disadvantage, and that this disadvantage is imposed on a particular entity rather than a group.[145]

In an influential article, "The New Property," Charles Reich argued that welfare payments and similar government benefits should be regarded as property akin to land or chattels.[146] But Reich was not arguing that these benefits should be transferable or devisable, which they are not, nor was he challenging the rule, unknown with respect to traditional forms of property, that when an individual obtains an income from another source, his claim to certain benefits is terminated. Rather, his sole demand was that individuals who were granted these benefits, like individuals who own traditional property, must not be deprived of them without due process of law. This demand is now universally accepted in American legal doctrine.[147] The recharacterization suggested here enables it to be formulated without the awkward interposition of the term 'property,' and thus without the indefensible implication that government benefits be granted any of the "sticks" that are granted to land or chattels. The allocation of benefits to people, like the allocation of transferable, devisable assets, is an advantage, and this advantage may not be taken from a particular individual without the procedures required by due process.

The Fifth Amendment does not limit the government to generally enacted provisions when economic assets are at stake, however. It also provides that such assets may be taken from specific individuals, in ways that are not prescribed by a general rule, so long as the government compensates the individuals for the market value of the asset. The reason for this alternative mode of justifiable government action, generally described as eminent domain, is that a particular economic asset that has been allocated to an individual or firm may be needed to effectuate a valid public policy. Land in a particular location is needed for a highway, or a particular structure is needed to preserve our historical or artistic heritage. As Edwin Baker, Louis Kaplow, and Frank Michelman have suggested, when the government imposes such disadvantages on specified individuals, it should be required to compensate them.[148] This alternative mode of governmental action can only be employed, however, if the disadvantage imposed on the individual or firm is one that can be adequately compensated by money, that is, an asset such as land or buildings for which a market exists, so that the individual or firm can use the government payment to obtain an equivalent asset.[149] Other assets or advantages that trigger due process protection, such as an individual's life, liberty of movement, or reputation, may only be taken by the government in accordance with a general enactment.

Public choice theorists have challenged the restriction of the compensation requirement to individual groups or firms. Government, they argue, should compensate small groups—and not just individuals—when it takes their property because such groups can mobilize politically and block the taking, thereby decreasing government efficiency.[150] But the idea seems to suffer from a confusion, addressed in the previous two chapters, between legal rights and human rights. Granting a statutory cause of action to small groups in order to blunt their political opposition may make good sense in terms of politics or policy, but the takings clause operates as a categorical constraint on government. Why should we impose such a constraint, and authorize courts to enforce it, for policy purposes? Rather, the constraint should be imposed in cases of genuine unfairness or oppression, and these concerns, according to our theory of government, arise when an individual is singled out for disadvantageous treatment.

It will often be the case that a government official can only exercise eminent domain if she is authorized to do so by a general enactment of some sort. Such an enactment, however, does not eliminate the government's obligation to compensate the individual; the enactment only establishes the parameters for the deprivation, while the decision leading to the deprivation itself remains particularized. The government can restrict development if it acts in accordance with some generally applicable rule—that factories should not be built near residences, or that ecologically sensitive wetlands should not be developed, as in *Lucas*. Such rules affect groups of people, and those groups must take their chances in the political process. When the government then forbids development of a particular parcel, all it needs to demonstrate is that this parcel fits the general rule. In contrast, an authorization to take land for a road by eminent domain does not specify the particular land to be taken. The government cannot demonstrate that any particular parcel fits the general authorization, because the authorization is not the sort of rule that permits this determination. When an administrator then selects the specific parcel, that action affects the person to whom that parcel is allocated individually, and the person has no access to the political process. To be sure, a group of people was potentially affected by the initial authorization to build a road, but between potential and actual effect lies the possibility of abuse.

Thus, the thought experiment of bracketing the concept of property reveals a basic principle of the administrative state, as it has evolved in modern Western nations. This principle is that the market is simply one mode of regulation that the government employs in its plenary authority over the economy, and that property rights, as they existed in pre-modern times, have been replaced by government authorized allocations of economic assets in those areas where regulation by the market is desired. With the concept of property thus displaced, there is no category of regulation for which compensation is required. Once economic assets have been allocated, however, their deprivation represents a real disadvantage, and thus contains the possibility of government oppression. This concern is not triggered by the concept of property, since it does not apply to generalized deprivations of allocated assets, but rather by the fact that the governmental action is directed against individuals. In many cases, oppression can be avoided by requiring that government action against individuals must be authorized by general regulatory programs, and that individuals receive procedural protection to enforce this requirement. Sometimes, however, the government needs to utilize particular assets that cannot be described by general regulation. In that case, to avoid oppression, it must compensate the individual for the market value of the utilized assets.

The Limits of Takings

There remains a final question to consider in this matter. May the government deprive an individual of any allocated asset for any reason, as long as it provides compensation at the market rate? Is there, in other words, any inherent limit on the government's exercise of eminent domain? The Fifth Amendment states that government may only take property for "public use," and our instinct is that this term imposes some discernible limit. The government may need a person's land and home to build a highway, but what public use could there be for a person's clothes, furniture, or souvenir collection? Joseph Sax points out,[151] however, that the development of the administrative state has expanded the notion of public use to the point where the term is of little value without further explanation.[152] This explanation cannot be provided by reference to the category of object that the government is taking. With respect to objects for which public purposes are easy to imagine, such as land or houses, a categorical approach provides too little protection for individuals, because we can imagine improper uses as well. With respect to other objects, the limitation is purely empirical, and does not provide us with a rationale. If we want to indulge in bizarre hypotheticals, we can imagine that someone's souvenir collection has unique historical value, that the fabric of someone's couch is saturated with a previously unknown substance that can cure hepatitis, or that someone has a unique skill that can save the country from a terrorist attack. In these cases, we might very well be willing to approve the use of eminent domain.

    To give content to the notion of a public use, it is necessary to refer to the purposes of the Fifth Amendment itself, not to the categories of objects that are being taken. Meir Dan-Cohen's phenomenological theory of ownership, which focuses on the connection between the objects that a person owns and the person's sense of self, provides the relevant consideration for this inquiry.[153] According to Dan-Cohen, some possessions are highly prized although they have no market value, such as bottle cap collections, souvenirs, or the family photo album. Others have market value, such as one's home, car, furniture, and clothing, but have an emotional value for the individual that exceeds their market value because these possessions are connected with an individual's identity. In these cases, compensation at the market rate does not provide full compensation, because the individual attaches some additional value, which Dan-Cohen describes as ownership value, to the object. In the case of services, most people attach some additional value, beyond the market rate, to their own services, because the circumstances of this service affects their quality of life. This might be described as liberty value. If the government compelled them to provide their services in some specified way, they may well feel that payment at their former salary level did not compensate them for their loss of liberty or choice. Bracketing the traditional concept of property, and considering the value that individuals attach to assets that have been allocated to them, brings these added values of ownership and liberty into focus.

Both the due process and just compensation clauses are designed to prevent government oppression, a purpose that remains completely relevant in the administrative state. The question, then, is whether the government is oppressing individuals by taking assets allocated to them, even if it compensates them at the market rate. Mere loss of ownership or liberty value is not necessarily oppression, but may be the collateral disadvantage that accompanies a valid governmental action. It is thus no worse than the disadvantage that occurs when one group loses out in the political process. In addition, loss of ownership cannot be deemed oppressive if the individual's ascription of value results from what Margaret Radin describes as commodity fetishism, such as, for example, an emotional attachment to investment property.[154] But loss of ownership or liberty value becomes oppressive when the government has no valid purpose, and is using eminent domain to discomfort the individual by depriving her of ownership or liberty value that, while difficult to measure, is predictably substantial and socially comprehensible. Suppose the government condemns a person's home because she is a Republican, or a Jew, or has spoken out against its policies. While the condemnation of homes is often valid, this particular condemnation would be invalid because it is being used to oppress the individual, and should be prohibited on that ground. If the government condemned the person's souvenirs, furniture, or services, we would be much more suspicious, but the government might be able to demonstrate that it had a valid purpose. Thus, the real determination would ultimately turn on the same issue of oppression.[155]

How is such a standard to be implemented? The answer, in our system, is through the courts. The courts should always be open to a claim that the government's use of eminent domain was designed to oppress the person to whom an asset was allocated, even though the government paid full compensation. Efforts to use eminent domain should be denied if the person can demonstrate that the object involved could reasonably be assumed to have ownership or liberty value, and that the government was using its authority to punish or oppress the person by depriving her of that uncompensated value. Such a demonstration is available in cases of eminent domain, but not regulation, because eminent domain is exercised against specific individuals, and thus demands the additional protection of due process and just compensation.

This book can thus be ended on a cheerfully anti-administrative note. Its general theme has been that we must accept the reality of the administrative state, that we must rethink many basic concepts in politics and law if we want to understand the government we actually possess. A further point is that we can only control the administrative state and combat its potential for oppression if we accept its reality and engage in the same process of reconceptualization. The result has an undeniably grim quality, however, precisely because the administrative state is our present reality, and social nostalgia paints that reality with grimy colors, while adding sparkle to the pre-modern concepts that we need to abandon or revise. But here, as in several other places, there is a continuing role for courts, our most traditional and non-administrative institution. Courts should scrutinize administrators' exercise of eminent domain. They should strike down any exercise of this authority that is designed to oppress individuals rather than implement a valid public purpose. We live in a highly regulated state, but the extent, complexity, necessity, and value of the government's authority to regulate should never stop other governmental actors, such as judges, from protecting individuals from the abuse of that authority.

Conclusion to Part II

PART I of this study argued that the inherited concepts that we use to describe the structure of our government—the three branches, power, discretion, democracy, and legitimacy—do not provide a satisfactory description of the government we actually possess. Each of its four chapters, aspiring like Twain's Connecticut Yankee to be "a champion of hard unsentimental common sense and reason," pursued the thought experiment of bracketing one of these concepts and proposing an alternative description based on the image of an interacting network. These chapters argued that the proposed alternatives better satisfy the stated criteria for a good political metaphor: reflecting our emotional commitments, revealing the heuristic character of theory, and facilitating microanalysis. The conclusion to Part I then suggested that these alternatives fit together to generate a unified image of government, whereas the inherited concepts that they were designed to replace do not. Thus, the alternatives satisfied a fourth criterion as well, that of metaphorical unity. It was argued that this serves as another reason to proceed with the thought experiment of bracketing our inherited concepts and replacing them with network-based alternatives.

It may appear that the alternative concepts suggested in the four chapters of Part II fail to satisfy this fourth criterion. They propose to bracket a unified image of law and rights, and offer instead the disparate metaphors of policy and implementation, causes of action, moral demands on government, and market-generating allocations. But the conceptual unity claimed for law is largely a rhetorical device designed to collect a divergent and unruly throng of ideas beneath a single banner, thereby concealing its heterogeneity. In contrast, the proposed alternatives achieve the virtue of metaphorical unity because they are all derived from the very same network model that generated the political alternatives presented in Part I. Thus, they replace law's alleged unity with a truly unified and coherent image. Moreover, they provide additional coherence because they describe the legal system and the political system, that is, the operations and structure of government, with the single image of the network. Here too, the criterion of metaphorical unity suggests that the thought experiment of bracketing the basic concepts that we used to describe our legal system is worth pursuing.

The first difficulty with law's claim to conceptual unity is that it is based

on a distinction between law and politics. This distinction is simply unsupportable. In fact, the assertion that law is separate from politics lacks
even surface plausibility unless one relies on a pre-modern concept of law.
Modern law consists primarily of statutory enactments, regulatory enactments, and regulatory enforcement, and no one argues that any of these
are apolitical. The only aspect of law, as the term is generally used, that
could possibly be described as separate from politics is adjudicatory decision making, that is, the function that dominated what we now call law
before the advent of the administrative state. Even that claim is hotly contested today. Virtually every political scientist who has addressed the subject, and many legal scholars as well, have concluded that judges, to say
nothing of administrative adjudicators, are predominantly motivated by
political considerations. There is no need to resolve this debate for present
purposes, however. The point is that the only category of governmental
action that can possibly be distinguished from politics is adjudicatory decision making, not law in general. Any concept of law that relies on law's
separate identity from politics, therefore, must be understood as a theory
of adjudication, not of legislation or administrative implementation. Such
a theory is of limited value in a modern administrative state, and, because
of these limitations, fractures the asserted unity of law rather than maintaining it.

Not only is the concept of law incapable of maintaining its asserted distinction from politics, but it also fails to achieve internal unity. The most
basic problem, described in Chapter 6, is the concept's amphibious character. Law refers both to a set of rules that control the government and to
the rules that the government employs to implement its goals. The rule of
law, not surprisingly, incorporates this identical ambiguity. Medieval scholars, from John of Salisbury through St. Thomas and beyond, were able to
assert the unity of these two sets of rules because they believed that both
were derived from the natural law established by God. In their view, the
entire universe embodied a series of reiterated structures, where the rules
that the king imposed on his subjects resembled and reflected rules that
God imposed upon the king.

Once these beliefs decayed, the connection between the controls on
government and the instrumentalities of government was severed and the
two concepts drifted apart from one another to lead independent existences. It is true that the requirement of acting through previously stated
rules is one control that might be imposed on government, but many
other controls are considered equally important, such as non-interference
with speech or the prohibition against torture. Conversely, one reason the
government might choose to act through rules is that it feels morally obligated or constrained to do so, but there are many other reasons why it
might adopt such an approach. Weber identifies rule-governed action as

an essential aspect of the rational-legal character of modern government, and he saw this as a mode of domination, not as a means of disciplining those in charge.

Rights are often regarded as organically related to law, and thus as a component of a unified concept, but they suffer from the same partially acknowledged divergence between law's two components. Everyone recognizes that legal rights, discussed in Chapter 7, and natural rights or human rights, discussed in Chapter 8, arise from different sources. Legal rights are created by the positive enactments of the government, or from contingently established customs, while natural or human rights stem from moral considerations that lie beyond the government's control. The two categories may overlap, of course, just as the categories of green objects and edible objects overlap, but they are distinctly different things. Many legal rights, such as the right to deduct one's business expenses from one's taxable income, are clearly not moral imperatives for government, while many broadly supported human rights, such as equal opportunity, are regularly denied or frustrated by positive enactments. To describe these separate concepts by using the same term, and to imply that they represent two versions of a single concept, is misleading at best.

Not only does the terminology of rights establish a misleading unity by conflating two separate concepts, but it also creates artificial divisions in each concept's underlying subject matter. Legal rights, as discussed in Chapter 7, provide the mechanism by which individuals or legally created entities can obtain an adjudicatory determination of the benefits to which they are entitled by virtue of positive enactment or Common Law, and then have that determination enforced against governmental officials or private parties. Such rights are thus part of the process by which modern government implements its policy objectives by means of adjudication. In the pre-modern state, this process merited special notice because adjudication, carried out by courts, was virtually the only implementation mechanism. In the modern state, courts remain important, but are joined by a variety of other mechanisms, such as administrative agencies, and other modalities that are characteristic of those agencies, such as guidance and negotiation. There is no reason to create categorical distinctions between these various modes of implementation, apart from social nostalgia. Rather, it would be preferable, from the perspective of metaphorical unity, to employ a single concept to describe the various and often interchangeable mechanisms by which modern government implements its policies.

Human rights, in contrast, are not positive enactments or Common Law, but an aspect of morality, as discussed in Chapter 8. They constitute an effort to impose controls on officials in positions of authority. While they may be adopted by government, they do not arise from government, but from civil society and individual conscience. From both a sociological

and a philosophical perspective, they are part of the norm-generating process that occurs in those arenas. To separate them from that process and
treat them as a part of a purely political or legal theory is to create an artificial distinction between aspects of moral philosophy and social psychology that are in fact organically connected. In addition, the prevailing
image of human rights as possessions of the individual tends to create a
categorical distinction between negative rights, that is, rights to avoid specific governmental actions, and positive rights, that is, rights to obtain specific governmental services. In the pre-modern state, where government
was not expected to provide very many services, there was no conception
of positive rights, so that this division did not arise. The advent of the
modern state, and the expectations that it generates, have fractured the
preexisting unity of human rights, which is in some sense natural rights'
successor concept. Again, the interest of metaphorical unity would be
served by a new approach that eliminated the categorical distinction between negative and positive rights, and provided a unified account of the
moral demands that citizens impose on governmental action.

The idea that property is a human right, discussed in Chapter 9, may
seem to unify protection for property with other rights, that is, other protections from state action, but it actually fractures the allocation of resources that we think of as property into different components. Because
control, a mode of governance, was the essence of property in the medieval world, property could be regarded as an inviolable right; government could not remove property, most notably land, from a person's control unless the person committed a crime. The gradual commercialization
of property undermined this notion, but it could still be plausibly maintained in the absence of extensive governmental regulation. Moreover,
property rights, as the essential right of the elite, were so central in the pre-
modern world that it seemed plausible to depict newly emerging concepts
of liberty as a form of property—a person's property right in his own body
and its liberty.

These unities have been dissolved by the modern administrative state
and its attendant transformations. The resources that legal enactments allocate to people are subject to innumerable regulations that increase or decrease their value; since we do not recognize any inherent limits on the potential scope of economic regulation, there is no category of possessions
that can be treated as a human right, and thereby shielded from such regulation, although particular possessions may be protected by the general
principle of due process. The effort to define some protected category
must then rely on the outmoded concept of control, thus dividing property into two separate types, protected and unprotected, that have very
different legal consequences but are virtually impossible to distinguish
from each other. Moreover, the idea of political liberty, which now in-

cludes so many protections against government, and extends to the poor as well as the wealthy, is no longer usefully described as a property right in one's body or one's liberty. And we would not want to describe it in this manner, for the vast incursions upon private resources that our modern regulatory state demands make property an unappealing template for protections that we genuinely treasure. Thus, the concept of property is deeply fractured from within, and conceptually divided from other protections against government that we currently conceive as human rights.

In place of this fractured idea of law and rights, the preceding chapters offer a unified metaphorical description based upon the network model. They reject the concept of law as a qualitatively distinct aspect of government, while simultaneously providing the conceptual resources needed to impose controls on the political process. Chapter 6 uses the same network image developed in Part I to conceptualize a modern government's effort to achieve its specified objectives. These objectives are viewed as policies adopted by an authorized governmental unit, such as the chief executive, the legislature, a court or an agency. Policies are communicated to other governmental units by specific signals or programmed into the unit as part of its design. Units that have been given policies in either manner must then put out a variety of signals in accordance with those policies, and the body of signals so produced can be described as implementation. What is generally called law is simply one such mechanism, that is, general rules addressed to private parties. These rules are important, but there are many other implementation mechanisms available in the administrative state.

When a general rule is chosen as the particular implementation mechanism for a given policy, that rule must be applied to specific situations. The most common way to do so is to establish a neutral, passive adjudicator and to authorize private parties to send a signal to that adjudicator. The content of this signal can be described as a cause of action, that is, a claim that triggers a response from the administrator. As discussed in Chapter 7, legal rights are nothing more than such causes of action. They are an important means of deploying the implementation mechanism of general rules, but they are not the only one available in an administrative state. Nonbinding complaints by private parties and active investigatory efforts by government officials can also be employed to apply general rules to specific cases.

Entirely apart from the implementation process, members of society send signals of various kinds to governmental units. Some of these are promises of electoral support or threats of electoral opposition, as described in Chapter 4, and some are grounded on considerations of efficiency or expediency, but some arise from moral concerns, and are stated in moral terms. Chapter 8 argues that these moral signals, currently described as human rights, are more accurately conceived as demands that the government must put out, or refrain from putting out, a particular signal. These demands, which can be termed obligations and constraints, constitute controls on governmental action. If the government responds by adopting them as positive enactments, they become part of the policy and implementation process. Quite often, this is achieved by enacting the moral demands as a general rule, at the constitutional or legislative level, and then applying that rule to specific situations by employing causes of action. But this mechanism is most useful for moral demands that government refrain from particular outputs, that is, demands that can be characterized as constraints. For demands that require a particular signal, and can thus be characterized as obligations, other means of implementation are typically more effective.

The concept of property, once bracketed, can be conceptualized within this same network model, as Chapter 9 describes. Most of the features we associate with a regime of property rights in a modern administrative state are the positive enactments that are needed to implement the policy of market regulation. The implementation mechanism for this policy generally resembles preexisting concepts of law, since it makes use of general rules and causes of action to enforce private claims. But the administrative state denies private parties any human or moral right to such a mechanism, and allows private control only where the market has been selected as a means of regulation. There are, quite separate from this market policy, certain human rights constraints on governmental action that involve the same sort of objects that were traditionally associated with property. But these can be fully described by the idea of due process, one of our basic moral demands on government.

This network model, as a comprehensive metaphor to describe our political and legal system, is the thought experiment recommended by this book. In the modern administrative state, it has been argued, the metaphor is a more accurate, coherent description than our prevailing concepts, and better satisfies the three criteria of embodying our emotional commitments, reflecting the heuristic character of thoughts, and facilitating microanalysis. In addition, as the conclusion to Part I and this conclusion argue, it better satisfies a fourth criticism of metaphorical unity. Finally, in its mechanistic modernity, the network metaphor enables us to disentangle our concepts from those that were developed to describe a previous and qualitatively different mode of governance. It thus protects us from our social nostalgia.

The purpose of developing this network metaphor is obviously not to extirpate our inherited concepts, such as the three branches, power, discretion, democracy, legitimacy, law, rights, and property, from either our language or our thoughts. That would lead to an excessively convoluted discourse and, besides, it is impossible. Instead, the idea is to convey a sense of caution to scholars, judges, and policy analysts whose task it is to think systematically about modern government. Before slapping down a term like property or discretion on a page, before condemning some administrative mechanism as undemocratic or unlawful, before assuming that one can simply clarify or alter the definition of terms like legitimacy or power that are hundreds or thousands of years older than we are, before assuming that government possess a particular shape or that morality imposes a particular demand, one should pause. Are we describing what is really there, surrounding us on all sides? Are we asserting what we genuinely believe, what we really feel? Are we thinking our own thoughts, or are we succumbing to thoughts that are thinking for us?

As stated at the outset, the underlying point is that we are entering this third millennium with a set of political and legal concepts that were developed in the first few centuries of the preceding one. We are linguistically bound to many of those concepts, but that is no reason to be conceptually bound to them as well. The millennium we are entering offers great opportunities and poses great dangers, opportunities and dangers we know—unlike our predecessors at the beginning of the previous millennium—that we can neither predict nor imagine. To prepare ourselves for these vast developments, we need, at the very least, a set of concepts that accurately depicts our current reality and reflects our genuinely-held values.

In the final analysis, as stated repeatedly throughout this book, the whole thing is merely a thought experiment. Our inherited terms will remain, and perhaps they will prove to be of use. But this book argues that it will often be more useful, more meaningful, to conduct the experiment, to bracket these terms and employ alternative conceptions. Experimentation, after all, is central to our modern outlook, and to our entire theory of knowledge. It reflects the same purposive approach to the world that surrounds us, the same rejection of the claim that tradition possesses an inherent truth, the same willingness to judge strategies on the basis of their pragmatic consequences, that characterizes the administrative state itself. Whether an experiment is successful, whether it truly generates meaningful or useful knowledge, can only be determined once the experiment has been performed. What justifies the effort is the promise of success, a dissatisfaction with the present state of knowledge, and an informed guess that the effort may produce results. That is the intent behind this book; the results are presented in its arguments.

Perhaps these arguments will ultimately be rejected, but what reason could there be for not attempting them? The only obvious one is the set of attitudes maintained by people in the early centuries of the previous millennium—the veneration of tradition, the unwillingness to innovate, the preference of symbolism to pragmatic consequences. This has its charm, and is one source of our social nostalgia for that bygone era, but we have definitively rejected it as an operative principle of theory or practice. As we look back on the era when it prevailed, we are more likely to see obduracy, social injustice, inefficiency, and self-destructiveness. Its embodiment is not the mythic grandeur of King Arthur that began the Middle Ages, but the very real failures that brought this era to a close.

A famous example of such failure can be found in the well-documented battle of Agincourt. Agincourt illustrates medieval aversion to experimentation with particular clarity, and also illustrates the sort of social nostalgia that keeps these altitudes alive in otherwise pragmatic, innovative times. The French knights who fought at Agincourt were fully committed to the concept of chivalry, a concept that was really as nostalgia-driven by the time of the battle as it is today. It was that unanalyzed commitment that led to their undoing.

The battle was one event in the prolonged struggle between England and France that become known as the Hundred Years War. The war began in 1337, when Edward III of England renewed the claim to the French throne that he had abandoned in 1328 to Philip VI, the first Valois king. At Sluys, in 1340, an English fleet, using archers armed with longbows, disastrously defeated the French fleet. Edward then invaded France in 1346 with an army composed largely of longbow archers and a relatively small number of troops equipped with plate armor, swords, and shields, generally called men at arms. Confronted by a much larger French force consisting almost entirely of men at arms, Edward tried to escape and, on being cornered at Crecy, in the county of Picardy, took up a defensive position. The French charged the English line in repeated waves and were slaughtered by the English longbow men. King Philip was wounded and barely escaped. The English army then moved on and captured the port of Calais, which the English were to hold for the next two hundred years.

A truce ensued, but when it expired in 1355, Edward invaded France once more, this time sending his son, Edward the Black Prince, at the head of an army composed largely of longbow archers and a relatively small numbers of men at arms. Confronted by a much larger French force consisting almost entirely of men at arms, Edward tried to escape and, on being cornered at Poitiers, in the County of Poitou, took up a defensive position. The French charged the English line in repeated waves and were slaughtered by the longbow men. King Jean II, successor to King Philip, was wounded and captured by the English forces.

To obtain the king's release, the French ultimately agreed to the treaty of Bretigny, which gave the English a ransom of three million gold crowns and about one-third of France's territory. During the half century that followed, several more English armies invaded France to enforce the terms of this treaty on the unwilling French territories that had been transferred to

English rule. King Charles V, Jean's successor, had learned at least enough from prior experience to avoid an open battle with the English, preferring to allow their armies to rampage through the French countryside, plundering, pillaging, and murdering the townspeople and peasants in the usual manner of a medieval army. His Fabian tactics, combined with the proclivities of the French territories, enabled him to regain most of the lands that his father had ceded. Long truces followed, but a final settlement could not be reached.

In 1415, King Henry V of England, newly risen to the throne, invaded France once more. He landed at Harfleur, in northern France, and captured the city with the help of artillery. It was at this point that he issued his challenge to the Dauphin to decide the outcome of the war by single combat. The Dauphin did not respond, however, and Henry, with his army now much weakened by disease, and with the campaigning season drawing to a close, was faced with the prospect of a somewhat crestfallen return to England. To avoid this, he decided to march overland to the English enclave of Calais, thus demonstrating his ability to move through the French countryside at will. Confronted by a much larger French force along his route, Henry tried to escape, but was cornered at Agincourt in the Pas-de-Calais.

On the morning of October 25, the two armies deployed for battle. They faced each other across a flat, ploughed field no more than 1200 yards wide, bounded by impassable woods on either side. The French army was led by the constable Charles d'Albret. Having contemptuously rejected an offer of 6,000 crossbow men from the Parisian militia, he commanded about 25,000 men at arms, nearly all dismounted. These forces, constrained by the narrowness of the field, were drawn up in three lines, with a relatively small number of mounted knights in the third line. The English army, commanded by King Henry, and now reduced to about 1,000 dismounted men at arms and 5,000 to 6,000 longbow archers, was drawn up in a single line.

Initially, the two armies stood at a distance of about 1,000 yards, and neither one advanced. The English devoted the time to arranging their line, with the men at arms placed in three blocks, under three different commanders, and the archers placed in four blocks, two between the blocks of knights and two on either flank. On the French side, the principal concern of the leading warriors was to get into the forward line to demonstrate the courage and obtain the glory that chivalry demanded. Perhaps they believed, as Shakespeare has them say, "let us but blow on them, The vapor of our valour will o'erturn them" (*Henry V*, Act IV, Scene II). Their enthusiasm produced a considerable amount of disorganized jostling and shoving, and succeeded in crowding out the French artillery. Whether distracted by this effort or as a result of some sudden accession of military judgment, the French did not advance. In fact there was no need for them to do so; the English had to break through their lines in order to reach Calais, or retreat into a hostile and increasingly frigid countryside. King Henry, equally aware of this dilemma, ordered his forces to advance to a distance of extreme bowshot—about 250 to 300 yards—and let loose a barrage of arrows against the forward French line.

Thus provoked, the French—some seventy years after Crecy and sixty after Poitiers—could think of no other tactic than to charge the line of English longbow men, sending cavalry along the flanks and their first line of chivalry-mad men at arms down the center of the field. The cavalry reached their opponents first; the English archers pulled back a few yards, revealing sharpened stakes that they had planted in the ground, and fired their arrows at the onrushing cavalry. Some of the French horses were hit by arrows, some were impaled on the stakes, and the remaining ones panicked and turned back in full retreat. By this point, however, the first line of French men at arms were advancing, and a number of them were trampled by the retreating horses while others fell onto the muddy ground in the confusion. The remainder grouped themselves into three narrow columns that advanced against the three blocks of English men at arms, apparently ignoring the longbow men, whom they regarded as unworthy opponents. Because their narrow columns denied them the advantage of their numbers, and because they were somewhat exhausted after advancing 250 yards over slippery, rough ground wearing fifty pounds of armor and dodging the retreating horses, they were brought to a halt by the English men at arms. Difficult as it may be to picture, the French were now so tightly packed, and so heavily armored, that they became locked into an immovable metallic mass. At this point, the unworthy, unarmored archers attacked the tightly packed French columns from the sides. They slipped their swords through the visor-slits or joint spaces of their opponents' armor, or simply banged their opponents' metal heads with the hammers they had used to drive their sharpened stakes into the ground. Before long, dead French men at arms lay in enormous piles, and the surviving ones retreated, only to crash into the advancing second line. More confusion ensued, more men at arms fell into the mud, and more were stabbed or hammered by the English archers. The remainder, still a large number, turned and fled. According to Shakespeare, the French suffered ten thousand casualties, while the English lost only four knights and twenty-five others (*Henry V*, Act IV, Scene VIII). These legendary-sounding numbers are actually confirmed by modern historians, who place the French dead at no fewer than seven thousand, and the English at no more than a few hundred.

King Henry completed this victory, and its attendant rejection of chivalry, by ordering his troops to begin killing the many French prisoners they had gathered up, apparently believing that these prisoners would turn on their captors when the third French line advanced. Since his own men at arms refused to do this, Henry had the longbow men carry out the order, and only countermanded it when he saw the third French line abandoning its position. He then marched on to Calais. The war, which the French might have ended at Agincourt, given their enormous numerical advantage, dragged on for forty more years, bringing continued destruction and despair to France.

Notes

Notes to Chapter One

1. For the "return to normalcy," see Francis Russell, The Shadow of Blooming Grove: Warren G. Harding in His Times (New York: McGraw-Hill, 1968).

2. E.g., Clint Eastwood, in Dirty Harry (Don Siegel, director) (Warner/Malpaso, 1971).

3. Star Wars (George Lucas, director) (TCF/Lucasfilm, 1977).

4. Regarding the sedimentation of ideas over time, see Edmund Husserl, The Crisis of the European Sciences (David Carr, trans.) (Evanston, Ill.: Northwestern University Press, 1970), at 52; Edmund Husserl, Experience and Judgment (James Churchill & Karl Ameriks, trans.) (Evanston, Ill.: Northwestern University Press, 1973), at 47–51.

5. Edwin Arlington Robinson, Miniver Cheevy, in Collected Poems (New York: Macmillan, 1929), at 347.

> Miniver loved the days of old
> When swords were bright and steeds were prancing;
> The vision of a warrior bold
> Would set him dancing.

6. Oliver Sacks, An Anthropologist on Mars (New York: Vintage, 1995), at 153–69; E. S. Howland, Nostalgia, Journal of Existential Psychiatry 10:197 (1962); David Werman, Normal and Pathological Nostalgia, Journal of the American Psychoanalytic Association 25:387 (1977). At some point in the midst of his life, the author realized that he would never recover from the Dodgers' departure from Brooklyn.

7. Raymond Williams, The Country and the City (New York: Oxford University Press, 1973), at 9–12.

8. Maurice Halbwachs, The Collective Memory (Francis Ditter & Vida Yazdi Ditter, trans.) (New York: Harper & Row, 1980).

9. According to Svetlana Boym, nostalgia is composed of *nostos*, the restorative desire to "rebuild the lost home," and *algia*, the reflective experience of loss and longing. Svetlana Boym, The Future of Nostalgia (New York: Basic Books, 2001). In political theory, we restore concepts so that we can have a space that our sense of loss and longing can inhabit.

10. Jacob Burckhardt, The Civilization of the Renaissance (S.G.C. Middlemore, trans.) (New York: Harper, 1958).

11. Charles Homer Haskins, The Renaissance of the 12th Century (Cleveland: Meridian, 1957).

12. R. W. Southern, The Making of the Middle Ages (New Haven, Conn.: Yale University Press, 1953), at 170–84.

13. R. R. Agrawal, The Medieval Revival and Its Influence on the Romantic

Movement (New Delhi: Abhinav Publications, 1990); Henry Beers, A History of
English Romanticism in the Nineteenth Century (New York: H. Holt and Co.,
1901); Paul Johnson, The Birth of the Modern (New York: HarperCollins, 1991),
at 281–82.

14. Irwin Edman described this as a deterioration complex. See Charles
Frankel, ed., The Uses of Philosophy: An Irwin Edman Reader (New York: Simon
& Schuster, 1955), at 151.

15. Hesiod, Theogony and Works and Days (M. L. West, trans.) (Oxford:
Oxford University Press, 1988), at 35.

16. Id. at 41.

17. Id. at 42.

18. On the social construction of the Middle Ages, see Norman Cantor, In-
venting the Middle Ages (New York: William Morrow, 1991); Jacques Le Goff
and Pierre Nora, eds., Constructing the Past: Essays in Historical Methodology
(Cambridge: Cambridge University Press, 1985).

19. Alan Harding, Medieval Law and the Foundations of the State (Oxford:
Oxford University Press, 2002); Joseph Strayer, On the Medieval Origins of the
Modern State (Princeton: Princeton University Press, 1970).

20. W. S. Holdsworth, A History of English Law, vol. 1 (London: Methuen,
1903); Antonio Marongiu, Medieval Parliaments: A Comparative Study (S. J.
Woolf, trans.) (London: Eyre & Spottiswoode, 1968); Charles McIlwain, The
High Court of Parliament and Its Supremacy (New Haven, Conn.: Yale University
Press, 1910); Strayer, supra, note 19.

21. J. C. Holt, Magna Carta, 2d ed. (Cambridge: Cambridge University Press,
1992); A. E. Dick Howard, The Road from Runnymede: Magna Carta and Constitutionalism in America (Charlottesville: University of Virginia Press, 1968).

22. Kenneth Fowler, The Age of Plantagenet and Valois: The Struggle for Su-
premacy, 1328–1498 (New York: Putnam, 1967); Bernard Guenée, States and
Rulers in Later Medieval Europe (Juliet Vale, trans.) (Oxford: B. Blackwell, 1985);
Robert Fawtier, The Capetian Kings of France: Monarchy and Nation, 987–1328
(Lionel Butler and R. J. Adam, trans.) (New York: St. Martin's Press, 1960);
Angus MacKay, Spain in the Middle Ages: From Frontier to Empire, 1000–1500
(London: Macmillan, 1977); Richard Mortimer, Angevin England, 1154–1258
(Oxford: Blackwell, 1994); W. L. Warren, Henry II (Berkeley: University of Cali-
fornia Press, 1977).

23. See Fernand Braudel, Capitalism and Material Life, 1400–1800 (Miriam
Kochan, trans.) (New York: Harper and Row, 1973); Catharina Lis and Hugo
Soly, Poverty and Capitalism in Pre-Industrial Europe (James Coonan, trans.)
(Hassocks: Harvester Press, 1979); Robert Lopez, The Commercial Revolution of
the Middle Ages, 950–1350 (Cambridge: Cambridge University Press, 1976);
Edward Miller and John Hatcher, Medieval England: Rural Society and Economic
Change, 1086–1348 (New York: Longman, 1978); Henri Pirenne, Medieval
Cities: Their Origins and the Renewal of Trade (Frank Halsey, trans.) (Princeton:
Princeton University Press, 1969).

24. Alan Cobban, The Medieval Universities: Their Development and Organization (New York: Harper & Row, 1975); Southern, supra note 12, at 203–18.

25. On the expansion of European culture, see Robert Bartlett, The Making of

Europe: Conquest, Colonization and Cultural Change, 950–1350 (Princeton: Princeton University Press, 1993).

26. S. B. Chrimes, An Introduction to the Administrative History of Mediaeval England (Oxford: Blackwell, 1959); Strayer, supra note 19; Charles Tilly, ed., The Formation of Nation States in Western Europe (Princeton: Princeton University Press, 1975); T. F. Tout, Chapters in the Administrative History of Mediaeval England: The Wardrobe, the Chamber and the Small Seals (Manchester: Manchester University Press, 1920–1933); W. L. Warren, The Governance of Norman and Angevin England, 1086–1272 (Stanford, Calif.: Stanford University Press, 1987), at 65–86, 125–33.

27. Initially, this literature was for the consumption of the noble classes, see Southern, supra note 12, at 115, who found themselves and their privileges under increasing pressure from the expanding royal regimes.

28. Whether Arthur actually existed is a matter of intense debate. For some leading theories, see Geoffrey Ashe, The Discovery of King Arthur (London: Guild Publishing, 1985); Geoffrey Ashe, The Arthurian Fact, in Geoffrey Ashe, ed., The Quest for Arthur's Britain (Chicago: Academy Chicago Publishers, 1994), at 27; Norma Goodrich, King Arthur (New York: Harper & Row, 1986); Michael Holmes, King Arthur: A Military History (London: Blandford, 1996); Jean Markale, King of the Celts (Christine Hauch, trans.) (Rochester, Vt.: Inner Traditions, 1994); John Morris, The Age of Arthur (New York: Barnes & Noble, 1996); Graham Phillips and Martin Keatman, King Arthur: The True Story (London: Arrow, 1992); John Rhys, Studies in the Arthurian Legend (Oxford: Clarendon Press, 1891). But there is no debate about when he existed, or is supposed to have existed. It was between A.D. 450 and 550, the period when the political and social structure of the Roman Empire was collapsing. Many of the theories identify him as the leader, whether king or general, who won the historically documented battle of Badon Hill, in about A.D. 510, where the Romanized Britons decisively defeated the invading Saxons and preserved their control of southern Britain for several generations.

29. An illuminating exception occurs in one of the leading Arthurian Romances, Chrétien de Troyes's Yvain, in Arthurian Romances (D.D.R. Owen, trans.) (London: J. M. Dent, 1993), at 281, 350–59, where the hero, Yvain, frees three hundred young girls who are being held in bondage as silk workers by the evil lord of Pesme Avanture and his two goblins. For Chrétien to portray an actual merchant would ruin the fantasy, but the evil lord can readily be seen as a stand-in for these distressingly wealthy parvenus.

30. Thomas Malory, Le Morte Darthur (R. M. Lumiansky, ed.) (New York: Collier, 1982).

31. William Entwistle, The Arthurian Legend in the Literatures of the Spanish Peninsula (London: J. M. Dent & Sons, 1925); Irving Leonard, Books of the Brave (Berkeley: University of California Press, 1992); Henry Thomas, Spanish and Portuguese Romances of Chivalry (London: Kegan Paul, 2003).

32. Miguel de Cervantes, The Adventures of Don Quixote (J. M. Cohen, trans.) (Baltimore: Penguin, 1950). In Bk. 1, Ch. 13, id. at 97–98, Don Quixote refers explicitly to Arthur, Lancelot, and Guinevere. His fellow travelers then conclude that he is insane.

33. Laurence des Cars, The Pre-Raphaelites: Romance and Realism (New York: Harry N. Abrams, 2000); Alicia Faxon, Dante Gabriel Rossetti (New York: Abbeville Press, 1989).

34. Richard Wagner, Parsifal, in Richard Wagner, Opera and Drama (William Ellis, trans.) (Lincoln: University of Nebraska Press, 1995); Tristan and Isolde, in id.

35. Alfred, Lord Tennyson, Idylls of the King (New York: New American Library, 1961).

36. Matthew Arnold, Tristram and Iseult, in The Poems of Matthew Arnold, 2d ed. (London: Longman, 1979).

37. Walter Scott, The Bridal of Triermain, in Poetical Works (London: Oxford University Press, 1964). A much more famous work by Scott, Ivanhoe (New York: Collier, 1962), is not explicitly Arthurian, but it is pervaded by the spirit of Arthurian romance. See Jerome Mitchell, Scott, Chaucer and Medieval Romance (Lexington, Ky.: University Press of Kentucky, 1987).

38. Algernon Swinburne, Tristram of Lyonesse and Other Poems (London: Chatto & Windus, 1909).

39. Benjamin Disraeli, Endymion (New York: Longmans, Green: 1900).

40. Mark Twain, A Connecticut Yankee in King Arthur's Court (New York: Washington Square Press, 1960).

41. Robinson, Merlin, supra note 5, at 235; Lancelot, supra note 5, at 365; Tristram, supra note 5, at 595.

42. Lord Robert Baden-Powell, Yarns for Boy Scouts (London: C. Arthur Pearson, 1909), at 117–20, 143–44; Lord Robert Baden-Powell, Lessons of a Lifetime (New York: Henry Holt & Co., 1933), at 261; Michael Rosenthal, The Character Factory: Baden-Powell and the Origins of the Boy Scout Movement (New York: Pantheon Books, 1986), at 120–23. The uniform, however, is not Arthurian; it is modeled on the uniforms of the South African constabulary.

43. E.g., Thomas Berger, Arthur Rex (New York: Delacorte Press, 1978); Marion Bradley, The Mists of Avalon (New York: Ballantine, 1982); C. S. Lewis, That Hideous Strength (New York: Scribner, 1996); Sharan Newman, Guinevere (New York: St. Martin's, 1981); Walker Percy, Lancelot (New York: Ivy Books, 1989); Mary Stewart, The Crystal Cave (New York: Fawcett Crest, 1970); T. H. White, The Once and Future King (New York: Ace, 1958). See generally Nathan Starr, King Arthur Today: The Arthurian Legend in English and American Literature, 1901–1953 (Gainesville: University of Florida Press, 1954); Raymond Thompson, The Return from Avalon: A Study of the Arthurian Legend in Modern Fiction (Westport, Conn.: Greenwood Press, 1985).

44. Alan J. Lerner and Frederick Lowe, Camelot (Majestic Theater, New York, 1960) (based on White, supra note 43).

45. Among the Arthurian movies are: Camelot (Joshua Logan, director) (Warner, 1967) (based on the Broadway musical, supra note 44); Excalibur (John Boorman, director) (Warner/Orion, 1981); King Arthur (Antoine Fuqua, director) (Touchstone, 2004); Knights of the Round Table (Richard Thorpe, director) (MGM, 1953); Lancelot and Guinevere (Cornel Wilde, director) (Emblem, 1962); Monty Python and the Holy Grail (Terry Gilliam & Terry Jones, directors) (EMI/Python [Monty] Pictures/Michael White, 1975); Perceval Le Gallois

(Eric Rohmer, director) (Gaumont, 1978); The Sword in the Stone (Wolfgang Reitherman, director) (Walt Disney, 1963) (based on White, supra note 43). The most recent release, King Arthur, claimed to provide "a more realistic portrayal of 'Arthur' than has ever been presented onscreen," and while it was set in the sixth century, some historians might cavil at the image of Guinevere leading the British troops into battle dressed in a leather bikini. There are some Arthurian references in Indiana Jones and the Last Crusade (Steven Spielberg, director) (UIP/Paramount/Lucasfilm, 1989).

46. The pizza chain is Round Table and the Las Vegas hotel is the Excalibur.

47. J.R.R. Tolkien, The Lord of the Rings (Boston: Houghton Mifflin, 1954–1956). The work is typically published as a trilogy, The Fellowship of the Ring, The Two Towers, and the Return of the King, but that was the publisher's decision; Tolkien regarded it as one unified novel.

48. Joyce Hoffman, Theodore H. White and Journalism as Illusion (Columbia, Mo.: University of Missouri Press, 1995), at 1–4; Sally Smith, Grace and Power: The Private World of the Kennedy White House (New York: Random House, 2004). The quoted language is from the source of Mrs. Kennedy's information about Camelot, the Lerner and Loewe musical, which was based on the novel by Theodore H. White's fellow fantasist, T. H. White. Hoffman reports that members of Kennedy's staff were scornful of the Camelot theme; Roger Hilsman, an undersecretary of state, said: "If Jack Kennedy heard this stuff about Camelot, he would have vomited." Hoffman, supra, at 3.

49. Raymond Williams, Keywords, rev. ed. (New York: Oxford University Press, 1983).

50. William Connolly, The Terms of Political Discourse, 3d ed. (Princeton: Princeton University Press, 1993); W. B. Gallie, Essentially Contested Concepts, in Max Black, ed., The Importance of Language (Englewood Cliffs, N.J.: Prentice-Hall, 1962), at 121.

51. Daniel Rodgers, Contested Truths: Keywords in American Politics Since Independence (Cambridge, Mass.: Harvard University Press, 1987).

52. Terence Ball, Transforming Political Discourse: Political Theory and Critical Conceptual History (Oxford: Blackwell, 1988).

53. Ludwig Wittgenstein, Philosophical Investigations, 3d ed. (G.E.M. Anscombe, trans.) (Englewood Cliffs, N.J.: Prentice- Hall, 1958), at 31–36, §§ 65–76.

54. For related arguments about the need to rethink our categories in the context of the regulatory state, see Cass Sunstein, After the Rights Revolution: Reconceiving the Regulatory State (Cambridge, Mass.: Harvard University Press, 1990); Cass Sunstein, The Partial Constitution (Cambridge, Mass.: Harvard University Press, 1993).

55. See Aristotle, On Generation and Corruption, in The Works of Aristotle (Robert Maynard Hutchins, ed.) (Chicago: Britannica, 1952), vol. 1 at 409, 428–41 (Bk. 2); Plato, Timaeus, in Complete Works (John Cooper, ed.) (Indianapolis: Hackett, 1997), at 1224, 1250–70.

56. Wittgenstein, supra note 53.

57. Hilary Putnam, Reason, Truth and History (Cambridge: Cambridge University Press, 1981), at 127–49.

58. See Jacques Derrida, Of Grammatology (Gayatri Spivak, trans.) (Baltimore: Johns Hopkins Press, 1974); George Lakoff, Women, Fire and Dangerous Things: What Categories Reveal about the Mind (Chicago: University of Chicago Press, 1987); Steven Winter, A Clearing in the Forest: Law, Life, and Mind (Chicago: University of Chicago Press, 2001); Steven Winter, Transcendental Nonsense, Metaphorical Reasoning, and the Cognitive Stakes for Law, University of Pennsylvania Law Review 137:1105 (1989).

59. Edmund Husserl, Ideas (W. R. Boyce Gibson, trans.) (New York: Collier, 1962), at 100 (italics omitted).

60. Id. (italics omitted).

61. The words 'government' and 'state' are not bracketed, for no other reason than doing so does not seem to be a useful thought experiment for this book's purposes. On the other hand, these terms are not used as analytic categories in this book, but simply as ordinary language referents. For purposes of clarity, however, it may be worth defining them at this initial point. 'Government,' as used here, refers to all public officials, that is, all the persons directly employed by the entity that wields ultimate authority within a given territory, and all its subsidiary divisions and agencies. 'State' refers to the government plus its citizens in relation to the government; in other words, it is the political system, as that term is used in systems theory. Thus, a political party is not part of the government, but part of the state; a private firm or religious organization, even though it is made up of citizens, is outside the state. What about a business firm that does all its work for the government, or an established church? The boundary questions here are so complex that one could devote a volume of this size merely to sorting them out. Instead, no attention will be paid to this question, because the division of entities and actions into government, state, or private action will not be used for analytic purposes. This book assumes that some distinction can be made between government and private parties, but none of its arguments would be affected if the definition of government is either very expansive or very constricted.

62. Alexander Bickel, The Least Dangerous Branch: The Supreme Court at the Bar of Politics (Indianapolis: Bobbs-Merrill, 1962), at 1.

63. Michael Mann, The Sources of Social Power, vols. 1–2 (Cambridge: Cambridge University Press, 1986, 1993); see vol. 1 at 6.

64. Amy Gutmann and Dennis Thompson, Democracy and Disagreement (Cambridge, Mass.: Belknap Press, 1996), at 26.

65. Jürgen Habermas, Between Facts and Norms: Contributions to a Discourse Theory of Law and Democracy (William Rehg, trans.) (Cambridge, Mass.: MIT Press, 1996), at 30 (italics omitted).

66. Theodore Lowi, The End of Liberalism: The Second Republic of the United States, 2d ed. (New York: W. W. Norton, 1979), at 92.

67. H.L.A. Hart, The Concept of Law (Oxford: Clarendon Press, 1961), at 80.

68. Ronald Dworkin, Taking Rights Seriously (Cambridge, Mass.: Harvard University Press, 1977), at xi. A few sentences later, Dworkin states that his definition "does not suppose that rights have some special metaphysical character," id. Apparently, he does not regard the quality of being something that can be "held by an individual" as metaphysical.

69. Robert Nozick, Anarchy, State, and Utopia (New York: Basic Books, 1974), at 171.

70. Edmund Husserl, Cartesian Meditations: An Introduction to Phenomenology (Dorion Cairns, trans.) (Dordrecht: Kluwer, 1993), at 7–55; Husserl, Crisis, supra note 4, at 73–81; Husserl, Ideas, supra note 59, at 96–100. See Herman Philipse, Transcendental Idealism, in Barry Smith and David Smith, eds., The Cambridge Companion to Husserl (Cambridge: Cambridge University Press, 1995), at 239; John Scanlon, Husserl's Ideas and the Natural Concept of the World, in Robert Sokolowski, ed., Edmund Husserl and the Phenomenological Tradition (Washington, D.C.: Catholic University Press, 1988), at 217; Paul Ricoeur, Husserl: An Analysis of His Phenomenology (Edward Ballard & Lester Embree, trans.) (Evanston, Ill.: Northwestern University Press, 1967), at 82–114.

71. René Descartes, Discourse on Method and the Meditations (F. E. Sutcliffe, trans.) (Harmondsworth: Penguin, 1968), at 53–60 (Discourse on Method 4).

72. Husserl, Cartesian Meditations, supra note 70, at 3–7, 18–25; Husserl, Ideas, supra note 59, at 96–100.

73. See Alfred Schutz, The Phenomenology of the Social World (George Walsh & Frederick Lehnert, trans.) (Evanston, Ill.: Northwestern University Press, 1967).

74. For contemporary Anglo-American statements of this view, see Peter Berger and Thomas Luckmann, The Social Construction of Reality: A Treatise in the Sociology of Knowledge (Garden City, N.Y.: Anchor Books, 1967); Richard Bernstein, Beyond Objectivism and Relativism (Philadelphia: University of Pennsylvania Press, 1983); Nelson Goodman, Ways of Worldmaking (Indianapolis: Hackett, 1978); Putnam, supra note 57; Richard Rorty, Philosophy and the Mirror of Nature (Princeton: Princeton University Press, 1979); Peter Winch, The Idea of a Social Science and Its Relation to Philosophy (London: Routledge, 1958).

75. Intersubjectivity refers to the relationship between people who interact with each other through a specific medium such as language, but whose experience of the world remains individual. See Husserl, Crisis, supra note 4, at 161–67, 244–57; Husserl, Ideas, supra note 59, at 94–95, 149–51.

76. This view is often associated with pragmatism, particularly in the United States. See Richard Bernstein, Community in the Pragmatic Tradition, in Morris Dickstein, ed., The Revival of Pragmatism (Durham, N.C.: Duke University Press, 1998), at 141; Rorty, supra note 74. But it is also a basic tenet of phenomenology. See Schutz, supra note 73.

77. On the role of the emotions in conceptual activities, see Antonio Damasio, Descartes' Error: Emotion, Reason, and the Human Brain (New York: Avon Books, 1994); Robert Frank, Passions within Reason: The Strategic Role of the Emotions (New York: W. W. Norton, 1988).

78. Robert Cooter, The Strategic Constitution (Princeton: Princeton University Press, 2000), at 10–13; Henry Shue, Basic Rights: Subsistence, Affluence, and U.S. Foreign Policy, 2d ed. (Princeton: Princeton University Press, 1996).

79. On the role of emotions in law, see Susan Bandes, ed., The Passions of Law (New York: New York University Press, 1999). See generally Frank, supra note 77.

80. See Edward Rubin, The New Legal Process, the Synthesis of Discourse, and the Microanalysis of Institutions, Harvard Law Review 109:1393 (1996).

81. Jeffrey Alexander et al., eds., The Micro-Macro Link (Berkeley: University of California Press, 1987); James Coleman, Foundations of Social Theory (Cambridge, Mass.: Belknap Press, 1990), at 21–23; Randall Collins, On the Microfoundations of Macrosociology, American Journal of Sociology 86:984 (1981); Joan Huber, ed., Macro-Micro Linkages in Sociology (Newbury Park, Calif.: Sage Publications, 1991); Thomas Schelling, Micromotives and Macrobehavior (New York: W. W. Norton, 1978), at 9–44.

82. Max Weber, Economy and Society (Guenther Roth & Claus Wittich, eds.) (Berkeley: University of California Press, 1978), at 1399–1403 (Appendix II: Parliament and Government in a Reconstructed Germany).

83. Jody Freeman, Extending Public Norms Through Privatization, Harvard Law Review 116:1285 (2003); Jody Freeman, The Contracting State, Florida State University Law Review 28:155 (2000). Freeman argues that privatization represents a different form of regulation, not the abandonment of regulation.

84. See Martha Derthick and Paul Quirk, The Politics of Deregulation (Washington, D.C.: Brookings Institution, 1985).

85. See Michael Dorf, Legal Indeterminacy and Institutional Design, New York University Law Review 78:875 (2003); Jody Freeman, The Private Role in Public Governance, New York University Law Review 75:543 (2000); Jody Freeman, Collaborative Governance in the Administrative State, UCLA Law Review 45:1 (1997); Susan Sturm, Second Generation Employment Discrimination: A Structural Approach, Columbia Law Review 101:458 (2001).

86. Philip Bobbitt, The Shield of Achilles: War, Peace, and the Course of History (New York: Alfred A. Knopf, 2002).

87. For the idea of a conceptual horizon, see Hans-Georg Gadamer, Truth and Method (New York: Crossroad, 1988), at 267–74; Husserl, Experience, supra note 4.

88. Weber, supra note 82, at 8–9; Max Weber, "Objectivity" in Social Science and Social Policy, in Max Weber, The Methodology of the Social Sciences (Edward Shils & Henry Finch, trans.) (New York: Free Press, 1949), at 50; Max Weber, The Meaning of "Ethical Neutrality" in Sociology and Economics, in id. at 1, 40–43. See Fritz Ringer, Max Weber's Methodology (Cambridge, Mass.: Harvard University Press, 1997), at 92–121.

89. Robert Musil, The Man Without Qualities (Sophie Wilkins, trans.) (New York: Vintage Books, 1996), at 199–200. Arnheim is very assimilated, and the reader is not definitively told that he is Jewish until fairly late in the novel. See id. at 592.

90. Twain, supra note 40.

91. Schelling, supra note 81. See also Malcolm Gladwell, The Tipping Point (Boston: Little, Brown, 2000)

92. Weber, supra note 82, at 215–16.

93. Id. at 24–25. This definition combines Weber's definitions of instrumental and value rationality. For a discussion of the relationship between the two, in the context of administrative governance, see Edward Rubin, It's Time to Make the Administrative Procedure Act Administrative, Cornell Law Review 89:95 (2003), at 146–62.

94. Weber, supra note 82, at 217.

95. Id. at 220–23, 958–63.

96. Id. at 956–58.

97. Id. at 973.

98. E.g., Gary Becker, The Economic Approach to Human Behavior (Chicago: University of Chicago Press, 1976); James Buchanan and Gordon Tullock, The Calculus of Consent (Ann Arbor: University of Michigan Press, 1962); Jeffrey Friedman, ed., The Rational Choice Controversy: Economic Models of Politics Reconsidered (New Haven, Conn.: Yale University Press, 1996); Donald Green and Ian Shapiro, Pathologies of Rational Choice Theory: A Critique of Applications in Political Science (New Haven, Conn.: Yale University Press, 1994); Howard Margolis, Selfishness, Altruism, and Rationality: A Theory of Social Choice (Chicago: University of Chicago Press, 1984); Richard Posner, The Economic Analysis of Law, 5th ed. (New York: Aspen, 1998); Cass Sunstein, ed., Behavioral Law and Economics (Cambridge: Cambridge University Press, 2000).

99. See, e.g., Alvin Gouldner, Patterns of Industrial Bureaucracy (Glencoe, Ill.: Free Press, 1954), at 15–29; Carl Friedrich, Some Observations on Weber's Analysis of Bureaucracy, in Robert Merton et al., eds., Reader in Bureaucracy (Glencoe, Ill.: Free Press, 1952), at 27.

100. See Peter Aucoin, The New Public Management: Canada in Comparative Perspective (Montreal: IRPP, 1995); Ian Ayres and John Braithwaite, Responsive Regulation: Transcending the Deregulation Debate (Oxford: Oxford University Press, 1992); Eugene Bardach and Robert Kagan, Going by the Book: The Problem of Regulatory Unreasonableness (Philadelphia: Temple University Press, 1982); Michael Barzelay, The New Public Management: Improving Research and Policy Dialogue (Berkeley: University of California Press, 2001); Michael Dorf and Charles Sabel, A Constitution of Democratic Experimentalism, Columbia Law Review 98:267 (1998); Neil Gunningham, Peter Grabosky, and Darren Sinclair, Smart Regulation: Designing Environmental Policy (Oxford: Clarendon Press, 1998); Christopher Hood, The Art of the State: Culture, Rhetoric, and Public Management (Oxford: Clarendon Press, 1998); Alain Lipietz, Towards a New Economic Order: Post-Fordism, Ecology and Democracy (Malcolm Slater, trans.) (Cambridge: Polity Press, 1992); David Osborne and Ted Gaebler, Reinventing Government (Reading, Mass.: Addison-Wesley, 1992); Charles Sabel, Work and Politics: The Division of Labor in Industry (Cambridge: Cambridge University Press, 1982); Susan Sturm, Second Generation Employment Discrimination: A Structural Approach, Columbia Law Review 101:458 (2001).

101. Martin Albrow, Bureaucracy (New York: Praeger, 1970); Eugene Kamenka and Martin Krygier, eds., Bureaucracy: The Career of a Concept (London: Edward Arnold, 1979), Fritz Morstein Marx, The Administrative State: An Introduction to Bureaucracy (Chicago: University of Chicago Press, 1957), at 16–17.

102. Wolfgang Mommsen, The Age of Bureaucracy (New York: Harper, 1974), at 1–21. It might appear that Weber was more historical in his studies of religion, specifically, as Mommsen suggests, in The Protestant Ethic and The Spirit of Capitalism, Mommsen, supra, at 12–13. In fact, this book also relies on the methodology of ideal types, linking Calvinism to capitalism as a fully developed

conceptual framework. See Max Weber, The Protestant Ethic and the Spirit of Capitalism (Talcott Parsons, trans.) (New York: Charles Scribner's Sons, 1958), at 98. As Roth and Wittich note, the controversy that erupted over the historical validity of this linkage struck Weber as "pretty unrewarding." "He left the historical treatment of Protestantism to his friend Ernst Troeltsch" and continued his own investigations on the subject in his Sociology of Religion, which explores the idealized linkage between religion and social structure for a variety of other cultures. Weber, supra note 82, at lxxvii.

103. See, e.g., Reinhard Bendix, Nation Building and Citizenship, rev. ed. (Berkeley: University of California Press, 1977); Samuel Huntington, Political Order in Changing Societies (New Haven, Conn.: Yale University Press, 1968); Theda Skocpol, States and Social Revolutions (Cambridge: Cambridge University Press, 1979); Tilly, supra note 26; Immanuel Wallerstein, The Modern World–System (New York: Academic Press, 1974).

104. Huntington, supra note 103, at 93–139.

105. Gilles Deleuze and Félix Guattari, A Thousand Plateaus (Minneapolis: University of Minnesota Press, 1987), at 39–74.

106. Derrida, supra note 58, at 229–68.

107. Michael Polanyi, Personal Knowledge (Chicago: University of Chicago Press, 1974), at 69–131.

108. Norman Chester, The English Administrative System, 1780–1870 (Oxford: Clarendon Press, 1981), at 14–67, 123–68; Helen Jewell, English Local Administration in the Middle Ages (New York: Barnes & Noble, 1972); Wolfram Fischer and Peter Lundgreen, The Recruitment and Training of Administrative and Technical Personnel, in Tilly, supra note 26, at 456; Henry Parris, Constitutional Bureaucracy (New York: Augustus M. Kelly, 1969), at 22–33; Weber, supra note 82, at 963–69.

109. Robert Shackleton, Montesquieu: A Critical Biography (London: Oxford University Press, 1961).

110. Chester, supra note 108, at 124.

111. See Ernest Baker, The Development of Public Services in Western Europe, 1660–1930 (Hamden, Conn.: Anchor Books, 1966); Chester, supra note 108, at 31–41.

112. Jonathan Dewald, The European Nobility, 1400–1800 (Cambridge: Cambridge University Press, 1996); George Huppert, Les Bourgeois Gentilshommes: An Essay on the Definition of Elites in Renaissance France (Chicago: University of Chicago Press, 1977); Hans Rosenberg, Bureaucracy, Aristocracy, and Autocracy: The Prussian Experience, 1660–1815 (Boston: Beacon, 1966).

113. Baker, supra note 111, at 9–11; Jonathan Dewald, Aristocratic Experience and the Origins of Modern Culture: France 1570–1715 (Berkeley: University of California Press, 1993); Fischer and Lundgreen, supra note 108, at 492–502; Ellery Schalk, From Valor to Pedigree: Ideas of Nobility in France in the Sixteenth and Seventeenth Centuries (Princeton: Princeton University Press, 1986).

114. Weber, supra note 82, at 958–63, 969–83; see Clive Church, Revolution and Red Tape: The French Ministerial Bureaucracy 1770–1850 (Oxford: Claren-

don Press, 1981); Morstein Marx, supra note 101; Fischer and Lundgreen, supra note 108.

115. Weber, supra note 82, at 215–16, 226–41.

116. Antony Black, Political Thought in Europe, 1250–1450 (Cambridge: Cambridge University Press, 1992), at 136–52; Joseph Canning, A History of Medieval Political Thought, 300–1450 (London: Routledge, 1996); Otto Gierke, Political Theories of the Middle Age (Frederic Maitland, trans.) (Cambridge: Cambridge University Press, 1938), at 30–37; Ernst Kantorowicz, The King's Two Bodies: A Study in Mediaeval Political Theology (Princeton: Princeton University Press, 1957); Janet Nelson, Kingship and Empire, in J. H. Burns, ed., The Cambridge History of Medieval Political Thought, c. 350–c. 1450 (Cambridge: Cambridge University Press, 1988), at 211; J. A. Watt, Spiritual and Temporal Powers, in Burns, supra, at 367.

117. Fritz Kern, Kingship and Law in the Middle Ages, 149–65 (S. B. Chrimes, trans.) (Westport, Conn.: Greenwood Press, 1985); McIlwain, supra note 20; J.G.A. Pocock, The Ancient Constitution and the Feudal Law (New York: W. W. Norton, 1957), at 30–69; R. Van Caenegem, Government, Law and Society, in Burns, supra note 116, at 174, 192–95.

118. John of Salisbury, Policraticus: Of the Frivolities of Courtiers and the Footprints of Philosophers (Cary J. Nederman, trans.) (New York: Cambridge University Press, 1990). Regarding John's precursory position, see Harold Berman, Law and Revolution (Cambridge, Mass.: Harvard University Press, 1983), at 276–77; Canning, supra note 116, at 111; D. E. Luscombe and G. R. Evans, The Twelfth-Century Renaissance, in Burns, supra note 116, at 306, 325–26; Reginald Poole, Illustrations of the History of Medieval Thought and Learning, 2d ed. (New York: Dover, 1960), at 204.

119. Dante Alighieri, Monarchy (Prue Shaw, trans.) (Cambridge: Cambridge University Press, 1996). Also St. Thomas Aquinas, Summa Theologica (Fathers of the English Dominican Province, trans.) (Westminster, Md.: Christian Classics, 1981), at 995 (I–II, Q. 90, A. 4); St. Thomas Aquinas, On Kingship, To the King of Cyprus (Gerald Phelan, trans.) (Westport, Conn.: Hyperion Press, 1979); Marsilius of Padua, The Defender of Peace: The Defensor Pacis (Alan Gewirth, trans.) (New York: Harper & Row, 1967); Arthur McGrade, The Political Thought of William of Ockham: Personal and Institutional Principles (London: Cambridge University Press, 1974). See Black, supra note 116, at 24–28.

120. Heinrich Fichtenau, Living in the Tenth Century (Patrick Geary, trans.) (Chicago: University of Chicago Press, 1991), at 161–64; Gierke, supra note 116, at 30; Nelson, supra note 116.

121. For discussions of this trend, stated in terms of rationalization, see, in addition to Huntington, supra note 103, and Weber, supra note 82, Jürgen Habermas, The Theory of Communicative Action, vol. 1: Reason and the Rationalization of Society (Thomas McCarthy, trans.) (Boston: Beacon Press, 1984); Jürgen Habermas, Between Facts and Norms: Contributions to a Discourse Theory of Law and Democracy (William Rehg, trans.) (Cambridge, Mass.: MIT Press, 1996), at 94–99.

122. See Matthew Adler and Eric Posner, Rethinking Cost-Benefit Analysis, Yale Law Journal 109:165 (1999), at 194–225; James Griffin, Well-Being:

Its Meaning, Measurement, and Moral Importance (Oxford: Clarendon Press, 1986); Shelly Kagan, The Limits of Morality (Oxford: Clarendon Press, 1989).

123. Baker, supra note 111; Howard G. Brown, War, Revolution, and the Bureaucratic State (Oxford: Clarendon Press, 1995); Chester, supra note 108; Church, supra note 114; Huntington, supra note 103; Rosenberg, supra note 112; Parris, supra note 108; Gianfranco Poggi, The Development of the Modern State (Stanford, Calif.: Stanford University Press, 1978). In addition, writers who focus on cultural trends, rather than the mechanics of government, also identify this era as a critical one. E. J. Hobsbawm, The Age of Revolution, 1789–1848 (New York: Mentor, 1962); Paul Johnson, The Birth of the Modern: World Society in 1815–1830 (New York: HarperCollins, 1991); Raymond Williams, The Long Revolution (New York: Harper & Row, 1961).

124. See note 113, supra, citing sources.

125. Church, supra note 114, at 69–111.

126. Id. at 86–89.

127. Baker, supra note 111, at 41–50; Brown, supra note 123.

128. Baker, supra note 111, at 7–11; Church, supra note 114, at 16–19; Fischer and Lundgreen, supra note 108, at 502–5.

129. Church, supra note 114, at 31.

130. Id.

131. Id. at 16–17.

132. Id. at 69–110.

133. Baker, supra note 111, at 34–36, 61–64; John Mackintosh, The British Cabinet, 3d ed. (London: Stevens & Sons, 1977), at 70–73; Parris, supra note 108, at 33–35.

134. Baker, supra note 111, at 63–64.

135. This was an enormous sum. Jane Austen, whose novels are contemporary with these developments, almost always gives the precise income of her heroines' suitors. The very wealthiest, Mr. Darcy, with his huge ancestral home and its park ten miles around, has 10,000 a year. Jane Austen, Pride and Prejudice (Oxford: Oxford University Press, 1980).

136. Chester, supra note 108, at 123–68; Emmeline Cohen, The Growth of the British Civil Service, 1780–1939 (London: G. Allen & Unwin, 1941); Ronald Nelson, The Home Office, 1782–1801 (Durham, N.C.: Duke University Press, 1969); Parris, supra note 108; Charles Edward Troup, The Home Office, 2d ed. (London: G. P. Putnam's Sons, 1925), at 7–25.

137. Baker, supra note 111, at 33–36; Chester, supra note 108, at 31–51, 222–81; Mackintosh, supra note 133, at 50–70.

138. Chester, supra note 108, at 169–237.

139. See Ferenc Feher, ed., The French Revolution and the Birth of Modernity (Berkeley: University of California Press, 1990); Patrice Higonnet, Class, Ideology, and The Rights of Nobles during the French Revolution (Oxford: Clarendon Press, 1981); Lynn Hunt, Politics, Culture, and Class in the French Revolution (Berkeley: University of California Press, 1984); John Markoff, The Abolition of Feudalism: Peasants, Lords, and Legislators in the French Revolution (University Park: Pennsylvania State University Press, 1996).

140. Church, supra note 114, at 50–109.

141. Michael Broers, Europe under Napoleon, 1799–1815 (London: Arnold, 1996), at 52–58. Robert Toombs, France 1814–1914 (London: Longman, 1996), at 97–100.

142. Derek Beales: Joseph II, vol. 1: In the Shadow of Maria Theresa, 1741–80 (Cambridge: Cambridge University Press, 1987).

143. See T.C.W. Blanning, Joseph II (London: Longman, 1994); Robert Kann, A History of the Habsburg Empire, 1526–1918 (Berkeley: University of California Press, 1974), at 183–207; Saul K. Padover, The Revolutionary Emperor: Joseph the Second (New York: Robert O. Ballou, 1934).

144. Blanning states that the aim of Joseph's reform of the Church was "the transformation of priests into civil servants." Supra note 143, at 97.

145. Padover, supra note 143, at 180–82.

146. Paul Bernard, From the Enlightenment to the Police State: The Public Life of Johann Anton Pergen (Urbana: University of Illinois Press, 1991), at 140–77.

147. Padover, supra note 143, at 182. See also Blanning, supra note 143, at 58–59.

148. Charles Seruzier, Historical Summary of the French Codes with French and Foreign Bibliographical Annotations Concerning the General Principles of the Codes Followed by a Dissertation on Codification (David Combe, trans.) (Littleton, Colo.: Fred B. Rothman, 1979).

149. Broers, supra note 141, at 52; René David, French Law: Its Structure, Sources and Methodology (Michael Kindred trans.) (Baton Rouge: Louisiana State University Press, 1972), at 11–16; James Gordley, Myths of the French Civil Code, American Journal of Comparative Law 42:459 (1994).

150. Seruzier, supra note 148, at 140–51.

151. Giles Macdonogh, Prussia: The Perversion of an Idea (London: Sinclair-Stevenson, 1994), at 40–43; Rosenberg, supra note 112.

152. Kann, supra note 143, at 179–80; Padover, supra note 143, at 193–98. This effort was ultimately unsuccessful, although Joseph did succeed in enacting a modernized matrimonial code.

153. Jeremy Bentham, A Fragment on Government (J. H. Burns & H.L.A. Hart, eds.) (New York: Cambridge University Press, 1988).

154. William Blackstone, Commentaries on the Laws of England (Chicago: University of Chicago Press, 1979).

155. Daniel Boorstin, The Mysterious Science of the Law (Cambridge, Mass.: Harvard University Press, 1941).

156. Bentham vented his fury in Jeremy Bentham, A Comment on the Commentaries (Darmstadt, Ger.: Scientia Verlag Aalen, 1976).

157. Edmund Burke, Reflections on the Revolution in France (L. G. Mitchell, ed.) (Oxford: Oxford University Press, 1993).

158. Joseph de Maistre, Considerations on France (Isaiah Berlin and Richard Lebrun, eds.) (New York: Cambridge University Press, 1994); Joseph de Maistre, On God and Society (Elisha Griefer, ed.) (Chicago: Henry Regnery, 1959).

159. Charles Lombard, Joseph de Maistre (Boston: Twayne, 1976).

160. David Klinck, The French Counterrevolutionary Theorist Louis de Bonald (New York: Peter Lang, 1996).

161. Id. at 74–77.

162. Richard Bensel, Yankee Leviathan: The Origins of Central State Authority in America, 1859–1877 (Cambridge: Cambridge University Press, 1990); William Nelson, The Roots of American Bureaucracy, 1830–1900 (Cambridge, Mass.: Harvard University Press, 1982); John Rohr, To Run a Constitution: The Legitimacy of the Administrative State (Lawrence: University Press of Kansas, 1986); Stephen Skowronek, Building a New American State: The Expansion of National Administrative Capacities, 1877–1920 (New York: Cambridge University Press, 1982); Sunstein, After the Rights Revolution, supra note 54, at 11–24.

163. Some scholars have argued that the United States did not establish a true regulatory agency until the creation of the Interstate Commerce Commission in 1887. See Brian Cook, Bureaucracy and Self-Government (Baltimore: Johns Hopkins University Press, 1996), at 79–86; Thomas McCraw, Prophets of Regulation (Cambridge, Mass.: Belknap Press, 1984); Nelson, supra note 162, at 127–33; Rohr, supra note 162, at 90–110.

164. Maurice Baxter, Henry Clay and the American System (Lexington, Ky.: University Press of Kentucky, 1995); Robert Remini, Henry Clay: Statesman for the Union (New York: W. W. Norton, 1991); Glyndon Van Deusen, The Jacksonian Era (New York: Harper, 1959); Leonard White, The Jacksonians: A Study in Administrative History, 1829–1861 (New York: Macmillan, 1954).

165. Eric Foner, Reconstruction: America's Unfinished Revolution (New York: Harper & Row, 1988), at 153–70; Claude Oubre, Forty Acres and a Mule: The Freedmen's Bureau and Black Land Ownership (Baton Rouge: Louisiana State University Press, 1978).

166. Skowronek, supra note 162, at 19–35. See also Samuel Beer, The Modernization of American Federalism, Publius: 3:59 (1973); Daniel Elazar, The Federal Partnership: Intergovernmental Relations in the Nineteenth Century United States (Chicago: University of Chicago Press, 1962).

167. Frederick Jackson Turner, The Frontier in American History (New York: H. Holt, 1920). The existence of a large, unorganized frontier, to which those who disliked government regulation could resort, may well have made those governments more reluctant to impose controls on valued business interests, while that same frontier, to which disaffected workers could flee, may well have made business less capable of the oppressions which motivated such controls.

168. G.W.F. Hegel, The Philosophy of History (J. Sibree, trans.) (New York: Dover, 1956), at 86. He says: "Had the woods of Germany been in existence, the French Revolution would not have occurred."

169. Brown, supra note 123; Brian Downing, The Military Revolution and Political Change (Princeton, N.J.: Princeton University Press, 1992); Charles Tilly, War Making and State Making as Organized Crime, in Peter Evans, Dietrich Rueschemeyer, and Theda Skocpol, Bringing the State Back In (Cambridge: Cambridge University Press, 1985), at 169.

170. A strong claim that American government was pre-administrative before the 1880s might exempt early American political theorists, such as Madison, Hamilton, and Story, from criticism for use of outmoded concepts, but such a claim would be rather extreme, and it would not apply to the twentieth-century theorists whom this study discusses.

Notes to Chapter Two

1. Harold Berman, Law and Revolution (Cambridge, Mass.: Harvard University Press, 1983), at 276–77; Joseph Canning, A History of Medieval Political Thought, 300–1450 (London: Routledge, 1996), at 111; D. E. Luscombe and G. R. Evans, The Twelfth-Century Renaissance, in J. H. Burns, ed., The Cambridge History of Medieval Political Thought c. 350–c. 1450 (New York: Cambridge University Press, 1988), at 306, 325–26; Reginald Poole, Illustrations of the History of Medieval Thought and Learning, 2d ed. (New York: Dover, 1960), at 204.

2. William Blackstone, Commentaries on the Laws of England (London: Cavendish, 2001); Jean-Jacques Rousseau, The Social Contract (Willmoore Kendall, trans.) (Chicago: Henry Regnery, 1954), at 41 (Bk. 2, Ch. 4), 66–67 (Bk. 2, Ch. 9).

3. Antoine de Baecque, The Body Politic: Corporeal Metaphor in Revolutionary France (Charlotte Mandell, trans.) (Stanford, Calif.: Stanford University Press, 1997).

4. John of Salisbury, Policraticus: Of the Frivolities of Courtiers and the Footprints of Philosophers (Cary Nederman, trans.) (New York: Cambridge University Press, 1990), at 66–67 (V. 2).

5. Id. at 67 (V. 2). See id. at 69–81 (V. 2–8).

6. Id. at 81–85 (V. 9).

7. Id. at 85–91 (V. 10). "Courtier," which is neutral in Castiglione, is used by John as a sort of imprecation, but he offers no other term for his "flanks." He does describe them, however, as "those who always assist the prince," id. at 67, or, alternatively, "those who ought to assist princes." Id. at 85.

8. Id. at 91–98 (V. 11, 15).

9. Id. at 104. See 104–25 (V. 1, 2, 6, 7, 8, 9, 18, 19).

10. Id. at 104. See 104–9 (V. 1).

11. Id. at 67 (V. 2).

12. Id. at 125–26 (V. 20).

13. Id. at 126. The term "centipede" is John's.

14. John Morrall, Political Thought in Medieval Times (New York: Harper & Row, 1958), at 44.

15. John of Salisbury, supra note 4, at 87 (V. 10). Chapter 10 is entitled: "Of the flank of the powerful, whose needs are to be satisfied and whose malice is to be restrained."

16. Id. at 193.

17. See Hans Liebeschutz, Mediaeval Humanism in the Life and Writings of John of Salisbury (London: The Warburg Institute, 1950), at 38–44; Quentin Skinner, The Foundations of Modern Political Thought, vol. 1 (The Renaissance) (New York: Cambridge University Press, 1978), at 33–35, 46–48.

18. On the prevalence of this metaphor, or concept, in Western thought, see Arthur Lovejoy, The Great Chain of Being: A Study in the History of an Idea (New York: Harper & Row, 1936). The concept of a hierarchy can be traced to the sixth-century Christian mystic who wrote under the name of Dionysus the Areopagite, and is consequently known as Pseudo-Dionysus or Pseudo Denis. See Dionysius, the Pseudo-Areopagite, The Ecclesiastical Hierarchy (Thomas L.

Campbell, trans.) (Lanham, Md.: University Press of America, 1981); Dionysius the Areopagite, The Celestial Hierarchy (Shrine of Wisdom, ed.) (London: Woking, 1935).

19. See Antony Black, Political Thought in Europe, 1250–1450 (New York: Cambridge University Press, 1992), at 16–17.

20. For John's biography, see Liebeschutz, supra note 17, at 8–22; Clement C. J. Webb, John of Salisbury (London: Methuen, 1932); Christopher Brooke, John of Salisbury and His World, in Michael Wilks, ed., The World of John of Salisbury (Oxford: Basil Blackwell, 1984), at 1.

21. David Knowles, Thomas Becket (Stanford, Calif.: Stanford University Press, 1971); W. L. Warren, Henry II (Berkeley: University of California Press, 1973), at 56.

22. John Appleby, The Troubled Reign of King Stephen (London: Barnes & Noble, 1970), at 11–13; H. A. Cronne, The Reign of Stephen, 1135–54: Anarchy in England (London: Weidenfeld and Nicholson, 1970); R.H.C. Davis, King Stephen, 3d ed. (London: Longman, 1990); Keith Stringer, The Reign of Stephen: Kingship, Warfare, and Government in Twelfth Century England (London: Routledge, 1993); W. L. Warren, Henry II (Berkeley: University of California Press, 1973), at 3–53; William of Malmesbury, Chronicles of the Kings of England (J. A. Giles, trans.) (London: G. Bell, 1889).

23. I. S. Robinson, The Papacy 1073–1198: Continuity and Innovation (Cambridge: Cambridge University Press, 1990); Brian Tierney, The Crisis of Church and State, 1050–1300 (Englewood Cliffs, N.J.: Prentice-Hall, 1964). On Becket's role in this struggle, see Frank Barlow, Thomas Becket (Berkeley: University of California Press, 1986); Warren, supra note 21, at 447–555.

24. Both Berman, supra note 1, at 282–83, and Luscombe and Evans, supra note 1, at 326–27, point out that John uses the classics to provide cover names for contemporary political figures, and thus to keep himself out of trouble (a goal at which he failed rather badly). While this seems plausible, John's enthusiasm for the classics goes far beyond such a pragmatic purpose. See Charles Homer Haskins, The Renaissance of the 12th Century (Cleveland: Meridian Books, 1957), at 99–101. Moreover, he could readily have found cover names in the Bible, a source that was far more familiar to his readers than the classics, and more likely to keep him out of trouble.

25. See Ralph Miliband, The State in Capitalist Society (New York: Basic Books, 1969); Nicos Poulantzas, Political Power and Social Classes (London: New Left Books, 1973); Nicos Poulantzas, Classes in Contemporary Capitalism (London: New Left Books, 1975).

26. See, e.g., Michael Kammen, A Machine That Would Go of Itself: The Constitution in American Culture (New York: Knopf, 1986).

27. Aristotle, Politics (Benjamin Jowett, trans.) (Oxford: Clarendon Press, 1905), at 176–86 (IV. 14–16).

28. M.J.C. Vile, Constitutionalism and the Separation of Powers (Oxford: Clarendon Press, 1967).

29. Aristotle, supra note 27, at 264–72 (IV. 11–12); Cicero, The Republic (Niall Rudd, trans.) (Oxford: Oxford University Press, 1998), at 30–33 (I,

65–70); Polybius, The Rise of the Roman Empire (Ian Scott-Kilvert, trans.) (London: Penguin, 1979).

30. Vile, supra note 28, at 33–43.

31. Id. at 87.

32. John Locke, The Second Treatise of Government (Indianapolis: Bobbs-Merrill, 1952), at 82–84 (143–48).

33. Montesquieu (Charles Louis de Secondat) The Spirit of the Laws (Anne Cohler, Basia Miller, & Harold Stone, trans.) (Cambridge: Cambridge University Press, 1989), at 156–66 (Bk. 11, Ch. 6).

34. Id. at 166–68 (Chs. 7–19).

35. Id. at 154–56 (Chs. 1–5).

36. Id. at 162–64 (Ch. 6).

37. William Gwyn, The Meaning of Separation of Powers: An Analysis of the Doctrine from Its Origin to the Adoption of the United States Constitution (New Orleans: Tulane University, 1965); Paul Spurlin, Montesquieu in America, 1760–1801 (New York: Octagon Books, 1969).

38. Woodrow Wilson, The State: Elements of Historical and Practical Politics (Boston: D.C. Heath, 1889).

39. Lynton Caldwell, Novus Ordo Seclorum: The Heritage of American Public Administration, Public Administration Review 36:476 (1976); A. F. Pollard, Factors in American History (New York: MacMillan, 1925); Samuel Huntington, Political Order in Changing Societies (New Haven, Conn.: Yale University Press, 1968), at 96–97; Richard Stillman, Preface to Public Administration (New York: St. Martin's Press, 1991). Even Gordon Wood, although he makes a convincing case for the novelty of American revolutionary thought, concedes that England exhibited many republican traits as early as the first half of the eighteenth century. Gordon Wood, The Radicalism of the American Revolution (New York: Vintage Books, 1991), at 95–109. As Wood says: "The Americans did not have to invent republicanism in 1776; they only had to bring it to the surface." Id. at 109.

40. Blackstone, supra note 2, at I *146–47, *250.

41. Alexander Bickel, The Least Dangerous Branch: The Supreme Court at the Bar of Politics (Indianapolis: Bobbs-Merrill, 1962).

42. Joseph Clark, Congress: The Sapless Branch (New York: Harper & Row, 1964).

43. William Banks, Efficiency in Government: Separation of Powers Reconsidered, Syracuse Law Review 35:715 (1984); James Landis, The Administrative Process (New Haven, Conn.: Yale University Press, 1938), at 89–122; Peter Strauss, The Place of Agencies in Government: Separation of Powers and the Fourth Branch, Columbia Law Review 84:573 (1984).

44. See Humphrey's Executor v. United States, 295 U.S. 602 (1935); Bowsher v. Synar, 478 U.S. 714 (1986); Strauss, supra note 43; Paul Verkuil, The Purposes and Limits of Independent Agencies, Duke Law Journal 1988:257 (1988); Paul Verkuil, The Status of Independent Agencies after Bowsher v. Synar, Duke Law Journal 1986:779 (1986).

45. John Rohr, To Run a Constitution: The Legitimacy of the Administrative State (Lawrence: University of Kansas Press, 1986), at 153.

46. One of the few such trees is the *ailanthus*, a deciduous tree, native to China, with an unpleasant odor.

47. Bradley Patterson, The White House Staff: Inside the West Wing and Beyond (Washington, D.C.: Brookings Institution, 2000); Nelson Polsby, Congress and the Presidency, 4th ed. (Englewood Cliffs, N.J.: Prentice-Hall, 1986), at 76–84.

48. Karl Deutsch, The Nerves of Government: Models of Political Communication and Control (New York: Free Press, 1963).

49. Paul DiMaggio, Structural Analysis of Organizational Fields: A Blockmodel Approach, Research in Organizational Behavior 8:335 (1986); John Meyer, Institutionalization and the Rationality of Formal Organizational Structure, in John Meyer and W. Richard Scott, eds., Organizational Environments: Ritual and Rationality (Beverly Hills: Sage, 1983), at 261; Walter Powell, Neither Market nor Hierarchy: Network Forms of Organization, Research in Organizational Behavior 12:295 (1990); W. Richard Scott, The Organization of Environments: Network, Cultural, and Historical Elements, in Meyer and Scott, supra, at 155. These authors are all associated with the new institutionalism movement. See Walter Powell and Paul DiMaggio, The New Institutionalism in Organizational Analysis (Chicago: University of Chicago Press, 1991). For recent applications of the network metaphor in legal scholarship, see Kal Raustiala, The Architecture of International Cooperation: Transgovernmental Networks and the Future of International Law, Virginia Journal of International Law 43:1 (2002); David Zaring, National Rulemaking through Trial Courts: The Big Case and Institutional Reform, UCLA Law Review 51:1015 (2004).

50. C. Nelson Dorny, Understanding Dynamic Systems: Approaches to Modeling, Analysis and Design (Englewood Cliffs, N.J.: Prentice-Hall, 1993), at 17–47.

51. Patricia Churchland and Terrence Sejnowski, The Computational Brain (Cambridge, Mass.: MIT Press, 1992); Philip Johnson-Laird, The Computer and the Mind: An Introduction to Cognitive Science (Cambridge, Mass.: Harvard University Press, 1988).

52. George Lakoff, Women, Fire and Dangerous Things: What Categories Reveal about the Mind (Chicago: University of Chicago Press, 1987); Steven Winter, A Clearing in the Forest: Law, Life, and Mind (Chicago: University of Chicago Press, 2001); Steven Winter, Transcendental Nonsense, Metaphoric Reasoning, and the Cognitive Stakes for Law, University of Pennsylvania Law Review 137:1105 (1989); Steven Winter, An Upside/Down View of the Countermajoritarian Difficulty, Texas Law Review 69:1881 (1991).

53. See Jody Freeman, Collaborative Governance in the Administrative State, UCLA Law Review 45:1 (1997).

54. Haskins, supra note 24, at 127–31. John's own experience emphasizes the point. His ecclesiastical career proceeded from England, where he was born, to France, where he was educated, to England, to Rome, and then back and forth between France and England several times, before his final appointment as bishop at Chartres cathedral. See Liebeschutz, supra note 17, at 8–22; Clement C. J. Webb, John of Salisbury (London: Methuen, 1932); Christopher Brooke, John of Salis-

bury and His World, in Michael Wilks, ed., The World of John of Salisbury (Oxford: Basil Blackwell, 1984), at 1.

55. J. L. Austin, How To Do Things with Words, 2d ed (Cambridge, Mass. Harvard University Press, 1962).

56. Jürgen Habermas, The Theory of Communicative Action, vol. 1: Reason and the Rationalization of Society (Thomas McCarthy, trans.) (Boston: Beacon Press, 1984), at 273–337.

57. See Dorny, supra note 50, at 117–25.

58. Id. at 212–37.

59. Id. at 534–37.

60. Paul DiMaggio and Walter Powell, The Iron Cage Revisited: Institutional Isomorphism and Collective Rationality in Organizational Fields, American Sociological Review 48:147 (1983), reprinted in Powell and DiMaggio, supra note 49, at 63; Marco Orru, Nicole Biggart and Gary Hamilton, Organizational Isomorphism in East Asia, in Powell and DiMaggio, supra note 49, at 361.

61. Michael Gabriel and John Moore, eds., Learning and Computational Neuroscience: Foundations of Adaptive Networks (Cambridge, Mass.: MIT Press, 1990); Donald Hebb, The Organization of Behavior (New York: John Wiley, 1949).

62. Bowsher v. Synar, 478 U.S. 714 (1986); INS v. Chadha, 462 U.S. 919 (1983); Northern Pipeline Construction Co. v. Marathon Pipe Line Co., 458 U.S. 50 (1982); Buckley v. Valeo, 424 U.S. 1 (1976); A.L.A. Schechter Poultry Corp. v. United States, 295 U.S. 495 (1935). The Court often upholds federal statutes against separation of powers challenges, two notable examples being Mistretta v. United States, 488 U.S. 361 (1989) (judicial sentencing commission); Morrison v. Olson, 487 U.S. 654 (1988) (removal of independent prosecutor by Congress). Commentators generally agree that the doctrine is confused. Rebecca Brown, Separated Powers and Ordered Liberty, University of Pennsylvania Law Review 139:1513 (1991); Erwin Chemerinsky, A Paradox without a Principle: A Comment on the Burger Court's Jurisprudence in Separation of Powers Cases, Southern California Law Review 60:1083 (1987); E. Donald Elliot, Why Our Separation of Powers Jurisprudence Is So Abysmal, George Washington Law Review 57:506 (1989); William Gwyn, The Indeterminacy of Separation of Powers and The Federal Courts, George Washington Law Review 57:474 (1989).

63. For the distinction between formal and functional separation of powers accounts, see Brown, supra note 62; Martin Flaherty, The Most Dangerous Branch, Yale Law Journal 105:1725, 1732–44 (1996); Harold Krent, Separating the Strands in Separation of Powers Controversies, Virginia Law Review 74:1253 (1988); Thomas Merrill, The Constitutional Principle of Separation of Powers, Supreme Court Review 1991:225 (1991); Strauss, supra note 43; Cass Sunstein, Constitutionalism after the New Deal, Harvard Law Review 101:421 (1987).

64. There are a number of cases where the powers clearly overlap—the president's veto, Congress's impeachment and removal power, the Senate's confirmation of appointments—and there is no clause specifically stating that the powers must be separate. To be sure, Articles I, II, and III use the words "legislative," "executive," and "judicial" in their introductory passages, but these terms may be

meant merely as organizing principles. Article I, unlike the others, uses the adjective "all" in the phrase "All legislative Powers herein granted," but it is also the only Article to pluralize "power" (the other references being the "executive Power" and the "judicial Power"). This pluralization, plus the words "herein granted," suggests that since the legislative powers of Congress are being specifically enumerated, unlike the power of the executive or judiciary, the drafters are simply stating that Congress can exercise all the powers that have been enumerated, not that all legislative powers are necessarily granted to the legislature.

65. Wood, supra note 39, at 150–51.

66. The very first sentence of The Federalist Papers reads: "After an unequivocal experience of the inefficiency of the subsisting federal government, you are called upon to deliberate on a new Constitution for the United States of America." James Madison, Alexander Hamilton, and John Jay, The Federalist Papers (Isaac Kramnick, ed.) (London: Penguin, 1987), at 87 (I).

67. Papers of James Madison (Robert Rutland et al., eds.) (Charlottesville: University Press of Virginia, 1984), vol. 12, at 202; Richard Kay, Adherence to the Original Intentions in Constitutional Adjudication: Three Objections and Responses, Northwestern University Law Review 82:226 (1988), at 271–72; Edward Dumbauld, The Bill of Rights and What It Means Today (Norman: University of Oklahoma Press, 1957), at 33–44.

68. 478 U.S. 714 (1986) (striking down portions of the Balanced Budget and Emergency Deficit Control Act [Gramm-Rudman], Public Law No. 99–177, 99 Stat. 1038 [1985], codified at 2 U.S.C. § 901 et seq.).

69. 424 U.S. 1 (1976) (striking down portions of the Federal Election Campaign Act, Public Law No. 92–225, 86 Stat. 3 [1972], codified at 2 U.S.C. § 431 et seq.).

70. 462 U.S. 919 (1983) (striking down legislative veto provisions in some 200 federal statutes). Chadha, strictly speaking, was decided on the basis of the Presentment Clause, not separation of powers, but both proponents and opponents of the decision recognize this as a virtually identical issue.

71. Mark Granovetter, Getting a Job: A Study of Contacts and Careers, 2d ed. (Chicago: University of Chicago Press, 1995), at 17–19.

72. See Steven Calabresi and Saikrishna Prakash, The President's Power to Execute the Laws, Yale Law Journal 104:541 (1994); Steven Calabresi and Kevin Rhodes, The Structural Constitution: Unitary Executive, Plural Judiciary, Harvard Law Review 105:1153 (1992).

73. Elena Kagan, Presidential Administration, Harvard Law Review 114:2245 (2001); Strauss, supra note 43.

74. See Bradley Patterson, White House Staff: Inside the West Wing and Beyond (Washington, D.C.: Brookings Institution, 2000). See also Joseph Bock, The White House Staff and the National Security Assistant: Friendship and Friction at the Water's Edge (Westport, Conn.: Greenwood Press, 1987).

75. Theodore Sorensen, Kennedy (Old Saybrook, Ct.: Konecky & Konecky, 1965), at 259. Sorensen was Special Counsel, which meant that he was a leading advisor for domestic affairs.

76. See Kagan, supra note 73, at 2247–48; Morton Rosenberg, Beyond the Limits of Executive Power: Presidential Control of Agency Rulemaking Under Ex-

ecutive Order 12,291, Michigan Law Review 80:193, 221–24 (1981). See generally Bronwen Morgan, Social Citizenship in the Shadow of Competition (Aldershot, Eng.: Ashgate, 2003) (comparative discussion of meta-regulation).

77. OMB's regulatory review authority was established by a series of executive orders: Executive Order No. 12,291, Federal Register 46:13,193 (Feb. 17, 1981) (Ronald Reagan); Executive Order No. 12,498, Federal Register 50:1,036 (Jan. 4, 1985) (Ronald Reagan), combined and amended by Executive Order 12,866, Federal Register 58:51,735 (Sept. 30, 1993) (William Clinton), amended by Executive Order 13,258, Federal Register 67:9,385 (Feb. 26, 2002) (George W. Bush). See Harold Bruff, Presidential Management of Agency Rulemaking, George Washington Law Review 57:533 (1989); Rosenberg, supra note 76.

78. James Blumstein, Regulatory Review by the Executive Office of the President: An Overview and Policy Analysis of Current Issues, Duke Law Journal 51:851 (2001); Bruff, supra note 77; Harold Bruff, Presidential Power and Administrative Rulemaking, Yale Law Journal 88:451 (1979); Christopher DeMuth and Douglas Ginsberg, White House Review of Agency Rulemaking, Harvard Law Review 99:1075 (1986); Rosenberg, supra note 76.

79. E. Donald Elliott, TQM-ing OMB: Or Why Regulatory Review Under Executive Order 12, 291 Works Poorly and What President Clinton Should Do About It, Law & Contemporary Problems 57:167 (1994); Alan Morrison, OMB Interference with Agency Rulemaking: The Wrong Way to Write a Regulation, Harvard Law Review 99:1059 (1986); Richard Pildes and Cass Sunstein, Reinventing the Regulatory State, University of Chicago Law Review 62:1 (1995).

80. See James Benze, Presidential Power and Management Techniques: The Carter and Reagan Administrations in Historical Perspective (New York: Greenwood Press, 1987); Richard Neustadt, Presidential Power: The Politics of Leadership (New York: New American Library, 1964).

81. Calabresi and Prakash, supra note 72; Calabresi and Rhodes, supra note 72; Geoffrey Miller, Independent Agencies, Supreme Court Review 1986:41 (1986).

82. Lawrence Lessig and Cass Sunstein, The President and the Administration, Columbia Law Review 94:1 (1994); Peter Shane, Conventionalism in Constitutional Interpretation and the Place of Administrative Agencies, American Law Review 36:573 (1987).

83. Colin Diver, Presidential Powers, American University Law Review 36:519 (1987); Susan Foote, Independent Agencies Under Attack: A Skeptical View of the Importance of the Debate, Duke Law Journal 1988:223 (1988); Terry Moe, Regulatory Performance and Presidential Administration, American Journal of Political Science 26:197 (1982); David Welborn, Governance of Federal Regulatory Agencies (Knoxville: University of Tennessee Press, 1977); David Welborn, Regulation in the White House: The Johnson Presidency (Austin: University of Texas Press, 1993), at 22–107.

84. See Flaherty, supra note 63; Lessig and Sunstein, supra note 82; Peter Shane, Independent Policymaking and Presidential Power: A Constitutional Analysis, George Washington Law Review 57:596 (1989); Strauss, supra note 43; Verkuil, Status, supra note 44.

85. John Ely, Democracy and Distrust (Cambridge, Mass.: Harvard University Press, 1980), at 131–34; F. A. Hayek, The Road to Serfdom (Chicago: University

of Chicago Press, 1967); Marci Hamilton, Representation and Delegation: Back to Basics, Cardozo Law Review 20:807 (1999); Gary Lawson, The Rise and Rise of the Administrative State, Harvard Law Review 107:1231 (1994); Theodore Lowi, The End of Liberalism: The Second Republic of the United States, 2d ed. (New York: W. W. Norton, 1979); Martin Redish, The Constitution as Political Structure (New York: Oxford University Press, 1995); David Schoenbrod, Power without Responsibility: How Congress Abuses the People through Delegation (New Haven, Conn.: Yale University Press, 1993).

86. Jerry Mashaw, Greed, Chaos, and Governance: Using Public Choice to Improve Public Law (New Haven, Conn.: Yale University Press, 1997), at 132–36; Jerry Mashaw, Prodelegation: Why Administrators Should Make Political Decisions, Journal of Law, Economics and Organizations 1:81 (1985); Peter Schuck, The Limits of Law: Essays on Democratic Governance (Boulder, Colo.: Westview Press, 2000), at 251–66; David Spence and Frank Cross, A Public Choice Case for the Administrative State, Georgetown Law Journal 89:97 (2000); Peter Strauss, Formal and Functional Approaches to Separation-of-Powers Questions—A Foolish Inconsistency?, Cornell Law Review 72:488 (1987); Cass Sunstein, Is the Clean Air Act Unconstitutional?, Michigan Law Review 98:303 (1999).

87. 38 Stat. 251 (1913), codified at 12 U.S.C. §§ 221 et seq.

88. See Whitman v. American Trucking Associations, Inc., 531 U.S. 457 (2001); Yakus v. United States, 321 U.S. 414 (1944); Amalgamated Meat Cutters v. Connally, 337 F. Supp. 737 (D.D.C. 1971).

89. Regarding legislative oversight in general, see James Bowers, Regulating the Regulators: An Introduction to the Legislative Oversight of Administrative Rulemaking (New York: Praeger, 1990); Morris Ogul, Congress Oversees the Bureaucracy: Studies of Legislative Supervision (Pittsburgh: University of Pittsburgh Press, 1976); Richard Lazarus, The Neglected Question of Congressional Oversight of EPA: Quis Custodiet Ipsos Custodes (Who Shall Watch the Watchers Themselves)?, Law & Contemporary Problems 54:205 (1991); Matthew McCubbins and Thomas Schwartz, Congressional Oversight Overlooked: Police Patrols Versus Fire Alarms, American Journal of Political Science 28:165 (1984).

90. But see Gary Lawson, Delegation and Original Meaning, Virginia Law Review 88:327 (2002). Lawson's argument is based on the premise that there is a constitutionally established presumption against the exercise of federal authority. On textual grounds, this argument seems untenable after the Fourteenth Amendment. See Bruce Ackerman, We the People (Cambridge, Mass.: Belknap Press, 1991). On practical grounds, it is untenable after the development of the administrative state.

91. The distinction with respect to the nondelegation doctrine is essentially the same as the one made with respect to separation of powers. See note 63 above, citing sources.

92. Peter Aranson, Ernest Gellhorn, and Glenn Robinson, A Theory of Legislative Delegation, Cornell Law Review 68:1 (1982); Brown, supra note 62; Redish, supra note 85.

93. Lisa Bressman, Schechter Poultry at the Millennium: A Delegation Doctrine for the Administrative State, Yale Law Journal 109:1399 (2000); Cynthia Farina, Statutory Interpretation and the Balance of Power in the Administrative

State, Columbia Law Review: 89:452 (1989); John Manning, Textualism as a Nondelegation Doctrine, Columbia Law Review 97:673 (1997); Cass Sunstein, Nondelegation Canons, University of Chicago Law Review 67:315 (2000). For a critique, see David Driesen, Loose Canons: Statutory Construction and the New Nondelegation Doctrine, University of Pittsburgh Law Review 64:1 (2002).

94. See James Barber, The Lawmakers: Recruitment and Adaptation to Legislative Life (New Haven: Yale University Press, 1965); Christopher Deering and Steven Smith, Committees in Congress, 3d ed. (Washington, D.C.: CQ Press, 1997); Richard Fenno, Congressmen in Committees (Boston: Little, Brown, 1973); John Kingdon, Congressmen's Voting Decisions, 3d ed. (Ann Arbor: University of Michigan Press, 1989); William Muir, Legislature: California's School for Politics (Chicago: University of Chicago Press, 1982).

95. Robert Cooter, The Strategic Constitution (Princeton: Princeton University Press, 2000), at 79–99. Cooter's analysis is based on economics, and the economic term for the problem of controlling subordinates such as administrative agencies is, conveniently enough, the agency problem.

96. See Terry Moe, Interests, Institutions, and Positive Theory: The Politics of the NLRB, Studies in American Political Development 2:236 (1987); Terry Moe, Control and Feedback in Economic Regulation: The Case of the NLRB, American Political Science Review 79:1094 (1985).

97. See Colin Diver, The Optimal Precision of Administrative Rules, Yale Law Journal 93:65 (1983).

98. David Driesen points out that aggressive reliance on the nondelegation doctrine as a principle of statutory interpretation violates the principle it is supposed to protect because it assigns excessive authority to the judiciary in its effort to avoid assigning such authority to the executive. Driesen, supra note 93.

99. M. Elizabeth Magill, Beyond Powers and Branches in Separation of Powers Law, University of Pennsylvania Law Review 150:603 (2001).

100. See Jerry Mashaw, Agency Statutory Interpretation, Issues in Legal Scholarship, Dynamic Statutory Interpretation (2002): Article 9, at http://www/bepress.com/ils/iss3/art9; Edward Rubin, Dynamic Statutory Interpretation in the Administrative State, Issues in Legal Scholarship, Dynamic Statutory Interpretation (2002): Article 2, http://www.bepress.com/ils/iss3/art2. The legislature is generally not bound by a preexisting statute in enacting a new one, but if the subject matter of two statutes overlaps, drafters of the new statute will be well advised to interpret the existing one.

101. Jerry Mashaw, Bureaucratic Justice: Managing Social Security Disability Claims (New Haven, Conn.: Yale University Press, 1983).

102. Malcolm Feeley and Edward Rubin, Judicial Policy Making and the Modern State: How the Courts Reformed America's Prisons (Cambridge: Cambridge University Press, 1998).

103. See Standard Oil Co. v. United States, 221 U.S. 1 (1911); Board of Trade v. United States, 246 U.S. 231 (1918); ABA Antitrust Section, The Rule of Reason, Monograph 23 (Chicago: American Bar Association, 1999); Richard Posner, Antitrust Law, 2d ed. (Chicago: University of Chicago Press, 2001), at 33–43.

104. In the federal system, this review is authorized by the Administrative Pro-

cedure Act, 5 U.S.C. §§ 701, 706, and by the substantive statute authorizing agency action.

105. 467 U.S. 837 (1984). On the importance of *Chevron*, see Cass Sunstein, Law and Administration After Chevron, Columbia Law Review 90:2071 (1990).

106. See Motor Vehicle Manufacturers Assoc. v. State Farm Automobile Ins. Corp., 463 U.S. 29 (1983); Greater Boston Television Corp. v. FCC, 444 F.2d 841 (D.C. Cir. 1970), cert. denied, 403 U.S. 923 (1971); Stephen Breyer, Judicial Review of Questions of Law and Policy, Administrative Law Review 38:363 (1986); Christopher Edley, Administrative Law: Rethinking Judicial Control of Bureaucracy (New Haven, Conn.: Yale University Press, 1990), at 96–130; Merrick Garland, Deregulation and Judicial Review, Harvard Law Review 98:505 (1985); R. Shep Melnick, Administrative Law and Bureaucratic Reality, Administrative Law Review 44:245 (1992); Sidney Shapiro and Richard Levy, Heightened Scrutiny of the Fourth Branch: Separation of Powers and the Requirement of Adequate Reasons for Agency Decisions, Duke Law Journal 1987:387 (1987).

107. See notes 33 and 81, citing sources.

108. For a more extensive discussion of this approach, see Edward Rubin, Independence as a Governance Mechanism, in Stephen Burbank and Barry Friedman, eds., Judicial Independence at the Crossroads (Thousand Oaks, Calif.: Sage, 2002), at 56.

109. See Gibson v. Berryhill, 411 U.S. 564 (1973); Ward v. Village of Monroeville, 409 U.S. 57 (1972); Tumey v. Ohio, 273 U.S. 510 (1927); Henry Friendly, "Some Kind of a Hearing," University of Pennsylvania Law Review 123:1267 (1975); Martin Redish and Lawrence Marshall, Adjudicatory Independence and the Value the Value of Procedural Due Process, 95:455 (1986); Paul Verkuil, The Purposes and Limits of Independent Agencies, Duke Law Journal 1988:257 (1988) (recommending that independence be used only as a means of shielding the adjudicatory process from elected officials).

110. Alberto Alesina and Roberta Gatti, Independent Central Banks: Low Inflation at No Cost?, American Economic Review 85:196 (1995); Ali al-Nowaihi and Paul Levine, Central Bank Independence: Gain without Pain?, in Nigel Healey and Zenon Wisniewski, Central Banking in Transition Economies (Torun, Poland: Torun Business School, 1999), at 55; Alex Cukierman, Central Bank Strategy, Credibility, and Independence (Cambridge, Mass.: MIT Press, 1992); Stanley Fischer, Modern Central Banking, in Forrest Capie, Stanley Fischer, Charles Goodhart, and Norbert Schnadt, eds., The Future of Central Banking (New York: Cambridge University Press, 1994), at 262; Susanne Lohmann, Optimal Commitment in Monetary Policy: Credibility versus Flexibility, American Economic Review 82:273 (1992); Geoffrey Miller, An Interest Group Theory of Central Bank Independence, Journal of Legal Studies 27:433 (1998); Kenneth Rogoff, The Optimal Degree of Commitment to an Intermediate Monetary Target, Quarterly Journal of Economics 100:1169 (1985); Carl Walsh, Optimal Contracts for Central Bankers, American Economic Review 81:150 (1995).

111. See Stephen Burbank, The Rules Enabling Act of 1934, University of Pennsylvania Law Review 130:1015 (1982); Jack Friedenthal, The Rulemaking Power of the Supreme Court: A Contemporary Crisis, Stanford Law Review 27:673 (1975); Howard Lesnick, The Federal Rule-Making Process: A Time for

Re-Examination, American Bar Association Journal 61:579 (1975); Catherine Struve, The Paradox of Delegation: Interpreting the Federal Rules of Civil Procedure, University of Pennsylvania Law Review 150:1099 (2002).

112. Strauss, supra note 43.

113. See Cooter, supra note 95, at 195–96.

114. For example, the election of state judges in the United States works poorly. See Phyllis Beck, Foreword: A Blueprint for Judicial Reform in Pennsylvania, Temple Law Review 62:693 (1989); Daniel Pinello, The Impact of Judicial-Selection Method on State Supreme Court Policy (Westport, Conn.: Greenwood Press, 1995); Stephen Croley, The Majoritarian Difficulty: Elective Judiciaries and the Rule of Law, University of Chicago Law Review 62:689 (1995).

115. Supposedly independent judges can be controlled by a legislature that determines the institutional budget of the courts, such as their budget for staff and building construction, even if it does not determine the salaries of particular judges. See Feeley and Rubin, supra note 102, at 111–28.

116. See Harold Bruff, On the Constitutional Status of the Administrative Agencies, American University Law Review 36:491 (1987).

117. See, e.g., McCubbins and Schwartz, supra note 89; McNollgast [Matthew McCubbins, Roger Noll, & Barry Weingast], Structure and Process, Politics and Policy: Administrative Arrangements and the Political Control of Agencies, Virginia Law Review 75:431 (1989); McNollgast, Administrative Procedures as Instruments of Policy Control, Journal of Law, Economics and Organizations 3:243 (1987); Barry Weingast and Mark Moran, The Myth of the Runaway Bureaucracy, Regulation May/June, 1982:33; Barry Weingast and Mark Moran, Bureaucratic Discretion or Congressional Control? Regulatory Policymaking by the Federal Trade Commission, Journal of Political Economy 91:775 (1983).

118. See Thomas Sargentich, The Contemporary Debate about Legislative-Executive Separation of Powers, Cornell Law Review 72:430 (1987), which points out that basic value choices lie behind the separation of powers debate.

119. Schoenbrod, supra note 85; David Schoenbrod, Goals Statutes or Rules Statutes: The Case of the Clean Air Act, UCLA Law Review 30:740 (1983).

120. Robert Katzmann Institutional Disability: The Saga of Transportation Policy for the Disabled (Washington, D.C.: Brookings, 1986); R. Shep Melnick, Regulation and the Courts: The Case of the Clean Air Act (Washington, D.C.: Brookings Institution, 1983); Thomas McGarity, Some Thoughts on "Deossifying" the Rulemaking Process, Duke Law Journal 41:1385 (1992); see also Richard Pierce, Two Problems in Administrative Law: Political Polarity on the District of Columbia Circuit and Judicial Deterrence of Agency Rulemaking, Duke Law Journal 1988:300 (1988); Patricia Wald, Regulation at Risk: Are Courts Part of the Solution or Most of the Problem?, Southern California Law Review 67:621 (1994).

121. James Q. Wilson, Bureaucracy: What Government Agencies Do and Why They Do It (New York: Basic Books, 1989), at 158–71. The other two types of agencies, according to Wilson, are those where both the procedures and the outcomes are observable, such as the IRS, and those where neither is observable, such as a public school.

122. Ralph Bryant, Controlling Money: The Federal Reserve and Its Critics

(Washington, D.C.: Brookings Institution, 1983); William Greider, Secrets of the Temple (New York: Simon & Schuster, 1987), at 450–94; Miller, supra note 110.

123. David Jones, The Politics of Money: The Fed Under Alan Greenspan (New York: New York Institute of Finance, 1991), at 16–22. In 1990, eight of the eleven members of the Federal Open Market Committee (there was one vacancy at the time) had a Ph.D. in economics, and another had an MBA.

124. Administrative Procedure Act, 5 U.S.C. 557(d)(1), see id. § (A) ("no interested person outside the agency shall make or knowingly cause to be made to any member of the body comprising the agency . . . an ex parte contact"); Professional Air Traffic Controllers Org (PATCO) v. FLRA, 685 F.2d 547 (D.C. Cir. 1982); Raz Inland Navigation Co. v. ICC, 625 F.2d 258 (9th Cir. 1980); Marathon Oil v. EPA, 564 F.2d 1253 (9th Cir. 1977). For restrictions on inputs from other government officials, see Portland Audubon Society v. Endangered Species Committee, 984 F.2d 1534 (9th Cir. 1993) (restriction on communication from President and White House staff); PATCO, supra (restriction on communication from Secretary of Transportation); Sokaogon Chippewa Community v. Babbit, 961 F. Supp. 1276 (W.D. Wis. 1997) (restriction on communication from members of Congress). See Alan Morrison, Presidential Intervention in Informal Rulemaking: Striking the Proper Balance, Tulane Law Review 56:879 (1983); Paul Verkuil, Jawboning Administrative Agencies: Ex Parte Contacts by the White House, Columbia Law Review 80:943 (1980).

125. Sierra Club v. Costle, 657 F.2d 298 (D.C. Cir. 1981); United Steelworkers of America v. Marshall, 647 F.2d 1189, cert. denied, 453 U.S. 913 (1981); Action for Children's Television (ACT) v. FCC, 564 F.2d 458 (D.C. Cir. 1977). See Gary Becker, A Theory of Competition among Pressure Groups for Political Influence, Quarterly Journal of Economics 98:371 (1983); Richard Stewart, The Reformation of American Administrative Law, Harvard Law Review 88:1669 (1975); Verkuil, supra note 124. But see D.C. Federation of Civic Assns v. Volpe, 459 F.2d 1231, 1245 (D.C. Cir. 1971), cert. denied, 405 U.S.1030 (1972) (improper influence by member of Congress).

126. Aranson, Gellhorn, and Robinson, supra note 92; Redish, supra note 85; Schoenbrod, supra note 85.

127. For examples of learning processes by agencies, see Richard Harris, Coal Firms under New Social Regulation (Durham, N.C.: Duke University Press, 1985); Jeremy Rabkin, Office for Civil Rights, in James Q. Wilson, The Politics of Regulation (New York: Basic Books, 1980), at 304.

128. Michael Dorf, Legal Indeterminacy and Institutional Design, New York University Law Review 78:875 (2003); Susan Sturm, Second Generation Employment Discrimination: A Structural Approach, Columbia Law Review 101:458 (2001); Cass Sunstein, The Supreme Court 1995 Term: Foreword: Leaving Things Undecided, Harvard Law Review 110:4 (1996).

129. See William Bechtel and Adele Abrahamsen, Connectionism and the Mind: An Introduction to Parallel Processing in Networks (Oxford: Blackwell, 1991), at 66–105; Churchland and Sejnowski, supra note 51, at 96–107; Teuvo Kohonen, Self-Organization and Associative Memory (Berlin: Springer-Verlag, 1984); David Rumelhart, James McClelland, and the PDP Research Group, Par-

allel Distributed Processing: Explorations in the Microstructure of Cognition (Cambridge, Mass.: MIT Press, 1986).

130. Bressman, supra note 93.

131. Ashutosh Bhagwat, Modes of Regulatory Enforcement and the Problem of Administrative Discretion, Hastings Law Journal 50:1275 (1999). Bhagwat's discussion focuses on the way administrative agencies supervise private parties, but executive, legislative, or judicial supervision of agencies follows a similar pattern.

132. McCubbins and Schwartz, supra note 89.

133. 462 U.S. 919 (1983).

134. The Court asserted that the Framers, by specifying these overlaps, had intended to prohibit any others (just as someone who says that she loves strawberry ice cream obviously means that she dislikes chocolate). For criticisms of the decision's formalism, see E. Donald Elliott, *INS v. Chadha*: The Administrative Constitution, the Constitution and the Legislative Veto, Supreme Court Review 1983:125 (1983); Peter Strauss, Was There a Baby in the Bathwater? A Comment on the Supreme Court's Legislative Veto Decision, Duke Law Journal 1983:789 (1983).

135. See Louis Fischer, Constitutional Dialogues: Interpretation as Political Process (Princeton: Princeton University Press, 1988), at 224–29.

136. The legislation requires each agency to submit the text of the rule, a cost-benefit analysis, and various other materials to Congress, and then wait sixty days, before implementing the rule. In addition, it authorizes Congress to disapprove the rule by joint resolution (which, in accordance with *Chadha*, must be signed by the president). Contract with America Advancement Act of 1996, Pub. L. No. 104–21, 110 Stat. 847, codified in part at 5 U.S.C. §§ 801–8.

137. Abraham Chayes, The Role of the Judge in Public Law Litigation, Harvard Law Review 89:1281 (1976); Colin Diver, The Judge as Political Pawnbroker: Superintending Structural Change in Public Institutions, Virginia Law Review 65:43 (1979); Owen Fiss, Foreword: The Forms of Justice, Harvard Law Review 93:1 (1979); William Fletcher, The Discretionary Constitution: Institutional Remedies and Judicial Legitimacy Yale Law Journal 91:635 (1982); Susan Sturm, A Normative Theory of Public Law Remedies, Georgetown Law Journal 79:1355 (1991).

138. See Bradley Chilton, Prisons Under the Gavel: The Federal Court Takeover of Georgia Prisons (Columbus: Ohio State University Press, 1991); Ben Crouch and James Marquart, An Appeal to Justice: Litigated Reform of Texas Prisons (Austin: University of Texas Press, 1989); Feeley and Rubin, supra note 102, at 27–143; Steve Martin and Sheldon Ekland-Olson, Texas Prisons: The Walls Came Tumbling Down (Austin: Texas Monthly Press, 1987); Ira Robbins and Michael Buser, Punitive Conditions of Prison Confinement: An Analysis of Pugh v. Locke and Federal Court Supervision of State Penal Administration under the Eighth Amendment, Stanford Law Review 29:893 (1977); Larry Yackle, Reform and Regret: The Story of Federal Judicial Involvement in the Alabama Prison System (New York: Oxford University Press, 1989).

139. Cooter, supra note 95, at 79–99.

140. For descriptions of this process, see Melvin Eisenberg, The Nature of the Common Law (Cambridge, Mass.: Harvard University Press, 1988), at 50–103;

Feeley and Rubin, supra note 102, at 204–52; Duncan Kennedy, A Critique of Adjudication: Fin de Siècle (Cambridge, Mass.: Harvard University Press, 1997), at 23–39; Joseph Raz, The Authority of Law: Essays on Law and Morality (Oxford: Clarendon Press, 1979), at 183–89; Martin Shapiro, Courts: A Comparative and Political Analysis (Chicago: University of Chicago Press, 1981), at 1–64; Cass Sunstein, Legal Reasoning and Political Conflict (New York: Oxford University Press, 1996), at 62–101.

141. See note 22, supra.

Notes to Chapter Three

1. Thomas Malory, Le Morte D'Arthur (R. M. Lumiansky, ed.) (New York: Collier Books, 1982), at 8; see id. at 11–12.

2. The term, and possibly the concept of power, can be traced to ancient Rome, at least. Whatever its origins, however, the Western world developed a largely distinctive concept of power. See Terrence Ball, Transforming Political Discourse: Political Theory and Critical Conceptual History (Oxford: Basil Blackwell, 1988), at 81.

3. See Matthew 16:19. Based on this text, the power of the keys was described as the power of binding and loosing.

4. Stanley Chodorow, Christian Political Theory and Church Politics in the Mid-Twelfth Century (Berkeley: University of California Press, 1972), at 154–64.

5. Malory, supra note 1, at 13, 129–30, 735–37.

6. Bertrand de Jouvenel, On Power (J. F. Huntington, trans.) (New York: Viking, 1949), at 63–91; James George Frazer, The Golden Bough (New York: Macmillan, 1963), at 96–105, 122–26, 169–84, 308–30; Henry Myers, Medieval Kingship (Chicago: Nelson-Hall, 1982), at 1–14.

7. Independence Day (Roland Emmerich, director) (Twentieth-Century Fox, 1996).

8. Air Force One (Wolfgang Petersen, director) Beacon/Columbia, 1997).

9. Ernst Kantorowicz, The King's Two Bodies (Princeton: Princeton University Press, 1957), at 194–206.

10. See Otto Gierke, Political Theories of the Middle Age (Frederic Maitland, trans.) (Cambridge: Cambridge University Press, 1938); Kantorowicz, supra note 9.

11. This was the divine right of kings theory. See Reinhard Bendix, Kings or People: Power and the Mandate to Rule (Berkeley: University of California Press, 1978), at 21–40; Antony Black, Political Thought in Europe 1250–1450 (Cambridge: Cambridge University Press, 1992), at 137–39; Joseph Canning, A History of Medieval Political Thought 300–1450 (London: Routledge, 1996), at 47–59, 93–95; Heinrich Fichtenau, Living in the Tenth Century (Patrick Geary, trans.) (Chicago: University of Chicago Press, 1991), at 161–64; Gierke, supra note 10, at 30–37; Kantorowicz, supra note 9; Fritz Kern, Kingship and Law in the Middle Ages (S. B. Chrimes, trans.) (Oxford: Blackwell, 1939); J. A. Watt, Spiritual and Temporal Powers, in J. H. Burns, ed., Cambridge History of Medieval Political Thought (Cambridge: Cambridge University Press, 1988), at 367.

As Kantorowicz describes, the same corporatist conception was applied to other entities, such as towns, trading organizations, and business firms, but in an even more secularized manner. Kantorowicz, supra note 9, at 291–314.

12. For a comprehensive discussion of the concept of power in Western political thought, see Ball, supra note 2, at 80–105.

13. Steven Winter, The "Power" Thing, Virginia Law Review 82:721 (1996).

14. Thomas Hobbes, Leviathan (C. B. Macpherson, ed.) (Harmondsworth: Penguin, 1981), at 150–51 (I, 10). Hobbes says: "Naturall Power, is the eminence of the Faculties of Body, or Mind: as extraordinary Strength, Fortune. . . . Instrumentall are those Powers, which acquired by these, or by fortune, are means and Instruments to acquire more."

15. Talcott Parsons, Power and the Social System, in Steven Lukes, Power (New York: New York University Press, 1986), at 94. For an incisive critique, see Jürgen Habermas, The Theory of Communicative Action, vol. 2: Lifeworld and System: A Critique of Functionalist Reason (Thomas McCarthy, trans.) (Boston: Beacon Press, 1987), at 267–77.

16. Max Weber, Economy and Society (Guenther Roth & Claus Wittich, eds.) (Berkeley: University of California Press, 1978), at 53.

17. Michael Mann, The Sources of Social Power (Cambridge: Cambridge University Press, 1986), vol. 1 at 6. Mann labels the type of power identified by his Weberian definition as authoritative. He contrasts this with diffused power that "spreads in a more spontaneous, unconscious, decentered way throughout a population." Id. at 8.

18. Bertrand Russell, Power (London: Routledge, 1960), at 25.

19. Robert Dahl, The Concept of Power, Behavioral Science 2:201–15 (1957), reprinted in Roderick Bell, David Edwards, and R. Harrison Wagner, Political Power: A Reader in Theory and Research (New York: Free Press, 1969), at 79, 80.

20. Michael Oakeshott, Talking Politics, in Michael Oakeshott, Rationalism in Politics and Other Essays (Indianapolis: Liberty Fund, 1991), at 438, 445.

21. Peter Blau, Exchange and Power in Social Life (New York: John Wiley, 1964), at 117. For critiques of Blau's theory, see Pierre Birnbaum, Power Divorced from Its Sources: A Critique of the Exchange Theory of Power, in Brian Barry, ed., Power and Political Theory (New York: John Wiley, 1976), at 15; Jack Lively, The Limits of Exchange Theory, in Barry, supra, at 1.

22. Wesley Hohfeld, Fundamental Legal Conceptions (Walter Cook, ed.) (New Haven, Conn.: Yale University Press, 1919), at 50–60. Hohfeld's theory is discussed at length in Chapter 7. As that chapter suggests, he was thinking largely in terms of matters that could be argued to a court of law. Thus, while some of the following discussion is not directly relevant to Hohfeld, the reason is that power, in his theory, is even less like a medieval monarch's command, and more clearly authorized action subject to constraint.

23. Carl Friedrich, Man and His Government (New York: McGraw-Hill, 1963), at 17–19.

24. This implicit categorization is itself medieval. A standard medieval interpretation of the Trinity is that it consisted of He who gives love (God, the Father), He who receives love (Jesus, His Son), and the bond of love that passes between them (the Holy Spirit).

25. See Jeremy Waldron, The Dignity of Legislation (Cambridge: Cambridge University Press, 1999), at 25–27.

26. Adolph Berle, Power (New York: Harcourt, Brace & World, 1969), at 59–83.

27. See de Jouvenel, supra note 6.

28. Thomas McGarity, Presidential Control of Regulatory Agency Decision-making, American University Law Review 36:443 (1987); Nelson Polsby, Congress and the Presidency, 4th ed. (Englewood Cliffs, N.J.: Prentice-Hall, 1986), at 73–78; Glen Robinson, Independent Agencies: Form and Substance in Executive Prerogative, Duke Law Journal 1988:238 (1988); Edward Rubin, Independence as a Governance Mechanism, in Stephen Burbank and Barry Friedman, eds., Judicial Independence at the Crossroads (Thousand Oaks, Calif.: Sage, 2002), at 56.

29. See Dennis Wrong, Power: Its Forms, Bases and Uses (New York: Harper & Row, 1979), at 93–99.

30. Ch. 6, 38 Stat. 251 (Dec. 23, 1913), codified as amended at 12 U.S.C. §§ 221 et seq.

31. Pub. L. No. 90–321, 82 Stat. 146 (1968), codified as amended at 15 U.S.C. §§ 1600–1613, 1631–1641, 1671–1677. The provision that assigned rule-making power to the Fed is § 105, 15 U.S.C. § 1604. See Edward Rubin, Legislative Methodology: Some Lessons from the Truth-in-Lending Act, Georgetown Law Journal 80:233–307 (1991), at 243.

32. Mann, supra note 17, at 18–28; Parsons, supra note 15, at 125–37.

33. Steven Lukes, Power: A Radical View (London: Macmillan, 1974).

34. See Peter Bachrach and Morton Baratz, The Two Faces of Power, American Political Science Review 56:947 (1962); Peter Bachrach and Morton S. Baratz, Power and Poverty: Theory and Practice (New York: Oxford University Press, 1970); Jean Elshtain, Power Trips and Other Journeys: Essays in Feminism and Civic Discourse (Madison: University of Wisconsin Press, 1990), at 136–38.

35. Michel Foucault, The Birth of the Clinic: An Archaeology of Medical Perception (A. M. Sheridan Smith, trans.) (New York: Pantheon, 1973); Michel Foucault, Discipline and Punish: The Birth of the Prison (Alan Sheridan, trans.) (New York: Vintage, 1979); Michel Foucault, The History of Sexuality (Robert Hurley, trans.) (New York: Vintage, 1980); Michel Foucault, Power/Knowledge (Colin Gordon, ed.) (Colin Gordon, Leo Marshall, John Mepham, Kate Soper, trans.) (New York: Pantheon Books, 1980), at 146–65. In an alternative but related image, Foucault states that power is "a machine in which everyone is caught, those who exercise power just as much as those over whom it is exercised." Id. at 156.

36. For an explication and defense of Foucault's view, see Winter, supra note 13.

37. Anthony Giddens, New Rules of Sociological Method: A Positive Critique of Interpretive Sociologies (London: Hutchinson, 1976), at 111. See also Anthony Giddens, The Constitution of Society (Berkeley: University of California Press, 1984). What is said in connection with Giddens could also apply to Stewart Clegg, Frameworks of Power (London: Sage, 1989).

38. Giddens, New Rules, supra note 37, at 111 (italics omitted).

39. The same critique can be applied to Hannah Arendt's idea that power is an agreement to engage in coordinated action; see Communicative Power, in Lukes,

supra note 15, at 59. While her point that violence is not the equivalent of power is well taken, her alternative view makes almost everyone a power holder.

40. See Alan Hunt, Explorations in Law and Society: Toward a Constitutive Theory of Law (New York: Routledge, 1993), at 267–301; Wrong, supra note 29.

41. Wrong, supra note 29, at 4. For other critiques, see Clegg, supra note 37, at 74, and Winter, supra note 13, at 778–80. Winter argues convincingly that authoritative governmental actors frequently experience a feeling of constraint or compulsion arising from role expectations, id. at 819–32. But if one fails to make a conceptual incision between this feeling and the structure of government, one will be unable to distinguish governmental action from the general flow of social relations.

42. See Judith Butler, Gender Trouble: Feminism and the Subversion of Identity (New York: Routledge, 1990); Judith Butler, The Psychic Life of Power: Theories in Subjection (Stanford, Calif.: Stanford University Press, 1997); Kathy Davis, Power under the Microscope: Toward a Grounded Theory of Gender Relations in Medical Encounters (Dordrecht: Foris Publications, 1988); Kathy Davis, Monique Leijenaar, and Jantine Oldersma, The Gender of Power (London: Sage, 1991); Maxine Sheets-Johnstone, The Roots of Power: Animate Form and Gendered Bodies (Chicago: Open Court, 1994).

43. Catherine MacKinnon, Toward a Feminist Theory of the State (Cambridge, Mass.: Harvard University Press, 1989); Robin West, Jurisprudence and Gender, University of Chicago Law Review 55:1 (1988); Joan Williams, Deconstructing Gender, Michigan Law Review 87:797 (1989).

44. It overinterprets the concept of a woman, for example. See Katherine Bartlett, MacKinnon's Feminism: Power on Whose Terms?, California Law Review 75:1559 (1987); Angela Harris, Race and Essentialism in Feminist Legal Theory, Stanford Law Review 42:581 (1990).

45. See Denis Galligan, Discretionary Powers: A Legal Study of Official Discretion (Oxford: Clarendon Press, 1986), which defines discretion in terms of power.

46. Christopher Edley, Administrative Law: Rethinking Judicial Control of Bureaucracy (New Haven, Conn.: Yale University Press, 1990), at 6; Theodore Lowi, The End of Liberalism: The Second Republic of the United States, 2nd ed. (New York: W. W. Norton, 1979); Timothy Wilkins and Terrell Hunt, Agency Discretion and Advances in Regulatory Theory: Flexible Agency Approaches Toward the Regulated Community as a Model for the Congress-Agency Relationship, George Washington Law Review 63:479 (1995), 479–81.

47. Kenneth Davis, Discretionary Justice: A Preliminary Inquiry (Baton Rouge: Louisiana State University Press, 1969).

48. Galligan, supra note 45, at 21.

49. Henry Hart and Albert Sacks, The Legal Process: Basic Problems in the Making and Application of Law (William Eskridge & Philip Frickey, eds.) (New York: Foundation, 1994), at 144.

50. Carl Friedrich, Authority, Reason and Discretion, in Richard Flathman, ed., Concepts in Social and Political Philosophy (New York: Macmillan, 1973), at 167.

51. Ronald Dworkin, Taking Rights Seriously (Cambridge, Mass.: Harvard University Press, 1978). On the similarity between Dworkin's approach and the

legal process approach of Hart and Sacks, see Vincent Wellman, Dworkin and the Legal Process Tradition: The Legacy of Hart and Sacks, Arizona Law Review 29:413 (1987).

52. Dworkin, supra note 51, at 31.

53. Id. at 32.

54. Id. at 31.

55. Id. at 32.

56. In addition, design decisions that are made for independent reasons may affect the type and intensity of regulation. As Ashutosh Bhagwat points out, the choice of comprehensive regulation, as opposed to regulation that prosecutes particular violations of a legislative rule, will restrict the ability of courts and agency superiors to supervise the officials who implement the regulation. Modes of Regulatory Enforcement and the Problem of Administrative Discretion, Hastings Law Journal 50:1275 (1999).

57. Keith Hawkins, On Legal Decision-Making, Washington & Lee Law Review 42:1161 (1986).

58. M. P. Baumgartner, The Myth of Discretion, in Keith Hawkins, ed., The Uses of Discretion (Oxford: Clarendon Press, 1992), at 129; Martha Feldman, Social Limits to Discretion: An Organizational Perspective, in id. at 163.

59. Martin Shapiro, Who Guards the Guardians? (Athens: University of Georgia Press, 1988).

60. For descriptions of this method, see John Friedmann, Planning in the Public Domain: From Knowledge to Action (Princeton, N.J.: Princeton University Press, 1987), at 137–79; Stuart Nagel, Policy Evaluation: Making Optimum Decisions (Brooklyn: Praeger, 1982); Carl Patton and David Sawicki, The Policy Analysis Process: Basic Methods of Policy Analysis and Planning, 2d ed. (Englewood Cliffs, N.J.: Prentice-Hall, 1993); Edward Quade, Analysis for Public Decisions (New York: American Elsevier, 1975); Edith Stokes and Richard Zeckhauser, A Primer for Policy Analysis (New York: W. W. Norton, 1978), at 5–6.

61. Matthew Adler and Eric Posner, Cost-Benefit Analysis (Chicago: University of Chicago Press, 2001); See Edward Mishan, Cost-Benefit Analysis: An Introduction (New York: Praeger, 1976).

62. Charles Lindblom, The Science of "Muddling Through," Public Administration Review 19:79 (1959); David Braybrooke and Charles Lindblom, A Strategy of Decision: Policy Evaluation as a Social Process (New York: Free Press, 1970).

63. Kent Greenawalt, Discretion and Judicial Discretion: The Elusive Quest for the Fetters That Bind Judges, Columbia Law Review 75:359 (1975).

64. Melvin Belli, The Story of Pardons, Case and Comment 80(3): 38 (1975); George Killinger, Hazel Kerper, and Paul Cromwell, Probation and Parole in the Criminal Justice System (St. Paul, Minn.: West Publishing, 1976), at 315.

65. Killinger, Kerper, and Cromwell, supra note 64, at 318–19; Samuel Stafford, Clemency: Legal Authority, Procedure, Structure (Williamsburg, Va.: National Center for State Courts, 1977). See Connecticut Board of Pardons v. Dumschat, 452 U.S. 458 (1981), which challenged an action by the Connecticut Board of Pardons, an administrative agency, functioning essentially as a parole board. The Court, somewhat confused by the historical association of the term 'pardon' and

sovereign executive power, held that the process was entirely discretionary, and thus not subject to due process requirements.

66. Pardon of Richard M. Nixon, and Related Matters: Hearings before the Subcommittee on Criminal Justice of the Committee on the Judiciary, House of Representatives, 93d Cong., 2d Sess. (September 24, October 1 and 17, 1974); The Controversial Pardon of International Fugitive Marc Rich: Hearings before the Committee on Government Reform, House of Representatives, 107th Cong., 1st Sess. (February 8 and March 1, 2001); President Clinton's Eleventh-Hour Pardons: Hearing before the Committee on the Judiciary, United States Senate, 107th Cong., 1st Sess. (February 14, 2001).

67. Regina Austin, Sapphire Bound!, Wisconsin Law Review 1989:539 (1989); Cynthia Farina, Conceiving Due Process, Yale Journal of Law & Feminism, 3:189 (1991); Joel Handler, The Conditions of Discretion: Autonomy, Community, Bureaucracy (New York: Russell Sage Foundation, 1986); Michael Lipsky, Street-Level Bureaucracy: Dilemmas of the Individual in Public Services (New York: Russell Sage Foundation, 1980), at 81–156; Roberto Unger, False Necessity: Anti-Necessitarian Social Theory in the Service of Radical Democracy (Cambridge: Cambridge University Press, 1987); Lucie White, Subordination, Rhetorical Survival Skills and Sunday Shoes: Some Notes on the Hearing of Mrs. G., Buffalo Law Review 38:1 (1990).

68. Handler, supra note 67, at 301.

69. Peter Aranson, Ernest Gellhorn, and Glenn Robinson, A Theory of Legislative Delegation, Cornell Law Review 68:1 (1982); Davis, supra note 47; F. A. Hayek, The Road to Serfdom (Chicago: University of Chicago Press, 1994), at 63–96; Lowi, supra note 46, at 92–126; David Schoenbrod, Power without Responsibility: How Congress Abuses the People through Delegation (New Haven, Conn.: Yale University Press, 1993).

70. See Jean-Luc Migue and Gerard Belanger, Toward a General Theory of Managerial Discretion, Public Choice 17:27 (1974); Paul Wycoff, The Simple Analytics of Slack-Maximizing Bureaucracy, Public Choice 67:35 (1990).

71. Weber, Economy and Society, supra note 16, at 956–1003.

72. Max Weber, The Protestant Ethic and the Spirit of Capitalism (Talcott Parsons, trans.) (New York: Charles Scribner's Sons, 1958), at 181–82.

73. Max Weber, Bureaucracy and Political Leadership, in Weber, Economy and Society, supra note 16, at 1393; discussion of escape-proof nature of bureaucracy at 1401–02.

74. A thoughtful exploration of these issues can be found in a series of articles by Joel Handler. See Joel Handler, Reforming Welfare: The Constraints of the Bureaucracy and the Clients, University of Pennsylvania Law Review 118:1167 (1970); Joel Handler, Dependent People, the State, and the Modern/Postmodern Search for the Dialogic Community, UCLA Law Review 35:999 (1988); Joel Handler, Continuing Relationships and the Administrative Process: Social Welfare, Wisconsin Law Review 1985:687 (1985); Joel Handler, Community Care for the Frail Elderly: A Theory of Empowerment, Ohio State Law Journal 50:541 (1989).

75. Clegg, supra note 37; Foucault, Discipline, supra note 35; Foucault, History, supra note 35.

76. Hans Kelsen, The Pure Theory of Law (M. Knight, trans.) (Berkeley: Uni-

versity of California Press, 1967), at 125–45. Kelsen uses the term for a somewhat different purpose, namely, the authorization of individuals to take legal actions such as making contracts or wills.

77. Myers, supra note 6, at 56.

78. Hannah Arendt, What Is Authority?, in Hannah Arendt, Between Past and Future (New York: Penguin, 1961); Ball, supra note 2, at 106–11; Richard Tuck, Why Is Authority Such a Problem?, in Peter Laslett, W.G. Runicman, and Quentin Skinner, Philosophy, Politics, and Society (fourth series) (New York: Barnes & Noble, 1972), at 194.

79. See Oakeshott, supra note 20, at 441–45. Oakeshott defines authority as an "antecedent right to prescribe," id. at 442, and states that power is "categorically distinguished from authority," id. at 445.

80. Arendt, What Is Authority, supra note 78, at 93; H.L.A. Hart, The Concept of Law (Oxford: Clarendon Press, 1961), at 18–25; Joseph Raz, Authority and Justification, in Joseph Raz, ed., Authority (New York: New York University Press, 1990), at 115; Robert Paul Wolff, In Defense of Anarchism, rev. ed., (Berkeley: University of California Press, 1998).

81. Weber, Economy and Society, supra note 16, at 212–15.

82. David Easton, The Political System (Chicago: University of Chicago Press, 1981), at 132.

83. Raz describes this as an exclusionary reason, that is, one that excludes other reasons in its demand for obedience. Joseph Raz, The Morality of Freedom (Oxford: Clarendon Press, 1986), at 23–69. See also David Easton, The Perception of Authority and Political Change, in Carl Friedrich, ed., Authority, Nomos I (Cambridge, Mass.: Harvard University Press, 1958), at 179.

84. Hannah Arendt, Communicative Power, in Lukes, supra note 15, at 59, quote at 65.

85. Ball, supra note 2, at 115–20; Richard DeGeorge, The Nature and Limits of Authority (Lawrence: University of Kansas Press, 1986); R. B. Friedman, On the Concept of Authority in Political Philosophy, in Flathman, supra note 50; H.L.A. Hart, Commands and Authoritative Legal Reasons, in Raz, supra Note 80, at 115; Raz, Introduction, in Raz, supra, at 1, 2; Wolff, supra note 80, at 6.

86. See Daniel Bell, The Coming of Post-Industrial Society (New York: Basic Books, 1976); Hans-Georg Gadamer, Truth and Method (New York: Crossroad, 1988), at 286–89; Friedrich, supra note 50; Heidi Hurd, Challenging Authority, Yale Law Journal 100:1611 (1991). For a critique, see Ball, supra note 2, at 115–21. As Ball suggests, the difficulty with these arguments is that they circumvent the democratic process (or, in the terms suggested here, the electoral and interactive process that makes government responsive to its citizens). Hurd partially avoids Ball's critique by relying on the wisdom of the democratic process to equate practical authority with theoretical authority. This, however, exaggerates the effect of the interactive process in the manner that was critiqued in Chapter 5. Hurd's argument might apply to ancient Athens, when the people themselves made the laws, but it seems unrealistic in an administrative state, where so many of the state's authoritative pronouncements come from agencies, or from the legislature's effort to control those agencies.

87. Jean Bodin, Six Books of the Commonwealth (M. J. Tooley, trans.) (New York: Macmillan, 1955).

88. Hans Kelsen, General Theory of Law and State (Anders Wedberg, trans.) (Cambridge, Mass.: Harvard University Press, 1945), at 252–65; Kelsen, Pure Theory, supra note 76, at 193–221.

89. Hart, supra note 80, at 26–96.

90. Melvin Eisenberg, The Concept of National Law and the Rule of Recognition, Florida State University Law Review 29:1229 (2002).

91. Foucault, Power/Knowledge, supra note 35, at 156; Giddens, New Rules, supra note 37, at 111; Mann, supra note 17, at 6–10; Weber, supra note 16, at 212–15. Russell describes the type of power that depends on force as "naked power," and treats it as an exception. Supra note 18, at 57–71.

92. Cornelius Kerwin, Rulemaking: How Government Agencies Write Law and Make Policy, 2d ed. (Washington, D.C.: CQ Press, 1999).

93. James Q. Wilson, Bureaucracy: What Government Agencies Do and Why They Do It (New York: Basic Books, 1989), at 179–95.

94. Christopher Deering and Steven Smith, Committees in Congress, 3d ed. (Washington, D.C.: CQ Press, 1997); Richard Fenno, Congressmen in Committees (Boston: Little, Brown, 1973); John Kingdon, Agendas, Alternatives, and Public Policies (Boston: Little, Brown, 1984).

95. This picture of the legislative process is well supported by studies of the way particular statutes were designed and enacted. See, e.g., Sheri David, With Dignity: The Search for Medicare and Medicaid (Westport, Conn.: Greenwood Press, 1985); Stephen Bailey, Congress Makes a Law: The Story Behind the Employment Act of 1946 (New York: Vintage, 1964); Eric Redman, The Dance of Legislation (New York: Simon & Schuster, 1973); Edward Rubin, Legislative Methodology: Some Lessons from the Truth in Lending Act, Georgetown Law Journal, 80:233 (1991).

96. See Philip Heymann, The Politics of Public Management (New Haven, Conn.: Yale University Press, 1987). David Welborn Governance of Federal Regulatory Agencies (Knoxville: University of Tennessee Press, 1977); David Welborn and Jesse Burkhead, Intergovernmental Relations in the American Administrative State: The Johnson Presidency (Austin: University of Texas Press, 1989).

97. See Graham Wilson, The Politics of Safety and Health: Occupational Safety and Health in the United States and Britain (Oxford: Clarendon Press, 1985); Heymann, supra note 96.

98. Peter Share, When Inter-Branch Norms Break Down: Of Arms–for–Hostages, "Orderly Shutdowns," Presidential Impeachments, and Judicial "Coups," Cornell Journal of Law and Public Policy 12:503 (2003).

99. See Burbank and Friedman, supra note 28; Stephen Burbank, The Architecture of Judicial Independence, Southern California Law Review 72:315 (1999); Edward Hartnett, Why Is the Supreme Court of the United States Protecting State Judges From Popular Democracy?, Texas Law Review 75:907 (1997); Peter Russell and David O'Brien, eds., Judicial Independence in the Age of Democracy: Critical Perspectives from Around the World (Charlottesville: University of Virginia Press, 2001).

100. Terry Moe, Congressional Control of the Bureaucracy: An Assessment of the Positive Theory of "Congressional Dominance," Legislative Studies Quarterly 12:475 (1987); Irwin Morris, Congress, the President and the Federal Reserve: The Politics of American Monetary Policy-Making (Ann Arbor: University of Michigan Press, 2000); Wilson, supra note 93, at 235–76; Dan Wood and Richard Waterman, Bureaucratic Dynamics: The Role of Bureaucracy in a Democracy (Boulder, Colo.: Westview, 1994).

101. This is the basis of the principal-agent model of Congress-agency relations. See Jonathan Bendor, Serge Taylor, and Roland Van Galen, Politicians, Bureaucrats and Asymmetric Information, American Political Science Review 80:1187 (1987); Randall Calvert, Mark Moran, and Barry Weingast, Congressional Influence over Policymaking: The Case of the FTC, in Matthew McCubbins and Terry Sullivan, eds., Congress: Structure and Policy (Cambridge: Cambridge University Press, 1987); Barry Weingast, The Congressional-Bureaucratic System: A Principal-Agent Perspective Public Choice 44:147 (1984).

102. Matthew McCubbins and Thomas Schwartz, Congressional Oversight Overlooked: Police Patrols versus Fire Alarms, American Journal of Political Science 28:165 (1984): Arthur Lupia and Matthew McCubbins, Learning from Oversight: Fire Alarms and Police Patrols Reconstructed, Journal of Law, Economics and Organization 10:96 (1994).

103. Harold Seidman and Robert Gilmour, Politics, Position and Power: From the Positive to the Regulatory State, 4th ed. (New York: Oxford University Press, 1980); Wilson, supra note 93, at 235–53.

104. Emmett Moore, The Environmental Impact Statement Process and Environmental Law (Columbus: Battelle Press, 1997); Serge Taylor, Making Bureaucracies Think (Stanford, Calif.: Stanford University Press, 1984).

105. See Robert Katzmann, Regulatory Bureaucracy: The Federal Trade Commission and Antitrust Policy (Cambridge, Mass.: MIT Press, 1980).

106. Lincoln Caplan, The Tenth Justice: The Solicitor General and the Rule of Law (New York: Knopf, 1987); David Strauss, The Solicitor General and the Interests of the United States, Law & Contemporary Problems 61:165 (1998); Neal Devins and Michael Herz, The Uneasy Case for Department of Justice Control of Federal Litigation, University of Pennsylvania Journal of Constitutional Law 5:558 (2003); Nicholas Zeppos, Department of Justice Litigation: Externalizing Costs and Searching for Subsidies, Law & Contemporary Problems 61:171 (1998).

107. See Wolff, supra note 80, at 3–12.

108. Although the term 'authorization' was borrowed from Kelsen, the problem that unauthorized acts by officials create for his pure theory of law—see Stanley Paulson, Material and Formal Authorisation in Kelsen's Pure Theory, Cambridge Law Journal, 39:172 (1980)—does not afflict the proposed alternative.

109. Weber, Economy and Society, supra note 16, at 266–71.

110. E.g., Philip Howard, The Death of Common Sense: How Law Is Suffocating America (New York: Warner Books, 1994).

111. See, e.g., Jameson Doig and Erwin Hargrove, Leadership and Innovation: A Biographical Perspective on Entrepreneurs in Government (Baltimore: Johns Hopkins University Press, 1987); Thomas McCraw, Prophets of Regulation (Cambridge, Mass.: Belknap Press, 1984).

112. Isaac Deutscher, Stalin: A Political Biography (New York: Vintage, 1960), at 231.

113. Id. at 228–34. See Sheila Fitzpatrick, The Russian Revolution, 2d ed. (Oxford: Oxford University Press, 1994), at 106–11.

114. Dworkin, supra note 51, at 31.

Notes to Chapter Four

1. It first appears in Herodotus. See Raphael Sealey, The Athenian Republic (University Park: Pennsylvania State University Press, 1987), at 98–102.

2. Aristotle's Politics (Benjamin Jowett, trans.) (Oxford: Clarendon Press, 1905).

3. R. R. Bolgar, The Classical Heritage and Its Beneficiaries (Cambridge: Cambridge University Press, 1954), at 508–11; Joseph Canning, A History of Medieval Thought, 300–1450 (London: Routledge, 1996), at 125–26.

4. Thomas Aquinas, On Kingship, in Political Writings of Thomas Aquinas (Dino Bigongiari, ed.) (New York: Free Press, 1997), at 175; Thomas Aquinas, Summa Theologica (Fathers of the English Dominican Province, trans.) (Westminster, Md.: Christian Classics, 1981), at (I–II, Q. 95, A.4); Marsilius of Padua, The Defensor Pacis (Alan Gewirth, trans.) (New York: Columbia University Press, 1951), vol. 2, at 27–28 (I.8).

5. Aristotle, supra note 2, at 115 (III. 7, 1279b).

6. Id. at 116 (III. 8, 1279b).

7. Id. at 239–40 (VI. 2, 1317b).

8. Id. at 166 (IV. 9, 1294b).

9. Id. at 114–15 (III. 7, 1279a-b). The Jowett translation uses the term "constitutional government." Other translations favor the English word "polity," e.g., The Politics of Aristotle (Ernest Barker, trans.) (New York: Oxford University Press, 1958); Aristotle, The Politics (T. A. Sinclair & Trevor Sauders, trans.) (London: Penguin, 1981). The word is left in transliterated form here to avoid confusion.

10. In fact, the Greeks used *politeia* the way we use polity. As Aristotle acknowledges, his usage of the term is his own neologism. Id.

11. Id. at 162–66 (IV. 8, 9).

12. Giovanni Sartori, Democratic Theory (Westport, Conn.: Greenwood Press, 1962), at 250–57.

13. Samuel von Pufendorf, On the Law of Nature and of Nations, in The Political Writings of Samuel Pufendorf (Cray Carr, ed., Michael Seidler, trans.) (New York: Oxford University Press, 1994), at 164 (III. 2.8); T. A. Sinclair, Translator's Introduction in Aristotle, The Politics, supra note 9, at 21–22; Roger Just, Women in Athenian Life and Law (London: Routledge, 1989), at 188–93; Raphael Sealey, Women and Law in Classical Greece (Chapel Hill: University of North Carolina Press, 1990), at 40–41.

14. Benjamin Constant, Political Writings (Biancamaria Fontana, trans.) (Cambridge: Cambridge University Press, 1988), at 313–28; Sartori, supra note 12, at 250–57. On Athenian democracy in general, see Aristotle, The Athenian Consti-

tution (P. J. Rhodes, trans.) (New York: Penguin, 1984); M. H. Hansen, The Athenian Democracy in the Age of Demosthenes (J. A. Cook, trans.) (Oxford: B. Blackwell Press, 1991); Sealey, supra note 1.

15. Maude Clarke, The Medieval City-State (New York: Barnes and Noble, 1966); Henri Pirenne, Early Democracies in the Low Countries: Urban Society and Political Conflict in the Middle Ages and the Renaissance (J. V. Saunders, trans.) (New York: Harper & Row, 1963); Daniel Waley, The Italian City-Republics (New York: McGraw-Hill, 1969); Quentin Skinner, The Italian City Republics, in John Dunn, ed., Democracy: The Unfinished Journey, 508 B.C. to A.D. 1993 (Oxford: Oxford University Press, 1992), at 57. In fact, citizenship in a Greek polis had a racial component; even free men were excluded if they could not demonstrate some ancestral link to the city. Cleisthenes may have relaxed this rule in Athens when he organized the ten tribes (demes) but it was subsequently re-asserted. See John Myres, The Political Ideas of the Greeks (New York: Green-wood Press, 1968), at 347-51.

16. Arthur Monahan, Consent, Coercion and Limit: The Medieval Origins of Parliamentary Democracy (Kingston, Ont.: McGill-Queen's University Press, 1987), at 97-133; Gaines Post, Studies in Medieval Legal Thought: Public Law and the State, 1100-1322 (Princeton: Princeton University Press, 1964), at 91-238; Gaines Post, A Roman Legal Theory of Consent, "quod omnes tangit," in Medieval Representation, Wisconsin Law Review 1950:66 (1950).

17. Thomas Ertman, Birth of Leviathan: Building States and Regimes in Medieval and Early Modern Europe (Cambridge: Cambridge University Press, 1997).

18. Jean-Jacques Rousseau, The Social Contract (Willmoore Kendall, trans.) (Chicago: Henry Regnery, 1954), at 140-53 (III. 12-15).

19. Aristotle, supra note 2, at 165-66 (IV. 9, 1294a-b). In discussing ways of mixing democratic and oligarchic institutions, Aristotle writes that "the appoint-ment of magistrates by lot is democratical, and the election of them oligarchical." Later on, he states that the Spartan constitution, which he takes to be an example of mixed government, has many oligarchical elements. That all offices are filled by election and none by lot is one of these oligarchical characteristics." See also his discussion of Plato's Laws, id. at 71 (II. 6, 1264b-1266a).

20. Marcus Tullius Cicero, The Republic, in the Republic and the Laws (Niall Rudd, trans.) (Oxford: Oxford University Press, 1998), at 19-33 (I. 39-69); Poly-bius, The Rise of the Roman Empire (Ian Scott-Kilvert, trans.) (London: Penguin, 1979), at 303-11 (VI. 3-10). See Neal Wood, Cicero's Social and Political Thought (Berkeley: University of California Press, 1988). Regarding "Tully's" in-fluence during the eighteenth century, see Peter Gay, The Enlightenment: An In-terpretation, vol. 1 (The Rise of Modern Paganism) (New York: W. W. Norton, 1966), at 105-9.

21. Raymond Williams, Keywords, rev. ed. (New York: Oxford University Press, 1983), at 93-99.

22. James Harrington, The Political Works of James Harrington (J.G.A. Pocock, ed.) (Cambridge: Cambridge University Press, 1977), at 161-64.

23. Baron Montesquieu (Charles Louis de Secondat), The Spirit of the Laws (Anne Cohler, Basia Miller, & Harold Stone, trans.) (Cambridge: Cambridge Uni-versity Press, 1989), at 10-15 (Bk. 2, Ch. 2).

24. Jennifer Roberts, Athens on Trial (Princeton: Princeton University Press, 1994), at 174–93; Gordon Wood, The Creation of the American Republic, 1776–1787 (New York: W. W. Norton, 1969), at 197–206, 574–80; Gordon Wood, Democracy and the American Revolution, in Dunn, supra note 15, at 91, 92–94.

25. Wood, Creation, supra note 24, at 222–35, 580–87.

26. Alexis de Tocqueville, Democracy in America (Henry Reeve, trans., Frances Bowen, Phillips Bradley, eds.) (New York: Vintage Books, 1945).

27. George Grote, A History of Greece from the Earliest Period to the Close of the Generation Contemporary with Alexander the Great (London: J. Murray, 1869–70).

28. Joint Association of Classical Teachers, The World of Athens: An Introduction to Classical Athenian Culture (Cambridge: Cambridge University Press, 1984), at 210–16; Donald Kagan, Pericles of Athens and the Birth of Athenian Democracy (New York: Simon & Schuster, 1991), at 54–56.

29. In fact, there was considerable discussion of the Spartan constitution at the time the U.S. Constitution was being drafted. Wood, Creation, supra note 24, at 64–65, 118, 232, 423–24. Wood quotes a contemporary newspaper as complaining: "While we are pleasing and amusing ourselves with Spartan constitutions on paper, a very contrary spirit reigns triumphant in all ranks. . . . Spartan constitutions and Roman manner, peculiar to her declining state, never will accord." Id. at 423.

30. For general discussions, see Anthony Birch, The Concepts and Theories of Modern Democracy (London and New York: Routledge, 1993); David Held, Models of Democracy, 2d ed. (Stanford, Calif.: Stanford University Press, 1996). See Dan Kahan, Democracy Schmemocracy, Cardozo Law Review 20:795 (1999), which argues that the very multiplicity of views about democracy raises suspicion about the coherence of the concept.

31. Carl Schmitt, The Crisis of Parliamentary Democracy (Ellen Kennedy, trans.) (Cambridge, Mass.: MIT Press, 1985). For discussions of Schmitt's analysis, see Jean Cohen and Andrew Arato, Civil Society and Political Theory (Cambridge, Mass.: MIT Press, 1992), at 201–10; Marci Hamilton, Discussion and Decisions: A Proposal to Replace the Myth of Self-Rule with an Attorneyship Model of Representation, New York University Law Review 69:477 (1994).

32. See Hamilton, supra note 31. Frank Michelman attempts to rescue the idea of self-government through the principle that each citizen should be willing to regard herself as the hypothetical author of all the laws. Frank Michelman, Brennan and Democracy (Princeton: Princeton University Press, 1999). This, of course, is not self-government and it is not possible. What it is, however, is an effort to deny the inevitable authority structure of government.

33. For general works on participatory democracy, see Amitai Etzioni, The Spirit of Community: Rights, Responsibilities and the Communitarian Agenda (New York: Crown Publishers, 1993); Michael Sandel, Democracy's Discontent: America in Search of a Public Philosophy (Cambridge, Mass.: Belknap Press, 1996); Philip Selznick, The Moral Commonwealth: Social Theory and the Promise of Community (Berkeley: University of California Press, 1992). For neo-Marxist works favoring this same idea, see C. B. Macpherson, The Real World of Democracy (Oxford: Clarendon Press, 1966); C. B. Macpherson, The Life and

Times of Liberal Democracy (Oxford: Oxford University Press, 1977); Ralph
Miliband, The State in Capitalist Society (New York: Basic Books, 1969); Nicos
Poulantzas, Political Power and Social Classes (Timothy O'Hagan, trans.) (London: New Left Books, 1973); Nicos Poulantzas, Classes in Contemporary Capitalism (David Fernbach, trans.) (London: New Left Books, 1975). A similar theme
appears in works on industrial democracy; see John Burnheim, Is Democracy Possible? (Cambridge: Polity Press, 1985); G.D.H. Cole, Self-Government in Industry (London: G. Bell & Sons, 1918); Robert Dahl, A Preface to Economic
Democracy (Berkeley: University of California Press, 1985); Carol Gould, Rethinking Democracy: Freedom and Social Cooperation in Politics, Economy and
Society (New York: Cambridge University Press, 1988); Paul Hirst, Associative
Democracy: New Forms of Economic and Social Governance (Amherst: University of Massachusetts Press, 1994).

34. See Bruce Ackerman, Social Justice and the Liberal State (New Haven,
Conn.: Yale University Press, 1980); John Dryzek, Discursive Democracy: Politics,
Policy and Political Science (Cambridge: Cambridge University Press, 1990); Amy
Gutmann and Dennis Thompson, Democracy and Disagreement (Cambridge,
Mass.: Belknap Press, 1996); Joshua Cohen, Deliberation and Democratic Legiti-
macy, in James Bohman and William Reg, eds., Deliberative Democracy (Cam-
bridge, Mass.: MIT Press, 1967), at 67; John Ely, Democracy and Distrust: A The-
ory of Judicial Review (Cambridge, Mass.: Harvard University Press, 1980); James
Fishkin, Democracy and Deliberation: New Direction for Democratic Reform (New
Haven, Conn.: Yale University Press, 1991); Jürgen Habermas, Between Facts and
Norms (William Rehg, trans.) (Cambridge, Mass.: MIT Press, 1996); John Rawls,
Political Liberalism (New York: Columbia University Press, 1993); Cass Sunstein,
The Partial Constitution (Cambridge, Mass.: Harvard University Press, 1993).

35. Aristotle, supra note 2, at 239–40 (VI. 2, 1317b).

36. Gaetano Mosca, The Ruling Class (Hannah Kahn, trans.) (New York:
McGraw-Hill, 1939); Robert Michels, Political Parties (Edan and Cedar Paul,
trans.) (Glencoe, Ill.: Free Press, 1949); C. Wright Mills, The Power Elite (New
York: Oxford University Press, 1956).

37. Joseph Schumpeter, Capitalism, Socialism, and Democracy (New York:
Harper & Bros., 1942).

38. Walter Lippmann, The Phantom Public (New York: Macmillan, 1927).

39. Aristotle, supra note 2, at 240 (VI. 2, 1317b).

40. Dahl, supra note 33, at 32–62; James Buchanan and Gordon Tullock, The
Calculus of Consent: The Logical Foundations of Constitutional Democracy (Ann
Arbor: University of Michigan Press, 1962).

41. Robert Dahl, Who Governs? Democracy and Power in an American City
(New Haven, Conn.: Yale University Press, 1961); Nelson Polsby, Community
Power and Political Theory (New Haven, Conn.: Yale University Press, 1963).

42. William Riker, The Theory of Political Coalitions (New Haven, Conn.: Yale
University Press, 1962).

43. Donatella della Porta, Social Movements, Political Violence and the State
(New York: Cambridge University Press, 1995); William Gamson, The Strategy of
Social Protest, 2d ed. (Belmont, Calif.: Wadsworth, 1990); Alberto Melucci, No-
mads of the Present (Philadelphia: Temple University Press, 1989); Anthony

Oberschall, Social Conflicts and Social Movements (Englewood Cliffs, N.J.: Prentice-Hall, 1973); Sidney Tarrow, Power in Movement: Social Movements, Collective Action and Politics (Cambridge: Cambridge University Press, 1994); Alain Touraine, The Voice and the Eye: An Analysis of Social Movements (Cambridge: Cambridge University Press, 1981). For general descriptions of this literature, see Marcy Darnovsky, Barbara Epstein and Richard Flacks, Cultural Politics and Social Movements (Philadelphia: Temple University Press, 1995); Donatella della Porta and Mario Diani, Social Movements: An Introduction (Oxford: Blackwell, 1999); Doug McAdam, John McCarthy, and Mayer Zald, Comparative Perspectives on Social Movements (Cambridge: Cambridge University Press, 1996).

44. Robert Dahl, Dilemmas of Pluralist Democracy (New Haven, Conn.: Yale University Press, 1982); Dahl, Preface, supra note 33; Dahl, Who Governs, supra note 41; Earl Latham, The Group Basis of Politics (Ithaca, N.Y.: Cornell University Press, 1952); Polsby, supra note 41; David Truman, The Governmental Process (New York: Alfred Knopf, 1951).

45. Dahl, Preface, supra note 33, at 4–33.

46. Peter Bachrach and Morton Baratz, Two Faces of Power, American Political Science Review 56:947 (1962); See Ely, supra note 34, at 135; Held, supra note, at 186–220; Jack Lively, Democracy (New York: St. Martin's Press, 1975), at 131–45; Steven Lukes, Power: A Radical View (London: Macmillan, 1974), at 16–35; Claus Offe, Disorganized Capitalism: Contemporary Transformations of Work and Politics (Cambridge, Mass.: MIT Press, 1985), at 259–99. Another body of criticism suggests that organizations do not necessarily represent the interests of their members. See Michael McCann, Taking Reform Seriously: Perspectives on Public Interest Liberalism (Ithaca, N.Y.: Cornell University Press, 1986); Terry Moe, The Organization of Interests: Incentives and the Internal Dynamics of Political Interest Groups (Chicago: Univerisity of Chicago Press, 1980).

47. See Ely, supra note 34; William Miller, Some Underpinnings of American Constitutional Democracy, in W. Lawson Taitte, ed., Democracy: Its Strengths and Weaknesses (Dallas: University of Texas Press at Dallas, 1988), at 61.

48. Cary Nederman suggests a somewhat more modern origin for polyarchial pluralism by linking it to the medieval corporatist thought of John of Salisbury and Marsilius of Padua. See Freedom, Community and Function: Communitarian Lessons of Medievel Political Theory, American Political Science Review 86:977 (1992). Nederman's explicit link is to communitarian thought, but polyarchic pluralists such as Dahl evince the same communitarian inclinations that Nederman claims for John and Marsilius. They differ from standard communitarians like Michael Sandel in their emphasis on participation through mediating institutions.

49. Cynthia Farina, The Consent of the Governed: Against Simple Rules for a Complex World, Chicago Kent Law Review 72:987 (1997). For an empirical critique of the popular will concept, see H. B. Mayo, An Introduction to Democratic Theory (New York: Oxford University Press, 1960), at 87–89.

50. Geoffrey of Monmouth, The History of the Kings of Britain (Lewis Thorpe, trans.) (London: Penguin, 1966), at 258–63; Thomas Malory, Le Morte D'Arthur (R. M. Lumiansky, ed.) (New York: Collier, 1982), at 10–38, 730–41.

51. Maury Klein, Days of Defiance (New York: Vintage, 1999); Kenneth Stampp, And the War Came (Chicago: University of Chicago Press, 1964).

52. 531 U.S. 98 (2000).

53. See Thomas Cronin, Direct Democracy: The Politics of Initiative, Referendum and Recall (Cambridge. Mass.: Harvard University Press, 1989); David Magleby, Direct Legislation: Voting on Ballot Propositions in the United States (Baltimore: Johns Hopkins University Press, 1984); David D. Schmidt, Citizen Lawmakers: The Ballot Initiative Revolution (Philadelphia: Temple University Press, 1989); Laura Tallian, Direct Democracy: An Historical Analysis of the Initiative, Referendum, and Recall Process (Los Angeles: People's Lobby, 1977).

54. E.g., Philip Frickey, Interpretation on the Borderline: Constitution, Canons, Direct Democracy, NYU Annual Survey of American Law 1996:477 (1996); Elizabeth Garrett, Who Directs Direct Democracy?, University of Chicago Law School Roundtable 4:17 (1997); Elizabeth Garrett, Money, Agenda Setting, and Direct Democracy, Texas Law Review 77:1845 (1999); Clayton Gillette, Plebiscites, Participation, and Collective Action in Local Government Law, Michigan Law Review 86:930 (1988). Hans Linde, When Initiative Lawmaking Is Not "Republican Government": The Campaign Against Homosexuality, Oregon Law Review 72:19 (1993); Magleby, supra note 53; Jane Schacter, The Pursuit of "Popular Intent": Interpretive Dilemmas in Direct Democracy, Yale Law Journal 105:107 (1995).

55. Edmund Burke, Speech to the Electors of Bristol, in The Writings and Speeches of Edmund Burke (Paul Langford, ed.) (Oxford: Clarendon Press, 1981); Hanna Pitkin, The Concept of Representation (Berkeley: University of California Press, 1967).

56. See Richard Fenno, Congressmen in Committees (Boston: Little, Brown, 1973); Richard Fenno, Home Style: House Members in Their Districts (Boston: Little, Brown, 1978), at 157–60; Christopher Deering and Steven S. Smith, Committees in Congress, 3d ed. (Washington, D.C.: CQ Press, 1997), at 83–116; Eric Uslaner, Policy Entrepreneurs and Amateur Democrats in the House of Representatives: Toward a More Policy-Oriented Congress, in Leroy N. Rieselbach, ed., Legislative Reform: The Policy Impact (Lexington, Mass.: Lexington Books, 1978), at 105–16.

57. See generally Richard Hasen, Voting Without Law?, University of Pennsylvania Law Review 144:2135 (1996).

58. Charles Tilly, The Contentious French (Cambridge, Mass.: Belknap Press, 1986); Chalres Tilly, From Mobilization to Revolution (Reading, Mass.: Addison-Wesley, 1978).

59. John Meyer, Institutionalization and the Rationality of Formal Organizational Structure, in John Meyer and W. Richard Scott, eds., Organizational Environments: Ritual and Rationality (Beverly Hills: Sage, 1983), at 261; Paul DiMaggio and Walter Powell, The Iron Cage Revisited: Institutional Isomorphism and Collective Rationality in Organizational Fields, in Walter Powell and Paul DiMaggio, eds., The New Institutionalism in Organizational Analysis (Chicago: University of Chicago Press, 1991), at 63.

60. See Ruy Teixeira, The Disappearing American Voter (Washington, D.C.: Brookings Institution, 1992).

61. National Voter Registration Act of 1993, Pub. L. No. 103–31, 107 Stat. 79, codified as amended at 42 U.S.C. § 1973gg.

62. See Anthony Corrado and Charles Firestone, eds., Elections in Cyberspace: Toward a New Era in American Politics (Washington, D.C.: Aspen Institute, 1996); Richard Hasen, Internet Voting and Democracy, Loyola (Los Angeles) Law Review 34:979 (2001); Eben Moglen and Pamela Karlen, Soul of a New Political Machine: The Online, the Color Line and Electronic Democracy, Loyola (Los Angeles) Law Review 34:1089 (2001). Ironically, the Internet could conceivably allow the restoration of certain elements of Athenian democracy in a mass society (see Moglen and Karlen, supra), but this is far from inevitable; see Ian McClean, Democracy and New Technology (Cambridge: Polity Press, 1989).

63. Telephone or Internet voting, however, might create other problems of social equity. See Jerry Kang, E-Racing E-lections, Loyola (Los Angeles) Law Review 34:1155 (2001); Moglen and Karlen, supra note 62.

64. Pub. L. No. 92–225, 86 Stat. 3 (1972), codified as amended at 2 U.S.C. § 431.

65. 424 U.S. 1 (1975).

66. Id. at 14–23, 45–50.

67. Id. at 18.

68. Edwin Baker, Campaign Expenditures and Free Speech, Harvard Civil-Rights, Civil Liberties Law Review 33:1 (1998).

69. Mayo, supra note 49, at 73–75.

70. Robert Biersack, Paul S. Herrnson, and Clyde Wilcox, eds., After the Revolution: PACs, Lobbies, and the Republican Congress (Boston: Allyn & Bacon, 1999); James Deakin, The Lobbyists (Washington, D.C.: Public Affairs Press, 1966); Michael Hayes, Lobbyists and Legislators: A Theory of Political Markets (New Brunswick, N.J.: Rutgers University Press, 1981); Ken Kollman, Outside Lobbying: Public Opinion and Interest Group Strategies (Princeton: Princeton University Press, 1998).

71. Fenno, Home Style, supra note 56.

72. E.g., Gordon Adams, The Politics of Defense Contracting: The Iron Triangle (New Brunswick, N.J.: Transaction Books, 1982); Eugene Bardach and Robert A. Kagan, Going by the Book: The Problem of Regulatory Unreasonableness (Philadelphia: Temple University Press, 1982); John E. Chubb, Interest Groups and the Bureaucracy: The Politics of Energy (Stanford, Calif.: Stanford University Press, 1983); Brian Cook, Bureaucratic Politics and Regulatory Reform: The EPA and Emissions Trading (New York: Greenwood Press, 1988); Martha Derthick, New Towns In-Town: Why a Federal Program Failed (Washington, D.C.: Urban Institute, 1972); Jeffrey Pressman and Aaron Wildavsky, Implementation: How Great Expectations in Washington Are Dashed in Oakland (Berkeley: University of California Press, 1973).

73. For arguments that administrative interaction contributes to democracy, see Marshall Breger, Government Accountability in the Twenty-First Century, University of Pittsburgh Law Review 57:423 (1996); Frank Fischer, Citizen Participation and the Democratization of Political Expertise: From Theoretical Inquiry to Practical Cases, Policy Science 26:165 (1993); Ernest Gellhorn, Public Participation in Administrative Proceedings, Yale Law Journal 81:359 (1972). For arguments that it derogates from democracy, see Theodore Lowi, The End of Liberalism: The Second Republic of the United States, 2d ed. (New York: W. W. Nor-

ton, 1979); Kay Lehman Schlozman and John Tierney, Organized Interests and American Democracy (New York: Harper & Row, 1986), at 386–410; Sidney Verba and Norman Nie, Participation in America: Political Democracy and Social Equality (New York: Harper & Row, 1972).

74. Peter Schuck, Delegation and Democracy: Comments on David Schoenbrod, Cardozo Law Review 20:775 (1999).

75. See, e.g., Jody Freeman, Collaborative Governance in the Administrative State, UCLA Law Review 45:1 (1997); Michael Dorf and Charles Sabel, A Constitution of Democratic Experimentalism, Columbia Law Review 98:267 (1998); Bronwen Morgan, Social Citizenship in the Shadow of Competition (Aldershot, Eng.: Ashgate, 2003).

76. Nicolai Gogol, The Overcoat, in Tales of Good and Evil (David Magarshack, trans.) (Garden City, N.Y.: Doubleday, 1957).

77. Franz Kafka, The Trial (Willa & Edwin Muir, trans.) (New York: Modern Library, 1956).

78. Ghostbusters (Ivan Reitman, director) (Columbia/Delphi, 1984).

79. Philip Howard, The Death of Common Sense: How Law Is Suffocating America (New York: Warner Books, 1994).

80. Habermas, supra note 34, at 352–59. As discussed in Chapter 5, pp. 159–60, Habermas envisions modern democratic government as three concentric rings consisting of civil society, the administration, and the elected officials. Civil society, in his view, communicates only with elected officials, and since he is aware that the administrative apparatus stands between civil society and these officials, he envisions this communication as flowing through narrow sluices that traverse the middle ring.

81. John Rohr, To Run a Constitution: The Legitimacy of the Administrative State (Lawrence: University Press of Kansas, 1986).

82. Id. at 28–53.

83. Max Farrand, ed., The Records of the Constitutional Convention of 1787 (New Haven, Conn.: Yale University Press, 1966), at 643–44.

84. Rohr, supra note 81, at 45–46.

85. For arguments that the Framers' goals cannot be described in terms of the concept of democratic self-rule, see Rebecca Brown, Accountability, Liberty and the Constitution, Columbia Law Review 98:531 (1998); Erwin Chemerinsky, Foreword: The Vanishing Constitution, Harvard Law Review 103:43 (1989); Lawrence Sager, The Incorrigible Constitution, New York University Law Review 65:893 (1990).

86. Freeman, supra note 75; Philip Harter, Negotiating Regulations: A Cure for Malaise, Georgetown Law Journal 71:1 (1982); Jerry Mashaw, Prodelegation: Why Administrators Should Make Political Decisions, Journal of Law, Economics and Organizations 1:81 (1985), Robert Reich, Public Administration and Public Deliberation: An Interpretive Essay, Yale Law Journal, 94:1617 (1985); Susan Rose-Ackerman, Progressive Law and Economics—And the New Administrative Law, Yale Law Journal 98:341 (1988); Mark Seidenfeld, A Civic Republican Justification for the Bureaucratic State, Harvard Law Review 105:1512 (1992).

87. Seidenfeld, supra note 86.

88. The U.S. Congress has made several efforts to facilitate administrative interaction in ways that go beyond traditional patterns. The Magnuson-Moss Act at-

tempted to provide funding for consumer groups to participate in Federal Trade Commission rule making. Federal Trade Commission Warranty Act, Pub. L. No. 93–637, Title II, 88 Stat. 2193 (1975), codified as amended at 15 U.S.C. 57. The Consumer Product Safety Act allowed citizens to petition the Consumer Product Safety Commission to initiate a rule-making proceeding, and to participate in Commission-initiated rule making by producing their own proposals. Consumer Product Safety Act, Pub. L. No. 92–573, § 10, 86 Stat. 1217 (1972) repealed by Consumer Product Safety Amendments of 1981, Pub. L. No. 97–35, § 1210, 95 Stat. 703, 721. Criticism of these innovations is often based on exaggerated expectations of them. They will not ensure fairness, or secure self-government, or conform to our inherited concept of democracy. All that they can be expected to achieve is to increase the quantity and quality of interaction at the administrative level. See Barry Boyer, Funding Public Participation in Agency Proceedings: The Federal Trade Commission Experience, Georgetown Law Review 70:51 (1981); Antonin Scalia and Frank Goodman, Procedural Aspects of the Consumer Product Safety Act, UCLA Law Review 20:899 (1973).

89. Freeman, supra note 75; Robert Healy and William Ascher, Knowledge in the Policy Process: Incorporating New Environmental Information in Natural Resources Policy Making, Policy Science 28:1 (1995); Cornelius Kerwin, Rulemaking: How Government Agencies Write Law and Make Policy, 2d ed. (Washington, D.C.: CQ Press, 1999), at 66–70; Jerry Mashaw, The Management Side of Due Process: Some Theoretical and Litigation Notes on the Assurance of Accuracy, Fairness and Timeliness in the Adjudication of Social Welfare Claims, Cornell Law Review 59:772 (1974); Douglas Michael, Cooperative Implementation of Federal Regulations, Yale Journal on Regulation 13:535 (1996); Eric Orts, Reflexive Environmental Law, Northwestern University Law Review 89:1227 (1995).

90. This is a major theme of the growing literature on regulatory implementation. See Ian Ayres and John Braithwaite, Responsive Regulation (New York: Oxford University Press, 1992); Bardach and Kagan, supra note 72; Lars Noah, Administrative Arm-Twisting in the Shadow of Congressional Delegations of Authority, Wisconsin Law Review 1997:873 (1997); Tom Tyler, Why People Obey the Law (New Haven, Conn.: Yale University Press, 1990); Pressman and Wildavsky, supra note 72.

91. Cary Coglianese, Assessing Consensus: The Promise and Performance of Negotiated Rulemaking, Duke Law Journal 46:1255 (1997); James Rossi, Participation Run Amok: The Costs of Mass Participation for Deliberative Agency Decisionmaking, Northwestern University Law Review 92:173 (1997).

92. This is discussed further in the following sections of the present volume: "Law's Normative Function, or the Rule of Law," in Chapter 6; "The Heuristic Character of Theory," in Chapter 7; "Moral Demands in General," in Chapter 8; and "Compensation for Takings," in Chapter 9.

93. See Stephen Breyer, Breaking the Vicious Circle: Toward Effective Risk Regulation (Cambridge, Mass.: Harvard University Press, 1993); Gerald Frug, The Ideology of Bureaucracy in American Law, Harvard Law Review 97:1276 (1984); Thomas Sargentich, The Reform of the American Administrative Process: The Contemporary Debate, Wisconsin Law Review 1984:385 (1984); Richard Stewart, The Reformation of American Administrative Law, Harvard Law Review

88:1669 (1975); Cass Sunstein, Interest Groups in American Public Law, Stanford Law Review 38:29 (1985).

94. See Lowi, supra note 73, at 175–76; Rossi, supra note 91; Richard Stewart, Madison's Nightmare, University of Chicago Law Review 57:335 (1990); Stewart, supra note 93.

95. Seidenfeld, supra note 86.

96. 5 U.S.C. §§ 551–59, 561–68, 570, 701–6.

97. See Colin Diver, Policymaking Paradigms in Administrative Law, Harvard Law Review 95:393 (1981); Kerwin, supra note 89; William Pederson, Formal Records and Informal Rulemaking, Yale Law Journal 85:38 (1975); Peter Strauss, The Rulemaking Continuum, Duke Law Journal 41:1463 (1992).

98. See Gellhorn, supra note 73; Jeffrey Lubbers, Federal Administrative Law Judges: A Focus on Our Invisible Judiciary, Administrative Law Review 33:109 (1981); Jerry Mashaw, Bureaucratic Justice: Managing Social Security Disability Claims (New Haven, Conn.: Yale University Press, 1983); Paul Verkuil, The Emerging Concept of Administrative Procedure, Columbia Law Review 78:258 (1978).

99. Pub. L. No 89–487, 80 Stat. 250 (1966), codified at 5 U.S.C. § 552.

100. Pub. L. No. 94–409 (1976), 90 Stat. 1241, codified at 5 U.S.C. § 552b. One of the earliest American laws with a cutesy name. The reference is to the famous line by Justice Brandeis that "sunshine is among the best of disinfectants."

101. For criticisms, see Michael Fitts, Can Ignorance Be Bliss? Imperfect Information as a Positive Influence on Political Institutions, Michigan Law Review: 88:917 (1990); Kimberly Krawiec, Cosmetic Compliance and the Failure of Negotiated Governance, Washington University Law Quarterly 81:487 (2003); Rossi, supra note 91, at 228–36; Antonin Scalia, The Freedom of Information Act Has No Clothes, Regulation March/April 1982:15; Thomas Tucker, "Sunshine . . ." A Dubious New God, Administrative Law Review 32:537 (1980); Patricia Wald, The Freedom of Information Act: A Short Case Study in the Perils and Paybacks of Legislating Democratic Values, Emory Law Journal 33:649 (1984).

102. See Stephen Breyer, Judicial Review of Questions of Law and Policy, Administrative Law Review 38:363 (1986); Christopher Edley, Administrative Law: Rethinking Judicial Control of Bureaucracy (New Haven, Conn.: Yale University Press, 1990); Merrick Garland, Deregulation and Judicial Review, Harvard Law Review 98:505 (1985); Thomas McGarity, Some Thoughts on "Deossifying" the Rulemaking Process, Duke Law Journal 41:1385 (1992); R. Shep Melnick, Regulation and the Courts: The Case of the Clean Air Act (Washington, D.C.: Brookings Institution, 1983).

103. For descriptions of this process, see Bruce Ackerman and William Hassler, Clean Coal/Dirty Air (New Haven, Conn.: Yale University Press, 1981); Adams, supra note 72; Bardach and Kagan, supra note 72; John Braithwaite, To Punish or Persuade: Enforcement of Coal Mine Safety (Albany, N.Y.: State University of New York Press, 1985); Derthick, supra note 72; Robert Kagan and John Scholz, The "Criminology of the Corporation" and Regulatory Enforcement Strategies, in Keith Hawkins and John Thomas, eds., Enforcing Regulation (Boston: Kluwer-Nijhoff, 1984); Paul Quirk, Industry Influence in Federal Regulatory Agencies (Princeton: Princeton University Press, 1981).

104. See sources cited in note 43, supra.

105. See Barry Adam, The Rise of the Gay and Lesbian Movement, rev. ed. (New York: Twayne Publishers, 1995); Rufus Browning, Protest Is Not Enough: The Struggle of Blacks and Hispanics for Equality in Urban Politics (Berkeley: University of California Press, 1984); Gary Delgado, Organizing the Movement: The Roots and Growth of ACORN (Philadelphia: Temple University Press, 1986); Susan Handley Hertz, The Welfare Mothers Movement: A Decade of Change for Poor Women? (Washington, D.C.: University Press of America, 1981); Robert Katzmann, Institutional Disability: The Saga of Transportation Policy for the Disabled (Washington, D.C.: Brookings Institution, 1986); Robert Mayer, The Consumer Movement: Guardians of the Marketplace (Boston: Twayne Publishing, 1989).

106. Katzmann, supra note 105; Melnick, supra note 102.

107. See Grant Jordan and William Maloney, The Protest Business? Mobilizing Campaign Groups (New York: Manchester University Press, 1997); Bron Taylor, ed., Ecological Resistance Movements: The Global Emergence of Radical and Popular Environmentalism (Albany: State University of New York Press, 1995); Andrew Szasz, EcoPopulism: Toxic Waste and the Movement for Environmental Justice (Minneapolis: University of Minnesota Press, 1994).

108. Freeman, supra note 75.

109. Pub L. No 101–648, 104 Stat. 4969 (1990) codified as amended at 5 U.S.C. §§ 561–70.

110. Coglianese, supra note 91; William Funk, When Smoke Gets in Your Eyes: Regulatory Negotiation and the Public Interest—EPA's Woodstove Standards, Environmental Law 18:55 (1987); William Funk, Bargaining toward the New Millennium: Regulatory Negotiation and the Subversion of the Public Interest, Duke Law Journal 46:1351 (1997); Susan Rose-Ackerman, Consensus Versus Incentives: A Skeptical Look at Regulatory Negotiation, Duke Law Journal 43:1206 (1994); Rossi, supra note 91. For more positive assessment, see Philip Harter, Points on a Continuum: Dispute Resolution Procedures and the Administrative Process, Administrative Law Journal 1:141 (1987); Kerwin, supra note 89, at 190.

111. Freeman, supra note 75. See also Dennis Hirsch, Bill and Al's XL-ent Adventure: An Analysis of the EPA's Legal Authority to Implement the Clinton Administration's Project XL, University of Illinois Law Review 1998:129 (1998).

112. Evelyn Brodkin, The False Promise of Administrative Reform: Implementing Quality control in Welfare (Philadelphia: Temple University Press, 1986); Naomi Gottlieb, The Welfare Bind (New York: Columbia University Press, 1974); Joel Handler, The Poverty of Welfare Reform (New Haven, Conn.: Yale University Press, 1995); Sar Levitan, Martin Rein, and David Marwick, Work and Welfare Go Together (Baltimore: Johns Hopkins University Press, 1972); David Macarov, Work and Welfare. The Unholy Alliance (Beverly Hills: Sage Publications, 1980); Lawrence Mead, Beyond Entitlement, The Social Obligations of Citizenship (New York: Free Press, 1986); Dorothy Miller, Women and Social Welfare: A Feminist Analysis (New York: Praeger, 1990); Charles Murray, Losing Ground: American Social Policy, 1950–1980 (New York: Basic Books, 1984); Francis Fox Piven and Richard Cloward, Regulating the Poor: The Functions of Public Welfare, 2d ed. (New York: Vintage Books, 1993).

113. Daniel Moynihan, Maximum Feasible Misunderstanding Community Action in the War on Poverty (New York: Free Press, 1969).

114. Kathryn Olmsted, Challenging the Secret Government: the Post-Watergate Investigations of the CIA and the FBI (Chapel Hill: University of North Carolina Press, 1996); Twentieth Century Fund Task Force on Covert Action and American Democracy: The Need to Know (New York: Twentieth Century Fund, 1992); Loch Johnson, America's Secret Power: The CIA in a Democratic Society (New York: Oxford University Press, 1989); Harry Ransom, The Intelligence Establishment (Cambridge, Mass.: Harvard University Press, 1970).

115. Of course, other governmental units are expected to supervise the intelligence apparatus. In the United States, Congress is the authorizing agency and structural superior of the Central Intelligence Agency, and the courts have some specific areas of jurisdiction. But because the electoral process is heavily affected by certain types of public anxieties, members of Congress have been too easily intimidated by CIA staff members, who naturally prefer to avoid supervision. The courts have been equally timid; in United States v. Richardson, 418 U.S. 166 (1974), for example, the Supreme Court refused to require the CIA to disclose its budget on the basis of a poorly argued procedural technicality, even though such disclosure is explicitly required by the Constitution. This is not to suggest that direct citizen interaction would necessarily have been more clear-headed or courageous during the difficult Cold War years, but it would certainly have given us one more opportunity to supervise an agency that had in fact spun out of control. For further discussion of the Richardson case, see Chapter 7.

Notes to Chapter Five

1. See, e.g., Rodney Barker, Political Legitimacy and the State (Oxford: Clarendon Press, 1990); William Connolly, ed., Legitimacy and the State (New York: New York University Press, 1984); Jürgen Habermas, Legitimation Crisis (Thomas McCarthy, trans.) (Boston: Beacon Press, 1973); Alan Hyde, The Concept of Legitimation in the Sociology of Law, Wisconsin Law Review 1983:379 (1983); Patrick Riley, Will and Political Legitimacy (Cambridge, Mass.: Harvard University Press, 1982); Robert Rogowski, Rational Legitimacy: A Theory of Political Support (Princeton: Princeton University Press, 1974); Tom Tyler, Why People Obey the Law (New Haven, Conn.: Yale University Press, 1990); Max Weber, Economy and Society (Guenther Ross & Claus Wittach, eds.) (Berkeley: University of California Press, 1978), at 31.

2. Geoffrey of Monmouth, The History of the Kings of Britain (Lewis Thorpe, trans.) (London: Penguin, 1966), at 205–7 (spelling used in text is Marlory's).

3. Id. at 207–8.

4. Id. at 208. The story that Arthur was brought up by Sir Ector, away from Uther's household, and without knowledge of his royal status, does not appear in Geoffrey. It is reported by Malory without explanation. Thomas Malory, Le Morte Darthur (R. M. Lumiansky, ed.) (New York: Collier, 1982), at 6. The second part of Mary Stewart's trilogy that retells the Arthurian legend from Merlin's perspective offers a plausible explanation: because of the doubts about Arthur's real

parentage, he is sent away in the hope that Igrayne will give birth to an unquestioned son by Uther, and held in reserve, as it were, in case no subsequent son is born. Mary Stewart, The Hollow Hills (New York: Fawcett Crest, 1973), at 94–118.

5. See Jenny Teichman, Illegitimacy: An Examination of Bastardy (Ithaca, N.Y.: Cornell University Press, 1982).

6. Malory, supra note 4, at 12. The passage reads as follows:

> Then all the kings were passing glad to see Merlyn and asked him, "For what cause is that boy Arthur made your king?"
>
> "Sirs," said Merlyn, "I shall tell you the cause: because he is King Uther Pendragon's son, born in wedlock, gotten on Igrayne the wife of the Duke of Tintagel."
>
> "Then he is a bastard," they all said.
>
> "Nay," said Merlyn. "After the death of the duke by more than three hours Arthur was begotten. And thirteen days later King Uther wedded Igrayne. Therefore have I proved that he is no bastard. . . ."

7. Reinhard Bendix, Kings or People: Power and the Mandate to Rule (Berkeley: University of California Press, 1978), at 21–40; Antony Black, Political Thought in Europe, 1250–1450 (Cambridge: Cambridge University Press, 1992), at 137–39; Joseph Canning, A History of Medieval Political Thought, 300–1450 (London: Routledge, 1996), at 47–59, 93–95; Heinrich Fichtenau, Living in the Tenth Century (Patrick Geary, trans.) (Chicago: University of Chicago Press, 1991), at 161–64; Otto Gierke, Political Theories of the Middle Age (Frederic Maitland, trans.) (Cambridge: Cambridge University Press, 1938), at 30–37; J. A. Watt, Spiritual and Temporal Powers, in J. H. Burns, ed., Cambridge History of Medieval Political Thought (Cambridge: Cambridge University Press, 1988), at 367. For the manner in which the conception of divine right evolved during the period, see Ernst Kantorowicz, The King's Two Bodies: A Study in Mediaeval Political Theology (Princeton: Princeton University Press, 1957).

8. Fritz Kern, Kingship and Law in the Middle Ages (S. B. Chrimes, trans.) (Oxford: Blackwell, 1939), at 12–27.

9. See Black, supra note 7, at 146–48; Marc Bloch, Feudal Society (L. A. Manyon, trans.) (Chicago: University of Chicago Press, 1961), at 383–89.

10. The Norman invasion of Britain in 1066 resulted from a dispute over the succession after the death of Edward the Confessor. Thereafter, Britain was not subject to external invasion. Nonetheless, it experienced civil war due to disputes over the succession to the throne in 1100–1106 (Henry I defends his throne against Duke Robert of Normandy after King Rufus's death), 1135–53 (Stephen and Matilda dispute the throne after Henry II's death), 1173–86 (Henry II's sons contest the succession in anticipation of his death), 1326–27 (Edward II deposed and murdered by supporters of Edward III), 1399 (Richard II deposed by Henry IV), and 1450–85 (the War of the Roses between the Lancastrians and the Yorkists). See Winston Churchill, The Birth of Britain (New York: Dodd, Mead, 1956).

11. Barker, supra note 1, at 11, see 23–24.

12. David Easton, A Systems Analysis of Political Life (Chicago: University of Chicago Press, 1979).

13. See Barker, supra note 1, at 11–24; David Beetham, The Legitimation of Power (Atlantic Highlands, N.J.: Humanities Press, 1991); Herbert Kelman and V. Lee Hamilton, Crimes of Obedience (New Haven, Conn.: Yale University Press, 1989); Riley, supra note 1; Tyler, supra note 1, at 25.

14. See Barker, supra note 1, at 24, which criticizes Rogowski, supra note 1, on the grounds that Rogowski comes close to defining legitimacy in terms of rational agreement with the actions of government, rather than acceptance of the government in general. Heidi Hurd, Challenging Authority, Yale Law Journal 100:1611 (1991), takes a position similar to Rogowski's with respect to the concept of authority. See Chapter 3.

15. As Alan Hyde notes, the term is used, in common speech, as a "simple description of positive legal doctrine" (the president legitimated the military action by explicitly approving it) or as "any sort of public relations which attempts to put political institutions or decisions in a favorable light" (the president tried to legitimate his invasion of Iraq by finding illegal weapons there). Hyde, supra note 1, at 381 n. 1.

16. Walter Ullmann, Principles of Government and Politics in the Middle Ages, 2d ed. (New York: Barnes & Noble, 1966) Walter Ullmann, Law and Politics in the Middle Ages (Ithaca, N.Y.: Cornell University Press, 1975).

17. See note 7, supra, citing sources. For an exception, see Marsilius of Padua, The Defender of Peace, The Defensor Pacis (Alan Gewirth, trans.) (New York: Harper & Row, 1967).

18. King James I of England (King James VI of Scotland), The Political Works of James I (Charles McIlwain, ed.) (New York: Russell & Russell, 1965); Robert Filmer, Patriarcha and Other Writings (Johann Sommerville, ed.) (Cambridge: Cambridge University Press, 1991). See James Daly, Sir Robert Filmer and English Political Thought (Toronto: University of Toronto Press, 1979).

19. Weber, supra note 1, at 212–99, 941–54. See Robert Grafstein, The Failure of Weber's Concept of Legitimacy, Journal of Politics 43:456 (1981); Jürgen Habermas, Between Facts and Norms: Contributions to a Discourse Theory of Law and Democracy (William Rehg, trans.) (Cambridge, Mass.: MIT Press, 1996).

20. Hyde, supra note 1.

21. Hans Kelsen, General Theory of Law and State (Anders Wedberg, trans.) (Cambridge, Mass.: Harvard University Press, 1945); Hans Kelsen, Pure Theory of Law, 2d ed. (Max Knight, trans.) (Berkeley: University of California Press, 1967). David Easton seconds this view. Easton, supra note 12, at 137.

22. H.L.A. Hart, The Concept of Law (Oxford: Clarendon Press, 1961), at 7.

23. Id. at 18–25.

24. Id. at 92–96. In simple societies, Hart notes, the rule of recognition might consist simply of a list of primary rules.

25. Id. at 97–107.

26. Alexander Bickel, The Least Dangerous Branch: The Supreme Court at the Bar of Politics (Indianapolis: Bobbs-Merrill, 1962); Charles Black, The People and the Court: Judicial Review in a Democracy (New York: Macmillan, 1960).

27. See Hyde, supra note 1.

28. Brian Tamanaha, Realistic Socio-Legal Theory (Oxford: Clarendon Press, 1997), at 131–37.

29. See, e.g., J. W. Gough, The Social Contract: A Critical Study of Its Development, 2d ed. (Oxford: Clarendon Press, 1957); David Gauthier and Robert Sugden, eds., Rationality, Justice and the Social Contract (Ann Arbor: University of Michigan Press, 1993); Don Herzog, Happy Slaves (Chicago: University of Chicago Press, 1989), Vicente Medina, Social Contract Theories: Political Obligation or Anarchy (Savage, Md.: Rowan & Littlefield, 1990).

30. Gierke, supra note 7, at 87–90. This political evolution was regarded as a human choice, not one ordained by God, although it was certainly subject to God's laws for human life.

31. Althusius, The Politics of Althusius (Frederick Carney, trans.) (London: Eyre & Spottiswoode, 1964); George Buchanan, A Dialogue of the Law of Kingship among the Scots (Roger Mason & Martin Smith, trans.) (Aldershot, Eng.: Ashgate, 2004). Otto von Gierke, The Development of Political Theory (Bernard Freyd, trans.) (New York: W. W. Norton, 1939); Quentin Skinner, The Foundations of Modern Political Thought, vol. 2: The Age of Reformation (Cambridge: Cambridge University Press, 1978), at 338–45.

32. See C. B. Macpherson, The Theory of Possessive Individualism; Hobbes to Locke (Oxford: Oxford University Press, 1962); Riley, supra note 1. The older idea of a contract between people and ruler is described by contemporary scholars as a governmental or constitutional contract, and the post-Reformation concept of a contract among equals is described as a social or a civil one. Martyn Thompson has observed, however, that most of the political writers of the late seventeenth and early eighteenth centuries did not distinguish clearly between these two themes, but tended to combine them. Martyn Thompson, Locke's Contract in Context, in The Social Contract from Hobbes to Rawls (David Boucher & Paul Kelly, eds.) (London: Routledge, 1994), at 73.

33. David Hume, A Treatise of Human Nature, 2d ed. (P. H. Niddich, ed.) (Oxford: Clarendon Press, 1992), at 540–45; David Hume, Of the Original Contract, in Essays, Moral, Political and Literary (Eugene Miller, ed.) (Indianapolis: Liberty Classics, 1985). For discussions of Hume's critique of contract theory, see D. Forbes, Hume's Philosophical Politics (Cambridge: Cambridge University Press, 1975); David Miller, Philosophy and Ideology in Hume's Political Thought (Oxford: Clarendon Press, 1981); Russell Hardin, From Power to Order, from Hobbes to Hume, Journal of Political Philosophy 1:69 (1993). For a different view of Hume's approach, see David Gauthier, David Hume, Contractarian, Philosophical Review 88:3 (1979).

34. Jeremy Waldron, John Locke, Social Contract Versus Political Anthropology, in Boucher and Kelly, supra note 32, at 51. Waldron states that Locke intended his theory to serve as "a moral template to be placed over historical events and over our present predicament."

35. Immanuel Kant, The Metaphysics of Morals (Mary Gregor, trans.) (Cambridge: Cambridge University Press, 1996), at 92–93 (§ 47).

36. G.W.F. Hegel, Philosophy of Right (T. M. Knox, trans.) (London: Oxford University Press, 1967), at 58–59 (§ 75), 155–59 (§ 258). See Frederick Neu-

houser, Foundations of Hegel's Social Theory (Cambridge, Mass.: Harvard University Press, 2000), at 175–224; Riley, supra note 1, at 163–99; Michel Rosenfeld, Hegel and the Dialectics of Contract, in Hegel and Legal Theory (Drucilla Cornell, Michel Rosenfeld, & David Carlson, eds.) (New York: Routledge, 1991), at 228.

37. John Rawls, A Theory of Justice (Cambridge, Mass.: Harvard University Press, 1971).

38. Id. at 136–42.

39. Id. at 137.

40. Id. at 54–117.

41. Michael Sandel, Liberalism and the Limits of Justice (Cambridge: Cambridge University Press, 1982).

42. John Rawls, Political Liberalism (New York: Columbia University Press, 1993), at 22–28.

43. Hegel, supra note 36, § 75, at 59.

44. Anonymous, Sir Gawain and the Green Knight, Pearl and Sir Ofeo (J.R.R. Tolkien, trans.) (New York: Ballantine, 1975). Tolkien's translation was published posthumously.

45. Id., § 17, at 30.

46. Id., § 35, at 44.

47. Id., § 45, at 53.

48. Id., § 49, at 57. Tolkien is possibly being a bit prudish here. Brian Stone's version (2d ed., London: Penguin, 1974) is: "My young body is yours, Do with it what you will."

49. Sir Gawain and the Green Knight, supra note 44, § 55, at 62.

50. Id., § 77, at 78–79.

51. Id., § 96, at 93.

52. Id., § 98, at 94. This breach of feudal morality is also associated with the Christian theme of humility and sin, for Gawain continues by saying that the girdle shall make him recall "the failure and the frailty of the flesh so perverse, so tender, so ready to take taints of defilement." See Maurice Keen, Chivalry (New Haven, Conn.: Yale University Press, 1984), at 44–63.

53. Kent Greenawalt, Promissory Obligation: The Theme of Social Contract, in Joseph Raz, ed., Authority (New York: New York University Press, 1990), at 268. See also Miller, supra note 33, at 79–80 (stating Hume's view).

54. Sir Gawain and the Green Knight, supra note 44, § 43, at 51.

55. See generally Keen, supra note 52, at 1–17, 162–78; For an account of an analogous ethos in the ancient world, see M. I. Finley, The World of Odysseus, rev. ed. (New York: Viking, 1965), at 114–54.

56. Dante Alighieri, Banquet (Richard Lansing, trans.) (New York: Garland, 1990).

57. Keen, supra note 52, at 174–75.

58. Virginia Held, Mothering versus Contract, in Jane Mansbridge, ed., Beyond Self-Interest (Chicago: University of Chicago Press, 1990); Linda Hirshman, Is the Original Position Inherently Male-Superior?, Columbia Law Review 94:1860 (1994); Carole Pateman, The Sexual Contract (Stanford, Calif.: Stanford

University Press, 1988). Susan Moller Okin argues that Rawls's original position is conducive to feminist arguments. See Justice, Gender and the Family (New York: Basic Books, 1989).

59. Rawls, supra note 37, at 145.

60. Jon Elster, Introduction, in Jon Elster, ed., The Multiple Self (New York: Cambridge University Press, 1985), at 1. See Jon Elster, Ulysses and the Sirens: Studies in Rationality and Irrationality, 2d ed. (New York: Cambridge University Press, 1984).

61. Thus, the argument against giving freedom of decision to the later self is that the person makes a more rational decision at the prior time. This envisions two actual decisions, each bearing the same relationship to the individual at the time it is made. Rawls is trying to undermine the validity of an actual decision with a hypothetical one, on the ground that the hypothetical decision is more rational, and that the only rational approach is to be bound by this hypothetical decision, rather than by an actual one. In fact, it is more rational to assume, as Elster argues (see Multiple Self, note 60, supra), that one will be altered by one's experiences, and that it would be unwise to make definitive commitments from behind the veil.

62. Dworkin argues, quite correctly, that an argument based on a hypothetical contract does not gain any force from our moral obligation to obey our promises, since such an obligation arises only from actual agreements. Ronald Dworkin, Taking Rights Seriously (Cambridge, Mass.: Harvard University Press, 1978), at 150–53. In fact, Rawls does not rely on this argument. Rather, he relies on the rational force of promise keeping. This is much more closely related to the medieval idea that promises are sacred, since for Rawls it is rationality, not morality, that plays the role that sacramental notions played in the medieval worldview, that is, as the organizing principle for thought.

63. See Alfred Cobban, A History of Modern France, vol. 1: Old Regime and Revolution, 1715–1799 (Baltimore: Penguin, 1957).

64. See T.C.W. Blanning, Joseph II (London: Longman, 1994); Robert A. Kann, A History of the Habsburg Empire, 1526–1918 (Berkeley: University of California Press, 1974), at 204–7; Saul K. Padover, The Revolutionary Emperor: Joseph the Second (New York: Robert O. Ballou, 1934).

65. See Hegel, supra note 36, at 155–79 (§§ 257–74).

66. Norman Cantor, The Civilization of the Middle Ages (New York: Harper Collins, 1993), at 464–73; Francis Gies, The Knight in History (New York: Harper & Row, 1984), at 196–204; Johan Huizinga, The Waning of the Middle Ages (Garden City, N.Y.: Doubleday, 1954), at 67–107. Keen, supra note 52, at 238–49, is partially in agreement, but treats chivalry's continuation in the Renaissance as somewhat more genuine.

67. Cantor, supra note 66, at 467; Gies, supra note 66, at 100–101, 146–50; Keen, supra note 52, at 229–32.

68. For arguments that a regime is legitimate by virtue of deliberation, see Jon Elster, ed., Deliberative Democracy (Cambridge: Cambridge University Press, 1998); Amy Gutmann and Dennis Thompson, Democracy and Disagreement (Cambridge, Mass.: Belknap Press, 1996); Habermas, supra note 19.

69. Robert Post, Constitutional Domains: Democracy, Community, Manage-

NOTES TO PAGES 158-162

ment (Cambridge, Mass.: Harvard University Press, 1995), at 268–89; Robert Post, Democracy, Popular Sovereignty and Judicial Review, California Law Review 86:429 (1998).

70. The Federalist Papers (Isaac Kramnick, ed.) (London: Penguin, 1987) No. 10, at 122 (attributed to James Madison); see also No. 9, at 118 (attributed to Alexander Hamilton). As the primary draftsman of the Constitution, Madison's views are of particular significance.

71. Id. at 123.

72. Habermas, supra note 19.

73. Jürgen Habermas, The Theory of Communicative Action (Thomas McCarthy, trans.) (Boston: Beacon Press, 1981, 1987).

74. Id., vol. 2 (Lifeworld and System: A Critique of Functional Reason), at 113–97.

75. Habermas, supra note 19, at 367; see generally at 366–73.

76. Id. at 367.

77. Id. at 354–59. Habermas derives this image from a book by Bernhard Peters. Peters's book does not appear to have been translated into English, and I have not read it. The German citation is Die Integration moderner Gesellschaften (Frankfurt am Main: Suhrkamp, 1993).

78. Richard McAdams, The Origin, Development, and Regulation of Norms, Michigan Law Review 96:338 (1997).

79. Douglas Baird, Robert Gertner, and Randal Picker, Game Theory and the Law (Cambridge, Mass.: Harvard University Press, 1994), at 122–58; Peter Ordeshook, A Political Theory Primer (New York: Routledge, 1992), at 234–41.

80. Lauren Edelman, Howard Erlanger, and John Lande, Internal Dispute Resolution: The Transformation of Civil Rights in the Workplace, Law & Society Review 27:497 (1993); Lauren Edelman, Legal Ambiguity and Symbolic Structures: Organizational Mediation of Civil Rights Law, American Journal of Sociology 97:1531 (1992); Lauren Edelman, Steven Abraham & Howard Erlanger Professional Construction of the Law: The Inflated Theory of Wrongful Discharge, Law & Society Review 26:47 (1992); Lauren Edelman, Stephen Petterson, Elizabeth Chambliss, and Howard S. Erlanger, Legal Ambiguity and the Politics of Compliance: Affirmative Action Officers' Dilemma, Law & Policy 13:73 (1991). However, it is also possible that the compliance procedures established as a result of these professionals' participation will be largely symbolic. See John Meyer, Institutionalization and the Rationality of Formal Organizational Structure, in John Meyer and W. Richard Scott, eds., Organizational Environments: Ritual and Rationality (Beverly Hills: Sage, 1983).

81. See Sarbanes-Oxley Act of 2002, Pub. L. No. 107–204, 116 Stat. 745 codified at 15 U.S.C. §§ 7201 to 7266.

82. See Alfred Aman, Administrative Equity: An Analysis of Exceptions to Administrative Rules, Duke Law Journal 1982:277 (1982); Robert Anthony, "Well, You Want the Permit, Don't You?" Agency Efforts to Make Nonlegislative Documents Bind the Public, Administrative Law Review 44:31 (1992); Seth Kreimer, Allocational Sanctions: The Problem of Negative Rights in a Positive State, University of Pennsylvania Law Review 132:1293 (1984); Lars Noah, Administrative Arm-Twisting in the Shadow of Congressional Delegations of Authority, Wisconsin Law Review 1997:875 (1997); Jim Rossi, Making Policy through the Waiver

NOTES TO PAGES 162-163

of Regulations at the Federal Energy Regulatory Commission, Administrative Law Review 47:255 (1995); Peter Schuck, When the Exception Becomes the Rule: Regulatory Equity and the Formation of Energy Policy through an Exceptions Process, Duke Law Journal 1984:163 (1984); Steven Spaeth, Industrial Policy, Continuing Surveillance, and Raised Eyebrows: A Comparison of Informality in Administrative Procedure in Japan and the United States, Ohio Northern University Law Review 20:931 (1994); Michael Young, Judicial Review of Administrative Guidance: Governmentally Encouraged Consensual Dispute Resolution in Japan, Columbia Law Review 84:923 (1984).

83. Weber, supra note 1, at 213.

84. Robert Cooter, Expressive Law and Economics, Journal of Legal Studies 27:585 (1998).

85. Beetham, supra note 13; E. Allan Lind and Tom Tyler, The Social Psychology of Procedural Justice (New York: Plenum Press, 1988); Tyler, supra note 1.

86. See Walker Connor, Ethnonationalism: The Quest for Understanding (Princeton: Princeton University Press, 1994); Clifford Geertz, The Interpretation of Cultures: Selected Essays (New York: Basic Books, 1973); Elie Kedourie, Nationalism, 4th ed. (London: Hutchinson, 1960). This position is sometimes described as primordialism. See Umut Ozkirimli, Theories of Nationalism: A Critical Introduction (New York: St. Martin's Press, 2000), at 64–83.

87. Karl Deutsch, Nationalism and Social Communication (Cambridge: MIT Press, 1966); Michael Hechter, Rational Choice Theory and the Study of Race and Ethnic Relations, in J. Rex and D. Mason, eds., Theories of Race and Ethnic Relations (Cambridge: Cambridge University Press, 1986); Dov Ronen, The Quest for Self-Determination (New Haven, Conn.: Yale University Press, 1979).

88. Otto Bauer, The Question of Nationalities and Social Democracy (Joseph O'Donnell, trans.) (Minneapolis: University of Minnesota Press, 2000); Paul Gilbert, The Philosophy of Nationalism (Boulder, Colo.: Westview Press, 1998); David Miller, On Nationality (New York: Clarendon Press, 1995); Ross Poole, Nation and Identity (London: Routledge, 1999); Anthony Smith, National Identity (Reno, Nev.: University of Nevada Press, 1991); Anthony Smith, Nations and Nationalism in the Global Era (Cambridge: Polity Press, 1995); Yael Tamir, Liberal Nationalism (Princeton: Princeton University Press, 1993); Charles Taylor, The Politics of Recognition, in Amy Gutmann, ed., Multiculturalism and the "Politics of Recognition" (Princeton: Princeton University Press, 1992), at 25.

89. Benedict Anderson, Imagined Communities: Reflections on the Origin and Spread of Nationalism, rev. ed. (London: Verso, 1991); Paul Brass, Ethnicity and Nationalism: Theory and Comparison (Newbury Park, Calif.: Sage, 1991); Basil Davidson, Black Man's Burden: Africa and the Curse of the Nation-State (New York: Times Books, 1992); Ernest Gellner, Thought and Change (London: Weidenfeld & Nicolson, 1964); Eric Hobsbawm and Terrence Ranger, The Invention of Tradition (New York: Cambridge University Press, 1983).

90. Beetham, supra note 13; Gerard Delanty, Loyalty and the European Union, in Michael Waller and Andrew Linklater, eds., Political Loyalty and the Nation-State (London: Routledge, 2003), at 123.

91. Davidson, supra note 89; Ted Gurr, Minorities at Risk: A Global View of Ethnopolitical Conflict (Washington, D.C.: Institute of Peace Press, 1993); Michael

Huysseune, Deconstructing and Reconstructing Loyalty: The Case of Italy, in Waller and Linklater, supra note 90, at 173; Michael Ignatieff, Blood and Belonging: Journeys in the New Nationalism (New York: Farrar, Strauss & Giroux, 1994); Will Kymlicka, Multicultural Citizenship (Oxford: Oxford University Press, 1995); Martha Minow, Making All the Difference: Inclusion, Exclusion and American Law (Ithaca, N.Y., Cornell University Press, 1990); Pinia Werbner, Divided Loyalties, Empowered Citizenship: Muslims in Britain, in Waller and Linklater, supra note 90, at 105. As these sources suggest, the opposition of ethnic groups to the nation can be regarded as positive or negative, depending on one's point of view.

92. See Isaac Deutscher, Stalin: A Political Biography (New York: Vintage, 1960), at 461–97; John Mackintosh, Juggernaut; A History of the Soviet Armed Forces (New York: Macmillan, 1967); Martin McCauley, The Soviet Union, 1917–1991, 2d ed. (London: Longman, 1993), at 145–74.

93. Sheila Fitzpatrick, Everyday Stalinism (Oxford: Oxford University Press, 1999); Alena V. Ledeneva, Russia's Economy of Favours: Blat, Networking, and Informal Exchange (Cambridge: Cambridge University Press, 1998).

94. One source of such variation is commitment to conflicting values, such as women's rights or cosmopolitanism. See Jill Stearns, Conflicting Loyalties: Women's Human Rights and the Politics of Identity, in Waller and Linklater, supra note 90, at 59; Jeremy Waldron, Minority Cultures and the Cosmopolitan Alternative, in Will Kymlicka, ed., The Rights of Minority Cultures (Oxford: Oxford University Press, 1995), at 93.

95. David Gauthier, Morals by Agreement (Oxford: Clarendon Press, 1986), at 113–56.

96. See Daniel Bell, Communitarianism and Its Critics (Oxford: Clarendon Press, 1993); Amitai Etzioni, The Spirit of Community: Rights, Responsibilities and the Communitarian Agenda (New York: Crown Publishers, 1993); Alasdair MacIntyre, After Virtue, 2d ed. (Notre Dame, Ind.: University of Notre Dame Press, 1984), at 204–25; Michael Sandel, Liberalism and the Limits of Justice (Cambridge: Cambridge University Press, 1982); Michael Smith, ed., Power, Community and the City (New Brunswick, N.J.: Transaction Books, 1988).

97. MacIntyre, supra note 96, at 221; Robert Putnam, Bowling Alone: The Collapse and Revival of American Community (New York: Simon & Schuster, 2000), at 273–76; Michael Sandel, Democracy's Discontents: America in Search of a Public Philosophy (Cambridge, Mass.: Belknap Press, 1996), at 201–49; Vernon Van Dyke, The Individual, the State and Ethnic Communities in Political Theory, in Kymlicka, supra note 94, at 31.

98. See Richard Rorty, Solidarity or Objectivity?, in John Rajchman and Cornel West, Post-Analytic Philosophy (New York: Columbia University Press, 1985); Iris Young, The Ideal of Community and the Politics of Difference, in Linda Nicholson, ed., Feminism/Postmodernism (New York: Routledge, 1990).

99. Fitzpatrick, supra note 93; Ledeneva, supra note 93.

100. Tyler, supra note 1, at 115–78; Tom Tyler and Yuen Huo, Trust in the Law: Encouraging Public Cooperation with the Police and the Courts (New York: Russell Sage, 2002). See also Karyl Kinsey, Deterrence and Alienation Effects of IRS Enforcement: An Analysis of Survey Data, in Joel Slemrod, ed., Why People

Pay Taxes: Tax Compliance and Enforcement 264 (Ann Arbor: University of Michigan Press, 1992).

101. See Richard McAdams, An Attitudinal Theory of Expressive Law, Oregon Law Review 79:339 (2000).

102. Marco Steenbergen, Kathleen McGraw, John Scholz, How Taxpayers Think about Their Taxes: Frames and Values, in Slemrod, supra note 100.

103. Paul Robinson and John Darley, The Utility of Desert, Northwestern University Law Review 91:453 (1997); Paul Robinson, Punishing Dangerousness: Cloaking Preventive Detention as Criminal Justice, Harvard Law Review 114:1429 (2001). See also Johannes Andenaes, Punishment and Deterrence (Ann Arbor: University of Michigan Press, 1974).

104. Ian Ayres and John Braithwaite, Responsive Regulation: Transcending the Deregulation Debate (Oxford: Oxford University Press, 1992); Eugene Bardach and Robert Kagan, Going by the Book: The Problem of Regulatory Unreasonableness (Philadelphia: Temple University Press, 1982); Michael Dorf, Legal Indeterminacy and Institutional Design, New York University Law Review 78:875 (2003); Daniel Farber, Revitalizing Regulation, Michigan Law Review 91:1278 (1993); Daniel Farber, Taking Slippage Seriously: Noncompliance and Creative Compliance in Environmental Law, Harvard Environmental Law Review 23:297 (1999); Jody Freeman, Collaborative Governance in the Administrative State, UCLA Law Review 45:1 (1997); Neil Gunningham, Peter Grabosky, and Darren Sinclair, Smart Regulation: Designing Environmental Policy (Oxford: Clarendon Press, 1998); Joel Handler, Dependent People, the State, and the Modern/Postmodern Search for the Dialogic Community, UCLA Law Review 35:999 (1988); Orly Lobel, The Renew Deal: The Fall of Regulation and the Rise of Governance in Contemporary Legal Thought, Minnesota Law Review 89 (2004); Lars Noah, Administrative Arm-Twisting in the Shadow of Congressional Delegations of Authority, Wisconsin Law Review 1997:873 (1997); Richard Pildes and Cass Sunstein, Reinventing the Regulatory State, Chicago Law Review 62:1 (1995); Susan Sturm, Second Generation Employment Discrimination: A Structural Approach, Columbia Law Review 101:458 (2001).

105. Robert Nozick, Anarchy, State and Utopia (New York: Basic Books, 1974), at 4.

106. Kelman and Hamilton, supra note 13. The example of the Holocaust, although perhaps overly dramatic in this context, is also relevant. See also Hannah Arendt, Eichmann in Jerusalem: A Report on the Banality of Evil (New York: Viking, 1963); Daniel Goldhagen, Hitler's Willing Executioners: Ordinary Germans and the Holocaust (New York: Alfred A. Knopf, 1996).

107. See Teichman, supra note 5.

108. See Barbara Tuchman, A Distant Mirror: The Calamitous 14th Century (New York: Alfred Knopf, 1978).

109. This remained true as late as the American Civil War. A Confederate soldier wrote: "Be [the] army friend or foe, it passes along like a withering scourge, leaving only ruin and desolation behind." David Eicher, The Longest Night (New York: Simon and Schuster, 2001), at 193.

110. See Hugo Grotius, The Law of War and Peace (Francis Kelsey, trans.) (In-

dianapolis: Bobbs-Merrill, 1925), I, III, VIII. 1–2; Thomas Hobbes, Leviathan (New York: Penguin, 1951), at 228–39, 261–74 (Chs. 18 & 21).

111. See sources sited in note 104, supra.

112. Farber, Taking, supra note 104.

113. Several recent commentators attribute this phenomenon to cognitive errors, rather than an emotional error such as social nostalgia. See Cary Coglianese, Bounded Evaluation: Cognition, Incoherence, and Regulatory Policy, Stanford Law Review 54:1217 (2002); Cass Sunstein, Daniel Kahneman, David Schkade, Ilana Ritov, Predictably Incoherent Judgments, Stanford Law Review 54:1153 (2002).

114. For programs that explicitly involved negotiated standards of compliance, see Charles Caldart and Nicholas Ashford, Negotiation as a Means of Developing and Implementing Environmental and Occupational Health and Safety Policy, Harvard Environmental Law Review 23:141 (1999); David Dana, The Uncertain Merits of Environmental Enforcement Reform: The Case of Supplemental Environmental Projects, Wisconsin Law Review 1998:1181 (1998); Freeman, supra note 104; Dennis Hirsch, Bill and Al's XL-ent Adventure: An Analysis of the EPA's Legal Authority to Implement the Clinton Administration's Project XL, University of Illinois Law Review 1998:129 (1998); Bradford Mank, The Environmental Protection Agency's Project XL and Other Regulatory Reform Initiatives: The Need for Legislative Authorization, Ecology Law Quarterly 25:1 (1998).

115. Malcolm Feeley, Coercion and Compliance: A New Look at an Old Problem, in Samuel Krislov et al., eds., Compliance and the Law (Beverly Hills: Sage, 1972), at 51.

116. Edmund Husserl, Ideas: General Introduction to Pure Phenomenology (W. R. Boyce Gibson, trans.) (New York: Collier, 1962), at 93.

117. See, e.g., William Van Alstyne, The Second Amendment and the Personal Right to Arms, Duke Law Journal 43:1236 (1994); Randy Barnett and Don Kates, Under Fire: The New Consensus on the Second Amendment, Emory Law Journal 45:1141 (1996); Don Kates, Handgun Prohibition and the Original Meaning of the Second Amendment, Michigan Law Review 82:204 (1983); Nelson Lund, The Second Amendment, Political Liberty, and the Right to Self-Preservation, Alabama Law Review 39:103 (1987).

118. See Malcolm Feeley and Edward Rubin, Judicial Policy Making and the Modern State: How the Courts Reformed America's Prisons (New York: Cambridge University Press, 1998), at 13–19, 30–39.

119. In other words, it is invented tradition. See James Fentress and Chris Wichham, Social Memory: New Perspectives on the Past (Oxford: Blackwell, 1992); Maurice Halbwachs, The Collective Memory (Francis Ditter & Vita Ditter, trans.) (New York: Harper & Row, 1980); Hobsbawm and Ranger, supra note 89.

120. Jürgen Habermas, The Theory of Communicative Action, vol. 2: Lifeworld and System: A Critique of Functionalist Reason (Thomas McCarthy, ed.) (Boston: Beacon Press, 1989), at 153–97, 332–73. Habermas describes this process as the "uncoupling of system and lifeworld" and he regards it as a negative development.

121. John of Salisbury, Policraticus: Of the Frivolities of Courtiers and the Footprints of Philosophers (Cary J. Nederman, trans.) (New York: Cambridge University Press, 1990), at 190–213 (VIII. 17–21).

122. Harold Berman, Law and Revolution (Cambridge, Mass.: Harvard University Press, 1983), at 281–82; Black, supra note 7, at 75–78, 148–52; Jean Dubabin, Government, in J. H. Burns, ed., The Cambridge History of Medieval Political Thought c. 350–c. 1450 (Cambridge: Cambridge University Press, 1988), at 477, 493–98.

123. Jürgen Habermas, The Theory of Communicative Action, vol. 1: Reason and the Rationalization of Society (Thomas McCarthy, trans.) (Boston: Beacon Press, 1984); Weber, supra note 1, at 641–1003. See Karl Lowith, Max Weber, and Karl Marx (London: Routledge, 1993), at 51–80.

124. See Habermas, supra note 1.

125. For the original, see Theodore Sorensen, Kennedy (New York: Harper & Row, 1965), at 248.

126. This is particularly clear from comparative historical analysis. See Jeff Goodwin, No Other Way Out: States and Revolutionary Movements, 1945–1991 (Cambridge: Cambridge University Press, 2001); Theda Skocpol, States and Social Revolutions: A Comparative Study of France, Russia and China (Cambridge: Cambridge University Press, 1979); Theda Skocpol, Social Revolutions in the Modern World (Cambridge: Cambridge University Press, 1994); Timothy Wickham-Crowley, Guerillas and Revolutions in Latin America: A Comparative Study of Insurgents and Regimes since 1956 (Princeton: Princeton University Press, 1992).

127. The classic examples are peasant rebellions, such as the Jacquere or Wat Tyler's, where the crowds slaughtered noblemen while proclaiming loyalty to the king. Yves-Marie Berce, History of Peasant Revolts: The Social Origins of Rebellion in Early Modern France (Amanda Whitmore, trans.) (Ithaca, N.Y.: Cornell University Press, 1990); Charles Oman, The Great Revolt of 1381 (Oxford: Clarendon Press, 1969).

Notes to Chapter Six

1. Black's Law Dictionary, 6th ed. (St. Paul, Minn.: West Publishing, 1990): "Law, in its generic sense, is a body of rules of action or conduct prescribed by controlling authority and having binding legal force"; Oxford English Dictionary, 2d ed. (Oxford: Clarendon Press, 1989): "a rule of conduct imposed by authority. . . . The body of rules, whether proceeding from formal enactment or from custom, which a particular state or community recognizes as binding on its members or subjects"; Webster's Third International Dictionary (Springfield, Mass.: Merriam-Webster, 1993): "A binding custom or practice of a community; a rule or mode of conduct or action that is prescribed or formally recognized as binding by a supreme controlling authority or is made obligatory by a sanction . . . made, recognized, or enforced by the controlling authority."

2. George Fletcher, Basic Concepts of Legal Thought (New York: Oxford University Press, 1996), at 11–14, 33–38. This dual meaning dates back to the Middle Ages. See Otto Gierke, Political Theories of the Middle Age (Frederic Maitland, trans.) (Cambridge: Cambridge University Press, 1938), at 73–79.

3. Jürgen Habermas, The Theory of Communicative Action, vol. 1: Reason and the Rationalization of Society (Thomas McCarthy, trans.) (Boston: Beacon

Press, 1984), at 243–71; Niklas Luhmann, A Sociological Theory of Law (Elizabeth King & Martin Albrow, trans.) (London: Routledge & Kegan Paul, 1985);
Max Weber, Economy and Society (Guenther Roth & Claus Wittich, eds.) (Berkeley: University of California Press, 1978), at 217–26, 839–76. With respect to Luhmann's work, some of which has not been translated, see Hugh Baxter, Autopoiesis
and the "Relative Autonomy" of Law, Cardozo Law Review 19:1987 (1998).

    4. St. Thomas Aquinas, Summa Theologica (Fathers of the English Dominican
Province, trans.) (Westminster, Md.: Christian Classics, 1981), at 995 (I–II, Q.
90, A. 4). See Gierke, supra note 2, 75–76; Kenneth Pennington, Law, Legislative
Authority and Theories of Government, in J. H. Burns, ed., The Cambridge History of Medieval Political Thought, c. 350–c. 1450 (Cambridge: Cambridge University Press, 1988), at 424, 424–30; Jacques Maritain, The Rights of Man and
Natural Law (Doris Anson, trans.) (New York: Gordian Press, 1971), at 39–43. As
Pennington notes, there was a subsidiary theme connecting law with will, but association of law and reason prevailed. See note 40, infra.

    5. See Joseph Canning, A History of Medieval Political Thought, 300–1450
(London: Routledge, 1996), at 129–30.

    6. Aquinas, supra note 4, at 966–97 (I–II, Q. 91, A.2).

    7. See John Austin, The Province of Jurisprudence Determined (Wilfrid Rumble,
ed.) (New York: Cambridge University Press, 1995), Lecture I. Austin describes
such things as gravity as "laws by remote analogy."

    8. Randy Barnett asserts this equivalence of gravity and enacted statutes in ar-
guing for the validity of natural law. A Law Professor's Guide to Natural Law and
Natural Rights, Harvard Journal of Law & Public Policy 20:655 (1997), at
656–57. See also Richard Epstein, International News Service v. Associated Press:
Custom and Law as Sources of Property Rights in News, Virginia Law Review
78:85 (1992); Warren Lehman, Rules in Law, Georgetown Law Journal 72:1571
(1984); Michael Moore, Moral Reality, Wisconsin Law Review 1982:1061 (1982).
Characterizing a position he partially accepts, Epstein writes, "Property comes
from the bottom up, and not from the top down. In other words the state does not
hand down the law or create property rights, any more than it decrees the laws of
physics or chemistry." Epstein, supra, at 85.

    9. Bentham makes fun of this idea at the beginning of his Comment on the
Commentaries. He ascribes to Blackstone the position that law is a command
given by one person to another, and then observes that Blackstone refers to the
law of optics. What command is involved in the optical law that the angle of reflection is equal to the angle of incidence? he asks. It is presumably, God saying
"hark ye, you rays. There are some surfaces you will meet in your travels that
when you strike upon them, will send you packing: now when in such a case, this
is what I would have you do: keep the same slope in *going* that you did in coming. Mind and do what I say: if you don't, as sure as you are rays it will be the
worse for you: upon this the rays (finding they should get into bad bread else)
made their bows, shrugged up their shoulders and went and did so." Jeremy
Bentham, A Comment on the Commentaries (Darmstadt, Ger.: Scientia Verlag
Aalen, 1976), at 32.

    10. The Mirror of the Justices (William J. Whittaker, ed.) (London: Selden So-
ciety, 1895). The *Mirror* is attributed to the archivist Andrew Horn, originally a

London fishmonger. Frederic Maitland, however, believes this to be an error. See supra, Introduction, at xii–xxv.

11. See Gierke, supra note 2, at 73–87.

12. Aquinas, supra note 4, at 997–98 (I–II, Q. 91, A. 3); see also id. at 1014 (I–II, Q. 95, A.2), 1022 (I–II, Q. 97, A.1).

13. Id. at 997–98 (I–II, Q. 91, A.3), 1014 (I–II, Q. 95, A.2). Thus, for example, natural law declares murder a crime and requires a murderer to be punished, but the particular measure of punishment is established by human law.

14. Id. at 1024 (I–II, Q. 97, A. 3). "When a thing is done again and again it seems to proceed from a deliberate judgment of reason"—that is, reason made manifest by deeds, rather than by speech.

15. Id. at 1019–20 (I–II, Q. 96, A. 4), id. at 1014 (I–II, Q. 95, A.2). An authorized promulgation by the sovereign that conflicts with natural law is simply not a law, according to St. Thomas, and need not be obeyed. If the promulgation contravenes divine law, and thus threatens people's salvation, it must not be obeyed.

16. For a contemporary version of St. Thomas's position, see Maritain, supra note 4, at 62–65, 80–81.

17. R. Van Caenegem, Government, Law and Society, in Burns, supra note 4, at 192–95; Canning, supra note 5, at 22–25; Janet Nelson, Politics and Ritual in Early Medieval Europe (London: Hambledon Press, 1986), at 62. As Van Caenegem states, supra at 193, with respect to the Norman regime in England, "Royal legislation was revived in a more humble, sporadic, even shame-faced way."

18. Aquinas, supra note 4, at 1010–11 (I–II, Q. 94, A. 4).

19. Id. at 1020–21 (I–II, Q. 96, A.5) ("as to the directive force of law, the sovereign is subject to the law by his own will, according to the statement that 'whatever law a man makes for another, he should keep for himself'").

20. Id. ("Hence, in the judgment of God, the sovereign is not exempt from the law as to its directive force, but he should fulfill it of his own free will and not of constraint").

21. Here, as elsewhere, St. Thomas is unifying disparate strands of thought. As Randall Collins notes, "The greatness of Thomas Aquinas is as an intellectual politician." Randall Collins, The Sociology of Philosophies: A Global Theory of Intellectual Change (Cambridge, Mass.: Belknap Press, 1998), at 479.

22. R. W. Southern, The Making of the Middle Ages (New Haven, Conn.: Yale University Press, 1953), at 109–10, 138, 146.

23. Marc Bloch, Feudal Society (L. A. Manyon, trans.) (Chicago: University of Chicago Press, 1961), at 370–74 (vol. 2); Georges Duby, The Chivalrous Society (Cynthia Postan, trans.) (Berkeley: University of California Press, 1977), at 15–58; F. L. Ganshof, Feudalism (Toronto: University of Toronto Press, 1961), at 158–67. England was something of an exception; as a result of the Norman Conquest, it developed a precocious unity, albeit one that was partially eroded in the years that followed. Thomas Ertman, The Birth of Leviathan (Cambridge: Cambridge University Press, 1997), at 156–223; W. L. Warren, The Governance of Norman and Angevin England 1086–1272 (London: Edward Arnold, 1987). The same was true for the Norman Kingdom of Sicily. See Charles Homer Haskins, The Normans in European History (New York: W. W. Norton, 1966).

24. Heinrich Fichtenau, Living in the Tenth Century (Patrick Geary, trans.) (Chicago: University of Chicago Press, 1991), at 262–83. On other voluntary acts of devotion, with at least some sense of submission to divine law, see Johan Huizinga, The Waning of the Middle Ages (Garden City, N.Y.: Doubleday Anchor, 1954), at 177–200.

25. Peter Goodrich, Law in the Courts of Love: Andreas Capellanus and the Judgments of Love, Stanford Law Review 48:633 (1996); Jean Markale, Courtly Love (Jon Grahams, trans.) (Rochester, Vt.: Inner Traditions, 2000).

26. Bloch, supra note 23, at 312–19: Frances Gies, The Knight in History (New York: Harper & Row, 1984), at 77–80, 104–5; Huizinga, supra note 24, at 67–107; Maurice Keen, Chivalry (New Haven, Conn.: Yale University Press, 1984), at 143–78; Sidney Painter, French Chivalry: Chivalric Ideas and Practices in Medieval France (Baltimore: Johns Hopkins University Press, 1940).

27. In addition, there were many social rituals, such as those of mourning, penance, humiliation, and reconciliation, that had their own associated set of rules. See Fichtenau, supra note 24, at 30–49.

28. Keen, supra note 26, at 174–75. As Keen states, "The insult was a very serious one. It implied a reproach that would be universal in knightly company, and that would set the guardians of chivalrous mores into action."

29. For medieval accounts of the chivalric rules regarding battlefield behavior, see Honore Bonet, The Tree of Battles (G. W. Coopland, trans.) (Cambridge, Mass.: Harvard University Press, 1949); Jean Froissart, Chronicles (John Bourchier, Lord Berners, trans.) (New York: AMS Press, 1967) (see, e.g., §§ 161–67, describing the Battle of Poitiers and the dinner that follows, where the victorious Black Prince serves and honors the King of France, who is now his captive); Lancelot of the Lake (Corin Corley, trans.) (Oxford: Oxford University Press, 1989) (the "Vulgate" Lancelot), at 277–82, 293–94, 304–07, 535–37; Raymond Lull, The Order of Chivalry (Hammersmith: Kelmscott Press, 1893).

30. Huizinga, supra note 24, at 67–69.

31. John Keegan, The Face of Battle (New York: Penguin, 1976), at 108–12.

32. Lancelot of the Lake, supra note 29. The work's intention to portray Lancelot as the embodiment of chivalry is announced at the beginning, when the young Lancelot receives extensive instruction on the subject from the Lady of the Lake. Her parting words to him as he sets off for King Arthur's court are one of the leading statements of the chivalric ideal. Id. at 51–57. See also the wise man's advice to the repentant Arthur, id. at 241–50. The Vulgate cycle is a series of Arthurian tales written in the first part of the thirteenth century. In addition to Lancelot of the Lake, it includes The Quest for the Holy Grail, The History of the Holy Grail, The History of Merlin and The Death of Arthur. The author or authors of these works are unknown. The attributions to Walter Map, archdeacon of Oxford, in The Quest of the Holy Grail and the Death of Arthur, and to Robert de Boron, author of an earlier Lancelot cycle, in The History of the Holy Grail and The History of Merlin, are generally regarded as false.

33. Id. at 61–62. The wounded knight's name is never given.

34. Id. at 62.

35. Id. at 72–75.

36. Id. at 205.

37. Id. at 207.

38. Hugo Grotius, The Rights of War and Peace (M. Walter Dunne, trans.) (Washington, D.C., 1901; reprint, Westport, Conn.: Hyperion Press, 1979), at 21–30 (1. I. 10–17), see id. at 21 (1. I. 10) ("Natural right is the dictate of right reason, showing the moral turpitude, or moral necessity, of any act from its agreement or disagreement with a rational nature, and consequently that such as act is wither forbidden or commanded by God, the author of nature"); Samuel Pufendorf, On the Law of Nature and of Nations in Eight Books, in The Political Writings of Samuel Pufendorf (Craig Carr & Michael Seidler, eds.) (New York: Oxford University Press, 1994); see id. at 149 (II.3.13) ("Most men agree that the natural law is to be derived from man's reason itself, and therefore from the injunctions of this faculty when it is functioning correctly. . . . [E]ven though the Divine Scriptures shed additional light to make the natural law more clearly known, it can nonetheless be investigated and firmly demonstrated even without that assistance, through the rational powers which the Creator has granted to and still preserves in us").

39. Thomas Browne, Religio Medici (Cambridge: Cambridge University Press, 1963), at 18 (I, 16) (originally published 1642).

40. There were, of course, dissenters from this general view. Perhaps the most notable is Hobbes. See Thomas Hobbes, Leviathan (C. B. Macpherson, ed.) (London: Penguin, 1968), at 201–17 (Ch. 15), 311–35 (Ch. 26) See 216–17: "These dictates of Reason, men use to call by the name of Lawes; but improperly: for they are but Conclusions, or Theoremes concerning what conduceth to the conservation and defence of themselves; whereas Law, properly is the word of him, that by right hath command over others." This notion of law as the ruler's will was found in Roman law; see Digest of Justinian, in Corpus Juris Civilis, The Civil Law (S. P. Scott, trans.) (New York: AMS Press, 1973), vol. 2, at 227 (Digest I.IV.I), and it was present in the Middle Ages as well. According to Pennington, supra note 4, at 427–28, the canonist Laurentius Hispanus introduced it, but without producing a decisive impact.

41. See sources cited in Habermas, supra note 3. The turning point may be Montesquieu, who pays a brief obeisance to natural law before proceeding to positive law, and the way it varies from one nation to the next. Baron Montesquieu (Charles Louis de Secondat), The Spirit of the Laws (Anne Cohler, Basia Miller, & Harold Stone trans.) (Cambridge: Cambridge University Press, 1989), at 6–7 (Bk. 1, Ch. 2). His treatment of religion is particularly naturalistic. Id. at 479–89 (Bk. 25, Chs. 1–12).

42. Michael Broers, Europe under Napoleon, 1799–1815 (London: Arnold, 1996), at 52–58. René David, French Law: Its Structure, Sources and Methodology (Baton Rouge: Louisiana State University Press, 1972), at 11–16; Charles Seruzier, Historical Summary of the French Codes: With French and Foreign Bibliographical Annotations Concerning the General Principles of the Codes Followed by a Dissertation on Codification (David Combe, trans.) (Littleton, Colo.: Fred B. Rothman, 1979). Scholars have concluded that The Napoleonic Code was not the Newtonian reconceptualization that it purported to be, but a relatively conservative compromise between Roman and medieval law that consolidated several prior projects. See Broers, supra, at 52; David, supra, at 14–16; James Gord-

ley, Myths of the French Civil Code, American Journal of Comparative Law 42:459 (1994). This only underscores the mythological nature of the claim that the Code is a coherent, orderly system of law.

43. Robert Kann, A History of the Habsburg Empire, 1526–1918 (Berkeley: University of California Press, 1974), at 179–80; Giles Macdonogh, Prussia: The Perversion of an Idea (London: Sinclair-Stevenson, 1994), at 40–43; Saul K. Padover, The Revolutionary Emperor: Joseph the Second (New York: Robert O. Ballou, 1934), at 193–98; Hans Rosenberg, Bureaucracy, Aristocracy, and Autocracy: The Prussian Experience, 1660–1815 (Cambridge: Harvard University Press, 1958). As might be expected, Joseph II was the driving force behind this effort in Austria and, as might be expected, he tried to do too much too fast, and the Austrian code was not adopted until after his death.

44. Morton Horwitz, The Transformation of American Law, 1780–1860 (Cambridge, Mass.: Harvard University Press, 1977), at 30.

45. Randy Barnett, The Structure of Liberty: Justice and the Rule of Law (Oxford: Clarendon Press, 1998); John Finnis, Natural Law and Natural Rights (Oxford: Clarendon Press, 1988); Robert George, In Defense of Natural Law (Oxford: Clarendon Press, 1999); Martin Golding, Philosophy of Law (Englewood Cliffs, N.J.: Prentice-Hall, 1975); Heidi Hurd, Moral Combat (Cambridge: Cambridge University Press, 1999); Alisdair MacIntyre, Whose Justice? Which Rationality? (South Bend, Ind.: University of Notre Dame Press, 1988); Maritain, supra note 4; Jacques Maritain, Natural Law: Reflections on Theory and Practice (William Sweet, ed.) (South Bend, Ind.: St. Augustine's Press, 2001); Michael Moore, Law as a Functional Kind, in Robert George, ed., Natural Law Theory: Contemporary Essays (Oxford: Clarendon Press, 1992), at 188; Henry Veatch, Human Rights: Fact or Fancy? (Baton Rouge: Louisiana State University Press, 1985); Lloyd Weinreb, Natural Law and Justice (Cambridge, Mass.: Harvard University Press, 1987).

46. David, supra note 42; George Fletcher, Truth in Codification, U.C. Davis Law Review 31:745 (1998); Gordley, supra note 42; Arthur Hartkamp et al., eds., Towards a European Civil Code, 2d ed. (The Hague: Kluwer Law International, 1998).

47. See Mitchell Lasser, Judicial (Self-) Portraits: Judicial Discourse in the French Legal System, Yale Law Journal 104:1325 (1995); Michael Troper, Christophe Grzegorczyk, and Jean-Louis Gardies, Statutory Interpretation in France, in D. Neil MacCormick and Robert Summers, eds., Interpreting Statutes: A Comparative Study (Aldershot: Dartmouth, 1991), at 171.

48. Zenon Bankowski and D. Neil MacCormick, Statutory Interpretation in the United Kingdom, in MacCormick and Summers, supra note 47, at 359; Elmer Driedger, The Construction of Statutes, 2d ed. (Toronto: Butterworths, 1983).

49. Benjamin Watt, Why French Law Rejects Judicial Precedent, International Business Lawyer 25:18 (1997).

50. J. B. Ruhl and James Salzman, Mozart and the Red Queen: The Problem of Regulatory Accretion in the Administrative State, Georgetown Law Journal 91:757 (2003); Peter Schuck, The Limits of Law: Essays on Democratic Governance (Boulder, Colo.: Westview, 2000), at 3–46.

51. William Buzbee, Recognizing the Regulatory Commons: A Theory of

Regulatory Gaps, Iowa Law Review 89:1 (2003). Buzbee argues that areas assigned to multiple regulators will be less regulated than society desires due to both client confusion and regulator neglect.

52. H.L.A. Hart, The Concept of Law (Oxford: Clarendon Press, 1961).

53. Austin, supra note 7; Hans Kelsen, General Theory of Law and State (Anders Wedberg, trans.) (Cambridge, Mass.: Harvard University Press, 1946); Hans Kelsen, Pure Theory of Law (Max Knight, trans.) (Berkeley: University of California Press, 1978).

54. Hart, supra note 52, at 38.

55. Id. at 40–41.

56. Id. at 125. Hart uses this example to make a different point, namely, that statutory language has an "open texture" that requires interpretation. However, it is precisely in his choice of examples that Hart reveals his pre-modern conception of law.

57. Hart describes laws intended to control citizen behavior as primary rules, and laws that give orders to public officials as secondary rules. Id. at 89–96.

58. Id. at 29–43, 77–78.

59. Ronald Dworkin, Taking Rights Seriously (Cambridge, Mass.: Harvard University Press, 1977), at 81–130; Ronald Dworkin, Law's Empire (Cambridge, Mass.: Belknap Press, 1986), at 225–75.

60. See Hart, supra note 52, at 121–32.

61. Dworkin, Law's Empire, supra note 59, at 225.

62. Id. at 91–107.

63. Id. at 1.

64. Id. at 176–84; see id. at 313–54.

65. Id. at 177–84.

66. Electronic Fund Transfer Act, 15 U.S.C. 1693g (2002).

67. Weber, supra note 3, at 24–26. See Edward Rubin, It's Time to Make the Administrative Procedure Act Administrative, Cornell Law Review 89: 95 (2003), at 146–62.

68. Weber, supra note 3, at 26.

69. Herbert Simon, Administrative Behavior: A Study of Decision-Making Processes in Administrative Organization, 3d ed. (New York: Free Press, 1976).

70. Steven Kelman, Making Public Policy: A Hopeful View of American Government (New York: Basic Books, 1987); Charles Lindblom, The Policy-Making Process, 2d ed. (Englewood Cliffs, N.J.: Prentice-Hall, 1980); Nelson Polsby, Congress and the Presidency, 4th ed. (Englewood Cliffs, N.J.: Prentice-Hall, 1986); Simon, supra note 69; Edith Stokey and Richard Zeckhauser, A Primer for Policy Analysis (New York: W. W. Norton, 1978); Aaron Wildavsky, The Art and Craft of Policy Analysis (London: Macmillan, 1979).

71. Ian Ayres and John Braithwaite, Responsive Regulation: Transcending the Deregulation Debate (New York: Oxford University Press, 1992); Cary Coglianese and David Lazer, Management-Based Regulation: Prescribing Private Management to Achieve Public Goals, Law & Society Review 37:691 (2003); Eugene Bardach and Robert Kagan, Going by the Book: The Problem of Regulatory Unreasonableness (Philadelphia: Temple University Press, 1982); Eugene Bardach, The Implementation Game: What Happens after a Bill Becomes a Law (Cam-

bridge, Mass.: MIT Press, 1977); Keith Hawkins, Environment and Enforcement: Regulation and the Social Definition of Pollution (Oxford: Clarendon Press, 1984); Robert Kagan, Adversarial Legalism: The American Way of Law (Cambridge, Mass.: Harvard University Press, 2001); Jeffrey Pressman and Aaron Wildavsky, Implementation (Berkeley: University of California Press, 1973); John Scholz, Cooperation, Deterrence, and the Ecology of Regulatory Enforcement, Law & Society Review 18:179 (1984).

72. For example, public choice scholars attribute the growth of government to the desire of elected officials to maximize their chance of reelection, and the desire of administrators to maximize their budgets, rejecting the idea that government has grown because society wants it to achieve an increased number of public policies. See Peter Aranson, Ernest Gellhorn, and Glen Robinson, A Theory of Legislative Delegation, Cornell Law Review 68:1 (1982); Morris Fiorina, Congress: Keystone of the Washington Establishment (New Haven, Conn.: Yale University Press, 1977); Dennis Mueller and Peter Murell, Interest Groups and the Size of Government, Public Choice 48:125 (1986); William Niskanen, Bureaucracy and Representative Government (Chicago: Aldine, Atherton, 1971); Sam Peltzman, The Growth of Government, Journal of Law & Economics 23:209 (1980).

73. See William Eskridge and Philip Frickey, The Supreme Court, 1993 Term: Foreword: Law as Equilibrium, Harvard Law Review 108:26 (1994); Peter Ordeshook, A Political Theory Primer (New York: Routledge, 1992); Daniel Rodriguez, The Positive Political Dimensions of Regulatory Reform, Washington University Law Quarterly 72:1 (1994); Daniel Rodriguez, The Positive Political Theory of Legislative History: New Perspectives on the 1964 Civil Rights Act and Its Interpretation, University of Pennsylvania Law Review 151:1417 (2003); Kenneth Shepsle and Barry Weingast, eds., Positive Theories of Congressional Institutions (Ann Arbor: University of Michigan Press, 1995).

74. Ronald Cass, Models of Administrative Action, Virginia Law Review 72:363 (1986); Colin Diver, The Optimal Precision of Administrative Rules, Yale Law Journal 93:65 (1983); Colin Diver, Policymaking Paradigms in Administrative Law, Harvard Law Review 95:393(1981); Jody Freeman, Collaborative Governance in the Administrative State, UCLA Law Review 45:1 (1997); Thomas McGarity, Regulatory Analysis and Regulatory Reform, Texas Law Review 65:1243 (1987); Mark Seidenfeld, A Civic Republican Justification for the Bureaucratic State, Harvard Law Review 105:1511 (1992); Peter Strauss, Rules, Adjudications, and Other Sources of Law in an Executive Department: Reflections on the Interior Department's Administration of the Mining Law, Columbia Law Review 74:1231 (1974); Cass Sunstein, After the Rights Revolution: Reconceiving the Regulatory State (Cambridge, Mass.: Harvard University Press, 1990).

75. Brian Tamanaha, Realistic Socio-Legal Theory: Pragmatism and a Social Theory of Law (Oxford: Clarendon Press, 1997), at 91–152.

76. On the prescriptive stance of legal scholarship, see Paul Brest, The Fundamental Rights Controversy: The Essential Contradictions of Normative Constitutional Scholarship, Yale Law Journal 90:1063 (1981); George Fletcher, Two Modes of Legal Thought, Yale Law Journal 90:970 (1981); Lawrence Friedman, The Law and Society Movement, Stanford Law Review 38:763 (1986); Edward Rubin, The Practice and Discourse of Legal Scholarship, Michigan Law Review

86:1835 (1988); Edward Rubin, Law And and the Methodology of Law, Wisconsin Law Review 1977:521 (1977); Mark Tushnet, Legal Scholarship: Its Causes and Cure, Yale Law Journal 90:1205 (1981).

77. Fritz Kern, Kingship and Law in the Middle Ages (S. B. Chrimes, trans.) (Westport, Conn.: Greenwood Press, 1985), at 149–65; Charles McIlwain, The High Court of Parliament and Its Supremacy (New York: Arno Press, 1979); J.G.A. Pocock, The Ancient Constitution and the Feudal Law (New York: W. W. Norton, 1957), at 30–69; R. Van Caenegem, Government, Law and Society, in J. H. Burns, ed., The Cambridge History of Medieval Political Thought, 350–1450 (Cambridge: Cambridge University Press, 1988), at 174, 192–95.

78. Bronwen Morgan, Social Citizenship in the Shadow of Competition (Aldershot, Eng.: Ashgate, 2003), at 18–22.

79. This characterization of speech acts follows J. L. Austin, How To Do Things with Words (Oxford: Oxford University Press, 1962); Habermas, supra note 3, at 273–337. See Chapter 2.

80. Michael Dorf, Legal Indeterminacy and Institutional Design, New York University Law Review 78:875 (2003); Freeman, supra note 74; Lars Noah, Administrative Arm-Twisting in the Shadow of Congressional Delegations of Authority, Wisconsin Law Review 1997:873 (1997); Susan Sturm, Second Generation Employment Discrimination: A Structural Approach, Columbia Law Review 101:458 (2001); Peter Strauss, The Rulemaking Continuum, Duke Law Journal 41:1463 (1992).

81. Ayres and Braithwaite, supra note 71; Bardach and Kagan, supra note 71; Daniel Farber, Revitalizing Regulation, Michigan Law Review 91:1278 (1993); Daniel Farber, Taking Slippage Seriously: Noncompliance and Creative Compliance in Environmental Law, Harvard Environmental Law Review 23:297 (1999); Freeman, supra note 74; Neil Gunningham, Peter Grabosky, and Darren Sinclair, Smart Regulation: Designing Environmental Policy (Oxford: Clarendon Press, 1998); Orly Lobel, The Renew Deal: The Fall of Regulation and the Rise of Governance in Contemporary Legal Thought, Minnesota Law Review 89 (2004 forthcoming); Morgan, supra note 78; Noah, supra note 80; Eric Orts, Reflexive Environmental Law, Northwestern University Law Review 89:1227 (1995); Richard Pildes and Cass Sunstein, Reinventing the Regulatory State, Chicago Law Review 62:1 (1995); Sturm, supra note 80.

82. Michael Dorf and Charles Sabel, A Constitution of Democratic Experimentalism, Columbia Law Review 98:267 (1998); Joel Handler, Dependent People, the State, and the Modern/Postmodern Search for the Dialogic Community, UCLA Law Review 35:999 (1988); William Simon, The Practice of Justice (Cambridge, Mass.: Harvard University Press, 1998); Sturm, supra note 80.

83. Neil Komesar, Imperfect Alternatives: Choosing Institutions in Law, Economics, and Public Policy (Chicago: University of Chicago Press, 1994); Peter Schuck, Law and Post-Privatization Regulatory Reform: Perspectives from the U.S. Experience, in Peter Schuck, The Limits of Law (Boulder, Colo.: Westview Press, 2000), at 180. For a case study of the shift from command and control to market regulation, see Carl Bauer, Siren Song: Chilean Water Law as a Model for International Reform (Washington, D.C.: Resources for the Future, 2004).

84. Judith Resnik, Managerial Judges, Harvard Law Review 96:374 (1982).

85. Alexander Bickel, The Least Dangerous Branch: The Supreme Court at the Bar of Politics (Indianapolis: Bobbs-Merrill, 1962).

86. Dorf, supra note 80; Charles Sabel and William Simon, Destabilization Rights: How Public Law Litigation Succeeds, Harvard Law Review 117:1015 (2004); Sturm, supra note 80; Cass Sunstein, The Supreme Court 1995 Term: Foreword: Leaving Things Undecided, Harvard Law Review 110:4 (1996); David Zaring, National Rulemaking Through Trial Courts: The Big Case and Institutional Reform, UCLA Law Review 51:1015 (2004). See also, with respect to Common Law, Melvin Eisenberg, The Concept of National Law and the Rule of Recognition, Florida State University Law Review 29:1229 (2002). For seminal works about the modern role of judges, see Abram Chayes, The Role of the Judge in Public Law Litigation, Harvard Law Review 89:1281 (1976); Colin Diver, The Judge as Political Powerbroker: Superintending Structural Change in Public Institutions, Virginia Law Review 65:43 (1979); Owen Fiss, Foreword, The Forms of Justice, Harvard Law Review 93:1 (1979). Malcolm Feeley and I, in a study of prison reform litigation, were primarily concerned with judicial decision making, rather than institutional litigation in its entirety, but came to similar conclusions about the judge's interaction with other parties. See Malcolm Feeley and Edward Rubin, Judicial Policy Making and the Modern State: How the Courts Reformed America's Prisons (Cambridge: Cambridge University Press, 1998).

87. See, e.g., Stephen Burbank and Barry Friedman, eds., Judicial Independence at the Crossroads: An Interdisciplinary Approach (Thousand Oaks, Calif.: Sage, 2002).

88. Alberto Alesina and Roberta Gatti, Independent Central Banks: Low Inflation at No Cost?, American Economic Review 85:196 (1995); Ali al-Nowaihi and Paul Levine, Central Bank Independence: Gain without Pain?, in Nigel Healey and Zenon Wisniewski, eds., Central Banking in Transition Economies (Torun, Poland: Torun Business School, 1999), at 55; Alex Cukierman, Central Bank Strategy: Credibility and Independence (Cambridge, Mass.: MIT Press, 1992); Stanley Fischer, Modern Central Banking, in Forrest Capie, Stanley Fischer, Charles Goodhart, and Norbert Schnadt, eds., The Future of Central Banking (Cambridge: Cambridge University Press, 1995), at 262; Susanne Lohmann, Optimal Commitments in Monetary Policy: Credibility versus Flexibility, American Economic Review 82:273 (1992); Geoffrey Miller, An Interest Group Theory of Central Bank Independence, Journal of Legal Studies 27:433 (1998); Kenneth Rogoff, The Optimal Degree of Commitment to an Intermediate Monetary Target, Quarterly Journal of Economics 100:1169 (1985); Carl Walsh, Optimal Contracts for Central Bankers, American Economic Review 81:150 (1995).

89. See Habermas, supra note 3, vol. 2: Lifeworld and System: A Critique of Functionalist Reason, at 361–73.

90. Kelsen, General Theory, supra note 53, at 58–64. According to Kelsen, a law consists of an instruction for a government agent to apply punishment under a set of defined circumstances, e.g., "If a person commits theft, the competent court shall imprison for five to fifteen years." See Joseph Raz, The Concept of a Legal System: An Introduction to the Theory of the Legal System, 2d ed. (Oxford: Clarendon Press, 1980), at 111–12.

91. Hart, supra note 52, at 89–96.

92. Colin Diver, The Optimal Precision of Administrative Rules, Yale Law Journal 93:65 (1983).

93. For my previous discussion of this idea, see Edward Rubin, Law and Legislation in the Administrative State, Columbia Law Review 89:369 (1989).

94. Meir Dan-Cohen, Decision Rules and Conduct Rules: On Acoustic Separation in Criminal Law, Harvard Law Review 97:625 (1984).

95. In American jurisprudence, this position is generally identified as formalism or conceptualism. See Neil Duxbury, Patterns of American Jurisprudence (Oxford: Clarendon Press, 1995), at 3–64; Thomas Grey, Langdell's Orthodoxy, University of Pittsburgh Law Review 45:1 (1983); Gary Minda, Postmodern Legal Movements (New York: New York University Press, 1995), at 13–20; Dennis Patterson, Langdell's Legacy, Northwestern University Law Review 90:196 (1995); Richard Pildes, Forms of Formalism, University of Chicago Law Review 66:607 (1999); Frederick Schauer, Formalism, Yale Law Journal 97:509 (1988); John Henry Schlegel, Langdell's Legacy or, The Case of the Empty Envelope, Stanford Law Review 36:1517 (1984); G. Edward White, Patterns of American Legal Thought (Indianapolis: Bobbs-Merrill, 1978).

96. Matthew Alder and Eric Posner, eds., Cost-Benefit Analysis: Legal, Economic, and Philosophical Perspectives (Chicago: University of Chicago Press, 2001); David Baybrooke and Charles Lindblom, A Strategy of Decision: Policy Evaluations as a Social Process (New York: Free Press, 1963) (incrementalism); Ajit Dasgupta and D. W. Pearce, Cost-Benefit Analysis: Theory and Practice (London: Macmillan, 1972); Charles Lindblom, The Science of Muddling Through, Public Administration Review 19:79 (1959); E. J. Mishan, Cost-Benefit Analysis, rev. ed. (New York: Praeger, 1976).

97. Kagan, supra note 71.

98. John Braithwaite, Peter Grabosky, and John Walker, An Enforcement Taxonomy of Regulatory Agencies, Law & Policy 9:323 (1987). See Ayres and Braithwaite, supra note 71, at 19–53.

99. Mirror of the Justices, supra note 10.

100. Aquinas, supra note 4, at 997–98 (I–II, Q. 91, A. 3); see also id. at 1014 (I–II, Q. 95, A.2), 1022 (I–II, Q. 97, A.1).

101. Lon Fuller, The Morality of Law, rev. ed. (New Haven, Conn.: Yale University Press, 1969).

102. Hart, supra note 52, at 18–25, 79–88. This norm attaches only to primary rules in Hart's scheme.

103. See note 118, infra (citing sources).

104. For efforts to rehabilitate this position, see note 45, supra (citing sources).

105. Finnis, supra note 45, at 85–97.

106. This distinction is essentially the same as the distinction between negative and positive rights. See Isaiah Berlin, Two Concepts of Liberty, in Isaiah Berlin, Four Essays on Liberty (Oxford: Oxford University Press, 1969), at 118: Maurice Cranston, What Are Human Rights? (London: Bodley Head, 1973); Alan Gewirth, The Community of Rights (Chicago: University of Chicago Press, 1996), at 31–70; Henry Shue, Basic Rights (Princeton: Princeton University Press, 1980).

107. The following discussion of Fuller is drawn from Rubin, supra note 93, at 397–408.

108. Fuller, supra note 101, at 39, 46–94.

109. Id. at 46; see id. at 38–44.

110. Id. at 91–92.

111. Agencies are often punished for past behavior that they had no reason to think was objectionable. See, e.g., Michael Pertschuck, Revolt against Regulation: The Rise and Pause of the Consumer Movement (Berkeley: University of California Press, 1982). We regard this as an acceptable part of the process by which administration is subordinated to politics. Contradiction is common in complex, regulatory statutes, and can be resolved by the agency, as a matter of implementation strategy. For example, the Federal Trade Commission has been assigned the dual role of promoting competition through antitrust law and limiting it through fair trade law. See Alan Stone, Economic Regulation and the Public Interest: The Federal Trade Commission in Theory and Practice (Ithaca, N.Y.: Cornell University Press, 1977), at 26–51. This may or may not be a good governance strategy, but it is not immoral; the agency's job is to resolve the contradiction by balancing the two policies.

112. Fuller is actually aware of this last problem, and takes a strong stand against this form of impossibility, but he thinks it affects only enactments providing for strict criminal liability, rather than the great majority of regulatory statutes. Fuller, supra note 101, at 71–79.

113. In American constitutional law, the generality and nonretroactivity principles are often not described as aspects of due process because they are explicitly forbidden by separate clauses in the original Constitution. United States Constitution, Article I, Section 9, Clause 2 ("No bill of attainder or ex post facto law shall be passed").

114. Hart, supra note 52, at 18–35.

115. See H.L.A. Hart, The Morality of Law (book review) Harvard Law Review 78:1281 (1965); H.L.A. Hart, Positivism and the Separation of Law and Morals, Harvard Law Review 71:593 (1958). For Fuller's responses, see Lon Fuller, supra note 101, at 187 ("A Reply to Critics"); Lon Fuller, Positivism and Fidelity to Law—A Response to Professor Hart, Harvard Law Review 71:630 (1958).

116. See Habermas, supra note 3, vol. 2, at 332–73 (the colonization of the lifeworld).

117. Id., vol. 1, at 243–71.

118. See Elizabeth Anderson and Richard Pildes, Expressive Theories of Law: A General Restatement, University of Pennsylvania Law Review 148:1503 (2000); Deborah Hellman, The Expressive Dimension of Equal Protection, Minnesota Law Review 85:1 (2000); Lawrence Lessig, Social Meaning and Social Norms, University of Pennsylvania Law Review 144:2181 (1996); Richard Pildes, Why Rights Are Not Trumps: Social Meanings, Expressive Harms, and Constitutionalism, Journal of Legal Studies 27:725 (1998); Cass Sunstein, On the Expressive Function of Law, University of Pennsylvania Law Review 144:2021 (1996); Cass Sunstein, Social Norms and Social Roles, Columbia Law Review 96:903 (1996).

119. See Emile Durkheim, The Division of Labor in Society (W. D. Walls, trans.) (New York: Free Press, 1984), at 31–44; Ferdinand Tonnies, Community and Society (*Gemeinschaft und Gesellschaft*) (Charles Loomis, trans.) (New

Brunswick, N.J.: Transaction Books, 1996), at 171–222 (Part 3: The Sociological Basis of Natural Law); Max Weber, Economy and Society (Guenther Roth & Claus Wittich, eds.) (Berkeley: University of California Press, 1978), at 641–895 (The Sociology of Law). Durkheim wrote: "wherever an authority with power to govern is established its first and foremost function is . . . to defend the common consciousness from all its enemies, from within as well as without. It thus becomes the symbol of that consciousness." Durkheim, supra, at 42. For a discussion of Durkheim's position, see David Garland, Punishment and Modern Society (Chicago: University of Chicago Press, 1990), at 28–35.

120. Matthew Adler, Expressive Theories of Law: A Skeptical Overview, University of Pennsylvania Law Review 148:1363 (2000). See also Jane Baron, The Expressive Transparency of Property, Columbia Law Review 102:208 (2002).

121. Adler, supra note 120, at 1376.

122. William Eskridge and John Ferejohn, Super-Statutes, Duke Law Journal 50:1215 (2001). Quoted language at 1216.

123. Fred Dallmayr, Hermeneutics and the Rule of Law, Cardozo Law Review 11:1449 (1990); Richard Fallon, "The Rule of Law" as a Concept in Constitutional Discourse, Columbia Law Review 97:1 (1997); Fletcher, Basic Concepts, supra note 2, at 11–26; Margaret Radin, Reconsidering the Rule of Law, Boston University Law Review 69:781 (1989); Judith Shklar, Political Theory and the Rule of Law, in Allan Hutchinson and Patrick Monahan, The Rule of Law: Ideal or Ideology (Toronto: Carswell, 1987), at 1. Fletcher describes the rule of law as "opaque even to legal philosophers." Id. at 11.

124. Despite the presence of the word "law" in the term, this is not necessarily the case. It is frequently asserted, for example, that the rule of law requires that justice be administered by impartial, independent judges. See Michael Dorf, Prediction and the Rule of Law, UCLA Law Review 42:651 (1995), at 679–90; Gerald Gaus, Public Reason and the Rule of Law, in Ian Shapiro, ed., The Rule of Law: Nomos XXXVI (New York: New York University Press, 1994), at 328; John Rawls, A Theory of Justice (Cambridge, Mass.: Harvard University Press, 1961), at 235–43; Joseph Raz, The Rule of Law and Its Virtue, Law Quarterly Review 93:195 (1977); Geoffrey Walker, The Rule of Law: Foundation of Constitutional Democracy (Carlton, Victoria: Melbourne University Press, 1988), at 1–45. But this standard, by itself, demands only fairness, not law; it is, for example, perfectly consistent with Weber's notion of khadi justice, that is, the Judgment of Solomon or of the village elder sitting under the tree. See Weber, supra note 119, at 813–14, 976–80.

125. See Scott Brewer, Exemplary Reasoning: Semantics, Pragmatics, and the Rational Force of Legal Argument by Analogy, Harvard Law Review 109:923 (1996), at 992–94; A. V. Dicey, Introduction to the Study of the Law of the Constitution, 10th ed. (London: Macmillan, 1987), at 202–3; Frederich Hayek, The Road to Serfdom, 15th ed. (Chicago: University of Chicago Press, 1994), at 80–81; Mortimer Kadish and Sanford Kadish, Discretion to Disobey: A Study of Lawful Departures from Legal Rules (Stanford, Calif.: Stanford University Press, 1973), at 40–45; Antonin Scalia, The Rule of Law as a Law of Rules, University of Chicago Law Review 56:1175 (1989); Robert Summers, A Formal Theory of the Rule of Law, Ratio Juris 6:127 (1993).

126. See Anthony Babington, The Rule of Law in Britain From the Roman Oc-cupation to the Present Day (Chichester: B. Rose, 1978), at 257–90; Neal Devins, Asking the Right Questions: How the Court Honored the Separation of Powers by Reconsidering *Miranda*, University of Pennsylvania Law Review 149:251 (2000), at 279–84; Fuller, supra note 101, at 33–41; Antal Orkeny and Kim Scheppele, Rules of Law: The Complexity of Legality in Hungary, in Martin Kry-gier and Adam Czarnota, eds., The Rule of Law after Communism (Aldershot: Ashgate, 1999), at 55; Radin, supra note 123; Walker, supra note 124, at 31–32.

127. The distinction is obscured by the common phrase that we have a gov-ernment of "laws, and not of men." See Frank Michelman, Law's Republic, Yale Law Journal 97:1493 (1988), at 1500. This could mean that the government, al-though otherwise unconstrained, must rule according to principles stated in ad-vance, or that rules constrain the government, but do not necessarily include the rule that the government must act through such pre-stated principles.

128. The well-known and now notorious exception of impeachment illustrates the point; legislatures in fact monitor high-ranking officials through the impeach-ment and removal process, but, when they do so, they function as a court.

129. As discussed above, in connection with Fuller, supra note 101, due pro-cess also incorporates the idea that rules applied to individuals may not be impos-sible to follow, that they may not be retroactive, and so forth. In *A Theory of Jus-tice*, Rawls, supra note 124, at 235–43, conflates the principles of due process with the rule of law.

130. Additionally, due process demands that judges be impartial, that is, not alter their decision based on the identity of the person before them. See Dorf, supra note 124, at 679–90. This can be regarded as a constraint on judicial deci-sion making. If the demand that government must act through rules is taken to mean only this, and the demand that there be constraints on government includes only this constraint, then the two meanings of the rule of law discussed above col-lapse into one. But that one is merely an aspect of due process, not a general prin-ciple of governance.

131. For discussions of legal formalism, see note 95, supra (citing sources).

132. See Jerome Frank, Courts on Trial: Myth and Reality in American Justice (Princeton: Princeton University Press, 1949); Karl Llewellyn, The Common Law Tradition: Deciding Appeals (Boston: Little, Brown, 1960). See generally Dux-bury, supra note 95, at 65–160.

133. See Stanley Fish, Doing What Comes Naturally: Change, Rhetoric, and the Practice of Theory in Literary and Legal Studies (Durham, N.C.: Duke Uni-versity Press, 1989); Duncan Kennedy, A Critique of Adjudication: Fin de Siècle (Cambridge, Mass.: Harvard University Press, 1997); Cass Sunstein, Problems with Rules, California Law Review 83:953 (1995); Cass Sunstein, Legal Reason-ing and Political Conflict (New York: Oxford University Press, 1996).

134. With respect to the interpretation of the Constitution, see Phillip Bobbitt, Constitutional Interpretation (Oxford: Blackwell, 1991); David Strauss, Common Law Constitutional Interpretation, University of Chicago Law Review 63:877 (1996); Harry Wellington, Interpreting the Constitution: The Supreme Court and the Process of Adjudication (New Haven, Conn.: Yale University Press,

1990), at 5–19. With respect to the interpretation of statutes by a court, see William Eskridge, Dynamic Statutory Interpretation (Cambridge, Mass.: Harvard University Press, 1994); Owen Fiss, Objectivity and Interpretation, Stanford Law Review 34:739 (1982). With respect to the interpretation of statutes by an agency, see Jerry Mashaw, Agency Statutory Interpretation, Issues in Legal Scholarship, Dynamic Statutory Interpretation (2002): Art. 9, http://www.bepress.com/ils/iss3/art9; Edward Rubin, Dynamic Statutory Interpretation in the Administrative State, Issues in Legal Scholarship, Dynamic Statutory Interpretation (2002): Article 2, http://www.bepress.com/ils/iss3/art2. This view of agency interpretation of statutes is embodied in Chevron, USA v. NRDC, 467 U.S. 837 (1984).

135. This is often described as a substantive theory of the rule of law; see Fallon, supra note 123, at 21–24; Allan Hutchinson and Patrick Monaghan, Democracy and the Rule of Law, in David Dyzenhaus and Arthur Ripstein, eds., Law and Morality (Toronto: University of Toronto Press, 2001), at 340; Brian Tomanaha, On the Rule of Law: History, Politics, Theory (Oxford: Oxford University Press, 2004).

136. Jack Donnelly, Universal Human Rights in Theory and Practice (Ithaca, N.Y.: Cornell University Press, 1989), at 12–21; Ronald Dworkin, Taking Rights Seriously (Cambridge, Mass.: Harvard University Press, 1977), at xi–xiii; Louis Henkin, The Age of Human Rights (New York: Columbia University Press, 1990), at 2–3; Michael Perry, Is the Idea of Human Rights Ineliminably Religious?, in Austin Sarat and Tomas Kearns, eds., Legal Rights (Ann Arbor: University of Michigan Press, 1997), at 205.

137. United States Constitution, Article I, Section 8, Clause 5; Article II, Section 2, Clause 3; Article III, Section 2, Clause 1.

138. See Bernard Bailyn, The Ideological Origins of the American Revolution, rev. ed. (Cambridge, Mass.: Belknap Press, 1992), at 198–229; Gordon Wood, The Creation of the American Republic, 1776–1787 (New York: W. W. Norton, 1969), at 524–47, 596–615.

139. See Thornton Anderson, Creating the Constitution: The Convention of 1787 and the First Congress (University Park: Pennsylvania State University Press, 1993); Richard Morris, The Forging of the Union, 1781–1789 (New York: Harper & Row, 1987); David Siemers, Ratifying the Republic: Antifederalists and Federalists in Constitutional Time (Stanford, Calif.: Stanford University Press, 2002); Carl van Doren, The Great Rehearsal: The Story of the Making and Ratifying of the Constitution of the United States (New York: Viking, 1961).

140. Jack Rakove, Original Meanings: Politics and Ideas in the Making of the Constitution (New York: Vintage, 1996), at 105–8.

141. Philip Frickey, Interpretation on the Borderline: Constitution, Canons, Direct Democracy, NYU Annual Survey of American Law 1996:477 (1996); Elizabeth Garrett, Who Directs Direct Democracy?, University of Chicago Law School Roundtable 4:17 (1997); Clayton Gillette, Plebiscites, Participation, and Collective Action in Local Governments, Michigan Law Review 86:930 (1988); Hans Linde, When Initiative Lawmaking is Not "Republican Government": The Campaign Against Homosexuality, Oregon Law Review 72:19 (1993); David Magleby, Direct Legislation: Voting on Ballot Propositions in the United States

(Baltimore: Johns Hopkins University Press, 1984); Jane Schacter, The Pursuit of "Popular Intent": Interpretive Dilemmas in Direct Democracy, Yale Law Journal 105:107 (1995).

142. Bruce Ackerman, We the People, vols. 1 & 2 (Cambridge, Mass.: Belknap Press, 1991).

Notes to Chapter Seven

1. The Mirror of the Justices (William J. Whittaker, ed.) (London: Selden Society, 1895). Regarding the authorship of the work, see id., Introduction (Frederic Maitland).

2. According to St. Thomas, if an authorized enactment violates natural law, it is actually not law at all, and need not be obeyed; if it contravenes divine law, and thus threatens people's salvation, it must not be obeyed. St. Thomas Aquinas, Summa Theologica. (Fathers of the English Dominican Province, trans.) (Westminster, Md.: Christian Classics, 1981), at 1019–20 (I–II, Q. 96, A. 4), id. at 1015 (I–II, Q. 95, A.2). For contemporary versions, see Randy Barnett, The Structure of Liberty: Justice and the Rule of Law (Oxford: Clarendon Press, 1998); John Finnis, Natural Law and Natural Rights (Oxford: Clarendon Press, 1988); Robert George, In Defense of Natural Law (Oxford: Clarendon Press, 1999); Heidi Hurd, Moral Combat (Cambridge: Cambridge University Press, 1999); Alisdair MacIntyre, Whose Justice? Which Rationality? (South Bend, Ind.: University of Notre Dame Press, 1988); Jacques Maritain, The Rights of Man and Natural Law (New York: Gordian Press, 1971); Michael Moore, Law as a Functional Kind, in Robert George, Natural Law Theory: Contemporary Essays (Oxford: Clarendon Press, 1992), at 188; Lloyd Weinreb, Natural Law and Justice (Cambridge, Mass.: Harvard University Press, 1987).

3. Hans Kelsen, General Theory of Law and State (Anders Wedberg, trans.) (Cambridge, Mass.: Harvard University Press, 1946); Hans Kelsen, Pure Theory of Law (Max Knight, trans.) (Berkeley: University of California Press, 1978). For leading contemporary versions, see H.L.A. Hart, The Concept of Law (Oxford: Clarendon Press, 1961); Joseph Raz, The Concept of a Legal System: An Introduction to the Theory of Legal System (Oxford: Clarendon Press, 1970).

4. See, e.g., Joel Feinberg, Rights, Justice and the Bounds of Liberty (Princeton: Princeton University Press, 1980); Rex Martin, A System of Rights (Oxford: Clarendon Press, 1993); Dennis Mueller, Constitutional Democracy (New York: Oxford University Press, 1996), at 209–24; Joseph Raz, The Morality of Freedom (Oxford: Clarendon Press, 1986), at 165–92; Hillel Steiner, An Essay on Rights (Oxford: Blackwell, 1994); Alan White, Rights (Oxford: Clarendon Press, 1984); Carl Wellman, A Theory of Rights: Persons under Laws, Institutions and Morals (Totowa, N.J.: Rowman & Allanheld, 1985). This is not to suggest that these authors do not distinguish between legal rights and human rights, but only that they assume there is some underlying, unified concept of rights themselves.

5. See George Fletcher, Basic Concepts of Legal Thought (New York: Oxford University Press, 1996), at 11–12.

6. J. H. Baker, An Introduction to English Legal History, 3d ed. (London:

Butterworths, 1990), at 14–33; F. L. Ganshof, Feudalism (Philip Grierson, trans.) (Toronto: University of Toronto Press, 1964), at 156–60; W. S. Holdsworth, A History of English Law (Boston: Little, Brown, 1931), vol. 1, at 64–193; W. L. Warren, Henry II (Berkeley: University of California Press, 1973), at 247–52.

7. Robert Bartlett, Trial by Fire and Water (Oxford: Clarendon Press, 1986); R. C. van Caenegem, The Birth of English Common Law (Cambridge: Cambridge University Press, 1973), at 64–65; George Neilson, Trial by Combat (London: Williams & Norgate, 1890), at 167–201; Edward Rubin, Trial by Battle, Trial by Argument, Arkansas Law Review 56:261 (2003). As Caenegem notes, "Distractions were not so plentiful as today."

8. Holdsworth, supra note 6, vol. 1, at 17–32; Ganshof, supra note 6, at 158–60; Frederic Maitland, The Constitutional History of England (Cambridge: Cambridge University Press, 1908), at 105–14; Anthony Musson and W. M. Ormond, The Evolution of English Justice (London: Macmillan, 1999); Warren, supra note 6, at 247–52.

9. Jeremy Bentham, Of Laws in General (H.L.A. Hart, ed.) (London: Athlone Press, 1970).

10. For discussions of Bentham's theory of legal rights, see David Lieberman, The Province of Legislation Determined: Legal Theory in Eighteenth-Century Britain (Cambridge: Cambridge University Press, 1989); H.L.A. Hart, Essays on Bentham (Oxford: Clarendon Press, 1982); Gerald Postema, Bentham and the Common Law (Oxford: Clarendon Press, 1986).

11. Wesley Hohfeld, Fundamental Legal Conceptions (Walter Cook, ed.) (New Haven, Conn.: Yale University Press, 1919).

12. Id. at 35–36, 65–67.

13. Id. at 38; see 36–38.

14. Id. at 38–50.

15. Id. at 50–60.

16. Id. at 60–63.

17. Id. at 23. Hohfeld's work originally appeared as two articles in the Yale Law Journal. In the first article, Yale Law Journal 23:16 (1913), the title begins with the word "Some" before the quoted language. The title of the second article, id. at 65, Yale Law Journal 26:710 (1917), and of the book is as quoted in the text.

18. Id. at 27–31.

19. Hart, supra note 3, at 26–41.

20. Hart, supra note 10, at 188–92.

21. Hart acknowledges that his characterization does not account for Hohfeld's category of immunities (see id.), but he gives, as an example of these excluded immunities, human rights, which he describes as rights that lie against the government in its entirety. This is difficult to understand; human rights are excluded in any event from a theory of legal rights since they are not within the government's positive control. A more serious problem with his characterization is that it also seems to exclude positive law immunities, such as Jill's immunity from taxation.

22. Ronald Dworkin, Hard Cases, in Taking Rights Seriously (Cambridge, Mass.: Harvard University Press, 1977), at 81, 91.

23. Id. at 89–100.

24. Id. at 105–23.

25. Id. at 123.

26. Raz, supra note 4, at 166.

27. Id. at 181. Ultimate values, according to Raz, involve the interests of the rights holder. See id. at 180–83.

28. Joseph Raz, Legal Rights, in Jules Coleman, ed., Rights and Their Foundations (New York: Garland, 1994), at 67. Raz recognizes that there are legal rights and duties that cannot be enforced, specifically certain rights against officials. His example is that the "law determines what appeals the highest Court of Appeals has a right to hear but if it decides to hear an appeal that it has no right to hear then no one can take legal action to stop it." He asserts, however, that this situation is "clearly exceptional and in a sense parasitical on rights and duties which are enforceable or which do give rise, when disregarded, to actions for remedies or sanctions."

29. Joseph Raz, The Authority of Law Essays on Law and Morality (Oxford: Clarendon Press, 1978), at 45.

30. For the English practice, see William Blackstone, Commentaries on the Laws of England (Chicago: University of Chicago Press, 1979), at 337–41; Henry de Bracton, On the Laws and Customs of England (Samuel Thorne, trans.) (Cambridge, Mass.: Belknap Press, 1968–77), vol. 2 at 385–403; Neilson, supra note 7, at 36–39.

31. Dante Alighieri, Monarchy (De Monarchia) (Prue Shaw, trans.) (Cambridge: Cambridge University Press, 1996); Frederick Pollock and Frederic Maitland, The History of English Law Before the Time of Edward I, 2d ed. (London: Cambridge University Press, 1968) vol. 1 at 74.

32. Bracton, supra note 30, vol. 2 at 403; Neilson, supra note 7, at 46–58; Pollock and Maitland, supra note 31, vol. 1 at 633; Theodore Plucknett, A Concise History of the Common Law, 5th ed. (Boston: Little, Brown, 1956), 116–17; R. C. Van Caenegem, The Birth of the English Common Law (Cambridge: Cambridge University Press, 1973), at 68. For a literary presentation, see Chrétien de Troyes, Yvain (The Night With the Lion), in Arthurian Romances (D.D.R. Owen, trans.) (London: Everyman, 1993), at 339–42 (ll. 4344–4565). The rationale for trial by ordeal was precisely the same. See Bartlett, supra note 7, at 71–102.

33. For a more extensive discussion, see Rubin, supra note 7.

34. Chris Sanchirico, Character Evidence and the Object of Trial, Columbia Law Review 101:1227 (2001). Sanchirico argues that the evidentiary rules that have evolved, specifically those involving character evidence, are better explained if the trial is viewed as an implementation mechanism.

35. See Robert Cooter and Thomas Ulen, Law and Economics (New York: HarperCollins, 1988), at 108–12; Edwin Mansfield, Microeconomics: Theory and Applications, 3d ed. (New York: W. W. Norton, 1979), at 470–94; Robert Pindyck and Daniel Rubinfeld, Microeconomics, 2d ed. (New York: Macmillan, 1992), at 661–69.

36. For the idea that statutes, creating what are commonly called rights, carry expressive significance, see Elizabeth Anderson and Richard Pildes, Expressive Theories of Law: A General Restatement, University of Pennsylvania Law Review 148:1503 (2000); Deborah Hellman, The Expressive Dimension of Equal Protec-

tion, Minnesota Law Review 85:1 (2000); Lawrence Lessig, Social Meaning and Social Norms, University of Pennsylvania Law Review 144:2181 (1996); Richard Pildes, Why Rights Are Not Trumps: Social Meanings, Expressive Harms, and Constitutionalism, Journal of Legal Studies 27:725 (1998); Cass Sunstein, On the Expressive Function of Law, University of Pennsylvania Law Review 144:2021 (1996); Cass Sunstein, Social Norms and Social Roles, Columbia Law Review 96:903 (1996). This notion is criticized in Chapter 6 as a claim for the inherent morality of law, but the criticism was not meant to suggest that statutes cannot fulfill symbolic functions.

37. See Jean Baudrillard, In the Shadow of the Silent Majorities (New York: Semiotext(e), 1983); Murray Edelman, Constructing the Political Spectacle (Chicago: University of Chicago Press, 1988); Max Horkheimer and Theodor Adorno, Dialectic of Enlightenment (John Cumming, trans.) (New York: Continuum, 1996), at 120–67.

38. Marc Galanter, Why the "Haves" Come Out Ahead: Speculations on the Limits of Legal Change, Law & Society Review 9:95 (1974); Stewart Macaulay, Elegant Models, Empirical Pictures, and the Complexities of Contract, Law & Society Review 11:507 (1977). See also Ian Macneil, The New Social Contract: An Inquiry into Modern Contractual Relations (New Haven, Conn.: Yale University Press, 1980); H. Laurence Ross, Settled Out of Court: The Social Process of Insurance Claims Adjustments (Chicago: Aldine, 1970).

39. See Samuel Gross and Kent Syverud, Don't Try: Civil Jury Verdicts in a System Geared to Settlement, UCLA Law Review 44:1 (1996); David Trubek et al., The Costs of Ordinary Litigation, UCLA Law Review 31:72 (1983).

40. George Priest and Benjamin Klein, The Selection of Disputes for Litigation, Journal of Legal Studies 13:1 (1984); John Gould, The Economics of Legal Conflicts, Journal of Legal Studies 2:279 (1973); Samuel Gross and Kent Syverud, Getting to No: A Study of Settlement Negotiations and the Selection of Cases for Trial, Michigan Law Review 90:319 (1991).

41. Einer Elhauge, Does Interest Group Theory Justify More Intrusive Judicial Review, Yale Law Journal 101:31 (1991); Galanter, supra note 38.

42. For a fuller discussion, see Edward Rubin, The Code, the Consumer, and the Institutional Structure of the Common Law, Washington University Law Quarterly 75:11 (1997).

43. Mauro Capelletti and Bryant Garth, Access to Justice: The Newest Wave in the Worldwide Movement to Make Rights Effective, Buffalo Law Review 27:181 (1978); Harold Krent, Essay: Explaining One-Way Fee Shifting, Virginia Law Review 79:2039 (1993); Phyllis Monroe, Financial Barriers to Litigation: Attorney's Fees and the Problem of Access, Alabama Law Review 46:148 (1982).

44. John Coffee, Understanding the Plaintiff's Attorney: The Implications of Economic Theory for Private Enforcement of Law Through Class and Derivative Actions, Columbia Law Review 86:669 (1986); Laura Nader, ed., No Access to Law: Alternatives to the American Judicial System (New York: Academic Press, 1980); Jonathan Macey and Geoffrey Miller, The Plaintiff's Attorney's Role in Class Action and Derivative Litigation: Economic Analysis and Recommendations for Reform, University of Chicago Law Review 58:1 (1996); Deborah Rhode, Class Conflicts in Class Actions, Stanford Law Review 34:1183 (1982); Christo-

pher Whelan, ed., Small Claims Courts: A Comparative Study (Oxford: Clarendon Press, 1990).

45. See, e.g., Civil Rights Act, 42 U.S.C. 2000a–3(b); Equal Credit Opportunity Act, 15 U.S.C. § 1691e(d); Truth in Lending Act, 15 U.S.C. § 1640(a)(3); Magnuson-Moss Warranty Act, 15 U.S.C. § 2310(d)(2).

46. 405 U.S. 727 (1972).

47. 504 U.S. 555 (1992).

48. 461 U.S. 95 (1983)

49. David Driesen, Standing for Nothing: The Paradox of Demanding Concrete Context for Formalist Adjudication, Cornell Law Review 89:808 (2004); William Fletcher, The Structure of Standing, Yale Law Journal 98:221 (1988); Cass Sunstein, Standing and the Privatization of Public Law, Columbia Law Review 88:1432 (1988); Cass Sunstein, What's Standing After *Lujan?* Of Citizen Suits, "Injuries," and Article III, Michigan Law Review 91:163 (1992). For an effort to mediate between this view and the court's position, see William Buzbee, Standing and the Statutory Universe, Duke Environmental Law and Policy Forum 11:247 (2001).

50. Examples of federal statutes that include such provisions are the Clean Air Act, 42 U.S.C. § 6972; the Clean Water Act, 33 U.S.C. § 1365(e); the Safe Drinking Water Act, 42 U.S.C. § 300j–8; the Noise Control Act, 42 U.S.C. § 4911; and the Federal Election Campaign Act, 2 U.S.C § 437g (a)(1). By stating that the restriction on citizen standing was constitutional, not prudential, the Supreme Court's *Lujan* decision implied that all these provisions might be struck down. However, the Court seems to have retreated from this questionable conclusion in *Federal Election Commission v. Atkins*, 524 U.S. 11 (1998), which upheld the provision in the Federal Election Campaign Act granting standing to any aggrieved party.

51. Lea Brilmayer, The Jurisprudence of Article III: Perspectives on the "Case or Controversy" Requirement, Harvard Law Review 93:297 (1979).

52. 262 U.S. 447 (1923). In *Frothingham*, taxpayers claimed that the federal grants to states to reduce infant mortality violated the Tenth Amendment.

53. See Ex parte Levitt, 392 U.S. 633 (1937); Schlesinger v. Reservists Committee to Stop the War, 418 U.S. 166 (1974); Valley Forge Christian College v. Americans United for Separation of Church and State, 176 U.S. 464 (1982).

54. Flast v. Cohen, 392 U.S. 83 (1968); Bowen v. Kendricks, 487 U.S. 589 (1988).

55. 418 U.S. 166 (1974). The political aspect of this case is discussed in Chapter 4, note 115.

56. Art. I, Sec. 9, cl. 7.

57. See Gibson v. Berryhill, 411 U.S. 564 (1973); Ward v. Village of Monroeville, 409 U.S. 57 (1972); Tumey v. Ohio, 273 US. 510 (1927); Henry Friendly, Some Kind of a Hearing, University of Pennsylvania Law Review 123:1267 (1975); Martin Redish and Lawrence Marshall, Adjudicatory Independence and the Value the Value of Procedural Due Process, Yale Law Journal 95:455 (1986).

58. Robert Kagan, Adversarial Legalism: The American Way of Law (Cambridge, Mass.: Harvard University Press, 2001); Robert Kagan, Adversarial Legalism in American Government, Journal of Policy Analysis & Management 10:369 (1991).

59. For critiques, see Malcolm Feeley, The Process Is the Punishment: Handling Cases in a Lower Criminal Court (New York: Russell Sage Foundation, 1979); Marvin Frankel, Partisan Justice (New York: Hill and Wang, 1980); Marvin Frankel, The Search for Truth: An Umpireal View (New York: Association of the Bar of the City of New York, 1975); Arthur Miller, The Adversary System: Dinosaur of Phoenix, Minnesota Law Review 69:1 (1984); Jeffrey Stempel, Cultural Literacy and the Adversary System: The Enduring Problems of Distrust, Misunderstanding and Narrow Perspective, Valparaiso Law Review 27:313 (1993); Lloyd Weinreb, Denial of Justice: Criminal Process in the United States (New York: Free Press, 1977).

60. Sean Doran, John Jackson, and Michael Seigel, Rethinking Adversariness in Nonjury Criminal Trials, American Journal of Criminal Law, 23:1 (1995).

61. Michael Seigel, A Pragmatic Critique of Modern Evidence Scholarship, Northwestern University Law Review 88:995 (1994); Michael Seigel, Pragmatism Applied: Imagining a Solution to the Problem of Court Congestion, Hofstra Law Review 22:567 (1994).

62. See Marc Galanter and Mia Cahill, "Most Cases Settle": Judicial Promotion and Regulation of Settlements, Stanford Law Review 46:1339 (1994); Herbert Kritzer, Adjudication to Settlement: Shading in the Gray, Judicature 70:161 (1986).

63. See Owen Fiss, Against Settlement, Yale Law Journal 93:1073 (1984); Judith Resnick, Managerial Judges, Harvard Law Review 96:376 (1982).

64. Alfred Alschuler, The Prosecutor's Role in Plea Bargaining, University of Chicago Law Review 36:50 (1968); Alfred Alschuler, The Trial Judge's Role in Plea Bargaining, Columbia Law Review 76:1059 (1976); Alfred Alschuler, The Defense Attorney's Role in Plea Bargaining, Yale Law Journal 84:1179 (1975); Alfred Alschuler, Plea Bargaining and Its History, Columbia Law Review 79:1 (1979); Ilene Nagel and Stephen Schulhofer, A Tale of Three Cities: An Empirical Study of Charging and Bargaining Practices under the Federal Sentencing Guidelines, Southern California Law Review 66:501 (1992); Stephen Schulhofer, Plea Negotiations under the Federal Sentencing Guidelines: Guideline Circumvention and Its Dynamics in the Post-Mistretta Period, Northwestern University Law Review 91:1284 (1997); Robert Scott and William Stuntz, Plea Bargaining as Contract, Yale Law Journal 101:1909 (1992).

65. Stephen Schulhofer, Plea Bargaining as Disaster, Yale Law Journal 101:1979 (1992). See Alfred Alschuler, The Changing Plea Bargaining Debate, California Law Review 69:652 (1981); Alfred Alschuler, The Supreme Court, the Defense Attorney, and the Guilty Plea, University of Colorado Law Review 47:1 (1975); David Lynch, The Impropriety of Plea Agreements: A Tale of Two Countries, Law & Social Inquiry 19:115 (1994); Stephen Schulhofer, Is Plea Bargaining Inevitable? Harvard Law Review 97:1037 (1984).

66. Gerard Lynch, Our Administrative System of Criminal Justice, Fordham Law Review 66:2117 (1998).

67. 5 U.S.C. §§ 551–808. The omission is significant, not only because the act is designed as a codification of the procedures that federal agencies are required to follow, but also because its specific mechanism of control is through private participation in the administrative process. See Edward Rubin, It's Time to Make the

Administrative Procedure Act Administrative, Cornell Law Review 89:95 (2003),
at 100–105.

68. E.g., Federal Communications Commission: How to File a Complaint with
the FCC: Regarding Telephone or Other Telecommunication Common Carrier
Services (Washington, D.C.: Federal Communications Commission, 1996).

69. E.g., Comptroller of the Currency, at www.occ.treas.gov/customer.htm
(OCC Customer Assistance); Environmental Protection Agency, at www.epa.gov/
epahome/hotline.htm (hot line phone numbers and further links); Federal Com-
munications Commission, at www.fcc.gov/contacts.html ("How to Contact the
FCC"); Federal Trade Commission, at www.ftc.gov/ftc/consumer.htm ("File a
Complaint" links to FTC Consumer Complaint Form).

70. E.g., Environmental Protection Agency, supra note 69; Whistleblower Protection Act of 1989, Pub. L. No. 101–12, 103 Stat. 16, codified at 5 U.S.C.
1201–22; Pennsylvania Whistleblower Act, 43 Penn. Statutes 1421–28.

71. Clive Chajet and Tom Shachtman, Image by Design: From Corporate Vi-
sion to Business Reality (Reading, Mass.: Addison-Wesley, 1991); Philip Kotler
and Gary Armstrong, Principles of Marketing, 9th ed. (Upper Saddle River, N.J.:
Prentice-Hall, 2001); Al Ries and Jack Trout, Bottom-up Marketing (New York:
McGraw-Hill, 1989); William Stanton, Fundamentals of Marketing, 7th ed. (New
York: McGraw-Hill, 1984).

72. Ibrahim al-Wahab, The Swedish Institution of Ombudsman (Stockholm:
LiberFörlag, 1979); Roy Gregory and Philip Giddings, Righting Wrongs: The
Ombudsman in Six Continents (Amsterdam: IOS Press, 2000); Walter Gellhorn,
Ombudsmen and Others: Citizens' Protectors in Nine Countries (Cambridge,
Mass.: Harvard University Press, 1966).

73. Marília Crespo Allen, European Ombudsman and National Ombudsmen
or Similar Bodies (Luxembourg: European Parliament, 2001); Gerald Caiden, ed.,
International Handbook of the Ombudsman: Evolution and Present Function
(London: Greenwood Press, 1993); Katja Heede, The European Ombudsman:
Redress and Control at the Union Level (The Hague: Kluwer Law International,
2000). New Zealand has also played an important role in the development of this
institution. See L. B. Hill, The Model Ombudsman: Institutionalizing New
Zealand's Democratic Experience (Princeton: Princeton University Press, 1976).

74. Roy Gregory and Peter Hutchesson, The Parliamentary Ombudsman: A
Study in the Control of Administrative Action (London: Allen & Unwin, 1975);
Roy Gregory and Philip Giddings, The Ombudsman, the Citizen and Parliament:
A History of the Office of the Parliamentary Commissioner for Administration and
Health Service Commissioners (London: Politico's Publishing, 2002); Carol Har-
low and Richard Rawlings, Law and Administration (London: Butterworths,
1997), at 391–455; Mary Seneviratne, Ombudsmen: Public Services and Admin-
istrative Justice (London: Butterworths, 2002); H.W.R. Wade and C. F. Forsyth,
Administrative Law, 8th ed. (Oxford: Oxford University Press, 2000), at 87–112,
137–38.

75. Patrick Birkenshaw, Grievances, Remedies, and the State (London: Sweet
& Maxwell, 1995), at 412–14 (prisons), 414–21 (police); Thomas Gibbons, Regulating the Media, 2d ed. (London: Sweet & Maxwell, 1998), at 264–74.

76. Morris Fiorina, Congress, Keystone of the Washington Establishment

(New Haven, Conn.: Yale University Press, 1977), at 41–70; John Johannes, To Serve the People: Congress and Constituency Service (Lincoln: University of Nebraska Press, 1984), at 95–118; David Mayhew, Congress: The Electoral Connection (New Haven, Conn.: Yale University Press, 1974), at 52–61.

77. Roy Gregory and J. Pearson, The Parliamentary Ombudsman after Twenty-five Years, Public Administration 70:469 (1992); Harlow and Rawlings, supra note 74, at 421–55; Richard Rawlings, The MP's Complaints Service, Modern Law Review 53:22 & 149 (1990).

78. 5 U.S.C. § 553(e): "Each agency shall give an interested person the right to petition for the issuance, amendment or repeal of a rule."

79. See Cellnet Communication, Inc. v. FCC, 965 F.2d 1106 (D.C. Cir. 1992); Professional Pilots Federation v. FAA, 118 F.3d 758 (D.C. Cir. 1997); William Luneburg, Petitioning Federal Agencies for Rulemaking: An Overview of Administrative and Judicial Practice and Some Recommendations for Improvement, Wisconsin Law Review 1988:1 (1988).

80. See Alden Abbott, The Case against Federal Statutory and Judicial Deadlines: A Cost-Benefit Appraisal, Administrative Law Review 39:171 (1987); Merrick Garland, Deregulation and Judicial Review, Harvard Law Review 98:507 (1985); John Graham, The Failure of Agency Forcing: The Regulation of Airborne Carcinogens Under Section 112 of the Clean Air Act, Duke Law Journal 1985:100 (1985); Sidney Shapiro and Robert Glicksman, Congress, the Supreme Court, and the Quiet Revolution in Administrative Law Duke Law Journal 1988:819 (1988); Sidney Shapiro and Thomas McGarity, Reorienting OSHA: Regulatory Alternatives and Legislative Reform, Yale Journal on Regulation 6:1 (1989).

81. See David Currie and Frank Goodman, Judicial Review of Federal Administrative Action: Quest for the Optimum Forum, Columbia Law Review 75:1 (1975), at 54–61; James Freedman, Summary Action by Administrative Agencies, University of Chicago Law Review 40:1 (1972); Rubin, supra note 67, at 123–31; Paul Verkuil, A Study of Informal Adjudication Procedures, University of Chicago Law Review 43:739 (1976); Keith Werhan, Delegalizing Administrative Law, University of Illinois Law Review 1966:423 (1996), at 442.

82. Hart, supra note 10, at 127–61; see Hart, supra note 3, at 49–76.

83. R.H.C. Davis, A History of Medieval Europe: From Constantine to Saint Louis, 2d ed. (London: Longman, 1988), at 285–301; Heinrich Fichtenau, Living in the Tenth Century: Mentalities and Social Orders (Chicago: University of Chicago Press, 1991), at 164–65; Richard Mortimer, Angevin England 1154–1258 (Oxford: Blackwell, 1994), at 41–51, 72–74; Warren, supra note 6, at 371–96.

84. Truth in Lending Act, 15 U.S.C. §§ 1632, 1640; Regulation Z, 12 C.F.R. § 226.18 (c)(iv).

85. When Common Law standards nonetheless persist, by influencing the design of the regulation, for example, they often cause the regulation to be ineffective. See Noga Morag-Levine, Chasing the Wind: Regulating Air Pollution in the Common Law State (Princeton, N.J.: Princeton University Press, 2003).

86. Jürgen Habermas, The Theory of Communicative Action, vol. 1: Reason and the Rationalization of Society (Thomas McCarthy, trans.) (Boston: Beacon Press, 1984), at 243–71.

87. See, e.g., Erin Brockovich (Steven Soderbergh, director) (DeVito-Shamberg-

Jersey, 2000); A Civil Action (Steven Zaillian, director) (Wildwood/Touchstone, 1988); Class Action (Michael Apted, director) (Interscope, 1991); To Kill a Mockingbird (Robert Mulligan, director) (U-I Alan Pakula, 1962); The Verdict (Sidney Lumet, director) (TCF/Zanuck-Brown, 1982).

88. Hart, supra note 3, at 49–76; Hart, supra note 10, at 127–61.

89. Daniel Farber, Reassessing the Economic Efficiency of Compensatory Damages for Breach of Contract, Virginia Law Review 66:1471 (1980); Jeffrey Perloff, The Effects of Breaches of Forward Contract due to Unanticipated Price Changes, Journal of Legal Studies 10:221 (1981); Mitchell Polinsky, Risk-Sharing through Breach of Contract Remedies, Journal of Legal Studies 12:427 (1977); Thomas Ulen, The Efficiency of Specific Performance: Toward a Unified Theory of Contract Remedies, Michigan Law Review 84:341 (1984).

90. E.g., Lochner v. New York, 198 U.S. 45 (1905); Adair v. United States, 208 U.S. 161 (1908); Coppage v. Kansas, 236 U.S. 1 (1915); Adkins v. Children's Hospital, 261 U.S. 525 (1923); Tyson & Brother v. Banton, 273 U.S. 418 (1927); New State Ice Co. v. Liebmann, 285 U.S. 262 (1932). See Roscoe Pound, Liberty of Contract, Yale Law Journal 18:454 (1909).

91. Home Building & Loan Association v. Blaisdell, 290 U.S. 398 (1934); West Coast Hotel v. Parrish, 300 U.S. 379 (1937); United States v. Carolene Products Co., 304 U.S. 144 (1938); Williamson v. Lee Optical of Oklahoma, 348 U.S. 483 (1955). See Howard Gillman, The Constitution Besieged: The Rise and Demise of Lochner Era Police Powers Jurisprudence (Durham, N.C.: Duke University Press, 1993); Morton Horwitz, The Transformation of American Law, 1870–1960: The Crisis of Legal Orthodoxy (New York: Oxford University Press, 1992).

92. 349 U.S. 294 (1954).

93. See Sanford Kadish, Methodology and Criteria in Due Process Adjudication—A Survey and Criticism, Yale Law Journal 66:319 (1957); Charles Reich, The New Property, Yale Law Journal 73:733 (1964).

94. McAuliffe v. New Bedford, 155 Mass.216, 220, 29 N.E. 517, 518 (1892).

95. See Home Building, supra note 91 (citing sources).

96. Classic statements of this notion can be found in Black & White Taxicab & Transfer Co. v. Brown & Yellow Taxicab & Transfer Co., 276 U.S. 518, 533 (1928) (Holmes, J., dissenting) (The Common Law is the enactment of a sovereign, not a "brooding omnipresence in the sky"); Erie Railroad Co. v. Tompkins, 304 U.S. 64 (1938) (abolishing the doctrine of federal Common Law, because the federal courts, having a specified and not a general jurisdiction, are not authorized to establish Common Law rules). The position is of course connected to positivism; see Kelsen, General Theory, supra note 3; Kelsen, Pure Theory, supra note 3. But see Anthony Sebok, Misunderstanding Positivism, Michigan Law Review 93:2054 (1995), which argues that the formalists, who championed the independence of Common Law, were positivists as well.

97. Barsky v. Board of Regents, 347 U.S. 442 (1954) (license to practice medicine); Beilan v. Board of Education, 357 U.S. 399 (1958) (employment); Nelson v. County of Los Angeles, 362 U.S. 1 (1960) (employment).

98. Our sense of fairness will be violated, however, if the political process fails to function properly. This is the import of the famous footnote 4, United States v.

Carolene Products Co., 304 U.S. 144 (1938). See Bruce Ackerman, Beyond Carolene Products, Harvard Law Review 98:713 (1985); Jack Balkin, The Footnote, Northwestern University Law Review 83:275 (1989); Lea Brilmayer, Carolene, Conflicts, and the Fate of the "Insider-Outsider," University of Pennsylvania Law Review 134:1291 (1986); John Ely, Democracy and Distrust (Cambridge, Mass.: Harvard University Press, 1980).

99. 210 U.S. 373 (1908).

100. 239 U.S. 441 (1915).

101. 397 U.S. 254 (1970).

102. 408 U.S. 564 (1972).

103. 408 U.S. 593 (1972).

104. 416 U.S. 134, 154 (1974).

105. Although Justice Rehnquist wrote the plurality opinion that decided the case, six members of the Court disagreed with his bittersweet theory. See 416 U.S. at 164 (Powell, J., concurring); id. at 177 (White, J., concurring and dissenting); id. at 206 (Marshall, J., dissenting).

106. For criticisms, see Jerry Mashaw, Administrative Due Process: The Quest for a Dignitary Theory, Boston University Law Review 61; 885 (1981); Frank Michelman, Formal and Associational Aims in Procedural Due Process, Nomos: Due Process 18:126 (1977); Henry Monaghan, Of "Liberty" and "Property," Cornell Law Review 62:405 (1977).

107. E.g., Memphis Light, Gas & Water Division v. Craft, 436 U.S. 1 (1978); Barry v. Barchi, 443 U.S. 55 (1979); Greenholtz v. Inmates of the Nebraska Penal and Correctional Complex, 442 U.S. 1 (1979); Vitek v. Jones, 445 U.S. 480 (1980).

108. This approach, moreover, led to the technical problem that federal courts, where due process complaints were regularly brought, found themselves interpreting the discretionary content of state statutes as matters of first impression, and thus with no previous interpretation from the state's own judiciary.

109. Bentham, supra note 9, at 10–12.

110. Niklas Luhmann, Social Systems (John Bednarz, trans.) (Stanford, Calif.: Stanford University Press, 1995), at 374–76.

111. Galanter, supra note 38; Stewart Macaulay, Law and the Balance of Power: The Automobile Manufacturers and Their Dealers (New York: Russell Sage Foundation, 1966); Macneil, supra note 38; Nader, supra note 44; Laura Nader and Harry Todd, eds., The Disputing Process: Law in Ten Societies (New York: Columbia University Press, 1978).

112. See note 40 (citing sources).

113. Feeley, supra note 59; Jerry Mashaw Bureaucratic Justice: Managing Social Security Disability Claims (New Haven, Conn.: Yale University Press, 1983); William Simon, Visions of Practice in Legal Thought, Stanford Law Review 36:469 (1984); William Simon, Rights and Redistribution in the Welfare System, Stanford Law Review 38:1431 (1986); Lucie White, Subordination, Rhetorical Survival Skills, and Sunday Shoes: Notes on the Hearing of Mrs. G., Buffalo Law Review 38:1 (1990).

114. Chrétien, supra note 32.

115. Id., at 344–46. This theme, where a knight who has committed some

wrong abandons his name, fights under a sobriquet, and in effect wins back his name, is common in Arthurian romances.

116. Id. at 363–66.

117. Id. at 366.

118. Id. at 367.

119. The image of these two armored men in thoughtless combat also supports the criticism of adjudication formulated by feminist scholars such as Cynthia Farina—that it represents an overly aggressive, male response to conflict resolution. See Cynthia Farina, Conceiving Due Process, Yale Journal of Law & Feminism 3:189 (1991).

Notes to Chapter Eight

1. Jack Donnelly, Universal Human Rights in Theory and Practice (Ithaca, N.Y.: Cornell University Press, 1989), at 12–21; Ronald Dworkin, Taking Rights Seriously (Cambridge, Mass.: Harvard University Press, 1977), at xi to xiii, 184–205; Louis Henkin, The Age of Human Rights (New York: Columbia University Press, 1990), at 2–3; Michael Perry, Is the Idea of Human Rights Ineliminably Religious?, in Austin Sarat and Tomas Kearns, eds., Legal Rights (Ann Arbor: University of Michigan Press, 1997), at 205; Joseph Raz, The Morality of Freedom (Oxford: Clarendon Press, 1986). As Raz points out, however, the converse is not true; rights are not the foundation of morality.

2. For a dissenting view, see Rex Martin, A System of Rights (Oxford: Clarendon Press, 1993), at 51–72. Martin argues that government recognition and maintenance are internal to our notion of rights. This chapter adopts the majority view. If Martin's position were adopted instead, however, the argument would be even stronger. See note 53, infra.

3. Of course, some rights may be limited to particular groups by virtue of their substantive features. Only a woman can assert the right to an abortion; only a group of Americans who speak a language other than English can assert the right to preservation of a minority language; only someone who works for a living can assert the right to a paid vacation. But these limits come from the substance of the rights, not from a restriction on the persons who can assert them. A right of Protestant women to have abortions, or Korean-speaking Americans to preserve their language, or of steelworkers to have paid vacations is not a human right according to the standard view.

4. Joel Feinberg, Rights, Justice and the Bounds of Liberty (Princeton: Princeton University Press, 1980), at 143–58 (rights are claims); H. J. McCloskey, Rights, Philosophical Quarterly 15:115 (1965) (rights are entitlements); James Nickel, Making Sense of Human Rights: Philosophical Reflections on the Universal Declaration of Human Rights (Berkeley: University of California Press, 1987), at 13–35 (both); Brian Orend, Human Rights: Concepts and Context (Peterborough, Ont.: Broadview, 2002), at 17–24 (both).

5. The most convincing and harrowing images of hell in the twentieth century depict totalitarian regimes. See Aldous Huxley, Brave New World (New York: Ban-

tam, 1958); George Orwell, 1984 (New York: Signet, 1949); Evgenii Zamiatin, We (Gregory Zilboorg, trans.) (New York: Dutton, 1959).

6. The general view is that Roman law lacked a conception of rights, at least in the modern sense. See John Finnis, Natural Law and Natural Rights (Oxford: Clarendon Press, 1980), at 205–20; H. F. Jolowicz, Roman Foundations of Modern Law (Oxford: Oxford University Press, 1957), at 66–72; Richard Tuck, Natural Rights Theories: Their Origin and Development (Cambridge: Cambridge University Press, 1979), at 708 (summarizing work of Michel Villey).

7. Antony Black, The Individual and Society, in J. H. Burns, ed., The Cambridge History of Medieval Political Thought c. 350–c. 1450 (Cambridge: Cambridge University Press, 1988), at 588; Marc Bloch, Feudal Society (L. A. Manyon, trans.) (Chicago: University of Chicago Press, 1961), at 113–16, 163–75; Jean Dunbabin, Government, in Burns, supra, at 477, 508–15; F. L. Ganshof, Feudalism (Philip Grierson, trans.) (Toronto: University of Toronto Press, 1996), at 81–87, 129–33; R. W. Southern, The Making of the Middle Ages (New Haven, Conn.: Yale University Press, 1953), at 98–117.

8. St. Augustine of Hippo, The City of God (Marcus Dods, trans.) (New York: Modern Library, 1950), XXII.22.4. See R. A. Markus, Saeculum: History and Society in the Theology of Saint Augustine (Cambridge: Cambridge University Press, 1970), at 197–230. St. Thomas does not argue to the contrary. Although he asserts, following Aristotle, that social and political relations are natural for man, and thus could have arisen before the Fall, he does not assert that they actually did so. Indeed, his important and original observation that the political system develops through social learning implies a primordial condition when this system did not exist. See Black, supra note 7, at 23–24.

9. Natural law is, of course, an older and broader concept than natural rights. Natural law tells us, at the very least, how to behave to each other in the political realm. Natural rights are a set of claims that are derived from natural law and determine some specific set of claims or entitlements. As Randy Barnett observes, natural rights determine an area of liberty, within which natural law specifies our behavior. Randy Barnett, A Law Professor's Guide to Natural Law and Natural Rights, Harvard Journal of Law & Public Policy, 20:655 (1997).

10. The leading advocate for Ockham's primacy is Michel Villey; see Tuck, supra note 6, at 22. See also Arthur McGrade, Ockham and the Birth of Individual Rights, in Brian Tierney and Peter Linehan, Authority and Power: Studies on Medieval Law and Government Presented to Walter Ullmann on his Seventieth Birthday (Cambridge: Cambridge University Press, 1980). Tuck argues that Ockham's approach did not represent a significant step beyond Aquinas's; the real creator of natural rights theory in his view was Jean de Gerson, Chancellor of the University of Paris, in the late fourteenth and early fifteenth centuries. Tuck, supra, at 25–29.

11. See Arthur McGrade, Rights, Natural Rights and the Philosophy of Law, in Norman Kretzmann, Anthony Kenny, and Jan Pinborg, eds., The Cambridge History of Later Medieval Philosophy: From the Rediscovery of Aristotle to the Disintegration of Scholasticism, 1100–1600 (Cambridge: Cambridge University Press, 1982); Tuck, supra note 6, at 15–31.

12. Quentin Skinner, The Foundations of Political Thought, vol. 2: The Age of Reformation (Cambridge: Cambridge University Press, 1978), at 239–41.

13. See Antony Black, The Juristic Origins of Social Contract Theory, History of Political Thought 14:57 (1993); Harro Hopfl and Martyn Thompson, The History of Contract as a Motif in Political Thought, American Historical Review 84:919 (1979); Martyn Thompson, Locke's Contract in Context, in David Boucher and Paul Kelly, The Social Contract from Hobbes to Rawls (London: Routledge, 1994), at 73.

14. C. B. Macpherson, The Political Theory of Possessive Individualism: Hobbes to Locke (Oxford: Oxford University Press, 1962), at 46–61.

15. Jean Hampton, Hobbes and the Social Contract Tradition (Cambridge: Cambridge University Press, 1986); Macpherson, supra note 14; J. B. Schneewind, The Invention of Autonomy: A History of Modern Moral Philosophy (Cambridge: Cambridge University Press, 1998), at 78–82.

16. Immanuel Kant, The Metaphysics of Morals (Mary Gregor, trans.) (Cambridge: Cambridge University Press, 1996), at 30–31 (Division of the Doctrine of Right, § B).

17. G.W.F. Hegel, The Philosophy of History (J. Sibree, trans.) (New York: Dover, 1956). See especially id. at 427–57 (Pt. 4, Sec. 3, Chs. 2 & 3); G.W.F. Hegel, The Philosophy of Right (T. M. Knox, trans.) (London: Oxford University Press, 1967), at 155–88 (§§ 257–86). See also G.W.F.Hegel, Natural Law (T. M. Knox, trans.) (Philadelphia: University of Pennsylvania Press, 1975); Frederick Beiser, Hegel's Historicism, in Frederick Beiser, ed., The Cambridge Companion to Hegel (Cambridge: Cambridge University Press, 1993).

18. See, e.g., Barry Adam, The Rise of a Gay and Lesbian Movement, rev. ed. (New York: Twayne Publishers, 1995); Dennis Chong, Collective Action and the Civil Rights Movement (Chicago: University of Chicago Press, 1991); John D'Emilio, Making Trouble: Essays on Gay History, Politics, and the University (New York: Routledge, 1992); Myra Marx Ferree and Patricia Martin, eds., Feminist Organizations: Harvest of the New Women's Movement (Philadelphia: Temple University Press, 1995); Ethel Klein, Gender Politics: From Consciousness to Mass Politics (Cambridge, Mass.: Harvard University Press, 1984); Doug McAdam, Political Process and the Development of Black Insurgency, 1930–1970 (Chicago: University of Chicago Press, 1982); Aldon Morris, The Origins of the Civil Rights Movement: Black Communities Organizing for Change (New York: Free Press, 1984).

19. Comprehensive political theories often aspire to the theoretical derivation of human rights. See Robert Nozick, Anarchy, State and Utopia (New York: Basic Books, 1974); John Rawls, A Theory of Justice (Cambridge, Mass.: Belknap Press, 1971). Other contemporary efforts to deduce human rights from a general theory include Feinberg, supra note 4; Finnis, supra note 6; Alan Gewirth, The Community of Rights (Chicago: University of Chicago Press, 1996).

20. John Rowan, Conflicts of Rights: Moral Theory and Social Policy Implications (Boulder, Colo: Westview, 1999). See also Richard Rorty, Human Rights, Rationality and Sentimentality, in Stephen Shute and Susan Hurley, eds., On Human Rights (New York: Basic Books, 1989).

21. E.g., Jean Bodin, Colloquium of the Seven about Secrets of the Sublime

(Marion Daniels, trans.) (Princeton: Princeton University Press, 1975); John Locke, A Letter Concerning Toleration (Indianapolis: Bobbs-Merrill, 1955). Bodin argues for toleration on the basis that all religions share an essential core that is more important than their variations. Locke's argument is that forcing religion on another person is inherently un-Christian and endangers the soul of both the public official and his subject. "If the Gospel and the Apostles may be credited, no Man can be a Christian Without *Charity*, and without *that Faith which works*, not by Force, but by *Love*." Id. at 23.

22. The initial attack on slavery came from the Spanish Thomists, most notably Bartolomé de Las Casas. Although they certainly believed in natural law and natural liberty, they did not draw their arguments against enslavement of the Indians from these philosophic principles. Rather, Las Casas argued that God has endowed the Indians with reason, and that forced conversion of reasoning human beings is morally impermissible. Lewis Hanke, All Mankind Is One (DeKalb, Ill.: Northern Illinois University Press, 1974), at 86–89; see also Hugh Thomas, The Slave Trade (New York: Simon & Schuster, 1997), at 125–27. Similarly, the opposition of the English and American Quakers was based on religious considerations, not on natural law or natural rights. Thomas Drake, Quakers and Slavery in America (New Haven, Conn.: Yale University Press, 1950); Thomas, supra, at 458–61.

23. Thomas Hobbes, Leviathan (C. B. Macpherson, ed.) (Harmondsworth: Penguin, 1981), at 192 (Pt. 2, Ch. 14) 269–71 (Pt. 2, Ch. 21). The right against self-incrimination was only beginning to be recognized by English courts at the time Hobbes wrote. See Leonard Levy, Origins of the Fifth Amendment (New York: Macmillan, 1986). So here Hobbes, statist though he was, was adopting a progressive position. See Blandine Kriegel, The State and the Rule of Law (Marc LePain, trans.) (Princeton: Princeton University Press, 2001), at 38–40.

24. John Locke, The Second Treatise on Government (Indianapolis: Bobbs-Merrill, 1952), at 77 (§ 136); 81 (§ 142).

25. For example, Locke's Letter Concerning Toleration, supra note 21, relies on religious and pragmatic arguments, barely mentioning and never relying on the social contract theory of his Second Treatise on Government, supra note 24. The Second Treatise does not propose a right to free exercise of one's religion. Similarly, Rousseau's arguments against slavery are to be found primarily in Jean-Jacques Rousseau, A Discourse on Inequality (Maurice Cranston, trans.) (Harmondsworth: Penguin, 1984), a policy-oriented work that does not rely on social contract theory. Rousseau's Social Contract (Willmoore Kendall, trans.) (Chicago: Henry Regnery, 1954), at 8–15 (I, iv) does disparage slavery, but the principal point of the passage is to refute Grotius's argument that people's ability to sell themselves into slavery suggests that they give up all their rights when they enter into the social contract.

26. One early-eighteenth-century effort to derive human rights from social contract theory was John Trenchard and Thomas Gordon, Cato's Letters, or, Essays on Liberty, Civil and Religious, and Other Important Subjects (Ronald Hamowy, ed.) (Indianapolis: Liberty Fund, 1995). Even at this relatively late date, however, such an approach was uncommon.

27. On the secularization of law and morality in the eighteenth century, see Peter Gay, The Enlightenment, vol. 1: The Rise of Modern Paganism (New York:

W. W. Norton, 1966); vol. 2, The Science of Freedom (New York: W. W. Norton, 1969); Schneewind, supra note 15.

28. Voltaire (François-Marie Arouet), Treatise on Tolerance (Brian Masters, trans.) (Cambridge: Cambridge University Press, 2000).

29. Cesare Beccaria, On Crimes and Punishments (David Young, trans.) (Indianapolis: Hackett, 1986). See id. at 10 (citing the inspiration of "the immortal Montesquieu"). Voltaire welcomed Beccaria's treatise enthusiastically, and wrote an introduction. M. D. Voltaire, Commentary, in Cesare Beccaria, An Esaay on Crimes and Punishments (Stanford, Calif.: Academic Reprints, 1953). See generally Gay, supra note 27, at 445–46.

30. See Keith Baker, The Idea of a Declaration of Rights, in Dale Van Kley, ed., The French Idea of Freedom (Stanford, Calif.: Stanford University Press, 1994); Daniel Rogers, Rights Consciousness in American History, in David Bodenhamer and James Ely, eds., The Bill of Rights in Modern America (Bloomington: Indiana University Press), at 3; Dale Van Kley, From the Lessons of French History to Truths for All Times and All People: The Historical Origins of an Anti-Historical Document, in Van Kley, supra, at 72.

31. See Hannah Arendt, Between Past and Future (New York: Penguin, 1977); Adam Seligman, The Idea of Civil Society (Princeton: Princeton University Press, 1992); Richard Sennett, The Fall of Public Man (New York: W. W. Norton, 1974). Seligman explicitly links the modern human rights movement to the collapse of the public sphere, and the consequent projection of private interests into public discourse. Seligman, supra, at 118–43.

32. See Leszek Kolakowski, Modernity on Endless Trial (Chicago: University of Chicago Press, 1990), at 214–15; L. W. Sumner, Rights Denaturalized, in R. G. Frey, ed., Utility and Rights (Minneapolis: University of Minnesota Press, 1984), at 20.

33. For the text of these documents, see Ian Brownlie, ed., Basic Documents in International Law (Oxford: Clarendon Press, 1967); Louis Henkin, Richard Pugh, Oscar Schacter, and Hans Smit, Basic Documents Supplement to International Law: Cases and Materials, 2d ed. (St. Paul: West Publishing, 1987).

34. Universal Declaration of Human Rights, Art. 23, cl. 2; see Brownlie, supra note 33, at 136.

35. Id., Art. 23, cl. 3. See also Art. 25, cl. 1; Brownlie, supra note 33, at 136 ("everyone has the right to a standard of living adequate for the health and well-being of himself and his family").

36. Id., Art. 22 (social security), Art. 24 (rest and leisure), Art. 26 (education). See also Art. 28 ("Everyone is entitled to a social and international order in which the rights and freedoms set forth in this Declaration can be fully realized"); Brownlie, supra note 33, at 136–37.

37. Donnelly, supra note 1, at 143–44; Adeno Addis, Individualism, Communitarianism and the Rights of Ethnic Minorities, Notre Dame Law Review 67:615 (1991); Judith Baker, ed., Group Rights (Toronto: University of Toronto Press, 1994); Robert Clinton, The Rights of Indigenous Peoples as Collective Group Rights, Arizona Law Review 32:739 (1990); James Crawford, ed., The Rights of Peoples (Oxford: Oxford University Press, 1988); Ronald Garet, Communality and Existence: The Rights of Groups, Southern California Law Review 56:1001

(1983); Natan Lerner, Group Rights and Discrimination in International Law (Dordrecht, Neth.: Martinus Nijhoff, 1991); Ian MacDonald, Group Rights, Philosophical Papers 28:117 (1991); Sharon O'Brien, Cultural Rights in the United States: A Conflict of Values, Law and Inequality 5:267 (1987); Jeremy Waldron, Can Communal Goods Be Human Rights?, in Liberal Rights: Collected Papers, 1981–1991 (Cambridge: Cambridge University Press, 1993), at 339.

38. Rawls, supra note 19, at 118–42.

39. Id. at 60.

40. Id. at 195–257.

41. Cass Sunstein, The Partial Constitution (Cambridge, Mass.: Harvard University Press, 1993), at 3–7, 68–92.

42. Nozick, supra note 19, at 10, quoting John Locke, Two Treatises on Government, 2d ed. (New York: Cambridge University Press, 1967), Sec. 4.

43. Id. at 49.

44. Id. at 50–51.

45. Edmund Husserl, Ideas: General Introduction to Pure Phenomenology (W. R. Boyce Gibson, trans.) (New York: Collier, 1962), at 387–88. See Nelson Goodman, Ways of Worldmaking (Indianapolis: Hackett, 1978); Alfred Schutz, The Phenomenology of the Social World (George Walsh and Frederick Lehnert, trans.) (Evanston, Ill.: Northwestern University Press, 1967), at 97–138; Max Weber, Economy and Society (Guenther Roth & Claus Wittich, eds.) (Berkeley: University of California Press, 1978), at 4–22.

46. Jerry Mashaw, The Supreme Court's Due Process Calculus For Administrative Adjudication in Mathews v. Eldridge: Three Factors in Search of a Theory of Value, University of Chicago Law Review 44:28 (1976); Frank Michelman, Formal and Associational Aims in Procedural Due Process, Nomos: Due Process 18:126 (1977); Tom Tyler, Why People Obey the Law (New Haven, Conn.: Yale University Press, 1990).

47. Rawls, supra note 19, at 387–88.

48. Thus, a government-centered approach is equally deontological as a human-centered approach. Although clearly more institutional in character, it is not consequentialist or utilitarian, and thus does not suffer from the difficulties that afflict rights theories based on these positions. See David Lyons, Utility and Rights, in Jeremy Waldron, Theories of Rights (Oxford: Oxford University Press, 1984); J. L. Mackie, Can There Be a Right-Based Moral Theory: in Waldron, supra; H. J. McCloskey, Respect for Human Moral Rights versus Maximizing Good, in Frey, supra note 32.

49. Jeremy Bentham, Of Laws in General (H.L.A. Hart, ed.) (New York: Oxford University Press, 1970), at 248–94.

50. Richard Fallon, Individual Rights and the Powers of Government, Georgia Law Review 27:343 (1993); Nozick, supra note 19, at 26–33; L. W. Sumner, The Moral Foundation of Rights (Oxford: Oxford University Press, 1987). For a critique, see Eric Rakowski, Conceptual Independence and Comparative Competence, Georgia Law Review 27:391 (1993).

51. Nozick, supra note 19, at 26–53.

52. Raz, supra note 1, at 183–85.

53. Roderick Hills, The Constitutional Rights of Private Governments, New

NOTES TO PAGES 271-272

York University Law Review 78:144 (2003); Martin, supra note 2, at 73–97. If one adopts Martin's view that government recognition and maintenance is internal to the concept of human rights, then the need for a theory phrased in terms of government becomes even more insistent.

54. Steven Ratner, Corporations and Human Rights: A Theory of Legal Responsibility, Yale Law Journal 111:443 (2001). As Ratner notes, such an approach represents a new departure in human rights thinking; id. at 458–60.

55. For arguments that there is no analytic distinction between the two, see Susan Bandes, The Negative Constitution: A Critique, Michigan Law Review 88:2271 (1990); Stephen Holmes and Cass Sunstein, The Cost of Rights (New York: W. W. Norton, 1999), at 39–43; Gerald MacCallum, Negative and Positive Freedom, Philosophical Review 76:312 (1976); Henry Shue, Basic Rights: Subsistence, Affluence and U.S. Foreign Policy, 2d ed. (Princeton, N.J.: Princeton University Press, 1996), at 35–51. For arguments in favor of the distinction, see Frank Cross, The Error of Positive Rights, UCLA Law Review 48:857 (2001); Gewirth, supra note 19, at 33–38.

56. Maurice Cranston, What Are Human Rights? (London: Bodley Head, 1973); Maurice Cranston, Human Rights, Real and Supposed, in D. D. Raphael, ed., Political Theory and the Rights of Man (Bloomington: Indiana University Press, 1976); Cross, supra note 55; Charles Frankel, Human Rights and Foreign Policy (New York: Foreign Policy Association, 1978); Shelly Kagan, Does Consequentialism Demand Too Much? Recent Work on the Limits of Obligation, Philosophy and Public Affairs 13:239 (1984); Nozick, supra note 19, at 26–53; Peter Singer, Famine, Affluence and Morality, Philosophy and Public Affairs 1:229 (1972); Carl Wellman, The Proliferation of Rights: Moral Progress or Empty Rhetoric: (Boulder, Colo.: Westview Press, 1999).

57. Isaiah Berlin, Two Concepts of Liberty, in Isaiah Berlin, Four Essays on Liberty (Oxford: Oxford University Press, 1969), at 118.

58. See Donnelly, supra note 1; Gewirth, supra note 19; Nickel, supra note 4, at 147–70; Carlos Nino, The Ethics of Human Rights (Oxford: Clarendon Press, 1991); Shue, supra note 55; Edward Sparer, The Right to Welfare, in Norman Dorsen, ed., The Rights of Americans: What They Are, What They Should Be (New York: Vintage, 1971), at 65.

59. Gewirth, supra note 19, at 81–87.

60. Seth Kreimer, Allocational Sanctions: The Problem of Negative Rights in a Positive State, University of Pennsylvania Law Review 132:1293 (1984).

61. See J. L. Mackie, Rights, Utility and Universalization, in Frey, supra note 32; Nickel, supra note 4, at 120–21; Jeremy Waldron, Rights in Conflict, in Waldron, supra note 37, at 203.

62. For general discussions of this concept, see Donnelly, supra note 1, at 143–44; Michael Hartney, Some Confusions Concerning Collective Rights, in Will Kymlicka, ed., The Rights of Minority Cultures (Oxford: Oxford University Press, 1995); Chandran Kukathas, Are There Any Cultural Rights?, in Kymlicka, supra, at 228; Will Kymlicka, Multicultural Citizenship (Oxford: Clarendon Press, 1995), at 34–48; Stephen Marks, Emerging Human Rights: A New Generation for the 1980s? Rutgers Law Review 33:435 (1981).

63. Dworkin, supra note 1, at xi.

64. Ludwig Wittgenstein, Philosophical Investigations, 3d ed. (G.E.M. Anscombe, trans.) (Englewood Cliffs, N.J.: Prentice-Hall, 1958), at 94–97.

65. Kymlicka, Multicultural Citizenship, supra note 62, at 45–46, 75–106.

66. Arguments favoring the concept of group rights or collective rights, are prevalent in modern scholarship. See Adeno Addis, Individualism, Communitarianism and the Rights of Ethnic Minorities, Notre Dame Law Review 67:615 (1991); Judith Baker, ed., Group Rights (Toronto: University of Toronto Press, 1994); Ivar Berg, Race, Stratification, and Group-Based Rights, in Elijah Anderson and Douglas Massey, eds., Problem of the Century: Racial Stratification in the United States (New York: Russell Sage, 2001), at 115; Robert Clinton, The Rights of Indigenous Peoples as Collective Group Rights, Arizona Law Review 32:739 (1990); Richard Falk, The Rights of Peoples (in Particular Indigenous Peoples), in Crawford, supra note 37; Garet, supra note 37; Darlene Johnston, Native Rights as Collective Rights: A Question of Group Self-Preservation, in Kymlicka, Rights, supra note 62, at 179; Kymlicka, Multicultural Citizenship, supra note 62; Will Kymlicka, Liberalism, Community and Culture (Oxford: Clarendon Press, 1989), at 135–61; Lerner, supra note 37; Ian MacDonald, Group Rights, Philosophical Papers 28:117 (1991); Sharon O'Brien, Cultural Rights in the United States: A Conflict of Values, Law and Inequality 5:267 (1987); Vernon van Dyke, Human Rights, Ethnicity, and Discrimination (Westport, Conn.: Greenwood, 1985); Vernon van Dyke, Justice as Fairness: For Groups?, American Political Science Review 69:607 (1975); Jeremy Waldron, Can Communal Goods Be Human Rights?, in Liberal Rights: Collected Papers, 1981–1991 (Cambridge: Cambridge University Press, 1993), at 339.

67. Efforts to reconcile the demands of universalism and cultural relativism include Kymlicka, Multicultural Citizenship, supra note 62; Alain Touraine, Can We Live Together: Equality and Difference (David Macey, trans.) (Stanford, Calif.: Stanford University Press, 2000).

68. See James Coleman, The Asymmetric Society (Syracuse: Syracuse University Press, 1982); Peter French, Collective and Corporate Responsibility (New York: Columbia University Press, 1984); Hills, supra note 53; Ratner, supra note 54, for the view that corporations can function as moral actors; see Meir Dan-Cohen, Rights, Persons, and Organizations: A Legal Theory for Bureaucratic Society (Berkeley: University of California Press, 1986), for the contrary view.

69. For an argument that unorganized groups are capable of collective action, see Larry May, The Morality of Groups (Notre Dame, Ind.: University of Notre Dame Press, 1987).

70. See Kymlicka, Multicultural Citizenship, supra note 62, at 163–70.

71. 406 U.S. 205, 241 (1972). The Court held that Amish parents must be granted an exemption from compulsory education laws for their fourteen- and fifteen-year old children because continued exposure to the public schools would undermine their religion. Justice Douglas noted that the child might "want to be a pianist or an astronaut or an oceanographer. To do so he will have to break from the Amish tradition." Id. at 244–45.

72. See John Ely, The Constitutionality of Reverse Discrimination, University of Chicago Law Review 41:723 (1974); Deborah Malamud, Values, Symbols and

Facts in the Affirmative Action Debate, Michigan Law Review 95:1668 (1997); Samuel Issacharoff, Can Affirmative Action Be Defended?, Ohio State Law Journal 59:669 (1998). Affirmative action need not be treated as being based on a group right, of course. There is also an individual rights justification for it, namely, that the benefited individuals have been disadvantaged, as individuals, because of their membership in a particular group, and are entitled to differential treatment to compensate for that particularized disadvantage. In that case, affirmative action implements a first-generation right (no discrimination) or second-generation right (equal opportunity to flourish), rather than a third-generation right.

73. Kymlicka, Multicultural Citizenship, supra note 62, at 152–72.

74. Susan Bandes, The Negative Constitution: A Critique, Michigan Law Review 88:2271 (1990); Mary Ann Glendon, Rights Talk: The Impoverishment of Political Discourse (New York: Free Press, 1991). See also Mary Ann Glendon, A Nation under Lawyers: How the Crisis in the Legal Profession Is Transforming American Society (Cambridge, Mass.: Harvard University Press, 1994).

75. Rawls, supra note 19, at 42–44.

76. 489 U.S. 189 (1989).

77. Holmes and Sunstein, supra note 55, at 88–98.

78. A verbal indication of the U.S. Constitution's progenerative status is that so many modern, i.e., postwar constitutions begin with the phrase "We the people" or a variant of that phrase. See Belarus (1994), Preamble; Cambodia (1993), Preamble; Congo Republic (1992), Preamble (follows a one-paragraph account of the nation's history); Eritrea (1996), Preamble; India (1950), Preamble; Japan (1946), Preamble; Mongolia (1992), Preamble; Russia (1993), Preamble ("We the multinational people"); South Africa (1996), Preamble; South Korea (1948), Preamble; Zambia (1991), Preamble.

79. Isaac Deutscher, Stalin: A Political Biography (New York: Vintage, 1970), at 565–70.

80. See generally Donald Downs, Nazis in Skokie (Notre Dame, Ind.: University of Notre Dame Press, 1985); Richard Lindley, Autonomy (Atlantic Highlands, N.J.: Humanities Press International, 1986); Raz, supra note 1, at 369–429; Schneewind, supra note 15; Thomas Scanlon, A Theory of Freedom of Expression, Philosophy & Public Affairs 1:204 (1972), reprinted in Frederick Schauer and Walter Sinott-Armstrong, eds., The Philosophy of Law: Classic and Contemporary Readings with Commentary (Fort Worth: Harcourt Brace College Publishers, 1996), at 362; Horacio Specter, Autonomy and Rights: The Moral Foundations of Liberalism (Oxford: Clarendon Press, 1992); Robert Paul Wolff, In Defense of Anarchism (Berkeley: University of California Press, 1998), at 12–18.

81. See Kathryn Abrams, From Autonomy to Agency: Feminist Perspectives of Self-Direction, William and Mary Law Review 40:805 (1999); Hilary Charlesworth, Human Rights as Men's Rights, in Julia Peters and Andrea Wolper, eds., Women's Rights, Human Rights: International Feminist Perspectives (New York: Routledge, 1995), at 103; Hilary Charlesworth and Christine Chinkin, Violence against Women: A Global Issue, in Julie Stubbs, ed., Women, Male Violence and the Law (Sydney: Sydney University Law School, 1994); Susan Kupfer, Autonomy and Community in Feminist Legal Thought, Golden Gate University Law Review 22:583 (1992); Catherine MacKinnon, Crimes of War, Crimes of Peace, in

Stephen Shute and Susan Hurley, eds., On Human Rights: The Oxford Amnesty Lectures 1993 (New York: Basic Books, 1993), at 83; Carol Smart, Feminism and the Power of Law (London: Routledge, 1989), at 138–44; Robin West, Jurisprudence and Gender, University of Chicago Law Review 55:1 (1988). MacKinnon puts the point as follows: "Women's rape becomes men's liberty, gang rape their fraternity, prostitution their property, forced pregnancy their family and their privacy, pornography their speech." Id. at 96.

82. Bradwell v. Illinois, 83 U.S. (16 Wall.) 130 (1872) (legal practice); Minor v. Happersett, 88 U.S. (21 Wall.) 162 (1874) (voting); Radice v. New York, 264 U.S. 292 (1924) (night workers in restaurants); Goesaert v. Cleary, 335 U.S. 464 (1948) (bartenders, unless women's husband or father owned the bar). A concurring opinion in *Bradwell* invoked natural law in favor of its conclusion: "The paramount destiny and mission of women are to fulfill the noble and benign offices of wife and mother. This is the law of the creator." 83 U.S. at 141 (Bradley, J., concurring).

83. 411 U.S. 677 (1973). The Court first struck down a statute for gender discrimination grounds two years earlier, in Reed v. Reed, 404 U.S. 71 (1971), but on the grounds that discrimination in the circumstances of the case (involving administrators of a will) lacked a rational basis. By the time *Frontiero* and *Reed* were decided, of course, the Civil Rights Act of 1964 had already outlawed certain forms of gender discrimination.

84. 410 U.S. 113 (1973).

85. This insight, now contested, was initially advanced by Carol Gilligan, In A Different Voice: Psychological Theory and Women's Development (Cambridge, Mass.: Harvard University Press, 1982).

86. See Annette Baier, A Progress of Sentiments, 2d ed. (Cambridge, Mass.: Harvard University Press, 1994); Carole Pateman, Feminist Critiques of the Public/Private Dichotomy, in S. I. Benn & G. F. Gaus, eds., Public and Private in Social Life (New York: St. Martin's Press, 1983), at 285; Virginia Held, Feminist Morality (Chicago: University of Chicago Press, 1993); Linda Hirshman, Is the Original Position Inherently Male-Superior? Columbia Law Review 94:1860 (1994); Margaret Thornton, ed., Public and Private: Feminist Legal Debates (Oxford: Oxford University Press, 1995).

87. Amitai Etzioni, The Spirit of Community (New York: Touchstone, 1994); Peter Gabel, The Phenomenology of Rights-Consciousness and the Pact of the Withdrawn Selves, Texas Law Review 62:1563 (1984); Glendon, Rights Talk, supra note 74; Mark Tushnet, An Essay on Rights, Texas Law Review 62:1363 (1984); Michael Sandel, Liberalism and the Limits of Justice (Cambridge: Cambridge University Press, 1982).

88. See Glendon, Rights Talk, supra note 74; Glendon, Nation under Lawyers, supra note 74; Robert Kagan, Adversarial Legalism: The American Way of Law (Cambridge, Mass.: Harvard University Press, 2001); R. Shep Melnick, Between the Lines: Interpreting Welfare Rights (Washington, D.C.: Brookings Institution, 1994); R. Shep Melnick, Regulation and the Courts: The Case of the Clean Air Act (Washington, D.C.: Brookings Institution, 1983); Stuart Scheingold, The Politics of Rights: Lawyers, Public Policy, and Political Change (New Haven, Conn.: Yale University Press, 1974).

89. Etzioni, supra note 87; Sandel, supra note 87; Seligman, supra note 31.

90. See note 81, supra (citing sources).

91. See William Eskridge, Gaylaw: Challenging the Apartheid of the Closet (Cambridge, Mass.: Harvard University Press, 1999); Andrew Koppelman, The Gay Rights Question in Contemporary American Law (Chicago: University of Chicago Press, 2002).

92. Kant, supra note 16, at 62 (Pt. 1, §§ 24 & 25).

93. See Eskridge, supra note 91; Lisa Duggan and Nan Hunter, Sex Wars: Sexual Dissent and Political Culture (New York: Routledge, 1998).

94. 478 U.S. 186 (1986). Bowers upheld the constitutionality of a Georgia sodomy statute on the grounds that homosexuality is unnatural, an argument the Court supported by asserting that prescriptions against homosexuality "have ancient roots."

95. 539 U.S. 558 (2003).

96. William Eskridge, The Case for Same-Sex Marriage: From Sexual Liberty to Civilized Commitment (New York: Free Press, 1996).

97. 539 U.S. at 604–5.

98. See Stephen Buckle, Natural Law and the Theory of Property: Grotius to Hume (Oxford: Clarendon Press, 1991); Knud Haakonssen, Natural Law and Moral Philosophy: From Grotius to the Scottish Enlightenment (New York: Cambridge University Press, 1996); Tuck, supra note 6, at 58–100; Jeremy Waldron, The Right to Private Property (Oxford: Clarendon Press, 1988), at 141–71; Edwin West, Property Rights in the History of Economic Thought: From Locke to J. S. Mill, in Terry Anderson and Fred McChesney, eds., Property Rights: Cooperation, Conflict and the Law (Princeton: Princeton University Press, 2003).

99. Lucas v. South Carolina Coastal Council, 505 U.S. 1003 (1992); Yee v. City of Escondido, 503 U.S. 519 (1992); First English Evangelical Lutheran Church v. City of Los Angeles, 482 U.S. 304 (1987). A wide range of scholars supports this view. See Richard Epstein, Takings: Private Property and the Power of Eminent Domain (Cambridge, Mass.: Harvard University Press, 1985); J. W. Harris, Property and Justice (Oxford: Clarendon Press, 1996); Stephen Munzer, A Theory of Property (Cambridge: Cambridge University Press, 1990); Nozick, supra note 19; J. E. Penner, The Idea of Property in Law (Oxford: Clarendon Press, 1997); Laura Underkuffler, The Idea of Property: Its Meaning and Power (Oxford: Oxford University Press, 2003).

100. Robert Dahl, C. B. Macpherson, Capitalism and the Changing Concept of Property, in E. Kamenka and R. S. Neale, eds., Feudalism, Capitalism and Beyond (London: Edward Arnold, 1975), at 116; Ralph Miliband, The State in Capitalist Society (London: Weidenfeld & Nicolson, 1969); Nickel, supra note 4, at 147–70; Joseph Singer, Entitlement: The Paradoxes of Property (New Haven, Conn.: Yale University Press, 2000). The strongest version of this point, of course, is Karl Marx, Capital: A Critique of Political Economy (Samuel Moore & Edward Aveling, trans.) (New York: Modern Library, 1906).

101. Eva Brems, Human Rights: Universality and Diversity (The Hague: Martinus Nijhoff, 2001); Tony Evans, U.S. Hegemony and the Project of Universal Human Rights (New York: St. Martin's Press, 1996); A.J.M. Milne, Human

Rights and Human Diversity: An Essay in the Philosophy of Human Rights (Albany: State University of New York Press, 1986); Adamantha Pollis, Human Rights in Liberal, Socialist and Third World Perspective, in Richard Claude and Burns Weston, eds., Human Rights in the World Community: Issues and Action, 2d ed. (Philadelphia: University of Pennsylvania Press, 1992), at 146.

102. See Daniel Bell, The East Asian Challenge to Human Rights: Reflections on an East-West Dialogue, Human Rights Quarterly 18:641 (1996); Joseph Chan, A Confucian Perspective of Human Rights, in Joanne Bauer and Daniel Bell, eds., The East Asian Challenge for Human Rights (Cambridge: Cambridge University Press, 1999), at 212; Bilahari Kausikan, Asia's Different Standard, Foreign Policy 24 (Fall 1993); Bilahari Kausikan, An Asian Approach to Human Rights, ASIL Proceedings 147 (1995); Tommy Koh, The United States and East Asia: Conflict and Cooperation (Singapore: Times Academic Press, 1995). See also Jefferson Plantilla and Sebasti Raj, eds., Human Rights in Asian Cultures: Continuity and Change (Osaka: Hurights, 1997).

103. This would include most of South America, Africa, and Asia (with the notable exception of Japan)—all together, about four-fifths of humanity.

104. See Marjorie Argosin, A Map of Hope: Women's Writings on Human Rights (New Brunswick, N.J.: Rutgers University Press, 1999); Rebecca Cook, ed., Human Rights of Women: National and International Perspectives (Philadelphia: University of Pennsylvania Press, 1994); Jack Donnelly, Cultural Relativism and Universal Human Rights, Human Rights Quarterly 6:400 (1984); Carol Gould, Feminism and Democratic Community Revisited, in Nomos 35:400 (1993); Nickel, supra note 4, at 68–81; Orend, supra note 4, at 155–88; Patricia Williams, The Alchemy of Race and Rights (Cambridge, Mass.: Harvard University Press, 1991).

105. Alan Gewirth, Are There Any Absolute Rights?, Philosophical Quarterly 31:1 (1981), reprinted in Alan Gewirth, Human Rights: Essays on Justification and Applications (Chicago: University of Chicago Press, 1982), at 218, 219.

106. 366 U.S. 36, 56 (Black, J., dissenting). See Alexander Meikeljohn, The First Amendment Is an Absolute, Supreme Court Review 1961:245 (1961).

107. Keith Whittington, Constitutional Construction: Divided Powers and Constitutional Meaning (Cambridge, Mass.: Harvard University Press, 1999).

108. Thomas, supra note 22, at 449–557.

109. Ronald Dworkin, Law's Empire (Cambridge, Mass.: Belknap Press, 1986); Ronald Dworkin, Hard Cases, Harvard Law Review 88:1057 (1975); Owen Fiss, Objectivity and Interpretation, Stanford Law Review 34:739 (1982); Herbert Wechsler, Toward Neutral Principles in Constitutional Law, Harvard Law Review 73:1 (1959).

110. Clare Dalton, An Essay in the Deconstruction of Contract Doctrine, Yale Law Journal 94:997 (1985); Lee Epstein and Jack Knight, The Choices Justices Make (Washington, D.C.: CQ Press, 1998); Morton Horwitz, The Transformation of American Law 1780–1860 (Cambridge, Mass.: Harvard University Press, 1977); Jeffrey Segal and Harold Spaeth, The Supreme Court and the Attitudinal Model (Cambridge: Cambridge University Press, 1993); Mark Tushnet, Red,

White and Blue: A Critical Analysis of Constitutional Law (Cambridge, Mass.: Harvard University Press, 1988); Roberto Unger, Knowledge and Politics (New York: Free Press, 1975).

111. See Ibrahim al-Wahab, The Swedish Institution of Ombudsman: An Instrument of Human Rights (Stockholm: LiberFörlag, 1979); Walter Gellhorn Ombudsmen and Others: Citizens' Protectors in Nine Countries (Cambridge, Mass.: Harvard University Press, 1966); Roy Gregory and Philip Giddings, eds., Righting Wrongs: The Ombudsman in Six Continents (Amsterdam: IOS Press, 2000), Donald Rowat, The Ombudsman Plan: Essays on the Worldwide Spread of an Idea (Toronto: McClelland & Stewart, 1973); Frank Stacey, Ombudsmen Compared (Oxford: Clarendon Press, 1978); Sam Zagoria, The Ombudsman: How Good Governments Handle Citizens' Grievances (Cabin John, Md.: Seven Locks Press, 1988).

112. Eric Orts, Reflexive Environmental Law, Northwestern University Law Review 89:1227 (1995).

113. 42 U.S.C. § 4332.

114. Michael Dorf and Charles Sabel, A Constitution of Democratic Experimentalism, Columbia Law Review 98:267 (1998); Jody Freeman, Collaborative Governance in the Administrative State, UCLA Law Review 45:1 (1997); Joel Handler, Dependent People, the State, and the Modern/Postmodern Search for the Dialogic Community, UCLA Law Review 35:999 (1988); Bronwen Morgan, Social Citizenship in the Shadow of Competition (Aldershot, Eng.: Ashcroft, 2003); William Simon, The Practice of Justice (Cambridge, Mass.: Harvard University Press, 1998); Susan Sturm, Second Generation Employment Discrimination: A Structural Approach, Columbia Law Review 101:458 (2001); Richard Pildes and Cass Sunstein, Reinventing the Regulatory State, Chicago Law Review 62:1 (1995).

115. Edward Rubin, Nazis, Skokie and the First Amendment as Virtue, California Law Review 74:233 (1986).

116. See Jeremy Waldron, Rights and Needs: The Myth of Disjunction, in Sarat and Kearns, supra note 1, at 87. Waldron argues that needs discourse is of value, but that it must be integrated into a framework of rights in order to be coherent.

117. 350 U.S. 879 (1955).

118. This constraint of generalized action is the one that Locke identifies as a means of ensuring that the natural right of property is not infringed. Because he approaches the idea from the natural rights tradition, however, he does not connect it with the concept of due process.

119. United States v. Carolene Products, 304 U.S. 144 (1938). See Bruce Ackerman, Beyond Carolene Products, Harvard Law Review 98:713 (1985); Jack Balkin, The Footnote, Northwestern University Law Review 83:275 (1989); Peter Linzer, The Carolene Products Footnote and the Preferred Position of Individual Rights: Louis Lusky and John Hart Ely v. Harlan Fiske Stone, Constitutional Commentary 12:277 (1995). For a discussion of the case's background, see Geoffrey Miller, The True Story of Carolene Products, Supreme Court Review 1987:397 (1987).

120. John Ely, Democracy and Distrust: A Theory of Judicial Review (Cambridge, Mass.: Harvard University Press, 1980).

121. NAACP v. Button, 371 U.S. 415, 433 (1963) ("Because First Amendment freedoms need breathing space to survive, government may regulate in the area only with narrow specificity"). See Baggett v. Bullitt, 377 U.S. 360 (1964); Houston v. Hill, 482 U.S. 451 (1987).

122. 297 U.S. 233 (1936). See Minneapolis Star & Tribune Co. v. Minnesota Commissioner of Revenue, 460 U.S. 575 (1983); Arkansas Writers' Project, Inc. v. Ragland, 481 U.S. 221 (1987).

123. Newspapers benefit, of course, from being able to avoid special taxation, but so would firms in any other industry. The rationale of the decisions must refer to the rights of a different party, namely, the newspaper's readers.

124. See, e.g., Boos v. Berry, 485 U.S. 312 (1988) (striking down a city ordinance restricting signs placed on the streets near foreign embassies); Board of Airport Commissioners v. Jews for Jesus, 482 U.S. 569 (1987) (striking down prohibition on political expression in airports); Schneider v. State of New Jersey 308 U.S. 147 (1939) (striking down a city ordinance prohibiting leafleting on public property); Greer v. Spock, 424 U.S. 828 (1976) (upholding restriction on demonstrations in nonrestricted areas of military base); Grayned v. City of Rockford, 408 U.S. 104 (1972) (upholding restriction on noise-making near school when school is in session); Adderly v. Florida, 385 U.S. 39 (1966) (upholding prohibition of speech in areas outside prisons and jails). For discussions, see Daniel Farber and John Nowak, The Misleading Nature of Public Forum Analysis: Content and Context in First Amendment Adjudication, Virginia Law Review 70:1219 (1984); Harry Kalven, The Concept of a Public Forum: Cox v. Louisiana, Supreme Court Review 1965:1 (1965); Robert Post, Constitutional Domains: Democracy, Community, Management (Cambridge, Mass.: Harvard University Press, 1995), at 199-267.

125. Post, supra note 124, at 1-20, 199-267.

126. United States ex rel. Atterbury v. Ragen, 237 F.2d 953 (7th. Cir. 1956), cert. denied, 339 U.S. 990 (1957); United States ex rel. Morris v. Radio Station WENR, 209 F.2d 105 (7th Cir. 1953); Garcia v. Steele, 193 F.2d 276 (8th Cir. 1951); Siegel v. Ragen, 180 F.2d 785 (7th Cir.), cert. denied, 339 U.S. 990 (1950); Powell v. Hunter, 172 F.2d 330 (10th Cir. 1949). See Note, Beyond the Ken of Courts: A Critique of the Judicial Refusal to Review the Complaints of Convicts, Yale Law Journal 72:506 (1963).

127. 247 F. Supp. 683 (E.D. Ark., 1965).

128. See Bradley Chilton, Prisons under the Gavel: The Federal Court Takeover of Georgia Prisons (Columbus: Ohio State University Press, 1991); Ben Crouch and James Marquart, An Appeal to Justice: Litigated Reform of Texas Prisons (Austin: University of Texas Press, 1989); Malcolm Feeley and Edward Rubin, Judicial Policy Making and the Modern State: How the Courts Reformed America's Prisons (Cambridge: Cambridge University Press, 1998), at 27-143; Steve Martin and Sheldon Ekland-Olson, Texas Prisons: The Walls Came Tumbling Down (Austin: Texas Monthly Press, 1987); Ira Robbins and Michael Buser, Punitive Conditions of Prison Confinement: An Analysis of Pugh v. Locke and Federal Court Supervision of State Penal Administration Under the Eighth Amendment, Stanford Law Review 29:893 (1977); Larry Yackle, Reform and Regret: The Story of Federal Judicial Involvement in the Alabama Prison System (New York: Oxford University Press, 1989).

129. Michel Foucault, Discipline and Punish: The Birth of the Prison (Alan Sheridan, trans.) (New York: Vintage Books, 1979).

130. Thorsten Sellin, Pioneering in Penology: The Amsterdam Houses of Correction in the Sixteenth and Seventeenth Centuries (Philadelphia: University of Pennsylvania Press, 1944); Thorsten Sellin, Slavery and the Penal System (New York: Elsevier, 1976); Pieter Spierenburg, The Prison Experience: Disciplinary Institutions and Their Inmates in Early Modern Europe (New Brunswick, N.J.: Rutgers University Press, 1991).

Notes to Chapter Nine

1. See A.M.A. Honore, Ownership, in A. Guest, ed., Oxford in Jurisprudence (Oxford: Clarendon Press, 1961), at 107; Stephen Munzer, A Theory of Property (Cambridge: Cambridge University Press, 1990), at 17; Jeremy Waldron, The Right to Private Property (Oxford: Clarendon Press, 1988), at 47. Honore's list of these attributes includes the right to possess, the right to use, the right to the capital, the right to manage, and the right to the income.

2. See Stephen Buckle, Natural Law and the Theory of Property: Grotius to Hume (Oxford: Clarendon Press, 1991); Knud Haakonssen, Natural Law and Moral Philosophy: From Grotius to the Scottish Enlightenment (New York: Cambridge University Press, 1996); Richard Tuck, Natural Rights Theories: Their Origin and Development (Cambridge: Cambridge University Press, 1979), at 58–100; Waldron, supra note 1, at 141–71; Edwin West, Property Rights in the History of Economic Thought: From Locke to J. S. Mill, in Terry Anderson and Fred McChesney, eds., Property Rights: Cooperation, Conflict and the Law (Princeton: Princeton University Press, 2003).

3. See Haakonssen, supra note 2, at 171, 252–53; West, supra note 2.

4. Hugo Grotius, De Jure Belli ac Pacis Libri Tres (Francis Kelsey, trans.) (Birmingham, Ala.: Legal Classics Library, 1984), at 53–54 (I,2.i.5); John Locke, The Second Treatise of Government (Thomas Peardon, ed.) (Indianapolis: Bobbs-Merrill, 1952), at 17 (V, § 27); Richard Overton, An Arrow against All Tyrants . . . in Andrew Sharp, ed., The English Levellers (Cambridge: Cambridge University Press, 1998), at 54, 55. See C. B. Macpherson, The Theory of Possessive Individualism (Oxford: Oxford University Press, 1962), at 137–48, 199–203; C. B. Macpherson, Human Rights as Property Rights, Dissent 24:72 (1977); Tuck, supra note 2, at 70–71; Laura Underkuffler, On Property: An Essay, Yale Law Journal, 100:127 (1990).

5. Restatement (First) of Property, Ch. 1, Introductory Comment (Philadelphia: American Law Institute, 1936); Felix Cohen, Dialogue on Private Property, Rutgers Law Review 9:357 (1954); Kevin Grey, Equitable Property, Current Legal Problems 4:157 (1994); Wesley Hohfeld, Fundamental Legal Conceptions (Walter Cook, ed.) (New Haven, Conn.: Yale University Press, 1919); Loren Lomansky, Persons, Rights, and the Moral Community (Oxford: Oxford University Press, 1987).

6. This intuition, however, is subject to many qualifications and complexities. Some writers argue that ownership itself can only be understood as a set of relationships among people. See John Christman, The Myth of Property: Toward an

Egalitarian Theory of Ownership (New York: Oxford University Press, 1994), at 15–27; Thomas Grey, The Disintegration of Property, in Roland Pennock and John Chapman, eds., Nomos XXII: Property (New York: New York University Press, 1980), at 69; Honore, supra note 1. If property is itself nothing more than a relationship among people, then the right to property, a fortiori, can be nothing more than a relationship. Some scholars have argued that ownership, or possession, is more corporeal, or definitive. See Richard Epstein, Takings: Private Property and the Power of Eminent Domain (Cambridge, Mass.: Harvard University Press, 1985); Thomas Merrill and Henry Smith, Optimal Standardization in the Law of Property: The *Numerus Clausus* Principle, Yale Law Journal 110:1 (2000); J. E. Penner, The "Bundle of Rights" Picture of Property, UCLA Law Review 43:711 (1996). The argument here is that even if this is true, the general right to acquire or retain such ownership is necessarily relational.

7. See Kaiser Aetna v. United States, 444 U.S. 164, 176 (1979); Loretto v. Teleprompter Manhattan CATV Corp., 458 U.S. 419, 433–36 (1982); Dolan v. City of Tigard, 512 U.S. 374, 393–94 (1994); Cohen, supra note 5; Kevin Grey, Property in Thin Air, Cambridge Law Journal 50:252 (1991); A.M.A. Honore, Rights of Exclusion and Immunities against Divesting, Tulane Law Review 34:453 (1960); J. W. Harris, Property and Justice (Oxford: Oxford University Press, 1996), at 13; Thomas Merrill, Property and the Right to Exclude, Nebraska Law Review 77:730 (1998); J. E. Penner, The Idea of Property in Law (Oxford: Clarendon Press, 1997), at 68–104.

8. G.W.F. Hegel, Philosophy of Right (T. M. Knox, trans.) (London: Oxford University Press, 1967), at 40–57 (§§ 41–70).

9. C. B. Macpherson, Capitalism and the Changing Concept of Property, in Eugene Kamenka and R.S. Neale, eds., Feudalism, Capitalism and Beyond (London: Edward Arnold, 1975), at 116.

10. Frank Michelman, Foreword: On Protecting the Poor Through the Fourteenth Amendment, Harvard Law Review 83:7 (1969); Frank Michelman, Welfare Rights in a Constitutional Democracy, Washington University Law Quarterly 1979:659 (1979).

11. Waldron, supra note 1, at 343–445. Waldron bases his approach on Hegel.

12. Hegel, supra note 8, at 40 (§ 41), 42 (§ 45). Note that this version of a right to property is diametrically opposed to the right to property advanced by its strong advocates in the Anglo-American tradition, such as Milton Friedman, Robert Nozick, and Richard Epstein; see Milton Friedman, Capitalism and Freedom (Chicago: University of Chicago Press, 1962); Robert Nozick, Anarchy, State and Utopia (New York: Basic Books, 1974); Epstein, supra note 6, because their idea of property precludes redistribution, whereas Hegel, Macpherson, Michelman, and Waldron virtually require it.

13. This is not, however, the way Hegel characterizes it. His view of the state's role seems to be the more conventional one of enforcing the commonly understood rules for possession and transfer of property. "In civil society," Hegel argues, "property rests on contract and on the formalities which make ownership capable of proof and valid in law." Hegel, supra note 8, at 139 (§ 217). Waldron criticizes Hegel for not translating his notion of property into a positive right to avoid poverty, supra note 8, at 377–82.

14. Grey, supra note 6.

15. 260 U.S. 393 (1922). Commentary on the case is voluminous. See, e.g., Bruce Ackerman, Private Property and the Constitution (New Haven, Conn.: Yale University Press, 1977), at 156–67; Robert Brauneis, "The Foundation of Our 'Regulatory Takings' Jurisprudence": The Myth and Meaning of Justices Holmes's Opinion in *Pennsylvania Coal v. Mahon*, Yale Law Journal 106:613 (1996); William Fischel, Regulatory Takings: Law, Economics and Politics (Cambridge, Mass.: Harvard University Press, 1995), at 14–47; Lawrence Friedman, A Search for Seizure: *Pennsylvania Coal v. Mahon* in Context, Law & History Review 4:1 (1986); Carol Rose, Mahon Reconstructed: Why the Takings Issue is Still a Muddle, Southern California Law Review 57:561 (1984); William Treanor, Jam for Justice Holmes: Reassessing the Significance of *Mahon*, Georgetown Law Journal 86:813 (1998).

16. If the mining company owned the surface rights, however, it was allowed to mine, regardless of whether the mining would cause subsidence. This suggests that the motivation behind the statute was not protection of the environment but protection of the surface owners, thus making the statute seem more like an effort to prefer one group to another than like a neutral social policy. Since the demise of substantive due process, however, American courts have ceased striking down statutes that possessed this character.

17. 260 U.S. at 413.

18. Id. at 415.

19. See Guido Calabresi, A Common Law for the Age of Statutes (Cambridge, Mass.: Harvard University Press, 1982).

20. Margaret Radin, The Liberal Conception of Property: Cross Currents in the Jurisprudence of Takings, Columbia Law Review 88:1667 (1988).

21. For an argument endorsing this position, see Epstein, supra note 6. For a less extreme, but still politically unviable argument along the same lines, see Fischel, supra note 15.

22. In Penn Central Transportation Co. v. City of New York, 438 U.S. 104 (1967), the Supreme Court held that "distinct investment-backed expectations" merited compensation. Frank Michelman endorses this approach on utilitarian grounds. See Property, Utility and Fairness: Comments on the Ethical Foundations of "Just Compensation" Law, Harvard Law Review 80:1165 (1967); see also Munzer, supra note 1, at 425–35. This is less intrusive than a comprehensive requirement of the sort Richard Epstein favors (see Epstein, supra note 6), but it remains incompatible with the administrative state. For example, many people whose real estate is down-zoned may have distinct, investment-backed expectations, but we do not compensate them under our current regime.

23. See Lucas v. South Carolina Coastal Council, 505 U.S. 1003 (1992); Yee v. City of Escondido, 503 U.S. 519 (1992); First English Evangelical Lutheran Church v. City of Los Angeles, 482 U.S. 304 (1987); Williamson City Regulatory Planning Comm. v. Hamilton Bank, 473 U.S. 172 (1985); Penn Central Transportation Co. v. City of New York, 438 U.S. 104 (1978). For an argument that the case is not particularly important, see Fischel, supra note 15, at 37–48.

24. 480 U.S. 470 (1987). The case involved a new statute very similar to the one that had been struck down in *Mahon*. This time, the Court upheld the statute.

25. See Paul Einzig, Primitive Money in Its Ethnological, Historical and Economic Aspects, 2d ed. (Oxford: Pergamon Press, 1966).

26. Lancelot of the Lake (Corin Corley, trans.) (Oxford: Oxford University Press, 1989), at 3–22. This is the first part of a five-part work. It is called the Vulgate Lancelot because it is written in French, not Latin.

27. The story possesses at least a modicum of historical accuracy. In the middle to latter part of the fifth century, when Arthur's father would have lived, Gaul was still nominally part of the Roman Empire. Britain, on the other hand, had become an independent realm after 410, when the Emperor Honorius had denied it any aid from Rome, and there was probably frequent dissension among the island's various Celtic kingdoms. A force of British soldiers entered Brittany, then known as Armorica, in 468 to defend it from Saxon incursions, and, after settling there, would give the region its current name. The social relationships in the story, however, are entirely medieval.

28. Id. at 6.

29. Id. at 18.

30. Id. at 20.

31. The author of the Vulgate Lancelot remains unknown. See Chapter 6, note 32.

32. J. H. Baker, An Introduction to English Legal History, 2d ed. (London: Butterworths, 1979), at 139–219; Underkuffler, supra note 4.

33. R. Van Caenegem, Government, Law and Society, in J. H. Burns, ed., The Cambridge History of Medieval Political Thought, c. 350–c. 1450 (Cambridge: Cambridge University Press, 1988), at 174, 194–98; Georges Duby, The Chivalrous Society (Cynthia Postan, trans.) (Berkeley: University of California Press, 1977), at 178–85; Heinrich Fichtenau, Living in the Tenth Century: Mentalities and the Social Order (Patrick Geary, trans.) (Chicago: University of Chicago Press, 1991), at 141–44; F. L. Ganshof, Feudalism (Philip Grierson, trans.) (Toronto: University of Toronto Press, 1996), at 106–49; R. W. Southern, The Making of the Middle Ages (New Haven, Conn.: Yale University Press, 1953), at 111.

34. Marc Bloch, Feudal Society (L. A. Manyon, trans.) (Chicago: University of Chicago Press, 1961), at 293–311; Jean Dunbabin, Government, in Burns, supra note 33, at 477, 509–10; David Herlihy, The History of Feudalism (New York: Harper & Row, 1970), at 78–79; J. R. Strayer, The Two Levels of Feudalism, in J. R. Strayer, Medieval Statecraft and the Perspectives of History (Princeton: Princeton University Press, 1971).

35. In the parley with Ban, Claudus declares that he did not take Ban's land "because of anything you have done to me, or out of any enmity towards you, but because of King Arthur, who is your lord, for his father, Uther Pendragon, drove me from my land." Lancelot, supra note 26, at 6. Given his character, Claudus might be lying, but his rationale had to seem plausible or the story would not have made sense to its audience. Moreover, he has no incentive to omit any important item from his list of grievances against King Arthur.

36. See Bloch, supra note 34, at 255–79; Georges Duby, Rural Economy and Country Life in the Medieval West (Cynthia Postan, trans.) (London: Edward Arnold, 1968); Frances and Joseph Gies, Life in a Medieval Village (New York: Harper & Row, 1990), at 67–105; Southern, supra note 33, at 101–2.

37. See Duby, supra note 33, at 186–215; Fichtenau, supra note 33, at 359–78; Francis and Joseph Gies, Life in a Medieval Castle (New York: Harper & Row, 1974), at 96–124.

38. As Marc Bloch notes, "Castles were not only a safe refuge for the master and sometimes for his subjects; they also constituted, for the whole of the surrounding district, an administrative capital and the centre of a network of dependencies." Bloch, supra note 34, at 401.

39. Bloch, supra note 34, at 145–240; Fichtenau, supra note 33, at 152–56; Ganshof, supra note 33, at 69–155.

40. These are not the only places in the story where feudal loyalty is emphasized. There is a lengthy passage, which is placed after the seneschal betrays the castle but before Ban sees it burning, which describes the courageous resistance of one of Ban's knights against Claudus's troops. This knight, who is described in the most laudatory terms, addresses the seneschal as a "whore's son" and compares him to Judas for his betrayal of King Ban. Lancelot, supra note 26, at 13.

41. See Fernand Braudel, Capitalism and Material Life, 1400–1800 (Miriam Kochan, trans.) (New York: Harper, 1975); Catharina Lis and Hugo Soly, Poverty and Capitalism in Pre-Industrial Europe (James Coonan, trans.) (Hassocks: Harvester Press, 1979); Robert Lopez, The Commercial Revolution of the Middle Ages: 950–1350 (Cambridge: Cambridge University Press, 1971); Edward Miller and John Hatcher, Medieval England: Rural Society and Economic Change, 1086–1348 (New York: Longman, 1978); Henri Pirenne, Medieval Cities: Their Origins and the Renewal of Trade (Frank Halsey, trans.) (Princeton: Princeton University Press, 1969). This process began as early as the twelfth century.

42. Carol Rose, "Takings" and the Practices of Property: Property as Wealth, Property as Propriety, in Carol Rose, Property and Persuasion (Boulder, Colo.: Westview Press, 1994), at 59–61.

43. See C. Edwin Baker, Property and Its Relation to Constitutionally Protected Liberty, University of Pennsylvania Law Review 134:741 (1986); Morris Cohen, Property and Sovereignty, Cornell Law Quarterly 13:8 (1927); Southern, supra note 33, at 146.

44. Jane Austen, Emma (London: Penguin, 1966); Johann Wolfgang von Goethe, Elective Affinities (R. J. Hollingdale, trans.) (London: Penguin, 1971).

45. Slavery is traditionally defined as the ownership of a human being as property. See M. I. Finley, Ancient Slavery and Modern Ideology (New York: Viking, 1980), at 73; Eugene Genovese, Roll, Jordan, Roll: The World the Slaves Made (New York: Vintage, 1972), at 3–7; H. J. Nieboer, Slavery as an Industrial System: Ethnological Researches (The Hague: Martinus Nijhoff, 1910), at 6; Kenneth Stampp, The Peculiar Institution: Slavery in the Ante-Bellum South (New York: Vintage, 1956), at 22–27; James Watson, Slavery as an Institution, Open and Closed Systems, in James Watson, ed., Asian and African Systems of Slavery (Oxford: Basil Blackwell, 1980), at 809. Of course, slavery involved many other issues, including racism, class stratification, subordination, and dishonor. Hegel's discussion emphasizes these features; see G.W.F. Hegel, The Phenomenology of Mind (J. B. Baillie, trans.) (New York: Harper & Row, 1967), at 234–40.

46. This is not to say that the serfs of the feudal era had a pleasant life. But, as noted above, the noncommercial character of their subordination conferred sev-

eral advantages that were denied to slaves, particularly the African slaves of a later period. They generally could not be displaced from their homes, they were partially protected by the force of local custom, and, as Christians, they were fully entitled to receive all the sacraments, including marriage.

47. Locke, supra note 4, Ch. 4. See Luis de Molina, Extracts on Politics and Government, From Justice, Tract II (George Moore, trans.) (Chevy Chase, Md.: Country Dollar Press, 1951); Grotius, supra note 4, at 345–47. Various aspects of slavery were debated, such as whether one could sell oneself into slavery (the issue Locke focuses on), or whether a particular group of people should be enslaved (Las Casas argued that the American Indians should be exempt; see Lewis Hanke, All Mankind Is One (DeKalb: Northern Illinois University Press, 1974), at 86–89; Hugh Thomas, The Slave Trade (New York: Simon & Schuster, 1997), at 125–27). But it is difficult to find a general condemnation by a political theorist prior to Montesquieu. See Baron Montesquieu (Charles Louis de Secondat), The Spirit of the Laws (Anne Cohler, Basia Miller, & Harold Stone, trans.) (Cambridge: Cambridge University Press, 1989), at 250 (Bk. 15, Ch. 5).

48. Honore, supra note 1.

49. See Munzer, supra note 1, at 91–93.

50. William Blackstone, Commentaries on the Laws of England (Chicago: University of Chicago Press, 1979), Bk. 2 at 2. See also id. Bk. 1 at 138: the right of property is "the free use, enjoyment and disposal of all [a person's] acquisitions, without any control or diminution, save only by the laws of the land."

51. Carol Rose, Possession as the Origin of Property, Chicago Law Review 73:73 (1985). Adam Mossoff explicitly connects the concept of possession to premodern natural rights theories. See Adam Mossoff, What is Property? Putting the Pieces Back Together, Arizona Law Review 45:371 (2003).

52. Adolph Berle and Gardiner Means, The Modern Corporation and Private Property (New York: Harcourt, Brace & World, 1932).

53. Guido Calabresi and Douglas Melamed, Property Rules, Liability Rules and Inalienability: One View of the Cathedral, Harvard Law Review 85:1089 (1972).

54. See Ian Ayres and Eric Talley, Solomonic Bargaining: Dividing a Legal Entitlement to Facilitate Coasean Trade, Yale Law Journal 104:1027 (1995); Ian Ayres and Eric Talley, Distinguishing Between Consensual and Nonconsensual Advantages of Liability Rules, Yale Law Journal 105:235 (1995); Jason Johnston, Bargaining under Rules versus Standards, Journal of Law, Economics and Organization 11:256 (1995); Louis Kaplow and Steven Shavell, Property Rules versus Liability Rules: An Economic Analysis, Harvard Law Review 109:713 (1996); James Krier and Stewart Schwab, Property Rules and Liability Rules: The Cathedral in Another Light, NYU Law Review 70:440 (1995); Madeline Morris, The Structure of Entitlements, Cornell Law Review 78:822 (1993). For an effort to go one step further, and view all options as a species of auction, see Ian Ayres and Balkin, Legal Entitlements as Auctions: Property Rules, Liability Rules and Beyond, Yale Law Journal 106:703 (1996).

55. See Kevin Bales, Disposable People: New Slavery in the Global Economy (Berkeley: University of California Press, 1999), at 12–31. According to Bales, modern slavery is characterized by forced, unpaid labor, not permanent owner-

ship. He discusses a fifth country, Mauritania, where the traditional form of slavery prevails, but the Mauritanians try to keep it secret, and very few people pay attention to Mauritania.

56. See Hanoch Dagan, Takings and Distributive Justice, Virginia Law Review 85:741 (1999); Munzer, supra note 1; Joseph Singer, Entitlement: The Paradoxes of Property (New Haven, Conn.: Yale University Press, 2000), at 95–139; Underkuffler, supra note 4, at 37–51; Waldron, supra note 1, at 5–24.

57. See Antony Black, Political Thought in Europe, 1250–1450 (Cambridge: Cambridge University Press, 1992), at 72–78; Arthur McGrade, Rights, Natural Rights and the Philosophy of Law, in Norman Kretzmann, Anthony Kenny, and Jan Pinborg, eds., The Cambridge History of Later Medieval Philosophy: From the Rediscovery of Aristotle to the Disintegration of Scholasticism, 1100–1600 (Cambridge: Cambridge University Press, 1982); Arthur McGrade, Ockham and the Birth of Individual Rights, in Brian Tierney and Peter Linehan, eds., Authority and Power: Studies on Medieval Law and Government Presented to Walter Ullmann on his Seventieth Birthday (Cambridge: Cambridge University Press, 1980); Tuck, supra note 2, at 20–22 (discussing work by Michel Villey). As noted in Chapter 8, Tuck identifies the real creator of natural rights theory as Jean de Gerson, id. at 25–29.

58. Black, supra note 57, at 72; Tuck, supra note 2, at 22–23. Jesus and His apostles had been property owners in this sense. Technically speaking, William was excommunicated for leaving Rome without permission prior to the papal ruling on his writing, but he left because condemnation was a foregone conclusion.

59. Overton, supra note 4, at 55.

60. For an incisive critique of Locke's theory, see Waldron, supra note 1, at 137–252. See also Buckle, supra note 2, at 153–61; Macpherson, Theory, supra note 4; Munzer, supra note 1, at 254–91; Nozick, supra note 12, at 178–82; Leo Strauss, Natural Right and History (Chicago: University of Chicago Press, 1965), at 202–51; James Tully, A Discourse on Property: John Locke and His Adversaries (Cambridge: Cambridge University Press, 1980).

61. Eric Foner, Reconstruction: America's Unfinished Revolution (New York: Harper & Row, 1988) Claude Oubre, Forty Acres and a Mule: The Freedmen's Bureau and Black Land Ownership (Baton Rouge: Louisiana State University Press, 1978). A particularly poignant case involved General Sherman's Field Order No. 15, which set aside a portion of the Georgia-South Carolina coast as an exclusive settlement for former slaves. This turned out to be a war-time expedient, however, not an act of social justice. Having established their own farms and communities on this land, the people who settle there were then ordered to return it to its former owners, and told that their only choice was to work as tenants of these owners or face eviction. Foner, supra at 70–71, 158–61.

62. Epstein, supra note 6, at 22–23.

63. Nozick, supra note 12, at 171. The constraints Nozick is referring to are the general rules of criminal and civil law: "My property rights in my knife allow me to leave it where I will, but not in your chest." Id. See note 77, infra.

64. Ackerman, supra note 15, at 10–20, 113–67.

65. Felix Cohen, Transcendental Nonsense and the Functional Approach, Columbia Law Review 35:809 (1935); Cohen, supra note 5; Cohen, supra note 43; Robert Hale, Bargaining, Duress, and Economic Liberty, Columbia Law Review

43:603 (1943). See Gregory Alexander, Commodity and Propriety: Competing Visions of Property in American Legal Thought, 1776–1970 (Chicago: University of Chicago Press, 1997); Neil Duxbury, Robert Hale and the Economy of Legal Force, Modern Law Review 53:421 (1990); Joseph Singer, Legal Realism Now, California Law Review 76:465 (1988).

66. Hohfeld, supra note 5.

67. See Lawrence Becker, Property Rights: Philosophic Foundations (London: Routledge & Kegan Paul, 1977), at 11–21; Cohen, Transcendental Nonsense, supra note 65; Honore, supra note 1; Munzer, supra note 1, at 22–36; Waldron, supra note 1, at 47–59.

68. Ronald Coase, The Problem of Social Cost, Journal of Law & Economics, 3:1 (1960); Ronald Coase, The Nature of the Firm, Economica N.S. 4:386 (1937), reprinted in George Stigler and K. E. Boulding, eds., Readings in Price Theory (Homewood, Ill.: Richard D. Irwin, 1952).

69. Armen Alchian, Some Economics of Property Rights, in Armen Alchian, Economic Forces at Work (Indianapolis: Liberty Press, 1977), at 127; Armen Alchian and Harold Demsetz, Production, Information Costs and Economic Organization, American Economic Review 62:777 (1972); Harold Demsetz, Toward a Theory of Property Rights, American Economic Review 57:347 (1967); Oliver Williamson, The Economic Institutions of Capitalism: Firms, Markets, Relational Contracting (New York: Free Press, 1987).

70. See David Westbrook, Administrative Takings: A Realist Perspective on the Practice and Theory of Regulatory Takings Cases, Notre Dame Law Review 74:717 (1999), which points out that takings cases almost invariably involve objections to administrative action.

71. Neil Komesar, Imperfect Alternatives: Choosing Institutions in Law, Economics and Public Policy (Chicago: University of Chicago Press, 1994); Neil Komesar, Law's Limits: The Rule of Law and the Supply and Demand of Rights (Cambridge: Cambridge University Press, 2001).

72. Coase, Problem of Social Cost, supra note 68.

73. This does not contradict Waldron's argument that transferability can be separated from property ownership, by which he means the ownership of a certain modicum of material resources. See Waldron, supra note 1, at 423–43. The argument here is simply that transferability is required if one wants to establish a market, and the creation of markets is the driving force for allocating resources to private persons in the modern state.

74. This is exactly what Michael Milken did when he made a market in junk bonds. See James Stewart, Den of Thieves (New York: Simon & Schuster, 1991), at 45–47.

75. See Nevins Baxter, The Commercial Paper Market, 2d ed. (Boston: Bankers Publishing Co., 1966); Dall Bennewitz, Introduction to the Secondary Mortgage Market: A Primer (Chicago: United States League of Savings Institutions, 1983); Tamar Frankel, Securitization: Structured Financing, Financial Asset Pools, and Asset-Backed Securities (Boston: Little Brown, 1991); James Kinney and Richard Garrigan, The Handbook of Mortgage Banking: A Guide to the Secondary Mortgage Market (Homewood, Ill.: Dow Jones Irwin, 1985); Robert Roche, Bankers Acceptances, Federal Reserve Bank of Richmond Economic Quar-

terly 79:75 (1993); Marcia Stigum, After the Trade: Dealer and Clearing Bank Operations in Money Market and Government Securities (Homewood, Ill.: Dow Jones-Irwin, 1988). If the obligation is embodied in a physical object, such as a piece of paper, the owner could also destroy the obligation. It is difficult to imagine that his ability to do so contributes very much to the operation of the market. In any case, it could be readily precluded by recording all obligations and transfers in electronic form, and providing that the owner's refusal to receive the income would be deemed an automatic transfer to some other entity, such as the issuer or the government.

76. Berle and Means, supra note 52.

77. Waldron, supra note 1, at 49, argues that prohibitions on the harmful use of property should be regarded as a general background constraint, rather than a specific aspect of property itself.

78. Courts have consistently refused to provide compensation for zoning changes. See Village of Euclid v. Ambler Realty Co., 272 U.S. 365 (1926); Gorieb v. Fox, 274 U.S. 603 (1927); Goldblatt v. Town of Hempstead, 369 U.S.590 (1962); Agins v. Tiburon, 447 U.S. 255 (1980).

79. See, e.g., Civil Rights Act of 1964, Pub. L. No. 88-352, 78 Stat. 244, codified at 42 U.S.C. § 2000a.

80. Visual Artists Rights Act of 1990, 17 U.S.C. sec. 106A (2002). For discussions of similar statutes enacted in New York State, California, and France, see Edward Damich, The New York Artists' Authorship Rights Act: A Comparative Critique, Columbia Law Review 84:1733 (1984). See also Gilliam v. American Broadcasting Companies, Inc., 538 F.2d 14 (1976).

81. See generally Robert Axelrod, The Evolution of Cooperation (New York: Basic Books, 1984), at 42-43; Peter Ordeshook, A Political Theory Primer (New York: Routledge, 1992), at 174-80; Richard Posner, Aging and Old Age (Chicago: University of Chicago Press, 1995), at 51-65; Edward Rock and Michael Wachter, The Enforceability of Norms and the Employment Relationship, University of Pennsylvania Law Review 144:1913 (1996), at 1932.

82. Underkuffler, supra note 4, at 21-24. See also Ugo Mattei, Basic Principles of Property Law: A Comparative Legal and Economic Introduction (Westport, Conn.: Greenwood Press (2000).

83. Clean Air Act Amendments of 1990, 42 U.S.C. §§ 7401-7671 (2002); Reduction of Fuel and Fuel Additives, 40 C.F.R. § 80 (1985); Protection of Stratospheric Ozone, 40 C.F.R. § 82 (1988); Emissions Trading Policy Statement: General Principles for Creation, Banking and Use of Emission Reduction Credits, Federal Register 51:43,814, 43,829 (1986).

84. For analysis of this claim, and other aspects of the program, see Robert Hahn and Gordon Hester, Marketable Permits: Lessons for Theory and Practice, Ecology Law Quarterly 16:361 (1989); Robert Hahn and Roger Knoll, Barriers to Implementing Tradable Air Pollution Permits: Problems of Regulatory Interactions, Yale Journal on Regulation 1:63 (1983); Robert Hahn and Robert Stavins, Incentive-Based Environmental Regulation: A New Era from an Old Idea?, Ecology Law Quarterly 18:1 (1991); Paul Joskow and Richard Schmalensee, The Political Economy of Market-Based Environmental Policy: The U.S. Acid Rain Program, Journal of Law and Economics 41:37 (1988); Thomas Merrill, Explaining

Market Mechanisms, University of Illinois Law Review 2000:275 (2000); Carol Rose, Rethinking Environmental Controls: Management Strategies for Common Resources, Duke Law Journal 1991:1 (1991).

85. See Too Rich Too Soon?: How Child Stars Are Coping With the Pressures of Fame, Weekly In Touch 2 (35):12 (2003).

86. See, e.g., West's Ann. California Code: Family Code § 7500 et seq.; McKinney's Consol. Laws of New York: Artists & Cultural Affairs § 35.03.

87. See Janos Kornai, The Socialist System: The Political Economy of Communism (Princeton: Princeton University Press, 1992), at 76–86, 216–24; Martin McCauley, The Soviet Union 1917–1991, 2d ed. (London: Longman, 1993), at 78–88; Alec Nove, The Soviet Economic System (London: G. Allen & Unwin, 1977); Jonathan Spence, The Search for Modern China (New York: W. W. Norton, 1990), at 574–90.

88. Underkuffler, supra note 4, at 24–28. Underkuffler is using these terms for property, of course, not markets. While the flexibility with respect to area of field fits well enough with the traditional idea of property, the flexible levels of stringency clash with this idea, but fit comfortably into the notion of market regulation.

89. Communications Act of 1934, Ch. 652, 48 Stat. 1064 (June 19, 1934), codified at 47 U.S.C. §§ 151 et seq. Although this statute is a product of the New Deal, it was based on a similar statute, the Federal Radio Act of 1927, that was designed by the Coolidge Administration with full support of the affected broadcasters. Ronald Coase argues that this approach is inefficient, and that full control and transfer privileges to portions of the spectrum should be auctioned off; The Federal Communications Commission, Journal of Law and Economics 2:1 (1959). Edwin Baker responds that the broadcast media are subject to unique forms of market failure that render such reliance on the market undesirable. C. Edwin Baker, Media, Markets and Democracy (Cambridge: Cambridge University Press, 2002). The important point, for present purposes, is that this debate proceeds in terms of policy. It questions how fully market forces should be employed in the broadcasting field without needing to rely on any ideas about the natural or human rights or the inherent character of property.

90. See Amusement and Music Operators Ass'n v. Copyright Royalty Tribunal, 676 F.2d 1144 (7th Cir.), cert. denied, 459 U.S. 907 (1982). Phonorecording licenses are still called mechanical licenses in the industry because of their origins in mechanical reproduction of music in player piano rolls.

91. See Copyright Act of 1976, 17 U.S.C. sec. 115 (sound recordings); 116 & 116 (A) (jukeboxes); 4E[4][e] (cable television); 118 (noncommercial broadcasting); 119 (satellite retransmission).

92. Pub. L. No. 105–304, 112 Stat. 2860 (1998) (codified in scattered sections of 17 U.S.C.).

93. Some intellectual property scholars associate property rights with the right to exclude. See, e.g., Frank Easterbrook, Intellectual Property Is Still Property, Harvard Journal of Law and Public Policy 13:108 (1990); Simone Rose, Patent "Monopolyphobia": A Means of Extinguishing the Fountainhead?, Case Western Reserve Law Review 49:509 (1999). But what is the point of using such a loaded term as the equivalent for the right to exclude, unless one is trying to generate

rhetorical force for purposes other than the creation of this right? And what about the owner of the performance right for music, who does not have the right to exclude because of the compulsory license, but nonetheless has something of great economic value?

94. Bales estimates that there are currently 27 million slaves in the world. Bales, supra note 55, at 8.

95. See Richard Posner, The Regulation of the Market in Adoptions, Boston University Law Review 67:59 (1987); Elizabeth Landes and Richard Posner, The Economics of the Baby Shortage, Journal of Legal Studies 7:323 (1978).

96. See Ronald Cass, Coping With Life, Law and Markets: A Comment on Posner and the Law-and-Economics Debate, Boston University Law Review 67:73 (1987); Jane Cohen, Posnerism, Pluralism, Pessimism, Boston University Law Review 67:105 (1987); Tamar Frankel and Frances Miller, The Inapplicability of Market Theory to Adoptions, Boston University Law Review 67:99 (1987); Carol Sanger, He's Gotta Have It, Southern California Law Review 66:1221 (1993) (book review); Robin West, Submission, Choice, and Ethics: A Rejoinder to Judge Posner, Harvard Law Review 99:1449 (1986).

97. Robert Cooter and Thomas Ulen, Law and Economics (New York: HarperCollins, 1988), at 108–12; Edwin Mansfield, Microeconomics: Theory & Applications, 3d ed. (New York: W. W. Norton, 1979), at 470–94; Robert Pindyck and Daniel Rubinfeld, Microeconomics, 2d ed. (New York: Macmillan, 1992), at 661–69.

98. See Penner, supra note 7, at 104–27, who points out that something must be separable from the individual in order to function as property: thus, a person's kidney could not be property until modern medicine found a way to separate it from the person without killing her. Penner correctly notes that separability is not the same thing as transferability, but a pre-condition for it.

99. Laura Underkuffler, The Idea of Property: Its Meaning and Power (Oxford: Oxford University Press, 2003), at 51; see id. at 46–63.

100. Singer, supra note 56, at 91–94.

101. John Christman, The Myth of Property: Toward an Egalitarian Theory of Ownership (New York: Oxford University Press, 1994), at 125–46.

102. See Michael Robertson, Reconceiving Private Property, Journal of Law and Society 24:465 (1997).

103. Neil Gunningham, Robert Kagan, and Dorothy Thornton propose the related idea that a corporation should not be viewed as having control over private property, but rather as having a "license to operate" in a particular way from its stockholders, its community, its employees, and government regulators. See Neil Gunningham, Robert Kagan, and Dorothy Thornton, Shades of Green (Stanford, Calif.: Stanford University Press, 2003).

104. See, e.g., The Private Property Rights Protection and Compensation Act, H.R. 9, 104th Congress, 1st Session (1995), S.R. 605, 104th Congress, 1st Session (1995) (not enacted); Private Property Protection Act, H.R. 925, 104th Congress, 1st Session (1995). See Frank Michelman, A Skeptical View of "Property Rights" Legislation, Fordham Environmental Law Journal 6:409 (1995); Joseph Sax, Takings Legislation: Where It Stands and What Is Next, Ecology Law Quarterly 23:509 (1996).

105. 505 U.S. 1003 (1992).

106. See also Loretto v. Teleprompter Manhattan CATV Corp., 458 U.S. 419 (1982); Hodel v. Irving, 481 U.S. 704 (1987). In *Loretto*, a government regulation requiring apartment owners to allow their tenants to obtain cable television services was held to be a taking because it constituted a "permanent physical occupation" of the small amount of space where the cable ran. In *Hodel*, a regulation preventing the inheritance of very small parcels of land on an Indian reservation and declaring that the land would revert to tribal ownership was similarly held to be a taking. The only thing that seems to distinguish these regulations from other, very similar ones that have not required compensation, such as rent control (see Pennell v. City of San Jose, 485 U.S. 1 [1988]), or restrictions on the transfer of eagle feathers owned by Indians (see Andrus v. Allard, 444 U.S. 51 [1979]), is that *Loretto* and *Hodel* involve a loss of physical control.

107. Personal Responsibility and Work Opportunity Reconciliation Act, Pub. L. No. 104–93, 110 Stat. 205, codified at 42 U.S.C. §§ 601–17. PRWORA replaced the grants to individuals under AFDC with block grants to states.

108. See Jane Baron, The Expressive Transparency of Property, Columbia Law Review 102:208 (2002), which argues that theories about property are not likely to affect social practices. While this may be somewhat extreme—ideas do matter in the long run—the point here, as elsewhere in this study, is to argue from practices to theory, not from theory to practice. The argument is not that the proposed alternative will actually change our social norms, but rather that it is consistent with those norms.

109. See, e.g., Frank Cross, Law and Economic Growth, Texas Law Review 80:1737 (2002); Demsetz, supra note 69; Eirik Furubotn and Svetozar Pejovich, eds., The Economics of Property Rights (Cambridge, Mass.: Ballinger, 1974); Gary Libecap, Contracting for Property Rights, in Anderson and McChesney, eds., supra note 2, at 142; Ugo Mattei, Basic Principles of Property Law: A Comparative and Economic Introduction (Westport, Conn.: Greenwood Press, 2000), at 51–71; Munzer, supra note 1, at 191–224; Hernando de Soto, The Mystery of Capital: Why Capitalism Triumphs in the West and Fails Everywhere Else (New York: Basic Books, 2000).

110. Nozick, supra note 12, at 170. See id. at 167–74.

111. Jean-Jacques Rousseau, The Social Contract (Willmoore Kendall, trans.) (Chicago: Henry Regnery, 1954), at 27–32 (Bk. 1, Ch. 9). In support of his position, Rousseau makes the rather convincing point that property acquired by the state is then distributed to individuals by exactly this procedure. Any theory that relies heavily on first possession to determine people's rights must then distinguish between property that people owned before the state was formed and property they obtained from the state after its formation. But no such distinction is apparent in modern legal systems.

112. See Waldron, supra note 1, at 253–83.

113. Nozick, supra note 12, at 160–64. Nozick uses this example for the closely related argument that no society can impose a fixed rule for property distribution because voluntary transfers will upset the balance, requiring continued redistribution. This point, like his taxation-as-forced-labor point, is a bit labored, since most redistributive schemes are only concerned with providing a minimum

amount for the poor, not a fixed amount for everyone, and this can be readily achieved with an ordinary income tax. People must pay the tax every year, and the revenue can then be used to ensure that each person has the required minimum, thus maintaining the end-state that the society desires.

114. Arguments that people are entitled to rewards for their productive labor are more convincing; see Becker, supra note 67; Alan Gewirth, The Community of Rights (Chicago: University of Chicago Press, 1996), at 181–203, but they can be satisfied by providing people with income and government benefits, rather than property.

115. Singer, supra note 56, at 68–81.

116. Stephen Holmes and Cass Sunstein, The Cost of Rights (New York: W. W. Norton, 1999), at 35–83.

117. J. Gregory Sidak and Daniel Spulber, Deregulatory Takings and the Regulatory Contract: The Competitive Transformation of Network Industries in the United States (Cambridge: Cambridge University Press, 1997).

118. For related criticisms of the deregulatory takings idea, see Herbert Hovencamp, The Takings Clause and Improvident Regulatory Bargains, Yale Law Journal 108:801 (1999); Jim Rossi, The Irony of Deregulatory Takings, Texas Law Review 77:297 (1998); Jim Rossi and Susan Rose-Ackerman, Disentangling Deregulatory Takings, Virginia Law Review 86:1435 (2000); Oliver Williamson, Deregulatory Takings and the Breach of the Regulatory Contract: Some Precautions, NYU Law Review 71:1007 (1996).

119. Theo van Banning, The Human Right to Property (Antwerp: Intersentia, 2001), at 182–85; Richard Epstein, Property as a Fundamental Civil Right, California Western Law Review 29:187 (1992); James Ely, The Guardian of Every Other Right: A Constitutional History of Property Rights, 2d ed. (New York: Oxford University Press, 1998); Munzer, supra note 1, at 81–87; Jennifer Nedelsky, The Madisonian Legacy: Private Property and the Limits of American Constitutionalism (Chicago: University of Chicago Press, 1990); Richard Pipes, Property and Freedom (New York: Alfred Knopf, 1999); William Van Alstyne, The Recrudescence of Property Rights as the Foremost Principle of Civil Liberties: The First Decade of the Burger Court, Law & Contemporary Problems 43:66 (1980).

120. Epstein, supra note 6, at 138–39; Friedman, supra note 12, at 16–21; Michael Oakeshott, The Political Economy of Freedom, in Michael Oakeshott, Rationalism in Politics and Other Essays (Indianapolis: Liberty Fund, 1991), at 384, 392–96; Cass Sunstein, On Property and Constitutionalism, Cardozo Law Review 14:907 (1993).

121. Edwin Baker argues that the competitive nature of the market constrains entrepreneurs, effectively denying them liberty. Baker, supra note 43, at 785–92. Nonetheless, they exercise control over those they employ, and over those assets, such as a large home and personal savings, that are insulated from market forces.

122. See Becker, supra note 67; Cohen, supra note 43; at 174–78; Gewirth, supra note 114, at 174–76; Anthony Kronman, Contract Law and Distributive Justice, Yale Law Journal 89:472 (1980); Charles Lindblom, Politics and Markets (New York: Basic Books, 1977), at 47–50; Carol Pateman, Rethinking Democracy (Cambridge: Cambridge University Press, 1988), at 172–75.

123. Baker, supra note 43, at 792–800.

124. Robert Dahl, Dilemmas of Pluralist Democracy: Autonomy vs. Control (New Haven, Conn.: Yale University Press, 1982), at 171–85; Robert Dahl, A Preface to Economic Democracy (Berkeley: University of California Press, 1985); Lindblom, supra note 122; Ralph Miliband, The State in Capitalist Society (London: Weidenfeld and Nicolson, 1969); Pateman, supra note 122, at 175–76.

125. See Marcy Darnovsky, Barbara Epstein, and Richard Flacks, eds., Cultural Politics and Social Movements (Philadelphia: Temple University Press, 1995); William Eskridge, Some Effects of Identity-Based Social Movements on Constitutional Law in the Twentieth Century, Michigan Law Review 100:2069 (2002); Edward Rubin, Passing through the Door: Social Movement Literature and Legal Scholarship, University of Pennsylvania Law Review 150:1 (2001); Sydney Tarrow, Power in Movement: Social Movements, Collective Action and Politics (Cambridge: Cambridge University Press, 1994); Alain Touraine, The Voice and the Eye: An Analysis of Social Movements (Cambridge: Cambridge University Press, 1981).

126. Hegel, supra note 8, at 40–57 (§§ 41–70).

127. See Macpherson, Theory, supra note 4, at 112–36; Dorothy Thompson, The Chartists: Popular Politics in the Industrial Revolution (New York: Pantheon Books, 1984).

128. Aristotle's Politics (Benjamin Jowett, trans.) (Oxford: Clarendon Press, 1905), at IV.4, 1291b30–1292a38; V.5, 1304b19–1305a36. As recent and sophisticated an observer of democracy as Tocqueville voices exactly the same concern. Alexis de Tocqueville, Democracy in America (Harvey Mansfield & Delba Winthrop, trans.) (Chicago: University of Chicago Press, 2000), at 200–201.

129. A dramatic and somewhat tragic illustration of this point involves the recent events in Zimbabwe. The argument for land redistribution there was an overwhelming one, since a large proportion of the valuable farmland was in the hands of a tiny minority of farmers, and these farmers, moreover, were immigrants from a different culture who had seized the land by force as part of a colonial regime. Yet the democratic voters of Zimbabwe were unwilling to support even a gradual land reform program. This gave Robert Mugabe the incentive and excuse to establish a dictatorship; he then proceeded to institute radical land reform, accompanied by all the corruption and inefficiency that dictatorships typically display. See Banning, supra note 119, at 332–34.

130. Ackerman, supra note 15; Kevin Grey, Equitable Property, Current Legal Problems 4:157 (1994).

131. Ackerman, supra note 15, at 12, 88–113. See also Joan Williams, The Rhetoric of Property, Iowa Law Review 83:277 (1998); Westbrook, supra note 70.

132. Jeremy Waldron, Property, Honesty and Normative Resilience, in Stephen Munzer, New Essays in the Legal and Political Theory of Property (Cambridge: Cambridge University Press, 2001), at 10.

133. See Jürgen Habermas, The Theory of Communicative Action, vol. 2: Lifeworld and System: A Critique of Functionalist Reason (Thomas McCarthy, trans.) (Boston: Beacon Press, 1987), at 153–97.

134. Robert Ellickson, Order without Law: How Neighbors Settle Disputes (Cambridge, Mass.: Harvard University Press, 1999).

135. Komesar, Law's Limits, supra note 71, at 126–35.

136. On the non-intuitive character of law, see Brian Tamanaha, Realistic Socio-Legal Theory: Pragmatism and a Social Theory of Law (Oxford: Clarendon Press, 1997), at 128–52.

137. See Penner, supra note 6.

138. Merrill and Smith, supra note 6; Thomas Merrill and Henry Smith, What Happened to Property in Law and Economics, Yale Law Journal 111:357 (2001). See also Thomas Merrill and Henry Smith, The Property/Contract Interface, Columbia Law Review 101:773 (2001). The term "rehabilitate" is not being used facetiously. Merrill and Smith specifically announce their theory as an argument in favor of the traditional idea of property, and in opposition to the prevailing modern view that they ascribe, quite correctly, to Coase. See What Happened to Property, supra, at 357–60.

139. For a similar argument, used to critique rather than rehabilitate the concept of property, see Rose, supra note 51.

140. See West Coast Hotel v. Parrish, 300 U.S. 379 (1937); United States v. Carolene Products Co., 304 U.S. 144 (1938); NLRB v. Jones & Laughlin Steel Corp., 301 U.S. 1 (1937). See Bruce Ackerman, Beyond Carolene Products, Harvard Law Review 98:713 (1985); Lawrence Tribe, American Constitutional Law, 3d ed. (New York: Foundation, 2000), vol. 1, at 1332–81; Paul Murphy, The Constitution in Crisis Times, 1918–1969 (New York: Harper & Row, 1972), at 70–110; G. Edward White, From Sociological Jurisprudence to Realism: Jurisprudence and Social Change in Twentieth-Century America, Virginia Law Review 58:999 (1972).

141. To take just one example, credit card companies own the income stream from the cards they issue, that is, the sum total of consumer payments for the credit card debts incurred. This is already a somewhat novel form of property. In recent years, the companies, which are generally banks, have begun to issue securities that entitle the buyer to a portion of that income stream. See Allen Berger and Gregory Udell, Securitization, Risk, and the Liquidity Problem in Banking, in Michael Klausner and Lawrence White, eds., Structural Change in Banking (New York: New York University Press, 1993), at 227; Dennis Campbell and Susan Meek, eds., International Asset Securitization and Other Financing Tools (Ardsley, N.Y.: Transnational Publishers, 2000); Frankel, supra note 75; Tamar Frankel, Securitization; Its Effect on Bank Structure, in Klausner and White, supra, at 309. These sui generis forms of property are created by specialized instruments, and marketed to professional investors who understand the nature of those instruments. For related examples, see note 75, supra.

142. Westbrook, supra note 70, at 743–64.

143. Edward Rubin, Due Process and the Administrative State, California Law Review: 72:1044 (1984).

144. For the proposition that due process protection does not apply to groups, see sources cited in note 140, supra.

145. For related views of the boundary between takings and regulation, based on an economic rather than a political rationale, see Rossi and Rose-Ackerman, supra note 118, at 1477–86, distinguishing between government as a buyer, when compensation is required, and government as a regulator, when it is not; Sax, supra

note 104, at 62–64, distinguishing between government as a market participant, when compensation is required, and government as a mediator of conflicting economic claims, when it is not. While these proposals are based on different rationales from the one presented in the text, they lead to similar results. When the government acts as a buyer or a market participant, it will typically purchase particular pieces of property; when it acts as a regulator or mediator, it will affect large groups of owners.

146. Charles Reich, The New Property, Yale Law Journal 73:733 (1964). For an effort to explain this article's value in systematic terms, see Edward Rubin, On Beyond Truth: A Theory for Evaluating Legal Scholarship, California Law Review 80:889 (1992), at 924.

147. See Goldberg v. Kelly, 397 U.S. 254 (1970) (welfare benefits); Bell v. Burson, 402 U.S. 535 (1971) (driver's license); Morrisey v. Brewer, 408 U.S. 471 (1972) (parole from prison); Perry v. Sinderman, 408 U.S. 593 (1972) (government employment); Gagnon v. Scarpelli, 411 U.S. 778 (1973) (probation in place of prison); Goss v. Lopez, 419 U.S. 565 (1975) (public school attendance); Vitek v. Jones, 445 U.S. 480 (1980) (prison instead of a mental institution).

148. Baker, supra note 43, at 764–67; Louis Kaplow, An Economic Analysis of Legal Transitions, Harvard Law Review 99:509 (1986); Frank Michelman, supra note 22.

149. The amount of compensation is the market value of the asset. See Kirby Forest Industries, Inc. v. United States, 467 U.S. 1 (1984); United States v. 564.54 Acres of Land, 441 U.S. 506 (1979).

150. Dagan, supra note 56; Hanoch Dagan, Just Compensation, Incentives, and Social Meanings, Michigan Law Review 99:134 (2000); Daniel Farber, Public Choice and Just Compensation, Constitutional Commentary 9:279 (1992); Glynn Lunney, A Critical Reexamination of Takings Jurisprudence, Michigan Law Review 90:1892 (1992).

151. Sax, supra note 104.

152. See Berman v. Parker, 348 U.S. 26 (1954); Hawaii Housing Authority v. Midkiff, 467 U.S. 229 (1984).

153. Meir Dan-Cohen, Harmful Thoughts (Princeton: Princeton University Press, 2003), at 264. See also Margaret Radin, Property and Personhood, Stanford Law Review 34:957 (1982).

154. Radin, supra note 153.

155. Some scholars have suggested that a community might be able to advance such a claim. See Frank Michelman, Property as a Constitutional Right, Washington & Lee Law Review 38:1097 (1981), at 1110–14; Joseph Sax, Do Communities Have Rights? The National Parks as a Laboratory of New Ideas, University of Pittsburgh Law Review 45:499 (1984). According to the analysis suggested here, the community would need to demonstrate that it lacked access to the political process—for example, that its members belonged to an otherwise oppressed minority group.

Author Index

Reformation (Protestant): 149, 183, 261–62
Reification: of branches of government, 47, 54–55, 72–73; defined, 15–16; of democracy, 111, 126–27; of discretion, 90–91, 95–98; of human body image, 40; of human rights, 228, 261–63, 284; of law, 193–94, 209; of legal rights, 251–56; of legitimacy, 144–45, 167–68; of power, 77, 95–96, 99–100; of property, 308, 321–22
Republic. *See* Interactive Republic
Revolutions (*see also* England; France; United States): 177–78
Rights (*see also* Causes of Action; Moral Demands)
  generally: defects of image, 11, 332; dual meaning, 9–10, 191–92, 227–28, 332; and duties, 270; nominal, 235
  human: 260–84 (primary discussion)
    forms of: absolute, 284; defined, 192, 260–61, 264, 265, 424n.3; first generation, 270–71, 275–77; group, 266, 272–74; language, 273–74; negative, 270–71, 275–77, 289–90; positive, 266, 271–72, 275–78, 289; second generation, 266, 271–72, 275–78; third generation, 266, 272–74
    idea of: Asian values, 283; autonomy, 280–84; bracketed, 268, 274–75; content of, 264, 287–94; critiques of, 281–84; defects of image, 261–68, 270–83, 289–90, 293–94, 332–33; European, 283; moral demands as alternative, 268–78; morality and, 260–61, 268–69, 271, 424n.1; and natural law, 261, 425n.8, 433n.82; and natural rights, 261–64, 265, 425n.8, 425n.9; origin of, 261–64, 265, 425n.8, 425n.10; quasi-Cartesian doubt and, 261; reification of, 228, 261–63, 284; social contract and, 261–62, 266–67; social nostalgia and, 265; terminology of, 227–28, 265–66
    idea of, in operation: and adjudication, 275–76, 284–87; agencies and, 285–86; dangers of, 278–84; and duties, 270; implementation of, 285–87; and institutions, 292–94; judicial review and, 175, 269, 276–

77, 285, 286; and protections against government, 264–65, 287–95, 426n.21, 427n.22, 427n.25; rule of law and, 223; and state action, 270–71
  legal: 228–37 (primary discussion); and adjudication, 230–37, 332; and adversarialism, 241–43; bracketed, 236–37, 252, 255, 257; dangers of, 232–37; defects of image, 232–37, 246–56, 332; defined, 192, 227–28; Hohfeld's theory, 229–30, 415n.21; as implementation method, 232, 237–38; in Middle Ages, 228; normativity of, 246–51; overinclusive, 235–36; and positive law, 227; quasi-Cartesian doubt regarding, 232; reification of, 251–56; social nostalgia and, 233, 237, 239, 241, 242; theories of, 228–32; truth-finding and, 232–33, 236; underinclusive, 233–35
Rulemaking (Administrative): agency role, 80, 140, 170, 210–13; negotiated, 141; notice and comment, 139–40, compliance and, 170; and transitivity, 210–13
Rule of Law. *See* Law
Rule of Recognition: 148

Sacerdotal Government. *See* Government, Pre-Modern; Medieval Thought
Scholarship (*see also* Concepts): on administrative state, 13, 67, 83–85, 133, 165, 205–6, 214, 256; on democracy, 116–20; effect of, 11; on judiciary, 331; legal, 84–85, 204–5, 256; legal process, 148; legal realism, 229–30, 308; nature of, 14, 205; New Institutionalism, 48, 54, 130, 358n.49; New Public Governance, 24, 133, 138, 165–66, 170, 206, 207, 287; on policy making and implementation, 204–5; pre-modern concepts in, 10–11, 81–83; on property, 308–9, 314–15, 322, 325; public choice, 138, 141, 161, 204–5, 326, 406n.72; and social nostalgia, 15
Security: 14
Separation of Powers (*see also* Branches of Government; Mixed Government), 43–45, 54–56, 179–80, 359n.64